N

TRYGVE LIE AND THE COLD WAR

OFFICE OF THE PRESIDENT
OF THE GENERAL ASSEMBLY

GA-2

TRYGVE LIE
AND
THE
COLD
WAR

The UN Secretary-General
Pursues Peace,
1946–1953

James Barros

NORTHERN ILLINOIS UNIVERSITY PRESS

DeKalb, Illinois   1989

© 1989 by Northern Illinois University Press
Published by the Northern Illinois University Press, DeKalb, Illinois 60115
Manufactured in the United States of America using acid-free paper ∞
Design by Julia Fauci

Library of Congress Cataloging-in-Publication Data
Barros, James.
    Trygve Lie and the cold war : the UN Secretary-General pursues peace, 1946–1953 /
James Barros.
       p.   cm.
    Bibliography: p.
    Includes index.
    ISBN 0-87580-148-X
    1. Lie, Trygve, 1896–1968. 2. World politics—1945– 3. United Nations—
Biography. I. Title.
D839.7.L5B37   1989
341.23′24—dc20
  [B]

89-9296
CIP

To Oliver J. Lissitzyn
Professor Emeritus of International Law
Columbia University
Gentleman, Teacher, Scholar

CONTENTS

PREFACE

Norway's Trygve Halvdan Lie was the first secretary-general of the United Nations. He was sworn into office in early February 1946 and was succeeded by Sweden's Dag Hammarskjöld in the spring of 1953. During these years the initial postwar idealism, euphoria, and hope for a better world quickly disappeared. The United Nations coalition that had won the war against the Axis powers soon disintegrated, and what has been euphemistically labelled the Cold War commenced. This world struggle had an ideological façade manipulated by both sides, but intrinsically it was a power struggle not dissimilar to what had occurred in the past, and enormously dangerous because of advances in science, technology, and weapon systems of mass destruction.

It was a period that would have taxed an Olympian god let alone a mere mortal. Lie, who was committed to everything the United Nations stood for, correctly held that the charter and the rules of the various organs of the United Nations bestowed upon him powers and rights not enjoyed by his predecessors in the League of Nations. He envisaged a public political role for himself that his league predecessors had eschewed. During the years that Lie served as secretary-general he grappled behind the scenes, like the league's secretaries-general, as well as publicly with the vexing political issues that inundated the United Nations.

The United Nations that Lie presided over during these years was a Western-dominated institution, and although a Westerner at heart, his political initiatives were often interpreted in Western capitals, at the minimum, as a nuisance. Initially, Soviet Russia's reception of Lie's political forays was friendly, hitting its nadir only with the Korean war. The ability to walk the line between the two camps, when assuming unsolicited public or private political initiatives, was far from easy. Even men far more gifted than Lie would have experienced similar difficulties. The problem that Lie faced and failed to surmount can be traced not only to its insoluble nature but to false assumptions by Lie as to the influence that a secretary-general can wield in world politics, keeping in mind the lack of real physical power in military terms. This was compounded by his modes of operation, by his defects in character and personality, by his perceptions, and lastly by ideological ambiguity.

ACKNOWLEDGMENTS

As the reader will observe, this volume is largely based on widely scattered, disparate documentation. Examination of these materials was made possible by the generosity of the Social Sciences and Humanities Research Council of Canada, a Connaught Fellowship from the University of Toronto, and the assistance of the university's Humanities and Social Sciences Committee, as well as support from the Earhart Foundation, Ann Arbor, Michigan.

A special thanks is owed to Dr. Ruth Russell for her sharp questions and even sharper red pencil and to Professor Leon Gordenker, The Graduate Institute of International Studies, Geneva, Switzerland, for his helpful comments and suggestions.

The personnel of the depositories, both public and private, who assisted and guided me through the archival sources was legion. These depositories are listed at the beginning of the Notes. To thank any specific individuals and inadvertently omit others would be churlish. Expressing my indebtedness to all of them now follows one of the oldest and most agreeable traditions of the academic community. The same cautions apply to my thanks to the personnel of the Reference Department of Robarts Library, University of Toronto, without whom any academic would be aimlessly afloat. Their expertise in tracing the arcane is exceeded only by their graciousness and good humor. The task of typing this volume was undertaken by Brenda Samuels and Anna Marchese of Erindale College, University of Toronto, whose perseverance equaled their patience.

I would also like to express my appreciation to the Masters, Fellows, and Scholars of Churchill College in the University of Cambridge for permission to quote from the diaries of Sir Alexander Cadogan. Likewise I thank the *Canadian Journal of Political Science* for permission to reproduce in an enlarged and very revised form the opening chapter to this volume, which initially appeared many years ago.

TRYGVE LIE AND THE COLD WAR

CONSENSUS CANDIDATE

Prologue

In the intra- and intergovernmental wartime discussions leading to the establishment of the United Nations, all sides accepted that some sort of executive leadership would be necessary to direct and administer the projected world organization. Never having been a member of the League of Nations, however, Washington seemed not as sensitive to the innate influence and power of the secretary-general's office as were London, Paris, and Moscow, which had been members of the Geneva organization. Nor was Washington as sensitive to the political importance of who actually held the office as London and Paris, which during the interwar period had respectively furnished Sir Eric Drummond and Joseph Avenol as secretaries-general of the league.[1] In turn, the pronounced anticommunist orientation of Avenol and the paramount role he played in having Soviet Russia expelled from the league following its attack on Finland in December 1939[2] must have instructed Moscow to the political importance of the office and especially to the person who held it.

Although differences developed during the wartime discussions between the Western powers and Moscow dealing with various aspects of the secretary-general's office and the secretariat under the projected United

Nations organization, these differences were never so sharp or so deep as to be irreconcilable. Moreover, most of the discussions occurred at a time when the war against the Axis powers was not yet terminated, and the pressure to continue the wartime collaboration and consensus made compromise and agreement over these questions imperative. This collaboration and consensus, however, did not repeat itself in the actual selection and appointment of the United Nations' first secretary-general. By the time serious discussion commenced on this issue, the Axis coalition had been defeated and the conflicting political and strategic-military desires of East and West, later to be garbed in an ideological cloak and labeled the *Cold War*, had begun manifesting themselves. In this encounter over the selection of the secretary-general, the Russians played their hand with consummate skill.

Moscow's actions throughout these negotiations show with some clarity that it perceived the projected world organization as essentially one more bulwark—and a lesser one at that—in protecting and guaranteeing its future security. One cannot help but note the similarity between this Russian approach and that of the French in 1919. Moscow regarded the value of the projected international organization as an organ for world cooperation and for peaceful settlement to be very secondary; it would have liked to rule it out of questions where Soviet Russia or its supporters were involved. To direct the organization along the lines desired, Moscow strove during these negotiations to acquire, in conjunction with the other Great Powers, control over both the secretariat and the secretary-general. In particular, Moscow sought the appointment of a secretary-general who would be at least understanding, if not sympathetic, to its postwar political-security desires.

In Washington, and to a somewhat lesser extent in London and Paris, the case was reversed. Although national security, as distinct from world security, was an omnipresent consideration, these Allied capitals envisaged the organization as one for world cooperation and conflict resolution. This largely explains the differences that developed during the wartime negotiations between the Western powers and Moscow over the nature of the secretariat and the secretary-general's office. It certainly explains the American desire, in the negotiations over selecting and appointing the secretary-general, to have someone chosen who had "broad interests, demonstrated intellectual ability and . . . experience in administrating large organizations." In addition, the secretary-general was to have "qualities of moral leadership and the ability to inspire his associates" as well as "a real understanding of international affairs" and a deep interest in the development of the world community. The person was to be "progressive on economic and social questions" and devoid of "racial or class intolerance or prejudice" and have "demonstrated his ability to lead organizations composed of persons drawn from divergent groups."[3] This seeming lack of concern by the Americans for the candidate's political orientation, except in the most obvious cases, was not repeated on the British side. British political leadership, especially because of London's interwar experience, was quicker to look at the prospective candidate's national and subsurface political values and attitude.

The United Nations Preparatory Commission

In view of the American desire that the secretary-general not be designated at San Francisco, no decision was made at the conference on this matter.[4] Discussions developed after the charter was negotiated and prior to the first meeting of the General Assembly, scheduled to convene in London in January 1946. In a memorandum prepared on August 23, 1945, following Japan's defeat, the American representative on the United Nations Preparatory Commission, Edward Stettinius (a person of the greatest naïveté) raised the question of the secretary-general's selection. According to Stettinius, the "Secretary-General should, if possible, not be a national" of one of the Security Council's permanent members, and furthermore, should be selected "because of his [personal] qualifications." The first choice of the American government, Stettinius contended, should be the Canadian under-secretary of state for external affairs, Norman Robertson. Other persons, however, might be considered: Lester Pearson, the Canadian ambassador in Washington; Adrianus Pelt, a Dutch national and former high official of the league secretariat; Stanley Bruce, Australia's representative to the league; Douglas Forsyth, the secretary to the prime minister of South Africa; and finally, Caracciolo Parra Pérez, Venezuela's foreign minister.[5] Stettinius's notion that the secretary-general should not be a national of one of the Big Five was not so novel an idea since it appears to have developed as a desirable policy in the league's last years.[6] On the other hand, the notion that the selection be based on the secretary-general's qualifications was optimistic in the extreme if one kept in mind league practice.[7] The secretary-general's greater political role, as spelled out in the charter, surely dictated that the selection be based primarily on political considerations, something that Stettinius's memorandum appears to have ignored.

Indeed, the political considerations manifested themselves as early as September 7, although Stettinius lacked the prescience to recognize them. When Stettinius queried his Russian opposite, Andrei Gromyko, as to whether Moscow had given any consideration to a candidate for the secretary-generalship, Gromyko responded he had no names to offer. Gromyko added, however, that if the assembly convened in the United States in the autumn and the London discussions had not led to the selection of a secretary-general, he "would be happy to see Alger Hiss [who had been secretary-general of the San Francisco Conference and was then director of the State Department's Office of Special Political Affairs, which dealt with United Nations questions] appointed Secretary-General." Gromyko explained that "he had a very high regard" for Hiss, "particularly for his fairness and impartiality."[8] Since altruism in world politics is even less a virtue in Moscow than elsewhere, one would be hard pressed to cite a similar instance in the postwar period where Moscow proposed a Western official for an important international post. The episode acquires added interest because of Hiss's subsequent trial and conviction involving charges that he was a long-time Russian agent. Gromyko was also shrewd in using Stettinius as the conduit for the Hiss proposal, in view of Stettinius's esteem and affection for Hiss.[9] Curiously, Stettinius does not appear to have conveyed Gromyko's suggestion to anyone else.

Hiss's name, interestingly, also surfaced within British ranks. Professor Charles Webster of the Foreign Office raised with Minister of State Philip Noel-Baker, who handled United Nations affairs for the Labour government, Hiss's possible candidature because of his fine work as secretary-general at San Francisco.[10] Noel-Baker does not appear to have replied to this proposal nor does it appear to have been examined in discussions within British official circles. This was an odd silence in view of the fact that, among the British, even the most improbable American candidate generated immediate interest. It would not be unfair to suggest that the reasons for this silence might be that Noel-Baker was informed that Hiss was a suspected Russian agent, based on information that had developed from the defection in Ottawa of Igor Gouzenko, the cipher clerk to the Russian military attaché.[11]

The first discussion of the secretary-generalship among the Big Five did not commence until September 17. While the Russians and the Americans stressed that no one could be recommended who was a national of the state where the United Nations would be situated, the British, French, and Chinese did not agree that this had to be an absolute condition. The British representative, however, did concede that anyone recommended for the position had to have the confidence of the Big Five.[12] According to Stettinius, it "was generally agreed" that the Big Five must select "their nominee" several weeks before the assembly convened, so that there would be time to sound out the person chosen to make sure that the appointment would be accepted. It was likewise agreed that the Big Five "should avoid if possible any [public] debate" on the matter and hence should attempt to come to a consensus "beforehand by informal discussions."[13]

Before the substance of this London meeting reached Washington, Dean Acheson, the acting secretary of state, emphasized to Stettinius that the secretary-general "should be a national of a middle or small power." Washington, he observed, attached the greatest importance to appointing a person of the "highest ability" as secretary-general. It wanted someone who would be completely devoted to the institution and the office be considered of "such importance, and dignity and prestige as to attract an out-

standing man." To get the best person for the job, it was felt that the contractual arrangement should be flexible and no restrictions placed on
reelection. If the American position on contractual flexibility proved unacceptable, Stettinius would be permitted to settle for a five-year contractual term for the secretary-general. Since the American position was that
the holder of the office be from a "middle or small power," he was to oppose any provision that the retiring secretary-general could not be reem-
ployed by his own country. The retiring secretary-general would have to
use his own judgment involving the propriety of reentering national service soon after the termination of the contractual term. Pension rights
were to be generous to prevent financial considerations being a determining factor. If the basic assumption that the secretary-general should be a
national of a small or middle power changed, the provisions regarding employment in one's national service would have to be reconsidered. Indeed,
the imposition of such a provision would be essential if a secretary-general
were a national of one of the Great Powers.[14]

On September 20 the question was examined again by Adlai Stevenson,
Stettinius's deputy, and Webster of the Foreign Office. To Webster, it appeared likely that the best candidates would be from America. Stevenson
seemed somewhat startled by this idea and replied that perhaps the holder
of the office ought not to be a national of one of the Great Powers.[15] It
became obvious some days later that Webster's comments were not personal but reflected British policy. When Stettinius and Stevenson called on
Noel-Baker and noted that the question of the secretary-general was urgent, Noel-Baker repeated the idea of an American nominee, saying that it
would give the world confidence in the United States' commitment to the
organization. Noel-Baker, who had raised General Dwight Eisenhower's
name with Stettinius as early as September 3, held that the general's name
was in the minds of most people who had studied the matter but admitted
that he himself had not specifically consulted his cabinet colleagues about
Eisenhower. Stettinius asked if the United Nations' site and the secretary-
generalship were not connected in the sense that one nation should not
have both. Noel-Baker did not know if this was absolutely true.[16]

The British position, as reflected in the comments of Webster and Noel-
Baker, was either a Delphic glimpse of the future Cold War and the desirability of having an American as secretary-general or most likely a reaction
to the events of 1919 and the interwar period: America's rejection of the
league covenant and its dash into isolation, actions that might not be repeated if an American sat as secretary-general. The fact that Noel-Baker
and Webster had been closely associated with the league during the interwar period lends weight to this supposition as the motivating force in
shaping the British position.

While these Anglo-American exchanges were going on, Acheson instructed Stettinius to place in nomination the name of Canada's Robertson
on the grounds that he possessed the qualifications Washington considered

essential for any secretary-general. Stettinius might then, if necessary, indicate other names. It was felt, Acheson explained, that there was a better chance of coming to an agreement on the national of a middle or small power as secretary-general if America threw its support behind a particular candidate and concentrated its attention on that person. As to Australia's Bruce, he was considered too old by the State Department and the question was posed why Stettinius had omitted the name of Belgium's Foreign Minister, Paul-Henri Spaak.[17]

Despite Acheson's instructions, Stettinius, at an "informal meeting" of the Big Five summoned by Gromyko on September 26, did not recommend Robertson. The British desire to nominate an American had obviously complicated Stettinius's task, and the fulfillment of any such British desire was in turn tied to the question of where the United Nations headquarters would be established. Since the United States was high on the list as a possible headquarters site, Stettinius argued that the secretary-general should not be a national of the state where the United Nations was established. Noel-Baker, as expected, maintained that the first secretary-general should be a national of one of the Big Five, preferably an American. They agreed that it would prove difficult to get the Security Council and the assembly to choose both the secretary-general and the headquarters site from the same state. Noel-Baker's suggestion was that everyone should prepare a list of possible candidates containing nationals of his own country, as well as nationals of other states, that might be considered by the Big Five.[18]

French support for an American secretary-general had surfaced earlier that day, when Jacques Fouques-Duparc proposed Stettinius himself, Eisenhower, or John Winant, the ambassador in London. He was certain that the Big Five would accept an American, although he admitted that the candidate's nationality and the headquarters site were interdependent issues.[19] At the Foreign Office several days later, in spite of Stettinius's comments, Noel-Baker continued to hold that a strong case could be made for offering the position to an American. Aside from those already mentioned, he had in mind Harold Stassen, the former governor of Minnesota and one of the delegates at San Francisco. Alternative candidates might be Australia's Bruce, Canada's Pearson, and Belgium's former under-secretary of state for national defense, Henri Rolin. Regarding someone from the United Kingdom, Noel-Baker observed that as yet no name had occurred to him, although he thought that anyone chosen should have parliamentary experience.[20]

In an attempt to explain his action, Stettinius informed Acheson that his previous moves on the matter had merely been intended to open a general discussion of the question and to get other states to offer names while avoiding the necessity of committing Washington to any particular candidate. He hesitated to place only Robertson's name in nomination for several reasons. First, Secretary of State James Byrnes had expressed doubt about the wisdom of having the headquarters site in the United States with a Canadian secretary-general, since this would overemphasize North America. Second, Stettinius was not certain Washington was aiming high enough and he did not want to give the impression to others that America's mind was made up that Robertson was the best available man. He preferred to leave the matter open to further discussion without committing Washington to one particular person.

Moreover, Stettinius did not consider Spaak suitable for the post. He thought it important to discover someone who was "thoroughly acquainted with the concept" of the new world organization and would "not merely try to perpetuate the doctrine of the League." If, by this, Stettinius meant a more politically active secretary-general, he would live to regret it.

Pelt of the Netherlands should also be eliminated from the American list of potential candidates, Stettinius noted, for it was not believed that he had the necessary stature. He asked what Acheson thought of Jan van Roijen, the Dutch minister of state, as a substitute, and what his reaction was to Richard Casey, Australia's former minister in Washington? He observed that the British had suggested that, if neither an American nor a British candidate could be found, a Chinese candidate might be chosen; the French had mentioned Wellington Koo, China's ambassador in London. He had played down an American candidate, Stettinius explained, in view of the tie-in with the headquarters site. Indeed, the British and French had suggested that Stettinius himself should be secretary-general, but he had replied that he was unavailable. Unless instructed otherwise, he would maintain in future discussions that Washington preferred a secretary-general from one of the middle or smaller states; that unless it became clear that the United States would not be the headquarters site, Washington did not think an American should be considered for the office; that although Washington had not yet chosen a candidate it was considering a person like Robertson, Koo, Parra Pérez, or Van Roijen; and lastly, that Washington was interested in hearing the suggestions of other states.[21]

Several days after Stettinius sent this message, he met Casey who, though he did not commit himself, Stettinius thought would be interested and also available. From this meeting Stettinius was "coming around to the view" that Casey might prove to be an excellent candidate.[22] In Washington on October 8, Hiss informed Paul Gore-Booth, the first secretary of the British embassy that he assumed that for the present no American national would be chosen. Personally his first choice, he explained, was Robertson, and he dismissed the candidature of the Dutch Foreign Minister, Eelco van Kleffens, on the grounds that he was an overly cold person.[23]

By the time Gore-Booth's version of this talk arrived in the Foreign Office, the views in Washington on both Casey and Robertson had crystallized further. Those in the State Department who knew Casey's record, Byrnes informed Stettinius, felt strongly that he was not qualified for the post. He did not appear to satisfy any of the qualifications for the secretary-generalship, including familiarity with the United Nations' development. As to Robertson, and in view of the fact that the United States would probably be selected as the site of the United Nations headquarters, the State Department felt that it would "not be proper to push any Canadian" for the secretary-generalship at this time. If Robertson was suggested as a candidate, Stettinius should not take any action which might discourage Robertson's selection since Washington still felt that he was "one of the most able men available."[24] This message reached London, however, only after the Big Five had met on Stettinius's invitation to discuss the matter. Stettinius, as we shall see, began to conduct his own personal foreign policy above and beyond that of Washington.

The Emergence of Trygve Lie

At the meeting called by Stettinius for October 8, Noel-Baker instructed Webster to procrastinate inasmuch as he had not yet discussed the matter with Foreign Secretary Ernest Bevin.[25] Stettinius emphasized the need for the Big Five to come to a decision in order that exploratory steps could be taken to ascertain whether their candidate would accept the invitation. He was ready to discuss specific persons and hoped that the others present were likewise ready. Accordingly Stettinius offered five names for "consideration and discussion": Pearson, Robertson, Parra Pérez, Casey, and Van Roijen. He pointed out that all of these men were nationals of "middle or small powers," and as he had previously explained to them, Washington felt it preferable to have a national from among these states appointed as secretary-general. He then observed that with the aid of his subordinates he had prepared another "purely personal" list that he would offer for the purpose of showing the kind of person they were contemplating.

Neither in his communication to the State Department about this meeting nor in his meeting with Byrnes on October 22 did Stettinius make any mention of this second list or that he had proposed any other names aside from those just mentioned. The reason for this becomes apparent as, although the second list began with Bruce (whose name Stettinius had been instructed to drop), it then surprisingly included mainly Great Power nationals. First were the Russians Maxim Litvinov, the former foreign minister; Ivan Maisky the former ambassador in London; and Arkadi Sobolev, the embassy's counsellor in London. The Russian names fell like a bombshell. To redress the balance Stettinius then proposed the Englishmen Anthony Eden; Lord Cranborne, the former Dominions' secretary; Richard Law, the former minister of state; and Oliver Franks, the ministry of supply's permanent under-secretary. He likewise included the Chinese Koo, and Tingfu Tsiang, representative on the United Nations Relief and Rehabilitation Administration. The list concluded with Norway's Socialist Foreign Minister Trygve Lie—the first time he had been mentioned—Erik

Boheman, the secretary-general of the Swedish Foreign Ministry, and Van Kleffens.

Stettinius's performance had been irresponsible, Webster noted in his diary, and the French representative, René Massigli argued that it was really a matter for the council whose nonpermanent members might be offended if the Big Five arrived with their own candidate. Furthermore, the United Nations headquarters site was not yet settled and the choice of secretary-general depended to a certain extent on this question. Webster had little to do but associate himself with Massigli and urged that more exploration of the matter was necessary. The Russians and Chinese observed that under the circumstances they did not want to nominate anyone at that time. Stettinius then proposed that, rather than dictate to the council, they narrow the names down to two or three on the assumption the site would be in the United States and another two or three names on the assumption the site would be outside the United States. Once the site was chosen, the Big Five would then be in a position to make a final choice. Neither Massigli nor Webster encouraged this proposal. Although Stettinius pressed for another meeting on the matter, he was "somewhat dubious," he informed Byrnes, "of reaching any conclusions" on the question.[26]

Stettinius's deceitful behavior toward his associates in the State Department and his crass performance during this meeting of the Big Five leaves one breathless. Far more important, however, are the origins of his purely personal list, which Stettinius claimed he had prepared with the assistance of his subordinates. The documentary evidence tells us little aside from the fact that the names on the list had been "suggested from time to time."[27] But who had suggested these names? No doubt some of them had been suggested by his subordinates. One can assume that, as Stettinius's deputy, Stevenson was one of them. Another probably was Hiss, who had "close and daily ties with Stettinius" and who admitted he had "helped in preparing instructions" from August 16 to December 23 for the American delegation at the Preparatory Commission.[28] This possible association of Hiss with the Russian candidates proffered by Stettinius, as well as with Lie, who as we shall see was Moscow's real choice for secretary-general, acquires interest in view of the subsequent charge against Hiss of being a Russian agent. What better way for Moscow to channel Lie's name into the general discussion about possible candidates for the secretary-generalship than through the State Department?

Stettinius's machinations the next day, October 9, annoyed the British even more. Without first consulting Noel-Baker, a member of Stettinius's staff approached Sir Gladwyn Jebb, presiding over the United Nations Preparatory Commission, and informed him that the United States delegation would support his candidacy as secretary-general. Webster thought this was a move by Stettinius, who did not want as secretary-general an eminent American that would detract from Stettinius's own importance. In rejecting the offer, Jebb replied that a British secretary-general would be a fine idea and suggested Law. Noel-Baker thought that although Jebb longed for the job he was unsuited to be secretary-general. Webster pressed Noel-Baker to do something about the matter before the whole position could be compromised. Accordingly, he instructed Webster to draw up a new cabinet paper dealing with both the site and the related question of the choice of secretary-general.[29]

Webster argued in his paper that if the site was in the United States, it would be impossible to appoint an American as secretary-general. His alternative suggestion was a Canadian. The selection of an American would, of course, reflect the present position of the United States in world affairs. Unlike the site decision, that of the secretary-general would be only a temporary one since the first secretary-general might serve only five years and certainly not beyond ten. His conclusion was that London should continue to press for establishing the United Nations site in Europe, simultaneously proposing that the first secretary-general be an American.[30]

In a long note to Bevin, Noel-Baker emphasized that Stettinius might at any time make a bargain with Russia and China on this question. An American appointment would be popular in the United States and also help to maintain the United States' "interest in Europe." The problem was that Stettinius would discourage an American appointment because it would detract from his own position, which he jealously guarded. Although Stettinius would support a British national for the office, Noel-Baker did not see any suitable candidate, a view shared by Sir Alexander Cadogan, the Foreign Office's permanent under-secretary.

Under these circumstances the best thing to do might be to advocate a Canadian. Accordingly, he proposed Pearson. Noel-Baker would have preferred someone of higher caliber, but it appeared that finding one would be somewhat difficult. He suggested that Canada's Prime Minister Mackenzie King be consulted about Pearson and Robertson and, without committing London, attempt to ascertain whether he would wish Great Britain to place either name in nomination, if London considered it possible to secure the assent of the rest of the Big Five. Bevin might also authorize Noel-Baker to explore the situation in Washington regarding both the site and an American or Canadian secretary-general, without committing himself except to say that London wished to discover the best possible person for the job. Perhaps, he concluded, Bevin might want to discuss the whole question with Prime Minister Clement Attlee.[31]

However, before the British even approached MacKenzie King, Stettinius called on him and asked for his views of Pearson and Robertson. Because of Robertson's exhausted state Mackenzie King thought Pearson might make a better secretary-general.[32] On the following day, October 13, Mackenzie King observed to Noel-Baker that an American should not be barred if the site were in the United States—a comment that undoubtedly pleased the Minister of State. Indeed, he maintained that having an American as the first secretary-general might be advantageous. His own choice was Winant. When Noel-Baker raised Pearson as a possibility if an American were not chosen, Mackenzie King was non-committal but obviously pleased.[33]

Almost two weeks later, however, when Noel-Baker raised the subject of an American secretary-general with Byrnes in Washington, he encountered a somewhat cold reception. Byrnes felt that somewhere "there should be found a capable, competent person" and, if the United Nations were located in the United States, his "common sense" would tell him that an American should not be appointed to the office. Byrnes did not think the new world organization should be dominated by the United States.[34]

This same day, October 24, the State Department's Division of European Affairs opined that because Robertson had "been of incalculable assistance" as under-secretary for external affairs, as well as for other reasons, his removal would be disadvantageous to United States–Canadian relations. However, if Pearson were removed from Washington, no matter how outstanding an ambassador, he was not irreplaceable. Deputy Director of the Office of European Affairs John Hickerson scribbled his agreement and added that, if the site was in the United States, obviously a European as secretary-general would be obligatory unless one wanted to label the United Nations as an exclusively American show.[35]

In a memorandum to the cabinet, Bevin pointed out Washington's opposition to establishing the site in the United States. The present situation, he explained, was largely due to Stettinius's personal desire. In this he had been assisted by Gromyko, who had other motives. Stettinius maintained that a site in the United States would cause the Americans to take a continuing interest in the world organization. Gromyko hoped that, with an American site, the United Nations would have less power in Europe, where Russia had its chief interests.[36] By October 30, Bevin and Attlee decided that the best candidate would be Pearson, provided that Mackenzie King agreed. For different reasons, therefore, the Americans and the British had converged on the same candidate. Cadogan, who was present during this meeting, presciently noted that the Russians might object to a North American secretary-general if the site were established in the United States. On the other hand, with the site outside the United States, it would be best to have an American secretary-general. If Eisenhower were unavailable, it seemed agreed that Stettinius would be suitable. It was believed undesirable, if not also impracticable, Cadogan concluded to Jebb, to pick a national of a small power as secretary-general.[37]

Jebb responded that the selection of Sobolev, raised by Cadogan as a possibility should there be Russian pressure, would not likely be acceptable to others. On the other hand, Stettinius's appointment would be a disaster and Eisenhower was far preferable. Stassen, Jebb thought, would be the best American candidate, but he also raised for consideration several senators, including Arthur Vandenberg of Michigan. How, Jebb queried, could Bevin and Attlee square Pearson's selection with the belief that it was undesirable, if not also impractical, to have a national of a small state as secretary-general? To Jebb, a national from one of the Big Five, or preferably from the Big Three, was better. Why the reluctance to nominate a British candidate? If the site were in the United States it was highly desirable to have an English-speaking secretary-general, though clearly not an American.[38]

Reading these communications years later, one stands in wonder that the names of Russians and Americans would be bandied about so freely as potential candidates for the secretary-generalship, especially considering that these were not the thoughts of novices but of experienced senior officials. It underscores as nothing else can the politization of both the office and the office holder that occurred during the intervening years. Similar communications among senior officials today would be unthinkable. On this question, however, Noel-Baker—unlike Stettinius, the Foreign Office's senior officials, or even his cabinet colleagues—appears to have been devoid of altruism. To Noel-Baker it was clear that the appointment of a Russian secretary-general was absolutely out of the question. And, if an American secretary-general became necessary, it should certainly not be Stettinius but Eisenhower or Winant.[39] Although these British discussions had not resolved the matter, they had spotlighted Pearson's name and narrowed the list of other potential candidates.

In mid-November, the State Department forwarded to the American delegation in London its tentative slate of candidates. Feeling that it would be extremely difficult for the Big Five to agree on one of their nationals, the State Department argued that a national of a middle or small state should be chosen. The selection should be based primarily on the person rather than on the country, since much would depend on the secretary-general's ability. Because objections might be raised to a candidate from the country where the United Nations was established, or even from a neighboring state, it was thought inadvisable to push Robertson's candidacy or that of any other North American. On the other hand, no opposition was to be offered to the selection of a qualified North American if broad support was to develop.

Spaak and Van Roijen, whom the State Department now proposed as candidates, appeared to satisfy the qualifications described. The fact that they were Europeans, Washington observed, might assuage the feelings of those who wished to see the United Nations established in Europe. Other candidates also acceptable to the State Department were Robertson, Pearson, Bruce, Auguste De Schryver (Belgium's minister without portfolio), and Jan Masaryk (Czechoslovakia's foreign minster).[40]

Curiously, in early December, the rumor began to circulate in London that Washington desired the United Nations site in Europe because it really wanted an American secretary-general. This had been preceded by private reports to the State Department of another London rumor that Stettinius desired the office. Because of this, Washington supposedly did not want the site in the United States. The State Department denied this, pointing out that Stettinius was not interested in the position and that he had made this clear to numerous people in London when they had casually raised with him the possibility of his candidacy. The American delegation therefore was instructed to point out that Washington had held the consistent view that the secretary-general should not be a national of any of the Big Five countries. Who started this rumor and whether it was some sort of trial balloon is unclear; but, considering the views of some on the British side, it probably originated within official British circles.[41]

In all these preliminary discussions,[42] the Russians, as we have seen, proposed no one for the position. On the morning of December 17, however, following the decision to establish the United Nations headquarters in the United States, Gromyko made his move. He called on Stevenson, who had replaced Stettinius as the American representative on the United Nations Preparatory Commission. Without wasting time, Gromyko pointed out to him that Soviet Russia had supported Washington in establishing the United Nations site in the United States. In an obvious bid for a quid pro quo, Gromyko now wished to know the American view on the candidacy of Stanoje Simić, Yugoslavia's ambassador in Washington and former ambassador in Moscow. Gromyko thought some Big Five discussion about the secretary-general might be in order. When Stevenson questioned him about second choices, like Van Kleffens, Gromyko gave no hint that he was interested in anyone except Simić.

Stevenson suspected that Gromyko had proposed Simić's name for "trading purposes," he signaled Washington, to enable him to "make an important concession to unanimity" among the Big Five, and particularly with the United States, in order to get a sympathetic hearing for "his candidates for General Assembly positions." Stevenson preferred, if possible, to have Simić removed from consideration by one of the other Big Five. Perhaps the State Department might inform him, Stevenson suggested to Acheson, that it was willing to consider the credentials of all candidates, including Simić, and hold off for the present from giving its most recent thoughts on the entire subject.[43] Several days later, Stevenson informed Acheson that the names of Jean Monnet, the league's former deputy secretary-general, and Sir Archibald Clark Kerr, the British ambassador in Moscow, had also been "seriously advanced" as possible candidates by Stevenson's London friends who were not connected with the United Nations.[44]

But Acheson was annoyed with Stevenson's comments to Gromyko, particularly his espousal of Van Kleffens's candidacy, and his instructions reflected it. The State Department had hoped that Stevenson would not—the negative repeated—consider Van Kleffens as a substitute for Van Roijen. Referring to Van Kleffens, Acheson felt the job of secretary-general was not one for a man about to be retired. Moreover, the State Department understood that Van Kleffens was in poor health. In the absence of more concrete evidence from the Dutch authorities that Van Roijen was unavailable, Washington did not wish to drop his name as a possible choice for secretary-general.[45]

Acheson also had some thoughts on Gromyko's attempt to acquire American support on the grounds that Soviet Russia had supported the establishment of the United Nations site in the United States. Stevenson, if he felt it useful, could inform Gromyko that Washington was grateful for Moscow's vote and support but that the American government was in no way obligated to any country by reason of its support in this question, since the United States had not sought the establishment of the United Nations on its territory.

As Stevenson knew, Washington's preference was for Spaak or Van Roijen. Acheson suggested that Stevenson might wish to inform Gromyko that the American preference was based upon the State Department's "judgment of their competence and the probable reaction of other countries to their candidacies, and not upon the fact that they were from a particular geographical area." However, this preference should not be interpreted to mean that the State Department "would oppose other competent candidates who might be proposed." Although it felt that no candidate from the Americas should be pushed, a candidate should be judged "upon his merits." It would be unfortunate if the secretary-general's position "should devolve upon some individual because he was from a particular geographical area rather than because of his competence"—a hope no doubt, that Robertson and Pearson would not automatically be excluded from consideration. In addition, Washington felt that the time had arrived to discuss candidates among the Big Five rather than bilaterally, and Stevenson's arrangement with Gromyko for a Big Five meeting to discuss possible candidates was approved.[46]

By December 24, Koo's preferred candidates for secretary-general were Pearson, Van Kleffens, and Spaak in that order. As to Gromyko, he was greatly disappointed that Washington's initial reaction to Simić had been "unfavorable and foresaw 'difficulties.'" Although there had been no "affirmative response" to Van Roijen's candidacy, Stevenson promised to continue to keep his name and Spaak's in the discussions. Three other names, Stevenson noted, had also been added to London's gossip: Sir John Anderson, Britain's wartime minister of the exchequer; Thanassis Aghnides, the Greek ambassador in London and former league undersecretary-general;

and finally, Sir Ramaswami Mudaliar, India's representative on the United Nations Preparatory Commission.[47]

Several days before Stevenson sent this information Acheson had informed him that, since the United States had been chosen for the United Nations' site, it was likely that there might be a preference for a European as president of the assembly. In that case the United States continued to favor Norway's Trygve Lie,[48] reflecting a decision that had been taken by the State Department in mid-November.[49] On this question, Stevenson reported that Noel-Baker was very partial to Spaak although, to satisfy Russian objections, he would be willing to accept Masaryk or Lie, in that order. Interestingly, Noel-Baker objected to Lie "on personal qualification grounds in contrast to Spaak's ability and elocution." Stevenson observed, however, that there appeared to be "little interest" in a Norwegian president for the assembly. Some concern was expressed that a Norwegian president might find himself in a "somewhat embarrassing position" vis-à-vis Soviet Russia—an allusion to Norway's contiguous border with that country. Leaving aside some Latin American support for Herbert Evatt, Australia's foreign minister—based on his leadership of the small states at San Francisco and Latin American fears of the assembly's domination by Soviet Russia—diverse official sentiment in London seemed rather "strongly to favor" Spaak as assembly president. Gromyko, to put it mildly, was "lukewarm" about the possibility of Spaak being elected as president. Yet, Spaak might accept the position since it would probably permit him to continue his involvement in Belgian politics.

At the same time, there was very little support for Spaak as secretary-general, since it was doubtful that he would be willing to divorce himself from Belgian politics. Moreover, it was thought that Russian opposition would be "far stronger" to Spaak as secretary-general than as assembly president. From these comments, it was obvious that Spaak's chances of being chosen secretary-general were slim. Stevenson's subsequent comments, moreover, were also discouraging. In London, he observed, there was now "little enthusiasm" for Van Roijen or Van Kleffens. The delegation had also discovered, without mentioning Simić's name, that there would be "strong opposition" to any Eastern European as secretary-general, especially from Latin American states. Although not inspired by the delegation, it would be so construed by the Russians.

On December 24 an informal and unofficial meeting was held at Gromyko's apartment. Stevenson noted all the names that had been offered during the preceding weeks, including Simić's, but explained that only Spaak and Van Roijen had received Washington's formal approval. The question was then raised whether the discussion should be one of "names or principles." Koo questioned whether an American was excluded from consideration and whether a North American or national of one of the Big Five countries might be considered. Gromyko suggested that a North

American be excluded, thus rejecting the candidacies of Robertson and Pearson. Webster countered that no one should be excluded and only the "best man" should be selected. As to Simić, he thought him insufficiently experienced. In Webster's judgment, Simić could not compare with Spaak in competence and experience or in the favorable reaction manifested by others. Gromyko "did not press hard" for Simić, and Stevenson thought he "was following instructions with [the] full realization of the futility [of Simić's candidature] but with the expectation that his bargaining position would be improved."

Webster then divulged that his government's first choice was Eisenhower. Gromyko asked if he had other choices, but Webster did not respond. Stevenson proposed that perhaps candidates from among the Big Five, aside from Eisenhower, be ascertained. The only name Webster casually mentioned was Tsiang. He then asked whether Stevenson could discover if Eisenhower would be available. If not, there appeared to be "general and tacit agreement" to proceed with the consideration of other names as no American except Eisenhower seemed to be under consideration. Webster and Gromyko then rejected Van Roijen. At the same time, Webster and Koo were keen on Pearson. Stevenson concurred but explained that, since Pearson was from North America, Washington was reluctant to press his candidature. He also expressed reluctance to dismiss from consideration all Big Five possibilities until every name had been canvassed. On his part, Webster rejected his fellow countrymen: Anderson, Eden, and Sir Arthur Salter, the former director of the league's Economic Section, as well as Monnet.

In a discussion of the assembly president there was greater consensus. Stevenson, Koo, and Gromyko all expressed a preference for Lie. Webster preferred Spaak and felt that this in no way excluded the Belgian from consideration as secretary-general. Some days later, Lie's possibilities further improved when he replied to a query from Stevenson that he would be receptive should movement commence to elect him president of the assembly.[50]

Eden's candidacy as secretary-general had been pressed by Winston Churchill and South Africa's Prime Minister Jan Christiaan Smuts, as well as by others. His rejection by the Americans and British disappointed Eden,[51] who traced it in part to personal hostility toward him harbored by certain high officials of the Labour party since the 1930s.[52] Webster's inquiry concerning Eisenhower for secretary-general moved Washington to instruct Stevenson that he should "endeavor informally to discourage" any further consideration of Eisenhower's name.[53] This stance was buttressed by a public statement from Byrnes on January 11.[54] It was a predictable position in view of Washington's consistent policy that nationals of the Big Five countries be avoided and that the person selected be someone from a small or middle power.

On the Russian side, Foreign Minister Vyacheslav Molotov raised the issue with Byrnes on Christmas Day at the Moscow Conference of Foreign Ministers. There was no American candidate for the office, Byrnes assured him. Molotov noted that Simić among others had been proposed, and he thought Simić "would be very suitable since he was a non-party man, an experienced diplomat and objective in his views." Byrnes explained that neither he nor President Truman was supporting any particular candidate.[55]

Since Mackenzie King was not keen on losing Pearson to the United Nations, and undoubtedly to head off such a move, he suggested in early January 1946 that the British high commissioner in Ottawa, Malcolm MacDonald, be nominated for the position.[56] In view of London's adamant attitude against the candidacy of a British national, the proposal was stillborn.[57] On January 5, 1946, the State Department reduced its candidates to Spaak, Van Roijen, Pearson, and Robertson.[58] Of the four, Spaak's chances were the strongest, but he was also the candidate Moscow opposed most strongly. With some justification,[59] they considered him "an exponent of a Western European bloc."[60] Spaak's election, however, as president of the first assembly would remove him from consideration as secretary-general. Moreover, if Lie, who was first mentioned by Stettinius and was Moscow's real choice rather than Simić, made a good showing against Spaak for the assembly post, his chances for the secretary-generalship would be greatly improved. For, with the United Nations site in the United States, a European, not a North American, would have to be chosen, and Lie's only competitor was Van Roijen, to whom even the British objected.

Trygve Lie's Recommendation and Appointment

In this setting, Spaak decided in late December to withdraw his name from consideration as secretary-general. He hoped to become Belgium's prime minister, which the presidency of the assembly would not preclude as would the secretary-generalship.[61] Although Lie had been confidentially approached by Stettinius in August and by Stevenson in late December as to whether he would consider the presidency of the assembly,[62] Spaak's decision moved the Americans, along with the British, French, and Chinese, to agree on January 9 to Spaak's candidacy for president of the assembly. Gromyko, during this discussion, warned he would formally oppose Spaak's election and would support only Lie. Cadogan thought that Gromyko had instructions on this point and could not be moved.[63] An embarrassed Noel-Baker then informed Spaak that his election was impossible: he was opposed by Moscow. The Americans in turn did not wish a conflict with the Russians over this question, whereas the British did not think it wise to agitate matters just prior to so important a meeting of the assembly.[64]

The next morning, January 10, Gromyko vigorously returned to the attack. He threatened he would vote and speak against Spaak. He complained that Spaak's candidacy had been "built up without consultation" with Moscow, and that this was an inauspicious way to commence the assembly. In the face of Gromyko's onslaught Stevenson caved in. He noted that he would recommend to his delegation to support Lie, despite his previous day's explanation that the general support that he found for Spaak dictated that he would endorse him for the presidency of the assembly. The French likewise "wobbled," Cadogan observed, while the Chinese, he thought, would also vote for Lie. Cadogan predicted it would be a close election and that Spaak might be beaten. Britain needed at least ten Latin American votes. This appeared possible, for Stevenson revealed that, while informing the Latin Americans that the United States would vote for Lie, "he would leave them to vote as they chose."[65] Stevenson in fact informed Webster that he thought most of the Latin Americans would vote for Spaak.[66] In actual fact they voted for Spaak, as we shall see, though it would appear that the American delegation despite Stevenson's statement had applied a "'five line whip'" against their Latin American counterparts to vote for Lie.[67]

Stevenson's voltes-faces, now one way, now the other, leave one dizzy. Understandably, the British were not amused, and the proverbial wash had to be hung out on the line. As Byrnes explained to Bevin, only minutes before the assembly convened, six weeks previously Stevenson had informed Gromyko that the United States favored Lie's election as president of the assembly. When it was recently decided not to press Spaak for secretary-general, but as president of the assembly, Stevenson advised Byrnes that it appeared that the majority of the states favored Spaak. However, Gromyko then told Byrnes that Stevenson had asked him six weeks previously to support Lie. After consulting Moscow, Gromyko was instructed to do so. In view of this agreement and in view of Stevenson's first approach to Lie in late December, Byrnes determined that it was America's duty to vote for Lie, regardless of how the vote went. Who presided over the assembly was not as important as keeping faith with Oslo and Moscow. Although he advised Gromyko that the United States would vote for Lie, at the same time it would not attempt to influence how other governments voted.[68] Byrnes noted to Bevin that America was honor bound to execute this arrangement, which he had known nothing about until Stevenson confirmed it when questioned by the delegation.

What had occurred was "unfortunate," Bevin observed, and also somewhat "improper." He thought it wrong to decide so important a post "on such a low level" and then keep the British government in "total ignorance." Regardless of what happened later that afternoon, he feared he would be placed in a very "embarrassing position." Bevin felt, however, that he had to stand by the decision to support Spaak. Byrnes responded that he would second Lie's nomination—he did not, as it later turned out—and promised, as had Stevenson, that the Latin Americans would not be pressed to vote for Lie. Bevin held that this kind of "wire-pulling" was wrong and would bring the United Nations down in exactly the same way as the league was destroyed.[69]

Bevin's restrained anger can well be appreciated. It certainly must have given him a jaundiced view of Byrnes, and especially of Stevenson. For Stevenson to have solicited an agreement with Gromyko about Lie as assembly president without consulting the British, French, and Chinese and without concluding a parallel agreement with Gromyko about who was to be secretary-general, was duplicity and ineptness of a high order. One suspects that, by the time Stevenson struck this agreement, the wily Gromyko was probably already aware of Spaak's decision to drop his candidacy for secretary-general—a suspicion not unreasonable in view of the fact that the British knew of Spaak's decision as early as December 30.

Stevenson's machinations, of course, also placed Lie in a quandary. His first impressions were that everyone wanted him as president of the assembly. However, he found the possibility of running against a British-supported Spaak unattractive, especially when the Americans informed him that Spaak would win by a wide majority and that they would refrain from pressuring the Latin Americans who were partial to Spaak. On the morning of the vote, however, Lie was cornered by the Russian ambassador in London, Feodor Gousev, who explained that Moscow and the Eastern European states wanted to nominate him. When Lie proposed that Dr. Eduardo Zuleta Angel, the assembly's temporary chairman, be allowed to continue as president, Gousev demurred. Instead, he divulged that, on hearing of Lie's withdrawal, the Russians had consulted the Americans and they had agreed to continue to support his candidacy. It was the opinion of the Norwegian delegation that refusal of the proffered assembly nomination might be misconstrued by Washington and Moscow and be detrimental to Norway's interests. Thus, Lie did not object to his nomination and explained what had developed to the British.[70] As far as Moscow was concerned, although Spaak would be a nuisance as president of the assembly, this would be limited to the duration of that particular session. Moscow's eyes were on the secretary-generalship, which entailed a longer tenure and was intrinsically a political post as great as, if not greater than, the presidency of the General Assembly. The Russian ploy therefore was to have Lie not elected as president of the assembly but to garner enough votes to make his subsequent candidacy for the secretary-generalship far more creditable. How could this be done?

When the election of the assembly's president commenced, Byrnes, despite his comments to Bevin and assisted by the unclear rules on balloting procedures, remained silent. Gromyko, however, immediately placed Lie's name in nomination and spoke of him in glowing terms. He was then seconded by Poland's Foreign Minister Wincenty Rzymowski, who in turn was followed by Dmitri Manuilsky of the Ukraine. Although Lie was also supported by the Danish foreign minister as a sign of Scandinavian solidarity, the whole procedure could only have appeared as a Russian steamroller, especially when Manuilsky, who had acquired from the San Francisco Conference "a reputation for charming ruthlessness," moved that Lie be elected by acclamation. This display of "more ruthlessness and less charm . . . caused a strong adverse reaction." Thus, Spaak's name was never officially offered in nomination, and when Manuilsky's acclamation motion was put to an open vote, it was rejected.[71] These Russian actions were undoubtedly calculated, for Moscow could not have been unaware, as Stevenson had reported to Washington, that the Latin American states were concerned that a Norwegian president of the assembly might not be able to hold his own against Soviet Russia.

Even if the Americans pressured the Latin Americans—something that Byrnes denied[72] and British information held had occurred—the Russians maneuvers could only have reinforced the suspicions of the Latin Americans and others and sealed Lie's fate when the secret balloting began. "'Soyez tranquille, tout ira bien, l'Amérique latine vote pour vous,'" whispered the Bolivian representative to Spaak.[73] During this period, about twenty states in a total United Nations membership of fifty-one were Latin American. Thus, if most of them voted for Spaak he would be elected and this is exactly what they did—one of the earliest examples of bloc voting in the assembly. When it was announced that Spaak had been elected by a vote of twenty-eight to twenty-three, there was a "gasp of surprise."[74] By their tactics, the Russians had garnered Lie twenty-three votes but likewise had guaranteed his defeat.

Lie himself was "furious" with the Americans for seemingly having abandoned him, while the Russian tactics, especially Manuilsky's, were not appreciated. John Foster Dulles, who was a member of the American delegation, thought the whole affair had been "handled very badly" and that the afternoon's proceedings had "lacked dignity."[75] They certainly had. If Lie had received limited support, Byrnes noted, the Russians doubtlessly would have been "humiliated." However, the votes that Lie received left them "agreeably surprised."[76] Unlike Byrnes, not all the participants in this Russian display were fooled. Webster, for one, was not taken in and noted that the great performance staged by the Russians and "their stooges" in Lie's favor had probably elected Spaak.[77] Similarly observant were the Turks, who believed that Moscow's "sponsorship of Lie against Spaak for President of [the] General Assembly was [a] maneuver to ensure Lie's election as Secretary General."[78] By the time this message arrived in the State Department, Lie was well on his way to being appointed to the office.

What followed Spaak's election was really an anticlimax. The State Department, flinging its net as wide as possible, asked twenty-two of its diplomatic missions to recommend anyone from their host country who might be considered as potential candidates for secretary-general. The names that flowed back to Washington were like the waters of a river in spate.[79] But it was too late.

In the interim between Spaak's election and the next informal meeting of the Big Five on January 20, the preferred candidate of the Anglo-Americans continued to be Pearson.[80] Although Gromyko continued to press for Simić,[81] Lie's pronouncements on international questions were quoted at length by the Russian press,[82] a not so subtle sign that his star was in the ascent.[83] At about the same time the French were "suggesting Lie as the European most likely to be acceptable to the Russians."[84] Discussing the situation in Washington, the perceptive Acheson informed Pearson that he thought it likely that Moscow would abandon Simić's candidacy and "might concentrate on Lie" though he did not consider Lie "a very impressive candidate."[85]

The Big Five meeting on January 20, however, continued the deadlock. While Byrnes, supported by Bevin and Koo, pressed Pearson's candidature, Gromyko rejected it on geographic not personal grounds and again proposed Simić. The French offered their ambassador in Washington, Henri Bonnet, for the post. It was then decided to have an informal meeting of all the council's eleven members on the following day. This meeting was also inconclusive, although eight of the members supported Pearson's nomination. The search for a consensus candidate continued at an informal meeting of the Big Five on January 23. The candidates examined were Pearson, Lie, Simić, and Rzymowski. Russia's Deputy Foreign Minister Andrei Vyshinsky maintained that, since the United Nations site was in the United States and the organization's basic activity and many of its branches would be in Western Europe, "the secretary-general should come from a Slavic country of Eastern Europe." Byrnes dismissed this argument and on grounds of personal competence pressed Pearson's candidature. Gromyko now pressed Rzymowski's candidature. Byrnes's comment that Washington had not sought the United Nations site and his suggestion that this matter might have to be reopened appeared to cause Vyshinsky some worry. He promised to ask Moscow for further instructions. It was agreed to hold an informal meeting that afternoon with all the council's members present in order to discuss other candidates and hear from its nonpermanent members. It was understood that if this informal meeting failed to produce a consensus, the council would then convene a formal session and vote, even if the lack of consensus among its permanent members made impossible the selection of a secretary-general. The council's informal meeting was accordingly held but with inconclusive results.[86] Since Byrnes was leaving for Washington, Stettinius needed authority to act. They decided that Stettinius was to support Pearson, then Lie, and finally, Koo. No one else mentioned was acceptable without additional consultation.[87] Byrnes then contacted Bevin who agreed to accept Lie, but he would not do so until he knew the Russians would accept a compromise. Vyshinsky, who had been approached by Byrnes, was willing to agree on Lie. Accordingly, as the satisfied Stettinius wrote, he now had "authority to bring Lie forward as our man when I think the time is ripe."[88]

Discussing the situation several days later with Pearson in Washington, Byrnes was less than candid. He thought that the Russians might put Lie's name forward as the consensus choice. If this were done, Washington would accept Lie rather than force Moscow into casting a veto against him. Since he was not seeking the post, and if it would ease the situation, Pearson was willing to announce that he was unavailable. Byrnes responded that he should let the situation crystallize and make no move to withdraw his name from consideration.[89]

In freewheeling discussions within the American delegation on January 22, 25, and 26, Pearson's candidature was not contested. However, some like Senator Vandenberg and Dulles argued that it had not been pressed with sufficient vigor. The question of Lie's candidacy was another matter. It evoked considerable discussion of whether Norway fell within Russia's sphere of influence, whether Lie himself was under Russian influence or could be dominated by Moscow. Dulles felt that Lie had been Moscow's candidate from the start. But Lie would obviously be less amenable to pressure than a Yugoslav, Pole, or Czechoslovak secretary-general; and the time had passed for considering new candidates. Moreover, it was doubtful that a national from any country other than Norway would satisfy both Washington and Moscow. Lie appeared to be the only candidate for second choice. It was therefore decided that Pearson's candidacy would be pressed with the Russians and, if he were unacceptable, Stettinius was to shift to Lie. It was likewise decided to resolve the whole issue at the next informal meeting of the Big Five and not embarrass the council's nonpermanent members by asking them to vote on competitive candidates.[90] The die for Lie's election had been cast.

Lie, of course, was aware that he was being considered for secretary-general,[91] although his own recall of these events in later years was imperfect and necessitated appeals to others for their recollections.[92] Because he was being seriously considered, the Norwegian delegation decided that Lie should return to Oslo to confer with the government about accepting the post if it were offered. Before his departure he consulted the Big Five. The Americans and Russians encouraged him to go to Oslo and made clear to him that they were favorably disposed to his candidacy,[93] although Eleanor Roosevelt thought that Lie resented being considered a Russian tool.[94]

Koo was firmly convinced that the Russians would not accept Pearson and would be prepared to veto his candidacy in a public session of the council if this proved necessary—obviously an inauspicious way to launch the United Nations. Koo thought the Russians were hoping that someone would propose Masaryk's nomination. If there were no consensus on Masaryk they would be willing to accept Lie. On January 28, Bevin, on

Stettinius's suggestion, arranged with Vyshinsky another informal Big Five session. Before the meeting was convened, however, Gromyko reiterated to Stettinius that Moscow would not agree to Pearson but intimated that the Russians might be amenable to accepting Lie. Stettinius made no reply.

The American decision therefore was to propose Lie as a compromise candidate in order to acquire the greatest possible advantage from unanimity and to avoid Lie's being publicly characterized as the Russian candidate.[95] The meeting was therefore a kind of pro forma performance. Vyshinsky made it clear that Moscow would no longer insist on Simić or Rzymowski, but it could not accept Pearson. Stettinius asked for reactions to Lie. After some discussion Vyshinsky said he would accept Lie on his own responsibility. The French and British also agreed, subject to confirmation from their governments,[96] which soon followed.[97] The Norwegian government raised no objection to Lie's selection though they were apprehensive that it might in some way "involve international complications for them."[98] Lie was contemplating the job, the State Department was informed from Oslo, because he felt "his and Norway's balancing act between east and west" in the previous months might become "increasingly difficult not to say impossible in the near future."[99] For a moment, Lie hesitated: as Norway's Foreign Minister, "'his present seat is smaller but safer,'" the Foreign Office was informed by the embassy in Oslo.[100] He then accepted: "I could hardly refuse," Lie wrote later.[101]

On the afternoon of January 29, the council in a private meeting informally recommended Lie for the office and several days later he was appointed by the assembly as secretary-general, though there were several abstentions and three votes were cast against him.[102] He was a "poor choice," Webster noted in his diary, and "on the verge of being a stooge—perhaps not consciously but subconsciously," because Norway was very frightened of Russia. He was vigorous but far from clever or well-educated. Lie's swearing in had had a certain dignity;[103] but Webster categorized his address to the assembly as "second rate."[104] Thus, the person Noel-Baker had described as "third rate"[105] and Acheson had called an unimpressive candidate had been made secretary-general.[106] On the very day Lie was recommended for the office by the council, the State Department was informed by its mission in Norway that Lie was "clearly not an ideal choice" for the position, though he could be "rated highly." The mission's superficial observation was that Lie was a "loyal and enthusiastic" supporter of international organization and cooperation. More to the point, though Lie had shifted away from the formation of a western European bloc and Norway's participation in such a bloc, the mission did not believe that he was fundamentally any more pro-Russian than he had ever been nor that he would be pro-Russian as secretary-general. Indeed, his inclination would be the other way around. Ebullient and somewhat mercurial, Lie's greatest drawbacks appeared to be a lack of experience in running a large organization and his lack of a wide educational and cultural background and training. He would, however, work hard and loyally to make the United Nations a success.[107]

What can be made of these extended and serpentine negotiations? On the Russian side, Western documents reflect an apparently firm and calculating desire to protect Russian interests: skill in tactics and strategy, as well as vigorous campaigning for what Moscow desired through negotiation and debate. The Western powers, especially the United States, appear in disarray, adopting and trying to implement contradictory policies. One would be hard pressed to point out more amateurish behavior than that manifested by Stettinius, and especially Stevenson. The Western powers were unable to act forcefully: as Bevin was unwilling to act,[108] when Russian tactics contributed to Lie's defeat and Spaak's election as president of the assembly; as Byrnes was unwilling to act, when the United Nations' site was established in the United States, thus destroying Pearson's chances and, as Hiss warned, when Spaak's election would encourage Lie's candidacy and "make it difficult, if not impossible" for Washington "to oppose it directly or indirectly."[109]

But this whole procedure was not to be repeated. Experience proved to be the greatest teacher. Lie's election and tenure taught Washington and the West in general, especially during the Cold War, that the office of secretary-general was intrinsically political and that the candidates' subsurface political values and attitudes were all important. Negotiations to elect Lie's successors were as extended and serpentine as those that led to Lie's selection; but altruism was a scarce commodity on both sides and Moscow's initial success with Lie was not repeated so blatantly.

PERSONA AND POLITICS

A Question of Suspicion

London's doubts about Lie's fitness to be secretary-general were shared with Ottawa only on the eve of his appointment, and hence too late to affect events.[1] The misgivings of a senior Foreign Office official were detailed to the State Department by John Winant. Lie, the senior official observed, had a limited knowledge of international relations. In particular, two of Lie's failings appeared to be his great self-confidence and ambition. Lately, "yielding to his ambitions" Lie had "consistently leaned toward the Soviet view on the issues of the day." It was the opinion of his friends, however, that now that he was secretary-general and certainly after he was ensconced on the eastern seaboard of the United States, he would "'find his balance'."[2] Christopher Warner, the Foreign Office's assistant under-secretary repeated somewhat similar information to Sir Laurance Collier, the ambassador in Oslo. Warner also noted that during the first General Assembly's proceedings Lie, on the surface at any rate, appeared to be in Russia's pocket. Apart from being Moscow's candidate for the presidency of the assembly, and also second on its list for the secretary-generalship, Lie's speech in the assembly's opening debate sounded like one from the "Slav bloc." At the tail end of his speech he "dragged in the Fascist bogey."

This last point, Warner had learned, was omitted in the initial draft of the speech prepared jointly by the Norwegian delegation, then reincluded at Lie's insistence. The British delegation's impression was that Moscow was subjecting Lie to a "mixed policy of pressure and prizes."

In fairness to Lie, it had been pointed out to Warner that Norway had supported Great Power hegemony at San Francisco, where Lie's work probably attracted the Russians' attention. One could also reasonably contend that the motives of Oslo's anti-bloc posture were not only that it could not afford to manifest an anti-Russian stance on any matter on which Moscow had strong views but also that Lie had arrived at a similar conclusion to one reached in London. This was that, in striving for cooperation among western Europeans, more could be achieved by concentrating without fanfare in setting up "practical links" in limited areas (economics and military, for example) and shunning more dramatic dispositions and publicity. Of course, Lie was a natural candidate for Moscow to run against Spaak. Once Lie knew that the Russians were thinking of him as a possible secretary-general, he would have been superhuman if he had not adjusted his conduct accordingly.[3]

Collier's own opinion was that Lie, "though not positively unscrupulous," did not offer the impression that he possessed a "firmness of moral character equal to the acuteness of his intellect or the width of his sympathies." He was more a Charles James Fox than a William Pitt, Collier observed. Like Fox, however, Lie was capable of attracting individuals who could not wholly approve of him. Collier himself admitted such an attraction. He regretted Lie's departure as foreign minister for personal as well as political reasons and was not likely in the future to be able to convey London's point of view to the Oslo authorities "through so understanding or sympathetic a channel."[4]

Although Collier paid tribute to Lie's abilities, noted Clifford Heathcote-Smith of the United Nations Department, he appeared to have doubts whether Lie was the appropriate person for the post. It was to be expected that Lie's appointment would be regarded as a compromise, he noted, but it was probably the best appointment that could be made under the circumstances. It was to be hoped that Lie would "tread the middle path without deviation" and that he would not be moved by considerations of Norway's physical proximity to Russia or by the remoteness of the American headquarters site from possible centers of conflict.[5] A "judicious commentary," Phillip Noel-Baker observed. Whitehall in the future had to attempt always to render Lie "full support" when he was right and, by doing so, display and "emphasize his best qualities."[6]

In his last word on the subject Collier noted that Lie had to consider Norwegian interests. According to Lie, he had decided to allow his candidacy for assembly president to proceed "when the Russians intimated that his refusal to stand might disturb Russo-Norwegian relations." In essence, Lie like other Norwegians feared Soviet Russia and that, Collier thought, largely explained his actions.[7] It was interesting, Warner cynically observed, "if literally true," that Moscow had threatened Lie with a disturbance of Russo-Norwegian relations, if he did not run for assembly president. Lie did not, Warner gathered, claim that he had to be "bullied" into accepting the secretary-general's office.[8]

All these Foreign Office comments were largely subjective. It is unclear to what extent they were influenced by the Oslo legation's 1937, 1938, and 1939 reports on Norway's leading persons contending that when Lie was legal adviser to the Trade Unions Federation (1922–1935) he "was said to be a communist."[9] Lie, however, would have found it harder to fend off the more objective and empirical observations of the State Department's Division of European Affairs. The division credited Soviet Russia's support of Lie's candidacy as stemming directly from his November 1944 trip to Moscow, which, as we will see, was only partially correct. During this Moscow trip, the division alleged, Lie had apparently made a very positive impression on the Russians. In the opinion of George Kennan, the counsellor of the embassy in Moscow, Lie's visit had been a wise step. It had aroused, at least in the Foreign Ministry, a distinct desire to show Soviet Russia's capacity for generosity toward states that approached it with confidence and welcomed Moscow's assistance and protection. Since the November trip, Lie had "made intensive efforts to improve Norwegian-Russian relations." Along these lines he had concluded an agreement in principle with Moscow, without consulting London or Washington, to establish a joint Russian-Norwegian defense of the Svalbard (Spitsbergen) archipelago; reiterated his conviction that Russian forces would evacuate northern Norway, which in fact occurred; succeeded in including two Norwegian Communists in the coalition government established after Norway's liberation; consented to the establishment of a large Russian power-station near the frontier that might cause serious flooding in Norway; eulogized Soviet Russia in a speech commemorating the Russian revolution; alluded to Oslo's dissociation from any possible Scandinavian bloc that Moscow frowned on; hushed up border incidents that involved the shooting of Norwegian peasants and livestock; and succeeded in appointing a Communist to Norway's United Nations delegation against Labor party opposition.

Despite his pro-Russian attitude, the division concluded that Lie on balance actually preferred Great Britain and especially the United States. He had felt free to show a seeming preference for the Russians because of his belief that Oslo's relations with London and Washington were on a far firmer footing.[10] Perspicaciously, Pearson later wrote that the socialist Lie "may have been the choice of the USSR from the beginning," which doubtless thought he "would be more amenable to their policies."[11] Or, as Lie saw it, Moscow had "to find a man who, without being committed to the East, was not hostile to it"; and Moscow felt he was such a man.[12] The Russians had good cause for this belief, having had their eyes on Lie for almost twenty-seven years. They had probably first noticed him in 1918 when Maxim Litvinov and his entourage were expelled from Great Britain and escorted to Norway, where they were "put up by their Socialist friends"[13] before being exchanged for the British diplomatic agent in Moscow, Robert Bruce Lockhart, an exchange that Lie appears to have had a hand in arranging.[14]

Lie's radical leftist orientation did not go unnoticed by the Americans and French either. In late September 1919, Lie's name was included in a list of over four hundred known and suspected Norwegian bolshevists sent to the State Department by the legation in Oslo. The list indicated that Lie was "well identified as a bolshevist and, usually, that further information [was] readily obtainable." The legation noted correctly that on the day of Norway's general strike, July 21, Lie had given a speech on Norwegian militarism at *Folkets hus*, the trade unions' cultural and social center. This information was identified as having been furnished by the French military attaché, who seemed "excessively pessimistic and disposed to include names of Socialists who are not at all bolshevistic."

However, the legation was unsure of their man. Was he the Trygve Lie, it queried, who was an employee of the Norges Bank and an auditor of the Norges Brandkasse living at 5 Kronprinsensgate? This Trygve Lie lived at that address throughout the interwar period, as the Oslo telephone directory shows. The legation, to identify their man, had simply turned to the telephone directory of May 1919, where the namesake had listed his occupation and address.

The name of the future secretary-general of the United Nations did not appear in the telephone directory until July 1923, where he was correctly identified as an "O[ver] r[etts] sakfører" (a barrister) living in Grorud, a suburb of Oslo.[15] The question of identification was not raised again in late February 1921, when the Lie name was included by the legation in a supplementary list sent to Washington of persons "engaged in bolshevik activities in Norway," but then neither was the question cleared up.[16]

The September 1919 list was conveyed by the American to the British legation, which in turn sent it to their Foreign Office.[17] Here, it was sent to the director of intelligence, Sir Basil Thomson,[18] who, in view of his penchant for opening dossiers on British "subversive" elements,[19] probably opened dossiers for everyone mentioned in the list—albeit, in Lie's case, for a namesake in a different occupation and at a different address.

Within postwar American official circles Lie's political orientation appears to have been first raised as early as January 1947. In a talk at the State Department, Ambassador Guillermo Belt of Cuba complained about Lie's recent visit to Latin America, which he tied to the newly established United Nations Associations. In Cuba, he claimed, the association was definitely under leftist, and perhaps communist, control. He alleged that Lie was a Communist.[20]

The assistant to the director of special political affairs, Robert McClintock, opined that Lie was "certainly far from being a Communist."

His trip had nothing to do with the United Nations Associations in Latin America and had simply been an attempt to stimulate government interest and support for the United Nations in the states he visited.[21]

The trip did show, however, Lie's lack of political sophistication. This was mirrored in his comments that he had been impressed by the great poverty in the area, especially because of its proximity to the United States, the world's richest nation. He could not fathom, Lie observed, why Washington continued to pour huge sums into remote areas of Europe (Norway, perhaps?) and Asia, while apparently overlooking deplorable conditions closer to home. He ruminated that Soviet Russia had received scant recognition for the great work it had accomplished in reducing illiteracy. Moreover, it seemed "inconsistent" that the United States should insist upon democratic governments in far-off Europe and the Balkans, while in the Americas it tolerated governments of the opposite persuasion.[22]

If nothing else, Lie's remarks showed his failure to understand the political struggle being waged around him. To Washington during this period, the perceived area of conflict and danger was not Latin America but Europe and Asia; and assistance to these two areas, especially of an economic nature, was of the highest political importance. Lie's remarks about Russia's conquest of illiteracy, as though this had been achieved without intrinsic losses in other directions, was a non sequitur since the Communist party's absolute internal control necessary to achieve this success, could never be wielded by the United States in Latin America.

His remarks also reflected the naive notion that somehow Washington's strength was limitless and its mere intervention in Latin America would be sufficient to roll back the historical, political, cultural, social, demographic, geographic, and other intangible factors that had contributed to the poverty of the area. It was a pedestrian view, divorced from the immediate priorities and choices that Washington had to tackle at this juncture. Equally naive was Lie's notion that somehow the struggle between East and West was basically ideological in nature, which exposed his own ideological underpinnings, rather than one of political, military, and strategic considerations, in which the ideological factor was manipulated by both sides, who in concrete situations were moved more by the adage that the enemy of my enemy is my friend.

This attitude helps to explain Lie's subsequent enthusiasm for President Truman's Point Four program of aid and assistance to underdeveloped areas. Here also, however, Lie appears to have missed the bus when he held that the program "could never be realized without UN leadership and guarantees,"[23] as though the program was some sort of worldwide humanitarian endeavor unmotivated by political considerations and hence to be generously funded but not controlled by the American government.

Lie's political activities during the interwar period did not come to the attention of the United States' Federal Bureau of Investigation until mid-July 1947. Fortuitously, in an examination of certain old bureau files, Lie's name was noted on a list of names and publishing houses each with a foreign address.[24] This document and others had been seized by the New York City police and made available to the bureau, following the arrest of several prominent communist leaders in April 1921.[25] According to the list, Lie was a law student residing at Grorud, Oslo, Norway.[26] Actually, by this point, 1921, Lie had already acquired his law degree. The discovery of this material led Director J. Edgar Hoover to alert the New York office and request that it "establish definitely the exact nature of this list by an examination" of its files. In view of Lie's position any additional inquiries were to be "handled in a most discreet manner" and nothing was to be said that would indicate that the bureau was investigating him.[27]

Because the New York office was unable to find the 1921 list in its own files,[28] Hoover instructed that it "discreetly attempt" to secure a copy of the court transcript since the list had been offered as a trial exhibit, in order to ascertain what witness identified the list, the nature of the identification, and the witness's testimony relating to the list. If this proved impossible, Hoover suggested that the page listing Lie's name be detached from the document, and the remainder of the list then shown to two individuals, one of whom was a bureau informant, in order to obtain their "separate opinions as to the nature or purpose of that list of names."[29]

The court transcript, however, shed little light on the list of names. The bureau's informant likewise was unable to give an "opinion as to the nature or purpose" of the list. The second person interviewed stated that he could only hazard a guess as to the list's purpose and nature. Based on its wide array of names and addresses he held that the list "had been compiled by American Communists in order to develop sources and contacts among Communists, Socialists and Laborites abroad, and that the list could, therefore, be labelled, in a sense, a mailing list." In line with this opinion, he "discounted the notion that there was anything secretive or sinister about the list."[30] Faced with this report, the bureau decided not to disclose to the State Department that Lie's name had appeared on the list, for the simple reason that the document "was not identified as being a list of Communist or Communist sympathizers."[31]

Lie's youthful political wonderings were then recounted in the October issue of the rabid anticommunist periodical *Plain Talk*. A copy was then sent, by whom it is unclear, to every Latin American delegation at the United Nations. Its comments about Lie as well as certain members of the secretariat staff sufficiently disturbed Cesar Acosta of the Paraguayan delegation that he queried a member of the American mission about the periodical. He was assured that *Plain Talk* had a limited circulation, "was very reactionary in character," and tended to see "*Red* in everything." These assurances appeared to satisfy Acosta who admitted that he had been "somewhat concerned over the article."[32]

There were no further developments for over a year. Then in early September 1948, Attorney General Tom Clark brought to the attention of Secretary of State General George Marshall a memorandum he had received from the deputy commissioner of the Immigration and Naturalization Service. The memorandum pointed out that during investigations the service had interviewed Ruth Fischer, a former secretary of the German Communist party, as well as Louis Budenz, a former editor of the Communist party's *Daily Worker*. Fischer declared that she was once called to Moscow. En route, she met Trygve Lie, who Fischer maintained was then a member of the Norwegian Communist party. As to Budenz, he claimed that Lie had long been known to him as a Communist party member. Since Lie had been in Moscow in 1921 and 1934, it is conceivable that Fischer indeed met him. However, there is absolutely no credible evidence to show that Lie was ever a member of the Norwegian Communist party.

The deputy commissioner then pointed out that in the headquarters agreement between the United States and the United Nations, deportation proceedings could not be instituted against anyone at the United Nations before obtaining the secretary of state's prior approval, which could be given only after consulting the secretary-general or the appropriate state if a representative of a United Nations member was involved.

Clark's letter was passed along to Dean Rusk, director of the Office of United Nations Affairs, who observed to Marshall that the deputy commissioner's report did "not contain sufficient facts on which to base an independent judgment." From this report it would be difficult to state whether Lie "was supposed to have been a Communist at some earlier date or is supposed to be one now." In addition, it would be difficult to ascertain whether Fischer and Budenz "were involved in a communist inspired grudge."

There were few people, Rusk continued, who operated as much in a "goldfish bowl" as Lie did. One of his closest associates was his American executive assistant, Andrew Cordier, whose loyalty could not be questioned. All of Lie's official acts were subjected to close examination by the diplomatic representatives accredited to the United Nations. Espionage activities by Lie would be very difficult to conduct for obvious reasons. Rusk's recommendation was that Marshall not respond to Clark's missive but simply take note of the information that it contained. Clark's information was an added reason to exercise the care that had to be exercised anyway in the conduct of American foreign relations in the United Nations.

Marshall took most of Rusk's advice to heart but replied to Clark and noted that the matter obviously required the "exercise of the utmost discretion." Before he could form an opinion on the matter he needed considerable additional information. When and where, he queried, was the testimony of Fischer and Budenz given? When was Lie a member of the Norwegian Communist party? On what did Budenz base this? It was also important to know whether there was "substantial and reliable evidence" that Lie had "engaged in any activity detrimental to the security of the

United States" since becoming secretary-general.[33] Marshall had neatly thrown the ball back into Clark's court. However, since this exchange occurred during the beginning of the Berlin crisis, it certainly must have cast doubts on Lie's creditability, especially in private, about his political initiatives to reach a peaceful settlement of the dispute.

Faced with proving its case, the Immigration and Naturalization Service approached the Federal Bureau of Investigation and requested a "name check" on Lie. The bureau recommended, however, that the request also be routed to its espionage unit for information though not for action.[34] Lie was slowly being enmeshed in the bureaucratic web of Washington's security services. The name check request was acted on and a memorandum drawn up based on a review of the bureau's records.[35]

The memorandum pointed out that no actual investigation of Lie had ever taken place. It then rehashed the discovery of his name on the 1921 list and noted that the bureau's files contained "considerable heterogenous information" about Lie from many divergent sources, although this data appeared to be of "little real evidentiary value" on Lie's status as a Communist. Nevertheless, the memorandum discerningly concluded that the bureau's information was of "sufficient value to suggest . . . the not too remote possibility that [Lie] is a tool of Russia and a man that the Soviets can rely upon in a crisis."[36] Even excluding the pejorative use of the noun *tool*, this description of Lie is not too far from the truth, in the sense that Moscow perceived Lie as a person malleable enough to be shaped and molded to apologize and explain away Soviet Russia's actions in world politics.[37]

In the years that followed all the bureau's information on Lie, some of it dubious, was passed on to the relevant government agencies, especially to the Security Division of the State Department.[38] The bureau, however, would have been derelict in its duties if it had not done so. In early 1952, the State Department's Division of Biographic Information was asked for any evidence to be used in refuting press charges that Lie was a Communist or had a pro-Soviet Russian record. By this point, the Korean War was in full-swing and Lie was firmly in the Western camp. In a balanced and thoughtful reply, the division correctly noted that there was "no evidence available that Lie, in either a private or public capacity, ha[d] ever expressed himself or acted in a manner indicative of views toward the USSR more favorable than that of the Norwegian Labor Party itself."[39]

With Lie's departure as secretary-general in spring 1953, he became the focus of attention not of the bureau but of the Immigration and Naturalization Service, especially when the press announced that he would return to the United States in the autumn to attend the assembly's debates as a private citizen and give a series of lectures.[40] After reviewing Lie's file, the Inspections and Examinations Division of the service did not think that sufficient information existed to exclude Lie under the Immigration and

Nationality Act. The file was then forwarded to the deputy commissioner for a decision on whether the case should be investigated further. The commissioner thought that the matter should be discussed with the Department of Justice.[41]

The service then decided to ascertain the State Department's attitude: whether it would deny Lie a visa and, if his admissibility were challenged at a port of entry, whether this would cause an "undesirable international incident."[42] The formula devised to avoid any awkward situation was to admit him under a special section of the Immigration and Nationality Act.[43] For a moment the service, it appears, may have dabbled with the idea of recruiting Lie as a possible informant, but one of its senior officials wisely advised against it.[44] In the end, the necessary instructions were issued, and Lie was duly admitted when he arrived in New York.[45]

In the years that followed, whenever Lie entered the country, the service dutifully informed the bureau as well as the Central Intelligence Agency of his presence.[46] Although Lie was never under physical or electronic surveillance, he certainly had not quenched the suspicions that some persons had of him.

What is one to make of Lie's early political career, which begins with leftist activism in the period before the First World War and continues into the interwar period with an attraction to the Russian Revolution? Family poverty explains the former, as we shall see, whereas in retrospect the latter can be traced to the impact of the First World War and the Russian Revolution on Lie's generation. To the young especially, the Russian Revolution appeared to be the dawn of a new age, although the realities that the revolution unleashed soon dissuaded many of its benignity. Whether Lie's activities were syndicalist, as claimed by some Norwegians as well as Bruce Lockhart, is open to discussion.[47] Suffice it to say that, viewed on a broad political spectrum, Lie's youthful leftist-oriented outlook with time developed into an ambivalent ideological attitude toward Soviet Russia. This is not to say that he was pro-Soviet Russia or a crypto-communist but merely, like many of his generation, sympathetic to the social engineering being attempted in Soviet Russia, although as a citizen of a free and open society he was probably appalled at the price in human freedom and suffering that this entailed. Indeed, Lie "referred to Communists in a derogatory fashion," the American ambassador in Oslo reported in summer 1949, denied that he had ever been a Communist, and "repeatedly emphasized [that] he [was] strongly opposed to communism now."[48] This was undoubtedly true, certainly by August 1949, and was reflected that October in Lie's satisfaction that the Norwegian Communist party's representation in the Storting had been reduced in the recent elections.[49]

Although Lie as a leftist was moved by horizontal class loyalty regardless of nationality, he was also moved by a vertical national loyalty to Norway. These coequal but diverse loyalties produced difficulties whenever

Norway's relations with her powerful Russian neighbor had to be considered. Norwegian governments attempted to have, if not intimate relations, at least "correct" relations with their great neighbor, to use diplomatic parlance. In 1922, Norway had been among the first to recognize the new communist regime. Because of their common boundary line Norway appreciated Russia's interests in northern Europe, especially in the Baltic area; and this appreciation persisted with the wartime Norwegian government sitting in London, whose foreign minister was Lie.[50] Accordingly, Lie had a healthy respect for the Russians, combined with "a mixture of awe and fascination,"[51] which partially explains his malleability as perceived by Moscow. The Kremlin was not unaware of these diverse ideological, personal, and national considerations in dealing with Lie and in justifying its actions and often knew which string to pluck and when, in order to seduce or to frighten him, as he attempted to steer the United Nations through the postwar world of international politics. Lie would always subject similar actions by the West to higher standards of conduct, greater suspicion, public criticism, and, even more important, to any public or private political pressure that his office could muster. He was to have, at least until the Korean conflict, two sets of norms; or, to put it another way, two sets of hurdles, in which the Russian one was always several pegs lower, despite Lie's denials that this was so.

Political Maturation

Lie's leftwing politicization began early and can be traced to what is euphemistically referred to as a deprived childhood. His father died when he was young and his widowed mother was hard pressed to make ends meet. By 1911 this family situation, no doubt influenced by the industrial milieu in which he was growing up, led to Lie's close association with the Labor party that continued during his years as a student at the University of Oslo.[52] At best, it was probably a dreary life of constant toil. What emotional scars or resentments it produced can only be imagined. As Lie stoically noted years later, he "had never been used to luxury and had had a hard life in his youth."[53] True enough.

During his years in the Labor party, as Lie subsequently admitted, he had "an entrée into the Kremlin which few non-Communists have had." He met Russia's top leaders during trips to Moscow in 1921, 1934, and 1944.[54] And, why not? The Norwegian Labor party was one of Europe's most leftist-oriented parties.[55] This background helps explain Lie's trip to Moscow in 1921 as part of a Labor party delegation to negotiate with Lenin, Trotsky, and Zinoviev the terms under which the Labor party would adhere to Moscow's-controlled Comintern.[56] The Labor party's honeymoon with Moscow continued until 1923, at which point it severed its Comintern connections although it failed to join the Second Socialist International.[57] It was probably during these honeymoon years that Lie, along with other prominent members of the Labor party, was a recipient of Moscow's largess.[58]

Between his 1921 trip to Moscow and his 1934 trip, which was to define the relationship between the Norwegian Workers Sports Association and the Russian-based Red Sports International,[59] Lie acquired increasing influence and power within the Labor party as he climbed its bureaucratic ladder; his activities did not go unnoticed and unreported by either the American or British legations in Oslo.[60]

Lie's most significant interwar experience with the Russians occurred in 1935–1936, when he was minister of justice. During the Moscow show trials of Stalin's old bolshevik associates in the late summer of 1936 Leon Trotsky, who had been given asylum in Norway by Lie and the Labor government the previous year, was accused as the defendants' main instigator.[61] Instructed to protest orally about Trotsky's activities in Norway the Russian minister in Oslo was somewhat embarrassed about how he was to proceed since he "was doubtful as to how the most important words" in his instructions should be translated. He first saw Lie, who was acting foreign minister and subsequently the foreign minister. However, the words the Russian minister used to the former "were a great deal stronger than those he used to the latter."[62] Lie and most of his cabinet colleagues appear to have panicked. Trotsky was put under house arrest on the charge that he had violated the conditions of his residence permit. Three days later the Russian minister requested that Trotsky be expelled from Norway. Since the official and written request had come three days after Trotsky's detention, Lie was able to claim that it was not because of Russian intervention that he had placed Trotsky under house arrest.

Understandably, Trotsky had nothing but contempt for the Labor government and especially for Lie. He called him "Stalin's accomplice" and compared Lie to Burgomaster Stockman, the villain in Ibsen's *Enemy of the People*. When Lie demurred, Trotsky retorted that the Oslo authorities had all the vices but none of the virtues of a bourgeois government and rejected his proffered hand.[63] Subsequently, the charge was raised that Lie had done "Stalin's bidding."[64] In light of the archival evidence now available, the charge appears to have greater substance than when Lie wrote his memoirs as secretary-general. Certainly in Moscow the whole episode, in line with its prior scrutiny of Lie, must have given the Kremlin a measure of the man that was less than flattering.

The credits, if any, that Lie had stored up in Moscow in his handling of Trotsky were soon expended when, as minister of supply, he publicly supported Finland during the Russo-Finnish war and repeatedly attempted to give the Finns material assistance.[65] Lie's actions should have alerted Moscow to the fact that, although he might have the greatest empathy for it, especially in trying to appreciate its interests in northern Europe and in other areas as well, an attack on a small state, either directly or through a client state, might not find Lie in its corner. As the State Department noted just prior to the San Francisco Conference, Lie insisted "upon [the] rights, privileges, and duties [of] small nations."[66] As secretary-general he stressed that small nations had equal rights with big ones as a principle of the United Nations and the establishment of this principle as necessary if peace and freedom were to be supported worldwide.[67] In Norway's case he was convinced that Oslo should not allow itself to be kicked about among the Great Powers,[68] "who collectively," Sir Gladwyn Jebb noted to the cabinet, "seem to arouse all his class-consciousness."[69]

Wartime: Lie and the Russians

When he assumed Norway's foreign ministry in the exiled London government in 1941, Lie soon discovered, as had his predecessors, that Russian interests and desires in the far north did not necessarily dovetail with those of Norway. The Svalbard (Spitsbergen) archipelago was a case in point. A Russian proposal in summer 1941, that the island group be occupied by an Anglo-Russian force in order to deny it to the Germans and protect any American-Russian supply route via Greenland-Iceland-Spitsbergen, drove Lie to object ostensibly on the grounds that Norwegian territory would be occupied without Norwegian military participation. Lie's suspicion that Moscow had ulterior designs on the islands in order to ensure the Russians an outlet to the Atlantic was probably the real basis of the Norwegian objection. Doubtlessly to assuage Lie on this point the Russians, reeling from the blows of the advancing Germans, assured him and the British that they had no designs on Norwegian territory.[70]

The Norwegians and Lie obviously had little faith in the Russians. This explains Lie's desire, expressed to Eden, that the government-in-exile be informed beforehand, in order to expedite Norwegian cooperation, should military operations be contemplated in Norway.[71] In step with this attitude he resisted successfully Moscow's desire for a Russian-Norwegian pact of mutual assistance, which was rejected as not necessary and ill timed in view of the fact that Finland had joined Germany and was at war with Russia.[72]

Lie's attempt to placate the Russians when possible caused Norwegian opposition elements to accuse him of "inadequate appreciation of the Soviet danger and undue subservience to Soviet interests." Naturally, Lie's Labor party colleagues were very sensitive to this charge.[73] The accusation was unfair, for Lie certainly appreciated the danger that emanated from Moscow. In fact, by early October 1942, the British ambassador accredited to the Norwegian government suspected that Lie now feared a Russian demand for bases in northern Norway.[74] In an attempt to obviate a Russian advance across northern Finland and hence to northern Norway, Lie tried to remove Finland from the war. During a trip to Washington in the early spring of 1943, Lie, at the request of Secretary of State Cordell Hull, willingly acted as a go-between with the Finnish minister in Washington to explore the possibilities of opening negotiations between Finland and the Allied Powers.[75] However, the attempt to remove Finland from the war failed.

By mid-January 1944, on the eve of the Russian drive into Finland and subsequently into northern Norway, Lie partially drew back from his previous policy of North Atlantic defense encompassing the littoral states. In a broadcast to occupied Norway—his comments appeared in the clandestine press—Lie noted that wartime experience had shown that a "free and independent Norway" was of the "same importance to the Soviet Union as to the other Great Powers, and we look forward to close and useful cooperation with the Soviet Union after the war." For the postwar period Norway naturally stressed "an international organization which could be supplemented by an agreement embracing the lands around the North Atlantic." This presupposed that any such agreement "would be subordinated to an international organization and accompanied by an extension of our good relations with the Soviet Union."[76] The head of the Foreign Office's Northern Department, Christopher Warner, noted that, whereas earlier Norwegian policy statements had "talked of regional arrangements *preceding*" the establishment of a world organization, Lie had admitted to him that this reversal in policy was to take account of British and American views. But Warner thought that it was "also probable that it was done with one eye on Russia."[77]

On January 24, Lie raised with Warner the danger of Russian forces moving into northern Norway but was assured of the physical difficulties involved and reminded that Moscow had "recognised that Norway lay within the Anglo-American military theatre."[78] Obviously unassuaged, Lie returned to the problem the following month in a conversation with Sir Orme Sargent, the deputy under-secretary. He attempted to ascertain whether the British government would elaborate plans to occupy northern Norway if and when the area was evacuated by the Germans. If not, it conceivably meant that the oncoming Russians might "break into Northern Norway and occupy the country indefinitely." The area was so sparsely settled, Lie observed, that the occupying Russians would outnumber the indigenous Norwegians. In addition, a German occupation of northern Norway, coupled with a possible Finnish surrender to the Russians, made it more important than ever that a liberation agreement for Norway should be signed by the British and American governments and accepted by the Russians. It could then be evoked should Russian troops enter northern Norway.[79]

In March, Lie then proposed to Moscow that about 1000 Norwegian troops fight alongside the Russians and under Russian command in northern Russia.[80] This ploy to establish a Norwegian military presence should Russian troops advance into northern Norway went no further. Stubborn

Finnish resistance delayed the Russian advance along the Arctic coast. It was not until October, after Finland withdrew from the war that the Russians crossed the border into Norway. Moscow's silence to the March offer of troops, however, made the government-in-exile increasingly uneasy.[81]

At this point, Moscow requested the government-in-exile to discuss questions relating to Russian military operations in northern Norway. After a ten year hiatus, Lie was once again in Moscow. In the course of this November 1944 visit, Foreign Minister Molotov raised the Svalbard question. He suggested a revision of the 1920 treaty, which had demilitarized and neutralized the islands and also recognized Norway's sovereignty over the archipelago. Molotov held that the treaty conflicted with Russian interests and that Moscow in 1920 had been in no position to partake in the treaty negotiations. He explained that Moscow's subsequent adherence to the treaty had been under pressure. Taking an essentially *rebus sic stantibus* tack, Molotov argued that, because of changes in the relative positions of the powers since 1920 and Moscow's role in the present war, as well as sentiments on the matter in Soviet Russia, his government felt it was imperative to abrogate the treaty. He proposed that Byørnøya (Bear Island), one of the smaller islands in the archipelago and originally Russian, be ceded to Russia and the rest of the island group be placed under a Russian-Norwegian condominium. Molotov maintained that the islands affected Russia's northern security as well as her economic interests, and Moscow intended to raise the matter with the other allied signatories of the 1920 treaty but first wanted to reach a settlement with Norway, since it primarily concerned their two countries. Pointing to a map, Molotov observed that Soviet Russia was bottled up at the Turkish Straits as well as the Öresund, which connected the Baltic with the Kattegat. He concluded with the menacing observation that it was always preferable to settle such questions in an amiable fashion and avoid an argument.

Rather than remind Molotov that three years earlier Moscow had assured him and the British that it had no designs on Norwegian territory, Lie merely noted that he had had no indication that the Svalbard question would be raised and thus was not prepared to discuss it. He pointed out that Norway's sovereignty over the islands was established and that the archipelago and its surrounding waters were of great economic importance to his country. He promised, however, to refer the question to the Norwegian government in London upon his return.[82] In view of Norway's weak diplomatic and military position at this time, Lie's Fabian stance was justified.

Upon his return to London, Lie quickly established a committee, which he chaired, to examine the question and posit the Norwegian position. It decided to recognize Russia's security interests but to avoid discussions on repeal of the 1920 treaty or on Russia's territorial desires. Accordingly the possibility of militarizing the archipelago, including Bjørnøya, was proposed to Moscow provided this revision of the 1920 treaty was acceptable to the allied signatory powers. In addition, it was emphasized that the government-in-exile had no constitutional power to come to any final settlement, which could only be done once Norway was liberated and the Storting could make the final decision. Molotov however, responded that the Norwegian "reply did not go far enough to satisfy the wishes of the Soviet Government."[83]

In the negotiations that followed the Russians renounced their claim to Bjørnøya and desisted from demanding a Russian-Norwegian condominium over the archipelago. Moreover, Moscow emphasized that prospective arrangements should not cause Norway any economic losses. By the end of March 1945, the committee members were jittery and felt that the Norwegian position was so insecure that a formal treaty should be proposed on joint Norwegian-Russian militarization of the islands to safeguard the concessions made by the Russians over their initial demands. The final decision, however, was to ask Moscow only for a joint declaration until Norway was liberated. Molotov agreed, provided that Norway and Soviet Russia came to an agreement before jointly referring the question of treaty revision to the other signatory states. Such an arrangement "severely inhibited Norway diplomatically" and in particular discriminated against third party signatories like Great Britain and the United States. Nevertheless, a joint secret declaration on April 9 agreed to the following: the 1920 treaty's neutralization of the islands was impracticable and conflicted with Norwegian-Russian interests; the defense of the archipelago would be a joint Norwegian-Russian concern; the defense measures would be in accordance with arrangements that might be made by a world organization to which both states were members; lastly, the declaration touched upon installations, equipment, costs, the composition of forces, and other military matters. As one student of these negotiations noted, the agreement seemed "an undue compliance" by the Norwegian government; but when viewed in its proper time frame it appears very different. Naturally "there could hardly be any doubt as to the consequences of the arrangement, if it were put into practice."[84]

Upon his return from Moscow and before he began his negotiations with Molotov, Lie informed Eden of what had occurred.[85] In January 1945, no doubt to strengthen Norway's military and diplomatic position with Great Britain, Lie accepted Eden's offer of equipment and training for the Norwegian military.[86] He likewise attempted to arrange for Swedish armed intervention in northern Norway under certain circumstances.[87] In May, during the San Francisco Conference, Molotov again mentioned the Svalbard question to Lie.[88] Finally in early July, following the return to Oslo of the government-in-exile, Lie disclosed in a secret session of the Storting the Russian demands on the Svalbard Archipelago. Understandably, the Storting was "much disturbed." Nevertheless it authorized the negotiations to continue on the basis of Molotov's offer to Lie at San Francisco: Norwegian-Russian defense arrangements in the archipelago with recognition of Norway's sovereignty over the area.[89]

Even if one assumes that Norway was negotiating from a weak diplomatic and military position, the key to the problem, as Sir Orme Sargent pointed out to Lie in early March 1945, was that any negotiations could not go far, since they would involve a fundamental revision of the 1920 treaty. No Russian-Norwegian consensus could take effect until the other signatories of the treaty had been consulted and had agreed to its being replaced by a new convention in which any Russian-Norwegian agreement would be fitted.[90] Lie's acquiescence to Molotov's demand that Norway and Russian come to an agreement before jointly referring the question to the other signatories, therefore, was a panic move unjustified in view of the veto held by London and Washington, not to mention Paris, Stockholm, and Copenhagen, to any revision of the 1920 treaty.

Unfortunately for Lie, in the long run his role in these negotiations dogged him during his tenure as secretary-general. Indeed, when he was scheduled to call for the first time on Secretary of State Marshall, he obviously was so sensitive about the issue that the State Department thought he might raise it with Marshall, although it had nothing to do with his activities as secretary-general. Marshall accordingly examined the pertinent file.[91]

Although there was no public criticism in Norway about Lie's role, it was well known that he was "regarded in many quarters as having shown insufficient firmness" when the Svalbard question was initially raised. It also appears to have been the view in 1944 of Prime Minister Johan Nygaardsvold who "had wished to repudiate the whole negotiation but had been over-ruled." Lie naturally defended himself publicly, the British ambassador pointed out, which did "not of course settle the question whether he had committed the Norwegian Government too far" in his initial conversation with Molotov.[92]

In the short run, however, Lie's popularity among the leaders of the Norwegian Home Front and Norwegians in general[93] made it possible for him to continue as foreign minister when the government returned to Norway. When Supreme Court Justice Paal Berg was asked to form a new government the recognition that there was no acceptable candidate aside from Lie "prevented widespread opposition" to his continuation as foreign minister.[94]

Lie's political reliability as far as the Russians were concerned was no secret in Norway's higher political circles. Although Berg seriously thought of yielding to the demands that Lie be excluded from the cabinet, he soon decided to resist this pressure supported by his colleagues as well as by the Labor party leaders. According to the British ambassador, he was also supported by King Haakon, who allowed Berg to let it be known that he considered Lie had conducted his ministerial duties in London successfully. Moreover, Lie's retention would be a pledge to the world, and particularly to Norway's wartime allies, of the continuity of Oslo's foreign policy. In addition, the king noted that Lie's departure as foreign minister "would be badly received in Great Britain and in the United States—to which the Crown Prince added: 'and in Russia, too.'"[95]

Although the Norwegian Communist party was strongly opposed to Berg's candidacy as prime minister, it supported Lie's appointment as foreign minister as denoting continuity in foreign policy.[96] The British ambassador suspected that Lie "may not perhaps be entirely innocent of having canvassed for this support." Indeed, Lie himself admitted that he had had "a busy time seeing representatives of all political parties, 'even the Communists.'" Since the communist press, according to Lie's own admission, was getting its instructions from Stockholm through the Norwegian communist leader Peder Furubotn, this presumably meant "from Moscow in the last resort."[97] Moscow's pound of flesh was no doubt an understanding that Norwegian communists would be appointed to the cabinet, whom Lie subsequently boasted he picked himself.[98] Lie continued as foreign minister in Einar Gerhardsen's coalition government and in his subsequent Labor government in early November.[99]

The autumn elections had been preceded by negotiations to fuse the Labor and Communist parties. Lie regarded the breakdown of the negotiations as an added sign of future difficulties with Soviet Russia. The British ambassador would see, Lie observed, what would happen now: the Communists had attacked, and would attack, other Norwegian political figures and then would attack him—"that being, of course, the climax, in his view," Ambassador Collier signaled the Foreign Office.[100]

Although a large vote was cast for the Communist party, which surprised and disappointed Lie and was of particular concern to him because of the party's ability to "foment illegal strikes,"[101] in fact Lie was not attacked personally. Instead, in early September before the election he queried the Russians when their troops would leave northern Norway and elicited the quick response that instructions had been issued to the military to commence withdrawal. The Norwegian chargé d'affaires in Moscow appeared "very relieved" by the news. On September 16, *Tass* carried an announcement that the withdrawal had already begun.[102]

No doubt in an attempt to show his appreciation, on November 7, Soviet Russia's national holiday, Lie gave a somewhat obsequious speech extolling the virtues of the Russian Revolution and Stalinist rule.[103] To further "soothe Soviet susceptibilities," Lie also granted an interview to Cyrus Sulzberger, the diplomatic correspondent of the *New York Times*. In line with his speech, Lie declared that Norway had no desire to join any international blocs or coalition. His country, he assured Sulzberger, based its foreign policy entirely within the United Nations framework. Although Norway desired to collaborate with other Nordic states, she opposed the idea of a northern bloc, which "would create misunderstanding and mistrust among the Great Powers." Lie later maintained that Sulzberger had "somewhat overemphasized his repudiation of *blocs* in general," which did not imply that he had abandoned his support of common defense arrangements for Western Europe. Nevertheless, Lie hoped that his interview with Sulzberger would "have a good effect in Moscow."[104] No doubt to grease the skids, Lie agreed to the proposal for a Russian power-station on the Pasvik river, despite "strong opposition" from interested authorities, particularly the Norwegian military.[105]

With the Svalbard question seemingly quiescent and to remove any possible Russian excuses for renewed pressure, Lie then hastened the American evacuation of the small Arctic island of Jan Mayen. The government-in-exile had allowed the United States Navy to establish electronic installations there with the understanding that they would be withdrawn after the war.[106] Likewise against the wishes of his Labor party colleagues, Lie included a Communist as an alternate delegate on Norway's United Nations delegation. It appeared to be an attempt to forestall communist criticism in Norway and another gesture toward Moscow, the American embassy noted to Washington.[107] Lie's remarks to the new Storting on foreign affairs, in which he emphasized the special position enjoyed by the three great powers, was an additional nod in Moscow's direction.[108]

One of his close associates wrote in 1946 that Lie had succeeded in winning Moscow's "confidence."[109] The Kremlin's communist statecraft, initially honed by the ideological struggles in Czarist Russia before the Communist party assumed power and by the political struggles of the interwar period, was little moved by intangibles like confidence. One could argue that Moscow had taken the measure of the man and found him weak and easily influenced. Lie's stance was no doubt a reaction partially based on a healthy respect for the Russians, or what Jebb called a "mixture of awe and fascination," and probably, although to a lesser extent, on Lie's ambivalent ideological attitude toward the new Rome of the working classes. His handling of the Svalbard question in line with his early leftist-oriented background, his trips to Moscow, and his action in the Trotsky affair must have assured the Kremlin that Lie was to be preferred over many others for his "understanding" and "acquiescing" to Russian desires. A pliant individual as secretary-general would go far toward fulfilling the Kremlin's postwar tactical needs. The Russians in the long run may have misperceived their man, but Lie's talents in so narrow a field as Norwegian-Russian relations, Moscow undoubtedly thought, should be put to use in a far wider arena.

Character, Personality, Values, and Perceptions

It would not be unreasonable to assert that Lie's character and personality partly negated his public and private initiatives as secretary-general. Although any attempt to sketch these or to examine his views and perceptions is at best subjective, certain features are commented upon so often that they cannot be ignored. According to the State Department's views of him just prior to the San Francisco Conference, Lie was "considered something of a political opportunist."[110] This view was reflected in the terse comment of an American diplomat that Lie was "a politician with a sense of expediency"—a remark that his obituary in *The Times* of London deemed a "judicious assessment."[111] The American view was shared by George Warr of the Foreign Office's Northern Department, who thought Lie a "westerner at heart, so far as his somewhat unstable and unreliable character allow him to have any consistent convictions."[112]

It was a view also subscribed to by Ambassador Collier in Oslo.[113] Indeed, the experienced Rasmus Skylstad, the secretary-general of the Norwegian Foreign Ministry assured Collier with a smile that Lie "was not strong on principle."[114] This view would have been echoed by other Norwegians.[115] It was best put in its United Nations setting in early 1950 by Cecil Parrott, the head of the Foreign Office's United Nations Department, who held that Lie was willing to accept "[a]ny compromise, any shoddy solution as long as the U.N. flag is still left flying at the mast head."[116] Or, as a former secretariat official and student of the office observed, Lie had an "undisguised interest in the substance of political questions" and, although a lawyer, "acted a politician."[117]

The State Department and the Foreign Office also noted Lie's lapses in accuracy as well as his limited foreign affairs background.[118] Lastly, the State Department characterized Lie as an "affable and forceful . . . direct, unpretentious man, with an energetic, enthusiastic manner; hearty and talkative,"[119] qualities noticed by others, including Byron Price, the American assistant secretary-general for administration.[120]

Some other traits made Lie less than endearing. For example, his directness was said to be "ponderous."[121] At the same time he was called vain,[122] a kink in his character that manifested itself in petty ways: he monopolized the use of one of the staff elevators,[123] was concerned with his creature comforts,[124] and was miffed whenever he thought protocol was not being followed and proper respect and deference shown to him and his office.[125] Being greeted by a sufficiently senior official upon arrival and addressed as "Your Excellency" went far to assuage Lie's vanity.[126] In an attempt to raise the symbolic prestige of his office beyond the prerogatives bestowed upon him by the United Nations Charter, Lie pressed hard to be accorded diplomatic precedence equal to, or greater than, the doyen of the diplomatic corp at official functions in national states—a desire that was not universally applauded, although some supported the request in view of the world organization's international importance.[127] His vanity was also reflected in his desire to entertain [128] and probably to be entertained in turn, a condition cleverly exploited at the first assembly session by the Russians, who had previously played up to this vanity,[129] through a number of lunches for him.[130]

Lie was also emotive, his American secretariat associates tell us;[131] but deep down and "thinly concealed," according to Price, "dwelt anxious concern."[132] This might explain what was considered his "touchy"[133] disposition, which was partially reflected in a quick temper that perhaps influenced people, especially in the secretariat, but did not make friends and limited the circle of those he consulted.[134] Woe to any secretariat official who crossed the secretary-general's path, for exile to Geneva would soon follow.[135]

Although he loved outdoor sports,[136] and was especially attracted to American baseball,[137] Lie's girth, traceable to his predilection for what the American embassy in Oslo called "high living,"[138] no doubt was also affected by Lie's interest in television and the sedentary regime it encourages.[139] Lie's excessive weight, however, did not disguise his facial emotiveness,[140] made him appear flabby, and did not project the image of a great leader.[141] With the change in life-style and the seductive glamour and excitement of New York, Lie's girth expanded continually as he socialized with the great, the near great, and the glitterati of Hollywood.[142]

Unfortunately for Lie, his heavily accented, imperfect command of English[143] and lack of French[144] probably hindered his ability to discuss abstract questions dealing with the expansion of the powers and prerogatives of his office. Lie was certainly not unaware of these linguistic shortcomings, for on one occasion he asked the British ambassador in Oslo to transcribe his arguments, "since his command of English was not good enough to enable him to be sure that he had said things in the right way."[145] Lie's imperfect command of English, Jebb informed the cabinet, was one of his "chief disabilities." It was difficult for him to find the right words in any language other than Norwegian,[146] which undoubtedly explains Lie's resistance to public speeches. These speeches were often platitudinous and poorly delivered, even though William Stoneman, his speech writer and adviser, was an experienced journalist. Time and necessity, of course, improved Lie's command of English,[147] but he was never really at home in the language.

Although his imperfect English may partially explain his difficulties in properly presiding over the United Nations and its secretariat, Jebb thought that Lie was "partly by temperament and partly by lack of experience, a bad administrator."[148] His American executive assistant, Andrew Cordier, guardedly described him as a less than "tidy person" when it came to administration or to the use of diplomatic methods and techniques.[149] Cordier himself has been taken to task for contributing to this state of affairs by his inability to organize Lie's mind.[150] Be that as it may, the Australian representative, Paul Hasluck, who was well disposed toward Lie, was perhaps closer to the truth when he noted that Lie was sometimes "clumsy" in the way he handled matters.[151] More specific were the comments of Adrianus Pelt, the Dutch assistant secretary-general of conference and services, who had also served in the league secretariat. He complained that Lie was "too prone to disregard the practical problems of day-to-day operations and too cavalier about the treatment afforded the operating staff in respect to demands put on them and the funds made available."[152] The long and the short of it was that Lie's ways of doing things were ineffective and often counterproductive.

Moreover, Lie's own work habits contributed to this state of affairs. He was not as hard a worker as his Swedish successor Dag Hammarskjöld, in the sense of time spent at the office and at the job, although one could argue that as a family man, which Hammarskjöld was not, Lie had competing obligations for his time.[153] Lie, Jebb noted in early 1947, was "working much harder now than he originally did," and as he informed Jebb in confidence, "'even after dinner.'"[154]

Since Lie did not consistently manage his office affairs, Cordier was somewhat at a loss as to Lie's interest in particular questions. This uncertainty about Lie's stance slowed up Cordier's own work to some degree.[155] The situation in turn was compounded by Lie's disinterest in the secretariat's organization[156] and his proclivity to change his "mind periodically" and fortnightly shift the body of advisers upon whom he relied.[157] Unlike Hammarskjöld, Lie's solution to the problem appears to have been to "delegate responsibilities,"[158] so that with time he "gave up holding regular meetings even of the assistant secretaries-general, who were left to their own devices and to building up their own courts."[159]

Once he made up his mind, however, Lie held steadfastly to his decision.[160] Important as this was, if the United Nations' bureaucratic apparatus functioned at all it was largely due to Cordier who, leaving aside any human failings, was an intelligent, indefatigable, hard-working subordinate. Lie may have had his qualms about Cordier, but he was the indispensable assistant who supplied the missing link among the documents and a necessary conduit between Lie and the State Department or other elements in American society. The Lie-Cordier relationship had its symbiotic aspects but was one from which the State Department also acquired advantages.[161]

Lie's linguistic shortcomings probably reinforced the impression that he lacked intellectual credentials. Jean Chauvel, the French representative at the United Nations, for example, thought that Lie was less than intelligent and that his cordiality was limited, while his frankness was circumscribed by caution.[162] Lie's seeming lack of intellectual substance was noted by others.[163] Provided their assessments were correct, it would go far to explain Lie's lack of an all-encompassing theoretical view, a Weltanschauung, of his office and the world organization that he served. To Lie, it was obvious that the charter did not intend to repeat in the United Nations the restrictive interpretation of the secretary-general's office, which had evolved under Drummond in the league. This view derived both from the charter and the rules of procedure of its different organs, in particular from Article 99 giving the secretary-general the right to bring to the council's attention any matter believed to threaten the maintenance of international peace and security.[164]

The French drew a distinction between the secretary-general's normal duties as the United Nations' impartial servant and what appeared to be the specific powers given to the office under the charter.[165] A reading of Article 99, however, would show that it has its limitations. Even if Lie invoked Article 99 there was no legal obligation for the council to convene, and even if it convened it was not legally obligated to act. Also, Article 99 was no great innovation but merely a public acknowledgment of what Drummond had done behind the scenes, especially during the latter part of his tenure.[166] Then there was the added question, which Lie ignored, of how long any secretary-general could maintain the confidence of a state against which he or she had invoked Article 99. Lie chose the public role for his office, one could suggest, not only for the reasons that he cites in his memoirs but also because it suited his temperament, values, prior experience, and personality. He probably was not unaware that, whereas Drummond eschewed a public role for his office, behind the scenes he was politically influential.

Although Lie had no conceptualized construct for developing the political powers of his office, he was nevertheless determined that in his public endeavors he would be a "force for peace," its application depending on developments.[167] Wisely the Great Powers loomed large in Lie's thinking, and he realized that his work would be unsuccessful if there was no "mutual trust among the big powers." It was here that small countries like Norway had their mission—and by implication Lie himself—to help remove "distrust among the big powers and build bridges between them."[168] The bridge's center span would be the United Nations and the structural engineer monitoring the stresses and strains upon the structure would, of course, be Lie himself. This explains his wish to make United Nations facilities available as a neutral ground for any conference between the top leaders of Soviet Russia and the United States,[169] and his unsolicited attempts to interject himself into questions that might have jeopardized his relations with a number of member states.[170] In a throwback to his Norwegian Labor party experiences,[171] Lie held that compromise, cooperation, and understanding in political questions were tied to democratic values,[172] but he failed to admit, at least publicly, that an important part of the membership did not share those values, a failure that would make bridge building difficult, if not virtually impossible.

One area that allowed Lie free rein to intervene with only moderate risk was over the admission of new states to the United Nations. This vexing issue was a surface manifestation of the political confrontation between East and West. He lobbied for, and publicly preached the notion of, the desirability of universal membership[173]—and correctly so, although he was jaundiced against prospective member states that were dictatorships of the right, like Portugal and Spain, while simultaneously seeming oblivious to the qualities of those that were dictatorships of the left.[174] This in turn led to his involvement in a host of questions that, superficially administrative or procedural, were also political in nature. Too numerous to be cited, they included everything from when the assembly should convene to representation on assembly committees and candidates for the council's nonpermanent seats.

To achieve his chosen public role, Lie assumed, behind the scenes or in public, a number of positions and attitudes that, viewed in isolation, appear dysfunctional yet collectively supported his attempt to be a "force for peace." Although he had a jaundiced view about the American press in particular,[175] Lie was obviously aware of the powers of the fourth estate. He went to some length to surround himself in the secretariat with a group of talented journalists,[176] through whom he could convey worldwide his political messages, and also establish contact with influential journalists at the United Nations and elsewhere, as well as with their newspapers and wire services. Some of these people like Stoneman, former European manager of the *Chicago Daily News*, and Tor Gjesdal, former head of the wartime Norwegian Information Service, were also close advisers on political questions.[177]

For Lie it was of enormous importance to maintain close contacts and good personal relations with important persons in American government and political life. This was not only because the United Nations was situated in New York but because, when all was said and done and despite any reservations Lie may have had toward the United States and its leaders, American support was the keystone to the United Nations edifice. It explains his desire to establish contact with Raymond Fosdick, president of the Rockefeller Foundation, and a former senior official of the league secretariat. His contacts and social position made possible introductions to American foreign-policy opinion makers, especially from the worlds of journalism, academia, and so on.[178]

This desire for contacts with Washington's power holders explains what can be viewed as Lie's obsequious-message syndrome. Examples of this are too numerous to be cited but made sense in the case of Clement Attlee[179] because Lie's relations with Bevin were very bad, and Alexander Cadogan, who had been assigned as permanent representative to the United Nations, held Lie in contempt,[180] while in the Foreign Office he commanded little respect.

In this setting Lie's contacts with the Russians were equally important. They were largely maintained through Russian Assistant Secretary-General of Security Council Affairs Arkadi Sobolev and in the very early period probably through Molotov, whom Lie found "'sympathetic.'"[181] Lie, Jebb observed, "sincerely believed" that the United Nations could only function "if the Russians were humoured and conciliated," and he was committed to making the world organization work.[182] This belief partially explains Lie's gyrations as secretary-general: his concern, for example, over the shrinking number of Russians serving in the secretariate,[183] as well as the importance to him that Moscow expand its commitments to the United Nations system. Moves by Lie in the latter direction were mainly behind the scenes, but in public he made no bones about the fact that he "wanted the USSR in all UN organs."[184] Keeping in mind the temper of the times, the notion that Moscow would extend its commitments even beyond those pledged in the charter was optimistic in the extreme.

Naturally his endeavors would succeed or fail depending on whether the Russians perceived their interests would be served by joining any additional United Nations–related institutions.[185] Obviously Moscow saw no advantages, for Lie's attempts to have Soviet Russia join more United Nations specialized agencies, like the United Nations Educational, Scientific, and Cultural Organization, proved unsuccessful,[186] and in early 1949 he also failed to prevent its withdrawal from the World Health Organization.[187] This did not stop him, however, from raising the issue during his visit to Moscow in May 1950, but to no avail.[188]

Lie's concern with the major powers, which is understandable, in turn seemingly led to a lack of concern with the smaller powers, which then as now formed the overwhelming majority of members. His attitude, which was paradoxical in view of his partiality to small states, already discussed,[189] was somewhat reminiscent of the expression *kleiner Staaten*, and the pejorative connotation associated with that interwar German phrase. In 1948 the West's desire was to expand the budgetary and financial powers of the Interim Committee, which was to operate when the assembly was not in session in order to assist it in discharging its functions in the fields of peace and security.[190] Lie opposed expanding the committee's powers, and his attempts to pressure the Chinese, and especially the Dutch, over this issue were resented. The Uruguayan representative, Enrique Fabregat, expressed the greatest admiration for Lie, but "conveyed the impression that the great man paid too little attention to lesser persons."[191] Lie's "heavy pressure" was depreciated by the American mission, which felt that if he wanted to express his point of view he "should do so with somewhat more tact." It thought Lie should develop a structured procedure to allow delegations from smaller states "to express their views on administrative and budgetary matters"; merely to be consulted by the secretary-general would make these states happier.[192]

The State Department was "disturbed" by what had occurred, since it was "genuinely interested" in developing Lie's "status" and in maintaining an atmosphere as conducive as possible to effective United Nations operations.[193] To nudge Lie in the right direction the American mission pointed out to the well-placed Stoneman that the "general feeling was that Lie had plenty of time for the Permanent Members [of the council] and the big budget contributors, but had very little time to give to the little fellows." Lie was also directly pressed to establish contact with the smaller states, perhaps through his staff.[194] He bent to the pressure and promised to organize quickly such a system of consultation.[195] No doubt to hasten this system of consultation additional pressure was applied on Lie, granted indirectly, through the strategically placed Cordier.[196] Washington's concern appeared to have its impact, for subsequently Lie held that "high-level consultation" with delegations—he made no exceptions—was just what he thought his function should be.[197]

Saddling Up

Lie's activist role as secretary-general was portended within days after his appointment, when he expressed to Stettinius his chagrin at being excluded from the Military Staff Committee, established by the charter to advise and assist the council in maintaining international peace and security. He argued that he had to have access to the committee's discussions.[198] That same day, February 8, 1946, he raised the matter with the British representative on the Military Staff Committee. Lie appreciated the fact that the committee's secretariat, for security reasons, had to be a self-contained body, divorced from the world organization's main secretariat. However, to ensure that he was fully informed of the committee's proceedings he proposed the appointment of a personal liaison officer to sit with the committee but not to partake in its discussions. Lie correctly held that he had a responsibility for the secretariat as a whole and thus had certain rights in maintaining contacts with the committee's proceedings.[199]

The British chiefs of staff opposed Lie's scheme and supported a draft procedure whereby the Military Staff Committee secretariat would provide liaison with Lie and the council on all questions within the committee's competence. Cadogan was not at all sure that this procedure would pass the council without criticism and thought that it might be necessary to compromise in order to assuage Lie's desires.[200] Then in late February Lie raised the ante when he proposed that, aside from himself, the assistant secretary-general of Security Council Affairs, who it had already been agreed would be a Russian, would in practice represent him. In addition, all documentation without exception produced by the committee should be made available to him or his surrogate. General liaison, he suggested, between the committee and the secretariat might be confided to a military officer selected by and responsible to him and the committee.[201]

By the spring of 1946, the council had still to approve the Military Staff Committee's draft proposals. At this point Lie extended his front to include the council itself. Cordier explained to the American mission that Lie had given a great deal of thought to his "status" with respect to the council's proceedings. Lie felt, Cordier divulged, that it would be desirable for the council to have a procedural rule analogous to Assembly Rule 48, which allowed Lie upon the invitation of the president to make either oral or written statements to the assembly concerning any question being considered by that body.[202]

In mid-May the council's Committee of Experts tackled the problem, the American representative suggesting that Assembly Rule 48 also be adopted by the council. The Russian representative however, proposed that the qualifying phrase, "upon the invitation of the president," be eliminated. The American demurred. The ubiquitous Sobolev, speaking in Lie's behalf, held that Lie found it embarrassing, even insulting, that in the council, unlike the other United Nations organs, there was no rule entitling him to present his views. Sobolev then ran his zag to Lie's previous zig, by stating that Lie preferred a rule akin to Rule 24 of the Economic and Social Council rather than Rule 48 of the assembly. The American representative, needless to state, was surprised. Economic and Social Council Rule 24 was wider than Assembly Rule 48 since it allowed the secretary-general or deputy at any time, upon the invitation of the Economic and Social Council's president, or any chairman of its committees and subsidiary bodies, to make either oral or written statements concerning any question under consideration. Although Sobolev explained that the phrase, "upon the invitation of the president," was acceptable to Lie, the Australian and Russian representatives objected. They argued that the secretary-general was coequal with the council, and had the right to present such statements. Nevertheless the draft finally agreed to was analogous to Council Rule 24. The question then raised was what effect this would have on Lie's rights in the Military Staff Committee, which was still unresolved. It was agreed that retention of the phrase "upon the invitation of the president" did not prejudice this matter.

Stettinius noted to the State Department that there had been "some resentment" at the way Sobolev, evidently with Lie's full support and that of the Russian representative, "appeared to be trying to 'railroad' this matter through." Likewise, Cadogan noted to the Foreign Office that, whereas the "principle underlying" Lie's proposal seemed "unobjectionable, [the] manner and timing of its presentation was the subject of critical comment in the Committee."[203]

Foreign Office reaction was mixed. Counsellor John Ward personally thought the difficulty was to get Lie "to intervene in any matter of importance," although he admitted that in the Iranian question (which we will examine) Lie had unfortunately already intervened. "Yes Poor Mr. Lie is being terribly unclever," Jebb scribbled. However, Minister of State Philip Noel-Baker was more disposed to Lie's position. He felt Lie had a "right" to present oral or written statements to the council rather than have to depend on the president's invitation. Ward responded that it was "unfortunate" that Lie had raised the question as a matter of principle, since it could hardly be imagined that the council president would deny the secretary-general the opportunity to speak if he so requested. He thought the Australian position was proper and should be followed. Assistant Legal Adviser Gerald Fitzmaurice did not dissent but pointed out that the necessity to procure the president's invitation might provide "some checks on interventions that [might] prove embarrassing."[204]

The instructions to Cadogan mirrored these discussions. The Foreign Office agreed that Lie had apparently handled the whole matter "rather clumsily." It thought Lie's position automatically gave him the right to express his views to the council and its subordinate bodies. He already enjoyed an important right under Article 99; and if he felt he needed specific authorization, then the council could meet his wishes. In addition, Cadogan was to support the Australian proposal to omit the phrase, "upon the invitation of the president." In view of the secretary-general's "commanding position" in the charter, it appeared "quite wrong and inconsistent" that he be obliged to obtain the president's invitation before expressing his views. Surely this was a right he enjoyed.

On the other hand, the Military Staff Committee was a special case; but here also the Foreign Office thought that Lie "should have the right to address the Committee without the need to angle for an invitation." It noted that a subcommittee, which was studying relations with the secretariat, was apparently ready to recognize the secretary-general's right to address the Military Staff Committee and to attend its meetings whenever he wished, provided the committee chairman was notified. Surely the secretary-general should have rights equal to those of the council and its nonmilitary bodies, with whose work he was very much associated.[205]

Composing a draft text did not prove easy, and a number of meetings of the council's Committee of Experts were needed before a consensus could be hammered out.[206] What emerged was that the secretary-general, or the deputy acting on his or her behalf, could make oral or written statements to the council concerning any question under consideration. The need to be invited by the president had been scrapped but so had any reference to subordinate bodies of the council, like the Military Staff Committee. Moreover, the secretary-general could be appointed by the council to act "as rapporteur for a specified question." This procedural rule, originally proposed by the Americans, was opposed by some, the British in particular, on the grounds that it might place the secretary-general in an awkward position toward a given state if appointed rapporteur in a dispute. There was such strong pressure for the rule that the British gave way, but only on the understanding that the secretary-general could always decline to act as rapporteur if difficulties were anticipated. For the British to have insisted on rejection of this rule might have entailed an open discussion in the council of the secretary-general's function, which seemed "clearly undesirable."[207] The arrival of this information in the Foreign Office caused Ward to minute cynically that "Lie w[oul]d suit the Russians as a *rapporteur*."[208]

Several days before the council was to pass on the recommendations of the Committee of Experts, Lie informed the American mission that he had "no desires" to attend the Military Staff Committee's meetings. He denied that he had written any letters requesting this right and, in fact, held that he had no time to attend such meetings. Lie divulged that the pressure to allow him or his deputy to attend the committee's meetings emanated from Sobolev, who was evidently anxious to attend the committee's meetings in order to "exchange political ideas." This was not the first, nor the last, time that Lie would allow Sobolev to elbow his way unchecked down the corridors of the United Nations. Lie noted, undoubtedly with some regret, that "his own opinions on political matters were probably less valuable than those already available to the U.S. Delegation."[209]

On June 6, the council heard the report of the Committee of Experts, which pointed out, in an obvious allusion to the Military Staff Committee, that although the text adopted did not refer to the council's commissions, committees, or other subsidiary bodies, the unanimous opinion was that Lie or his deputy acting on his behalf, "should have the same power in relation to these organs as in relation to the Security Council." However, no such provision was stipulated "because it was considered undesirable to risk anticipating the question, which might appear premature in the present state of establishment of the organs related to the Security Council." The report and recommendations were then adopted without discussion by the council.[210] To Lie's disappointment the Trusteeship Council proved less generous, which he suspected was due to the attitude of the colonial powers that had reservations about his or his deputy's possible approach to issues facing it.[211]

In the end, Lie also acquired qualified entrée into the Military Staff Committee, whose chairman was to act as liaison between the committee and Lie and whose principal secretary was to be a liaison between the committee and Lie's office. Lie was to receive advance copies for his information and files of committee reports approved for submission to the council. The secretary-general, or the assistant secretary-general of Security Council Affairs, to wit Sobolev, acting on Lie's behalf, "normally" would have the right to attend all the committee's meetings and could make "oral or written statements concerning matters within the scope and the functions and powers of the Secretary-General." In line with this, the secretary-general would be furnished with a copy of the committee's provisional agenda and all the papers referred therein, except those relating to the committee's internal matters.[212]

Lie's earliest assertion of his newly won procedural prerogatives and the powers of his office was during a council debate in August 1946 dealing with the admission of new members. After recapitulating previous statements in behalf of universality, Lie concluded by noting that in his capacity as secretary-general he wished to support the admission of all states applying for membership.[213]

Cadogan wished to avoid raising the propriety of Lie's concluding remark but took the opportunity privately to tell Lie that his comment had been startling and "suggested that it was improper" for Lie to support the proposal of a council member. Lie responded that perhaps use of the word "support" had been unfortunate but argued that his office was very different from that in the league and he "was entitled to participate in the discussion of any subject." Lie based his stance on Article 99 of the charter, the council's rules of procedure, and discussions in London with which Cadogan was not familiar. Cadogan insisted that he was unconvinced and hoped that Lie would allow him, "in a friendly and personal way," to suggest that if he really had this "right, he should in his own interest, be very careful in his exercise of it." This was sound advice from Cadogan, but Lie "remained quite obstinate on the point of principle." The conversation was friendly, however. Indeed, Lie did not take it amiss when Cadogan, in a jocular aside, warned that in future he was going to keep a sharp eye out to prevent Lie from voting.[214]

Within the Foreign Office it was agreed that Cadogan's warning was well taken. Clearly Lie "should be very careful about exercising his right," John Peck of the United Nations Department scribbled on the minutes sheet. More detailed were the observations of the Chief Legal Adviser, Sir William Beckett. He thought the question was not Lie's right to intervene but rather the sort of statements he made when he did intervene. Lie's duty, he claimed, was to carry out other people's policies. Therefore, he had to be very careful how he intervened on any question of disputed policy. Lie clearly could intervene to give information, to explain mistakes and misunderstandings, and if necessary, to explain that a particular course of action would be administratively difficult and suggest another way of doing it. Conversely, according to Beckett, Lie could not intervene to speak for the United Nations as a whole in opposition to any United Nations body. Cadogan was right in privately admonishing Lie, who was in effect holding that United Nations interests (of which he was not a judge) required a specific course of action that he therefore supported. Lie was even more wrong, Beckett maintained, when he offered excuses. He did not think Lie's position was any different from that of his league predecessors except that under Article 99 he had certain rights, but these did not apply to this situation. One, he was not bringing to the council any matter affecting peace; and two, bringing the matter to the council's attention was one thing and suggesting a solution, or supporting proposals to solve the matter, was something entirely different.[215]

It all seemed, Assistant Head of the United Nations Department Paul Gore-Booth wrote to Jebb, "to boil down to a question of the exercise of personal judgement." Just as long years of tradition and experience made it very obvious to the secretary of the cabinet what he should and should not say, the same kind of tradition should develop in the United Nations. One feared, however, that Lie had not the "natural gift of discretion in a matter of this kind and that even when he chose the right moment for intervention, he [did] not always do it in the right way."[216]

Jebb supposed that Lie's prerogatives under the council's rules of procedure should be interpreted in line with Article 99, because the rules could not go beyond the charter itself. Article 99 provided that Lie could bring to the council's attention any matter threatening peace. It therefore appeared to follow that Lie's right to oral and written statements, as stipulated in the rules of procedure, should apply to remarks designed to bring to the council's attention such a matter that, in Lie's opinion, had either escaped attention or had not been considered sufficiently.

Of course, in practice without violating this general principle a clever man could phrase his remarks in such a way "as to give a twist in favour of any particular solution which he favoured." Likewise, an intelligent secretary-general, who had "gained the confidence of all concerned, could make tendentious statements of this kind without rousing the fury of one side or the other." As things were, however, Lie would have been wise to hold to the interpretation of Article 99 and the general principle Jebb had ventured to give. Jebb felt that the secretary-general, as the chief official of the United Nations, was something more than the secretary to the cabinet. Custom was the rule that applied to that position, which would prevent the secretary from "gratuitously drawing" the attention of his superiors to any great danger that threatened the British Empire's security and from making an extended speech propagating his point of view. Jebb's recollection was that the charter's drafters intended to give substantially greater power to the secretary-general of the United Nations than was given to his league predecessors. He felt that Whitehall would be well advised not to attempt to curtail more than was really necessary of Lie's powers, real or imagined. If Lie abused those powers, or strained the natural interpretation of Article 99 and the rules of procedure, it would be his "own funeral," and Jebb doubted "whether our own interests are likely to suffer very much." If, however, London clipped Lie's wings "we may be prejudicing," Jebb prophetically observed, "the position of his successor who may, for all we know, be an infinitely wiser and more powerful personality who will be able to get away with much more than the present Secretary-General."[217]

Reading this exchange in the Foreign Office, Peck suggested that it be sent to Cadogan, since it seemed "neither possible nor desirable to adopt a hard and fast line on the subject." This was done.[218]

Lie's next assertion of his political prerogatives was in September 1946, during a debate over the Ukrainian complaint that Greece's policies constituted a danger to peace and security in the Balkans because of incidents along the Albanian border provoked by the Greeks. An American draft resolution to establish a three-member council commission of investigation provoked Lie to make clear his "own position as Secretary-General and the rights of this office under the Charter." Should the American draft resolution be rejected, Lie hoped that the council would "understand that the Secretary-General must reserve his right to make such enquiries or investigations" as he might think necessary in order to "determine whether or not he should consider bringing any aspect of this matter to the attention" of the council under the charter's provisions. Obviously interested in expanding Lie's powers, Gromyko, as president of the council, thought that Lie "was right in raising the question of his rights"; that in the present "case, as in all other cases the Secretary-General must act." He had no doubt that Lie would do so in "accordance with the rights and powers" of the secretary-general as defined in the United Nations Charter.[219]

Cadogan's deputy, Valentine Lawford, informed the Foreign Office some days later that Lie had argued with a New York journalist that "Article 99 gave him the right to appoint and send investigators of his own to any area" without obtaining the council's prior consent. He specifically maintained that he could appoint his legal counsellor, the American Abraham Feller, or a group of private individuals to make inquiries in his behalf. When pressed as to whether he would do this in respect to the situation in Greece, "Lie's reply was a repeated 'Maybe.'" When the Greek ambassador to London, Thanassis Aghnides, spoke of the dangers to Greece of autimist and communist agitation supported by Greece's northern neighbors, Lie pressed him for an investigation. The idea of an investigation authorized by Lie and executed by Feller and Sobolev, Lawford observed, "would be a nightmare"—since neither, because of his political orientation, generated confidence in the British mission. Lawford concluded that if the council's dispatch of a commission of inquiry could be vetoed, it appeared doubtful whether Lie could really send one on his own initiative. It would be a surprise if the Russians agreed to this, despite what Gromyko said at the council meeting about Lie's prerogatives. Indeed, if the Russians agreed to Lie's commission of inquiry it "would be a serious reflexion on Lie."[220]

The Foreign Office was unimpressed by Lie's threats. The principal objection was that neither Article 99, nor any other article, specifically gave him the right to establish on his own initiative an investigatory commission. In addition, the receiving country would be under no legal obligation to give Lie's investigators facilities to expedite their investigation, and their authority might well be questioned either by the states concerned or by the council, or both.[221]

Perhaps the British attitude was best summed up in early May 1948, during the height of the Palestine crisis. The British delegation depreciated the "illusion (already present in Lie's mind)" that as secretary-general he was a "kind of arbiter of international business."[222] The opinion some months later of Paul Mason, head of the United Nations Department, was even stronger: "He really is a silly old man," he noted. Minister of State Hector McNeil's rejoinder was probably closer to the truth: "I'm never sure that he is silly, I'll agree he is never wise."[223]

Although it is clear that both Washington and London were willing to accept, up to a certain point, Lie's desire to expand his powers and prerogatives, it is likewise clear that initially Moscow supported Lie in this endeavor however and whenever it could. Within the secretariat itself Sobolev worked behind the scenes and in committees to see that this was achieved, and he was in turn supported by Gromyko and other members of the Russian delegation. Why so? one may ask. Why were the Russians interested in expanding Lie's powers and prerogatives? Because their initial assumption, that Lie as secretary-general would be their man, appeared to come to fruition when Lie intervened in the Iranian question in a manner that seemingly supported the Russian stance. Indeed, when the Iranian problem was winding down Sobolev raised informally "the question whether it might not be a good plan . . . to consider drawing up some rules relating to the functions of the Secretary General."[224] Accordingly, to have Lie's powers expanded would dovetail with Russian interests, especially if in the future Lie continued to support the Russian position. It was a ploy they would subsequently regret.[225]

The Secretariat

Keeping in mind Lie's deficiencies, it takes no imagination to visualize the situation that developed initially when the secretariat was being recruited. The move from London to New York, plus the temporary and inadequate original accommodations for the United Nations, only complicated the problem for Lie who within a short period of time was forced to establish a staff capable of serving the organization's members as well as dealing with the wide array of vexing and urgent political problems presented to the United Nations. The Australian Hasluck and others sympathized with Lie's plight.[226] Jebb put it succinctly: faced with this situation, Lie "had no choice but to recruit quickly, extensively and indiscriminately."[227]

The end result showed it, for the secretariat grew too rapidly, in too short a time, and included too many officials of mediocre quality. The ill-advised introduction of American managerial methods and techniques only added to the chaos. Lie's personal office, for example, had fifty-four employees. Fortunately, a handful of former members of the league secretariat were appointed, for without them the United Nations secretariat would have been hard pressed to make available the necessary technical services, such as interpreting, translating, and producing the verbatim and other records.[228] The repercussions of this headlong rush to hire, come what may, were still being felt when Hammarskjöld became secretary-general. Fellow Norwegians who had seen service with the league secretariat complained about Lie's inept management.[229] The point was also raised early on by the British,[230] who in October 1946 investigated the secretariat structure to see what could be done to improve its performance and reduce its expense.[231]

In fairness to Lie, it should be pointed out that the position of assistant secretary-general for administration, reserved for the United States,[232] was one that Lie initially wanted to bestow on the high-powered Chester Bowles, Adlai Stevenson, or Milton Eisenhower, the general's brother.[233] But this was not to be. Selected instead was John Hutson, under secretary of agriculture, a devoted Democratic party member, and a friend of President Truman and Secretary of State Byrnes.[234] Unfortunately, according to Jebb, Hutson was a "complete dud."[235] He resigned under pressure in early January 1947, which once again opened the search for another American.[236]

Bowles, whom Lie approached because of the world organization's administrative chaos, studied the problem and became "increasingly appalled by the built-in confusion." He felt assembly procedures made it virtually impossible to transform the secretariat into a well-run organization and declined Lie's offer. He did agree to act as Lie's special assistant on administrative matters and did so for over a year, handling specific administrative and management questions.[237] Lie raised again the names of Stevenson, Milton Eisenhower, and a number of others.[238] Finally, with Washington's consent, Byron Price, a former senior official in a number of government and nongovernment offices, accepted the assignment.[239]

Throughout these months of administrative bumbling and shortsightedness the secretariat's morale began to sag. There were still no definitive salary schedules and no contracts aside from the initial eleven contracts offered to Lie, the eight assistant secretaries-general, the legal counsellor, and Lie's executive assistant.[240] The administrative labyrinth appeared to occupy Lie's every moment.[241] It obviously also bothered him subconsciously, for at an intimate lunch given for him by Attorney General Sir Hartley Shawcross, who made a short approbatory speech, Lie's short non sequitur response was "'It'"—meaning the secretariat—"'will be better.'"[242] Trying to assess the situation, the Cabinet Steering Committee on International Organisations concluded, in early March 1947, that although Lie was personally popular to a certain degree, he was neither a good leader nor a good administrator, being "inclined to take wrong decisions, or, more often, to take no decision at all on matters which a directive is needed."[243] This lack of leadership Minister of State McNeil subsequently traced to Lie's prior commitments; or as he quaintly put it, Lie had "given too many hostages."[244]

The dam finally burst on March 11, 1947, when Lie had to face an agitated mass meeting of the secretariat that raised some of the more conspicuous grievances regarding salaries, working conditions, and so on.[245] Lie spoke with "obvious personal sincerity," staved off some of the more insistent complaints, but "did not reveal a very strong grasp of the administrative problems and tended to lay the blame for all difficulties" on the assembly's financial decisions and Hutson's personality.[246] Price, who Lie assured the secretariat would handle the complaints, soon tackled the administrative problems;[247] but as late as December 1947, secretariat morale was low and Lie "was [still] not held in high esteem." The secretariat thought that basically Lie was a "small town politician" who did not defend its rights, and Price likewise was viewed as a cold person when it came to human relations.[248]

One of Lie's persistent problems during this period was that, in the initial selection of secretariat personnel a very large proportion of Americans, Canadians, and English was hired. The fact that major secretariat hirings occurred immediately after the United Nations arrived in New York explains this state of affairs. Understandable as this was, it nevertheless did not soothe others—the French and Belgians, for example—who felt that there was an uneven distribution of secretariat positions by nationality. Although Lie regretted the number of Americans in the secretariat, he complimented their work.[249] Actually this question was mainly political rather than administrative in nature; the problems of the distribution of secretariat staff by nationality and the importance of the functional positions assigned were not peculiar to Lie's secretary-generalship but arose as early as 1919, when Drummond established the League of Nations multinational secretariat.[250]

For the British, at least, the only way to remedy the problem was to appoint a deputy under Lie, a "strong and able man" who would assume most of Lie's administrative tasks and act as a kind of super under-secretary to coordinate many of the secretariat's economic and social activities. Initially the British were thinking of a possible Scandinavian for the post in order to avoid difficulties with the Russians.[251] Molotov, however, objected to any deputy and Lie "curled up."[252] Because Bevin persisted and "impressed" upon Lie the "desirability" of appointing a deputy, Lie eventually succumbed but warned that there were "certain difficulties" to be ironed out with the Russians.[253]

When Jebb raised the issue with the Americans in the autumn of 1947, he explained that the individual selected would assume some of Cordier's burdens, allowing him to concentrate on assembly matters, including the

secretariat of the Interim Committee. Jebb raised the name of the Australian Robert Jackson, who had a reputation as a good administrator and was
a former deputy director of the United Nations Relief and Rehabilitation
Administration.[254] The Americans were concerned and made it clear that
they would be unsympathetic to any scheme that "would interfere with
Mr. Cordier's intimate and confidential relations with Mr. Lie." Jebb assured them that London had nothing "like this in mind."[255]

In the end, Lie yielded to London's pressure and, in December, agreed to
Jackson's appointment as assistant secretary-general for general coordination.[256] It was only natural that Cordier was disturbed over Jackson's appointment, which he thought reflected dissatisfaction with his work and a
lack of confidence in him by Lie. In particular Jackson's "aggressive personality" caused Cordier singular unease since he anticipated some disputes
within Lie's office, from which Jackson would work. Strong objections
were likewise raised by Byron Price, who had an understanding with Lie
that Jackson "would not be given authority" in Price's field. As Cordier's
position was not jeopardized, the Americans made no formal objection to
Jackson's appointment.[257]

In the manner of bureaucrats who see their territory infringed, in addition to Price, the other assistant secretaries-general were also hostile to
Jackson's appointment.[258] Lie credited Sobolev's objections and annoyance
to Moscow's instructions and to his subsequent loss of face because he had
failed to prevent the appointment.[259] The rub was that the suspicions of
the assistant secretaries-general had been aroused.[260]

One can argue that the cardinal mistake made by the British was that
they never tied Lie down on the exact perimeters of Jackson's jurisdiction,[261] spelling out clearly Jackson's powers. In fact, Minister of State
McNeil was informed that Jackson's powers were "somewhat undefined,
[including] coordination over the general range and programme of the Secretariat's activities."[262] In view of this and the hostility of the various
assistant secretaries-general, others correctly saw the potential danger.
"All we have is a promise from a notoriously weak Mr. Lie," noted Sir
Edmund Hall-Patch, the deputy under-secretary.[263] He was right.

In April 1948, Jackson discussed with Bevin and McNeil a wide array of
questions stemming from his appointment and the jobs Lie visualized for
him, but they did not touch the important issue of the perimeters of Jackson's jurisdiction.[264] On Jackson's urging, Bevin explained to the State Department the reasons for Jackson's appointment.[265] Previous to this Brian
Urquhart, Lie's English assistant, had approached Feller who favored Jackson's appointment. Urquhart asked him to explain to the American mission that the appointment was no London plot, as maintained in some
quarters.[266] The State Department's reaction to Jackson's appointment was
perceptive. It understood that Jackson was a "very able person, possibly so
able that he will be too aggressive in his activities in Mr. Lie's office. We

will hope for the best on this score."[267] Under-Secretary Robert Lovett assured Bevin that Jackson could count on Washington's fullest cooperation and agreed that coordinating United Nations activities was important.[268]

The problem of the secretariat, however, especially its higher direction, had initially surfaced in London soon after Lie became secretary-general. Lie, Stettinius reported to Washington, intended to make a "thorough canvass of talent" and approached his new job with "great modesty" and with the "realization that he had much to learn." Moreover, he recognized the "high moral demands" of the office, and it was felt that he would display shrewdness and not be pressured so easily by member states "particularly with respect to appointments."[269] Unfortunately, this did not prove true.

It would appear that Lie never consulted the league's first secretary-general, Sir Eric Drummond, who as Lord Perth was then sitting in the House of Lords as a Liberal peer, about the problems of establishing a multinational secretariat.[270] Likewise, offers of help and advice to Lie by the able Sir Arthur Salter, the former director of the league secretariat's Economic and Financial Section, were not picked up.[271]

Lie's attitude was probably dictated by the adverse criticism of the league that had surfaced during the San Francisco Conference, save for the pro-League of Nations remarks of South Africa's Jan Christiaan Smuts.[272] The anti-League of Nations comments by Lie's entourage no doubt contributed to this attitude.[273] Since Lie and others perceived that they were building a new Jerusalem, contacts, no matter how helpful, with a defunct and failed predecessor were to be avoided.[274] Even as late as 1951 an assembly session in Geneva, it appears, was unpalatable.[275] Far more important, Lie was probably averse to consulting former Geneva officials because the league, thanks to the exertions of Secretary-General Avenol, had expelled Soviet Russia from the world organization following her attack on Finland;[276] therefore, the league was persona non grata as far as Moscow was concerned. This was mirrored in the Russian desire for a new world organization and not the old league or a remodeled version,[277] and steering clear of Drummond, Salter, et al. was probably conceived by Lie as a wise policy.

Despite this stance there was pressure to consult. It came from Bevin, who recommended that Lie see the Greek Ambassador Thanassis Aghnides, a long-time member of the league secretariat who became director of the important Disarmament Section and finally under secretary-general. When they met, Lie produced a sheet of paper that bore the names of eight assistant secretaries-general. Were these persons candidates, Aghnides asked Lie, or had they already been appointed? They had already been appointed, Lie responded. Aghnides observed that he had nothing further to say, since the Czechoslovak, Ivan Kerno, who would handle legal affairs and who had been his league secretariat colleague, had been expelled from the Political Section by Drummond, who requested the Czech government withdraw him. Had Lie, Aghnides queried, appointed Kerno on Moscow's recommendation? The answer was in the affirmative. Obviously, Lie had felt it necessary to appease Moscow, for it appears Kerno, had flirted with the Russians in the past.[278] As Roger Allen, the assistant head of the Foreign Office's United Nations Department, noted in 1948, Kerno was "presumably tainted."[279] Although the Foreign Office lacked hard evidence regarding Kerno's political sympathies—one official in fact denying that he was a Communist[280]—nevertheless he was described as "'weak and subject to Soviet influence.'"[281] The State Department was equally suspicious,[282] even though Kerno on his retirement from the United Nations did not return to Czechoslovakia but remained with his family in the United States.[283]

Although Aghnides never related to Bevin his discussion with Lie,[284] it would be fair to say that it would merely have reaffirmed Bevin's negative opinion of Lie, for personal relations between them were bad. Bevin despised Lie enormously.[285] Lie offered no really cogent reasons for this state of affairs except the somewhat lame explanation that they shared the "strong sense of antagonism," so often characteristic of trade unionists, each of whom liked to boast that he had done a good job.[286] Although Bevin, unlike Lie, gave no explanation whatever about their personal relations, one can speculate that to someone like Bevin, who fought the Communists in the British Labour movement, the views and political background of a trimmer like Lie were highly suspect. Bevin's own "socialism was a very pragmatic kind" and untied to "theoretical justification." Never a Marxist, Bevin regarded communism as a "vicious and dangerous creed."[287] He therefore probably considered Lie as no more than a communist dupe, partially reflected in his "friendly personal basis with Gromyko, Vishinsky and the younger Russians,"[288] as well as in a marked anti-British orientation. Lie's anti-British remarks over an extended period of time[289] would certainly support the latter observation and were buttressed by Lie's disguised anti-American propensity.[290]

Bevin's attitude might well explain why Lie's relations with Eden were warmer.[291] Of course, Lie had worked closely with Eden during the war.[292] Moreover, the upper-class, foreign-policy experienced Eden could condescend and overlook the political waywardness of the leftist trade unionist. Such relationships might explain Bevin's objections to Molotov's suggestion that Lie attend a meeting of the Council of Foreign Ministers[293] and why Lie awkwardly requested in 1948 that when he arrived in London he would like to see Eden, then shadow cabinet foreign affairs critic, which was arranged with Minister of State McNeil acting as duenna.[294]

In addition to the choice of Kerno, Lie's relations with Russian Assistant Secretary-General Sobolev could only have contributed to his bad relations with Bevin. Based on an informal agreement between Washington and Moscow, subsequently approved by the Security Council's five permanent members, it was understood that the post of assistant secretary-general of Security Council affairs would be held by a Russian, while that of assistant secretary-general for administration would go to an American.[295] Lie initially wanted to appoint Alexei Roschin, a member of the secretariat of the first assembly session in London, but Stettinius objected. Lie was obviously unaware of the informal Great Power agreement, for it would appear that he interpreted Stettinius's objection as based on Roschin's nationality rather than on his personal qualities. Lie thought that if the position was given to the Russians "they would be easier on other matters."[296] Vyshinsky, however, also had doubts about Roschin. A week later Lie held that the Russians had to be given this position, showing he was by then aware, thanks to Vyshinsky, of the informal agreement. Vyshinsky then proposed Sobolev. Lie, after inquiry, quickly appointed him to fill the slot.[297] From Moscow's point of view no better man could have been picked.

Sobolev, who had been trained as an engineer, was both very intelligent and very likeable,[298] and he was also, Jebb admitted, the "most able"[299] of the assistant secretaries-general. Like Gromyko, he was well versed in procedural matters, which though seemingly formal on the surface, are often substantive in content in international organizations.[300] Thus, one reflection of Sobolev's abilities was that, when he substituted for Lie, the whole administration of the world organization ran like "clockwork." This was not an unimportant consideration for Lie in evaluating Sobolev's talents, in view of the general administrative chaos that permeated the United Nations. A good conversationalist, Sobolev was far from loquacious, but he always knew what he wanted and was usually successful in acquiring it.[301] Lie held that he was pleased with Sobolev.[302] In fact, of all the assistant secretaries-general, only Sobolev satisfied him.[303] Accordingly, the Lie-Sobolev relationship was close, and, in view of Sobolev's intelligence and likeableness, it was only natural that Lie should perhaps see in him the son he never had, mirrored in his claim that he had become Sobolev's "godfather."[304] Sobolev therefore became "the most powerful personality" within the secretariat and had "great influence" with Lie.[305]

Lie, of course, was not blind to the fact that Sobolev was a committed Communist.[306] Sobolev never really diverged from the Communist party line. The Australians, in particular, were convinced that behind the scenes he always maneuvered in favor of Moscow. There were rumors that during the assembly he attended meetings of the Russian mission, although other missions did not share this view nor did members of the secretariat. Jebb thought that Sobolev would not likely do anything that he believed was against Russia's interests, but within these strictures he thought Sobolev did try to execute his duties as a secretariat official. One could, however, criticize Sobolev for his unimpressive staff, which Jebb held could be traced to the "Upas Tree effect" of Sobolev's character.[307]

In line with Moscow's belief in a nonactivist secretariat, Sobolev viewed its functions as limited. It was to be restricted to circulating papers and organizing the United Nations machinery and never, if possible, allowed to partake in any substantive work.[308] Naturally, as we have already seen, Sobolev did not feel that this restriction applied to himself. He certainly had no inhibitions on immersing himself in the sensitive political question of the membership logjam that had developed by the summer of 1946.[309]

By the following year, Sobolev's activities were such that Cadogan reported to the Foreign Office that, while he was one of the best of the assistant secretaries-general and a good administrative director of his department, he could not be said to be a "good international civil servant and his activities [were] marked by political bias."[310] Jebb also, in the autumn of 1947, voiced his concern that, if the assembly established an Interim Committee, it would be very unfortunate if Lie assigned Sobolev to tend to its administrative needs. He urged efforts to see that Lie assign someone else, specifically Cordier.[311] Jebb's apprehensions can be well appreciated, for the Russians objected to the Interim Committee as a violation of the charter that would undermine, they claimed, the council's primary responsibility for the maintenance of international peace and security.[312]

British pressure appears to have had its impact for Lie ruled that his office, rather than Sobolev's, would service the Interim Committee. Sobolev agreed that this was a preferable arrangement;[313] but no sooner had he done so than he reverted to the notion that his office should be in charge. It would appear that Sobolev's about-face was based on instructions from the Russian mission, which probably decided that his administration of the Interim Committee would be an excellent way of keeping it under continuous surveillance. Lie, however, resisted Sobolev's renewed demand on the grounds that he had made his decision and was not going to change it.[314]

By mid-1948 it was alleged by the former Czechoslovak representative that Sobolev exercised a "much greater influence" in determining Russian policy in the United Nations than Gromyko. This claim was supported by others. A secretariat official personally knew of occasions where memoranda submitted by staff members in Sobolev's office had gone "astray" until, weeks later, pages only slightly altered had resurfaced in the statements of Russian representatives at the United Nations.[315]

Obviously Sobolev's role as a conduit with the Russian mission and Moscow was helpful to Lie, but why did he accept or ignore these more blatant political activities by Sobolev? The answer probably lay in Lie's belief that Sobolev had "more standing and influence with the Kremlin" than Gromyko.[316] He felt that through Sobolev he could fathom Moscow's reactions to events. It was his only private channel to the Russians, and Lie regretted Sobolev's absence and counsel during a number of crises, like the discussions on the North Atlantic Pact and the Berlin blockade. He attributed Sobolev's relative freedom to the "high esteem in which he was held by the Kremlin."[317] Indeed, after Sobolev resigned from the secretariat and returned to the United Nations as number three man in the Russian delegation to the assembly, Lie thought that through him he would have a "better understanding with the Soviet delegation." It was obvious Lie had a "high opinion of Sobolev," Warren Austin informed the State Department, "and of his own ability to deal with him."[318] So he had, but in view of Sobolev's many qualities and communist dedication—it was reported from Berlin that he had been connected with Russian atomic energy espionage in the United States[319]—one can speculate who was using whom. By the autumn of 1951 Lie was very bitter that Sobolev, "who had been so close" avoided speaking to him during the assembly session.[320] Lie, who now supported the South Koreans following the North Korean invasion, was detested by Moscow, and it must have been obvious to Lie that their prior close personal association, certainly on Sobolev's part, had been dictated solely by political considerations.

Equally disturbing to Bevin must have been the orientation and activities of Lie's legal counsellor, Feller. While still a member of the United Nations Relief and Rehabilitation Administration, Feller approached Stettinius and asked to be considered for a possible position in the United Nations secretariat.[321] Accordingly, when on the eve of his appointment a somewhat bewildered Lie was looking for competent personnel to organize the secretariat, Stettinius offered him the services of Feller.[322] Feller, who has been described as very "adroit," was undoubtedly one of the "most powerful" of the American secretariat officials around Lie,[323] reflected in Lie's heavy dependence on him for advice.[324] Like Cordier, Feller was an important conduit between Lie and the America mission to the United Nations as well as to the Washington authorities.[325]

The difficulty, as perceived by others, was that Feller, who was Jewish, was viewed as pro-Zionist.[326] This was not unreasonable, as a perusal of the minutes of the Executive of the Jewish Agency attests.[327] Likewise Feller's leftist loyalties, anti-British stance, and seeming "fair mindedness" toward the Russians raised doubts about his loyalties and proclivities. Certainly, Cordier, Price, and other American secretariat officials did little to counter Feller's influence.[328] Bevin's Gethsemane over the partition of Palestine, however, and Lie's endeavors in behalf of the Zionists, which we will examine, could only have raised the suspicion that Lie's stance was in part a product of Feller's coaching and advice. The fact that Feller was suspected of communist leanings[329] was added grist for Bevin's mill. The latter charge had surfaced when Lie was attacked in the October 1947 issue of *Plain Talk*. Feller denied the charges in the article, that he had been a member of the National Lawyers Guild or the Washington Committee for Democratic Action, which had been cited as communist front organizations by the Un-American Activities Committee of the House of Representatives and by the United States Attorney General, respectively. Feller likewise denied Communist party sympathy, sympathy for its front organizations, its policies, or its leaders, as well as membership in any organization with even the remotest communist connections.[330]

However, reports to the Federal Bureau of Investigation raised suspicions about Feller,[331] although there was no concrete evidence to associate him with any Communist, pro-communist, or subversive organization. Despite all of this, Feller's routine at the United Nations inspired no confidence. Cadogan in particular had his doubts. In March 1947, months before the article in *Plain Talk* appeared, he observed to Jebb that a memorandum the latter had written to the cabinet about the secretariat appeared to concentrate inordinately on its efficiency and to "ignore the question of ideological bias," which the previous year's experience showed as an "important factor" in its activities. Sobolev, Feller, and the Norwegian Colonel Roscher Lund, one of Lie's special advisers, who Jebb had described as an "absurd figure," seemed to Cadogan "to represent a real danger, rather than merely an element of weakness and obstinacy." Cadogan held that there was in general "within the Secretariat a large number of 'starry-eyed' left-wing sympathisers who, while doubtless well-intentioned themselves, [were] apt to become instruments of intrigue in the hands of some of their more hard-hearted colleagues."[332] In this matter, Lie was of no help, since he was occupied with administrative questions and did not supervise "adequately the political activities of his subordinates not all of whom [were] free from ideological bias."[333] One can criticize Cadogan for these harsh Cold War comments, but unfortunately they were not far from the truth,[334] as we shall see.

POSTWAR FISSURES

Unwelcome Guests: Bornholm and Iran

Lie's desire to build bridges between East and West was manifested even before he was appointed secretary-general. The first problem that elicited it was the continued Russian occupation of the Danish island of Bornholm in the Baltic. The island, which is considerably east of the Danish coast, covers the approaches to the Öresund and thus entrance into the Baltic and exit from there into the Kattegat. Sensitive to its strategic value, in May 1945 London was keen on British forces to accept the surrender of the German garrison. Instead, Russian forces landed on the island and accepted the German surrender. This fait accompli made the Foreign Office uneasy and Churchill was assured that a close watch would be kept on the situation, as it was "possible that the Russians will be in no hurry to evacuate Bornholm."[1]

By the summer of 1945 the Danes thought that the Russians would probably not depart from Bornholm until British forces departed from the Faroe Islands, which had been occupied in April 1940.[2] Indeed, the Danes feared that the Russians "might seek bases on Bornholm," especially if the United States sought postwar bases on Greenland.[3] Lie's desire to build bridges was buttressed by the fact that Soviet Russia's continued occupation of Bornholm was regarded by the Norwegians "as something of a test case."[4] Criticism of Moscow's policies in the Balkans, East Germany, and Bornholm had also appeared in Sweden and elsewhere.[5] Settling the issue would therefore contribute in a positive manner to returning the postwar world to a more stable state and easing the tensions that racked it.

Since the island lies close to Sweden—which was uneasy and suspicious about the Russian occupation of Bornholm—it was only natural that the Swedish minister in London should query Lie, in late January 1946, as to whether he had approached the Russians about Bornholm. Lie responded that he had "a definite impression" that the Russians would evacuate Bornholm once the question of the Kiel Canal and the Baltic's entrances had been settled.[6] Secretary of State Byrnes, unlike Lie, was not optimistic that the Russians would evacuate Bornholm once these questions were settled and preferred to postpone the definitive solution of both problems until the peace settlements.[7]

In line with Lie's optimism, and despite Byrnes's doubts, the Russians settled with the Danes and commenced their troop withdrawal from the island about mid-March 1946 and completed it by early April.[8] Jebb credited Lie as "largely instrumental in getting the Russians to evacuate . . . Bornholm," and speculated that the Russians had the erroneous impression that if they withdrew the British and the Americans would rush to replace them and fortify the island.[9] Though Lie's endeavors behind the scenes no doubt served to expedite the Russian withdrawal, these endeavors were predicated on the belief that the Russians could be persuaded to evacuate Bornholm provided they could do so without being subjected to excessive embarrassment.[10] In actual fact however, the evacuation itself was undoubtedly triggered by British actions: as Bevin subsequently admitted, Soviet Russia had been assured that Great Britain intended that the Kattegat-Öresund-Baltic passage should remain an open sea lane, and this had been done "at the time in order to get the Russians out of Bornholm."[11]

It was during this period that Churchill made his now famous "Iron Curtain" speech on March 4, 1946, at Fulton, Missouri. Lie viewed the speech as a mistake and more likely to increase Moscow's uncooperativeness than otherwise. Although he admitted that "he largely shared the sentiments expressed" in the speech, Lie thought it had aided Moscow's anti-Western elements and the thousands of Russia's unemployed generals.[12] In line with this somewhat sophomoric analysis of the foreign policy process in Stalin's Russia, Lie called on Bevin to complain about the speech. He claimed that a satisfactory reply from Moscow concerning Russian troop withdrawal from Iran, a question we will soon explore, could have been obtained had it not been for the Fulton address. Bevin disagreed.

Lie then related Sobolev's hope, on behalf of Russia's officials, that Bevin would publicly repudiate Churchill's address. The source of Sobolev's message could not have inspired confidence in Lie's political acumen. "I did not rise to this bait," Bevin noted to the British ambassador in Moscow. To Lie, he restricted himself to the comment that the basis of British foreign policy had been spelled out in his February comments to the House of Commons, which held that he could not imagine any circumstances that would lead England and Russia to war. This "unequivocal" policy statement, Bevin observed, was available to everyone and for the moment he had nothing further to add.[13] Bevin's refusal to repudiate Churchill was simple enough: though he would not admit it to Lie or publicly, he knew that what Churchill had spoken at Fulton was unchallengeable.[14]

The Iranian question also surfaced before Lie had been appointed secretary-general. The question was first brought to the Security Council's attention by the Iranians on January 19, 1946, who requested that it be investigated and the council recommend appropriate settlement terms. Iran contended that the Russians had interfered in her internal affairs contrary to international law and treaty arrangements. In particular, Iran maintained that Moscow prevented her from exercising authority in the province of Azerbaijan, part of the Russian zone established by the Tripartite Treaty of Alliance (Soviet Russia, Great Britain, and Iran) of January 1942. In late 1945, Teheran had protested to Moscow about this Russian interference and the Iranian Prime Minister had offered to go to Moscow to negotiate a settlement. Iran's United Nations' representative held that his government had sought a negotiated settlement in accordance with the charter, but that Moscow had refused to accept that his country's complaints were well taken.

Naturally, the Russians denied any interference in Iranian affairs. Moscow was, however, willing to hold direct talks with Teheran. By a unanimously adopted resolution on January 30, the council requested Iran and Soviet Russia to inform it of any results achieved by direct negotiations, which both sides claimed they desired. At the same time, the council retained the right to request information concerning the progress of the negotiations.[15]

Several weeks after this resolution was passed, Lie divulged to the American ambassador in Oslo that the Russians were convinced that London had egged Teheran to bring the question before the council and indicated that he shared this Russian conviction. Lie's opinion was that Moscow wanted at this juncture to extend its influence as far as possible before the United Nations began to function effectively.[16] Lie was disturbed by what had occurred. He felt that Iran should have expended greater time on direct negotiations with Soviet Russia. In fact, this was what he had recommended, pointing out that Norway, when he was foreign minister, had undergone "a very positive and satisfactory experience" with Russian

troop withdrawal.[17] Quite so; but then again northern Norway was devoid
of the oil resources that blessed Iran.

The Iranian question then took a new twist on March 18, when Lie
was approached in Washington by Iran's ambassador, Hussein Ala. That
morning Ala had again appealed to the council, complaining that Soviet
Russia was maintaining troops in his country beyond March 2, contrary
to the provisions of the Tripartite Treaty of Alliance of January 1942. Despite the new appeal, Lie's views were unchanged though he was disturbed
by the Russian delay in evacuating the troops. Nevertheless, Lie held that
a council debate "would probably intensify rather than ease the dispute."
He believed that the Russians "could be persuaded" to withdraw their
troops as they had done from northern Norway and Bornholm, provided
this could be accomplished without their being embarrassed. Though Russian policy might be cynical it was unwise to assume that Moscow was
not moved by prestige considerations. Lie felt that if again brought before
the council Moscow might prove intransigent; but by private negotiations
the Russians might be induced to withdraw their troops. Lie promised to
assist such private discussions. He pointed out that Sobolev enjoyed Moscow's confidence and would provide an excellent channel for these negotiations—a comment that could only have raised doubts in Ala's mind
about Lie's political sagacity. According to Lie, Ala then conveyed these
confidential thoughts to the State Department, which was not amused.

Lie nevertheless placed Iran's appeal on the council's provisional agenda
for March 25. This was soon followed by a request from Gromyko that Lie
postpone the council meeting until April 10, in order to give Moscow time
to prepare its response. Stettinius then informed Lie that, when the council convened on March 25, he would move to have the Iranian appeal
placed as the first item on the agenda. Lie took no steps to urge postponement of the council's meeting of March 25;[18] rather, he proposed to Stettinius that they "find some way over this hurdle." Byrnes, however, was
adamant that the council had to act and would brook no delays.[19] In the
end, Lie along with Sobolev persuaded Gromyko to agree to the council
convening ceremonially on March 25,[20] with actual discussion of the
question not to commence until the following day. Gromyko was present during this session, despite prior threats to boycott if the Western
powers pressed Iran's appeal. He explained that, pursuant to the council's
resolution of January 30, negotiations with Iran had led to an agreement
on the withdrawal of Russian troops. The complete withdrawal, he assured the council, would be accomplished within five or six weeks unless
"unforeseen circumstances" arose. He therefore proposed that the item
not be placed on the agenda, but the council rejected this and decided to
inscribe it.[21]

Lie took seriously Gromyko's threat not to participate in the council's
discussions of the question until April 10. It appeared to justify Lie's fears

that a public debate would exacerbate the question. In addition, it would damage United Nations prestige. Accordingly, Lie saw Gromyko in private and "urged him not to carry out his threat." He made it clear that he disapproved of boycotts as a means of settling political differences. Gromyko, however, could not be moved.[22]

At the council's next meeting, on March 27, the inevitable occurred. Gromyko proposed that consideration of the appeal be postponed until April 10. This was not accepted. Gromyko then noted that he was unable to participate in the discussion of the Iranian question and dramatically departed from the chamber. He failed to attend the next three meetings at which the question was discussed. The gist of these discussions led to Lie's being asked to ascertain from both sides the status of the Russian-Iranian negotiations and, in particular, whether the reported Russian troop withdrawal was conditioned upon the conclusion of an agreement between the two sides on other subjects, an allusion to possible Russian pressure on Iran for oil concessions.

The replies, when read to the council on April 3, were not consonant; but it was obvious from what was divulged that the Russians had raised the matter of an oil concession. In response to a question, Ambassador Ala stated that if Gromyko would withdraw the qualification of "unforeseen circumstances" that might delay withdrawal and give assurances that the troops would leave by May 6, his government would not further press the question, provided it remained inscribed on the council agenda. The council's decision, on April 4, was to pass a second resolution on the Iranian question, deferring until May 6 any further discussion of the matter. Gromyko then proposed that the question be removed from the agenda in view of a recent joint communique that an understanding had been reached on all points.[23] The possibility of removing the question from the council agenda, out of the limelight and into the discreet bilateral negotiations that Lie had initially wanted, now presented itself. Privately, but in Sobolev's presence, Lie suggested to the council's Chinese president that Iran "volunteer to call it all off." Quo Tai-chi thought that would be wrong. Stettinius was more than annoyed at Lie's suggestion: "He made it in front of Sobolev who will now repeat it," he telephoned Byrnes.[24]

Iran, Ala informed Lie on April 9, desired that the question remain on the agenda. By mid-April, however, because of categorical and repeated assurances to Teheran that Russian troop withdrawal would be completed by May 6, Ala was instructed that Teheran had "complete confidence in the word and pledge" of the Russian government and for this reason withdrew its appeal to the council. Naturally when the council received this communication, Gromyko, supported by the French and Polish representatives, attempted to have the question stricken from the agenda. Stettinius demurred: only when the council was informed on May 6 that the troop withdrawal had been completed could it drop the Iranian question from the agenda.[25]

In view of the Russian assurances and Iran's withdrawal of its appeal, Lie, in line with his prior thoughts on the matter, saw no advantage in keeping the question on the agenda. The world organization, he felt, should strive to settle disputes not to aggravate them. If both states agreed that their differences had been settled, the council should not raise doubts. Of course, any subsequent difficulties could be tackled immediately by the council. He was disturbed that the council majority did not agree with him. Lie desired to convey these views to the council in a private meeting, but the Australians had instructions not to attend private meetings and the Americans did not appear to favor one. He felt that he could not allow the Iranian precedent to be established, one which might be very influential in later years, without expounding what he, as secretary-general, saw as the wiser approach for the world organization.[26] Although Lie may have been oblivious to his own politicking, it was exhausting his credit and aggravating Stettinius. One suspects that Lie must have broached some of these thoughts with Stettinius on the afternoon of April 15, for Stettinius "had a little tiff" with Lie whose "face got very red."[27]

Nevertheless Lie decided to present his views to the council's president, who could do with them as he wished, although he anticipated that the president would convey them to the council. At the same time, he did not expect that his views would sway the majority's stand. Lie perceived the matter as a legal question of precedent rather than as a political matter of influencing the immediate course of the Iranian question. One is perplexed as to how he could conceive that the legal and political aspects of the question could be divorced. It was a serious mistake. Early on the morning of April 16, he conferred with the assistant secretaries-general and explained his views. There was a mixed reaction. Some concurred with Lie, including Sobolev, as one would expect. Others did not. However, with the assistance and urging of his legal counsellor, Feller, a memorandum was drafted for the council's president.[28]

It set forth the council's powers under Chapter VI of the charter (Articles 33 to 38) dealing with the peaceful settlement of disputes. In it Lie suggested that following Iran's withdrawal of its plea, the matter was automatically removed from the agenda unless the council voted an investigation, or a member brought it up as a dispute or situation, or the council found that a dispute or situation of a like nature existed and proceeded to recommend methods of adjustment. He also recognized that when an appeal was brought to the council's attention, it was no longer a matter involving only the disputing states, but one in which the council had a collective interest. Lie suggested, however, that the council would have to exercise that collective interest by invoking the charter's relevant articles. If this were not done, he concluded, it might well be that there was no way in which the council could "remain seized of the matter."[29]

Later that morning Lie chanced to meet Stettinius and enigmatically noted that he had a legal opinion to render.[30] His reticence to discuss it was perhaps a subconscious tit to Stettinius's tat of the previous day. When the council convened Lie conveyed his memorandum to Quo Tai-chi, who appeared surprised and questioned Lie's interest in the matter. When he did not accept the memorandum, Lie conveyed it to him through a third party.[31] Quo Tai-chi's attitude caused Lie to ruminate that the charter's intent and Article 99 gave him the authority to intervene in the proceedings; to submit legal opinions to the council's president; and to address the council on any matter. Quo Tai-chi's stance appeared to question this concept of the office's authority. If Quo Tai-chi did not acknowledge to the council receipt of his memorandum, Lie had decided that he would ask to speak and read it into the official record. All this proved unnecessary for Quo Tai-chi read the memorandum to the council. It was decided that it be referred to the Committee of Experts for study and report. Therefore, a vote on the question was delayed pending the committee's findings.[32]

In conversation with Charles "Chip" Bohlen, one of the State Department's Russian experts and an adviser to the mission, Lie proposed that Washington "should trust in Moscow and drop the case." Although some in the mission disagreed, Bohlen maintained that it was "ridiculous" to do so.[33] By this point the Cold War's tensions were rising, assisted no end by Russian actions in Iran; and Lie's comment to Bohlen could only have raised additional misgivings about the secretary-general's political acumen. Obviously he failed to see that keeping the question on the council agenda, despite all his political rationalizations, was one way of peacefully pressuring Moscow to expedite Russian troop withdrawal. In addition, Lie appeared not to appreciate that, for a weak and underdeveloped state like Iran dealing with a very powerful neighbor willing to engage in a high-risk foreign policy, appeals to world morality and world public opinion, to the tenets of international law, and to the procedures of international institutions were among the meager weapons in her diplomatic arsenal.

Lie's political acrobatics propelled Stettinius into a cold fury. The mission, he informed the State Department, felt that Lie's memorandum "was drafted with other than purely legal considerations in mind." Indeed, it was "considered extremely dubious practice for the Secretary-General to put in an unsolicited interpretation concerning a matter which should be decided by the Council alone." According to Stettinius, this was particularly true since eight of the council's eleven members held opinions contrary to those espoused by Lie.[34]

Stettinius pointed out to Byrnes that Lie had not been approached to give a legal opinion, but had "just jumped in." Moreover, he cryptically noted, "there were several other disturbing things" that had occurred with Lie and that Bohlen would relate them to Byrnes when they met. Byrnes responded that he already had suspicions about the situation. He queried whether Lie had consulted anyone on the council and was assured he had not but had apparently closeted himself with Feller and Sobolev before the memorandum was written.[35] In view of these hostile comments to Washington, the "hot words" rumored to have passed between Stettinius and Lie in the Delegates' Lounge of the United Nations were probably more than a mere rumor.[36]

Byrnes felt that Lie's memorandum, although maintaining that the council was prevented under the charter from taking further action in the Iranian question, was itself proposing action: namely, striking the question from the agenda, contrary to the council's resolution to desist from action until May 6.[37] In a closed session of the Senate Foreign Relations Committee, Byrnes indicated that he and other American officials believed that Lie had exceeded the limits of his authority, in suggesting that the council could not keep the question on its agenda after Iran had withdrawn it.[38]

Lord Halifax, the British ambassador in Washington, reported to London that Lie's memorandum had "surprised and irritated the bulk of middle-of-the-road and Right-Wing commentators." Their almost unanimous opinion was that Lie's legalistic arguments had "completely ignored" the case's merits and that acceptance of Lie's thesis "would set a precedent which might well make a mockery of the purposes" for which the world organization was established. Some observers recalled the League of Nations' capacity to lose sight of the "moral issue in a welter of procedural manoeuvres" and warned that the new organization must not be allowed to slip into the same evil ways. There was no question that Lie's reputation had "seriously suffered" from the episode. Leaving aside the Communists and their fellow travellers, who naturally were delighted, "even liberal-minded commentators conceded that he had not shown the impartiality" his office required. Those further to the right had "forthrightly damned him as unprincipled" and viewed his "performance as an act of frightened obeisance" to Soviet Russia by a citizen of her contiguous Norwegian neighbor. In the State Department, Halifax concluded, officials were speculating on Sobolev's role in preparing the Lie memorandum.[39]

Legal opinion within the State Department about Lie's memorandum was that a "fair construction" of the charter's relevant articles supported the view that the council had "complete control over its agenda." Thus, it had "wide discretion" in inscribing, not inscribing, or in maintaining agenda items. The exercise by the council of its discretion was in no way restricted by the "requests of parties to a dispute or a situation to place items on the agenda or to remove them," or when the secretary-general held that the situation had altered.[40]

Similar views were voiced by the Foreign Office's assistant legal adviser, Fitzmaurice. He had no doubt that Lie's argument was "wrong in substance." However, removal of the inscribed agenda item might result automatically from a council decision in which it reached some conclusion on the matter at issue, so that there was nothing more to do. It also might result from some specific council decision that the matter was regarded as disposed of or taken off the agenda. Nevertheless, Fitzmaurice thought, "whether by implication or expressly, . . . the decision must be the decision of the Council."[41]

During these days the Committee of Experts convened five times to examine Lie's memorandum. The committee was composed of advisers to the council's representatives. Those states wishing to retain the Iranian question on the agenda (Australia, Brazil, China, Egypt, Great Britain, the Netherlands, and the United States) rejected Lie's legal arguments. They contended, for example, that Lie's memorandum had placed the problem on too narrow a basis, that it implied an inexact understanding of the council's functions and the nature of its competence. Conversely, those states wishing to remove the item (France, Poland, and Soviet Russia) found legal grounds to agree with Lie, arguing, for example, that if the parties to a dispute reached agreement, the threat to the peace thereby disappeared; and if they asked that the item be withdrawn from the agenda, the council had to comply; and so on.[42] When word of the committee's majority report reached the Foreign Office, Counsellor John Ward observed that Lie had "received a rebuke for his very feeble and defeatist" memorandum.[43]

On April 22, Byrnes observed to Stettinius ironically that he had talked to his "friend Lie," who thought the question would be solved.[44] By this point, of course, Lie was aware of the Committee of Experts' report. The following day the council decided to retain the question on the agenda, though Gromyko maintained it was contrary to the charter and his delegation would not partake in further discussions of the matter.[45]

In the Foreign Office, as in the State Department, the genesis of Lie's memorandum left some uneasy. Could the background to the memorandum be given, Lawford, Cadogan's counsellor, was asked? Was it known whether the memorandum "derived from the legal brain" of Feller, from an authentic concern by Lie that a "dangerous precedent" might be established, or from Lie's "pure appeasement" of Gromyko promoted by Sobolev? Likewise, Lawford was asked for his current estimate of Lie's capacity for the job.[46] Before Lawford could respond an unsolicited report from the British mission to the United Nations held that Lie's intervention had been "entirely on his own initiative" and contrary to secretariat advice. Lie felt duty bound to draw the council's attention to the situation that had developed. Moreover, he was "generally held to have shown good intentions but poor judgment" in the manner in which he presented his position.[47]

Lawford's reply confirmed that the author of Lie's memorandum was Feller. Manifestly, Feller's general line of argument dovetailed with Lie's expressed desire to avoid a widening of the gap between Soviet Russia and the council's majority. One could conceive that Lie embraced the opportunity to prevent further ill will. What role Sobolev played in advising Lie along these lines, it was difficult to say. Sobolev, as the Foreign Office knew, was "one of those 'nice' Russians" whom everyone liked and "who for that very reason may be all the more useful to the Soviet Government." Certainly Sobolev had followed with great interest the Committee of Experts' discussion of Lie's memorandum, a committee whose proceedings he did not normally audit.

On Lie's capacity for the job, Lawford pointed out that it was unfair to assume that Lie was an enemy or that he was "consciously or unconsciously a Soviet stooge." Even so, one found traces occasionally of a "tendency at all costs to appease the Russians." As an example, Lawford divulged that just prior to the council meeting of March 27, when Gromyko left the chamber, Lie approached him and complained of Great Britain's "uncompromising attitude" over the Iranian question: he claimed that there was room for compromise but that British policy "would drive the Russians out" of the United Nations.

Lawford admitted that Lie's point of view was not difficult to fathom. Understandably, Lie did not want the world organization as well as his important international position to terminate after so short an existence. Like most people, he realized that the "doubtful quantity" in this whole matter was Russia's attitude. However, unlike everyone else, Lie "for his part [was] prepared to go to almost any lengths to keep her in."[48]

Lawford's report provoked considerable Foreign Office reaction. Ward confessed that he had "greatly over-rated" Lie as a candidate for the office. He thought that recently Lie had "declined a good deal personally." Because unanimity was needed among the council's permanent members to select a replacement for Lie or to reappoint him for another five year term, Ward thought that it would be extremely difficult to replace Lie "if he continued to suit the Russians." Jebb's "humble opinion" was that Lie was not the "right man for the job," which Jebb was willing to admit was the world's most difficult. He doubted whether Lie would want another five year tour, in view of the fact that he received a handsome retirement pension. The Northern Department's George Warr's pithy notation was that Lie's "unstable character" had "not stood up well" to Soviet Russia's flattering attentions. Assistant Under-Secretary Warner guessed that Lie was "an 'appeasing Westerner,' both on personal grounds connected" with his job and on national grounds. Warner did not believe that Lie's "actions or views at any given time [were] generally based on principle or basic conviction." As he had observed after Lie was appointed secretary-general, it would pay the Foreign Office, "to play up to his vanity a little," a comment Bevin endorsed, and he hoped that the Americans also would "not ignore or slight him."

Feller's prominent role in authoring Lie's memorandum did not go unnoticed. The head of the United Nations Department, Paul Mason, based on his prior dealing with Feller, "thought him a pretty amoral type of lawyer." "I shouldn't wonder," he reflected, "if he was a fellow traveller."

Equally pungent were the words of Deputy Under-Secretary Hall-Patch, who knew Feller well. He was a "smart and unscrupulous New York lawyer. I need say no more," he scribbled. From what he had seen of Lie since his appointment he appeared "very much more puffed up with his own importance," than when the Foreign Office knew him as Norway's foreign minister.[49]

While the council waited, in line with its resolution to defer the Iranian question until May 6, behind the scenes Lie again interjected himself into the question by proposing to Cadogan establishment of an investigatory commission, including a secretariat official, to be sent to Iran should there be conflicting reports from the parties about the promised Russian troop withdrawal.[50] Noel-Baker was obviously intrigued by the idea, though Ward had no doubt that Lie's proposed commission was a substantive matter and subject to the veto.[51] Was the proposed commission "Lie's own idea" and had Lie discussed it with other council members? Cadogan was queried.[52]

The Foreign Office considered it obvious that the Russians would do everything possible to prevent the council's establishment of such a commission. Since it was from the province of Azerbaijan that the Russians might fail to withdraw, any commission dispatched there might have difficulties with the local authorities. However, confronted with conflicting evidence, unless it wished to appear ridiculous, the council must surely make an attempt, at the minimum, to discover the facts. Although it might prove impossible to establish a commission, on the other hand, it might be worth pressing the proposal. The onus would be placed on the Russians for blocking it and thus attract world attention to Moscow's attempt to turn Iran into a satellite through the actions of its satraps in Azerbaijan.[53]

Cadogan responded that Moscow was sure to oppose the commission and could veto it, unless the Russians were declared to be parties to the dispute. But this would involve the council, Cadogan observed, "in a maze of controversy" that it had assiduously avoided: namely, determining what was a dispute. It was best to wait and see, and also oppose removal of the question from the agenda.[54] Noel-Baker thought that Lie's proposal "must have been most unwelcome to the USSR, tho' in itself a right and proper proposal for the SG to make."[55]

It depended, of course, on whose ox was being gored, and Lie's proposed commission certainly would have placed the Russians in an awkward position. But there is no evidence to suggest why Lie made this proposal or that he ever proffered it to the Russians. On the contrary, Lie's activities in the days that followed were attempts to placate the Russians by delaying any council meeting beyond May 6, to give them ample time to withdraw their troops from Iran.[56]

On the appointed day, May 6, Ambassador Ala informed the council that though there had been troop withdrawal from the Russian zone established by the Tripartite Treaty of Alliance of 1942, his government had been unable to confirm by direct observation reports of troop withdrawal from Azerbaijan. Several days later the council, with Gromyko absent, resolved to defer further proceedings on the question to give Teheran time to ascertain whether there had been total Russian troop withdrawal. Teheran was to submit a complete report once it had acquired the pertinent information and, if not able to do so by May 20, was to report whatever information it had acquired by that date.[57]

When May 20 arrived, Lie expressed to Stettinius his disbelief that Teheran would file any report by midnight and thought that, when the council convened as scheduled on May 22, it would find itself in a difficult situation. Lie then must have rocked Stettinius back on his heels when he observed that he did not see how the Iranian question could be removed from the agenda until Teheran had furnished the requested troop-withdrawal information. Even more incredibly, Lie then added that when he had submitted his legal memorandum he had not meant to infer that the question was to be removed from the agenda! What he had in mind at that juncture, he claimed, was that the question should be dropped by Iran as a complaint "but would be resumed as a complaint by the Security Council against the Soviet Union." In view of Lie's prior statements and actions, these comments boggle the imagination. Obviously weary, he complained that the entire Iranian question was complicated, especially as civil war seemed to have erupted in Iran. He did not know where the question would end.[58] Certainly Lie was aware from the Old and New Testaments that the meek would inherit the earth, but it was never said that it would be accomplished without toil and trouble.

Lie proved to be overly pessimistic. Although Ambassador Ala on May 20 stated that it had not been possible to establish total Russian troop withdrawal, he reversed himself the following day with information from the Iranian prime minister. Prior to the council's scheduled meeting of May 22, Lie then reverted to his previous stance that the question should be removed from the agenda. The council, however, again resolved to adjourn discussion of the Iranian question to an unspecified date but to convene at the request of any member. Never having been so reconvened, technically the council is still seized of the question.[59]

In London, Iran returned to Lie's idea of an investigatory commission; however, there appears to have been no British response.[60] With the Russians out of Iran, no useful purpose would be served by pursuing further the idea of a commission.

Lie's last word on the question was in early June, with Benjamin Cohen, the State Department's counsellor. Consistent in his inconsistency, Lie now queried "whether it would not be helpful to find a means of dropping Iran from the agenda." If doubt persisted about Russian troops in Iran, could not the secretariat be asked to render a report? Lie offered to send his American assistant, Stoneman, to Iran in such an event. Cohen had his doubts and thought it best to do nothing. He appreciated Lie's desire to draw the council's members closer together; however, it was important for Lie to be sure that his endeavors had a chance of success, or his actions might only widen the differences. In this connection, he noted Lie's unsolicited memorandum. Lie admitted that his memorandum "had not worked out well." He explained that he had considered it necessary to act, as Moscow "rightly or wrongly had felt that members of the council had not shown the same regard for Russian susceptibilities as they had shown for British susceptibilities in the case of Greece and Syria." Likewise, he had feared that Moscow might take some precipitous step that might have done the United Nations irreparable harm.[61]

Lie's comments bordered on the mendacious. In the Iranian question, as we have seen, he desired direct negotiations between the parties, though one was far more powerful than the other, and the avoidance of council pressure on Moscow that might, he theorized, complicate Russian troop withdrawal from Iran. In the contemporaneous and somewhat analogous complaint by Syria and Lebanon against Great Britain and France, Lie eschewed direct negotiations and wanted to involve the council. He "sympathized" with the Syrian and Lebanese complaint, Lie tells us; and when approached for advice, he confessed to his Arab suppliants that he felt that "the willingness of France and Britain to depart from the Levant could do with a little prodding." Accordingly, he advised that Syria and Lebanon bring their case to the council, for he was confident that England and France would respond.[62] If the Quai d'Orsay was alerted to Lie's advice that might partially explain Paris's hostile attitude toward him. His actions in these two episodes showed bias. Lie certainly did not cover himself with glory in the Iranian question as far as the West was concerned, and he squandered whatever remaining credits he had in the Spanish question as well.

Franco's Spain in the Dock

Of those states that remained neutral during the Second World War, none was despised more or held in greater contempt in the immediate postwar period than General Francisco Franco's Spain. The overthrow of the Spanish Republic by Franco's Falangist forces, the fratricidal civil war that followed, and the Nazi German and fascist Italian support for Franco, as well as his cordial relations with the Axis during the war, branded his regime as an outlaw government in the world community. The feelings against Franco's Spain were especially strong on the democratic left, a rubric that covered Lie, as well as on the dictatorial left, whose standard-bearer was Soviet Russia. It was only a matter of time, therefore, before Franco's government would become a topic of discussion at the United Nations.

Rather than raise the issue itself, in early April 1946, Moscow had its Polish surrogate place it on the council agenda. The Polish representative, Oscar Lange, argued that the actions of Franco's government were a danger to the maintenance of international peace and security and the United Nations was duty bound to take steps to compel Madrid to comply with the charter's principles and purposes. He proposed that all United Nations member states maintaining diplomatic relations with Madrid sever them immediately.

As one would expect, Gromyko supported Lange's stance. The American position favored the elimination of Franco's government and the restoration of democracy in Spain but without the eruption of another civil war in the Iberian peninsula. Cadogan observed that, before any collective action was taken, the council had to be sure it was not interfering with matters essentially within Spain's domestic jurisdiction. He maintained that Franco's Spain did not constitute a threat to the peace such as would warrant the collective severance of diplomatic relations.[63]

These words aggravated Lie; one of his assistants "obviously speaking on instructions" voiced to Lawford the "greatest anxiety" over the British position. When Lawford sharply disagreed, Lie's assistant suggested that it might be wise if Lie and Cadogan could see more of each other outside office hours. Several talks followed, which Cadogan thought had been helpful, but Lawford had his doubts, for he noted that "talks with Lie are not very profitable or productive."[64]

On April 25, the Australians offered an amendment to Lange's proposed resolution. The amendment called for the establishment of a five member subcommittee to determine whether the Spanish situation contributed to international friction and endangered international peace and security.[65] A vote on this amendment, however, would have led to a Russian veto, for Moscow's "position was unalterable." Lie's ploy was to delay the council proceedings while trying to have Gromyko's instructions altered. As Lie admitted, Gromyko had long meetings with Sobolev, presumably about the Russian stance. Gromyko, it appears, had asked Moscow to allow him to vote for the Australian amendment or, at the minimum, to be allowed to abstain. Lie felt that for the Russians to cast a veto at this juncture, "would have a very harmful effect on the Security Council."[66] Lie was likewise "surprised" by Argentina's intention to loan Spain $7.5 million, since Buenos Aires condemned Madrid at the General Assembly meetings in London.[67] The ideological symmetry between Juan Perón's Argentina and Franco's Spain, which might partially explain Buenos Aires's reversal of position, appears to have escaped Lie's attention.

Slightly revised by the French, the Australian resolution was unanimously adopted by the council on April 29, with Gromyko abstaining. Lie's delaying tactics had worked. The subcommittee comprised the representatives of Australia (chairman), Brazil, China, France, and Poland. It submitted its unanimous report on May 31 and concluded that no breach or threat to the peace had occurred, and no act of aggression had been proven. Therefore, the charter's enforcement measures could not be activated by the council. However, the subcommittee claimed, the Spanish situation was one whose continuance should be handled by the charter's procedures for peaceful settlement. The subcommittee urged that the council transmit to the assembly its recommendation that unless the Franco regime were withdrawn and steps toward political freedom satisfactory to the assembly be taken, a resolution be passed by it "recommending that diplomatic relations with the Franco regime be terminated by each member of the United Nations."[68]

During the subcommittee's deliberations Lie did little to disguise his commitment to expedite its task. His request on the subcommittee's behalf to the American mission for copies of the reports and analyses of materials broadcast by Spanish radio stations and monitored by American agencies smacked of a brusqueness that prompted Stettinius to decide that Lie's note would merely be "given a simple acknowledgement." In fact, the previous day Lie had warned Stettinius that he had "signed a rather rude and abrupt letter" to him, "the tone of which he regretted." Lie explained that it had been conveyed to him "from another office, and he had decided to sign it rather than redraft it."[69] He took a somewhat similar tack when he approached General Sir William Morgan, the chief commissioner of the Allied Commission in Rome, and requested all information and Italian documentation at his disposal concerning the attitude of Franco's regime toward the Axis and Allied Powers during the war.[70]

Once the subcommittee's report was made public, Lie attempted to ascertain the State Department's reaction. The only part of the report that Counsellor Cohen thought might produce difficulties was the proposed council recommendation to the assembly for the severance of diplomatic relations with Spain. Lie's rejoinder was that the subcommittee did not itself recommend the immediate severance of diplomatic relations but gave time, until the assembly convened in September, for the necessary steps to be taken in Spain. Lie feigned that he was unsure that American fear that this procedure "would help the communists was justified" and doubted whether Washington "appreciated the intensity of feeling of noncommunist European labor on the Franco issue." He was concerned that the growing tension between Soviet Russia and the West "might imperil the existence of [the] UN before it had a chance to develop."[71]

Lie indicated his own support for the subcommittee's recommendation in a talk with the acting American representative, Herschel Johnson. He explained to Johnson that, at a meeting of Scandinavian prime ministers and foreign ministers just prior to his appointment as secretary-general, he had proposed that, if one of them severed diplomatic relations with Spain, Norway would immediately do so, too. Lie's bold suggestion that others take the initiative certainly showed a lack of political grit. Sweden's Prime Minister Per Hansson, according to Lie, personally had no objection to severing relations with Spain but felt it was a step that should be taken by the United Nations, a clear intimation that Sweden would not act independently. It was an attitude no doubt shared by Denmark.

From another comment to Johnson, it was apparent that Lie had collaborated with the Australian foreign minister, Herbert Evatt, in preparing the subcommittee's report, although Lie admitted, keeping in mind his imperfect command of English, it had actually been drafted by Evatt and Paul Hasluck, the Australian representative. Although unaware of the State Department's view, Johnson personally was opposed to any collective diplomatic rupture with Spain. He did not believe it would prove effective. Indeed, its tendency would be to unite Spain in opposition to what would be perceived as an affront to Spanish "dignity and pride." Any such action would indirectly serve Franco's cause. The Egyptian representative, Hafaz Afifi Pasha, Johnson noted to the State Department, had learned of Lie's attitude and was displeased that "Lie was stepping outside his proper functions" in this question.[72]

Lie's collaboration with Evatt is of particular interest. They were bound together by similar but negative personality traits. Stettinius had scrutinized Evatt's behavior during the San Francisco Conference, and noted to President Truman that it could be "explained primarily in terms of [Australian] domestic politics." Evatt's support of varied Russian positions was considered in no way based on ideological factors, and even less on substantive ones, but on the political desirability in "Australian politics of being considered relatively Left Wing."[73] Evatt moreover, one astute observer of the United Nations scene has written, "was a contentious man . . . [who] did not suffer fools—or for that matter wise men— gladly." He "expected deference and was seldom inclined to regard any praise of himself as excessive. . . . [and any] injury to his vanity or sense of hierarchy might evoke vindictive reaction."[74] The epoxy binding Lie and Evatt was the Australian's idea that his country "could act as a bridge between the conflicting ideologies" of the United States and Soviet Russia—a belief that New Zealand Prime Minister Peter Fraser, who knew Evatt well, dismissed as "'crazy.'"[75] Lie, as noted before, also shared the penchant for bridge building, and, as we shall see, Lie and Evatt in alliance would shoulder their way through the corridors of the United Nations attempting to be the Roeblings of world politics.[76]

Meanwhile, meeting on the subcommittee's report, the council found it impossible to agree on a resolution acceptable, especially, to its permanent members.[77] When Poland's Lange proposed, on June 18, a compromise resolution, behind the scenes Lie urged him "in forceful terms to withdraw" it "on the ground that it would help Franco."[78] The council, however, was unable to hammer out a consensus resolution and the stalemate continued into the autumn and the convening of the assembly.[79] In mid-August, a visit by Cadogan gave Lie the opportunity to ruminate on the question. Franco had to be gotten rid of, he explained to Sir Alexander, who agreed, but correctly pointed out that there was no accord as to the procedure to be followed.[80]

Undoubtedly frustrated at the lack of Anglo-American support, Lie made his move on October 24, in a speech to the assembly supplementing his annual report on the work of the world organization. The Spanish question had already been discussed in the Security Council and Economic and Social Council, and he thought it probable that other organs of the United Nations and the autonomous specialized agencies would likewise become involved with it. In these circumstances, Lie argued, the assembly could "do a valuable service by giving comprehensive guidance" to the United Nations organs and member states "regarding their relationship" with Franco's regime. As long as this government continued in Spain it would be a cause of friction among the United Nations' founders.[81]

Who propelled Lie to make these comments and assume a public stance in the Spanish question is open to conjecture; but it would probably not be unfair to assume that it was prompted by Moscow, which wished to circumvent the stalement in the council. Using the everpresent and influential Sobolev, Lie was brought to express publicly what he had already expressed behind the scenes. Sobolev made no attempt to disguise his partiality. He was emphatic that a resolution be adopted severing diplomatic relations with Madrid. If the Franco government continued in power, the council should impose economic sanctions. When queried by Adlai Stevenson how the council could invoke sanctions if there was no threat to the maintenance of peace and security, Sobolev responded, in a leap of logicality, that Franco's very continuance in office after the severance of diplomatic relations would constitute such a threat. He had no doubt that the council could arrive at such a finding, to legitimize the application of economic sanctions.[82]

After his speech, in response to questions, Lie made it clear that he was not invoking Article 99 and had no intention of doing so; nor was he submitting the question to the assembly. Instead, he was attempting to bring to the members' attention the fact that the council was seized of the Spanish question and at the same time deadlocked over it. Lie insisted that as secretary-general "he felt deeply concerned" over the question and was asking for guidance from the world organization's members in order that a solution may be devised.[83]

The Foreign Office's reaction to Lie's statement was predictably unfriendly. John Wilson of the Western Department thought it very unfortunate that Lie should have chosen to make his declaration just at that moment. He was unsure whether Lie's action, in precipitating the question and making public comments before the matter was formally raised in the assembly, was entirely correct. In line with what had occurred in the council, Wilson envisaged Russian tactics designed to get the assembly to agree to a resolution recommending that United Nations members reduce their relations with the Franco government and possibly isolate it completely. Lie was clearly playing the Russian game, and unless London was fortunate, it might be placed in an awkward position in New York. Since Washington was assuming the same stance as London, Wilson thought the Russians could be prevented from doing what they wanted. The position of other states, particularly the Latin American ones, was unclear. Unfortunately, the result of an assembly discussion with all its accompanying publicity would probably be the strengthening of Franco and the turning back of the clock in Spain by six months. "This will not, however, be our fault," Wilson concluded.

William Hogg, also of the Western Department, thought that the Russian group's intent would be to obtain diplomatic recognition of José Giral of the Spanish Republican government in exile. Even if no guidance was enunciated the effect of this agitation would be to strengthen Franco and "therefore to prevent or defer the emergence of a solution on the lines which we would like to see."[84]

The reaction of Franco's controlled press to Lie's comments—censorship had been relaxed to permit full reporting on the discussion of the Spanish question abroad—was one of deep hostility. It held that Lie had "grossly exceeded his functions." His move was characterized as "apparently Communist-inspired" and Lie himself denounced as a "traitor" and a "fool," as well as Moscow's servant and the straw man of its policy.[85] Danish Foreign Minister Gustav Rasmussen was very much surprised by Lie's statement. He could understand the anti-Franco stance of his Norwegian counterpart, Halvard Lange; but Rasmussen's private opinion was that policy statements of this nature by the secretary-general "were not authorized by the Charter."[86]

Somewhat similar thoughts were held by Sir Victor Mallet, the British ambassador in Madrid, who admitted that he had been "rather shocked" by Lie's move at a time when the United Nations had "more important fish to fry." Furthermore, it appeared to Mallet that Lie showed an "almost frivolous disregard" toward the charter's strictures, which he was duty bound to protect. Reopening the Spanish question in the United Nations was certain to widen the differences and check any tendency of the country's civil war opponents to come together. Outside interference in Spain's affairs stiffened the Right and Center and aroused, in the Left, hopes that were unlikely to come to fruition. Any such action tended to discourage moderate elements from striving toward a rapprochement between democratic forces and the monarchists, about which Mallet had heard much recently.[87]

In forwarding Mallet's letter to Deputy Under-Secretary Sir Oliver Harvey, the head of the Western Department, Frederick Hoyer Millar, expressed fear that the more said about Spain, and especially at the United

Nations, the less likelihood there would be of the "internal opposition to Franco gaining strength" and the more likelihood that Franco could "consolidate his own position."[88] John Wilson's minutes for the Western Department noted that Mallet's views dovetailed with those of the Foreign Office. He thought that Great Britain was facing a "ruthless attempt" to defeat her aims in Spain. Moscow could not want a broadly based, liberal government in Madrid moving toward Western-style democracy. It would certainly do all it could to get a wholly left-wing government in power— the result of which would be chaos and perhaps civil war. Wilson did not know why Lie was playing with the Russians. Perhaps other departments could shed some light on this. Ever since the Norwegian traitor Vidkun Quisling went to his death claiming that Lie was in Russian pay, "there have been constant whispers of his link with Moscow."[89]

Mallet's report that the Spanish press was in "full cry" but reserved its "most biting criticisms" for Lie, who they maintained had "grossly exceeded his functions,"[90] provoked additional observations. Hoyer Millar thought Lie was justified in calling the assembly's attention to the Spanish question. Where Lie had gone very much astray, however, was in attacking Franco and suggesting that steps be taken to replace his regime. Hoyer Millar thought Lie had exceed his role as an "impartial and neutral Secretary-General." From a purely Spanish angle, there was little doubt that Lie's comments had been unfortunate. As the Madrid embassy had reported, they had given "Franco just the opportunity that he wanted of posing once again as the defender of Spain against foreign intervention." Inevitably, it would also have lowered the United Nations' prestige in the estimation of most Spaniards. Again, the United Nations appeared to be a tool of Russian and communist policy. All this was unfortunate when many in Spain were beginning to feel the country's "moral isolation" and were becoming more and more unhappy at Madrid's exclusion from the various activities organized by the United Nations. This favorable impact would be dissipated if Spaniards were allowed to think that the United Nations was run primarily in Russian interests or that the secretary-general was far from neutral. Hoyer Millar had no doubt that Lie, as a socialist in good standing, had a "perfectly genuine dislike for Franco and a real desire to see him kicked out," and this could be best achieved through United Nations action. On the other hand, Hoyer Millar supposed that Lie might be deliberately assisting Moscow, which wanted to complicate the Spanish question and make matters worse by charging Spain at the United Nations, and so ensuring that no moderate government could replace Franco in the near future.

The United Nations Department's views were recorded by John Peck, who noted that the question of Lie's prerogatives had been raised in the past. The line taken was that, although he had, on occasion, clearly gone beyond his rights, it would nevertheless be a mistake to challenge him since Article 99 of the charter gave him very wide powers. Moreover, a restrictive interpretation of the secretary-general's functions at this juncture might not be to London's advantage in the future, if Lie were replaced by someone of "greater authority and judgment"—a prophetic assessment. The difficulty with Lie, Peck observed, was that his diverse initiatives beyond the strict perimeters of the secretary-general's responsibilities had generally been unfortunate in their timing, their substance, and their method of presentation. Most likely in this matter responsibility could be traced to Sobolev, who "could be relied upon to reflect faithfully the Soviet view-point"; Lie might well have accepted Sobolev's advice on the Spanish problem without any thought or question. Peck admitted that these thoughts were "pure conjecture"; but if Lie was becoming a "menace," it might be worth investigating whether wise counsels could be whispered into his ear, possibly through Cadogan.

Hoyer Millar cautioned that London had enough trouble over the Spanish question as it was, without commencing an argument with Lie. The last word was from Warr, who could not explain Lie's actions either. The Norwegians, he observed, were interested in Spain. Perhaps they hoped that by showing interest they would be able to "curry favour with the Russians."[91]

A head-on collison by the State Department and the Foreign Office with Lie over the Spanish question was avoided, so that when Poland, on October 30, asked the council to remove the item from its agenda so the matter could be considered by the assembly, the council acquiesced and placed all its records and documents at the assembly's disposal. In the plenary organ the question was referred to the First Committee (Political and Security) for examination.[92]

When Lie subsequently raised the question of Great Britain's attitude with Jebb, the latter responded, in an obvious attempt to forestall additional initiatives by him, that the Spanish question was very difficult and that Lie should not "take the lead about any particular course."[93] Jebb's comments, unfortunately, had no impact on Lie. On the contrary, Lie noted to Adlai Stevenson that he felt the United States should support an assembly resolution to sever diplomatic relations. Lie disagreed with the council's contention that Franco's Spain was not a threat to the peace; fascism, he held, had been the seed of war and was a cancer in the world community and an unending threat.

Although Lie suggested to Stevenson a meeting of the five great powers, he was apprehensive that an exchange of views might only highlight their differences. He appeared greatly "agitated by the question and confused" as to what should be done aside from exploring the possibilities of an agreement among the Big Five. His alternate suggestion was that the United States and Great Britain directly pressure Franco's government, as the best method outside the United Nations, to attain its withdrawal. Lie thought that both countries should threaten oil embargoes, prepared to impose them unilaterally if Franco failed to step down, and call upon all other states to do likewise. Lie argued that Franco would be immediately toppled and the Republican government in exile would assume control of Spain until free elections could be held. Lie was confident that American economic help could control the character of the new Madrid government and that there was little likelihood of communism in Spain. He felt that the exclusion of Franco's Spain from the United Nations' autonomous specialized agencies was valuable but desired stronger measures against Franco that would have American support.[94]

Since the Americans and the British opposed any assembly resolution proposing radical measures against Franco's Spain, Lie struggled to keep the issue in the limelight. Over 64,000 postcards, he announced in a press release, had been received since September 1, arguing for the severance of diplomatic relations with Franco's Spain and the recognition of a Giral government.[95] When Sir Hartley Shawcross and others explained to Lie that serious unemployment would develop in England, especially in the steel industry that was largely dependent on Spanish iron ore, if economic relations were severed, Lie and others then discussed with some serious-ness the possibility of United Nations compensation to Great Britain for such losses.[96] He was becoming frustrated and rapidly losing his patience, which in part explains his outburst to the correspondent of the Oslo daily *Aftenposten*: that the greatest difficulty at the moment was the unfriendly American attitude toward Russia; pro-Russian comments, he observed, were sometimes sufficient to be branded as a "Red or Communist." This made daily life somewhat "boring," he complained.[97]

During this period, he was willing to grasp at any possibility that presented itself. His "grave concern" over the question[98] explains his initial attraction to a plan proposed by Cuba's Guillermo Belt—who in his assembly address of October 29, opposed coercive measures—that the Latin American, Spanish-speaking states make a special appeal to Franco to resign and open the way to Spain's admission to the United Nations.[99] By November 21, Lie's "orginally enthusiastic" reaction to Belt's proposal, "now seemed less so."[100] What led to Lie's about-face is only conjecture: perhaps a talk with Sobolev may have gotten Lie back on the right track, at least as far as Moscow was concerned; or he may have considered the mere stepping down of Franco as inadequate. What Lie and the anti-Franco camp wanted was not a mere resignation of the Caudillo but a complete removal, kit and caboodle, of the government structure in Spain, which the Belt-inspired solution would not guarantee.

Consideration of the question did not commence in the assembly's First Committee until December 2. The past arguments were largely repeated; draft resolutions and amendments were tendered by those wishing to coerce the Franco regime and those favoring a policy of nonintervention. The

First Committee discussed these proposals at length and decided, on December 4, to accept a Cuban suggestion to establish a subcommittee to draft a resolution based on the proposals it received.[101]

Lie was now disturbed because the Spanish question "had become a point of contention" in the assembly, conveniently ignoring his own contribution to this state of affairs. He told Senator Vandenberg, a member of the delegation to the assembly, that the intention of his original statement of October 24 denouncing the Franco government had been to have the question handled by the conference of foreign ministers.[102] This comment strains one's credulity and equaled in deceptiveness his statement to Stettinius in May that his memorandum on Iran had not meant to infer that the Iranian question should be removed from the council agenda.

On December 9, the First Committee considered its subcommittee's report. Due to the strong opposition of Senator Tom Connally of Texas, also a member of the delegation, it did not include proposals to break diplomatic relations or to impose economic sanctions. The draft resolution finally accepted by the First Committee was an admixture of the subcommittee's draft with Belgian and British amendments. The assembly discussed and adopted it on December 12. Its salient portions recommended that Spain be debarred from being a member of any United Nations–associated international agency and from participation in United Nations–sponsored activities until a new regime was established. In addition, it recommended that United Nations members "immediately recall" their diplomatic chiefs of mission accredited to the Madrid government and report action taken to the secretary-general at the next session of the assembly.[103] The Anglo-Americans by their actions, both inside and outside the United Nations, had prevented any recommendation for economic sanctions and had scaled down the severance of diplomatic relations to the less objectionable recall of senior diplomatic staff.

A week later, Lie requested the British mission to inform him as soon as possible of action taken by London in accordance with the resolution.[104] The Foreign Office was annoyed. A communication on this matter had been expected, wrote R. K. W. Sloan of the Western Department, possibly with a request from Lie for suitable action; instead, Lie asked what London had done about it. Sloan observed that there "may or may not be a dig," in Lie's communication, at Mallet's continued residence in Madrid. If so, it would be answered by Mallet's departure the following day. Nevertheless, Sloan observed, the United Nations Department might wish to take Lie up "on his apparently elliptical procedure."[105]

Whether this was done is unrecorded. Lie's haste in contacting the Foreign Office can probably be traced to the fact that he was "troubled" by the "lack of response" to the assembly's resolution[106] and allegedly disappointed "with [the] inadequate action"[107] taken by the assembly against Spain—and rightly so from his point of view.

The actual effect of the assembly resolution was meager. Only three states recalled their chiefs of mission (Great Britain, the Netherlands, and Turkey); thirty states had no diplomatic relations with Spain; nineteen states had no ambassador or minister plenipotentiary in Madrid; and one state, Perón's Argentina, merely acknowledged receipt of the resolution and responded by accrediting an ambassador to Madrid where there was none before.[108] By April 1947, with Bolivia's reestablishment of diplomatic relations with Spain,[109] it was obvious that the high point of United Nations action had come and gone.

The possibility that the Spanish question might be brought to the fore at the 1947 assembly session, however, prompted the State Department and the Foreign Office to "pursue the idea of defensive lobbying." As a first step, the State Department proposed that there be a "concerted informal approach" to explain to Lie London's and Washington's attitude and to ascertain whether he had received any indications of the intentions of other states on the Spanish question. Although Hogg of the Western Department suggested that the question be simultaneously broached with Lie, France, and China and preparations made to approach others at the first leakage, Jebb disagreed. Lie was "peculiarly unsound" on the Spanish question, he pointed out, and if told of any lobbying plans, he would "at once start lobbying in the opposite direction." There would be no harm in finding out what Lie knew regarding recent comments by others on the question, Jebb thought, but that was all that should be done.[110]

The fuse on the Spanish question was obviously sputtering, and to rekindle it, Lie again brought it to everyone's attention as he had the previous year, except this time he restricted himself to a comment in the introduction to his annual report. The problem of Franco's Spain, he wrote, could not "yet be said to be satisfactorily resolved in the spirit"[111] of the assembly resolution of December 1946. The United Nations' interest, however, was beginning to lag. An assembly resolution, of November 1947, was anodyne, and attempts to reintroduce the question in the council led nowhere.[112] Lie's comments to the council on the assembly resolution, however, were construed by Madrid, which took them to mean that the 1947 resolution had not affected the power of the 1946 resolution, as manifestly hostile.[113] Naturally, as one would expect, Lie was opposed to Spain's inclusion in the Marshall Plan.[114]

By 1949 Lie had to adjust his anti-Franco orientation in line with the changing forces in international politics. He tried to use the still stalemated Spanish question to help score gains in another direction: an increase in United Nations membership. He observed to the Americans that, although he did not like Franco, he no longer opposed Spain's admission to the United Nations; Franco was certainly no worse than Perón. Lie believed that the principle of universality should prevail and proposed an understanding with the Russians. He suggested that Spain be admitted along with fourteen other states, including some of the Russian satellite states of Eastern Europe[115] that the United States had opposed. The Americans, however, demurred. They thought it would be "unfortunate to raise [the] Spanish question at this time."[116]

Lie shifted his ground slightly in March 1950, when he was pressing Communist China's right to occupy the Chinese seat in the United Nations. He felt that China's countless millions had the right to be represented in the world organization. Moreover, Spain's twenty million shared this right and, whatever thoughts one had about Franco, Spain should be admitted to the United Nations.[117] A year later, Lie reiterated his desire to see Spain admitted along with other states. When Spain was finally admitted as a member in 1955, it was as part of a package deal like the one Lie had proposed in 1949, including some of the Eastern European states.[118] But by this point Lie was no longer secretary-general.[119]

In retrospect one can argue with some cogency that the Anglo-Americans were correct in resisting Lie's desire that the United Nations intervene against Franco's Spain, in their fear that it would stiffen support for Franco and his dictatorship and in their hope that, with time, internal developments would lead to a metamorphosis of the regime. Not until the mid-1970s did this occur, long after Spain became a United Nations member. It was a fate that Spain and her people, who had suffered so much, richly deserved.

4

WAR
BY
OTHER
MEANS

The Balkan Cockpit: Greece

The Greek question was already being discussed when Lie was appointed secretary-general. It had been brought to the Security Council's attention in January 1946 by Soviet Russia, which claimed that the continued postwar presence of British troops in Greece meant interference in her internal affairs, caused tensions, and adversely affected the Greeks and the maintenance of international peace and security. The Greek question, therefore, at least in this initial phase, was viewed by Lie as one more irritant between Moscow and the West that had to be treated quickly, before it caused greater inflammation. The debate between Bevin and Vyshinsky, both public and private, was bitter. He asked them to curb their inflammatory speech and to cool their passions; Lie sometimes advised the council president to adjourn public meetings and reconvene in the privacy of Lie's office to attempt to devise a settlement. Stettinius's attempt, in early February 1946, to draft a resolution acceptable to both sides elicited Lie's support. The whole episode was Lie's first brush with what has been called parliamentary diplomacy. It was a frustrating period, and at one point Lie "appeared to have had two or three highballs" to fortify himself during the discussions before he exclaimed to Stettinius that it was the "God damndest performance he had ever seen in his life." He was probably right. The council, in terminating this first discussion of the Greek question, merely noted the declarations of those states that had spoken on the question and considered the matter closed.[1] It was a British-Russian standoff.

The question remained quiescent until August when the Ukrainians complained that Greek policies were a threat to peace and security because of incidents along the Greek-Albanian border provoked by Athens. A procedural wrangle then developed over whether the Ukrainian complaint, which it was claimed was a series of unsupported accusations, could be inscribed on the council agenda. Led by the United States, which contended that no state could be denied the opportunity to present its case that a situation was likely to threaten peace and security, the council decided that the Ukrainian complaint should be heard. In a series of meetings all sides presented their views. Draft resolutions offered by a number of states, however, failed to gain acceptance. The consensus was to accept a ruling by the council president, Gromyko, that the council would move to the next item on its agenda. Asked for his opinion, Lie held that the council was no longer seized of the Greek question and that it was automatically removed from the agenda.[2]

In the midst of these discussions, as we have seen, the Americans proposed that a three-person investigatory commission be established. This propelled Lie to observe to the council that, should the American proposal be rejected—which it was—he reserved his right to make such inquiries or investigations. Lie held that he had this right under Article 99 and had no need for the council's prior consent. Lawford of the British mission doubted that Lie could do this on his own initiative, and the Foreign Office rejected the whole idea.[3] Cadogan's pithy observation to Lie was that, if he acted on his threat, "he would undermine his own position and would have to go."[4]

Lie did nothing officially. However, the initial American response was less clear-cut. When Lie told the Americans privately that he would establish a three-person secretariat mission of investigation, "provided he was assured" of American support, opinion in the State Department differed. Some thought Lie had such authority and should be supported although, in view of the fact that a "commission" could be vetoed, the "distinction between a commission and a committee" should be emphasized to Lie. But the State Department finally decided that it was inappropriate for Lie to investigate a matter that the council had already examined.

Like the Foreign Office, the State Department believed that any mission Lie might appoint would probably not be permitted to enter Albania, Bulgaria, or Yugoslavia and therefore no real inquiry could be conducted. This prospect made it "unwise to run the serious risks of impairing Lie's effectiveness in his relations with the Russians and of perhaps adversely affecting the Russian relationship to the United Nations as a whole."[5]

In November, despite American and British rejection of Lie's proposal, Alger Hiss, who handled United Nations matters, pointed out to Under-Secretary Acheson that, if a commission of investigation composed of the council's permanent members proved impossible, an alternative scheme might be for the council to direct Lie to have the secretariat investigate in its behalf. Hiss recalled Lie's previous proposal to dispatch an investigatory mission to Greece's borders; accordingly this proposal would not be novel and presumably would be agreeable to Lie. It would avoid protracted delay by the council in selecting personnel or countries to be represented on it. Hiss argued that there was also the advantage of establishing a precedent for "impartial" secretariat commissions of investigation. However, in view of how secretariat personnel were later chosen for the council commission of investigation in Greece and how those personnel behaved, the tenor of Hiss's remarks may be interpreted as supporting the subsequent accusation that he was a Russian agent.

At about this same time the Greek Ambassador in Washington, Kimon Diamantopoulos, inquired of the State Department whether Athens should bring the question to the General Assembly or get Lie to invoke Article 99 and bring it to the Security Council; while the American Ambassador in Athens was simultaneously informed, Lie had indicated a willingness to dispatch an investigatory commission.[6] The Greek request to Lie, on December 3, asked him to bring before the council a situation leading to friction between Athens and its neighbors who were supporting the violent guerrilla fighting in northern Greece against public order and Greek territorial integrity. The government also drew council attention to the urgent need for an on-the-spot investigation to discover the causes of this situation.

At its meeting of December 18, Herschel Johnson proposed an American draft resolution (modified and expanded by others) to establish a commission to ascertain the facts relating to the alleged border violations, with the right to conduct any necessary investigations in situ in areas of Greece, Albania, Bulgaria, and Yugoslavia. The commission would be composed of the council members and would have liaison officers accredited from Albania, Bulgaria, Greece, and Yugoslavia. Lie would furnish any necessary staff and other assistance. The commission would report to the council, making proposals to avert a recurrence of the border violations and disturbances. The resolution establishing the Council Commission of Investigation Concerning the Greek Frontier Incidents was adopted unanimously on December 19, 1946.[7]

Secretary of State Byrnes on the following day instructed Johnson that if any Albanian, Bulgarian, or Yugoslavian official of the secretariat were seconded to the commission staff then a Greek secretariat official should also be assigned. If no nationals of these countries were assigned, then Athens would not insist on the appointment of one of its own nationals.

"I just want to make sure there is a balanced staff," Byrnes wisely observed.[8] Lie, however, assured Johnson that no national of any concerned country would be put on the commission secretariat. In fact, he planned to appoint as principal secretary, Colonel Roscher Lund, a Norwegian and one of his special advisers.

Byrnes had seen the obvious hole, but there were other ways to "load" the commission secretariat and deny it that balance that Byrnes was so keen on achieving, thanks to the fact that Sobolev actually assigned secretariat officials to the commission staff. Lie apparently was unable to control or to see through the machinations of his Russian assistant secretary-general of Security Council affairs.[9]

The Commission Secretariat

The first indication that the activities, as well as the personnel, of the commission secretariat would cause a storm was on January 9, 1947, when Vassili Dendramis, the Greek representative at the United Nations, learned that the advance party of the commission secretariat would be led by a Ukrainian, Konstantin L. Volokhov, who was Sobolev's personal assistant. Dendramis admitted to the British that although Volokhov was an international civil servant and in no way a representative of the Ukrainian government, nevertheless he felt that it would have a deplorable effect in Greece if the advance party was led by a Ukrainian, in view of the very offensive accusations against the Greek government by the Ukrainian foreign minister in the United Nations.

On Cadogan's instructions, Lawford suggested to Lie that it should be possible to avoid offending Athens in this manner. Lie saw the point. He confirmed that the plan to send Volokhov as the leader of the advance party had originated with Sobolev, but Lie insisted that he had always thought Volokhov was Russian not Ukrainian—as though, with legal Russian identity, Volokhov would have been more acceptable to the Greeks.

Lie immediately ordered that Lund head the advance party. Lawford hoped that Athens would not attach great importance to the fact that Volokhov would still be in the advance party, albeit now in a very junior position. What had occurred, Lawford noted to Paul Mason, head of the United Nations Department, was another example of the kind of problem that the mission was up against thanks to Sobolev's position. Lawford did not know, he admitted, whether Sobolev was not fully cognizant of the impact that Volokhov as leader of the advance party would have in Greece or whether he deliberately wanted to treat the Greeks in this fashion. Be that as it may, Lawford felt it was "rather gratuitous" on Sobolev's part to have picked a Ukrainian as his personal assistant, as well as a member of the commission secretariat. It was no doubt part of Sobolev's policy of "sprinkling Slavs everywhere," of which the Foreign Office was well aware.

The mission had nothing specific against Volokhov, although it was true that throughout the discussions of the Greek question in August and September, he had not believed it inappropriate to sit with members of the Ukrainian delegation. Lawford described him as a "large, swart, gloomy individual, with a shambling gait." He had first met him during the Moscow Conference in 1943, but did not consider him a "person of outstanding ability." Volokhov's task on the commission secretariat would presumably be to act as a "spy for his master," at which assignment he would undoubtedly be competent. Suffice it to say, Lawford concluded, Volokhov had a "suitably N. K. V. D. appearance," and had "rarely been known to speak."[10]

In the Foreign Office, it was suggested that Cadogan be asked whether the personnel and composition of the commission secretariat could not be changed. The fear, however, was that the British government could not justify such a step unless a secretariat member could be caught "red handed in some infamy." Norway, it was pointed out, was "very subservient" to the Russians, Lund being to Volokhov what Lie was to Sobolev. Any such effort at the United Nations, without an excellent and incontrovertible reason, would be doomed to failure.[11]

The Foreign Office was stymied. It appreciated Lawford's "swift and effective action" regarding Volokhov and assumed that Lawford had seen the message from Athens that the second ranking member of the commission secretariat, Gustav Gottesman (a Pole dubbed by the commission's Australian representatives as Gustav Devilman), and Volokhov were "influencing Lund in quite the wrong way." Far greater damage might have occurred, it was noted, had Volokhov played the role for which he was originally groomed but had been denied thanks to Lawford's representations.[12] The Greeks thought Gottesman's and Volokhov's abilities to influence Lund could be partially traced to the Norwegian's limited intellectual make-up, to his inexperience in running such a body, and to his weakness for libations.[13]

Difficulties developed from the moment the commission arrived in Athens, largely because the secretariat undertook to run it. Many commissioners were angry over this and quickly prevented its success; but the secretariat deviously persisted in its attempt. Indeed, at one point, Gottesman told Mark Ethridge, the American commissioner, that he believed the secretariat should provide "'political guidance'" to the commission. Ethridge responded that Gottesman "was crazy and on dangerous ground and that he had better not try it." Gottesman, however, never lost an opportunity to embarrass the Greek authorities. The commission's press officer, a Canadian, Stanley Ryan, also had to be curbed, particularly over press reports he transmitted through the United Nations, of which nobody had been aware, including the commission's rotating chairmen. There was also evidence that Ryan leaked confidential documents to the Greek communist press.[14]

In fact, the press officer of the Canadian mission in New York had been forced to complain to the secretariat about how "Ryan had handled publicity of the Canadian point of view." The Canadian embassy in Athens admitted to its British counterpart that although Ryan was "definitely anti-Greek," this was partly due to Ryan's reaction to the Greek press campaign against him, which he felt was an attempt to make him line up with Athens's position. Since Ottawa was suspicious of "Ryan's pro-Soviet prejudices" the Canadian embassy sought more information about his attitude.[15]

In discussions with Canadian embassy officers, Ryan admitted that he had been born and lived in Russia until he was five years old, although he gave the impression that his parents were Canadian. He divulged that he had worked as an Associated Press correspondent during the 1930s in Germany, France, and Spain during the civil war. Ryan's general approach appeared to be "pro-Soviet." He emphasized his dislike for Mediterranean states because they were inefficient. Greece he disliked from the first instant, as it smelled of a police state; he was familiar with that smell based on his interwar experience in fascist countries. He had been branded a warmonger in the 1930s, he alleged, because he denounced Nazi Germany's expansionist policies. He believed that the Western states could and should reach an understanding with Soviet Russia based on spheres of influence, as agreed during the war for the Balkans, and then not to interfere in each other's assigned areas; but he failed to note that this very agreement had assigned Greece to the British sphere. Moreover, he professed the naive belief that Soviet Russia was concerned merely with her security and had no aggressive designs or economic frustrations like those that impelled Nazi Germany to invade other European countries.

Ryan admitted he was an admirer of America's former vice president Henry Wallace, who was critical of the Truman administration's policies toward Soviet Russia. His Canadian discussants noted that Ryan had been involved in deciding what groups the secretariat recommended as witnesses to the commission. Ottawa had been informed that the commission had been criticized in Greece for examining mostly witnesses of the extreme Left. While Ryan partly shared the responsibility for this bias, Ambassador Leo LaFleche informed Ottawa "other senior members of the Commission's Secretariat [were] still more pro-Soviet" than he. The American and British embassies in Athens had inquired about Ryan, and the alternate British commissioner, Edward Peck, "was quite openly antagonistic to the manner in which Mr. Ryan had handled press conferences in which the proceedings at secret sessions had been reported to the public." For instance, Ryan had publicly referred to executions of those involved in guerrilla activities, as political; and privately, he vehemently denounced official Greek actions. The condemned, he claimed, were prisoners of war and were being butchered; such actions were driving people into the hills and complicating the commission's task. Ryan denied Athens's need either to prevent the shipments of food into guerrilla-held areas or to take other "strong measures against a ruthless minority." He likewise denied the "evidence of foreign intervention" presented to the commission by the Greek liaison officer, the experienced diplomat, Alexis Kyrou. In addition, Ryan denied that there was a greater freedom in Greece than in Albania, Bulgaria, and Yugoslavia; only in Athens, he maintained, was there a façade of political freedoms. Ambassador LaFleche concluded that Ryan appeared either to be "pro-Soviet or so intent on maintaining an unprejudiced attitude in the face of pro-Greek propaganda that he [was] falling over backwards."[16]

Ryan's comments to his Canadian discussants had been deceptive in the extreme, a smoke screen to disguise both his background and his orientation. As the Greek embassy in Washington pointed out to the State Department (no doubt from information supplied by the Royal Canadian Mounted Police), Ryan's real name was Gerschun, his parents Jewish, and he had been born in Leningrad in 1902. Ryan had worked in Germany and in 1933 emigrated to New York. During the Spanish civil war he fought on the Loyalist side. Then in 1940, he established himself in British Columbia, where he joined the army, becoming a naturalized Canadian citizen in 1944. He had been appointed to the United Nations secretariat during the Preparatory Commission meetings in London.[17] Ryan's attitude, sympathies, and perceptions would have made it difficult for him to hold any other position than the one he had assumed. Even more important, however, it spotlighted him as the type of person easily amenable to possible recruitment into the Russian intelligence network, which followed, as the files of Western counterintelligence agencies clearly show. Whether the talent spotters and recruiters were Gottesman and Volokhov is unclear. Suffice it to say that like them he served his master diligently.[18]

The first questionable action by the secretariat occurred within a week after the commission convened in Athens. On the night of February 5, Lund was approached by three representatives of the ELAS (National Popular Liberation Army, the military arm of the communist-controlled EAM, the National Liberation Front) as well as the defense attorneys of five Greek guerrillas sentenced to death. The harsh sentences reflected a situation in which the legal government of Greece was fighting for its survival against a concerted communist, guerrilla-directed rebellion supported by her three northern neighbors as well as Soviet Russia. Lund, under the influence of Gottesman and Volokhov, especially in the matter of EAM petitions, summoned an informal meeting of some of the commission representatives. With their agreement, but without seeking formal permission of the whole commission, he handed Kyrou copies of the letters of appeal received for the condemned. He informed Kyrou that, since the question of the executions would be discussed by the commission, the secretariat considered it opportune for the government to suspend the sentences until after such discussion since it was possible that the commission might request some of the condemned to appear as witnesses.[19] Kyrou "very emphatically declared" that he was not in a position to convey any such message to his government concerning Greece's "domestic affairs." Tellingly, he inquired whether the five commission members who had met had been authorized to do so by the rest of them. Moreover, Kyrou noted, Lund was merely tendering a recommendation, and he hoped that the commission would avoid getting involved in this "purely domestic affair, so that it might not jeopardize in advance the success of its work."

That same night the cabinet convened and Kyrou was instructed to repeat to Lund his prior protest and to state that, as a gesture of goodwill to facilitate the commission's task, the government would postpone the executions for forty-eight hours, although the sentences had been properly decided by judicial tribunals with the exclusive right to do so. Concurrently, Dendramis was instructed to protest strongly to Lie the commission's interference in Greece's "domestic affairs" as contrary to the charter and the commission's terms of reference. Lund's antics, moreover, which had provoked the Greek authorities had been preceded several days before by a misleading announcement by Ryan that some members of the commission had called on the foreign minister, Constantine Tsaldaris, to recommend postponement of four of the executions. In fact, although two members of the commission had called to "make a friendly request" to Tsaldaris for postponement of the executions, he was unavailable, and Kyrou took note of their request. Ryan's action led to a semiofficial press release denying the whole story.[20]

Sir Clifford Norton, the British ambassador in Athens, reported that Lund had shown an "excess of zeal" in summoning some commission members on the night of February 5.[21] When Prime Minister Demetrios Maximos and Tsaldaris protested about what had occurred to Norton and American Ambassador Lincoln MacVeagh, they pointed out that the question concerned the United Nations and not their individual governments. According to MacVeagh, Moscow desired to involve the commission in the question of Greece's internal strife, which it alleged was the only and sufficient cause of the frontier disturbances. The presentation of petitions by the EAM had caused several commissioners to feel that it was in Athens's own interests to postpone any executions while the commission was sitting. However, MacVeagh observed, when the secretariat "gave wholly unwarranted and inaccurate publicity to their privately communicated and well meaning advice," additional complications developed including "excited protest" by the Greek authorities and "misinformation" to the press that the commission had intervened in Greece's internal affairs. Ethridge felt that the attempt to convey friendly advice to the Greeks "was injudicious in view [of the] apparent tendency of . . . Lund and press officer Ryan to cooperate with [the] Soviets." In fact, their breach of "secrecy and [their] misrepresentation" had "diverted public attention from [the] main objective of [the] Commission in [a] manner favorable to [the] Russian cause."[22] So they had.

The State Department agreed that Athens would commit a "grievous tactical error" if it continued its present attitude. World attention would focus on the executions rather than on the issue of frontier violations. Accordingly, MacVeagh was to suggest that Dendramis inform the council that his government had decided to postpone all executions in connection with guerrilla activities, until the commission had completed its investigations.[23] The Greeks saw the point, and Dendramis gave Lie the desired assurances.[24]

The Foreign Office, also, was "concerned over [the] improper activities and bias of [the] Secretariat." Accordingly it solicited the view of the British commissioner, Robert Windle, on whether there was a case to be made to the council or to Lie for changes in secretariat personnel.[25] After discussing the matter with Ethridge, Windle responded that, while they were "not happy" with the secretariat, they preferred to deal with the problem in Greece and would only invite the Foreign Office's assistance if absolutely necessary.[26]

The inevitable confrontation with the secretariat occurred within a week of Windle's message. In Salonika on the morning of February 25, French Commissioner Georges Daux, while presiding over the commission, was handed a newspaper by Gottesman reporting that two men, whose stay of execution the commission had requested, had been shot. Daux merely called it to the commission's attention. The Russian commissioner, Alexander Lavrishchev, quickly proposed a resolution, to be released to the public, that the Greek authorities had broken faith with and defied the commission. Ethridge refused to be rushed into action on the basis of a newspaper story and said he thought the commission would look foolish if it did so. He proposed an investigation, and this was accepted. Gottesman then informed the commission that he had conveyed a letter to Kyrou at 9 o'clock on the night of February 23, requesting a stay of execution. Kyrou maintained that he had not received the letter until 5 o'clock on the afternoon of February 24, from one of the Greek interpreters on the secretariat. He had immediately telegraphed Athens to request the stay of execution, but the guerrilla forces had severed the telegraph line to the little town where the executions would take place. The Greek interpreter, in turn confirmed that he delivered the letter on the afternoon of February 24, by 2 o'clock at the earliest, maybe an hour or two later. Lund's secretary likewise confirmed that she had given the letter to the Greek interpreter sometime on the afternoon of February 24, immediately after receiving it from Gottesman.

Ethridge had heard enough: "'It's obvious you have lied about this,'" he told Gottesman and demanded that the commission examine the telegram from the attorneys of the condemned men. Ethridge declared it "was obvious to me and certainly must be to other members of the Commission that [Gottesman] was more interested in embarrassing the Greek government than he was in saving the lives of the men." Windle demanded a closed commission session, restricted to its principal members, which did not occur until February 28.[27]

The main charges levelled against the secretariat were "insolent conduct" toward Greek liaison personnel; the incident of Gottesman's letter to Kyrou and his attempt to give "'political guidance'" to the commission; Ryan's biased press releases; and various other complaints. There was no doubt in Ethridge's mind that Lund, Gottesman, and Ryan sympathized "strongly with [the] Slavic bloc" and permitted "their sympathies to influence their actions." However, he reported, there was no proof that they were directly under Lavrishchev's influence, and they had not been "implicated in any action sufficiently flagrant" to convince a majority of the commission that one or all of them should be dismissed.[28] Windle also held that it was difficult to prove that the three were under Lavrishchev's influence, but he thought Deputy Assistant Principal Secretary Volokhov, who appeared "too dull to play an active political part," nevertheless acted "as [a] messenger box for [the] Soviet Delegation."[29]

When the commission convened to examine the members, "Lund was so abject under the tongue lashing" to which he was subjected that Windle then decided not to press the matter of his recall. Lund promised to control Gottesman. Russian Commissioner Lavrishchev was greatly chagrined by the whole business. The commission had no faith that the secretariat would execute its assigned task. However, it felt that there "would be a very bad scandal" if the United Nations' first investigatory commission asked for the recall of its principal secretariat personnel.[30] In practical terms, the secretariat's reputation reflected on the commission's work. Its failure because of the secretariat's bias and behavior, which had already been aired by the Greek press, could not be risked. Windle thought that this "shake up" of the secretariat had "had a beneficial effect" and would enable the commission to exercise greater control. However, if there was a second round, Gottesman's and Ryan's replacement should be seriously studied.[31] Thus, the secretariat had gotten its own stay of execution, and a generous one at that.

In his report to the State Department, the Balkan specialist and assistant to Ethridge, Cyril Black, pointed out that it would have been desirable if one or two secretariat members had been drawn from national civil services or been veterans of the League of Nations secretariat. Despite the complaint regarding Lund and Gottesman the majority of the staff were trained and faithful in executing their duties. In addition, neither Lund, Gottesman, nor Ryan had satisfactory command of French, which was the majority language of the commission and the liaison representatives. This problem was exacerbated by Lund's poor command of English, which left the Anglophone members of the commission unsure that he fully understood everything said to him. The lack of training of the senior personnel was matched by their "deviousness and Byzantinism which made them unsuitable for high administrative positions in an international organization." Many regarded their shortcomings as the "result of political bias" and felt that the threesome "were pro-Soviet in their outlook." It was clear that they "strongly disliked" the Greek government's political orientation, in contrast to those of Albania, Bulgaria, and Yugoslavia, but lacked the "sense or tact to treat all four countries on an equal basis." They took an "inordinate interest" in Greece's domestic affairs, whereas such an interest "was not displayed in other aspects of the subject" under investigation. From remarks by the three it appeared that in "their personal view the Soviet Union had a legitimate right to be interested" in Greece, while the United States "was making unwarranted" use of the United Nations machinery in trying to maintain in power an unpopular Greek administration.

Black concluded that the State Department should give serious consideration to making representations to Lie. The British commissioner, Windle, had informally suggested that Cadogan and his counterpart, Senator Warren Austin, speak to Lie jointly on this matter. An alternate scheme, Black suggested, would be for Austin to write Lie an appraisal of the secretariat, informing him that this experience was not taken lightly by Washington, which regarded the appointment of highly trained individuals for all United Nations work as indispensable to the organization's success.[32]

Truman Doctrine

It was in this setting that President Truman, on March 12, proposed to Congress a $400 million program of military aid and economic assistance to Greece and Turkey, what subsequently became known as the Truman Doctrine. Lie desired to funnel any American assistance to Greece through the Economic and Social Council's Economic Commission for Europe. His stance can be partially traced to the fact that his appointee as executive secretary of the commission was the well-known Swedish economist and subsequent Nobel Prize Laureate, Gunnar Myrdal. Like Lie and Evatt, Myrdal had his own theories of bridging the gap between the blocs. "He probably nurtures an ambition," the deputy American representative to the commission wrote in late 1948, "to be the great mediator between the East and the West."[33] This view of Myrdal was shared in the Foreign Office, which also pointed out in early 1950 that, as executive secretary of the commission, Myrdal "tended unduly to consider the susceptibilities of Eastern European countries in order, if possible, to make the Commission an effectively working organisation."[34] It would not be unfair to say that

Myrdal's perception of the East-West struggle was myopic in the extreme. The struggle was largely political, military, and strategic, though cloaked in an ideological garb, and the gap would be bridged or reduced, if at all, not by closer economic relations—also desired by Lie[35]—but by political accommodation based on countervailing military considerations.

Myrdal was so committed to his policy that the Foreign Office's assistant under-secretary, Eric Berthoud, had reason to believe that he was "anxious that the East and West should come to terms at almost any sacrifice, to be made rather by the latter than the former" as the West had to "pay the price of being more reasonable and civilized."[36] Similar comments had been voiced in the Foreign Office as early as January 1948.[37]

In addition, Myrdal's personality appeared to compound the problem. According to the deputy American representative to the commission, although Myrdal was intelligent, he was "extremely naive." If the Russians wanted to dupe him, they could probably do so, at least initially. There was, however, "no indication that he [was] sympathetic to the Communist philosophy or to Soviet aims in Europe." Myrdal was certainly "not a fellow traveller"—a view shared by the British. Indeed, Myrdal was a "man of great good will. He [was] generous, impulsive and talkative, often indiscreet and generally tactless." He had "very little guile, but [had] a pronounced capacity for deceiving himself." He liked everybody and wanted to be liked in return. Myrdal was "almost childlike in his enthusiasms." He could also be "irrationally stubborn." Unquestionably he was a fine economist.[38]

At least on the surface, Lie appeared to be wary of Myrdal and worried that he "would not keep himself out of East-West politics." He also feigned that he had appointed Myrdal only because Great Britain, France, and Soviet Russia had been unanimous on his selection, an interpretation to which Minister of State McNeil took exception.[39] Lie's worries were well taken for Myrdal's appointment, without consultation, of a Russian deputy executive secretary raised the ire of both the State Department and the Foreign Office. Actually, when the commission was being organized, Lie himself had recommended that Moscow designate someone to act as Myrdal's deputy. Its initial nominee, however, was rejected by Myrdal. The State Department feared that a Russian deputy, in line with Moscow's general lack of cooperation, meant either it would attempt further to obstruct effective action by the commission or wanted "to play up to Myrdal's vanity and expansionist ambitions" by claiming for the commission jurisdiction over all economic cooperation in Europe.[40]

Myrdal's action caused McNeil to raise with Lie the British government's "general dissatisfaction with Myrdal personally." While anxious to give the commission its full backing, London found "Myrdal a most difficult man to deal with and quite unpredictable in his actions." It seemed that he had "no political sense and no organising ability." McNeil wanted

Cadogan to inform the secretary-general that, while the Foreign Office recognized that the appointment of a Russian deputy was Myrdal's prerogative, this episode was an additional "example of Myrdal's lack of political judgment and of his muddle-headed approach to hard facts." London was not opposed to the commission, he noted to Cadogan, his complaint was "against the activity of Myrdal," which in McNeil's view was "not suited to command that degree of support" for the commission that the British government wanted to give.[41] Lie maintained to Cadogan, quite rightly, that he was unable to exercise complete control but "promised to do his best to put the brake on Myrdal in a general way."[42] Some sort of promise was better than none.

The Truman Doctrine was, of course, a jolt to the postwar system of international relations and a fair warning to Moscow that Washington would not stand idly by and allow the legal Greek government to be overthrown by a well organized minority element, using guerrilla tactics and supported by Greece's northern neighbors as well as Soviet Russia. Since the Greek question, however, was being handled by the council Lie felt that, in view of Washington's strong support of the United Nations, it was incumbent upon it to announce first to the council its intended program in Greece and Turkey and its reasons for it.[43] He was keenly disappointed with Truman's decision to aid Greece and Turkey directly, which bypassed the Economic Commission for Europe.[44] However, Myrdal's role in that body would partially explain Washington's reticence to use it. Lie correctly noted that Austin was "neither consulted nor informed in advance"[45] of this new American policy stance. In fact, Austin was informed of Truman's message to Congress only twenty-four hours before it was delivered.[46] Austin's exclusion from the inner circle was based almost entirely on security considerations. By this point Truman, Acheson, and a very small group within the government had become convinced that Alger Hiss, who handled United Nations matters and who would normally have been consulted about this new policy stance, was a Russian agent. His exposure as a mole within the State Department had become known to them through the defection in Ottawa of Igor Gouzenko, the cipher clerk of the Russian military attaché. In fact, Acheson himself, Hiss's former mentor, issued the order that Hiss's office was to be bypassed in any intra–State Department discussions of America's intended line in Greece and Turkey. Acheson, it appears, feared lest Hiss's office "do something to upset the applecart." Hiss, when he discovered what had been done, "was, it seems, furious."[47]

Lie's mounting burdens, compounded by Truman's new policy in the eastern Mediterranean, caused him to declare in private that he would rather be Norway's foreign minister than secretary-general.[48] He spoke in the "strongest terms" to Christopher Mayhew, the parliamentary undersecretary for foreign affairs, about Truman's circumvention of the United

Nations. He claimed that Truman's new policy would do the world organization the "utmost harm" and was a "prize example of clumsy diplomacy." He contrasted Washington's approach with London's "own tactful handling" of the Greek question and queried Mayhew why the United Nations had not been asked "to send an international force to Greece." He favored Truman's policy "on its merits" but believed the president's "manner of presentation [was] disastrous." Mayhew correctly noted the problem's urgency; and as to an international force, he raised the likelihood of a Russian veto in the council. Lie's confused reply was that Moscow's use of the veto had declined recently.

Lie also touched upon the work of the Balkan commission. He alleged, based on information supplied by Lund, that the British Commissioner, Windle, was obstructive, although he did not explain how. The surprised Mayhew retorted that London thought that the "Slav members of the Secretariat" were not contributing to a well-run operation. Lie had been friendly in their discussions, but Mayhew's "first impressions of him [had] been a bit disappointing." In fact, Lie had appeared "rather excitable and parochial about his job."[49]

As so often in the past, the Foreign Office's minutes were critical. The United Nations Department's Edward Tomkins had no doubt that the Russians would have invoked the veto and that Lie knew as well as anyone why the world organization could not send an international force to Greece. However, since Lie thought it possible, "it might be interesting to find out how it should be done." The Southern Department's Daniel McCarthy scribbled that it was interesting that the secretary-general should quote Lund on Windle. The truth of the matter was that Windle considered Lund a "weak man in the hands of the 'Slav' Secretariat," but Lund's comments suggested that he was also dishonest. After all, it was Windle who, sometimes to the Foreign Office's annoyance, had from time to time made "concessions to avoid clashes or deadlock on the Commission." At any rate, it showed that Windle had been a "thorn in the Slav side!"[50]

As the pressure mounted to have the Truman administration explain to the council its new stance in the eastern Mediterranean, the State Department approved Austin's proposal that he make such a statement.[51] Close questioning of Acheson by Senator Vandenberg as to why the United Nations had not been "notified and consulted" undoubtedly contributed to expediting Austin's statement.[52] However, both before and after Austin's statement to the council on March 28,[53] Lie declined to comment publicly on the proposed program of aid to Greece and Turkey.[54] Gromyko naturally proposed that all aid to Greece should be rendered through the United Nations, which he claimed would "exclude all possibilities of any foreign influence in that country."[55] It was a less than subtle stance and no one was receptive, except perhaps Lie and Myrdal.

Investigating the Commission Secretariat

Between the enunciation of the Truman Doctrine on March 12 and Gromyko's speech on April 7, Lie had done little to enhance his image in Athens, London, and Washington, and probably contributed to a Greek decision to protest officially about the antics of the Balkan commission secretariat. On March 25 in the council, Gromyko protested that Russian and Polish members of the Balkan commission, as well as the Albanian, Bulgarian, and Yugoslavian liaison officers, on arrival in Trikala on their way to Salonika, were delayed by the local authorities who "could not guarantee their safe passage." The group was able to continue only after the intervention of the Russian ambassador in Athens with Prime Minister Maximos.[56] In conveying this complaint to Foreign Minister Tsaldaris, Lie drew his attention to the fact that the Greek government had undertaken to make available all necessary facilities and assistance for the commission's work and stated that he hoped there would be no recurrence of similar incidents.[57]

Cadogan pointed out to London that, to the best of his knowledge, Lie had consulted no one on the council before sending this message. Lie's action appeared "improper," since the Balkan commission was the council's servant not the secretary-general's. Furthermore, if any action were warranted, it could only emanate from the commission itself and not, as in this case, from the complaints of one state represented on the commission. He requested instructions.[58] They followed immediately: it was left to Cadogan's discretion whether to protest in the council or to protest in concert with Austin in a personal interview with Lie. He was to remonstrate with Lie, pointing out that should there be any repetition of what had occurred, the British government would have "no alternative" but to express its "indignation forcibly in public session." In that situation Cadogan might find it convenient to cite, among other incidents, "the biased and irresponsible attitude and inefficiency of the [commission] Secretariat," reported by the British diplomatic missions in Athens and Salonika, as well as other "instances of partiality and impropriety" by the commission secretariat reported by Windle.[59]

Cadogan waited. Almost three weeks later, after alerting the Americans[60] but acting alone, he informally protested to Lie. Cadogan noted that when he called on him "to curse him for [this] performance," Lie "was quite contrite"[61] about the episode, which a follow-up conversation showed was "very much on his conscience."[62]

Cadogan's delay in approaching Lie was probably caused by the leaks that began to appear about the activities of the commission secretariat and doubtless monopolized Cadogan's attention. They first surfaced at Lie's news conference on March 26, the same day that he conveyed to the Greeks Gromyko's complaint.[63] On March 29, Austin was informed of the secretariat's activities by Secretary of War Robert Patterson, based on information from Ethridge's military assistant. It was clear enough to this officer that "Lund, and most of the members of the Secretariat under him were unreliable, were Russian in sympathy, and were not making the proper efforts to forward the work of the Commission."[64] Additional leaks, some spurious—for example that Gottesman had been caught trying to enter Windle's room—surfaced some days later. In an obvious attempt to save the situation by deflecting attention from the actions of Lund, Gottesman, Volokhov, and Ryan, Sobolev pointed out that twenty-five United Nations personnel drawn from many nationalities were accredited to the commission secretariat.[65] His efforts convinced no one, and the proverbial fat was in the fire.

In Washington, Dean Rusk, who handled United Nations matters, suggested that the State Department admit it had been informed of "certain irregularities" in the secretariat's conduct but that it preferred to wait for a complete report before deciding on additional action. The commission's responsibility was to investigate the disturbances along Greece's northern frontier and to report about them to the council. Accordingly, the State Department did not think that the irregularities raised would be "allowed to affect the nature" of the commission's final report and was reluctant to interrupt its substantive work in order to tackle a personnel problem. The State Department, however, would insist that "any irregularities substantiated be dealt with by the Secretary-General."[66] Rusk's eye remained riveted to the main issue, the secretariat's antics notwithstanding.

Ethridge was then informed by Acheson of the press comments and that some were direct criticisms of Lie himself. An informal request by the secretariat for the State Department to supply whatever facts it had so that they could be submitted to Lie had been rejected, Ethridge was told, as this was a matter that the secretariat should handle, based on its own investigation. Washington was to avoid involvement and not provide information even on an informal basis.[67]

Ethridge agreed. He believed that an investigation of the secretariat would delay the commission's work. Since Lund had been admonished, no serious difficulties had developed. "Personal qualifications and [the] objectionable attitude" of certain personnel had, however, been serious hindrances to the commission's work. Once its work terminated, Ethridge intended to report on this matter, and the information could be used to prevent a similar occurrence. He would suggest that similar reports be filed by other commissioners with their governments. Ethridge thought this would be more constructive than attempting to get the commission to act officially about the secretariat, either as part of its final report or in a separate report.[68]

Since the campaign to discredit the commission secretariat—akin to shooting fish in a barrel—was well orchestrated, the question might be raised: by whom? Cadogan, it appears, had information that pointed to the State Department,[69] and this may have been so, although there is no documentary evidence to support his allegation. At the same time others may also have been involved. Since the Foreign Office's attitude was not dissimilar from that of Rusk and Ethridge,[70] and it was not in Soviet Russia's interest to have the commission discredited, any speculation would have to concentrate on elements within the Greek government. Their anger and frustrations in dealing with Lie and the awesome foursome of Lund, Gottesman, Volokhov, and Ryan can be imagined.

On March 22, the State Department informed the American embassy in Athens that the Greek representative at the United Nations, Vassili Dendramis, had received instructions to approach Lie and request the recall of the secretariat attached to the Balkan commission, including Lund, for "incorrect attitudes and activities." Dendramis had not acted on these instructions but requested additional instructions from Athens. He had observed that Athens had to have "irrefutable evidence to back up its request." Washington believed a protest at that moment would be very "injurious to [the] Greek case" and would have a serious impact on the positions of the secretary-general and the United Nations. Moreover, it would handicap the commission's work. Therefore, the State Department had suggested that Dendramis delay execution of his instructions until Washington had consulted with Athens.

The State Department believed that the American embassy should impress upon the Foreign Ministry that Washington was "aware of [the] difficulties and irregularities" of the commission secretariat; that, pending advice from Ethridge to the contrary, the State Department preferred the issue not be taken up with Lie until completion of the commission's work; and finally, that under current conditions Athens should attempt to look at the broader issue involved and not attach inordinate importance to relatively minor questions.[71]

In the days that followed, Lie's opposition to the Truman Doctrine could not have gone unnoticed either by the Greek embassy in Washington or by the Greek mission at the United Nations. Certainly Lie's avoidance of any public comments about the doctrine, although pressed by journalists, and his decision to convey to the Greeks Gromyko's complaint must have added to the fury in Athens about Lie and the commission secretariat. American advice and admonitions in this setting had their limitations. This is reflected in the fact that, over a week after the State Department had contacted the American embassy in Athens, the British ambassador there could still report to the Foreign Office that he understood that the Greek government contemplated raising at the United Nations the matter of "biased messages" by Ryan and the question of the commission secretariat.[72] Washington's overtures to Athens appear to have had little impact.

Cadogan doubted the wisdom, from the Greek point of view, of raising this question at the United Nations and especially in the council. Indeed, the Greek case had been helped rather than hindered in the arena of public opinion by reports that the secretariat was biased. As the plaintiff in this dispute, it would surely be "somewhat invidious" for the Greeks to raise the question of the secretariat and, by doing so, incur the suspicion that they were trying to divert attention from their own weak case. Other delegations would probably show little sympathy to an attack on the secretariat, unless the Greeks supported it with "more concrete evidence of actual bias"—as opposed, let's say, to mere "weakness or incompetence." Cadogan agreed with the Foreign Office's previous instructions: that it would be preferable to protest to Lie in a private talk or in concert with Austin, when the commission's work was concluded. He claimed to have reliable information that some of the antisecretariat leaks were from the State Department, a reaction to Lie's privately expressed complaints about America's new tack in Greece and Turkey. Cadogan accordingly requested an updated statement from Windle that he could use "as chapter and verse" should he make any formal complaint to Lie. His impression, however, was that things had improved since Lund had been admonished. If this was so, perhaps the best approach would be to point out to Lie that the actions of some secretariat personnel appeared "to have given rise to legitimate criticism," at least in the initial stages of the commission's work, and to "impress upon him that in choosing future parties of this kind more care should be exercised as regards personal and national affiliations of [the] individuals concerned."[73]

In an obvious attempt to head off any moves by Cadogan and Austin, Lie himself made the initial approach to discuss the activities of the commission secretariat. On April 7, ostensibly to discuss the Palestine question, Lie asked both of them to come to his office. In what appears to have been a chagrined performance, Lie explained that he had instituted an investigation of all charges leveled against him that had appeared in the press and that he had discovered that they had no basis in fact. He cited a United Press release, quoting a State Department spokesman, that the State Department would insist that in this question "any substantiated irregularities be dealt with by the Secretary-General," since Lie had appointed the secretariat. This was, of course, a rendition of Rusk's comment to Acheson and did not differentiate between charges of secretariat partiality and other charges published by the press. It could be applied to all charges. Therefore, Lie asked Austin who spoke for the United States in the United Nations and what State Department official, if any, he should appeal to for the purposes of acquiring information that would help him investigate these charges. Austin could offer no names but assured Lie that everything would be done that could be properly done to help him acquire such information.

If he were in Lie's place, Austin observed, he "would grasp the nettle firmly and investigate thoroughly the facts," and if secretariat personnel should be discharged, Austin would do so immediately and divulge publicly what care had been exercised in selecting them. As to the allegations against the commission secretariat, if they were untrue, Austin would certainly offer proof that this was so. He pointed out that this was a matter that affected the United Nations' welfare and should be handled promptly by Lie.[74]

Cadogan strongly endorsed Austin's advice. Although London had heard the rumors about the secretariat it had few facts. As Lie already knew, the British government "had been exercised for some time about the staffing" of the commission secretariat. "It had a too distinct Slav tinge," Lie had been told and Cadogan recalled Lawford's objections against sending Volokhov to Athens as leader of the advance party. Although the mistake had been rectified it "had been a bad slip-up" and should not have occurred. London was "necessarily on the alert" though Lie could be confident that it would base itself on ascertained facts.[75] Cadogan and Austin's advice, Daniel McCarthy of the Foreign Office's Southern Department wrote, "could hardly be bettered." Lie appeared to be uneasy. The snag was that even if Lie was "eventually convinced he [might] still lack the will, or even courage, to act in any way which would bring him into conflict with the Slavs."[76]

The following day Assistant Secretary-General Byron Price asked the American mission whether Washington had any information that would be helpful to Lie "in investigating himself," since he had no organization like the Federal Bureau of Investigation to assist him. The mission felt that Washington ought to communicate to Lie informally all the information pertaining to the charges made in the press, that the "situation would be untenable and very embarrassing if we failed to do so."[77]

The State Department accordingly made available to Austin the information received from Salonika on March 6, detailing the main charges raised with Lund. Disingenuously, it declared that it did "not know the results of these representations," but assumed that Lie had been fully advised about them by Lund.[78] This same day, April 9, Lie in New York announced, after consulting Sobolev and Price, that he had decided to send Stoneman to Geneva, where the commission had gone to write its report, to investigate the commission secretariat and simultaneously to ascertain the source of the press "rumours." Lie felt that he had to protect secretariat personnel and denied that he had instituted an investigation into their political affiliations. He stated that he had not consulted any governments about Stoneman's report, which would be for his eyes only, and claimed he had received no official complaint from any government, from the commission itself, or from its members. He likewise denied he was going to resign.[79] The State Department noted to Ethridge that it had given the

United Nations secretariat only the main charges against the commission secretariat received from Salonika. Stoneman's report, therefore, would be in line with State Department wishes already made known to Ethridge. Washington hoped that he would, at his discretion, offer Stoneman whatever aid he thought would be helpful.[80] Moreover, Ethridge was also informed that Stoneman had the New York mission's "full confidence" and believed it of the greatest importance that Lie acquire all the information that "would assist in determining [the] correctness and competence" of the commission secretariat.[81] The State Department, as we have seen, was opposed to ascertaining the former point but agreeable on the latter.

If no official protest had ever been made, as Lie claimed, about the commission secretariat, the omission was soon remedied. On April 12, Dendramis delivered to Lie a secret and personal *aide-mémoire*. The document, the British embassy in Athens reported to the Foreign Office, appeared "to go a good deal further than was suggested" to a Greek official. The important point, however, was that the Greeks "raised the matter confidentially" with Lie and "not in public."[82] Anglo-American pressure had no doubt turned the Greeks away from any public confrontation with Lie over the secretariat and had probably assuaged their angst.

The *aide-mémoire* was a restrained, carefully drawn up, detailed litany of the offences, abuses, and machinations of the commission secretariat, concentrating on the activities of Gottesman, Lund, Ryan, and Volokhov. The most interesting part of the document, however, was two lines of comment at the end, seemingly deleted by five spaced ink strokes but easily readable. They noted that Lie, in his press conference of April 9, was reported to have stated that no complaint had ever been lodged with him about the secretariat's activities.[83] The apparent deletion of the two lines was a polite way of telling Lie that he had been mendacious and had been lucky in not being publicly challenged either by Dendramis and the Greek mission to the United Nations or by the Greek government. Lie, walking on thin ice, was counting on Western not to mention Greek restraint and was willing to risk the fury of patient men. He could afford to take the risk, for the Western states, rightly so, wanted the commission to issue its report and not be sidetracked into settling accounts with the awesome foursome. There would be plenty of time for that, as Lund was to discover in the years ahead; the Americans had long memories and an even longer reach.

Naturally McCarthy, of the Foreign Office's Southern Department, was pleased with the Greek *aide-mémoire*, which he optimistically wrote, coupled with Stoneman's report, should leave Lie in "little doubt about the partiality and improper activities" of the commission secretariat.[84]

Whether fortuitous or by design, the truth of the matter was that Stoneman's report was indecisive, since he avoided making subjective judgments and criticisms. On the other hand, his general remarks, when divorced from evidential testimony, were often subjective. In addition, his report was marred by an unspoken premise that somehow secretariat personnel, like Caesar's wife, were above reproach,[85] unless they were caught flagrante delicto. He appeared to ignore the fact that those in the commission secretariat, when partial along ideological lines, undermined their sworn loyalty to the United Nations. Stoneman's approach can in part be explained by what was conveyed to him when he questioned the commission and its secretariat in Geneva and especially by his interpretation of his assigned role.

Seven commissioners, he pointed out to Lie, (the American, Australian, Belgian, Brazilian, British, French, and Syrian) had charged the secretariat with partiality in its attitude toward the Greek government and had also leveled other complaints. The Chinese and Colombian commissioners had been less severe in their complaints; while the Russian one had no complaint of substance and the Polish commissioner's absence precluded being interviewed. All those who had voiced complaints generally agreed that it would be "unfortunate and undesirable" for Lie to take any further steps. Most of them also explained that they had complained to assist Lie in improving the secretariat's work. This attitude no doubt buttressed Stoneman's own thinking and approach.

The commission's charges, Stoneman noted, were both general and specific. Only extensive cross-examination and confrontation of commission members and secretariat personnel would lead to the truth. Stoneman held that it was not his "purpose to undertake a judicial enquiry" unless "formal and specific" charges were made by the United Nations members. He construed his assignment as allowing commission members "to voice their views" regarding the secretariat and satisfying them of Lie's "personal and official determination" to have the secretariat "function in an objective and correct manner." Stoneman then summarized the more serious complaints raised. One was that there had been a lack of "proper balance by nationality" in the secretariat's upper ranks. It included too many persons from countries involved in the dispute: Gottesman, the secretariat's leading figure, was Polish; Lund, a Norwegian whose country shared a common frontier with Russia, could not be completely independent; Volokhov was a Russian citizen; and Ryan had Russian antecedents. Reiterated were the often-heard complaints about these four men; Stoneman maintained they would be difficult either to prove or disprove. Those against Ryan would not be accepted in a court of law. He noted that the commission and its secretariat operated in an extremely difficult political situation, marked by a sharp division between Soviet Russia and most of the other commission members, in which suspicions were rife; and the Greeks, he claimed, encouraged suspicion of anyone who did not openly support their cause. In this setting it was very difficult for the secretariat to avoid being criticized. This was particularly so because secretariat members, in a number of cases, "happened to be outright liberals or citizens of countries which were closely concerned with the outcome" of the commission's work. Stoneman then alleged that many of the charges that had been leveled against the secretariat appeared to arise from a general suspicion of all those who fell under the rubric of liberal or Red. Stoneman's comment was extraordinary if it meant that partiality had occurred and should be excused, and a frank admission that perhaps criticism of the secretariat's lack of "proper balance by nationality" was well taken. Nevertheless, it was clear, Stoneman reported that nine of the eleven commissioners (except perhaps the Colombian) were of the "conviction that the Secretariat conducted itself with bias." This he concluded was the "only fact upon which it [was] possible to judge."[86]

Stoneman's report did little to pin down the question of the secretariat's activities. On April 23, in criticism of the report rather than of Stoneman himself, Lie informally admitted to journalists that he "was not completely satisfied" with it, meaning that "his curiosity" about the complaints raised had not been satisfied.[87] However, for varied reasons Lie, the Russians, and the Anglo-Americans wished to have the question fade away. For the Anglo-Americans especially, it was far more important that the Balkan commission issue its report.

This stance probably explains the placidity of the British mission to a proposal by George Clutton that his memorandum dealing with the secretariat's activities, along with a slightly revised version of Cyril Black's, should be conveyed to Lie in an informal interview by Austin and Cadogan. Both memoranda, he felt, could be left with Lie and the "matter go no further than his own ears." This would be preferable to a formal approach, in view of the secretariat's marked improvement in subsequent field commissions. Unless the mission, Lawford was instructed, had "any reason to the contrary," it was suggested that Clutton's proposal be implemented.[88] There appears to be no evidence that this was done.

Finally on June 25 the commission issued its report and, by a vote of eight to two (the Russians and the Poles disapproving and the French abstaining), concluded on the information gathered that Yugoslavia and to a lesser extent Albania and Bulgaria had supported the guerrilla forces in Greece; that Bulgaria and Yugoslavia had supported the separatist movement among Slavophones in Greece; that frontier violations unconnected with guerrilla activities were unprovoked by either side and the incidents were dismissed as lacking evidence of aggressive intentions on the part of any states concerned but mirrored strained relations between them; that there was in Greece a general condition of unrest, which, though not a civil war, helped explain the situation investigated by the commission; and lastly, that the reiteration of territorial counterclaims by Greece and Bulgaria, as well as Greece's claims against Albania, increased the tension between all these states including Yugoslavia. The commission's salient recommendation, the Russians and Poles objecting, was that the council establish a new commission or appoint a single commissioner for the purpose of restoring normal conditions along Greece's northern frontiers. If a small commission were established, it should consist of government representatives; whereas a single commissioner and staff should be nationals of states that were neither permanent members of the council nor directly interested in the affairs of the countries involved.[89] The commission's report, as one would expect, produced the inevitable Russian veto in the council, which finally led to the question's being submitted by the United States to the assembly for consideration.[90]

During the course of these council discussions Lie, like the old dog incapable of learning new tricks, informed Cadogan that council inaction on the question of a commission, or commissioner, would cause him to "claim [the] right to send out observers to satisfy himself as to what was happening in Northern Greece." Cadogan reminded the Foreign Office that Lie had first broached this right when the Ukrainians had raised the Greek question. Whether Lie, was "constitutionally empowered to send observers" into a sovereign state, seemed "dubious" to Cadogan. He thought, as previously, that Lie could dispatch observers only with the consent of the involved states, which in the present case he presumed Athens would give.[91] Nevertheless, it appears Lie never returned to the suggestion of appointing observers; perhaps he foresaw that they would be appointed by the assembly, whereas sending them on his own authority against Russian desires would have been a high risk policy, one that Lie might perhaps have been willing to assume if matters had been reversed and the Western powers saddled with Russia's role.

Mediation Endeavors

During this period Lie "was badly overstrained." With tears running down his cheeks he repeated to Julian Huxley, the director-general of the United Nations Educational, Scientific, and Cultural Organization, that he had had a "terrible time."[92] The Greek and Palestine questions, as well as other matters, had no doubt contributed to this state of affairs. Despite Russian objections, the report of the Balkan commission was included on the assembly's agenda. In the discussions that followed the Americans proposed that it establish a special committee to observe compliance by the involved states with suggested peaceful procedures spelled out in Washington's draft resolution. Moscow proposed instead that foreign troops and military missions be withdrawn from Greece, which was defeated. The assembly accepted the American idea of a United Nations Special Committee on the Balkans, to be composed of nine members, on which seats were reserved for Soviet Russia and Poland despite their rejection of the proposal and their insistence that they would neither partake in electing the committee's members nor participate in its work.[93]

The difficulties with the secretariat of the council's Balkan commission did not appear to have produced in Lie a healthy respect for the old adage of once bitten, twice shy. Information that Lie intended to appoint a French national as the principal secretary of the assembly's Special Committee on the Balkans, and a Russian as the deputy principal secretary, moved the alert Kyrou (now the Greek representative to the assembly) to threaten that he would protest the intended Russian appointment. He maintained that it "would lead to the same trouble" that had bedeviled the Balkan commission.

Stoneman confirmed Kyrou's story that a Russian would be appointed, except that he would not be deputy principal secretary. According to Stoneman the proposed Russian did not appear "very bright and would not be given substantial responsibilities in the political field." He was optimistic that the experience with the Balkan commission would not be repeated.[94]

Lie affirmed that the principal secretary would be French, Raoul Aglion, although he failed to mention that he did not like Aglion and had found him unsatisfactory as a member of his executive office. Lie's understandable desire was to avoid the appointment of an American or English national as principal secretary and believed that Aglion would be the best choice under the circumstances; he could handle the job, though "not ideal and . . . no administrator." Minister of State McNeil agreed with Lie that a French national would be a fine choice but disagreed that Aglion was the right person for the job. In his opinion, Aglion would be unacceptable to the British government. As regards the deputy principal secretary, Lie had in mind a Dutch national or even a Swede but neither could probably be spared, and accordingly he had instructed Price to find a suitable person, preferably an American.

Lie admitted that he was "under heavy pressure from Vyshinsky" to give the deputy principal secretaryship to a Russian, in spite of Soviet Russia's boycott of the special committee. As Lie saw it, although Moscow was not going to participate in the special committee's work, it was determined "to have a Soviet 'rapporteur' on the Secretariat." Cadogan understood that Lie was thinking of appointing a Russian to the secretariat's third slot, alongside a second American. Obviously, Kyrou's concern had had some impact on Lie. Although Lie realized that London would be displeased by such a Russian appointment, he was in a difficult position as director of the world organization's multinational secretariat. Cadogan remarked to Lie that if Moscow refused to cooperate with the assembly's prescribed action "it was unsuitable for Vyshinsky to try to force a Russian into the [special committee] Secretariat." Cadogan had little doubt, however, that Lie would succumb to Russian pressure on this matter.[95]

The "unfortunate nature" of Lie's appointment of Aglion was discussed by senior members of the American and British missions after the former's "unsuccessful informal talks" with Lie about this question. They agreed that this "very serious matter" should be taken up jointly with Lie and that he be handed a positive alternative. Moreover, a number of secretariat personnel were discussed as satisfactory possibilities.[96]

The British feared that any Russian national on the special committee secretariat would be a leak to the communist-controlled EAM and a conduit for Russian intelligence. A Russian might also impede the secretariat's operations. Lawford suggested that this was the moment to recall to Lie what occurred in the council's Balkan commission and raise a protest, as previously suggested.[97] In the end, Lie bent to the Western winds. As a sop no doubt to the Russians, Assistant Secretary-General Kerno was assigned the task of heading the special committee secretariat. On the other hand, Aglion was the principal secretary, but glaringly absent among the prominent officers of the special committee secretariat was any Russian national.[98]

As it reported in June 1948 to the assembly, however, the special committee failed to execute its assigned task because of the refusal of the governments of Albania, Bulgaria, and Yugoslavia to cooperate with it. The special committee held that these states had provided moral and material assistance to the Greek guerrillas on a scale that justified the conclusion of government knowldege about this assistance. It maintained that a threat to Greece's political independence and territorial integrity would persist and Balkan security would be in danger as long as this aid to the Greek guerrillas continued. The special committee recommended that surveillance of the relations of these Balkan states with Greece and the attempt to solve peacefully their differences should continue to be entrusted to a United Nations body. Moreover, it recommended that the assembly seek to secure the cooperation of Albania, Bulgaria, and Yugoslavia with the special committee.[99]

Bulgarian feelers to the Greeks, in June 1948, to resume diplomatic relations found Lie favorably disposed to Athens's receptiveness. He opined that the Bulgarian proposal was clearly meant to do away with the special committee.[100] In fact, the American consulate general in Salonika feared that Lie's activities in facilitating the Greek-Bulgarian exchanges, thus bypassing the special committee and without reference to it, would support the charge that a United Nations conciliatory body was unnecessary, since the states involved were already in direct contact. Indeed, Lie's action was in line with his previous attitude.[101]

Nothing developed, however. In November, in an attempt to bridge the gap, the assembly's First Committee (Political and Security) unanimously accepted an Australian proposal requesting as conciliators Evatt, president of the General Assembly; Lie; Spaak of Belgium, chairman and rapporteur of the First Committee; and Selim Sarper of Turkey. They were to convene a meeting of the government representatives of the four Balkan states to explore the possibilities of agreeing among themselves on the methods and procedure to be adopted in order to resolve their present difficulties.[102] Initially the Australian proposal, tendered by Evatt and suggested by Lie, had been unacceptable, as it had stipulated that the conciliation talks were to be "left to the somewhat doubtful combination" of Evatt and Lie. Based on Evatt's personal desire, this stipulation was considered "to savour of sharp practice."[103] An American amendment had therefore broadened the Evatt-Lie combination to include Spaak and Sarper.

Nevertheless, from Lie's remarks, the Greek representative, Panayiotis Pipinelis, drew the inference that there was friction between Lie and Evatt and that Lie was anxious over the dangers involved in delay. In addition Pipinelis believed that Lie felt Evatt was "trying to usurp some of his functions, and suspected" that Evatt desired to succeed him as secretary-general.[104] Lie, as we shall see, was protective of his office, and his subsequent denigration of Evatt might in part be traced to these supposed designs.[105] Without waiting for the assembly to approve the First Committee's draft resolution, Evatt commenced the conciliation endeavors. At the first meeting, with Lie and Sarper in attendance, Evatt handed the representatives of the four states a list of questions. Spaak had not been notified of the meeting, in an obvious attempt to destabilize the Evatt-Lie and Spaak-Sarper balance. Naturally Spaak was angry, an anger compounded by the fact that neither he nor Sarper were consulted in advance on the questions to be posed to the Albanian, Bulgarian, Greek, and Yugoslavian representatives. The Americans questioned the legality of the whole procedure, since the assembly had not yet ratified the First Committee's resolution. Their attitude was even stronger over the exclusion of Spaak.[106] By December, the main stumbling block in the discussions was Albania's insistence that Greece renounce her claims to northern Epirus. Lie suggested that, if Albania and Bulgaria accepted the agreement proffered, it would help them to become United Nations members and that he personally "would exert his influence in that direction."[107] Albania's continued refusal to accept it caused Bulgaria and Yugoslavia to likewise withhold their signatures. The stalemate continued.

The conciliation discussions did not resume until April 1949. Lie's interest appeared to lag, for, as Sarper observed to the Americans, Lie was then represented by Cordier and on one occasion by Sobolev.[108] Less than a week after these comments, Lie spoke alone to the Albanian representative. When Dendramis subsequently asked the experienced Sarper what had transpired at this meeting, the Turkish representative "very vehemently" replied that the entire conduct of the discussions "was a scandal"; he did "not know what was going on and was not being kept informed." He suggested that the Greeks should protest against Evatt's and Lie's independent course, in view of the fact that the resolution established a committee of four.[109] Lie and Evatt were regularly excluding the pro-Western Spaak and Sarper from the deliberations.

The assembly's Special Committee on the Balkans in particular deeply resented the "cavalier treatment received from Lie." Some members held that Lie's stance was inspired by Evatt and was an "endeavor to further strip [the] Committee of its conciliatory functions." The American embassy in Athens was especially concerned by a statement attributed to Lie that the special committee should avoid any moves at conciliation until after Evatt had submitted his report to the assembly on the conciliatory conversations he had chaired. If this approach were accepted, the embassy noted, Evatt's line would have succeeded, to wit, that the "functions of conciliation and observation should be exercised by two separate organs." Thus Evatt's and—although the embassy did not say it—Lie's, "usurpation of the Committee's conciliatory role would be complete and final."[110]

The gathering storm, however, was sufficient to cause Lie to change his tack. Evatt's conciliation efforts, he finally had to admit, terminated with the assembly's last session. Lie wanted to return the conciliation endeavors to the special committee as quickly as possible. Indeed, he no longer encouraged Evatt to continue his conciliation endeavors or to assume a prominent role in the world organization's affairs. His "bitter experiences" of the previous weeks, with Evatt attempting to deal personally with almost all United Nations questions as well as major world problems, explained his attitude.[111] The possibility that Evatt's activities in these matters might establish his credentials as a viable candidate for the secretary-generalship could not have escaped Lie's attention.

Despite his remarks Lie approached Gromyko to discuss the Greek question.[112] To remove the Albanian obstacle, he pointed out to Gromyko that Tirana acted only on Moscow's orders. Gromyko "was as cold as ice" to Lie's feelers and gave no response.[113] A *Tass* report on May 20, that Gromyko had made some sort of proposal about Greece, distressed Lie a great deal, since he felt that Washington might have been withholding vital information from Evatt's conciliation group. The American decision to keep the Greek question within the United Nations framework and to reject Russian offers for a settlement outside the organization dissipated his distress.[114] This episode might explain Lie's feeling that the Greek question was being considered at higher levels and that somehow "it might be settled there, if at all." The finale to the Evatt-Lie conciliation endeavors was less than edifying. Evatt's proposed release of a press statement about what the discussions had accomplished was unacceptable to the other members of the group, including Lie. After some angry exchanges over the telephone between Evatt at the airport and Lie in his office, it was agreed that Evatt would issue his statement only over his own signature.[115] In his contribution to these conciliation endeavors Lie had not covered himself with glory or distinction.

Suspicion of Lie, in Athens and at the Greek mission, were strong. Comments purportedly made by Lie to the journal *European Affairs* on the wartime genesis of the Greek question[116] caused Kyrou to ask Lie to clarify his remarks. Lie denied that the quoted statement covered his opinions on the question; nor did he recognize the statement as made by him at any time to the correspondent of that or any other journal.[117] Lie complained that Kyrou "was a difficult person who wrote too many letters about a lot of little matters" but admitted that it "was probably better for Kyrou to err on the side of doing too many things than to fail to cope with various little incidents as they came along."

Desperate, Lie admitted that he was unhappy about the situation in Greece. He queried the American representative on the assembly's special committee if Gromyko's proposals of May 20 could be used to help settle the Greek question. The only settlement that would satisfy Moscow, he was informed, would be for Athens to surrender to the guerrillas. How about United Nations supervised elections, as Gromyko had suggested? Lie asked, but he had to acknowledge that elections were an internal Greek matter.[118]

By August 1949, Lie felt that, although Greek internal reform was still necessary, the question would settle itself in the near future and all Greece's neighbors would be amenable to the settlement except Albania, which was then more under Russian domination than Bulgaria or Yugoslavia.[119] About a week later, in a discussion with members of the American mission, it was suggested to Lie—perhaps in the pious hope that his standing in Moscow might help break the log jam—that it "would be appropriate" if he "were to explore the [Greek] question and use his influence to try to steer the Russians to let the matter be peacefully arranged within the United Nations." He replied that he had already undertaken to sound out the Greeks and would sound out the Russians. If Athens encouraged him, he would then approach Belgrade. Lie hoped that with the Yugoslavs it might be possible to arrange a reasonable settlement in view of the widening split between Tito and Stalin.[120]

Lie pointed out to Kyrou that it was his "moral compulsion" to do whatever he could to conciliate the Greek question; he would not reveal to the Yugoslavs that he had consulted the Greeks. He would inquire whether Belgrade would now accept Evatt's spring proposals relating to the resumption of Greek-Yugoslav diplomatic relations, as well as to economic matters. Kyrou's reaction, however, was guarded; understandably, Lie's past track record inspired little confidence. Kyrou cautioned that the greatest care would have to be taken. He opined that, having failed militarily, Moscow would now attempt to take the lead in a political settlement, as evidenced by Gromyko's recent activities, and begged that nothing be done before he could obtain Athens's views. Lie responded that he had learned a lesson about care from the way Evatt had conducted the conciliation discussions. He expected a positive reply from Belgrade, Lie noted, and the same technique would be used with Sofia.[121] Kyrou then approached Cadogan and informed him of Lie's proposal. He pointed out that he had not encouraged Lie, and Cadogan, in turn, did not encourage Kyrou.[122]

Athens's reaction was as guarded as Kyrou's. Although it did not reject Lie's proposal, Athens thought it premature and preferred to wait and see how matters would develop. It was unsure of Yugoslavia's position and intentions. Accordingly, if Lie decided to make his approach, great care had to be exercised. At the same time, Kyrou was to emphasize to Lie that these views were "unofficial, informal, and off-record." The Greeks did not wish the Yugoslavs to ascertain that Lie had consulted them. Kyrou was "impressed by Lie's sincerity" but was pessimistic as to what would develop. He was confident that Lie would not reveal that he had consulted Athens.[123] In view of these Greek reactions, Lie concluded that the time had not yet arrived to approach the Yugoslavs; he would wait until the assembly convened. Kyrou thought this was the best solution.[124]

Lie's proposal and the Greek reaction to it ruffled Foreign Secretary Bevin. "Watch this. We must keep Lie off spoiling this Greek matter. He is a danger," Bevin scribbled. He thought that Lie had no right to conciliate the question using Evatt's mandate.[125] Bevin's view was echoed in the Southern Department and the attention of the mission in New York was drawn to this matter and to the Foreign Office and State Department views that Greek-Yugoslav economic relations be initiated directly.[126]

Second thoughts soon developed, however. Jebb pointed out that nothing in the charter really prevented Lie from "attempting on his own initiative to reconcile the differences between two member States." On the other hand, Jebb thought that with Evatt's group dissolved, Lie had no right to continue conciliation negotiations in the group's name. Although reservations were raised to these comments, Jebb held his ground. Personally, he felt the Foreign Office would have "no *legal* ground" against Lie if he attempted to conciliate the question on his own, "however misguided that might be."[127]

By late August, Lie thought that some movement in the Greek question would be possible during the coming assembly session. Although the possibility was very small and depended on the Russian position, it was "one which he wished to explore." The Americans encouraged him to do so.[128] Obviously the Foreign Office and the State Department were not coordinating their policies on this matter. The Foreign Office's attitude about Lie was shared by the Danish representative, William Borberg, who in a hypothetical discussion with the Americans was "not sure that it was a healthy thing to get the SYG 'enmeshed' in political problems." On this question, Borberg contrasted the office's evolution under the United Nations with its seeming nonpolitical character under the league. He frankly admitted that he did not know which was preferable but felt that Washington should proceed cautiously before establishing an inordinate number of precedents.[129]

When approached by the Americans as to possible conciliation scenarios, Lie "expressed a strong preference" for a conciliation effort by the president of the assembly, the chairman of the First Committee, and himself. They would consult with Greece and her three neighbors, as well as the council's permanent members other than China. If there appeared any prospect of achieving a settlement, then the four permanent members would be convened to confirm the arrangement. Lie had had in mind Philippine General Carlos Romulo and Canada's Pearson—whom he especially stressed[130]—as most likely to become president of the assembly and chairman of the First Committee, respectively. However, when Lie raised with the Russians Pearson's candidacy for chairman of the First Committee, their reaction was negative.[131] Nevertheless, Pearson became its chairman with Sarper as vice chairman and Romulo as president of the assembly.

In subsequent discussions with the Americans, Lie agreed to expand the conciliation group to include Sarper, which, with Pearson and Romulo, seemingly gave it a pro-Western tilt. Lie also agreed that neither Greece's internal problems nor complex territorial questions (an allusion to the problem of northern Epirus) should incumber the conciliation discussions. As to the Russians, he consented to tackle Vyshinsky in order to discover "very privately and informally" whether Moscow was "really in the mood for some consultation on the Greek question."[132]

Lie discussed this with Vyshinsky on September 25. Vyshinsky, unmoved, thought the Evatt endeavour had exhausted itself; he maintained that the Russian position continue to be the *Tass* report of May 20: free elections under United Nations supervision; an amnesty for Greek guerrilla forces; withdrawal of foreign troops from Greece; and international control of Greece's frontiers, including Russian participation. Although Vyshinsky had no instructions, he made it clear that this was not his final word on the matter. Indeed, the following day Assistant Secretary-General Konstantin Zinchenko (who had replaced Sobolev) conveyed a message from Vyshinsky that he expected instructions in several days. During the conversation Vyshinsky referred to Soviet Russia's possession of the atom bomb, which he thought would put his country in a "better bargaining position."

If this was the Russian position, Lie saw little prospect of conciliation and held correctly that the settlement of issues dealing with Greece's frontier security was the primary problem. Even if Moscow "might be in a bargaining mood," Lie, Romulo, and Pearson were convinced that the conciliation discussions should not be based on the *Tass* report of May 20.[133]

Finally on September 28, the First Committee appointed the conciliation group (Lie, Pearson, Romulo, and Sarper) with the right to consult any states that might be helpful. It was to report by October 17.[134] By October 5, complaints were filed about Romulo's and Lie's "naivete . . . regarding the Russian approach to the question." They were considered "extremely anxious to negotiate a settlement" and "too prone to accept Russian promises literally." While Romulo had somewhat limited experience in dealing with the Russians, no excuse was offered for Lie. It was suggested that Secretary of State Acheson (who had replaced Marshall) have a brief talk with Romulo based on the former's recent experience with the Russians in the discussions about Austria. Romulo might then comprehend that Vyshinsky, while adamant on Austria and violating other pledges, was "pouring blandishments" on himself and Lie with indications that the Russians "would be conciliatory on Greece and other matters." Romulo should thus be better equipped to take on the Russians—since Lie was not mentioned, one must assume that little hope was held in his direction.[135]

Lie's talks with the Russians left him pessimistic, and he thought that the conciliation group might present its report prior to October 17, especially if Moscow's position remained adamant.[136] Elections in Greece under international (now including Russian) supervision appeared to attract his attention. Sarper, with the upcoming Turkish elections probably in mind, held that international supervision of Greek elections "would set a very dangerous precedent." When Lie noted that the situations of Greece and Turkey were not analogous, Sarper responded that, although Greece was going through difficult times, Athens nevertheless had an established government and it would be difficult to ask for electoral supervision.[137]

The conciliation group, however, failed to devise a conciliation formula.[138] As Pearson and his Canadian associate Robert Riddell pointed out to the Americans, "the report was so favorable to Greece that Lie was worried about this fact."[139] Lie still hoped to fish in troubled waters, however, by discussing, before the assembly adjourned and the Albanian and Bulgarian representatives departed, the repatriation of children kidnapped by the Greek guerrillas, Greek-Yugoslav relations, and the Greek-Albanian frontier problem. A member of the American mission cautioned Lie on the last two points, a stance that Cordier seconded.[140] The advice appears to have had its impact, for only the repatriation of the kidnapped Greek children was tackled by the assembly.[141] Although deterred from examining the other two issues, Lie had no qualms in stressing to Pipinelis the necessity for Greece to press ahead with its policy of leniency; he felt that the lack of executions by Greek military courts during the previous two months "had been very helpful." Lie hoped that the current situation would continue in the interest of Greece and all other concerned parties.[142]

It was sound advice, but there appears to be no evidence that Lie ever spoke in a similar vein to Greece's neighbors, who, like Soviet Russia, Lie subjected to less stringent moral and political standards. The commencement of the Korean War changed Lie's perceptions drastically. Greece, which had been treated by Lie and the secretariat in a lamentable manner, was no longer center stage thanks to American aid and Greek resistance to outside attempts to otherthrow the government by a guerrilla-inspired war. Athens was no longer a pariah whose government was to be criticized in sotte voce. Indeed, by 1951, even though Lie was a little ambivalent, he could envisage a Greece as part of the Western military alliance. That he strove to repatriate the kidnapped Greek children there can be no doubt, and it will be to his everlasting credit that he attempted to do so.[143] When Lie visited Athens he was received by the government in a manner befitting his high international office. The Greeks held no hard feelings against him for what had occurred.[144] It would appear that Athens during these years had forgotten its League of Nations experience and been mesmerized by the idealism and optimism generated by the United Nations. It proved to be a painful lapse in memory.

5

A
PLUNGING
MERCURY

The Marshall Plan

Following the Truman Doctrine, the next important postwar step against the perceived Russian threat was Washington's decision to assist Europe to recover economically and thus resume its important role in world affairs. Secretary of State Marshall's commencement address at Harvard University on June 5, 1947, proposing this action[1] was favorably received in congressional and other circles. Subsequent statements by Marshall and Truman on the need for an integrated program of European economic recovery, encouraged Lie. He thought that Under Secretary William Clayton would discuss such a program with Myrdal whose Economic Commission for Europe would formulate the necessary plans.[2] This was wishful thinking at its worst, keeping in mind the need to execute a recovery program as quickly as possible and conceivable Russian obstruction either in the United Nations or in the Economic Commission for Europe. Moreover, Lie's handling of the Iranian, Spanish, and especially the Greek questions had generated little confidence in his political acumen in the State Department and in the Foreign Office; whereas Myrdal's views and orientation,[3] made unacceptable the use of the commission.

Indeed Myrdal felt the Marshall Plan would fail, secure the iron curtain, and bring on a war. The work envisaged under the plan had to be turned over to the commission. A program of recovery under the aegis of the commission, he believed, would have made Moscow's participation, as a commission member, "more likely, if not assured."[4] The fly in the ointment, of course, was that Russia's participation depended on whether Europe's economic recovery was considered to be in Moscow's interests. It obviously was not, something that Moscow perceived immediately, even if Myrdal did not.

In an obvious attempt to influence Whitehall's actions rather than to ascertain them, Lie contacted Gore-Booth at the Foreign Office through his English assistant, Martin Hill. Lie observed that Myrdal's Economic Commission for Europe "appeared to be [the] appropriate body," already established, to handle Marshall's proposal and pointed out that Myrdal wanted to know what was developing before he spoke to people in Moscow. The American attitude on this matter, specifically the use of Myrdal's commission obviously left Lie uneasy.

When asked by Hill whether the Foreign Office saw any objection to Myrdal placing the matter on the agenda of the commission's next meeting, Gore-Booth neatly parried the query by observing that urgent high-level talks were being conducted with the French and no doubt that similar talks would be conducted with the Americans. Therefore he did not think that a firm response about the commission's precise role could be given until these talks had occurred. He hoped very much that "Myrdal could be persuaded" to desist from any action until there had been consultation in London. It was obvious that Lie had gotten the "message" for, when Hill contacted Gore-Booth a second time, he appeared "less impatient" than earlier. Lie, Hill explained, was willing to tarry and understood that it served no useful purpose to place on the commission's "agenda a half baked item or one that did not command support from the leading members."[5]

Lie also approached the Americans. He wanted to discuss with Marshall, he explained, the implications of Marshall's Harvard proposals. Some had urged him to place the matter on the Economic and Social Council agenda, which would permit discussion of whether it conformed with the provisions establishing the Economic Commission for Europe's terms of reference.[6] Lie's request was then followed by a visit from Assistant Secretary-General Price to a senior member of the American mission. Since the Harvard address made no mention of either the United Nations or the Economic Commission for Europe, he conveyed the concern of Lie and others as to whether, in implementing Marshall's offer, Washington intended to abandon the commission in favor of unilateral action. Indeed, no mention of either body had been made by any government spokesman in connection with the question of European recovery.[7] Lie's concern encountered a less than friendly reception in the State Department. It was proposed that Marshall make it clear to Lie, either directly or through Austin, that it was the set policy of the American government that any steps leading to the preparation of a program for European economic recovery had to be taken by the European states themselves and that the Secretary of State was pleased to see that moves had already been made in this direction.

Undoubtedly the Economic Commission for Europe would be, and should be, one of the instruments considered by the European states in determining the best procedure for instituting a recovery program. Nevertheless, Washington felt it "would be unfortunate to place exclusive reliance on this agency to such an extent that, if the Commission were unable to produce a program, none would be forthcoming from other sources." (This comment was obviously made with Russian obstructionist tactics in mind.) In addition, it was the American view that the Economic Commission for Europe, as established by the Economic and Social Council and authorized by it to initiate and facilitate concerted action for Europe's economic recovery, was not required to be the sole organ for a recovery program—an allusion to Myrdal's pressures and endeavors.

The State Department assumed that if the European states desired to establish reconstruction machinery outside the United Nations' framework, this would not hinder other appropriate steps being taken by the commission or other United Nations organs. Because Washington thought it important that the European states take the initiative themselves, it suggested that, if Lie wished to urge the use of any United Nations facilities, he might discuss the matter with the United Nations representatives of the concerned European states.[8]

Lie took the hint and quickly asked to see Cadogan.[9] A brief was then prepared by R. L. Hall, Director of the Cabinet Office's Economic Section, who thought that Cadogan's approach to Lie should be that he had no instructions but thought that the paramount consideration was speed. Bevin's suggestion that Myrdal preside over the body to assess Europe's needs could be cited to show that London did not want to exclude the Economic Commission for Europe. Hall admitted, however, that London was "on a very sticky wicket," for there was no possible response to the statement that the commission was the obvious organ to use. Cadogan's best tack would be to say that he would transmit Lie's representations and was very sure that Great Britain was most anxious to take complete advantage of the Marshall offer, in full cooperation with other concerned states.[10]

Bevin in his message to Cadogan tried to assure Lie that both he and French Foreign Minister Georges Bidault were "anxious to utilise the machinery" of the world organization to the "maximum extent possible." However, they both felt that the urgent task they faced made it necessary to assume an initiative in advance of the Economic Commission for Europe's July meeting. Thus, they invited Molotov to join them in discussions the following week, an invitation that the pressure of time did not allow them to inform Lie about. They now awaited Molotov's reply, on which the next step necessarily depended. Bevin would keep Lie informed of developments.[11] Faced with a fait accompli, Lie could do nothing except to signal that he would be grateful if he could be kept informed of future moves.[12]

Bevin's explanations to Lie were less than candid, for in point of fact, as he explained to the British ambassador in Moscow, both he and Bidault were convinced that any initial moves must be outside the Economic Commission for Europe. They hoped that the commission at its July session would note and approve the steps taken and, assuming the Russians cooperated, that full use of the commission could be made at a later period. Bevin thought Molotov might ask whether it was proposed to use the commission or to establish separate organs. Presumably Myrdal would have informed the Russians that he and Lie thought the commission was the proper institution to bring together the experts needed to provide the basis for a response to Marshall's proposal. However, the new commission had not yet developed its secretariat, and despite "full confidence" in Myrdal, Bevin and Bidault were convinced that his staff "could not organise the initial steps needed to provide the basis for a reply."[13] The arguments to bypass the Economic Commission for Europe initially were plausible, but the comment about full confidence in Myrdal was not true and exposed Bevin and Bidault's desire to avoid the United Nations, Lie, the commission, and Myrdal for reasons already discussed. American and Anglo-French desires without any prior exchange of views had converged.

Illusions die slowly and Lie clung to the hope, nurtured by Bevin's deceptive comments, that appropriate instruments of the United Nations would be used to implement the Marshall Plan,[14] though Lie had to admit that he had not been invited to, contacted, or consulted about the contemplated meeting with Molotov in Paris.[15] The Foreign Office feared that any suggestion that London was "wedded to the use of U. N. machinery at all stages" and that Lie was informed on a daily basis of developments in Paris would injure British prospects during the talks.[16] This fear was unnecessary, for Russian rejection of the plan at Paris made agreement impossible. Naturally, Lie greatly regretted that the Paris discussions had broken down. In view of Europe's urgent needs and the nature of Marshall's proposals, Lie could not believe that this was the last word on the subject.[17]

In his own message about the Paris talks, Bevin assured Lie that he and Bidault had "made every effort and used every argument to assure" Molotov that the Anglo-French proposal embraced no interference in Russia's internal affairs or those of any other European state. The debate there had "made it crystal clear" that cooperation with Moscow in this matter "was impossible except on terms which would have been unacceptable" to the Anglo-French and to the Americans and contrary to Europe's interests. London and Paris therefore had to proceed without Moscow, and Bevin hoped Lie would "appreciate that in these circumstances there could be no questions of making full use" of United Nations machinery. Bevin assured Lie that every attempt would be made to see that it was "not bypassed," and he would keep Lie completely informed of future moves, "but we cannot afford to risk further delay and obstructions when so much is at stake."[18] Thanks to Moscow's tack, the avoidance by Bevin and Bidault of United Nations involvement could be justified. Lie acquiesced, pragmatically observing that the essential thing was to get relief to Europe quickly since "all other considerations were subordinate."[19]

Lie expanded on this view privately when he observed that the United Nations' purpose "should be one of helpfulness to the extent of the help required or requested"; it "should [not] be imposed upon any group" of member states. If a member state, specifically Russia, wished to obstruct the execution of plans contemplated by other member states, then according to Lie those states had the inherent right to associate with each other to pursue their objectives without reference to the United Nations.[20] Lie then publicly committed himself to the Marshall Plan and thus to Russian censure.[21] By this action, the Americans, not to mention the English and French, had the aura of Lie's support without the liability of his participation. Lie subsequently claimed that, as soon as he heard of Marshall's offer, he had urged the Norwegian authorities, who the British and French ambassadors in Oslo thought needed little urging, to accept it without condition and without regard to the United Nations' prestige, because the entire economic situation both in America and in Europe was more precarious than most people realized. Norway, Lie held, could not afford to introduce political considerations into such a question. If Moscow believed it could do so, that was Moscow's funeral. For other states, he believed the only "safe and sensible attitude" was to proceed without any thought of politics[22]—although Lie himself, as we have seen, opposed the inclusion of Franco's Spain in the Marshall Plan.[23]

Toward this end, and no doubt in a nod to Myrdal, Lie decided that the Economic Commission for Europe had to be careful to avoid any moves that the Russians could use in their campaign against the Marshall Plan. Indeed, he issued firm orders that no secretariat official should speak critically of the plan.[24] By the spring of 1948, Lie looked forward to the plan's impact on western Europe's economy and likewise its political stability[25]—a euphemism, it would appear by Lie, for a restructured global balance of power.[26] In a mid-April speech at President Roosevelt's home in Hyde Park, New York, although criticizing American and Russian policies, the Marshall Plan was supported.[27] By August 1949, Lie could exclaim with satisfaction that the plan had done wonders for Norway and Denmark and praise its concept and execution.[28] During his retirement years he pointed to the Marshall Plan's value despite its not being channeled through the United Nations.[29] In 1967, Lie was keen on celebrating the plan's twentieth anniversary, as the least that could be done to remind Norwegians of postwar American efforts to restore Europe after bailing it out of two world wars.[30] Alas, it was not to be. Lie and others "sadly concluded" that a ceremony might be self-defeating, since it might trigger anti-American feelings that would mar the event and be distorted by the press even though the incidents were minor.[31] It was not a matter of Norwegian ingratitude, peoples' memories are notoriously short in interstate relations.

The Coup in Prague

In the immediate postwar period Czechoslovakia's ability to maintain her independence and avoid falling into the Russian sphere of influence was a benchmark by which one could gauge the tensions of the Cold War. This precarious existence, the delicate balance of assuaging the Russians while avoiding their bear hug yet maintaining Prague's Western contacts, partially explains Lie's visit to the Czechoslovakian capitol in late January 1948. Czech Foreign Minister Jan Masaryk appealed for American and British economic support and was bitter about the West's seeming abandonment of his country to the Russians. He begged Lie to urge that they end their defeatist attitude, an appeal that Lie conveyed to both London and New York. President Eduard Beneš, Lie concluded after talking with him, appeared to be very much disillusioned and gave the impression of being a "voluntary prisoner."[32]

In New York, Lie told a meeting of the assistant secretaries-general that during his European trip he had encountered only fear, and not merely in Prague. There was no doubt that he was alluding to Soviet Russia; but probably to strike a proper balance and also keep Sobolev at bay, he added that the United States was also feared economically. The gist of the discussion that Lie then led was the possibility of war between the United States and Soviet Russia, which weighed heavily on his mind, especially if anything happened in Czechoslovakia. Within a month of Lie's visit the Czechoslovak democratic state fell victim to a well prepared and executed coup d'état, which was buttressed by Russian troop movements along the border. Lie was shocked by the news, as were countless others.[33]

Several days later on February 25 he was visited by the Czech representative, Jan Papánek, who asked Lie to accept an official note from him and present the Czech case formally to the Security Council—an oblique request that he invoke Article 99. Lie refused, advising him to await further developments. Papánek's request had placed Lie in an awkward position, since it required that he do something counter to Soviet Russia. Lie wanted to appease Moscow: his perceived task was to reconcile East and West, and Papánek's desired intervention had to be avoided. Nor did Lie want Papánek to leave his note, because if he took no action this would be interpreted as an anti-Western move. He therefore pressed Papánek not to ask him to do anything. Because of Lie's pleas and Papánek's momentary political myopia and because he lacked sufficient information to present to the council, Papánek withdrew his note. He told Lie he disagreed with him, that he was unconvinced, and that in several days time he would probably return.[34]

This encounter was a clear signal of dangers ahead; so on March 1, with the Communists now firmly ensconced in Prague, Lie had another conference with the assistant secretaries-general at his home. This long meeting dealt solely with the Czech crisis and what could be done to mend the United Nations' ripped fabric. Specifically, Lie's initial question was whether the hour had not arrived for him to resign. As we shall see this would not be the last time that the threat of his resignation would be flashed to all and sundry. The second question he posed was more immediate. Should he not issue a statement about the situation, pointing out that the "supreme crisis" had arrived and that the United Nations was headed for extinction. Various opinions were expressed, but that of Sobolev was the most important, in view of what subsequently was to occur and Lie's personal relations with him.

Sobolev chose his words carefully and confined himself to whether Lie should issue a statement. He made no defense of what Moscow had accomplished in Czechoslovakia and indicated in a bland manner that he did not consider it any business of the United Nations secretariat. Simultaneously, Sobolev developed the thesis that the charter "imposed no responsibility or right upon" Lie to intervene in political matters, which certainly was not the Russian attitude regarding the Iranian question. Sobolev held that it was the secretariat's duty to serve the world organization's member states "not to direct them." Indeed, it "would be wrong and very unfortunate" if Lie unilaterally involved himself "in those strong forces which were sweeping the world." Price, who thought he knew Lie's strong views on what had occurred in Prague, was surprised when he made no response to the thesis advanced by Sobolev.[35]

To Price, Lie divulged that he had convened the meeting largely for Sobolev's benefit and that Sobolev had exposed his Russian proclivities.[36] So he had. On the other hand, if Lie's talk of resignation was an attempt to pressure the Russians, it appears not to have made the slightest dent on Sobolev. Lie had placed a high price on his friendship with Moscow, and Sobolev failed to nibble at the bait. Sobolev, was obviously less interested in absorbing Lie's message than in clearly conveying Moscow's, which as seen from his conversation with Papánek Lie had already committed himself to, despite his comments to Price. Lie would now subject Russian actions in Czechoslovakia to a lower crossbar and thus an easier leap, than that to which he had subjected Anglo-French actions in the Syrian-Lebanese question several years before. It was a stance made easier by Western reticence to confront the Russians over their Czech success, a stance no doubt based on military considerations that hastened the formation of a Western defense alliance.

The initial astonishment over the Czech coup was followed by the trauma of Masaryk's death on March 10 under peculiar circumstances—it was suicide, Prague explained. Lie was convinced that Masaryk had been murdered. As he graphically described to Sulzberger of the *New York Times*, no man of Masaryk's bulk could have had "so few bumps on his body" if had leaped out a high window and queried how he, Lie, would look—keep in mind his girth—if he were to defenestrate himself.[37]

On the same day that Masaryk died, Papánek again called on Lie. Naturally Lie's attitude was unchanged. He did not want Papánek to insist on presenting his note, which had been redrafted in line with new information; he wanted him to withdraw it. Papánek flatly refused; regardless of what Lie did, Papánek would hold a press conference. Faced with this threat, Lie succumbed and read the note. Because it mentioned the first interview of February 25, Lie found the note unacceptable. He would be willing, Lie asserted, to help Papánek present the case to the council if the note were redrafted and any reference to the February 25 meeting, deleted. Papánek agreed.[38] Nevertheless the note mentioned the February meeting though its details were suppressed. The sanitized version finally accepted by Lie denounced the communist seizure of power and requested that the question be considered by the council.[39] Cadogan's initial reaction was that, if he were Lie, he would feel obligated to ask whether Papánek had addressed him on instructions from Prague.[40] It was a prophetic comment.

Papánek's own gyrations complicated the situation. It appears that he first told Lie that he was resigning his position. Then he tendered his note requesting that the question be considered by the council and insisted he would oppose any attempt by Prague to revoke his credentials, on the grounds that any such orders were not issued by the Czech government. Lie explained that if Prague made a new appointment and the credentials were signed by Beneš and the new prime minister, Klement Gottwald, he would have no choice but to place them before the council.

Lie then instructed Cordier to take Papánek's note immediately to Sobolev, as secretary of the council. Cordier, Feller, and Philip Jessup, Columbia University's renowned professor of international law and a senior member of the American mission, all agreed that Sobolev would immediately contact Gromyko who would then contact Moscow, with the likelihood that Prague would quickly terminate Papánek's status. Feller insisted that the secretariat was obligated to distribute Papánek's note before Prague revoked his credentials. They agreed that when Papánek transmitted his note he was the accredited Czech representative and that his note therefore had to be treated as an official communication. Sobolev held, however, that he had to discuss with Lie something in Papánek's note before he could process it as a council document. Cordier and Feller therefore endeavored to contact Lie to direct Sobolev to proceed.[41]

That afternoon the State Department was informed that Lie intended to distribute Papánek's note to the council and that it was the secretariat's position that it would be the council's decision whether to consider the note.[42] The final word from the American mission was that Lie had decided that Papánek's note should be considered a non-governmental communication and thus one he was not obligated to transmit to the council.[43] It had been a confused and hectic March 10.

Once the dust settled, the official explanation filtered through. Feller observed that events had moved too quickly for him to write a legal opinion, although he had discussed the question with Lie on several occasions. The key to Lie's ruling, he explained, was Papánek's statement that he submitted his note in his "private capacity." Accordingly, Lie had to look beyond the note in order "to make an essentially political judgment." This was that Papánek was acting in his personal capacity and not as the Czechoslovakian representative. Feller, who in this episode, as well as in the Iranian question, gives the impression of being a trimmer, now concurred with Lie's view, despite his initial reaction the previous day.[44]

Lie admitted to Rusk that it was Sobolev who raised the question whether the note "could properly be regarded as a communication from a member state." Lie then talked with China's Tingfu Tsiang, the council president, who held that on the face of it the note could not be regarded as an official communication. Lie confessed that he had received conflicting advice: Sobolev and Kerno holding that the communication was not official; Cordier and Feller holding that it should be conveyed in the regular fashion to the council.

Lie explained that he had asked whom Papánek represented. Not the present government, Papánek responded; he represented Masaryk. Lie retorted that Masaryk was not a government, he was not of this world. Papánek replied that then he represented Beneš. The note, Lie pointed out, indicted the present government, which Papánek was ostensibly representing. He therefore did not see how he could accept his note as a government communication merely because Papánek was formally accredited as the representative of the Czech government.[45]

An added consideration, the British mission noted to the Foreign Office, was that Lie held if he had accepted the note and placed it on the agenda, the council would have rejected it on the grounds that Papánek was acting only on his own initiative and did not recognize the government he was indicting. Lie's decision had "created or aggravated a sense of frustration" among secretariat personnel, though they admitted the legal basis for his action.[46] Although Lie's position was no doubt correct, the Canadian mission observed, what had occurred had given rise to internal controversy reflected in the New York press and in radio comment, which generally concluded that Lie had "'pigeon holed'" Papánek's note.[47] Austin's pithy comment summed it up: Lie felt, he signaled Washington, that "he could not ignore the realities of the situation and therefore had made a political rather than a legal ruling."[48] Indeed, he had.

If Lie had been intent on making some sort of statement about the Czech crisis, as he had mentioned to the assistant secretaries-general in the discussion of March 1, certainly Papánek's note to the council was a heaven-sent opportunity for Lie to make such a statement through another party and thus avoid the onus of acting on his own initiative. He failed to do so. One can well imagine the assault that Sobolev must have mounted to dissuade Lie from doing so, when Lie consulted him, if we are merely to judge from Sobolev's comments at the meeting of March 1. Kerno, in turn, whom Lie had also consulted was, as we have seen, Moscow's stooge or at the least someone very much open to Russian influence. In fact, during the discussion of March 1, Kerno, considering that he was Czech and that the Prague take-over should have moved him as much as it had moved every other Czech committed to democratic government and its value system, never mentioned his homeland and restricted himself to anodyne comments. For all intents and purposes he had seemingly caved in. His virtual silence during the discussion of March 1, considering that during the war he had fled Czechoslovakia to continue the anti-Nazi struggle in France, reinforces the Foreign Office's negative impression of him. Sobolev had won the initial skirmish and Lie had acquired no laurels.

Price, in particular, was disturbed by what had transpired. Well-meaning and something of an idealist in political matters, he had not been consulted about Papánek's note. When Lie claimed that the *New York Times* had been unfair in writing that he had reached his decision to reject the note on the advice of a Czech and a Russian—he subsequently pleaded that the press eliminate references to nationality in future comments about the secretariat—and insisted that the council's rules of procedure were very clear on the matter, Price interjected that sometimes there were too many rules and that the secretariat was tied down too much by them. He pointed out that Papánek's note was addressed to Lie but intended for the council. He saw nothing that precluded Lie from handing the note to Tsiang and pointing out that it was meant for him. The council could then have made its own ruling. Lie, already nervous, became agitated by Price's comments. He left Price's office and returned armed with the council's rules of procedure. He pointed to the rule requiring that he circulate to the council government communications. Price fatuously remarked that there was nothing in the rules of procedure that prevented Lie from conveying anything else he desired. He still did not understand why Lie took the responsibility of making so important a decision, which Price felt belonged to the council. Lie was not convinced,[49] but it would not be unfair to say that Price's comments had touched a troubled zone in Lie's psyche, which explained his understandable urge to clarify his actions.

Within the State Department it was pointed out that the propriety of Lie's ruling could be questioned by a council member. Or, Austin could request from Lie that the matter be placed on the agenda. Whichever procedure was used, Washington would have to press the matter through the council's proceedings. It would have to show that the Czech situation was of sufficient import and urgency to endanger the maintenance of international peace and security and that the country's territorial integrity and political independence had been intimidated by the threat or use of force.[50] The advice offered was clear enough: avoid entanglement over the Czech question in the United Nations. Before the matter was decided at higher levels, however, on March 12 Chile requested that the issue raised in Papánek's note be included on the council's agenda.[51]

The State Department's instructions to the American mission supported the Chilean request. At the same time, it instructed the mission that, if the propriety of Lie's handling of Papánek's note should arise, it was to take the general line that Lie's decision was within his discretion. Since the matter of Chile's complaint was now properly before the council, it appeared unproductive to discuss the correctness of Lie's decision, which in this case he was clearly competent to make. Then the mission was informed that Washington was not disposed to be an active proponent in the Czech case as it was in the Iranian case in 1946. Rather, the United States should act as a loyal council member faced with a difficult case on which it would speak frankly but avoid carrying the main burden.[52]

There was unease, however, over these instructions. The United Nations adviser to the Office of Far Eastern Affairs pointed out that the position on Lie's action did not appear "to have been cleared very widely." Indeed, there seemed "to be room for doubt concerning the propriety" of his action. Because of the political consequences that might flow from his episode it was suggested to Walton Butterworth, director of the Office of Far Eastern Affairs, that he might wish to approach Rusk on the matter. Clearly the International Security Division's view was that Lie was not required by the council's rules to consult with Tsiang and that Lie would have been completely within his rights if he had not done so. Moreover, the instructions to the mission in New York were not cleared with the Legal Adviser's Office, which entertained "grave doubts concerning the propriety" of Lie's action. Some in the United Nations Affairs Division shared this view. In addition, Hayden Raynor, special assistant to the director of the Office of European Affairs, although agreeing with the mission's instructions, admitted that he had been "troubled about the possibilities of the Papánek case as a precedent," but felt that the particular instructions given the mission circumvented this problem. Likewise, Jessup was also worried about the situation and had suggested that, if there were sufficient department support, consideration might be given to devising a procedure whereby the council would consult the assembly's Interim Committee in the case of a conflict over credentials. The adviser's personal view was that the question was of potential importance as a precedent and that steps "should be taken to prevent the secretariat from assuming political functions" properly belonging to the organs of the world organization.[53]

Butterworth's memorandum to Rusk noted that leaving aside legal interpretation the concern was over the political implications of Lie's action. Such an important political question appeared to call for a decision by a competent United Nations organ.

Lie's decision in effect passed on the substance of the very question that Papánek, whose credentials had not been questioned, was attempting to place before the council. If Lie doubted Papánek's status, the obvious step would have been to refer the note to the council, leaving that organ the task of deciding the matter[54]—Price's point, but not an undisputed one.

Rusk's reply was an attempt to fend off Butterworth. He held that the circumstances surrounding the Papánek case were "unique." Although the propriety of the secretary-general's action had been questioned, he thought there were particulars that supported Lie's decision; for example, Papánek's gyrations and circumlocutions which induced Lie to conclude that the note was a private communication despite the Czech's still satisfactory credentials.[55] It would be interesting to speculate what Rusk's attitude would have been if he had been made privy to the two Papánek-Lie talks as well as Sobolev's remarks at the meeting of March 1 and the inferences that could be drawn from them to reconstruct the probable conversation that took place between Sobolev and Lie when the Russian tarried in processing Papánek's note despite pressure from Cordier and Feller.

Naturally the Russians protested against the Chilean request that the Czech situation be included on the council's provisional agenda. They lost on a procedural vote and Chile, as well as Papánek, were invited to participate in the discussions that continued through May. An attempt to establish a special committee to investigate the Czech question failed to pass because of Russian vetoes. The matter went unresolved.[56]

As these discussions commenced, Pierre Ordonneau, counsellor of the French delegation, approached a member of the American mission and expressed the opinion that Lie "was showing increasing signs of adopting pro-Soviet attitudes," and recommended that the "United States should be 'on guard.'" He specifically mentioned several secretariat legal decisions regarding the council's powers and duties, including Lie's handling of Papánek's note. Ordonneau noted that all these decisions, which had been taken under Lie's direct instructions, had adversely affected the Western powers' positions and had assisted Soviet Russia. "Ordonneau speculated that *Lie still showed the effects of the collaboration with the Communists which he had carried out during his early political career in Norway.''* Ordonneau likewise suggested that Lie was striving to maintain a bridge between America and Soviet Russia and felt that Moscow "should continue to obtain advantages from its membership in the United Nations."[57] Although Ordonneau did not say it, these membership advantages might have to be paid for by the West and others. Ordonneau had the right scent. In Lie's world of hurdles, the Russian crossbar had been placed very low, for which in this question the Czechs had paid a very high price.

Lie admitted that he had thought it "still possible to work with the [Russian] Communists, but the Czechoslovak developments had convinced him" that this was no longer true. If Communists were brought into the government it was only a matter of time before they would attempt, on Moscow's orders, to take it over. Lie now worried about "Russian rumblings and threats regarding Norway." These comments naturally were made when Sobolev was not present.[58] Cordier was present, however, and Lie was thus sure that his comments would be reported to Washington. But they appear to be only so much window dressing, if one keeps in mind his subsequent reticence to speak up on whether he believed there were human rights violations in the trial of Hungary's Cardinal Mindszenty[59] as well as his subsequent reaction to Soviet Russia's blockade of Berlin and the West's attempt to build a defense alliance.

Berlin Confrontation

Berlin, deep within the Russian zone of Germany, was an international enclave, divided like all Germany, into four occupation zones. Western and Russian inability to agree on Germany's future led, in early 1948, to Russian restrictions on the Western powers' free access to the city, despite their rights there. The Russian action interfered with the Western powers' contact with their garrisons and the several million Berliners subject to their control. The action was taken after unsuccessful Four Power negotiations over a proposed currency reform, announced by the Western powers to be instituted in their occupation zones, though not in their Berlin zones. On June 24 the Russians halted, because of "technical difficulties," all land and water traffic between the Western occupation zones and Berlin. The Western riposte to this Russian blockade was the commencement of an airlift to supply their garrisons in the city as well as the Berliners who resided in their zones. The Berlin question was now center stage in world affairs.

The possibility of physical confrontation and all that it portended moved Lie to suggest to the assistant secretaries-general that he quickly invoke charter Article 99.[60] Testing the waters, Lie approached Cadogan who observed that he saw no hope for such an action in the present situation.[61] Likewise Jessup, who was approached by Price on Lie's instructions, noted that Article 99 bestowed on Lie "a privilege but did not impose a duty." Rebuffed, Lie then took another tack. He indicated to Jessup that even if the decision were not taken to raise the question under Article 99, his inquiry perhaps still served a useful purpose in showing the Russians that "he was on the job" and had raised the matter. Jessup thought that Lie was more intent on "making a gesture" than in actually getting the question inscribed on the council agenda.[62]

Cadogan correctly observed to London that Article 99 was meant to guarantee that "no dispute or situation be overlooked simply because no one felt it his business to bring the matter before" the council. In the Berlin question everyone was quite aware of what was occurring and presumably committed to solving it. Furthermore, he noted, under the chairmanship of the irrepressible Ukrainian Manuilsky, the council was perhaps not an appropriate body to examine the matter, and Lie himself anticipated that the Russians would reject his proposal. Cadogan was sure that Lie was trying to help, feeling that if he was inactive now, he might subsequently be reproached for his failure to act.[63] Although Cadogan had been more generous than Jessup in explaining Lie's motives, the Foreign Office and Bevin were suspicious.

The head of the United Nations Department, Paul Mason, rejected any reference of the question to the council, since he failed to see what it could accomplish. If it were brought up, this might be done in the next assembly session. Jebb agreed.[64] Bevin's stance reflected the Foreign Office consensus: London should prevent the Berlin question from being "transferred to a controversial international [political] level" provided it could be handled as a technical problem.[65] Keeping in mind Bevin's antipathy toward Lie, his suspicions about the antecedents of Lie's initiative can be appreciated. As he noted to the British military governor of Berlin, incorrectly as it turned out, Lie "usually never moves without Soviet concurrence."[66] He replied therefore to Cadogan that he fully endorsed his advice that this was not a matter where Article 99 should be applied. In time Lie would have his views on whether the Berlin situation warranted other United Nations action.[67] Bevin, however, was purposely vague on how this reference to the United Nations should be made, if at all. Should it be to the council and under what articles? Alternatively, should it be submitted to a regular or special session of the assembly, with advance notice to Moscow that London intended to do this?[68]

The reception of Lie's proposal fared no better in Washington. He was to be told, the mission was informed, that the State Department greatly appreciated the role the United Nations "might play" should the situation deteriorate further, that the discussions would continue, and that every possible means was being explored to arrive at a peaceful settlement of the problem.[69] Paris likewise thought that any United Nations action then would be "premature."[70] The Canadians correctly surmised that the question would not come before the council "until efforts to take the matter up direct in Moscow had proved fruitless."[71] The negative reaction of all the council's permanent members, including China, had thwarted Lie's initiative. The gist of the Russian reaction was that charter Article 107 (that nothing in the charter invalidated or precluded action relating to any former member of the Axis coalition, taken or authorized as a result of the war by the responsible governments) excluded the Berlin question from the United Nations' purview.[72] By June 29, Lie could see that the jig was up. He announced that he had been monitoring events in Berlin and would continue to do so, but for the moment he had no plan to invoke Article 99.[73]

No sooner was this initiative put to sleep, than the alarm bells again rang in the State Department. Like a jack-in-the-box, Lie this time proposed that he dispatch his Norwegian confrere, Colonel Roscher Lund, to report on the situation. Initially this offer had been Feller's brainchild, but Feller subsequently alleged great shock and surprise at Lie's proposal, which he denigrated.[74] When Robert McClintock of the Office of United Nations Affairs was informed by John Ross of the American mission of Lie's proposal, his instant reaction was that Lund's dispatch to Berlin at this juncture "would be highly prejudicial." Lund's memorable performance as the principal secretary of the Balkan commission in Greece in 1947, McClintock held, "damned him on the most charitable terms as being at least gravely negligent, if not actively pro-Soviet." To dispatch an "uncertain instrument" like Lund to Berlin at this period of extreme tension would be unfortunate from both Washington's and Lie's points of view. He imagined that Moscow might perhaps issue Lund a visa to enter Berlin based on its "knowledge of his known nuisance value." McClintock personally hoped Washington could discover some excuse to avoid issuing Lund a visa. Accordingly Ross was to consult with the British and French before informally suggesting to Cordier that the State Department did not believe that Lund's arrival at that moment would be useful. McClintock thought it had to be obvious to Cordier that if London, Paris, and Washington refused Lund admittance to Berlin, while Moscow allowed him entrance, it would put both Lund and Lie "in a somewhat rosy light."[75]

No doubt to appear reasonable on this issue, the State Department then informed Ross it did not want to give the impression of discouraging the notion of sending United Nations emissaries to Berlin at Lie's discretion. Accordingly the secretariat should not be approached on this matter but wait the arrival of Lie's note regarding Lund.

However, Ross had already approached the British mission, which was "highly allergic" to the Lund suggestion. In addition, he had informally suggested to Cordier that, in view of Washington's resistance to invoking Article 99, it was perhaps "premature" for Lie to contemplate sending a special emissary to Berlin. Lie took the hint. Cordier subsequently informed Ross that Lie would probably not, after all, send his contemplated note regarding Lund, but "reserved 'his right' to send his own man to Berlin when he wanted to." Cordier explained that Lie "was considerably miffed" at the State Department's negative stance.

Ross "did not know whether it was the [New York] heat or what, but he had the impression that Lie was feeling restive and was inclined to throw his weight around." McClintock's snappy retort was that Lie "had a great deal of corporeal weight but not too much else to balance it." He declared Washington wished to avoid getting into "any position of mutual acerbity" with Lie, but he saw no reason for the State Department to alter a well-considered position simply because Lie "was reacting unfavorably to the [New York] heat."[76] The proposal to dispatch Lund to Berlin died quietly; but in view of the complaints about his performance on the Balkan commission, Lie's notion to send him to Berlin without even considering possible Anglo-American objections boggles the imagination.

Shortly after this episode, the Western powers affirmed to Moscow their legal rights to remain in Berlin, protested against the blockade, and suggested quadripartite conversations on Berlin's administration provided the blockade was lifted. Although the Russians agreed to participate in Four Power discussions, they did not agree to lift the blockade. Departing for Europe Lie observed that "he did not expect to intervene in the Berlin situation." It was up to the powers themselves to come to an agreement on what was to be done. When asked whether any of the Four Powers, as parties to the Berlin dispute, would be allowed to vote on the issue if it came before the council, Lie wisely sidestepped a direct reply by noting that inscription of the Berlin question on the council's agenda "would bring complexities in its wake."[77] Indeed it would have.

Quadripartite discussions commenced in Moscow in late July. The Western representatives emphasized to Stalin and Molotov that the essential conditions for an agreement were an end to the blockade and Four Power control of Berlin's currency. In London Lie broached the Berlin question with the Foreign Office's permanent under-secretary, Sir Orme Sargent. Sobolev who had returned from home leave, according to Lie, reported there was no feeling of crisis and the Berlin question had not been allowed to interfere with accustomed holiday arrangements. Lie then mischievously observed to Sargent that "it would not in his opinion be quite disastrous if the Western powers were to leave Berlin." (It must have taken all of Sargent's self-restraint to hide his emotive reaction.) He had stopped in London, Lie explained, for he harbored the notion that if the deadlock were to continue he might propose to visit Berlin himself to examine the situation—the Lund proposal under another guise—since such a visit "might have a healthy effect" upon the Russian government. As the Western powers were now in contact with Stalin, Lie thought it would be unsuitable to proceed; but if the situation worsened, he was prepared to go if a visit would do some good. "I did not encourage him to think that his services would be required for this purpose," Sargent laconically noted.[78]

Publicly in the Introduction to his Annual Report Lie urged a resumption of Four Power negotiations on Germany's future. Nothing would "contribute more" to the United Nations' effectiveness, he held, than a settlement of this question, although Lie admitted that it was difficult to judge whether council and assembly conciliation and mediation machinery could assist in bridging the outstanding differences.[79]

The Russians were annoyed. In an unpleasant discussion with the Deputy Foreign Minister Yakov Malik, Lie was taken to task. Malik claimed that Lie sided with Washington and that the Introduction to the Annual Report in a number of places conveyed an anti-Russian animus. Lie rightly foresaw that he would now be subjected to a violent Russian press assault. However, he was not going to allow such press attacks to disconcert him, he wrote to his family; his square dealing with both sides left him serene. Perhaps the Russians would realize that there was no difference between being branded Stalin's stooge in Washington and the reverse in Moscow the next day.[80]

Lie's radio address on September 4, in which he held that the Germans had to be "given tolerable conditions" that could ensure democratic development,[81] must have been viewed in Moscow as an added injury. The expected press storm erupted on September 11 [82] and not to be outdone, the Bulgarian and Polish satraps followed suit.[83] Lie, *Pravda* noted, had attempted to deal with matters that fell outside the United Nations' purview. Thus, he acknowledged the possibility of examining the German question in the United Nations, although he knew very well that it was exclusively a matter for the Council of Foreign Ministers. It appeared, according to *Pravda*, that Lie was prepared to place himself in the hands of the Anglo-Americans who, unable to dictate settlement terms on the German question in the Council of Foreign Ministers, had already attempted to appeal to the world organization with demagogic ends in mind.[84] The reaction to *Pravda*'s comments in the German and the United Nations Departments of the Foreign Office, was that in any referral of the matter the world organization would be faced not with the German question but with a threat to the peace generated by Russian actions in Berlin.[85]

During this same period exploratory discussions among the Four Powers continued in Moscow. In late August there appeared to be grounds for cautious optimism: Berlin's four military governors were directed to implement simultaneous measures to lift the blockade and to introduce the Russian mark as the city's only currency. Berlin's currency was to be regulated from the Russian zone under the control of a financial commission governed by the Four Powers. From this it appeared that a solution to the question had been reached by which the lifting of the blockade would be matched by Anglo-American-French acceptance of the Russian mark in Berlin, provided the Four Powers could agree on joint currency control, banking arrangements, and trade facilities in the city. Likewise, the Western powers would lift the counterblockade that they had instituted between their zones and the Russian zone. However, the effort to work out the details of the Four Power control in Berlin led nowhere: the Russian military governor could not agree with his Western counterparts on the powers of the contemplated financial control commission; insisted on Russian control of Berlin's trade; and lastly, proposed added restrictions on Western access to the city by air. When additional exchanges failed to resolve the problem, the Western powers on September 29 referred the question, because of the Russian actions, to the council as a threat to the peace.

That same afternoon, Jessup called on Lie and recalled the Introduction to his Annual Report and his earlier suggestion to invoke Article 99. The question, Jessup noted, was now before the world organization as Lie had previously thought it should be. Lie observed that the "Russians were furious," that according to Sobolev, Moscow held that the appeal to the council was a deliberate attempt by the United States to destroy the United Nations. The Russians would resist placing the question on the agenda and would invoke charter Articles 106 and 107. Jessup responded that the problem's core was that Russian actions in Berlin threatened the peace. This stemmed from their attempts to pressure the other three powers to comply with their demands by the use of duress and force or the threat to use force. London, Paris, and Washington, however, simply were not going to kowtow to that kind of threat.

Lie strongly agreed; if the Western powers evacuated Berlin, it meant surrendering the city to the "communists and that would be a threat to [the] Scandinavian countries"—the reverse of what he had told Sargent in London. Jessup thought the remark important since Lie appeared to be speaking more as a Norwegian than as secretary-general. Lie then added that "Sobolev had suggested that the only solution was to have all Four Powers agree to withdraw their troops from Berlin." To which Jessup quickly retorted that the result would be a Berlin encircled by Russian forces. He pointed out to Lie that the Western powers were prepared to declare once more their readiness to discuss all questions with Moscow. If the blockade were lifted, all subjects were open to discussion. Lie then asked whether Jessup saw "any possibility for mediation." Jessup cautiously replied that the Western powers had brought the question to the United Nations in accordance with their understanding of their charter duties, and they hoped the processes of the world organization could succeed. Lie now divulged that some of his staff had pressed him to make a strong public statement when the matter surfaced, but he had decided not to do so. Jessup believed that this had been a wise decision. Lie was apprehensive of Bevin's and Spaak's public utterances and the reaction to them. He held that the reaction of the European press, including Scandinavian, suggested that these speeches portended the West's departure from the United Nations. Personally, Lie did not agree; but they could be thus interpreted and would be coupled with the assertion that the Western powers were intent on destroying the United Nations by bringing the Berlin question to the council. Lie concluded the conversation by "offering to be of any assistance at any time."[86]

Although there appears to be no official documentary evidence to support it, Lie subsequently asserted in his memoirs that Jessup and Rusk in early October visited him and inquired whether he was willing to explore an exit from the impasse. Lie responded that naturally he would do what was within his power and directed Feller, Sobolev, and Stoneman, separately, to come up with suggestions. In view of Jessup's guarded response to Lie's comments during their September 29 conversation, as well as Rusk's general circumspection in dealing with Lie, and based on evidence in Lie's papers, it would appear that Lie confused the conversation of late September with Jessup as occurring in early October.[87] He probably likewise confused the substance of the American reaction, whether by Jessup or Rusk, to any proposal on his part to mediate the Berlin question. Certainly in Lie's mind, the only contribution that the United Nations could offer toward resolving the question had to be restricted to mediation endeavors, for the world organization was unable to act forcefully against Moscow because of the veto in the council. The salient point was whether both sides sincerely desired mediation.[88] Lie's approach was sound, but the crux was who would mediate and how.

Since the Russians held that the question was excluded by charter Article 107, they requested that the Council of Foreign Ministers be convened. Moscow's arguments fell on deaf ears, and the council decided on October 5 to place the Berlin question on its agenda. The immediate Russian reaction was that they would not partake in the discussion, as inscription of the item was contrary to Article 107.[89] The previous day, Australia's mischievous Evatt, now assembly president, called on Secretary of State Marshall. Evatt's orientation and personality, and the belief that his country could act as a bridge between East and West, have already been described.[90] Evatt who already had a high opinion of his status as assembly president[91] and a propensity to interject himself into sensitive matters, proposed to Marshall that he and Lie were ready to be of service behind the scenes.[92] Lie now had a cohort that one suspects was uninvited.

For the moment, Lie stayed his hand as he awaited the outcome of efforts by the council president, Argentina's Foreign Minister Juan Bramuglia, to devise a resolution of the question. Sobolev then presented a memorandum dealing with a possible basis for settlement that Lie and Feller discussed with the American mission's Benjamin Cohen. Like Jessup, Lie held Cohen in high regard, no doubt traceable to Cohen's and Lie's shared pro-Zionist orientation. If Bramuglia failed, Lie felt that he "might come forth uncompromised" with his own formula for settlement.[93] Accordingly, Lie cautiously and wisely waited in the wings and conveyed the impression that he was anti-British and anti-Russian.[94] The former could probably be traced to the events in the Middle East following the partition of the Palestine Mandate and the establishment of Israel; while the latter was doubtlessly stoked by the Berlin question. When invited by Dulles to give the concluding lecture in a series sponsored by the Carnegie Endowment for International Peace, Lie declined, very much convinced that no useful purpose would be rendered by public comments on his part at so difficult a juncture. Dulles saw the point.[95]

His guardedness was well taken, for Bramuglia's initiative was vetoed by the Russians, though it had attempted to strike a balance by calling on both sides to remove their respective blockades immediately and simultaneously; to hold an immediate meeting of the military governors in order to bring about the unification of Berlin's currency by November 30, on the basis of the Russian mark as stipulated in the agreement of late August; and lastly, to commence negotiations in the Council of Foreign Ministers on the outstanding aspects of the German problem.[96]

The day following the Russian veto, October 26, Lie raised with Jessup the possibility of formulating a proposal concerning the circulation of the German mark in Berlin, which was proving to be the main stumbling block in the negotiations. To secure the necessary information and documentation Sobolev could contact the Russians and Feller the Americans; they could then devise a statement or, if desired, a more detailed technical proposal dealing with the currency question. If Lie could submit to both sides this statement or proposal, then perhaps the blockade could be lifted and the issuance of the Russian mark in Berlin could occur simultaneously. Through this process the prestige of both sides would be protected. Lie observed that he planned to talk with Deputy Foreign Minister Vyshinsky. Lie had to decide for himself, the skeptical Jessup responded, on how much the Russians really wanted a settlement.

The problem that Lie skirted was that with the onset of winter the Russians thought that the airlift might prove inadequate in supplying Berlin and accordingly extended negotiations and procrastination would vastly improve their bargaining position. He also appeared somewhat oblivious to the fact that the Berlin currency question was not only a technical matter but fundamentally a political question as well; and the details of settlement would have far-reaching political effects in Berlin, in all of Germany, as well as between the Western powers and Soviet Russia.

Lie discussed his proposal with Feller and Sobolev. Feller opined that never before had he seen so small a difference as now existed in the currency question. The thought that so small a difference of opinion over technical questions could be the cause of another world war shocked him—like Lie he was on the wrong path. Not so Sobolev. He was most reserved, but he was on terra firma when he expressed great doubt that anything would emerge from their work.[97]

Feller subsequently suggested that the Four Powers be approached by an intermediary and queried whether they would accept a proposal that would require the simultaneous lifting of the blockades and the introduction of the Russian mark into Berlin. The latter move would be based on the Moscow agreement of late August, as well as a statement spelling out the conditions of its introduction. If the powers accepted, a revision of Bramuglia's rejected resolution would be tabled in the council. The entire endeavor depended on Lie's ability to draft a statement on the currency question agreeable to both sides. Feller thought it would prove difficult, but he also thought it should be attempted, if all parties gave Lie the green light, and might just succeed.[98]

The immediate reference of the question to the assembly, Jessup warned Lovett, would make settlement of the question more difficult. Lie's "present flexibility and potential" as well as that of "other influential delegates would be lost." Jessup envisaged a number of scenarios in which the council used Lie or experts to help implement a solution of the currency question. Because of the variations and possibilities that existed within the framework that Jessup suggested, he thought it desirable to discuss the procedure immediately with the British and French so that their general reaction might be ascertained and work commence on the elaboration of the plan's details.[99]

Lovett, however, was uneasy. Although he expressed great interest in what Jessup proposed, the timing and progress of the discussions by Lie or the experts on lifting the Berlin blockade had to be very carefully considered, to avoid placing Washington in a "position of risking a questionable currency recommendation without obtaining corresponding advantages in [the] relaxation of [the Russian] blockade measures." In particular, Lovett questioned the "political desirability [of the] prominent role suggested" for Lie.[100] The State Department, like the Foreign Office, cast a wary eye wherever Lie was concerned.

With Sobolev's assistance, Lie approached Vyshinsky on the evening of October 28. He outlined his proposal, which presupposed the use of mutual experts. If Feller and Sobolev succeeded, a statement or a closely drawn technical plan could be presented to both sides. Lie was reasonably sure that both sides would accept such a plan, which could be presented without revealing that Lie and his associates had devised it. Vyshinsky, whose behavior during this discussion can be described as correct but not warm, repeatedly declared he did not believe that the Americans and British wanted a settlement of the question. He admitted lacking instructions on Lie's proposal and accordingly thought Sobolev's and Feller's endeavors were unnecessary. Indeed, in Sobolev's case, Vyshinsky looked askance at the idea that a Russian national should negotiate with Russian experts. Sobolev, he held, would be placed in an awkward position and some might hold it was incorrect to use a Russian secretariat official for this task. Vyshinsky's comment was indicative of Russian notions pertaining to the international character of secretariat officials. Lie responded that Sobolev's functional position in the secretariat made him responsible for the Berlin question; his Russian nationality was an added advantage. Feller was chosen because he was a close political consultant, had a legal background, and was skilled in drafting. Likewise, he had good contacts with the Americans. Moreover, both men were among the secretariat's most talented members. It was obvious that Vyshinsky did not welcome Lie's initiatives. Lie calmly accepted the rebuff. His impression was that Vyshinsky did not wish for the present any solution of the question.

Despite Vyshinsky's cool reception Lie asked Feller and Sobolev to continue their work on the currency question. Then on October 30, Vyshinsky requested to see Lie. From Vyshinsky's demeanor it was obvious that he had received instructions. He was now interested in Lie's proposal, asked if he was thinking of a special solution, and queried on what basis Lie assumed that the Americans likewise desired a settlement. Lie described his talks with Jessup and Rusk and offered two options that could lead to lifting the blockade and simultaneously introducing the Russian mark into Berlin. The first one involved isolating the "essence" of the Moscow agreement of late August, lifting the blockades and introducing the Russian mark, leaving to later discussions the details of Four Power control of the mark in the city.

Vyshinsky thought this would be easier to accomplish than the second option Lie proffered, which involved lifting the blockades and simultaneously introducing the Russian mark preceded by a detailed plan in which, with Lie's good offices, all the technical questions would be tackled. What Lie had proposed to Vyshinsky was not exactly what Feller had envisaged initially. Lie's first option did not commit the Russians to the details of currency control, which explains why Vyshinsky was partial to it. Indeed, Vyshinsky doubted that an agreement on Lie's second option could be worked out without extended discussions. Lie observed, and Vyshinsky agreed, that he now had a Russian go-ahead signal. Naturally, following in Vyshinsky's wake, Sobolev's demeanor likewise changed. Feller was ecstatic; but for all his vaunted drafting talents, he initially failed to see the important difference. Lovett's unease about dealing with Lie was not imaginary.[101]

Could Lie's proposed statement on the conditions governing the introduction of the Russian mark "be confined to fairly general principles," Feller asked Ernest Gross of the American mission, "or would it have to be fairly detailed and elaborate?" He realized that "unless the conditions were spelled out with reasonable adequacy, the western powers would not wish to agree to introduction of Soviet zone currency simultaneously with the removal of traffic restrictions." Precisely the point.

Lie and Feller were aware, Gross observed to Jessup, that "if Lie goes too far or too fast he might be mouse-trapped" by Moscow, as had occurred to Bramuglia and the neutral members of the council. In addition, Feller realized that there was danger to the United States if it leaked out that Lie's "official efforts to 'mediate' were being rebuffed."[102]

On November 2, Lie recounted to Jessup his talks with Vyshinsky. Jessup doubted that Lie could execute his plan without publicity and thought that French and British financial experts would have to be consulted. Lie pleaded for secrecy until he could decide whether a solution was possible. If he saw that a solution was possible, Lie had no objection to having it voiced publicly. He underlined that he had directed some of the secretariat's foremost people to study the question and bring their conclusions to him. Lie held that they were involved in ascertaining facts, and Jessup concurred.

Later that evening the Lie-Jessup conversation continued. In the interim Jessup had spoken to Marshall and, according to Lie, was more reserved. He believed that Jessup's recent trip to Berlin and his conversations with the Americans on the spot had reoriented him, so that he was no longer interested in a solution as he had been before. Lie agreed that he would inform the French and English of what was developing, but it would diminish the chances of keeping the plan a secret.[103] Lovett's unease about any intended role for Lie in the Berlin question was having its impact.

The next day, November 3, Jessup likewise informed Lovett of Lie's conversations with Vyshinsky. Although the odds that the Russians desired a Berlin settlement were miniscule, the mission felt that the situation required "further acquiescence in any neutral effort productive of some result" that Washington could accept without prejudicing its fundamental stance and as a final test of Moscow's willingness to come to an agreement. Cadogan had raised no objection with Jessup to the "general approach" that Lie had in mind.[104]

When approached by Lie, the French representative, Alexander Parodi, agreed to his plan, promised to inform Foreign Minister Robert Schuman, and assured him that Paris would support all his efforts to resolve the question. However, Cadogan's reaction, once he got the details from Lie, was very reserved. As Lie subsequently wrote, he "reflected the Foreign Office's traditional coolness toward any independent United Nations initiative." Cadogan raised the matter of technical problems and noted that what Lie proposed could be viewed as negotiations with the Russians contrary to the Western position against such negotiations as long as the Berlin blockade continued. Lie responded that it was precisely these negotiations that he wished to avoid. He found it difficult to fathom why the British government would refuse to make available experts and information to the world organization if this was needed to place him in a position to form a view respecting the disagreement over the Berlin currency question.[105]

"Poured a little cold water" on Lie's proposal, Cadogan noted in his diary.[106] He poured additional cold water in his message to the Foreign Office. It would also appear that Lie was less than candid in telling Cadogan the substance of his second conversation with Vyshinsky, especially his partiality to Lie's first option, which entailed discovering the "essence" of the Moscow agreement of late August. As Lie explained to Cadogan, what was needed was a document clarifying the agreement's scope and intentions and explaining why it had led nowhere. This proposal, Cadogan thought, might prove dangerous. He did not discuss it fully with Lie, although he reminded him of what had occurred in Berlin immediately following the August agreement, something that Stalin and Vyshinsky conveniently ignored.

Regarding Lie's second option of a detailed four-power plan tackling all the currency control questions, Cadogan pointed out that he personally lacked expert knowledge. British experts, however, had assured him that the Berlin situation complicated the issue so much, that no plan could be drafted without experts knowledgeable about those peculiar conditions. If a workable plan could be drafted in the secretariat by neutral experts, that was different; but Cadogan did not believe that in reality this could be achieved.

Lie had warned Cadogan that Evatt "was becoming active in the matter." He had raised with certain assembly members the desirability of invoking the Berlin question before that body, but Lie had attempted to persuade him to wait. In view of Evatt's track record, Cadogan naturally urged Lie to redouble his efforts. Cadogan inquired whether he should discourage Lie's initiative or whether London thought there was some harmless channel into which he could attempt to guide his endeavors. Cadogan thought the Berlin question had been referred to the council and should remain with that body. He observed, however, that the State Department had toyed with the idea of asking a body of independent banking experts to work out a Berlin currency plan and consequently that it might not want to reject Lie's proposal out of hand. As to Lie's plea for secrecy Cadogan was unsympathetic, since he felt a leak would inevitably develop.[107]

Bevin's reply was based largely on the advice of Patrick Dean, the Foreign Office helmsman on the Berlin question, who viewed Lie's proffered initiative as "undesirable and somewhat dangerous." Bevin accordingly noted to Cadogan that he did not like either of Lie's proffered options: in view of Russian attitudes, the first would lead nowhere and the second would be impossible. It was not, Bevin correctly observed, a question of devising a formula acceptable on the surface, but of devising a detailed arrangement satisfying the powers involved that their basic conditions would be met.

The present issue was not concocting an acceptable currency plan but lifting the Berlin blockade so that direct negotiations could commence. The West had made it clear that none could commence under duress. The development of a currency plan, whether undertaken directly or by the secretariat, went contrary to this "vital principle." Bevin agreed that, once the secretariat became involved, secrecy could not be preserved; and the lack of secrecy would destroy any chances of success.

While he would welcome any "reasonable settlement" that tackled the immediate lifting of the blockade, Bevin did not wish to seek an immediate settlement. If Moscow thought that the West was anxious for a solution, the Russians would retain their present stance and all chances of lifting the blockade in the immediate future would disappear. Because of all this, he was strongly opposed to bringing the Berlin question to the assembly. Nor did he favor Jessup's suggestion that the council president might ask Lie to study the question; fresh moves should emanate from the council itself. The proper move would be for its president, if he thought it desirable, to discuss with the council's members whether any useful purpose would be served by reopening the Berlin question at the present moment. The advantage of keeping the question solely within the council was that London could exercise some control over what happened, with the assistance of others. Bevin would see Bramuglia and warn him against being overoptimistic, believing that a solution was possible merely by discovering some simple formula. He would stress the principle against negotiating under duress and point out that his recent resolution, vetoed by Vyshinsky, represented the "absolute limit" to which the West was prepared to go to meet Moscow's point of view. He also would speak to him about Lie's suggested initiatives. If Lie's proffered initiative was to be taken seriously by either Jessup or Parodi, or by any of the council's six neutral members, an "informal and unobtrusive consultation" with Marshall and Schuman might be called for to reach agreement upon the line to be assumed.[108]

When given Bevin's negative response, Lie agreed that he would say nothing until Cadogan returned from London, where he would attempt to ascertain what had occurred between Bevin and Bramuglia.[109] Jessup, however, still appeared to favor the idea of the council president inviting Lie to study the question.[110] His stance reflected the position of State Department Counselor Bohlen who felt that, although there was much danger in Lie or the council's neutral members working on the currency question, it "would be difficult and probably unwise" to attempt to discourage their efforts.[111] Bevin was certainly willing, Marshall was informed, to consider initiatives emanating from within the council, but Patrick Dean pointed out that this did not apply to Lie "who is not 'reliable.'"[112] The State Department likewise shared the Foreign Office's "apprehensions" regarding the "risks involved" in Lie's "formulation . . . of proposals concerning the Berlin question."[113] Lie had been labeled.

On November 6, Cadogan called on Parodi and conveyed Bevin's negative response to Lie's suggested initiative. Parodi claimed, as had Jessup, that Lie had not mentioned the first option, clarification of the scope and intention of the late August agreement, which the Frenchman thought potentially dangerous. As Cadogan expected, Parodi and Schuman were predisposed to accept "in principle" the second option, a detailed Four Power control of Berlin's currency.[114]

The same day an agitated Evatt called on Lie. He had learned about Lie's suggested initiative. Evatt reproached Lie for keeping him in the dark about his conversations with the Four Powers. Lie retorted that as secretary-general and the chief administrative officer he possessed the right to engage in this activity and without informing anyone. The Berlin question was before the council not the assembly. Moreover, Lie pointed out, Evatt had himself assigned personnel to study the currency problem.[115]

Hopeful that a currency plan could be devised, Cadogan was instructed to stave off Lie's suggested initiative, which he thought would be far from easy.[116] Foreign Office activities, however, would make this unnecessary. On November 8, Evatt was again in top form, and Lie reviewed for him his talks with the Four Powers. Evatt's interest heightened, and he conjured up the possibility of using Lie's proffered initiative as a link in a larger scheme. He suggested that Lie, he himself, or both of them might bring the recent resolution unanimously adopted by the assembly, entitled "Appeals to the Great Powers to Renew Efforts to Compose Differences and Establish Lasting Peace," to the attention of the Four Powers, requesting that they quickly take steps to resolve the peace settlements and all questions flowing from them. This obviously also included the Berlin question. Evatt found it difficult to see how Bevin could reject the idea.[117]

That same day Lie spoke with Jessup, who asked how the council's six neutral members, and Bramuglia in particular, would be handled. Lie had no answer but assured Jessup that he intended to include them in his initiative. Neither could he answer Jessup's query as to how an eventual proposal could be worked out without bestowing on it a negotiated character. Lie attributed Jessup's increasing reserve to the American need to avoid conflict with the British.[118] That American doubts might have existed from the very beginning does not appear to have crossed Lie's mind. He certainly was less than candid about Evatt's proposal and his reaction to it.

However, by the following day, November 9, the fat was in the fire. It appears the Foreign Office had divulged Lie's suggested initiative to the Dominion governments, which, of course, included Australia. This explains how Evatt had discovered Lie's negotiations with the Four Powers and his annoyance at having been kept in the dark. By this point the story had also leaked into the press, and the indispensable secrecy had evaporated. As the leak presumably followed from informing the Dominions, Cadogan was naturally placed in an awkward situation, compounded by his need to inform Lie that Bevin's attitude had not changed and any settlement of the question required action through the council. Jessup and Parodi were present during this exchange, and although Lie remarked that Evatt was preoccupied with bringing the question to the assembly or making a direct appeal to the Four Powers, he made no comment about his own budding cooperation with Evatt.

Jessup feared that in unfriendly quarters the whole episode would be presented as showing that Moscow was ready to resolve the question while the West was being "intransigent." Jessup's fears were echoed by the Foreign Office's German Department.[119] In view of Cadogan's specific request that the entire matter be treated as very confidential, one can muse whether the Foreign Office's transmission to the Dominion governments was an inadvertent mistake or an attempt by elements antagonistic to Lie's whole approach to undercut him, knowing that the inevitable leak would follow. Whichever, it fused Lie with Evatt and led to even greater difficulties.

Lie explained his suggested initiative to Bramuglia, who appeared very pleased. Because Bevin desired that the neutrals continue their attempt to secure a resolution of the question, Bramuglia intended to convene them that day, November 10, to work out a proposal, requesting information on the various questions that divided both sides. He promised to keep Lie informed.[120]

By this point, of course, Lie was welded to Evatt's plan.[121] Consequently, one must greet as so much sop to the Americans Cordier's subsequent observation that Lie and Evatt had been encouraged in their scheme by a visit from Vyshinsky, who called to "express his appreciation of Lie's efforts" in the Berlin question. This undocumented and unreported visit apparently contrasted sharply with Vyshinsky's earlier attitude, when he had held that he could do nothing.[122]

Despite Bramuglia's comments to Lie, in discussions with the other council neutrals, he "indicated . . . some resentment" at Lie's intervention. He had made it clear to Lie that while technical studies by the secretariat would be useful to him "it would be inappropriate for Lie himself to play a part in diplomatic negotiations." Lie seemingly agreed with him. In fact, on November 12, Bramuglia informed Lie that the neutrals had agreed that as council president he should undertake on their behalf the diplomatic steps needed to help resolve the Berlin question. Although Bramuglia asked Lie to have the Feller-Sobolev studies continue, Lie had now been effectively displaced from any operational role, except the tangential one of expediting the Feller-Sobolev study and communicating it to Bramuglia.

Evatt's scheme now must have loomed larger than ever. At this point, Lie showed Bramuglia a copy of the draft letter he and Evatt had composed to the four government heads. Bramuglia observed that, in view of the task delegated to him by the six neutrals, he was in no position to sign the letter—although Bramuglia held, according to Lie, that it was a good move and should be sent. When Lie expressed doubt whether as secretary-general he should sign the letter along with Evatt, Bramuglia repeatedly opined that he should, since Lie, because of his functional position, stood equal to Evatt who was the assembly president.[123] Feller, Gjesdal, and Wilder Foote, the American director of the secretariat's Press and Publication Bureau, likewise urged Lie to share in the appeal. Stoneman, who had not been consulted and did not agree with the letter, resigned. The Evatt-Lie letter was the proverbial straw that broke the camel's back, but Stoneman's disillusionment with Lie had been building up since the Prague coup.[124] Perhaps Lie's momentary hesitation in signing the letter, and his discussion with Bramuglia about it, occurred because he felt that Evatt was "trying to usurp some of his own functions" and suspected him of wanting to be the next secretary-general.[125]

The joint Evatt-Lie appeal to the Four Powers pressed for "immediate conversations," with the necessary steps to solve the Berlin question, thus preparing the way for a quick renewal of negotiations to conclude the remaining peace treaties. Evatt and Lie held that the Four Powers should fully support Bramuglia's mediation efforts. Simultaneously, they stood ready to lend additional assistance, as in the currency studies being made by Lie.[126]

Evatt dispatched this missive in his capacity as assembly president without consulting his experienced diplomatic adviser, Australia's ambassador to Moscow, who was "dismayed" at Evatt's action.[127] Although his biographer claims that Evatt thus cut through the Gordian knot of the Berlin question,[128] this is misleading in the extreme. The Americans were furious, and apprehensive over the possible impact of the Evatt-Lie appeal.[129] Secretary of Defense James Forrestal, in particular, observed that the letter had "succeeded in giving the impression that, after all, the Russian demands [were] not so extreme and unmeetable."[130] The Americans correctly believed that the letter could be traced to Evatt's "personal desire" to assume a leading role in all United Nations matters, while Lie's desire was to "inject" the secretary-general's office into the Berlin question.[131] Evatt, Marshall noted to Lovett, was "wholly unpredictable, publicity seeking, and undependable." Indeed, Marshall feared that Evatt might cause immense difficulties in the Berlin question by his "quite evident effort for kudos" and feared that Washington's relations with the council might "be wrecked through Evatt's ill advised and in effect unauthorized actions."[132]

Equally strong were the observations of the experienced secretary-general of the Norwegian Foreign Ministry, Rasmus Skylstad, who had also served for many years in the League of Nations secretariat. Skylstad "strongly deprecated" the Evatt-Lie appeal since the council was seized with the Berlin question. Based on his league experience, Skylstad observed that the "desire to please all and offend none" had been the league's undoing. If the new world organization was to avoid the pitfalls of the old, leaders had to adopt a "realistic attitude toward world problems."[133]

Evatt's ploy, moreover, of sending the letter directly to the government heads rather than through their foreign ministries was resented. With undisguised annoyance, Marshall noted that Evatt admitted he "had bypassed [him] and gone direct to the President and was confident of success."[134] Bevin was likewise annoyed and found the whole procedure in "principle undesirable." He thought it had possibly been done at Sobolev's suggestion. "The Russians are fond of playing the Stalin/Molotov combination to our disadvantage," noted William Strang, the head of the German Department.[135]

Lie's complaints during this period centered on the British. He erroneously claimed that they perceived his and Evatt's appeal as primarily underpinning Russia's peace initiative, which he rightly denied. Lie believed that there were vested interests that stood to gain by a continuation of the East-West struggle. Ever the King Solomon, he admitted Moscow's unpardonable political miscalculations but also felt the Western powers had committed equally serious miscalculations. The greater the exposure to these antics backstage, he observed, the greater was one's contempt for methods of power politics. He found it terribly difficult to spotlight the guilty parties to the world at large.[136]

Within the British Cabinet, the objection raised to the Evatt-Lie letter was that it treated the "Berlin question as the only major outstanding issue between the Great Powers," and "obscured the point that this dispute was only one symptom of the world-wide tension between the Soviet Union and the Western Powers."[137] Moscow, of course, accepted the call for immediate conversations, but said nothing on lifting the blockade. The Western powers reiterated that conversations could only commence once the blockade was lifted. On the other hand, they supported Bramuglia's efforts to seek a solution. There was no agreement, however, between the parties to a meeting of the heads of government.[138]

Lie conceded that on the surface the rejection of his and Evatt's appeal appeared like a defeat, but he maintained that in reality their initiative was a move forward as all the parties had declared willingness to seek a solution within the council.[139] That was certainly true; but it had also been their stance when the question was initially appealed to the world organization.

As the smoke cleared, Bramuglia's proposal was to establish a committee of experts to study the currency question including the neutral council members and a representative of the secretary-general. The Four Powers accepted.[140] Bramuglia accordingly, on November 30, constituted the Technical Committee on Berlin Currency and Trade, with instructions to complete its study in thirty days, subsequently extended another thirty days.[141] Lie in turn informed Jessup that for the present he had terminated all secretariat studies dealing with the currency question.[142] He then appointed Myrdal as his representative on the committee, a choice that probably scored no points in the three Western capitols.[143] The committee labored through December 1948 and January 1949.

On February 11 the committee submitted a report to the council president, by then China's Tingfu Tsiang, stating that it had been unable to come to any solution acceptable to both sides.[144] No sooner was the committee report in Tsiang's hands than the Foreign Office was informed that Myrdal had recommended to Lie early publication of the report on the grounds that incorrect accounts had appeared in the press.[145] "We see no advantage whatever in publication of the report at the present time," Sir Ivone Kirkpatrick, the deputy under-secretary, wrote to Bevin. The committee's work had been technical and structured to discover whether a resolution of the currency question was technically feasible along lines initially suggested in view of Berlin's current conditions. Since the American and Russian experts held opposing views on this matter, it was clear that agreement was impossible. He saw no advantage therefore in publishing the experts' comprehensive investigations and discussions. Indeed, he thought, to publish the report would only heighten "undesirable public interest and controversy" in the question, which would not serve the interests of the Four Powers and would further strain East-West relations. The Canadians, Kirpatrick believed, shared this view. He proposed to instruct Cadogan to place these considerations immediately before Lie and to urge him, for the present, not to publish the report. Kirkpatrick feared that, unless the Foreign Office acted quickly, the Evatt-Lie combination might "raise the whole matter again with the maximum publicity and cause us difficulty and embarrassment." He asked for Bevin's approval of his draft instructions, in which case he would ask the American and French embassies to send identical instructions to their council representatives. The instructions were duly sent, with a concluding observation from Bevin for Cadogan's own information, that the report's publication would make it very clear that the committee's failure was mainly caused by the stance of the American expert.[146] The Americans were duly informed,[147] and Cadogan conveyed the Foreign Office misgivings. Lie observed he had discussed the problem with Tsiang, who intended merely to communicate the report to the Four Powers and to the council representatives of the states represented on the committee. Publication at the time was not contemplated. Tsiang's decision, Lie divulged, had resulted from advice tendered to him by the Americans.[148] The report was finally made public by Tsiang on March 15 in the form of a press release;[149] but by this point, as we shall see, steps had commenced to resolve the Berlin deadlock and confidentiality no longer served any useful purpose.

Sobolev's absence in Moscow during this period moved Lie to wire his assistant secretary-general to return immediately because he wanted his advice on the Berlin question when it came before the council. Through Sobolev, Lie felt, he could get some indication of Moscow's reaction to the unfolding events, the lack of which he had lamented during Sobolev's absence for part of the crisis the previous autumn.[150] It appears that during this period Lie also approached Russia's Deputy Foreign Minister Yakov Malik and suggested that if Moscow desired a settlement of the question Malik might approach Jessup.[151] The reverse actually occurred, when Stalin on January 31, 1949, declared that the Berlin problem could be resolved; his statement omitted any mention of the currency question that ostensibly had triggered the blockade. When queried by Jessup in mid-February, whether the omission was premeditated and significant, Malik responded that he would check with Moscow. His reply on March 15, that omission of the currency issue was no mistake, commenced a series of secret negotiations between the two, at least one informal session apparently taking place in Lie's home in Forest Hills, New York.[152]

As the secret Jessup-Malik negotiations commenced, press stories about the United Nations' failure to resolve the Berlin currency issue irritated Lie no end. With some justification he pointed out the importance for people to understand where the responsibility lay in such a question, which was certainly not with the United Nations. He praised the work of the organization's experts and others who had attempted to resolve the currency question. Then Lie slipped into his role of King Solomon, observing that it was not the fault of the experts that the great powers were, for various reasons, not then prepared to resolve the question by the means offered.[153] The British held strongly that Lie's comment was "wholly uncalled for," since it appeared to link the Western powers with Soviet Russia. Lie knew very well that Moscow was responsible for the Berlin situation. He thus gave the world the impression that the Western powers were in the same boat with Soviet Russia. When queried whether Washington intended to comment or make any representations on the statement, the Americans replied, perhaps with a touch of resignation, that it did not seem "desirable to inflate Lie's statement by taking any public notice" of it. At most, it might be remarked to one of Lie's assistants that the statement "attributed to him seemed somewhat gratuitous."[154]

By April, as the Jessup-Malik conversations were grinding away, the everrestless Evatt began to fidget, exactly as Kirkpatrick had feared. Evatt, Cordier informed the Americans, "was suffering an unusually aggravated attack of ambition" and intended to contact the American mission. The Berlin question loomed large among the questions he wanted to discuss, and in particular he wanted to partake in the Jessup-Malik conversations, which he thought might be held at the United Nations in order to associate it with their success. He hoped to contact both Rusk and Dulles. Cordier considered Evatt's "activities to be in the realm of the fantastic." He and Lie surmised that Evatt had failed to make a headline for some days and feared that these world problems would be solved without his contribution. Cordier had "never seen Evatt with such a melange of vaulting ambitions and desires to cure the troubles of the world within a few hours." Although he and Lie appreciated the "somewhat farcical nature" of Evatt's activities, they were also very much "concerned at the damage he might do."[155] Whether it was an attempt to acquire information and assuage Evatt or a question of Lie's curiosity getting the better of him, Lie some days later alluded to the Jessup-Malik conversations at the end of a dinner at his home with Rusk, Gromyko, and McNeil. Rusk sharply suggested, and Gromyko and McNeil agreed, that the Berlin question be left to Jessup and Malik and "expressed the hope that the rumors, leaks and public statements which had thus far been made would not complicate their talks on the following day."[156] Lie's reaction is unrecorded, but he must have gotten the message.

In early May an agreement was concluded on all the main questions of principle emanating from the Berlin problem. This included a mutual lifting of the blockades and a meeting of the Council of Foreign Ministers to consider questions relating to Germany and the currency situation in Berlin.[157] The Berlin crisis was ended, but the German problem persisted.

In August, Lie assured the American ambassador in Oslo that he "would enthusiastically welcome" West Germany's membership in the United Nations. It was a stance in keeping with his notion of universal membership—though, as we have seen, there were still lepers like Franco's Spain. In addition, Lie opposed the "dismantling" of Germany and thought that "world progress" would be delayed until that country was rebuilt.[158] It was perhaps not the best of all possible worlds, but it certainly was one that Lie must have sensed was, at least for the moment, less tense. This, in part, might explain his sense of euphoria and his belief, expressed in his annual report, that the United Nations was "helping to bring the world toward an era of more stable conditions."[159] The détente over Berlin had certainly contributed to that state of affairs. At the same time, Lie's own activities had in no way contributed to that détente. Lie rightly surmised in his memoirs that Moscow had climbed down from its previous position because of the airlift's success, the effectiveness of the West's counterblockade, and the propaganda and prestige defeats that it was suffering.[160] What he failed to note was that the West had also begun to organize militarily. The possibility of another Prague in Berlin was not as sure a bet in the winter of 1949 as it had been in the spring of 1948. In fact, Lie had opposed this very Western military organization that in part had contributed to a détente in the Berlin question, something he handled very gingerly in his less than candid and sometimes misleading memoirs.

Western Defense

As the military-strategic-political confrontation began to intensify, it was garbed in an ideological cloak and labeled the Cold War. Moves on the Western side toward a western European bloc, especially by Bevin, did not find Lie receptive. Queried in mid-February 1948 whether Bevin's moves were within the charter's spirit, Lie responded in the tradition of a good Talmudic scholar, by in turn asking whether a similar proposal for an eastern European bloc by the Bulgarian Communist Georgi Dimitrov, was likewise within the charter's spirit.[161] Nevertheless Russian "rumblings and threats regarding Norway" left Lie uneasy.[162] Accordingly, he was concerned by Russian misperceptions of the West. As he wrote to Norwegian Prime Minister Einar Gerhardsen in early April 1948, these misperceptions were aggravated by irresponsible talk in the United States about preventive war. Both sides were increasingly moved by national interest and shortsightedness. Though they had much to lose by an armed conflict, they appeared equally terrified and hysterical. He thought some of the American reaction to the Russians was part of a pronounced move to the right in the United States. Washington's seeming superiority through control of the atomic bomb was offset by Moscow's superiority in armed forces, which in any conventional war could soon control the important areas of Europe and Asia. Therefore, Lie regarded general American rearmament essential, for it would lead to a balance in conventional forces, and thus to a broader understanding.[163]

Lie's view that both sides were equally at fault was developed further in a talk on the third anniversary of President Roosevelt's death. He rebuked both states for pursuing nonconciliation policies and blamed them for the world's condition. There was fear in Russia and in small countries like his own, and the governments acted accordingly. Likewise the endless talk of war should cease. Although he praised the Marshall Plan as one way to strive for peace, Lie maintained that another way was for the Big Five to attempt to settle their differences, rather than engage in mutual threats. Even in the United Nations they tended to assume rigid positions rather than seriously explore a settlement of their differences. Contrary to popular conception, he declared, the United Nations was not dying. Indeed, the world organization was doing quite well, except when the great powers failed to employ it properly and to live up to the charter's terms.[164]

The reaction in Washington to Lie's speech was a controlled fury, and its conduit was Arthur Krock, political columnist of the *New York Times*.

Lie's position was "delicate and difficult," he wrote, and the charter described his office in terms that left room for "honest disagreement." He alluded to Lie's prior intervention in the Iranian question, which had led to a polite dissent by some states. However, his Hyde Park utterances had generated in Washington government circles an attitude less than polite. If these objections extended from the Executive branch to Congress, as they probably did, then Lie might have committed a disservice to both his office and to the United Nations by his public comments. There was in Washington "a strong official feeling" that, while Lie had the right to his opinion, he damaged and stretched his office when he left the strong impression that he was a "partisan for one group of nations." If Lie's comments were divorced from the East-West conflict within the United Nations and meant to be a condemnation of both sides, Krock believed they were proper and constructive. However, his comments adjudged the West, and especially the United States, as guilty of the very actions they charged against Soviet Russia and deemed Washington as responsible as Moscow for the war threat hanging over the world. The implication that both sides were equally guilty was neither the judgment of many United Nations members nor, according to the "rising belief" in Washington, a matter for Lie to pronounce judgment on, even if the world environment were less threatening. In his speech Lie had not differentiated, Krock maintained, between states that had labored for the United Nations' ends of human rights, the repudiation of force in interstate relations, and so on, from states that had subverted those ends.[165] It was a tough column.

Some days later the column was discussed by Hayden Raynor of the American mission and the secretariat's Foote, who was disturbed by it and Krock's disingenuous deletion of Lie's favorable comment about the Marshall Plan. Raynor replied that the "speech had been unfortunate." Foote held that Lie had to maintain a "neutral attitude." No one, Raynor retorted, could voice objection to a neutral stance from a person holding Lie's office. On the other hand, it appeared to many American officials that the total effect of Lie's "interventions in political matters, in speeches or in the UN itself, had been unneutral in that they tended to be against our positions." In defense of his chief, Foote, in what Raynor thought was a sincere statement, swore that there was no person more opposed to communism than Lie.[166]

Rusk also "strongly objected" to the speech. While he did not question Lie's right to be heard, he observed to Foote that Lie should evince no surprise if Hyde Park–type speeches drew a strong reaction from the American mission. "If he expected us to leave him alone, he must not attempt to engage in one-sided political debate," Rusk asserted. Foote violently objected, repeated what he had told Raynor, defended his chief's attempt to point to the serious situation dividing the great powers, and held that he possessed the right and duty to do so. Direct objections were raised with Lie by Austin, who indicated that certain portions of the address had been "unfortunate and it would not help his relations" with the American mission.[167] Lie's Philippic address, one can argue, had gained him nothing, except American enmity.

What impact this episode had on Lie is unknown, but for about the next two months he kept his peace. Paradoxically, although he had no objections to American rearmament, which he believed necessary, the coalescing of interests among the Western states led by the Anglo-Americans and the establishment of an alliance, even a defensive one, found him opposed. He probably held that any Western alliance would lead to a deepening of the division between East and West and a hardening of their respective positions—which was to be avoided at all costs. Certainly he viewed any Western alliance including Norwegian membership as one that would only increase his difficulties as secretary-general.[168] His remarks at a press conference in Detroit, on June 9, reflected this position when he emphasized that he would not like any British-American combination, though he did not believe such a bloc now existed.[169] Lie's desires notwithstanding, and thanks largely to the communist coup d'état in Prague and the Russian blockade of Berlin, the very combination that he deplored began to develop rapidly by late 1948 and early 1949. By mid-February 1949 the pregnancy was there for all to see and Lie felt forced publicly to expound on regional arrangements and alliances. They were provided for in the charter, he correctly noted, but subordinate to the United Nations itself. Likewise the charter recognized the inherent right of self-defense if the council failed to act. Regional arrangements could be useful in constructing the United Nations' system of collective security, provided those involved recognized the charter's supremacy. However, and here was Lie's salient point, regional arrangements could never be satisfactory substitutes for the United Nations. If alliances were accepted as a substitute for genuine collective security, then the hope for world peace would be very much endangered. Lie hoped, in an obvious allusion to the yet unborn North Atlantic Pact, that whatever was done on a regional basis, would be done so as to strengthen, not weaken, the world organization.[170] In Paris his statement was warmly supported by the communist and dissident socialist press but received scant notice from the moderate and right-wing press. However, the prestigious Le Monde questioned the soundness of Lie's position. It claimed that regional understandings were completely compatible with the United Nations' principles and, indeed, did not have to be subordinated to the charter since certain of its articles were outdated. Le Monde followed the official French view, which held that it was not a matter of replacing collective security by a regional arrangement but of recourse to regional arrangements because collective security was not yet assured.[171]

On March 17, 1949, Austin delivered to Lie an advance copy of the North Atlantic Pact.[172] At the next day's press conference Lie refused to comment on the treaty except to note that the necessary formalities had been observed.[173] Since release of the treaty's text, Lie explained to the American mission, coincided with his press conference, he had not thought it appropriate to comment on the treaty. He was pleased that it was well within the charter's framework, a point that had concerned him. Shaking his head, however, Lie questioned "the political wisdom of the move" but did not go into details. It would appear that in previous discussions with the American mission Lie had opined that Norway should join the North Atlantic Pact, a disingenuous comment if there ever was one, but criticized the way in which Norway's Foreign Minister Halvard Lange had handled the matter. Lie contended that Lange followed Norwegian public opinion rather than striking out on his own in the formulation of foreign policy.[174] Lie's interlocutor, however, failed to question him about his comment on Lange. This might have exposed the fact that, contrary to what he had previously said, Lie after all was strongly opposed to the treaty.

In a message to Parliamentary Under-Secretary Christopher Mayhew, Lie referred to a previous talk when he had noted his feeling that changes were pending in Moscow's hierarchy, which had now come to fruition—an allusion to Molotov's departure as foreign minister. He feared Moscow's next move would be to depart from the United Nations. Lie's message, however, was misleading. First, Mayhew noted to Bevin his "very low opinion of Lie's judgment." Lie's suggestion that he had foreseen Molotov's exit, Mayhew observed, was devoid of truth. Actually when Mayhew had inquired whether Lie saw any significance in the turnover of "Slav personnel" in the United Nations missions as well as the secretariat, Lie had responded that these changes were only routine. However, Lie then had commented that if the Western powers persisted with the North Atlantic Pact, "he thought that the Soviet Union would leave the United Nations." Mayhew had challenged Lie's view when they spoke earlier and would do so again. In his view, if Moscow did leave the United Nations it would not do so because of the North Atlantic Pact. It regarded the organization as a useful tool of "political warfare and propaganda," which would be increased, not decreased, by the treaty's signature. Moscow, he held, would leave the United Nations only when the world organization ceased to be of value to it in continuing its anti-Western campaign. Bevin scribbled his accord.

Similar conclusions had been reached by Robert Hankey, head of the Foreign Office's Northern Department. He thought it conceivable that if a Russian onslaught in the assembly against the treaty failed, Moscow might consider that exit from the United Nations would be the best blow it could strike. Such a move, however, would appear from Moscow's own interests to be very shortsighted. The treaty's signature, Western union, and so on had shown that Russia's council veto was not absolute in obstructing Western recovery, although it was a tool of considerable value. It was not likely that Moscow would abandon these advantages for the sake of a single display, especially after its persistent claim to be the world organization's main supporter, which would be augmented in face of the West's "imperialist aggressions." Hankey wondered why Lie feared a Russian departure: was it anything beyond Sobolev's continued absence in Moscow? [175]

Lie at this point again raised the specter of his resignation, which he confided to Myrdal, who naturally shared his opposition to the North Atlantic Pact. Myrdal thought the mood was fleeting, but Lie appeared "depressed" by what he viewed as the United Nations' decline and the achievement of the treaty. He bemoaned that he was no longer Norway's foreign minister in order to fight his country's participation in the North Atlantic Pact.[176] By early April Lie's opposition to the treaty was clear and the generally cautious Kerno tried to assure Ross of the American mission that the secretariat did not oppose it. Ross took this with a grain of salt for, as he noted, Kerno never missed "an opportunity to softsoap us." More interesting were the comments of Feller, who admitted to Ross that, although he had "been opposed to our policy towards the Soviet Union," he thought that given Moscow's stance the North Atlantic Pact was a "logical, necessary, inevitable and desirable accomplishment." Ross explained that personally he was greatly disturbed by the "depressing, pessimistic, defeatist attitude" that a large body of correspondents appeared to have absorbed from secretariat channels. He inquired about Lie's attitude toward the treaty, since he was often alleged to be very much opposed to it. Feller pirouetted past that one by noting that Lie shared Dulles's view concerning Norway—Dulles initially had not been inclined to include Norway in the treaty—and Feller implied that his chief resented the pressure put on Norway to join. Ross retorted that Oslo was able to decide this matter on its own, which it had done, and wisely in Ross's opinion. Feller noted that Lie favored a genuine North Atlantic Pact and had likewise been strongly partial to a Scandinavian one. Lie was depressed by the Norwegian-Swedish split over the treaty and the position Sweden was left in as a result. Ross had heard Lie offhandedly support two pacts,[177] but neither Lie nor Feller defined what was meant by a genuine North Atlantic Pact. If it meant Russian inclusion in any such treaty it was a reductio ad absurdum; and if it meant a North Atlantic Pact without Scandinavian participation, which was more likely the case, but a separate Scandinavian Pact tied in to the United Nations system, it was likewise absurd, since such a regional arrangement not tied to a more powerful grouping of states would be militarily worthless, as Scandinavian events had clearly shown during the opening phases of the Second World War.

In an obvious attempt to assuage Lie that the policy Oslo adopted was in the nation's interests, Minister of Justice Oscar Gundersen held several talks with him on the subject. The Norwegian embassy in Washington held that Gundersen had succeeded in "convincing" Lie of the "correctness" of Oslo's position concerning the treaty despite his opposition to it.[178] The embassy's view proved optimistic, although for a while Lie bided his time. Interviewed in Norway during his July holiday, Lie opined that although the United Nations had not yet fulfilled everyone's expectations, no regional arrangements could replace the international organization. As to the North Atlantic Pact, Washington on numerous occasions had emphasized that the world organization was the cornerstone of its foreign policy and that the North Atlantic Pact would commence to function only if the United Nations should fail.[179] Then in August Lie noted in the introduction to his annual report to the assembly, without mentioning the North Atlantic Pact or Russia's security arrangements with the satellite states of eastern Europe, that it was impossible to achieve durable security against war by an arrangement that excluded any of the great powers—a not too subtle allusion to the North Atlantic Pact. While Lie was willing to admit that regional security arrangements might on occasion redress the world's balance of power, collective security could be achieved only by accommodation among the great powers so that they might live together peacefully under the charter, however long this process might take.[180] *The Times* ironically noted that the difficulty was to know what should be done in the interim.[181] Such an attitude, the secretary-general of the Turkish Foreign Ministry suggested, could well assist Moscow to advance its main objective, which was to block cooperation and to divide the West.[182] Lie's report naturally pleased Moscow and Warsaw.[183]

Concurrent with its release Lie gave a speech at Bergen reviewing the United Nations' work during the previous four years—a speech that the British ambassador in Oslo subsequently characterized as "notorious."[184] The notion that regional cooperation was as important, perhaps more important, than work within the world organization, Lie dismissed as short-sighted. Regional or local cooperation was often very helpful, but it could not be a substitute for the United Nations. Although the charter permitted such regional cooperation, he correctly pointed out, it also prescribed limitations. The charter allowed regional arrangements for the peaceful settlement of local disputes. They could employ no force without the council's special authorization. That the United Nations was superior to regional arrangements was clear and any question of comparison was illogical. Regional cooperation, if initiated in conflict with the United Nations, might cause great harm; if conducted in cooperation with the United Nations, it would benefit all humanity. As to charter Article 51, which permitted collective self-defense until the council was able to take the necessary steps should there be an armed aggression against a member state, Lie observed that the provision was clearly of a temporary character. He did not think it ever actually would be invoked, regardless of any special arrangements concluded under this article. Such arrangements could not be called regional arrangements in the United Nations sense.[185] Although Lie did not say it, obviously the North Atlantic Pact was included. Indeed, it would appear that his remarks were directed specifically toward the treaty.[186] To cap his anti-North Atlantic Pact offensive, it appears that Lie then wrote to Prime Minister Gerhardsen suggesting that Foreign Minister Lange be dismissed from office because of his unwise decision to have Norway adhere to the treaty. The reaction was unfriendly.[187] This clash goes far to explain the mutual enmity that characterized the Lange-Lie relationship, which was of sufficient intensity that Lange refused to be considered as assembly president while Lie served as secretary-general.[188] The Swedes and Danes laid down no fast rule, but they likewise were "reluctant" to have one of their nationals assume the post while Lie remained in office.[189]

The response to Lie's Bergen speech soon manifested itself. The communist press, of course, approved asserting, incorrectly, that the speech clearly stated that the North Atlantic Pact was a regional arrangement contrary to the Charter and thanked Lie for having said so.[190] It would appear that Lie became alarmed at the strong international reaction, including Norway's, generated by his comments. After consulting Tor Gjesdal, political adviser and secretariat public relations officer, and Finn Moe, foreign editor of *Arbeiderbladet*, the Norwegian Labor government's mouthpiece, Lie arranged to give a special interview to the paper. In it, he refuted statements that he had criticized the North Atlantic Pact, maintaining that he considered the treaty a proper and legal arrangement under charter Article 51. He added his wish to avoid political comments on the treaty, which he at no time had "advocated or criticized."[191] Lie was correct that he had never advocated the North Atlantic Pact, but the latter comment was barefaced mendacity.

The most generous view of Lie's antics was by the Canadian ambassador in Copenhagen, who noted to Ottawa that Lie's Bergen speech with its careless phrasing played into the hands of the communist propaganda apparatus.[192] The British ambassador in Oslo, Sir Laurence Collier, was less generous. He held that Lie's reputation, which was already declining in Norway, had suffered another blow by his Bergen speech and by the publication in Norway of the adverse comments of *The Times* and other foreign newspapers on the tone of his annual report to the General Assembly. The Labor government, and Foreign Minister Lange in particular, regarded Lie "as an embarrassment." In opposition quarters, Collier observed, it was "freely whispered" that Lie had "allowed himself to fall under Russian influence." Despite this, there was a general reticence to comment openly in the press what was whispered in private. A Norwegian secretary-general was still considered an asset to "national prestige," even though the value of the asset was rapidly depreciating.[193]

Arriving in Stockholm, Lie, still sensitive to the international criticism of his Bergen speech, reiterated that he had been misunderstood, not having had the North Atlantic Pact specifically in mind when he criticized regional security arrangements. He hoped international developments would make such regional arrangements unnecessary. Journalists present at the press conference, however, "got [the] strong impression [that] he was unfriendly to [the North] Atlantic Pact."[194] The liberal *Dagens Nyheter*, however, rejected his explanations and correctly pointed out that his annual report could be interpreted in no way other than as criticism of the North Atlantic Pact. Lie's speech in Stockholm was described as "largely a platitudinous panegyric of the deeds and virtues" of the United Nations and bestowed special praise on Myrdal but avoided any comments about the North Atlantic Pact.[195] It was no Gettysburg address, and the critical reaction of the Swedish press showed it.[196]

Lie's odyssey across the Scandinavian landscape soon brought him to Copenhagen. His comments in Bergen had preceded him and led to a rumpus between the noncommunist press and the Communist party organ, *Land og Folk*. As in Oslo and Stockholm, Lie gave his version of the Bergen speech at a press conference and denied that he had attacked the North Atlantic Pact. This treaty, he now maintained, was not in the strictest sense a regional arrangement, since it was based on charter Article 51 dealing with collective self-defense. He denied saying that the North Atlantic Pact was in conflict with the charter but emphasized that regional arrangements could only bestow benefits if they dovetailed with the wider interests of the United Nations. In his Copenhagen speech, Lie covered more or less the same ground as in Bergen. As the Norwegian chargé d'affaires in Copenhagen informed his American counterpart, although those parts of Lie's speech dealing with regional arrangements and collective self-defense were identical with the Bergen address, several additions had been made to circumvent the difficulties that had arisen from the Bergen speech. The most important alteration was his comment that nothing he had said was directed at the North Atlantic Pact; until it was raised in the United Nations, it was an affair among governments. In addition, whereas Lie had stated earlier that the North Atlantic Pact could not be called a regional arrangement since it was based on Article 51 in Chapter VII of the United Nations Charter, he now declared it could not be a regional arrangement with reference to Chapter VIII, which deals with such matters. As he departed for New York, Lie left in his wake, as he had at Stockholm, a less than approving press.[197]

The whole Scandinavian experience had been a bitter pill for Lie to swallow. Safely ensconced once more at the United Nations, he complained that he had been subjected to "deliberate misinterpretations" of his Scandinavian speeches, as well as to harsh attacks in Sweden and especially in Denmark, where his visit had coincided with an election campaign and become an electoral issue. The Swedish press comments particularly upset him. He recounted to the Americans some of its less than complimentary descriptions, including accusations that he had turned into an American, which disqualified him for the secretary-generalship, and that he was nothing more than a loquacious toastmaster.[198] This was misleading; as the American embassy in Stockholm reported after a careful scrutiny of the Swedish press, it could find no such press statements.[199]

Lie returned to the issue some days latter, again denying opposition to the North Atlantic Pact. He had wanted the Scandinavian states to conclude their own regional arrangement and then join the North Atlantic Pact as a group, he explained. His criticism of the Scandinavians had been only a question of timing. They should have moved together and somewhat behind the other signatories. "We made no comment on this," the American reporting officer dryly noted in his memorandum of the conversation. Lie had introduced the matter himself, he observed, as he had on almost every occasion when he talked with senior officers of the American mission since his return from Scandinavia.[200] The whole business clearly bothered Lie, and, if his comments were attempts to make amends, they were useless. It also bothered Sweden's alternate representative at the United Nations, Sven Grafström, who admitted that Lie had made a deplorable impression during his Scandinavian tour, especially by his Bergen speech.[201] In line with this admission how could Lie's credit rating in the State Department's ledgers have been anything else than nil?

In a belated attempt to redress the balance, when the Ukrainian Manuilsky raised the North Atlantic Pact, Lie supposedly told him and the Russian Semyon Tsarapkin in no uncertain terms that the pact was Russia's own doing. Lie claimed to believe that Stalin wanted peace, but even firmer was his belief that so did Truman, Acheson, and all Americans.[202] Nevertheless, Lie voiced his concern to the Americans, as late as March 1950, lest the North Atlantic Pact be utilized as a political instrument, making it possible to ignore the United Nations. The organs of the world organization should not be inactivated, which would be dangerous for the United Nations' future and would buttress Moscow's arguments against the pact.[203] He feared that the organization spawned by the North Atlantic Pact would compete with the United Nations and lead to overlapping jurisdictions and perhaps to concentrating high-level political discussions in the pact's organization rather than in the world organization.[204] Whether these views were a post-factum rationalization to justify his opposition to the North Atlantic Pact is unclear.

Later events, however, especially the fighting in Korea, would lead Lie to assume a strong pro-North Atlantic Pact posture.[205] The price paid was abandonment of his bridge-building efforts. This about-face was no doubt an attempt to save the United Nations' position in world affairs in what was a blatant act of aggression, although one can claim it was also an attempt to board the bandwagon when there was no choice but to face concrete reality. He had failed to appreciate, especially after the 1948 spring events in Prague and the Russian blockade of Berlin, that military defense and the organization of a countervailing force was the only way to maintain the status quo and the peace that Lie and others so ardently desired. The moves to build a Western defense were not of choice but of necessity. They were meant to prevent a repetition of the events that had led to the shifting balance of power and the outbreak of the European war in the summer of 1939. Lie's mistakes, in the case of the North Atlantic Pact, were chiefly ones of perception, distorted perhaps by ideological ambiguity.

By June 1953 Lie, now retired in Oslo, held that West Germany's admission into the North Atlantic Pact was necessary because of the important military contribution it could make to the defense of Europe, including Scandinavia. The general thrust of Lie's remarks was "markedly" anti-Russian, although the impression of his British host was that Lie "was rather over-playing his hand in attempting to shew that this had always been his attitude."[206] Indeed.

6

PALESTINE
The
Children
of
Abraham

The Setting

It is a paradox that Palestine, the Holy Land that gave rise to three of the world's great monotheistic religions, should also be the land of endless strife. Its acquisition by the British from the Turks after the First World War and London's governance under a mandate from the Council of the League of Nations, saw an increase in the political turmoil that pitted the Arab majority against the Jewish minority.

The Jews had certain rights under the mandate agreement, including the right to immigrate to Palestine, stemming from British promises to Zionist leaders during the First World War. These promises, in the now famous Balfour Declaration of November 1917, committed the British government to "favour the establishment in Palestine of a national home for the Jewish people" and to facilitate its achievement. This was qualified only by the stipulation that nothing would be "done which may prejudice the civil and religious rights of existing non-Jewish communities in Palestine, or the rights and political status enjoyed by Jews in any other country." In order to mend fences with the Arabs who were hostile to this commitment to the Zionists the British had the council's 1922 mandate stipulate a special status for Transjordan. Although part of the mandate it was exempted from the provisions of the Balfour Declaration enshrined in the mandate agreement. Naturally the Zionist leaders opposed this provision; Jewish-British prewar relations hit their nadir with the White Paper of 1939, which placed severe limitations on Jewish immigration just as the war and the Holocaust was to begin.

The interwar struggle in Palestine between Arab and Jew was political, social, economic, and organizational. The Jews, represented by the Jewish Agency, which one can argue was the quasi-government of the Jewish community in the mandate, largely reflected Western values, especially its leadership. Accordingly, the struggle for Palestine during the interwar period can be perceived as one between a Western-oriented minority community and all that goes with it—social cohesion and mobility, economic integration, and interdependence, and especially organization—and a tradition-oriented majority lacking almost all of these qualities but under the impact of British rule and in a reaction to the Jewish presence in Palestine undergoing rapid transformation. The major expression of such socio-economic-political transformation is nationalism. Therefore two competing nationalisms vied for power in Palestine; and the British were saddled with the unattractive task of governing and attempting to maintain law and order, especially against the extremist elements in both camps. Thus, the interwar decades in Palestine were marked by riots, rebellion, and civil unrest. The prewar achievement of statehood by Iraq and its postwar acquisition by Lebanon and Syria, as well as the independence of Arab states like Egypt, Saudi Arabia, and Yemen naturally contributed to the developing nationalism of the Palestine Arabs. This was in turn fanned, especially during the 1930s, by a large-scale influx into Palestine of Jews fleeing the racial anti-Semitism of a Europe succumbing to Nazi Germany and of the postwar survivors of a devastated continent. By early 1947, Palestine was becoming ungovernable, as British attempts to bridge the gap between all parties proved futile. Unilateral British action, however, was also difficult. On the one hand, London had to consider both its short- and long-term relations with the Arab and Islamic worlds, for the Middle East was a pivotal area in British strategic thinking. On the other hand, groups within the Labour government were sympathetic to the Zionist cause, especially because of the unimaginable horrors visited upon the Jews during the Second World War, equal to the Turkish genocide of the Armenians during the first one. There was also world public opinion to consider and Britain's relations with the United States, which had an alert, politically active Jewish community with access to image makers and power holders. Lastly there was British public opinion, a not unimportant element in a parliamentary democracy. In the last analysis the struggle would be decided not by morality or justice but by the talents of a well-organized minority against the confusion of a disorganized majority, if one may paraphrase American Secretary of State Elihu Root.[1]

In this setting Lie's initial moves in the Palestine question were probably meant to increase the powers of his office and to have the United Nations play an expediting role in what was obviously a tangled web of politics and emotion. In time he saw the Palestine question as one that, if handled successfully by the world organization, would bestow needed prestige to the United Nations, which Lie perceived had not cleared many hurdles successfully since its inception. Or, as Abba Eban, the Jewish Agency's representative in New York, put it, "he badly needed an achievement for the United Nations that would give it some resonance in world opinion."[2] Indeed, Lie's pro-Zionist orientation understandably gave rise to the United Nations rumor that he had "become biased in favor of Israel."[3] The Zionists were not unaware of this, and Eban was instructed to "maintain the closest possible relations" with Lie because of his influence as secretary-general; which he did, especially during the crucial period of May through July 1948.

Lie, although he maintained a "strict organizational impartiality," took a propartition stance and disingenuously justified it on the grounds that, once the General Assembly's United Nations Special Committee on Palestine had tendered its report, he was obligated to "support and protect the committee's findings." The United Nations' fragility was an additional consideration, and he thought it would benefit immensely if the world organization "performed some historic act" like bringing the Jews, the Nazi's principal victims, once more into the community of nations. On numerous occasions, as we shall see, the struggle to partition Palestine "might have sunk into a slough of procedural complications" if it were not for Lie. Under these conditions it was only natural that Eban would have "an amiable relationship" with Lie.[4]

Lie's stance thus explains the effusive letter of thanks, prompted by Eban and dispatched by Chaim Weizmann, Israel's first president, for Lie's efforts in behalf of the Zionist cause within the limitations and prerogatives permitted by the secretary-generalship, as reported by Eban.[5] What Eban had first cultivated, others would prune if we can judge by Lie's subsequent warm relations with the Israeli mission to the United Nations.[6] There was also an anti-British element in all of this, which sometimes floated to the surface. The British attitude toward the United Nations had improved, Lie ventured to say in a weak moment, "'since we and the Americans licked them on Palestine.'"[7] Although Lie was not without "some deep-seated religious and racial biases," the sufferings of the Jews, both in history and in the recent past, partially explain his propartition policy,[8] but his lack of knowledge of, and sensitivity to, the Arab cause were appalling.

"About the Arab fellahin, I know only that they were frequently oppressed by the absentee landlords and would no doubt benefit from the great Zionist development projects already launched in the land: an orderly solution would provide for the fullest protection of their rights," he wrote in his memoirs.[9] When the book appeared in 1954 the Arabs, Cordier informed him, were irritated by his treatment of the Palestine problem, as well as by his full support for Israel through many appearances in behalf of the United Jewish Appeal. Others were likewise irritated, although not to the same degree: they thought it bad form for a former secretary-general to take a partition stance, thus raising the question of his objectivity on the problem while in office. The Arabs were so incensed that, during the 1954 assembly session, Secretary-General Hammarskjöld and Cordier had to intervene with their delegations on at least four occasions to persuade them not to raise the question of Lie's pension in the Administrative and Budgetary Committee.[10]

On the Agenda

The Zionists' initial interest in Lie's office was to secure various courtesies and privileges to facilitate Jewish Agency contacts in the United Nations. Thus they found "disquieting" comments of the Bolivian representative, Carlos Salamanca, regretting Lie's choice as secretary-general, whom he described as "pig-headed and stupid" and not a man of stature. When these comments were "unfortunately corroborated" by the secretariat's Raoul Aglion, who was pro-Zionist, they must have led to some unnecessary anxiety in Jewish Agency ranks.[11]

The actual involvement of Lie and the United Nations in the Palestine question commenced in mid-February 1947, when Bevin announced publicly that the question would be referred to the United Nations. He however foresaw difficulties in having it considered before the assembly convened in September. The distinct possibility was therefore raised that the assembly would be confronted with the question without any available study or recommendation from a United Nations organ. Some in the State Department held that the assembly could handle the matter more effectively on the basis of such studies and recommendations. The six months before the assembly convened would give ample time for such studies by other organs of the United Nations. The assembly, not being in session, could not undertake the work itself, as it had no appropriately authorized standing committee to make such studies prior to the September session.

As to Lie, State Department officials argued that he had the right and probably the duty to institute factual investigations of any problems, including the Palestine question, likely to be raised before any United Nations body. Charter Article 98, it was noted, provided that the secretary-general should perform functions entrusted to him by United Nations organs. Accordingly Lie could be required to investigate the Palestine question and report to the assembly if requested by either the Security or Trusteeships Councils. Lie could then presumably bring the question to council attention under Article 99, if any such factual studies should lead to the conclusion that the matter might endanger international peace and security. Whether such a step was feasible politically, in view of the British desire to avoid the council and take the issue to the assembly, was not raised in the State Department. However, the practical consideration was raised of whether Lie should be dragged into reporting or recommending anything about so controversial a question "where regardless of its content, he would be subject to attack." [12] True enough.

When approached by Cadogan about what procedure he should follow, Lie was very much opposed to a special assembly session. He proposed, provided Bevin agreed, that London request that the Palestine question be inscribed on the assembly's September agenda. He pointed out moreover that, during the assembly's six week session, it would also have to deal with other matters and thus probably be unable to decide on the question without considerable preparatory work. Lie thus offered to summon a special committee as quickly as possible to do this work. Lie and his staff were satisfied that these actions would not be ultra vires, although Lie realized that he would require the consent of all the principal states involved. He tendered that the special committee be composed of permanent and several nonpermanent council members, as well as one representative each for the Arabs and the Jews. The choice and status of the Jewish representative would have to be looked into but should not pose an impossible obstacle. The special committee's work would be preparatory and advisory in nature, with any conclusions subject to assembly approval. It would take no substantive decisions.

Cadogan was partial to the proposal, which would provide a body somewhat similar to the council—minus the veto—but would be concerned with only one question. He felt that any assembly session, whether ordinary or special, without such preparatory work "might wallow" for an indefinite period. If Bevin could agree to this proposed procedure, Lie would want to know soon, as he would have to approach and sound out a number of member states. The secretary-general thought that reference of the question to the Trusteeship Council was not appropriate, and Cadogan had not discussed reference to the Security Council, which he assumed was to be ruled out. [13]

To keep Washington at bay, the information fed by the secretariat to the American mission was that Lie had raised objections to the cost of a special assembly session, estimated at $750,000, but failed to mention Lie's proposal for a special committee. [14] Although a special assembly session would obviously cost money, and the estimated sum by standards of the day was not inconsiderable, certainly the issue at stake was of such importance that one can question whether the cost factor alone motivated Lie. There was, of course, a certain cogency to what Lie said. At the same time, his initiative in this matter, especially his appointment of the members of the special committee would have contributed in a not insignificant way to his attempt to expand the powers and the influence of his office. It would also redress some of the damage that the office, and Lie personally, had suffered as a result of his activities in the Iranian-Russian dispute and the issue of Franco's Spain.

London pondered Lie's proposal. Finally on March 3, Bevin signaled his acceptance, since it appeared to be the "most convenient provided it [was] practicable." As to the special committee's composition, Bevin disagreed with Lie's contemplated membership: a Jewish member would establish a "dangerous precedent for the participation of non-governmental organisations" in United Nations committees. The Arabs would likewise have to be excluded. Since the special committee would have a fact-finding mandate, it would be suitable for both Arabs and Jews to be invited to give evidence through representatives with expert knowledge of Palestine. If desired, these representatives could be accessible for consultation by the special committee rather than partake in its work. Beside the council's permanent members, Bevin wanted included in the special committee Brazil, Czechoslovakia, and the Netherlands. He left to Cadogan's discretion whether this should be proposed in a note to Lie or merely discussed with him. Similarly, either in writing or orally, he was to mention that London desired the committee's proceedings as far as possible to be in camera: the "glare of publicity" was to be avoided, especially as the proceedings would probably take place in New York.[15] When informed of Bevin's acceptance, Lie asked Cadogan to stall until he had approached the council's other permanent members.[16]

Lie then explained to Austin the proposed procedure and suggested that he poll the organization's members to see whether they would consent to his appointing a special committee of eight states. If a majority assented, Lie felt he would have the authority to appoint the committee to include the British suggestions, except that Sweden would replace the Netherlands. He had rejected Holland on the basis of the Netherlands' oil interests. Lie had discussed this point with Gromyko, who appeared to favor it personally and had asked Moscow for instructions. In point of fact, as Cadogan observed to the Foreign Office, it was only when Gromyko had expressed doubts about the Dutch that Lie suggested the Swedes as an alternative. Lie suggested to Cadogan that his legal advisers and those of the British mission jointly draw up the projected British note to ensure that the proposal to establish the special committee and Lie's appointment of its members should "not give rise to juridical objections" on the part of other United Nations members. Lie was obviously uneasy over whether his intended actions were based on firm legal, procedural, and constitutional foundations.

This was also of concern to Austin, who raised the question whether Lie was empowered under the charter and the assembly rules of procedure to appoint such a committee. Lie responded that his action the previous autumn in postponing the assembly after a correspondence poll was a precedent. Austin did not commit himself and merely noted that he would contact Lie as soon as possible about Washington's reaction to his proposal.[17]

The substitution of Sweden caused Edward Tomkins of the Foreign Office's United Nations Department to note that, from London's point of view, Holland would be greatly preferred as Sweden's fear of offending Soviet Russia made her a virtual Russian stooge. The Dutch were no worse than the French; in many ways they were better. What was needed was a recommendation on how to settle the differences between Arabs and Jews, to which Dutch oil interests appeared completely irrelevant. The American stooge was Brazil; the Russian, Czechoslovakia. If the special committee was to be established London should certainly push for a state satisfactory to the British government, which Sweden was not. His superior, Paul Mason, agreed but doubted whether the point should be pressed if Moscow was otherwise prepared to accept the special committee.[18]

Then on March 4, Lie was visited by a three-man group from the Jewish Agency led by Moshe Shertok [Sharett]. With the pro-Zionist Feller present, Lie explained the negotiations in progress. On the question of Arab or non-Arab representation on the contemplated special committee, he "emphatically advised" Shertok to issue no public statement. He asked his guests to trust him: he would not press his proposal if the Arabs were to acquire any unfair advantage over the Jews. Lie maintained that "he was acting as an impartial, objective, international civil servant." Naturally, he observed, he had "his own opinion," which it was nervously pointed out to the Jewish Agency he did not volunteer to give to his guests, an understandable apprehension on their part. He was taking them into his confidence, Lie explained to Shertok, which he asked them not to violate. In fact, no one was to be told that he had seen a Jewish Agency spokesman, and only Shertok's closest collaborators could be informed. Shertok, who was no one's fool, must have had the measure of the man but restricted himself to thanking Lie for receiving them and taking them into his confidence.[19] Based on this interview as well as information supplied by Aglion, the officials of the Jewish Agency by this point had a fairly good inkling as to Lie's orientation.[20]

The immediate problem to be faced, however, was the legality of the whole procedure. Since Austin was unable to discover in the charter or in the assembly rules any provision for action by polling member states through correspondence, he feared a legal dispute might develop if a minority opposed Lie's appointment of the special committee. Indeed, if its personnel was unacceptable to any group of member states, they could broach the legal question without revealing their real objection. Moreover, if a majority, excluding the Arab states, approved and Lie appointed the committee, would it be able to ascertain the viewpoint of a minority of interested member states that might yet oppose the special committee's action? In the absence of express authority, would not opponents be justified in holding that it was contrary to custom, general practice, and the laws of various nations on consultative and legislative organs?

If one assumed, Austin observed, that no law applied to the United Nations except international law, were there sufficient precedents to prove and justify a vote and a decision by correspondence? Would the American position be tenable, he queried, if it approved of this proposed procedure based solely on the one precedent cited by Lie: but Austin personally saw no precedent in the example cited by Lie except to expedite procedural matters. The Palestine case involved more than procedure. It involved a written poll of fifty-four states, for the appointment of eight, some of whom might be objected to, which was certainly a substantive matter. It also involved defining the authority of an assembly special committee—a substantive question, Austin posited. Then again, the question was not of a temporary nature. Once action was taken, that stance would have to be defended at the next assembly session. If the stance proved unsound, the United States would be in a difficult position before the world. On the other hand, if Washington rejected Lie's proposed procedure, it had to be in a "position that [was] practically infallible," or it would "suffer the denunciation of the world for having obstructed the proposal."[21] Unbeknownst to Austin he had allies within the Foreign Office.

Tomkins in the United Nations Department also found nothing in the charter, in the assembly rules of procedure, or in the Preparatory Commission report giving Lie the right to establish a special committee without an assembly recommendation. The doubts of Austin and his French counterpart therefore seemed justified, Tomkins observed. Lie, however, was prepared to proceed if London initiated the action. Perhaps Lie might be asked if he could suggest another procedure for establishing the kind of committee London desired. Gore-Booth thought that when the assembly convened it could retroactively legitimize the proposed special committee by a two-thirds vote. Failure to secure this vote would lose nothing but time.

Chief legal adviser William Beckett saw other problems. If Lie's authority to convoke the special committee was not raised in the assembly, the Foreign Office had to ponder the precedent's desirability. It would mean, he thought, that any member state could ask the secretary-general to establish a committee for preliminary consideration of any particular matter. Beckett presumed that the secretary-general would decide who would serve on the committee. He thought the whole procedure was completely outside the secretary-general's prescribed powers, especially the right to decide its composition. It might be a good precedent, although it could turn into a "tiresome one." If Lie's authority to act thus was discussed in the assembly, that body itself might adopt some rule defining the conditions for constituting such committees. Jebb pithily summed up: it was unclear what would happen if Lie polled the member states and a number of them, for example, those belonging to the Arab League, did not agree to the special committee. Jebb supposed that if Lie got thirty-six of the fifty-four member states to agree, "he *could* go ahead; but his action might subsequently be challenged in the General Assembly as *ultra vires*."[22] The whole landscape was pitted with traps and referral of the question to the United Nations had to be, like Caesar's wife, above suspicion.

The news from London that the British were partial to the creation of a special committee to prepare a basis for subsequent assembly action dovetailed with one procedure suggested within the State Department, namely, preparatory work under Lie's auspices. Accordingly, the American mission was informed that a quick and substantive political consideration of the Palestine problem in the world organization was greatly desired.[23] The arrival of Austin's message describing Lie's proposed procedure prompted McClintock to object to the selection of France and Sweden for the special committee, since they would be forced, it was felt, to act as the "uneasy umpires" in a dispute not affecting their national interests. A more logical membership would be the states on the Security, Trusteeship, and Economic and Social Councils, which would make a total membership of twenty-nine, including three Arab states, although McClintock did not mention the unwieldy nature of such a membership and the lack of Jewish representation. He opined that the acid test in the Palestine question was whether Lie's proposed procedure would be a useful instrument at the present time. If the answer was yes, as he believed it was, McClintock was sure that ways could be found within the charter to justify the establishment of the special committee. He felt that those things "not expressly forbidden by the Charter can be done, if they conduce to improve relations among states and to maintain international peace and security."[24] The legal adviser, Charles Fahy, subsequently observed that, although he thought Lie's proposed procedure was "legally permissible," it was perhaps not practicable. In the end, however, Loy Henderson, the director of Near Eastern and African affairs, approved the instructions finally sent Austin to reject Lie's proposed procedure.[25]

The rejection was based on two considerations: that it was "legally of very doubtful validity" and that it "would not accomplish the purposes intended." Washington desired that the British communicate to Lie a formal indication about what they wanted the United Nations to do regarding Palestine. Austin was to ask Cadogan whether London had considered asking Lie to "analyze this whole problem in a completely objective way." Lie could use the secretariat, augmenting it when deemed necessary, especially in connection with the immigration problem and so on. In instituting these studies, which the State Department thought was perfectly proper, Lie would naturally be free to advise and consult with any government he desired. He could, for example, consult with the United States and might even ask Washington to designate someone, an expert on Palestine, with whom he could confer.[26]

McClintock still had his "misgivings" about this procedure. His alternative was to allow Lie to poll the member states on what work could be accomplished, saving both time and money, before the assembly convened in September. Lie could outline the alternatives: his own proposal for a special committee, reference to the Trusteeship Council, and so on. The responses would give the State Department a valuable initial breakdown of opinion among the member states and might conceivably lead to such an impressive majority attitude favoring one particular alternative as to give that alternative real viability.[27] McClintock's sortie led nowhere, and the negative instructions to Austin, as already noted, were dispatched on March 6.[28]

The American mission emphasized that the important point was for the British to commit themselves as to how the United Nations should tackle the Palestine question. Procedures to hear the Jewish side would have to be found. Although Washington might not advocate a special assembly session, it would not oppose one.[29] Lie's proposed procedure for various reasons had been neatly shot down.

The American objections were soon conveyed to Cadogan, who conceded that the legality of Lie's proposed procedure was "debatable." London's formal statement to Lie, he observed, would be the basis for using the secretariat to produce a detailed analysis of the question. The study would offer no recommendations but form the foundation of the assembly discussion and so on. Lie agreed that he would follow in the British wake, if it proceeded along the course suggested by Washington. He wisely maintained that he wanted to take no action that did not have consent of all the council's permanent members. Lie apparently accepted without resentment the State Department's view that his proposed procedure was legally questionable. To Cadogan, however, he explained that the American approach would not contribute a great deal toward resolving the question. Indeed, according to Lie, Austin's deputy, Herschel Johnson, had remarked confidentially that Washington's difficulties "were really political (i.e., Jewish pressure)." The Russians approved of Lie's proposed procedure, provided Sweden was substituted for the Netherlands; and the French representative also approved, subject to Paris's confirmation; while the Chinese representative, although personally in favor, admitted that his government's attitude would depend on that of America. Washington's position was odd, Harold Beeley of the United Nations Department wrote, if as Lie suggested it was "due to Zionist pressure." He thought it might be indirect, for it was difficult to fathom why the Zionists would oppose the special committee, unless the State Department feared that an American representative on such a committee "would be in a too dangerously exposed position."[30]

McClintock remained uneasy. There was no logic to the view, he held, that Lie and the secretariat should be used to analyze the Palestine situation, following Washington's rejection of the special committee. If the British, in turn, objected to using Lie and the secretariat but showed a preference for Lie's procedure, or even for a special Assembly session, the American government had to be ready with a stance thereon. McClintock saw two possibilities. One was his previously proffered suggestion of a Palestine Committee composed of states on the United Nations' three major councils, whose subcommittee of investigation would visit Palestine and take testimony. The subcommittee and full committee would report to the assembly in September. The second possibility could be the convening of a special assembly session to consider appointing a special body to investigate the Palestine question and report back to the assembly. McClintock was partial to the second. If limited to the Palestine question, the assembly could be convened quickly, its membership composed largely of the personnel from diplomatic missions in Washington, who could vote on the issue and then return to Washington. Such a special session could be arranged, he thought, at a fraction of the cost calculated by Lie.[31]

The Foreign Office agreed with Lie that a secretariat report would contribute little toward a solution of the Palestine question. In fact if there was no action until September, it was noted to Bevin, the assembly's appointment of a committee then would postpone a decision until 1948. The Foreign Office was willing to admit that there was no specific authorization for the secretary-general to establish the type of committee proposed. Yet neither was Lie "explicitly precluded from doing so," particularly if he obtained the assent of the majority, or better still a two-thirds majority, of the members. The question appeared to be "whether it would be wise or unwise to allow him to create the precedent."[32]

Jebb conveyed this view to the Americans. He was blunt about using the secretariat: "who cared what the members of Lie's Secretariat might think of Palestine, and besides, nobody wanted some of the members of his Secretariat nosing around Palestine at this time." Jebb likewise dismissed the belief that the constitutional aspects of Lie's proposed procedure would be raised. Provided Lie followed the British request and obtained the prior agreement of a sufficient number of member states "to assure that the constitutionality of his action would not be formally questioned," he foresaw no difficulties. The absence of a preparatory committee between then and the assembly convening in September would defer action until 1948, and in the meantime the British were being shot at in Palestine. "This was my original line," McClintock marginally observed about Jebb's comments on the constitutional aspects.[33] The British had a strong case based on practicality.

Acheson, however, explained to the British that any report emanating from a special committee constituted in the manner suggested by Lie might be criticized in some United Nations and other quarters as lacking any foundation under the charter. Any serious questions anywhere along the way, regarding the legality of the United Nations' handling of the Palestine question would be unfortunate. Washington envisaged, he explained, a brief special assembly session, restricted to the Palestine question. It could establish a special committee on the question, composed of states represented on the United Nations' three councils, to make recommendations to the regular assembly session. A subcommittee could hold hearings, visit Palestine, and so on. The special assembly need not be expensive as Lie feared, since over half of the member states had missions in New York and others could furnish representatives from their diplomatic missions in Washington.[34] McClintock's persistence had paid off. His recommendations were now policy.

The British, however, continued to press the special committee and question the efficacy of any secretariat involvement. They sought a way to reconcile their desire to have the question examined before the assembly convened in September with Washington's objections to the creation of Lie's special committee.[35] In an attempt to reconcile differences, discussions were held on March 21 between the State Department and the British embassy. They informally agreed that the American mission would obtain Lie's opinion of a special assembly session in order to create a special committee.[36]

Lie's initial reaction was that he considered it improper under the rules to suggest to any member state that it limit its representation, or use its diplomatic personnel in the United States, in order to convene a special assembly quickly and economically.[37] If this was an argument to frustrate the convening of a special session, it was soon torpedoed by the Arab states' protests to Lie about the establishment of any special committee without a special assembly session.[38] Acheson's fears had proved wellfounded and would be hammered home in a memorandum to the British embassy a few days later.[39]

Faced by the Arab protests and warned by Feller that his proposal "was illegal,"[40] Lie had no choice but to agree to a special assembly session to consider a single agenda item and appoint a special committee. Once he had London's formal request to convoke the special session, Lie would poll the member states. When twenty-eight replied affirmatively, he would then convene the special session in two weeks time, which would automatically preclude the dispatch of expensive delegations and dovetail with Washington's belief as to how a special session could be quick and cheap. The question that remained, however, was how the Jews could present their side of the problem.[41]

The British request for a special assembly session soon followed.[42] The Zionists, however, were dissatisfied for they feared that the special committee to be appointed would have to include an Arab representative, putting the Arabs in an advantageous position. They felt that if Lie's proposed procedure had been followed this problem would not have surfaced.[43]

The problem that now developed, although seemingly procedural, was politically substantive. It dealt with the mechanics of assembly organization for handling the Palestine question. According to Lie, the procedure could be either regular or special, since the assembly's provisional rules of procedure allowed, for example, the establishment of a special steering committee to consider important questions, like the role the Jewish Agency might play in the assembly's deliberations. Simultaneously, a special plenary committee might be established to actually consider the British request on Palestine. But one could also make a strong case, Lie thought, for the regular procedure, especially in using the General Committee (steering committee). Since Arab and Jewish bodies would undoubtedly request hearings before the assembly, he thought it important that policy on such requests be framed by a committee "whose composition and competence have been well established and are widely understood." The move, moreover, to create a special steering committee to deal with these delicate questions would provoke extended debate on its terms of reference and composition. Lie preferred that the Palestine question be discussed as far as possible in plenary session; while certain aspects might be referred to committees, he definitely preferred to avoid their use.[44]

Cadogan was inclined to agree with Lie's approach. Although Jebb was inclined to disagree, he admitted that it might be advantageous.[45] London desired, it was explained to Cadogan, a short and speedy assembly session, concerned only with establishing and instructing a special committee on Palestine. Provided this was achieved, the Foreign Office would "not quarrel with the means adopted to achieve it." Since Cadogan considered Lie's proposed procedure would do this, the Foreign Office was content to rely upon Cadogan's judgment after he had taken the sense of other delegations. Likewise, it approved of Lie's idea that the British request should, if possible, be examined in plenary session.[46]

The reaction to Lie's proposal by Austin, the American mission, and the State Department was warmer. Lie's plan, although "cumbersome," had the virtue of closely following the assembly rules of procedure. It would minimize procedural wrangles. Indeed, improvisation offered more disadvantages than regular procedure, as it might incite debate and wander into substantive matters. On the other hand, there were "substantial doubts" whether the General Committee should decide on Arab and Jewish bodies being heard by the assembly. In the past, Washington had maintained that the General Committee be confined to rather narrow procedural matters. Austin felt that this would be the case in the present question; as most delegations would agree that both parties should be heard, the only question was in what manner.[47]

Rusk's office, however, thought that only member states could partake in assembly discussions. Accordingly, the General Committee should not be utilized to arrange hearings for Arab and Jewish bodies. A clear distinction, it suggested, should be drawn between whether nongovernment organizations should be heard by the assembly, which was a problem with political implications, and how such organizations might be heard. The assembly itself, not the General Committee, should decide the necessary procedures. The General Committee was limited merely to making suggestions.[48]

On the eve of the General Committee meeting, both Austin and Cadogan received from Lie a draft resolution, which Cadogan thought emanated from the assembly's Brazilian president, Oswaldo Aranha. Under the draft resolution, the General Committee would recommend that the assembly instruct the First Committee (Political and Security), to which the Palestine question had been referred, to admit the Arab Higher Committee of Palestine and the Jewish Agency to its discussions. In view of Lie's attitude it would be safe to say that Lie, not Aranha, was the instigator of the draft resolution. Cadogan signaled the Foreign Office that, if asked, he would sponsor only the Jewish Agency. Lie, Cadogan explained, was inclined to share his doubts about the propriety of nongovernment organizations appearing before the First Committee. He preferred, if they were to be heard, it be by some subcommittee, which Cadogan agreed would be preferable.[49]

When the General Committee convened on May 2, Lie opposed allowing the Jewish Agency to address the assembly's plenary session; such an "unprecedented" step, he pointed out correctly might lead to similar pressure from other private bodies in future. At the same time, despite his doubts expressed to Cadogan, he argued that there "was a clear precedent" for a nongovernment organization addressing an assembly committee, misleadingly citing the World Federation of Trade Unions' approach to the General Committee during the first assembly session in London, requesting representation on various United Nations organs.[50]

The General Committee proceeded to recommend that the assembly refer these Zionist petitions, as well as other similar ones that might be submitted, to the First Committee for decision. This was accepted by the assembly and subsequently by the First Committee, which extended an invitation including the Arab Higher Committee. On May 8, the Jewish Agency representative addressed the First Committee, followed by the Arab Higher Committee representative on May 9. By his public comments and endeavors behind the scenes Lie had given the Zionist cause a needed political boost.[51] The Jewish Agency's access to the forum of the First Committee helped diffuse its message within the organization and worldwide. Although matched by giving the Arab Higher Committee access to the First Committee, too, this was not, it would appear, of Lie's doing. Within the political and practical limitations and prerogatives of his office, Lie would use the United Nations to further Zionist aims.

After extended debates in the First Committee and the plenary assembly, an eleven-member United Nations Special Committee on Palestine was established. Its terms of reference were broad, and it was composed of Australia, Canada, Czechoslovakia, Guatemala, India, Iran, the Netherlands, Peru, Sweden, Uruguay, and Yugoslavia.[52] For obvious reasons the Arab states had been excluded, but Iran represented Islamic interests, as did India with its large Muslim minority. Anglo-American-Russian surrogates were evenly divided; for London: Australia, Canada, and the Netherlands; for Washington: Guatemala, Peru, and Uruguay; for Moscow: Czechoslovakia, Sweden, and Yugoslavia. Lie pressed Stockholm to appoint its deputy representative, Gunnar Hägglöf, to the Palestine Committee and also hoped to arrange his appointment as chairman. Lie's desire was no doubt based on Hägglöf's chairmanship of the First Committee's Sub-Committee 5, which had unanimously advised the full committee not to grant a hearing to organizations other than the Jewish Agency and Arab Higher Committee. This, however, did not exclude any rejected organizations from being heard subsequently by the Palestine Committee. Cadogan noted to the Foreign Office that Hägglöf had been "useful and sensible" as chairman of the subcommittee, but doubted whether the Swede "was sufficiently firm to be [an] ideal chairman" of so important a committee as the Palestine one.[53] Obviously he was not thought to be so; although Sweden was chosen to chair the Palestine Committee, it was represented by Chief Justice Emil Sandström.[54]

No sooner was the Palestine Committee established, than the British pointed out to Lie how undesirable it would be for the committee to commence taking evidence in New York, because of the adverse reaction it would have on the Arabs—an undisguised allusion to the large Jewish community in the area.[55] Lie saw the point and promised to support it; in due course, the Palestine Committee decided against hearing any organizations in New York.[56] Lie tried hard to appear impartial, and he was wherever he could without jeopardizing Zionist interests. He placed some of the secretariat's ablest personnel at the committee's disposal,[57] while excluding Jewish and Muslim members from serving with it;[58] and, undoubtedly with the Balkan commission secretariat experience in mind, admonished the Palestine Committee secretariat to be scrupulously objective.[59]

There was some minor friction with the Jewish Agency, which protested Lie's action in circulating a British note requesting that member states discourage illegal Jewish immigration to Palestine. Lie, of course, had no leeway but to circulate London's note; but the Jewish Agency thought he should likewise circulate its protest to member states. Lie, however, distributed copies only to the Palestine Committee. He magnanimously held that he "was not greatly concerned" about the complaint since he "felt there was bound to be Jewish criticism."[60] He displayed no similar attitude, as we shall see, toward Arab complaints. He kept completely clear of the Palestine Committee, Lie subsequently maintained, and held his thoughts about what would be a fair solution to both sides.[61] There is no evidence to suggest differently.

Partition

The Palestine Committee held sixteen public and thirty-six private meetings. It visited Palestine, where it heard representatives of the mandate government and the Jewish Agency and other Jewish bodies, including religious ones, giving a special hearing to Chaim Weizmann, titular head of the Zionist movement. It also heard the views of the Arab states of Iraq, Jordan, Lebanon, Saudi Arabia, and Syria. It visited Beirut, Amman, and informally Damascus. A subcommittee visited the displaced persons' camps in Austria and Germany and met with the American, Austrian, and British officials involved. The most serious flaw in the committee's proceedings, not of its own making, was the decision of the Arab Higher Committee to abstain from collaboration. Its decision was based on several objections, including assembly refusal to include on its special session agenda the question of terminating the Palestine mandate and declaring the country independent. This abstention was a serious tactical mistake for it surrendered the field of oral confrontation, and thus the chance to influence public opinion, to the Jewish Agency and its Zionist allies.

On August 31, 1947, the Palestine Committee's exhaustive report and recommendations were completed and conveyed to Lie. The majority proposal (Canada, Czechoslovakia, Guatemala, the Netherlands, Peru, Sweden and Uruguay) envisaged Palestine's partition into Arab and Jewish states, their boundaries sketched, with Jerusalem under international trusteeship and the United Nations as administering authority. There would be a system of economic union and collaboration established for the whole area. The minority proposal (India, Iran, and Yugoslavia) envisaged an independent federal state, comprising Arab and Jewish areas, boundaries defined, with Jerusalem as its capital. There would be a federal government as well as governments of the Arab and Jewish areas. The federal government would control national defense, foreign relations, immigration, currency, and so on; the Arab and Jewish areas would exercise local self-government, including authority over education, police, rights of residence, and so on. Provisions dealing with the distribution of executive, legislative, and judicial powers were spelled out, and an international body would supervise and protect the holy places. Australia abstained from voting for either report.[62]

Lie was ecstatic with the majority proposal. Did he not say it was going to happen? he exclaimed to Shertok. He was sure that the majority proposal would be accepted; that there was no other solution; and that the world could no longer tolerate the current status of the Jewish question.

There had to be an independent Jewish state.[63] He had unambiguously nailed his flag to the Zionist mast, and there was no turning back. He did not think Lie an enemy, Shertok laconically observed to the leaders of the Jewish Agency.[64]

Lie deceptively wrote later that the majority report manifested "a clear victory for the principle of partition." As chief executive officer of the United Nations, he "took the cue and, when approached by delegations for advice, frankly recommended that they follow the majority plan." What delegations he so advised is unknown. Some Arabs attacked him in public, but he "could not yield." The responsibility to resolve the Palestine question, he later mischievously wrote, had been transferred to the United Nations and the world organization had to act in line with "its best judgment."[65] But the British note of April 2, 1947, had devolved no such responsibility on the United Nations, specifically requesting only a recommendation from the assembly, under charter Article 10, on Palestine's future government. Assembly recommendations of this nature are exactly that, acted upon only as the member states see fit. One can, of course, cogently argue that assembly resolutions have a moral authority, but that is not to say that they are legally binding. More important, in a practical and in a legal-political sense the British government, not the assembly, had ultimate responsibility for setting policy in a violence-racked Palestine. In fact, at the time, Lie publicly admitted all this.[66]

In line with Lie's recommendation a special committee on Palestine was established to avoid reference of the Palestine Committee's report to the First Committee, so its deliberations on the other question would not be delayed.[67] The tense debates in the assembly on the Palestine Committee's report waxed long and bitter. Finally, on November 29, with thirty-three votes in favor, thirteen opposed, and ten abstentions, the assembly recommended adoption of the majority partition plan. Faced with a Hobson's choice, the British government, unlike Lie, abstained. A Palestine Commission was simultaneously established to arrange for the transfer of power from the mandate authorities to the envisaged Arab and Jewish government organs.[68] In Palestine, news of the vote was followed by theretofore unmatched intercommunal violence.

The State Department, however, like the Foreign Office wanted Lie to go slow with the Palestine Commission. They did not want the commission to enter Palestine before May 1, 1948, although this would not preclude the commission commencing detailed conversations with the British on taking over once London officially withdrew on May 15.[69] Lie's announcement that he might personally go to Palestine as director of the Palestine Commission secretariat must have confirmed London and Washington in the wisdom of pressing him with a go-slow signal.[70]

The Arabs, both in and out of Palestine, now proclaimed that they would resist partition, with armed force if necessary. Communal violence took an upswing. Even before the partition resolution was voted, doubt-lessly in anticipation of its acceptance, Lie instituted secretariat studies on the possibilities of forming an international force to implement the resolution, despite what he later wrote. After the partition vote, he commenced exploratory talks on the subject with various member states[71]— probably the Scandinavian and Benelux countries. Naturally, the Jewish Agency representatives "had close and cordial relations" with the secretariat, and Shertok had many meetings with Lie, who labored "to promote the execution of the [partition] resolution."[72]

Thus Lie's comments to Cadogan, that the commission early on would probably become conscious of the "need of some force to implement" the partition recommendation and "he thought it likely that they would appeal to the Security Council," should have alerted the wary that Lie was ready to fish in troubled waters.[73] In fact, Shertok was erroneously informed by Sobolev, as early as December 26, that Lie had queried the Big Five whether they would agree to participate in such an international force. By January 3, 1948, Eban was fed the story that "serious discussions" on the matter were taking place in Washington.[74]

Lie's approach to various states about the possibilities of an international force for Palestine was soon leaked by the New York Times. Lie denied any consultations with member states, although some had raised the matter, he admitted; and of course, he had discussed it with senior secretariat officials—no word that he had instituted secretariat studies himself. However, the problem of security was solely the responsibility of the Palestine Commission; if interested in a military force the commission would have to broach the question with the council.[75] The Foreign Office was uneasy and asked Cadogan for assurances, which he quickly gave, that the British mission was not involved in any such discussions.[76] The American mission was also uneasy; when it queried Lie about the story, he again denied it and claimed that the only time he had raised the subject was during a dinner for the council's permanent members, where he had casually mentioned the necessity of discovering some way of solving the security problem. Feller, however, proved indiscreet. When questioned, he first observed that Lie had denied the story, but when pressed he finally admitted that the secretary-general had indeed discussed the matter with the representatives of a number of small states.

Lie's argument justifying some sort of an international force was that the Palestine Commission would not be willing to depart for the Holy Land unless guaranteed suitable military protection. He and Byron Price felt that an American and Russian regiment under a neutral commander, like a Canadian or an Australian, would be sufficient to keep the peace in Palestine. This was a preposterous proposition if there ever was one, when thousands of well-trained, experienced British troops and police, familiar with the terrain and its people, were incapable of keeping the peace.

Whether the proposal was even feasible politically does not appear to have phased Lie in the least.

When questioned by the Americans whether any particular significance was to be attached to papers he had informally sent to Austin concerning precedents for establishing international forces (prepared by the secretariat on October 17 and 22, 1947, before the partition resolution was approved) Lie, without batting an eyelash, replied in the negative. They were merely secretariat working papers, he disingenuously explained, and conveyed to Austin merely as a matter of information.[77] In view of Feller's admissions, Lie's explanations must have led to some anxious glances among American officials.

At the first meeting of the Palestine Commission on January 9, Lie's desire to enforce the partition resolution was no longer disguised. The commission, he observed, could be "confident" that, should it be necessary, the council would "not fail to exercise, to the fullest and without exception, every necessary power entrusted to it by the Charter" so as to assist the commission in executing its mission. Lie thus committed himself, no doubt fearing that the council might not act. This was understandable, for none of the great powers wished to get involved in the chaos of Palestine, with the exception of Soviet Russia. Moscow's past denunciation of Zionism was more than matched by a new pro-Zionist, propartition, anti-Arab stance, no doubt dictated by its desire to see another British bastion in the Middle East disappear. Aside from this short-term gain, tensions would develop in the area allowing Moscow to both sow and reap long-term political advantages. Lie, like others, perceived none of this. The commission invited the British, the Jewish Agency, and the Arab Higher Committee to attend its meetings. The latter refused on the grounds that it rejected the partition. The firm British stance, which Lie felt did not dovetail "with either the letter or spirit of the partition plan," was that they would not progressively surrender authority to the commission but would do so only as of May 15.[78] Lie's orientation during this period was well reflected in Byron Price's comment to the American mission that, if the world organization failed to meet the Palestine challenge, it would signal the United Nations' demise "as an Organization to 'enforce' peace." This was "muddy thinking," McClintock marginally scribbled, since the "UN is being asked to enforce [the] partition of Palestine, not peace."[79]

To sound out the British, Lie visited London in late January. When he raised the question of an international force, Minister of State Hector McNeil responded that he did not think the partition plan could be forcibly implemented; were this feasible, the British government would have done it. The truth of the matter "was that no reasonable security force" could effect the partition. The only solution possible, as Bevin had repeatedly emphasized, was through Arab-Jewish agreement. Lie then queried if London would contribute to an international force; if not, what would be its attitude on the council toward such a force? McNeil saw no possibility of

London contributing forces except by the agreement of both sides. As for a British use of the veto, he was in no position to respond since Bevin had not yet come to a decision. Lie then shifted the conversation: since the Palestine Commission could not enter the mandate before May 1, could it come to London prior to then? McNeil had no answer, but promised to bring the query to Bevin's attention. He saw some advantages to such a visit by the commission.[80] It was the only concession that the British gave to Lie, and some days later Cadogan informed the Palestine Commission that it would be welcomed in London whenever it wished to come.[81]

At this point, Lie indiscreetly voiced to Shertok and other senior Jewish Agency officials his pent up hostility toward the British, whom he described as the worst "street thieves" he had ever set eyes on, and vehemently castigated British actions as a conspiracy to obstruct the partition resolution. The Palestine problem, he claimed, was basic to the world organization's survival as well as world peace, and he saw it as his responsibility to use all his strength and influence to implement the partition scheme. He regarded the officials of the Jewish Agency as "his collaborators" and wanted "close cooperation" with them. If the partition decision was foiled he would resign as secretary-general. He would impress on President Truman and Secretary of State Marshall that the United States had to blaze the path to implement partition and that there would be dangers involved should this not be achieved. There was no doubt among his attendant Jewish listeners that Lie's support would considerably strengthen the Zionist cause. Lie had harsh words for Bevin, whom he categorized as anti-Semitic and anticommunist. Although it was noted that Lie did not admire the Communists, neither did he think that policy could be based on hatred alone. Lie therefore was prepared to fight and looked upon the Jewish Agency as an ally in victory or defeat.

Lie claimed that in the initial discussions of the Palestine question he tried to be neutral; but once the partition resolution was passed, there was no longer room for neutrality, and he wanted to "implement loyally and fully the decision." He hinted that he was under surveillance by the American and British security services; therefore, the Jewish Agency and he should avoid their respective offices in contacting each other. As to an international force, it could not consist of units drawn only from small states; in fact a large force would be needed. Lie rejected Washington's argument that Moscow's participation in any international force would interject Russians into Palestine and that they would never be withdrawn. Based on his Norwegian experience, Lie opined that this was not the case: although the Russians would not evacuate a place unless obligated to do so, when so obligated they were punctilious. Lie was ready to ask both the Americans and the Russians to serve in an international force.[82] Norway's experiences with the Russians, which were sui generis, still dogged Lie but the rude shock of the Prague coup was only around the corner. In view of the United Nations' less than sterling performance in some of the issues before it, Lie's desire to have the world organization score some great success that would place it on the crest of the incoming waves of world politics can be well appreciated.

In the wake of this discussion and in compliance with a request from Lie, Shertok jotted down a summary memorandum for him of six points requiring urgent action. The most significant one referred to interviews with Truman and Marshall on the matter of an international force, during which Lie intended to indicate that the United Nations' "whole machinery" might collapse if the partition resolution was not executed.[83] Lie's position that the Palestine problem was "a basic one for [the] UN" was soon revealed to the Americans, as well as his intention "probably [to] make a strong statement on the need for effectively carrying out" the partition plan when the council took up the matter.[84]

The Palestine Commission's special report of February 16 to the council appeared to give Lie his opportunity. The commission's conclusion was that British forces in Palestine had to be replaced by an adequate force to help law-abiding Arabs and Jews, in conjunction with the commission, to maintain law and order and thus allow implementation of partition. Its only motivation, the commission declared, was to obtain from the council the necessary assistance without which it could not execute the great task entrusted to it.[85] Naturally, Lie thought the commission's view was very sound since it responded to the Arab threat to invade Palestine and overturn the partition plan. Lie ordered the secretariat to draw up a statement to the council, which he would hold in abeyance. This draft statement that Lie hammered out with the secretariat stressed that, despite the inability of East and West to provide the United Nations with armed forces as stipulated in the charter, there was enough agreement to allow the establishment of an emergency international force. It could be composed of those minimum military units that the five great powers were committed to make available to the council, which would be more than enough to maintain order in Palestine. In addition, the statement held that the United Nations could not allow violence directed against its decisions and bodies; if its moral force was insufficient, military force would have to be employed. Cautious, Lie refrained from presenting the statement until he could better gauge the trend of the council's debates and action. Correctly, he saw that it would be futile if he spoke only for the official record, even if he acted on the good possibility that the council might follow.[86]

During this period, Lie was "exceedingly depressed" about United Nations developments and "apprehensive" that the council's coming exchanges on Palestine would further dispirit him. The draft statement, however, soon leaked out, and it was "rumoured" that Lie might unveil some unusual formula for the immediate institution of an international force for Palestine. Canada's Pearson suggested to him the "dangers and difficulties of any such proposal coming from the Secretary-General on his own initiative," especially if Lie favored a particular type of force. Pearson's wise words appear to have made an impact.[87] They certainly gave Lie an inkling of what the reaction might be in the council if he issued the statement. He stayed his hand, at least for the moment.

In private, Lie stressed to British Colonial Secretary Arthur Creech Jones that the Palestine problem should not be allowed to destroy the United Nations' prestige.[88] From the initial council discussions on the Palestine Commission's special report, it was clear, however, that no international force would be instituted. Indeed, the Americans, who Lie hoped would carry the ball, held that the council was not empowered to enforce a political settlement recommended by either itself or the assembly. Instead, Austin proposed that the council establish a committee of its permanent members to examine whether the Palestine situation constituted a threat to international peace and security. It was obvious that the American position was to avoid enforcing implementation of the partition resolution and to restrict discussions of the whole matter to the permanent members.[89]

Lie was absolutely furious with the American stance. He tore into Austin, asking whether Washington supported the partition resolution and whether Austin believed it would be implemented.[90] Lie now repeated in public what he had said only in private; namely, that the United Nations' failure to execute the partition resolution would be a body blow to the world organization's prestige.[91] He might have felt that going public would evoke support for his position from others, since somewhat similar sentiments were echoed by Eleanor Roosevelt, a member of the American mission.[92] Roosevelt's public action, however, formidable as it was, was not in direct proportion to her political influence either within the mission or with the Truman administration. If Lie's public comments were an attempt to promote a crescendo in support of his international force idea, it never rose above a whimper.

Queried whether a conference among the Big Five on Palestine would be of assistance, Lie refused to answer, and skated away with the anodyne explanation that he was always pleased to see the Big Five consult on any matter. When pressed further, he observed that he was undecided whether to offer the council his own views on Palestine.[93] Pearson's advice was probably still on his mind; it was wise restraint, for the council decided on March 5 to ask its permanent members to "consult and inform" it with recommendations for guidance that the council might tender the Palestine Commission to help implement the partition resolution. Simultaneously, it appealed to everyone in Palestine and adjacent to it to reduce the violence sweeping the area.[94]

At their first meeting the permanent members—the British declined to partake—invited Lie and Cadogan to attend their discussions.[95] In these private discussions, the Russians appeared prepared to implement partition while the Americans were not. The rumors, according to Lie, were that Washington wanted to moderate the Arab position in exchange for relinquishing the partition plan. In such a situation, an international force to implement the partition resolution was a nonstarter.[96] Lie was very depressed by developments and divulged to Shertok that he had approached every member of the Palestine Commission urging implementation of partition.[97] No doubt to ginger up the Americans and undercut their position, Lie informally submitted a working paper by secretariat legal experts, probably Feller, affirming the council's "legal authority" to execute the partition plan recommended by the assembly. It opined that the Palestine Commission would become the Holy Land's "legally constituted government" after London terminated the mandate on May 15. The working paper was then leaked to the *New York Times*, undoubtedly on Lie's instructions.

Rusk pointed out that the leaked paper had been requested by the Palestine Commission and was dated February 3. McClintock correctly observed that "it was unfortunate for the public impression" to develop that the secretariat had "prepared a refutation" of Austin's council statement of February 24 that the charter did not bestow on the council power to enforce a recommended political settlement. Furthermore because the paper ruminated on the question of who was responsible for Palestine after May 15, McClintock suggested that "Lie had better set the record straight" as to when the paper was written and its origins. He also proposed that Lie be informed, since the paper had been distributed to the United States as a council member, that Washington "did not concur in his legal opinion."[98]

Several days later, the permanent members decided to make another attempt to get the representatives of the Arab Higher Committee to appear and answer questions. Lie, they agreed, would present these questions to Esa Nakkleh, the Arab Higher Committee representative in New York. Lie and Nakkleh accordingly met in the offices of the American mission. Nakkleh promised that he would transmit the questions posed by Lie to Jerusalem, but that in doing so he was not participating in any consultations. During this brief meeting there "was a very unpleasant" exchange between the two, Nakkleh charging "Lie and the secretariat with a prejudiced position in favor of the Jews" and Lie responding that "he had not come [there] to be insulted." On departing he remarked to the Americans privately that he was convinced of Washington's sincere desire to implement peacefully the partition plan and that he was doing everything possible to support these efforts. However, he feared that the Americans would find the plan could not be implemented by peaceful means but only by force. "Otherwise the UN would go downhill rapidly to nothing."[99] Lie's indignation was a good act, considering that he soon conveyed to Shertok confidential reports from the advance party of the Palestine Commission secretariat about political conditions in the mandate.[100] When informed of the run-in between Lie and Nakkleh, the Egyptian representative, Mahmoud Fawzi Bey, disapproved the latter's comments. He generously held that it had been inappropriate in all respects for Nakkleh to tell Lie "what he thought of the actions of Mr. Lie and the Secretariat, no matter how strongly the Arab Higher Committee might dislike these actions."[101]

The permanent members' report by China, France, and the United States on March 19 (Soviet Russia did not sign and Great Britain did not participate) called on the council to make clear to all concerned its determination not to allow Palestine to become a threat to international peace. Concurrently, the council should make every attempt to restore peace and order in Palestine.[102] At the midday recess, the permanent members met separately. Austin, faced with new instructions from Washington, now proposed to everyone's surprise that a special assembly session be called immediately to consider the establishment of a trusteeship for Palestine without prejudicing either the rights, claims, or position of any concerned party or any eventual political settlement. Pending the convening of the special session the council was asked to instruct the Palestine Commission to suspend its efforts to implement partition. Washington's reversal of position stunned everyone, especially Lie. He pointed out that the Palestine Committee had examined and rejected the idea of trusteeship. Lie maintained that it would require greater military effort than partition. He enquired whether the permanent members would be prepared to maintain the peace in Palestine should the council or the assembly reach a new decision. Of course, Austin responded, his government would be ready to support a United Nations decision.[103]

Lie, understandably, was skeptical. The American turnabout moved him immensely. The following day he saw Austin and revealed his "sense of shock and of almost personal grievance." Washington, he observed, knew very well where he stood on the question of partition; it had struck a blow to the United Nations and to himself, because of his "direct and deep commitment." Fulfilling his comments to the Jewish Agency representatives in February, Lie proposed that he and Austin both resign. Austin gave Lie his sympathy but declined to resign and advised Lie to hold back as well and not take Washington's new stance in a personal way. Since Austin does not appear to have reported the incident to Washington, he probably dismissed it as the reaction of an emotional person under stress.

Obviously dissatisfied, Lie trudged off to see Gromyko. Speaking personally, he likewise advised Lie not to resign. Unlike Austin, however, Gromyko asked for time to consult Moscow, which as one would expect seconded him.[104] Because up to this point Lie had more or less been on the Russian side in a host of questions before the United Nations—the Iranian-Russian dispute, the Spanish question, the coup in Prague, and so on—the advice was clearly in Russian interests. One can argue, perhaps not unfairly, that the American reversal, whether wise or unwise, was predicated on perceived national interests by senior officials in Washington.[105] If Lie thought that by his threat to resign he could shame the Americans into changing their new policy, he was naive in the extreme.

Austin's presentation of the trusteeship idea to the council produced a strained debate. It decided to call for a truce in Palestine, as well as to instruct Lie to convoke a special assembly session to consider further the question of Palestine's future government.[106] In the interim before the special session convened, Lie's pessimism was conveyed to Secretary of State Marshall by Byron Price, who noted that he and Lie felt strongly that Washington's actions on the Palestine question were "seriously threatening" the life of the United Nations.[107] Lie personally believed that no truce would be achieved but that increased fighting would again erupt in Palestine. In this, he mirrored the views of the Spaniard Pablo de Azcárate y Florez, a longtime senior member of the league secretariat then serving as chief of the United Nations secretariat in Palestine, as well as those of the ubiquitous pro-Zionist Colonel Roscher Lund, also in Palestine[108] where, as in Greece, his activities generated American protests.[109]

Although Lie was careful not to comment publicly on what the assembly might do in reacting to the American trusteeship proposal, in private he did not conceal the fact that the trusteeship idea had been proposed to the Palestine Committee and rejected.[110] Behind the scenes he continued his contacts with the Jewish Agency and expedited contacts between Chaim Weizmann and the Norwegian mission.[111] He found the situation confused and lacking leadership.[112] When the special assembly session convened on April 16, the American mission knew that Lie thought the situation hopeless and that no action could avert the impending chaos.[113]

Nevertheless, Lie kept up appearances; although devoid of optimism, he appeared pleased that Washington had submitted to the First Committee a working paper on trusteeship for Palestine. He felt that the paper might short-circuit a great deal of dispiriting debate.[114] In fact, under these circumstances the trusteeship proposal and the convocation of the special session were easy targets for a well placed Demosthenean volley, which was ably delivered on May 1 in the First Committee by Eban. A comparable encomium for partition by New Zealand's Sir Carl Berendsen so moved Lie that he dispatched "an admiring bouquet of roses." The trusteeship proposal generated only a modicum of support. Its stillbirth made Lie and the generally dour Gromyko "similarly ebullient."[115]

By this point, however, Lie was at the end of his tether, and as he admitted to the Jewish Agency's American leader, Nahum Goldmann, he was in an extremely difficult position. The Arabs hated him, but that did not bother him. Now the Americans were saying that he had sold himself to the Zionists. They held that as secretary-general he was obligated to partake in truce proposals, but Lie had responded that it was not his responsibility, a stance that Goldmann supported.[116]

The assembly went through motions, but they lacked immediate substance and appeared unreal as the countdown to May 15 continued unabated. The violence in Palestine mounted with each passing day leading, as the British finally withdrew, to an invasion by the Arab states and a de facto partition of the former mandate between Arabs and Jews. The assembly's efforts led to the passage of three resolutions: the first affirmed its support of council endeavors to secure a truce; the second empowered a United Nations mediator in Palestine, chosen by a committee (the Big Five), to use his good offices in cooperation with the Truce Commission established by the council on April 23, to promote a peaceful settlement, to arrange for continual functioning of necessary public services, and to assure protection of the holy places. Lastly, it gently relieved the Palestine Commission of its fruitless task, but it said nothing about the partition resolution of November 29, 1947, technically still on the books.[117]

There was understandable jubilation within Zionist ranks, which multiplied as Washington, in another abrupt about-face, announced recognition of the provisional government of Israel as the de facto authority of the new Jewish state. This precipitant action was much to Lie's surprise and to the consternation and embarrassment of the American mission.[118] Simultaneously, as the British evacuated the intercommunal fighting plunged into an undeclared war, with irregular and regular forces from surrounding Arab states invading Palestine. The chaos foreseen by many, including Lie, had come to fruition. He described the situation succinctly as a "fiasco," which indeed it was.[119]

Failure of a Mission

Even before the Arabs invaded Palestine, Lie had requested a legal examination of charter Article 99 and was dutifully assured that he could invoke it to bring any invasion to council attention as a threat to international peace and security.[120] He then had a letter drafted to the council president invoking the article, which was ready to use when Arab forces crossed into Palestine. He held his hand, however, to see Washington's reaction: if the Americans were prepared to bring the issue to the council, thus indicating a willingness to spearhead a move to halt the Arabs, then it would be wiser to surrender the initiative to them. On the actual day the Arabs invaded, May 15, however, the United States remained mute, as did the rest of the council with the exception of the Russians. Late that day Lie collected his closest advisers (including Cordier, Feller, Gjesdal, Jackson, and so on) at his home to examine the situation. The decision was to use Cordier and Jackson to approach the Americans and the British.[121] The opinion of these men, as Cordier explained, was that with Washington's sudden recognition of Israel London had become crucial in initiating any proposals to the Arabs. However, before approaching London, Lie wanted to learn more of Washington's policy.[122]

Lie wanted to send Assistant Secretary-General Jackson to Washington, Cordier explained to the American mission, to discover what might be done. He felt that he should use his office "as an impartial world civil servant" to do anything possible to discover a solution to the situation and that, "if the tide were not reversed," the current fighting would lead inevitably toward World War III. Collective action by member states might avert total hostilities. Top officials of the secretariat had no hope for council action, leaving a vacuum that Lie wanted to fill; if the council remained as inactive as the assembly in responding to the Arab attacks, its "prestige and authority" and ultimately that of all the United Nations would be harmed irreparably.

Cordier then telephoned Rusk in Washington and outlined Lie's views. Rusk claimed that policy on the current Palestine situation had not been, and probably would not be, formulated for several days. Until then, it appeared "futile to engage in any discussions" with Jackson. After further discussion with Lie, Jackson, and others, Cordier again called Rusk, but he could not be moved. For a third time Cordier contacted Rusk on the morning of May 16, and it was finally agreed that Jackson and Austin should meet.[123] However, nothing was likely to come from a situation where Lie saw Armageddon while the State Department saw merely a critical situation that in no way directly threatened the East-West balance of power, which alone could spring World War III.

When Jackson called on Austin he hinted that Lie might invoke Article 99, feeling that if the council failed to act decisively it would create an undesirable precedent that might encourage other nations to take aggressive measures when it suited their purposes. Governments that had heretofore accepted the United Nations' authority might now have second thoughts. To do nothing was to admit that the council and the United Nations were useless for preserving the peace. In view of this, Lie desired to see Marshall and Lovett, since there clearly were difficulties between Washington and London and Lie might initiate discussions with London if his good offices could be helpful in effecting a closer understanding between the two governments, especially over bringing the Palestine question under the council's effective control. Austin explained his own position and the difficulties that Washington had had with London on this question. He then telephoned Rusk and they agreed that the best approach was to delay in order to see what would happen and that a meeting with Marshall and Lovett was impossible.

From this talk with Austin, it was clear that there was a wide gap between the American and British positions on Palestine, because of which effective council action could hardly develop. The secretariat would have to work hard, according to Jackson, to try and bring both governments together if council action was desired. After discussion with Lie, Cordier, and Feller, it was decided to dispatch an official letter to the council's permanent members making clear Lie's position. Another would be sent to Marshall pointing out why Lie had looked forward to personal discussions to ease the position between the American and British governments. After talking with Cadogan, Cordier might visit Washington to emphasize Lie's stance, and possibly also prepare the ground for talks with Marshall and Lovett.[124]

Lie's letter to the council's permanent members declared that, because the question was now before the council, he had no need to invoke Article 99. Lie emphasized moreover that this was the first time since the charter was adopted that member states—Egypt and states of the Arab League—had openly declared themselves engaged in a foreign military intervention. This had occurred after the council established a Truce Commission and only hours after the assembly appointed a United Nations mediator. Lie then reiterated all his arguments in favor of quick action by the organization in this extremely serious situation.[125] Austin's reply cautiously avoided substantive comment and merely noted that the United States had decided to take no action because of lack of adequate information necessary to a decision.[126]

When Jackson delivered Lie's letter to Cadogan he repeated to him his prior arguments to Austin. Jackson drew analogies between the current situation and the Manchurian and Ethiopian episodes, which had led to the league's collapse, no doubt to provoke Cadogan's subconscious sympathies since he had lived through these interwar traumas when he served in the Foreign Office. Lie, Jackson explained, was willing to try to bring the Americans and British together, since the longer action was delayed, the greater was the danger. Cadogan appreciated Lie's position and admitted that the league's experience might be repeated. He regretted that the United Nations' armed forces had not been established; but, for the moment, one had to concentrate on the practical. Cadogan criticized American actions in some detail. He saw difficulties in constructing a common American-British line but realized the dangers that could flow from council delay. He assumed Lie's first practical step would be to suggest an immediate "standstill order to all concerned," which Jackson confirmed. Cadogan pointed out the danger if the council's order was ignored by the concerned parties. Jackson replied it was better to invoke the proper procedure even if it failed, in which case responsibility would fall where it belonged and not be shifted to either the council or Lie. Cadogan agreed.

They then discussed the possibility of making British and American military forces available to implement a standstill order. Washington's position, Cadogan realized, would depend on its willingness to see Russian forces in the area. This aspect had to be considered carefully since it related directly to the council's ability to take firm action. Jackson noted that Lie, at that stage, had not thought it appropriate to raise the question of the needed military force. Cadogan noted to the Foreign Office that a standstill order would give the opportunity for mediation. This faced the British government with a dilemma: an inactive United Nations would be a confession of failure, but a standstill order that was ignored and could not be enforced might involve it in "still greater humiliation." Cadogan recommended that, if a standstill proposal were made, he should vote for it on the grounds that mediation was being attempted, though it might fail if serious fighting erupted. An attempt should nonetheless be made at once to find a mediator. The "gamble" or failure was no greater than the harm done by ignoring the situation. London would have done its best and exhausted its last efforts. Similar thinking, Cadogan observed, explained Lie's letter.

Lie now decided that Cordier should proceed to Washington. Once Cordier ascertained where the difficulties lay between the American and British governments, Jackson could depart for London and possibly Paris. Personal contact with Marshall and Lovett was an essential first step, since it would be very dangerous to undertake discussions in London "unless specific points of disagreement could be made clear."[127]

Cordier would have departed for Washington with less optimism had he been aware of London's reaction to Cadogan's plea. While the British government shared Lie's concern that the United Nations must be made to function, Cadogan was informed, it thought it equally important that it function justly. London could not agree to action that singled out the Arabs for censure by ordering a standstill, which would almost certainly not be respected, but that would place the Arabs in the wrong if they ignored it. Furthermore, it would not agree to any United Nations action that, either in theory or practice, tilted in favor of one side or the other. Instructions on how to argue the British case were spelled out; but if there was an attempt to push through a standstill order, Cadogan was to ask for adjournment. If this were impossible, he was to let it be known that he would veto any resolution rather than accept one contrary to British policy.[128] "Perfectly bloodyminded" instructions, Cadogan angrily wrote.[129]

On May 17, Cordier delivered to the State Department a copy of Lie's letter to Austin as well as the one to Marshall. His now-standard arguments were repeated, especially his concern about the difficulties between London and Washington and his desire to consult and possibly use his good offices in this serious matter.[130] Rusk's advice to Marshall was that Washington should not "encourage" Lie to contact the State Department directly on political matters before the United Nations. Moreover, Austin's hand should be strengthened in every way, and he should be left to decide "as to when it would be useful and proper" for secretariat personnel to discuss such matters with the State Department.[131] Indeed, such instructions had been sent to Austin, but with the proviso that the State Department did "not wish to make it difficult for you by refusing requests on which Lie is insistent."[132] Marshall's reply to Lie on May 21 conveyed this attitude but in gentler syntax.[133]

Cordier's discussions with Rusk and others quickly established that a draft council resolution had been prepared and cleared at all levels, declaring Arab military moves into Palestine a breach of the peace. Rusk then outlined for Cordier additional measures that senior officials were contemplating, including a universal arms embargo and, if the British did not cooperate and cease arms shipments to the Arabs, lifting the American embargo on arms shipments to the Jews, a move that might have serious complications for London and Washington. Trade sanctions were another possibility, but this was still in the discussion stage. Military sanctions were also possible. The Americans, however, objected to possible zonal divisions of the area, whose unfortunate consequences could still be seen in Austria and Germany. This idea had developed with that of possible Russian participation. There was also the idea that aircraft carriers might be placed off the Palestine coast, to prevent an air war and thus retard hostilities. This, plus an arms embargo, could effectively strengthen the mediator's hand.

State Department officials emphasized, according to Cordier, the rapid deterioration in American-British relations, which "could be regarded as having reached a breaking point." If Congress and the public were aware of the whole story, it would have a serious impact upon the future of the European Recovery Program (the Marshall Plan's legal nonemclature), perhaps undercutting implementation of the recovery program or even forcing Washington to use it as leverage on the British. The Americans repeatedly observed that, in view of their proposed initiatives to the council, the crux of the problem was in London. If Washington could be charged with inconsistency, the charge against the British was obstructionism. They would have to modify their Arab policy before any settlement could be made in Palestine. They asked Cordier to make certain that Lie's strong weekend initiative would not be interpreted to imply that Washington was inactive. They had made moves—granted, some inconsistent—in the Security and Trusteeship Councils and the assembly. Cordier responded that Lie's moves were not for public consumption and his letters were confidential, but his proposed steps sought to safeguard world peace and to strengthen the United Nations.

The talks then touched on Lie's role and that of his representatives. It was agreed that Lie should always have access to the Secretary of State and, in given situations, through a personal representative. Lie wished to use the official permanent representative as much as possible, Cordier assured his hosts, not to by-pass him. He needed, however, to retain his right to contact foreign ministers and, through the official permanent representative, exchange views with more junior officials.[134]

Following Cordier's return, Lie asked to see Cadogan. He divulged that he wanted to send Jackson to London to explain "all his misgivings and fears." Cadogan thought that London should be forewarned of Jackson's visit. Lie responded that he would mull it over and let Cadogan know what he decided. For some unexplained reason, Lie teetered on the fence. Not until the next day, May 19, did he decide to send Jackson, so Cadogan signaled the Foreign Office "explaining this antic."[135] It was an inauspicious beginning. This was not the first time, however, that Cadogan had had to deal with the frustrations and disappointments, real or imagined, of some secretary-general: he had had extensive dealings with Drummond and Avenol during the league's years. At the same time, there was a thread of sympathy for Lie's pleas in Cadogan's message, based on this very interwar experience.

Lie had poured "out his heart" to him, Cadogan noted to London, about how discouraged he was at the United Nations' prospects. The immediate obstacle was Palestine, but Lie's disquiet was in general based on what he considered the unremitting decline of the United Nations since 1945. Cadogan responded with his customary arguments, correct ones at that: the world organization was an instrument to be used wisely and whenever possible by the member states, but as long as the East-West rift continued, it could not be expected to perform miracles. The world's best automobile could not travel a straight course if the steering wheel was turned in different directions simultaneously by two people. In the Palestine question especially, did Lie know whether Washington or anyone else was ready to use force? Would not the failure be greater if everyone ran out when asked to use force rather than adopting initially more modest measures that might evolve into something effective? Lie did not entirely agree.

Cadogan, however, had to admit that the United Nations was showing the same symptoms attributed to the league's demise. Perhaps it was inevitable, as he was inclined to think. He had watched the league closely for ten years from the Foreign Office and the United Nations since San Francisco. His experience had perhaps made him a "cynic." Governments, it appeared to Cadogan, with alacrity accepted all the slogans about leagues and United Nations and lived up to them until a conflict developed between their national interests and the principles of these organizations, at which point the former prevailed. Therefore, Cadogan failed to see the value of a covenant or a charter. There was a further rub: to fail to restrain the Arab member states from forcible resistance to an assembly recommendation would be an invitation to Yugoslavia, Pakistan, India, and of course, Soviet Russia to do the same. The league's failure in Manchuria, Cadogan observed, gave Mussolini the green light in Ethiopia, and Mussolini's unchecked action there was a call to all aggressors to proceed.

He had told Lie, Cadogan reported, that the United Nations' misfortune was that it had encountered problems it could not tackle. What was the use trying to apply international force when the world organization, after two years, could not establish its own military units? Jackson, who knew Lie's mind, would now come to London to place before Bevin Lie's views on Palestine. Cadogan had warned the secretary-general that he "did not think this a fruitful line of approach," that Lie should convey "any new or practical ideas" through him, and that nothing Jackson said would influence British policy on Palestine. It appeared that Jackson would also talk to Bevin on the European Recovery Program and American-British relations generally, but Cadogan did not discover with what particular aspects Jackson would deal.[136]

The reaction of Paul Mason, head of the United Nations Department, was that Lie's comments need not be taken "too tragically," as Lie was "notoriously temperamental" and inclined to oscillate from extreme optimism to extreme pessimism. In any case, it was "unnecessarily melodramatic" of Lie to send Jackson to London. On the other hand, Mason contested the United Nations' worth as reflected in the conversation. The council alone, he argued, had effectively intervened in two cases where war would almost certainly have erupted: Iran and Kashmir. In the Indonesian case, it helped prevent the spread of a situation that could have led to war. In unresolved matters like Greece and Korea, Mason had no doubt that its existence had contributed to preventing major hostilities. When people were exasperated, all this was forgotten because of the council's acrimonious debates and inability, thanks to Russian tactics, "to produce clear cut and tidy results." At the same time, he was sure Cadogan was correct, that there was serious risk of the United Nations succumbing, if it had not done so already, to the same malady that eventually throttled the league: world opinion's assumption that the organization was unequal to its primary task of preventing aggression and the consequent concentration on other aspects of its work, hoping to tide matters over and save something from the wreck. Mason recommended that Bevin, like Marshall, publicly profess confidence in the United Nations' future without dwelling on the difficulties then being experienced. Jebb agreed in general with Mason. Although sending Jackson over was a very inept move, Jackson apparently was "acting as a salutary check" on Lie, preventing him from committing some major indiscretion such as a public utterance under Article 99. Permanent Under-Secretary Sargent was less generous: Cadogan's message gave a "misleading picture" of Jackson's task; that Jackson might speak about the European Recovery Program and Anglo-American relations was the message's main drift. This link between the Recovery Program, which was not Lie's concern as secretary-general, and the Palestine question gave Jackson's trip "an unpleasant character."[137]

It is difficult to pinpoint whether Lie or Jackson had pressed the use in London of the comments to Cordier, which were not those of the State Department's most senior members, about Anglo-American relations and the European Recovery Program. The American mission reported at the time that Jackson had been encouraged to try the personal approach in London, based on information that Cadogan was instructed not to support the United States position. Lie, Washington was told, "had become philosophical" toward Jackson's eagerness for direct Foreign Office contact—a mission he partially acquiesced to in the hope of improving matters through personal exchange.[138] So far so good. Left unstated, however, was what arguments Jackson would use. Jackson subsequently wrote Cadogan that Lie had ordered him to see Bevin and Chancellor of the Exchequer Sir Stafford Cripps in order to alert the latter of the "major economic consequences" of the current situation. Jackson alleged that, although Lie realized his trip to London might be "misinterpreted," he thought that danger less important than carrying out his duty to assist agreement between the two governments. According to Jackson, Lie was concerned that, even if the United Nations did not sink because of East-West differences, the success of the recovery program was essential "to create a new world balance of power." Any Anglo-American misunderstanding over Palestine would reduce the recovery program's chances of success.[139] Jackson's allegations implied that Lie had wanted to use the European Recovery Program arguments. They were buttressed by Eban's message to Shertok that the American ambassador in London had apparently been instructed to emphasize to Bevin that a continuation of the present situation "*would prejudice [the] European Recovery Programme.*"[140] Since Lie and Eban were cheek by jowl, it is not unfair to suggest that Lie conveyed this erroneous information to Eban and also instructed Jackson to use the recovery program arguments in London. Jackson, from all private accounts, was a straightforward Australian devoid of subterfuge, his loquacity often peppered with cricket jargon incomprehensible to Lie,[141] and a man seemingly without a mendacious bone in his body. As Jackson months later observed to Jebb, he may have been a "fool" during his London mission, but he was certainly no "knave."[142] No indeed, but he would pay dearly for what was to occur.

Arriving in London on the evening of May 19, Jackson first called on Foreign Office Assistant Under-Secretary Sir Roger Makins, whose conversation should have alerted Jackson to the treacherous rapids that lay ahead. When Jackson laid Lie's anxieties on Palestine, and its possible effects on both the United Nations and the European Recovery Program, before Makins, his reaction was swift and to the point: Makins called raising the recovery program in connection with Palestine a "red herring." If Palestine were to cause a deterioration in British-American relations, Makins had no doubt a wide range of issues would be affected. The recovery program, however, would be the last of these, since it was generally agreed American policy toward a large grouping of states. Doubtlessly American Jewish organizations would attempt to influence Truman administration officials in a manner unfavorable to Great Britain. They might try to persuade Washington to reduce, or threaten to reduce, London's share of aid under the program. Whether these officials would be influenced by such moves was a matter of conjecture. Personally Makins doubted it. Palestine would no doubt be examined within the general context of Anglo-American relations, but Makins saw no purpose in examining it with special reference to the European Recovery Program.[143]

Late that night Jackson contacted Foreign Office Deputy Under-Secretary Sir Edmund Hall-Patch, in view of his special relationship with Bevin and Cripps. Hall-Patch, according to Jackson, appeared to be "fully alive" to the situation and the state of Anglo-American relations on the recovery program. Ominously, Hall-Patch offered no substantive comments. Later, Jackson called on Sir Edward Bridges, the Treasury's permanent secretary, and confirmed that the political aspects of his mission would be handled by Bevin, while the recovery program aspects would be handled by Chancellor of the Exchequer Sir Stafford Cripps. Since Cripps was departing from London, Jackson saw him immediately, but it was a tactical mistake, for Bevin, as we shall see, resented that Jackson's initial cabinet contact was with Cripps rather than him. According to Jackson, Cripps "grasped" the implications of the situation as he described it and its implications for the chancellor's work. He thought that Cripps was an "understanding and willing ally."

Later that same day, Jackson saw Sargent with Jebb and Martin Wright, head of the Middle East Department, present. Jackson presented Lie's views and noted his meeting with Cripps. Sargent was extremely cautious during the discussion and queried whether Lie was actually "issuing a 'warning' to His Majesty's Government." Not so, Jackson retorted. Could it be said, Sargent asked, that Lie was speaking officially and as a friend of the British government? This was so, Jackson answered. It was clear to Jackson that Sargent was sensitive that Washington might be manipulating Lie as a means of pressuring London to modify its Palestine position. Did Lie have specific proposals to handle the present situation, Sargent wondered. Not at that stage, Jackson explained, Lie's first concern being to make his own position clear and receive any guidance from London, especially in executing his responsibilities under Article 99. Jackson cautiously dwelt on Lie's desire to have the Americans and British survey their current divergent policies and reduce the possibilities of the United Nations "being caught in a cross fire." Sargent suggested that Jackson put Lie's views in writing. When the Australian hesitated, he asked if Jackson could at least embrace Lie's concern about the present situation under some broad headings? Jackson agreed.[144]

The next day Jackson's untitled memorandum was given to the Foreign Office to be read by Bevin upon his return to London. The memorandum spelled out Lie's anxieties on how the Palestine situation might affect the United Nations, Anglo-American relations, and the European Recovery Program.[145] Before Jackson's interview with Bevin, Martin Wright met with the American ambassador, who "took the opposite view from that advanced" by Jackson and Lie: that the Palestine question was affecting Washington's thinking about the recovery program and military assistance to western Europe.[146]

Unsuspecting, Jackson entered the lion's den on the morning of May 22. For his interview with Bevin, Jebb and Wright were present. With Wright's information under his belt Bevin began with a cannonade, telling Jackson that if Lie had a message to convey, the proper course would have been to deliver it to the foreign secretary, who could decide whether it should be forwarded to the cabinet. The procedure of approaching different cabinet ministers directly on such a matter was incorrect. Wright interjected that Lie was involved in reading the British government a "lecture" on British-American relations, and the place for that was in Washington not London. Jackson denied this. Lie, he pointed out, was not "allocating responsibility" to any country for the present crisis and his concern had already been conveyed to Washington. Bevin indicated that Lie's concern had resulted from American pressure. Jackson explained that, although Lie was under pressure from various quarters including American ones, this initiative was entirely his own. On all matters except Palestine, Bevin observed, Washington and London worked in "close harmony." On Palestine, the Americans had acted without consulting the British, which made Anglo-American cooperation very difficult. If Lie was implying that divergences between the two over Palestine had negative repercussions on the United Nations, he should approach both capitals but especially Washington.

Moreover, Bevin found it difficult to fathom Lie's thought processes in linking the Palestine question with the recovery program. He rejected the implication that, unless London modified its stance in Palestine and in a manner unacceptable to London, American aid under the recovery program would be affected. The British government would formulate what it believed to be a correct policy on Palestine from which it would not deviate because of a threat that the recovery program might be affected. Bevin was surprised that Lie would even advance such an idea and replied in the negative to Jackson's query whether he wished to convey any specific message to Lie. Furthermore, he made no reply when Jackson observed that Lie was under heavy pressure to make some public comment on Palestine and might be forced to do so if the current situation continued. Bevin explained that the British government opposed the use of force in Palestine at that juncture, which would open the road to Russian intervention in the Middle East; and since no one appeared prepared to implement the use of force, proposing it would only discredit the United Nations.[147]

The Foreign Office signaled Cadogan that Jackson, a "newcomer to high politics," would probably be returning slightly disgruntled. If the opportunity presented itself, he was to tell Lie that Bevin fully understood his "difficulties and apprehensions." Lie should not think that Bevin resented being approached, except in linking the recovery program with London's Palestine policy. That raised the impression, which Bevin was sure Lie had not wished to convey, that pressure could be placed on London to do something it knew was wrong.[148] These comments, however, had been added to Bevin's original message by Jebb, as "a little soft soap," in view of Jackson's mood when he departed and in the fear that he might "not exactly act as a sedative" with Lie.[149]

In point of fact, Jackson was not disgruntled. Before departing he again touched base with Bridges, Cripps, and Hall-Patch and spoke with Noel-Baker.[150] On his return, Jackson warned Lie that Bevin was "undoubtedly suspicious and resentful" of what had occurred in Palestine and had no real appreciation of the difficulties faced by Lie, Marshall, or the United Nations. Moreover, he was "obsessed by a fear" that the recovery program would be used to pressure him to change British policy in Palestine. Bevin had not been helpful in the least, but this was not true of Cripps or Jebb. Bevin was jealous of Cripps; and although Attlee understood the situation, his difficulty was that Bevin enjoyed "an immense influence in the country." The situation, Jackson warned, was "exceedingly delicate and must be handled with the utmost care and discretion."[151] If anything, Jackson admitted to Cadogan, he regretted his "own personal inability to convince" Bevin of the "honesty and objectivity" of Lie's motives. In fact, he had thought it "unwise" to inform Lie that his "integrity had been challenged." His personal experience was that Lie was a friend to both Great Britain and the United States. While noting that his own personal position was unimportant, Jackson denied the London suggestion that he was an innocent dispatched to execute a subtle plan concocted by the secretary-general. He had proceeded to London though he and Lie were both aware that the mission might be misconstrued, which was exactly what happened.[152]

Cadogan's reaction was sympathetic. As he observed to Jebb, he gathered that Jackson "had been a bit knocked about in London." Back in New York he was somewhat "chastened but not repentant." He was sure that Jackson thought it his duty to place before London the secretary-general's doubts about the United Nations' future, which naturally depended on continued cooperation between Washington and London. Cadogan was convinced that this was what Lie had in mind and dismissed the notion that Lie was a "catspaw of the Russians" or "merely self-seeking." In fact, Cadogan knew that Lie had come to the point of resigning several times during the previous months.

Nevertheless, as he had noted to Jackson, Lie was "misguided as to his proper powers and functions." In the London conversations, reference had been made several times to Lie's powers under Article 99, which were restricted to merely bringing a matter to the council's attention. As that organ was already seized with the Palestine question, there was nothing additional that Lie "could or should do about it." The problem was that Lie had consistently envisaged himself as "playing a dramatic" personal role in international politics. Cadogan had told Jackson that the British accepted that Lie had no ulterior motives in this episode but had merely been concerned for the United Nations' future. However, linking the European Recovery Program to London's Palestine policy had been unwise.

In his notes about this letter, Jebb agreed with Cadogan but felt that there would be a time lapse before Jackson again volunteered "to act as a

lightning-conductor." Wright's comment was pithy and less understanding: he doubted that Lie had been well-intentioned. Sargent was equally
negative. The trouble was that Lie had tried to combine helpfulness with
drama, a very difficult combination in the situation in which Lie found
himself.[153]

Jackson's mission had been an unmitigated disaster. Lie had fallen into
the same trap as others had, and it would snare them in the future; namely,
the notion that summit diplomacy through personal exchanges, directly
or through surrogates as in this case, can be more effective than exchanges
through established channels. It is a misconception that diplomacy can be
accomplished in a helter-skelter fashion, without the meticulous preparation necessary to avoid misunderstanding and to assure that subsequent
discussions and the grammatical construct of any agreements will flow
along convergent lines. Syntactical divergency on verbs, nouns, and tenses,
euphemistically referred to as semantic arguments, disguises fundamental
substantive disagreements difficult to bridge. The use and importance of
established channels had been pressed on Cordier by the State Department
and on Lie by Cadogan, but to no avail.

The fuse on Jackson's mission, however, sputtered for a few days longer,
much to everyone's annoyance. A press leak about Jackson's visit spurred
Bevin to query Cadogan on the story's source.[154] When Cadogan called on
Lie he was shown a copy of the *New York Sun*, which cited the story under
a London date line, reported by the Associated Press, and attributed to the
Foreign Office. Lie had been placed in a very embarrassing position with
the press, Jackson informed Jebb, the very situation he had wanted to
avoid. The fat was in the fire. Jebb denied that the leak originated in the
Foreign Office and maintained the story appeared inspired by someone
from the United Nations, published in the London *Daily Telegraph* of May
27. The Foreign Office's public admission that Bevin had indeed received a
message from Lie raised the secretary-general's blood pressure even more.
Bevin was in turn furious and threatened, if further leaks occurred, to publicly disclose all the exchanges during Jackson's visit. The leak, he claimed,
had placed the British government in an awkward position. Cadogan, however, would have none of that and pulled Bevin up short, pointing out that,
from the *New York Sun* story, it appeared the information originated in
London from the Foreign Office. Unless Bevin could offer evidence that the
story originated at the United Nations, Cadogan did not see how he could
again approach Lie. The impression conveyed is that Cadogan was getting
just a bit weary of it all. A detailed investigation by Jackson caused him to
conclude that, although the information originated in New York, it had
not come from a member of the secretariat.[155]

The press leak naturally made it necessary for Bevin to cover himself,
and Jackson's mission was divulged to the American ambassador. Lie had
been under pressure regarding Palestine, it was explained to him, from dif-

ferent sources including Zionists and unnamed members of the Truman administration. The European Recovery Program aspect was of particular concern to the ambassador, who asked Washington for more details.[156] Under-Secretary Lovett described the events leading to Jackson's departure for London and denied that Lie had been under pressure by any member of the Truman administration or that he had been informed that Washington would withhold recovery program aid unless British policy changed. The State Department feared Jackson was a "meddler" who apparently believed that he should "act as a mediator among the Big Five on political questions." He had not been "entirely discreet" and had probably exceeded his instructions, and what had happened could be "explained by Jackson's own personality and temperament."[157] These comments about Jackson's role were grossly unfair. There might not have been administration pressure on Lie, as Lovett claimed, but the possibility cannot be dismissed, since Truman's adviser on minority affairs, David Niles, had applied such pressure on the American mission during the partition debates in November 1947. Niles was Jewish, an avid Zionist born in Czarist Russia, identified by the FBI as a Soviet Russian agent,[158] and the Jewish Agency's direct conduit to Truman's office.[159] Although he was not aware of it, Jackson's days were now numbered.

Understandably, Jackson decided to get back in Bevin's good graces[160] and by mid-July he felt he was.[161] The same did not apply to his status with Lie. From the beginning they had taken an "instant dislike to each other."[162] He was "very annoyed" with Jackson's handling of his May mission to Bevin, he told Sargent on August 4. Moreover, it had now dawned on him that Jackson was relatively inexperienced in diplomacy or in understanding foreign policy. Otherwise, Lie was pleased with Jackson's work in the administration of the United Nations.[163] Two weeks after these words, however, Lie complained that he could not mesh with the other assistant secretaries-general and would have to be dismissed. It would cause talk, but Lie said he saw no way to avoid the decision.[164]

The boom was lowered on Jackson on the night of August 19. His functional position as assistant secretary-general for general coordination was all wrong and it would not work, Lie held. Jackson was bewildered as he later admitted. When Cadogan took up the matter with Lie on the following day, his account of what had led to the dismissal differed from Jackson's. In his conversation with Jackson, Lie let slip that his appointment would contribute to difficulties with senior secretariat staff. When Jackson later queried whether this meant in the future or in the past, Lie disingenuously replied in the future. But Lie was obviously guilt ridden, for he simultaneously exclaimed with emotion that Jackson had been a victim of Lie's own defective judgment and had been struck a low blow.[165] Technically Jackson was not dismissed; the new position was merely abolished in line with Lie's initial understanding that it and Jackson's appointment would be provisional and subject to review.[166] Jackson generously skirted any "personal conjecture" to Cadogan as to what had occurred.[167] Cordier, to his "astonishment," was informed by Lie that Jackson's appointment would be terminated. Cordier thought the decision "regrettable" since Jackson had much to offer; although Lie and Jackson were "temperamentally" so different that he did not see how they could have worked in tandem for any extended period of time.[168] Ever loyal to Lie, Cordier gave the American mission Lie's version of what had transpired and emphasized that Jackson's stay in the secretariat had been "stormy"; he had refused to conform to Lie's workstyle and had also "upset," in particular, Assistant Secretaries-General Price and Sobolev.[169]

The influence of the latter with Lie needs no additional comment. As to Price, it appears that somehow he had latched onto what the State Department knew of Jackson's mission and then used the information to undermine Jackson's position with Lie.[170] To have had the initiative go askew with Bevin was bad enough; to learn of Washington's negative reaction through Price was to add insult to injury and explains Lie's delayed and negative comments about Jackson's London mission to Sargent. Indeed, as late as June 29 Lie attempted to arrange through the American mission to have Jackson received by Ambassador Lewis Douglas in London. McClintock naturally denied the request and aborted an apparent attempt to generate a second London mission.[171] Then, or subsequently, the State Department views on Jackson and the London mission were apparently leaked to Price. Under these conditions, Jackson's inability to mesh with his colleagues or with Lie, mirrored in Cordier's comments, was the façade presented for the decision taken;[172] but the real and undetected reason was Lie's real or imagined political embarrassment over Jackson's handling of his mission. London's real annoyance had been, not so much the mission itself, and certainly not Jackson's behavior, but the suspicion that the British government was being threatened with a loss of European Recovery Program aid if it did not mend its policy on Palestine. In such a situation the Foreign Office's attempt to have Lie reconsider his decision to abolish Jackson's post had no chance of success, but London went through the motions anyway.

McNeil tried, in a pressing message on August 28; but Lie responded with a firm but polite no.[173] Jackson was not involved in this effort, which disturbed him as he harbored no ill-will toward Lie.[174] McNeil made another attempt in a personal letter on September 22. It did not appear to be a sound decision, either from Lie's interests or those of the Foreign Office, McNeil argued. Certainly it appeared to him personally not the most judicious way to end the relationship. Jackson was a senior civil servant, a man of drive and some influence; although he had not complained, it would be surprising if he did not think he had been somewhat curtly handled. If Lie's decision was final, McNeil would accept it, since he had always believed that London should not attempt to pressure anyone in Lie's position. Nevertheless, he found it very difficult to agree with him.[175]

Although Lie had obviously not so intended, Jackson's dismissal had reflected on the British government, as McNeil's bitter letter clearly showed. The incident was tucked away in the human memory banks at the Foreign Office. Whitehall, however, had conveniently forgotten its League of Nations experience. Jackson was not the first, nor would he be the last, secretariat official terminated for reasons of state, or to assuage the amour-propre of some secretary-general. Whatever his shortcomings, Jackson, as Cordier correctly pointed out, had had much to contribute.

Aftermath

On Lie's suggestion the council on May 20, 1948, appointed Count Folke Bernadotte as its mediator in Palestine. He was a member of the Swedish royal family and president of Sweden's Red Cross.[176] Lie claimed him as a close friend.[177] He subsequently held that Bernadotte and the Swedish royal family were friendly to the Zionist cause and that all the count desired was to win the Nobel Peace Prize.[178] Or, as Lie maintained to the *New York Times'* Cyrus Sulzberger, himself Jewish, Bernadotte "was pro-Jewish by bias."[179] Whether or not true, these views no doubt explain Lie's suggestion of him for the post; but being pro-Jewish was a far cry from being pro-Zionist and an unquestioning supporter of all Israeli actions and desires. This probable dichotomy might partially explain Lie's initial "misgivings" over Bernadotte's "intentions" and "tendencies" and his impression that the Israelis would have to show the "utmost firmness, [and] tenacity" in dealing with Bernadotte as his actions tended toward "appeasement" of the Arabs.[180] Lie's later views were more generous,[181] perhaps because he perceived Bernadotte as more pro-Zionist and less pro-Arab than he had originally judged, but this early undercutting of Bernadotte's endeavors with the Israelis startles the imagination. It is no wonder that when Eban wanted to terminate Bernadotte's mediatory role he considered Lie as a potential ally in any such endeavor.[182]

Nevertheless Lie was deeply affected when Bernadotte and a French companion, Colonel André Serot, were murdered on September 17 by unidentified Jewish terrorists in a well-planned assassination in Israel-controlled Jerusalem.[183] Naturally Lie delivered a eulogy for Bernadotte, written by Stoneman, which correctly noted that Bernadotte and Serot's unidentified killers had been dressed in Jewish uniforms. Stoneman also privately recommended that Lie sever his Israeli contacts until the assassins were arrested, tried, and executed. Feller and Foote as well as others were angry with Stoneman, and Lie likewise felt that Stoneman had over-done it.[184]

As Eban pointed out to Weizmann, Lie had "been a tower of strength" to the Israelis and they continued to retain "his full sympathy and coop-eration" even in the days following Bernadotte's assassination.[185] Indeed, even before Bernadotte's murder Lie showed no discontent regardless of the stance assumed by Israel on a number of issues, and when informed by one Israeli representative that "his 'baby Israel' [was] growing very well," Lie retorted " 'It grows very fast and has already learned to talk, in fact, it talks very much and particularly likes to say 'no.' ' "[186]

No sooner was the state of Israel established than Lie was tendering advice on the procedure to be followed to overcome the political and ad-ministrative obstacles to its admission to the United Nations. He rendered particular assistance with the Scandinavian states, who for various reasons had their qualms about admitting Israel to the world organization.[187] In view of his commitment to universality of membership—there were some pariahs, of course—it was an easy role to assume. Likewise, in the negotia-tions that continued after Bernadotte's assassination, Lie was solidly in the Zionist camp on the question of ceding the Negev and Beersheba to Israel. Specifically, when asked to suggest Israel's withdrawal from Beersheba, Lie held that a simple glance at the map made it obvious that the area was vital for Israel and not for Egypt. Accordingly, he instructed Acting Media-tor Ralph Bunche, in line with Eban's desire, to side with Israel's position on the question.[188] Israeli downing of British planes in January 1949 again moved Lie to render Tel Aviv assistance, largely based on the desire of Bunche to avoid council recriminations that might have had a negative impact on the negotiations being conducted on the Greek Dodecanesian island of Rhodes. Lie urged the British not to appeal the matter to the council. The quid pro quo was that Lie would urge the Israelis not to appeal to that same organ British moves in the area as military threats. Lie and Cordier feared these British moves might harden the Egyptian position to-ward the Rhodes negotiations, where they hoped to secure a settlement.[189]

By mid-January 1949, Lie's endeavors in the Palestine and other ques-tions had made him a marked man. The possibility of using him as an "impressive neutral" to help bridge the gap between Washington and Lon-don over the Arab-Israeli problem was discounted by Minister of State Hector McNeil, who held that Lie would be unacceptable to Whitehall and was "ineffective at any rate."[190] By this point, the Israeli-Egyptian negotia-tions had commenced on Rhodes under Bunche's chairmanship and on Feb-ruary 24 both sides signed an armistice agreement. Lie lauded the "ability and skill" of Bunche in these negotiations. Since Lie was not a self-effacing person he was inclined to bestow upon himself some of the credit for their success because he had given Bunche, he claimed, "a considerable amount of wise political advice." Having previously been an "extraordinary 'Number Two man'" in the secretariat, Bunche, according to Lie, "was now demonstrating that he could be a good 'Number One man.'" In Lie's mind, "Bunche and Feller were the two most capable Americans in the Secretariat, and perhaps the two most capable of any nationality." There were moments, Lie admitted, when "he was undecided as to which was the better all-around man." With Sobolev poised to depart from the secretariat for seemingly greener fields as chief of the American desk in the Russian Foreign Ministry, a vacuum was in the making, and it was only natural that others would move up to fill it.

Lie worried that the American government might soon steal Bunche away from him because of his notable qualifications, but he was assured on that score. As to the coming armistice negotiations with Jordan, Lie hoped that everything would go well, but feared that London "might throw some monkey wrenches into the machinery." He noted that the British had "always played 'a dirty game' in Palestine." Lie suspected that at this point the Jordanians would be used as the wrecking instrument.[191] He was wrong and must have realized it when he learned from Bunche of secret Israeli-Jordanian negotiations. He approved of these, which soon led to an armistice agreement on April 3.[192] Damascus's procrastination, however, in withdrawing to the Syrian-Palestine mandate frontier line caused some in Tel Aviv to suggest that Lie be urged to pressure the Syrian authorities to withdraw, mobilize American efforts in this direction, and dispatch Bunche with instructions to press the Syrians to pull back forthwith.[193] Whether this was done is unclear. Nevertheless, Lie persisted in his anti-British animus in the Palestine question and in other matters.[194] From Lie's comments one gets the impression that his view of Bunche was Olympian. In fact, it was probably more of a mixed bag, for as in Bernadotte's case, Lie waffled when fending off Eban's criticism of Bunche. It was probably a relatively painless stance to assume since Sobolev, who had previously supported Bunche, now joined the Israeli chorus of complaint.[195] The subsequent award of the Nobel Peace Prize to Bunche for his work filled him with pride, Lie later claimed, and was a tribute to the world organization and its secretariat for their role in settling international disputes.[196] But the fact of the matter was that Lie found it difficult to "accept that one of his officials had become the focus of world attention."[197] Lie no doubt resented that his perceived contributions to peace in Palestine, unlike those of Bunche, had gone publicly unacknowledged.

Lie's attitude toward Bunche was less than friendly.[198] It was partially reflected in denying Bunche the mediator's salary he was entitled to, claiming that Price had blocked it, and Price claiming the reverse, with the ever discreet Cordier having to admit that the great man did "not like to raise the salary of a member of his staff to a point higher than his own." It was a reaction, Thomas Power of the American mission observed, "based on emotion more than on administrative principle." In fact Bunche did not receive his due remuneration until June 1949, after many months.[199] With Bunche's reputation established Lie now attempted to use him to lobby for Israel's early admission to the United Nations. Bunche felt that it was inappropriate for him to do so because of his mediatory role; he also had some preconditions to Israel's admission: a report on Bernadotte's assassination; Tel Aviv's attitude toward Arab refugees and Jerusalem's internationalization; and lastly, Israel's boundary demands.[200] Lie's reaction is unknown. He attempted also to meddle, through Cordier and Dragon Protitch, a Yugoslav secretariat official in the Department of Security Council Affairs, in the task of the Palestine Conciliation Commission established by the assembly in December 1948 and composed of the Big Five. This irritated the French no end.[201] The Americans, perhaps because of their greater experience with Lie, were less irked than the French when he expressed a desire to help. Based on the suggestion of the conciliation commission's principal secretary, Azcárate y Florez, Lie wished to use his influence with both the Arabs and Israelis to compromise the stalemated negotiations of the conciliation commission in Lausanne. In view of the hostile Arab attitude toward him, what influence Lie thought he had with them remains a mystery. Lie's desire no doubt rang the State Department's alarm bells, if one can judge from previous reactions to Lie's desires to assume initiatives. Lie, however, was gently fended off with the message that the American representative on the conciliation commission would suggest that it adjourn for a few weeks—which it did—during which time Washington intended to conduct strenuous diplomatic endeavors to have the conciliation commission come to a solution before the assembly convened. The State Department promised to keep Lie informed of its plans after it had heard from the American representative on the conciliation commission, when Lie might perhaps join Washington in a "mutual effort to achieve a successful solution."[202] Obviously, it would be a safer endeavor if it were mutual endeavor, and Lie floated under the fantail of an American man-of-war.

Since he was clearly being kept at arm's length, Lie suggested that Jessup, whom he admired and for whom he had a soft spot, be appointed as the world organization's representative to devise a solution for the assembly to the whole Palestine question. Lie expected that the conciliation commission would be unable to offer a proposal acceptable to both sides and that the stalemate would be repeated in the assembly. Jessup, in Lie's mind, would in effect be Bunche's identical twin in the Palestine question's second phase. Power, to whom Cordier had reported all this, restricted himself to the ironic comment that he had sympathy for his ambassadorial colleague "faced with a problem which had so long defied solution."[203] Lie was clutching at straws. Almost a month later, July 20, the Syrian-Israeli armistice agreement was signed.

By August, it was probably beginning to dawn on Lie that what had sprouted in a partitioned Palestine was not a desert flower but a burning bush. It was his personal opinion, he casually observed to the American ambassador in Oslo, that Palestine would be a long-term problem.[204] So true. A week later he had occasion to discuss the work of the conciliation commission with the American representative, Paul Porter, who explained that Washington would seek to effect a political solution through economic measures. It wanted the conciliation commission to establish an Economic Survey Mission to study and recommend specific projects to help resettlement of the Palestine Arab refugees and also to devise a plan for the whole area's general economic development. Settling the refugee problem would go far in removing one of the major obstacles to a political settlement. Naturally Lie was receptive to the idea, and instructed Cordier to recruit for the survey mission the best people possible. He had always thought, he observed to Porter, that the Palestine problem needed patience. The peace treaties could not be obtained in a few months time; rather, each specific problem should be settled between the parties through the conciliation commission or directly. He then pressed on Porter Eban's prior proposal for direct talks between the Arabs and Israelis, which Eban alleged the conciliation commission had discouraged. Porter denied the allegation and gave Lie a detailed account of what had transpired. He held that Eban's contention was only an attempt to place the onus on the conciliation commission for a situation that in large part could be traced to Israeli "intractability."[205]

This latter quality caused Lie to protest strongly to Eban about Israeli violations of the armistice, which he considered "particularly unjustified" since machinery existed to settle the matter peacefully.[206] Lie's step was wise for matters were to be considered where restraint would assist him to defend Tel Aviv's interests. The report of the conciliation commission's Economic Survey Mission was a case in point. Its contemplated recommendation of a development authority for the area, divorced from a United Nations framework, disturbed Lie immensely. Any development authority for the area not tied to the United Nations, he argued, "would lead to confusion and misunderstanding." Within the organization's framework, although he did not say so, the development authority might equally assist Israel and also be under Lie's constant surveillance. Accordingly, he maintained, the survey mission had to consider the "long-standing and considerable" involvement by the United Nations in Palestine. Cordier, no doubt echoing his master's unconveyed thoughts, added that it was not in Washington's interests to do otherwise for it would open itself to the charge of imperialism and disregard of the world organization.[207] Lie won his point, for the end product was the establishment of the United Nations Relief and Works Agency for Palestine Refugees in the Near East[208]—which, however, had no regional economic development functions.

Conversely, Lie was disinclined to have the United Nations assume any administrative responsibility for the Palestine Arab refugees. As early as August 1948, he observed to Foreign Office Permanent Under-Secretary Sir Orme Sargent that he "saw no reason" why the International Refugee Organization could not tackle the matter provided it was given financial assistance.[209] Lie justified his resistance on the grounds that "he was strongly opposed to any extension of the Secretariat's operating activities." Based on prior experience, Lie was convinced, he said, that operational activities like handling the Arab refugees were "detrimental" to the United Nations' main political task.[210] The question of the refugees, however, was as much humanitarian as it was political. Viewing it as an administrative burden on the secretariat could be justified provided the underlying political aspects were always kept to the fore. He argued, for example, with the Egyptians and the Arab League, who were disappointed with the United Nations over the refugee issue, that the world situation had to be kept to the fore and priorities established; and the principal priority, he maintained, was to resist communism—the Korean war was by then in earnest—and they had to be patient.[211] Although Lie did not totally ignore the political problems bedeviling settlement of the refugee issue, he no doubt thought that somehow, and with time, the refugees would be absorbed by the surrounding Arab states.[212] It was not to be. What Lie and perhaps others failed to see was that the dialectics of nationalism had concocted a new Diaspora catalyzed by the noncooperation of the Palestine Arabs with the Palestine Committee and the Arab world's rejection of the partition plan, which envisaged a Zionist state much smaller than the one finally established after the partition fighting. And how could one logically deny to the Palestine Arabs the very thing that had been demanded by the Zionists for the Jews, namely, a national state?

The status of Jerusalem, which came before the assembly's Ad Hoc Committee in the autumn of 1949, was another matter that required Lie's attention. Initially in the summer of 1948, supported by the Americans, Lie opposed the internationalization of Haifa on the basis that it was totally Jewish and saw Jerusalem as the "only proper object [of] international control."[213] As early as April 1949, however, with the Israelis controlling one half of Jerusalem Lie opposed its internationalization.[214] It was an "impractical approach," he argued, that would not be accepted either by the Israelis or the Jordanians, who controlled the other half of the city. The United Nations, he pointed out, lacked the two army divisions needed to impose any such solution on both sides.[215] An Australian draft resolution proposing that the Palestine Conciliation Commission be instructed to reconsider urgently a permanent international regime for Jerusalem in closer harmony with the partition resolution of November 29, 1947, disturbed Lie. He very much "regretted" the draft resolution, he told the Australian mission. He thought Evatt had unwisely introduced it and it had caused him, Lie observed, much trouble. The Israelis had protested to him; and Lie held that while Evatt meant well, he was being badly advised; and he asked that Evatt be contacted about the matter. This was done, but Evatt was so annoyed he instructed that the Australian mission press ahead with its earlier instructions.[216]

Lie was pleased by the American stance, which paralleled his own;[217] but the Ad Hoc Committee nonetheless forwarded to the assembly a draft resolution recommending an international regime for Jerusalem. Although a joint draft resolution by the Netherlands and Sweden provided for the appointment by the secretary-general of a Jerusalem commissioner,[218] Lie informed Cadogan that it would be absolutely impossible to find anyone to assume the post.[219] However, Lie's endeavors behind the scenes to assist the Israelis by thwarting any assembly resolution recommending the internationalization of Jerusalem came to naught. The requisite resolution was passed on December 9, 1949.[220] The decision left him dissatisfied and he had "very real doubts" about it, he informed the Americans; but he would instruct the secretariat to accept loyally the assembly's decision.[221]

Two years later Lie officially visited the Middle East and saw at first hand the places and peoples who had merely been names to him.[222] Damascus and Tel Aviv were initially included in the itinerary. To make certain that the former was visited, Lie was nudged by the Western powers; a wise step also dictated in the hope that he would counsel moderation to both sides, since Syria and Israel were going at each other hammer and tongs.[223] The Damascus government received him with the courtesy and respect befitting his high office. The same did not hold true for the opposition press, which labeled him as pro-Jewish and was matched by a bitter parliamentary debate where he was branded an enemy of the Arab peoples.[224] In Lebanon, the American legation reported, "Lie gave the impression of not having hitherto been fully aware of the impact of the refugees on the Lebanese economy and the intense local political feeling on the subject."[225] He visited some of the Palestine Arab refugee camps but fortunately missed the one at Baalbek where it appears a land mine had been planted on the road leading to the camp entrance so that Lie's car would run over it.[226] Lie emphatically assured Shertok that in going to Egypt he would not miss Israel either on his way in or on his way out. In preparation for Lie's visit, and keeping in mind that during this period he was under attack from various quarters, arrangements were made to gear up the Israeli press for a rash of editorials extolling the United Nations and Lie's own position.[227] Naturally Weizmann viewed Lie's visit with pleasure.[228] During his stay in Israel Lie counseled "greater moderation" to the Israelis, and especially to the military.[229] The metamorphosis of interstate relations in the Middle East eroded whatever impact his advice had and following the 1967 Arab-Israeli war, the retired Lie was uneasy over Tel Aviv's "post-victory attitudes." Likewise, he was highly critical of the way the crisis leading to the war had been handled by the United Nations, and especially by Secretary-General U Thant, who certainly, Lie held, could have discovered "ways of delaying the withdrawal" of the United Nations Emergency Force from Suez.[230] The latter comment was well taken, but when it comes to the Palestine problem Thant is not the only secretary-general who can be criticized.

It is odd that Lie who spent the first years of his tenure as secretary-general trying to build bridges between East and West should, when faced with the Palestine question, have attempted no bridge building whatsoever. If there were ever a question facing the United Nations that needed someone to span the gap between the parties, this was it. Lie's reasons for hurtling himself into Zionist ranks, first surreptitiously, then openly and perceivably from Arab ranks, was due to many factors some of which have been touched upon earlier. Whether any bridge-building efforts by a secretary-general could have been in any way effective is open to serious doubts, for the gap between the parties was wide and deep. His pro-Zionist stance, however, destroyed whatever chances Lie might have had of being a bridge between Jews and Arabs, or of subsequently developing an Arab constituency. It was perhaps this bitter experience that caused him in 1951, during a procedural wrangle in the assembly over the Moroccan and Tunisian questions, to remark that "the Arabs were always bad Parliamentarians"[231]—a less than generous observation.

Nevertheless, by assuming the position of one side in this question, ostensibly but insincerely based on the partition resolution of November 29, 1947, Lie committed one of the cardinal sins that should be avoided by any secretary-general; namely, to so ally himself to one camp that it feels, in conjunction with other political advantages it may possess, that it is superfluous to search for an accommodation with its opponent. In the last analysis, only accommodation makes it possible for competitors to live in relative peace. Several wars later, and after many undeclared ones not to mention countless acts of violence and terrorism by both sides, social dislocation, lives ruined, and the endless expenditures of treasure, it can be legitimately asked whether some solution other than the one devised was not only more desirable but feasible. The possibilities were limited. For obvious political reasons the British wanted to withdraw from Palestine and relinquish the mandate. The evolution of the mandate into a United Nations trusteeship was unattainable, for with the exception of Soviet Russia, no other member of the Big Five, alone or collectively, because of local and international political conditions, was willing to assume the unappetizing task of enforcing such an arrangement. These same political conditions explain the desire to avoid an enforcement of the partition resolution. The Jews and the Arabs were left to their own devices, and this entailed the clash of arms. Not counting the social-political changes and undesirable political phenomenon that the endemic anarchy of the Palestine question breeds within the immediately concerned states, one can question whether the anarchic subsystem that it has spawned can be curbed; an anarchy that threatens in everwidening ripples other peoples and nations who are drawn into its vortex. Even in 1948 there were Cassandras, but others who, though well-meaning, were also unthinking about what the future might hold once Palestine was divided—and Lie was among them. The old adage still holds that the road to hell is often paved with good intentions.

7

INITIATIVES
EVERYWHERE
1949-1950

Seating Yugoslavia in the Security Council

The problem of Yugoslavia and Soviet Russia developed when Marshal Tito broke with Stalin and the Cominform in June 1948. By the summer of 1949, Yugoslav-Russian relations were fast approaching their nadir. Since the General Assembly selected the Security Council's nonpermanent members, rumors were rife about possible candidates for these seats. In an obvious attempt to needle Russian Assistant Secretary-General Konstantin Zinchenko, Lie mischievously inquired whether it was correct that Moscow favored Tito's Yugoslavia for one of the nonpermanent seats. Personally, Lie thought Belgrade's candidacy would be very advantageous and "would be quite embarrassing to the Soviets," he told the Americans.[1]

The Yugoslavs made their move in late September when Lie was approached by Aleš Bebler, the deputy foreign minister, who very strongly urged Lie to support Belgrade's candidacy. Despite his prior comments Lie did not commit himself but simply asked if Belgrade could not liquidate immediately its role in the Greek guerrilla war. The whole question of a nonpermanent seat, Lie noted to Ross, "was a very complex matter of world politics," and he felt that he lacked the competence to express an opinion until he had ascertained the American viewpoint. Ross explained that the Yugoslav approach to Lie was a surprise, that Washington had played no role in this initiative, and that the American mission's position on the matter had not yet crystallized.[2] Several days after this conversation, Lie was informed by Zinchenko that the Russians were greatly troubled by the Yugoslav candidacy. Concurrently Vyshinsky added some "vague and obscure threats,"[3] all of which caused Lie to shift gears. He now suggested that the American mission "should consider this problem carefully."[4] When John Hickerson, the assistant secretary of state for United Nations affairs, called on Lie on September 27 to inform him that the United States would vote for Yugoslavia's candidacy but would not campaign for it, Lie responded that as secretary-general he could only observe that the American decision would make the assembly's work even more onerous. To Hickerson's surprise, Lie then added that speaking solely as Trygve Lie, he fully understood Washington's decision and that he sympathized with Yugoslavia.[5] Maybe so, but his behind-the-scenes endeavors, it appears, did not dovetail with his proclaimed sympathies.

Two days later Lie unburdened himself to Eleanor Roosevelt, who he perhaps thought would be more understanding than Hickerson. Speaking with emotion he expressed serious anxiety that Moscow might abandon the United Nations because it was under the quickening pressure of American positions on China and the Yugoslav candidacy. American actions "were a direct affront to Stalin who hated the Yugoslavs more than anyone else." Lie considered the Russian-Yugoslav embroglio Stalin's most serious challenge in years, since it was basically a battle for mastership of the communist movement and an attack on Stalin's prestige. Accordingly, Washington's support of Belgrade's candidacy and Peking's complaints against Moscow for interfering in its affairs were very dangerous. Lie held that the Americans did not understand the Russians and were therefore mistakenly pressing Moscow too hard. Eleanor Roosevelt's retort, however, was merely that very many states like the United States had difficulty in fathoming the Russians.

In a long monologue Lie maintained that, while he was in accord with the ends of United States policy toward Soviet Russia, he feared that the Western states were moving too quickly. Although he agreed that Belgrade should attempt to free itself from Moscow's shackles, similarly, he had told Belgrade that it had been unwise to press its candidacy for the council. Lie had been frightened by the Berlin blockade, the Western airlift, and Norway's adherence to the North Atlantic Pact, the most serious episodes in the postwar period. The current crisis frightened him more so, in that the Russians might exit from the United Nations, and he strongly urged that Washington carefully consider its position on Belgrade and Peking's complaint against Moscow. Did he fear Soviet Russia would go to war?

Roosevelt asked. No, Lie responded, only that Moscow would withdraw from the United Nations. Nor was there danger of war between Russia and Yugoslavia: Moscow was merely executing its previous policy, attempting to foment an internal rebellion as in China. He did not want to see that occur and was surprised that Tito had not yet been murdered. He felt that China, the United States, and Yugoslavia were equally to blame for the situation that had developed, since they had not considered adequately the reactions that might develop from their actions.

Russian feelings on this matter, Secretary of State Acheson admitted, were intense. Tito's defection was an internal heresy that had to be suppressed. Nevertheless, Lie had grounds for being alarmed. However, once Belgrade presented its candidacy Washington had to come to a decision, and Acheson considered it most important that Belgrade be the "preferred candidate." This would place both Belgrade and Moscow in the council when discussion of their relations took place. Less generous than Acheson was Norway's representative at the United Nations, Arne Sunde who made "rather uncomplimentary remarks" about Lie to the Americans and indicated that he felt "Lie's sympathies were not wholly with the West." He thought that, at the minimum, Lie tended to be "jittery."[6]

Following his talk with Roosevelt, Lie was exposed again to Russian animus toward Yugoslavia at a dinner hosted by Vyshinsky: his impression was that hatred of the Yugoslavs was the Russians' "dominating passion" at the current assembly,[7] which could only have reinforced his belief that the Russians were being pushed too far, too fast. Ross personally thought "it was a mistake to adopt a timid posture when confronted with Russian opposition to some measure." He did not think problems could be solved by avoiding them: unlike Lie, Ross did not believe even for a moment that Yugoslavia's election to the council would destroy the United Nations. Suggestions by General Carlos Romulo of the Philippines, which were an attempt to assuage the Russians and sidetrack the Yugoslav candidacy, Ross considered based on erroneous information and tended to confirm his suspicion that Lie was "probably lobbying very actively against the Yugoslav candidacy."[8]

His presumed lobbying led nowhere: Yugoslavia was elected on the first ballot. Lie, although pleased at the Yugoslav-Russian split, was still concerned at the possible Russian reaction and reiterated that Belgrade had been most unwise to push its candidacy and others to support it. He thought the Russians should have been warned that if the eastern European bloc had no consensus candidate, the assembly would select a state from outside the area. This procedure, he naively told the Americans, would not have challenged Moscow—as though the caucus for the eastern European seat was something less than a Russian dictat. Lie was upset when his conversation with Roosevelt leaked to the press, although he was able to deny it since it had been reported somewhat inaccurately. He suspected that the leak had occurred in the State Department in an attempt to embarrass him—a not unreasonable suspicion.

Lie found it difficult to understand how Moscow could be so foolish as to believe that it could elect Czechoslovakia over Yugoslavia while Prague was in the middle of a purge. He had warned the Russians through Zinchenko that they would lose the vote. Lie agreed with an American interlocutor that the Russians would not depart from the world organization, particularly the council, from anger over a lost electoral struggle, but only as a deliberate step. He felt, however, that a series of defeats might have accumulative effects, persuading Moscow that the United Nations was of little value to it. Lie thought the Russian response would occur at the latest in a year's time. When he mentioned to Zinchenko that the Russians might take some quick action in response to Yugoslavia's election, the latter retorted that Moscow "moved very slowly in important matters."⁹

As so often in the past, Lie had seemingly worried only about Russia's reactions and amour-propre; that his stance might generate Western hostility appeared to escape him as did the fact that the West also had interests to protect. Certainly in the matter of Yugoslavia's candidacy, he failed to perceive that his intervention could have, at best, only minimal impact and might be resented, adding considerably to any jaundiced views held about him, especially in American ranks—which the leak about his conversation with Roosevelt clearly evidenced.

Which China?

Asian affairs, in which Lie had little interest or knowledge, did not monopolize his attention during his first years as secretary-general.¹⁰ Although Far Eastern matters, as in Indonesia, Kashmir, as well as Korea, intruded on his schedule during this period, the real vortex of world politics was western Europe. The tensions between East and West in this arena drew his primary attention, and the only time, it appears, he used his office to intervene in Asian affairs was at the start of Indonesia's attempt to acquire independence from the Netherlands.¹¹

Thus the civil war in China, even as it increased in intensity, failed to attract Lie's attention. Unofficially the fighting between the Nationalist government forces led by General Chiang Kai-shek and the Kuomintang party and the Communist party forces led by Mao Tse-tung was brought to Lie's attention by a private Chinese organization as early as May 1948, but it appears to have evoked no response.¹²

The issue was again raised unofficially, but this time publicly, when Lie was asked during a press conference in early January 1949, whether he and Foreign Minister Evatt intended to intervene to stop the fighting in China. He could not speak for Evatt, Lie responded, but confessed that the problem had not been on his mind and he did not see how he could stop it. He was skeptical and unsure whether Article 99 could be used.[13] Lie's official response soon followed. He doubted his authority to intervene in the civil war; moreover, it did not appear that such a move could be of assistance under current conditions.[14] Within a month, however, a Chinese press report claimed that Lie had contacted the Nationalist government, stating that the United Nations was willing to use its influence to mediate between the parties to promote peace, and that Lie alleged London and Washington agreed to support the world organization in this endeavor.[15]

Lie immediately denied the story. The previous week the irrepressible Evatt had telephoned suggesting that he and Lie mediate the Chinese civil war, the American mission reported, but Lie had wisely replied that "he would not do so."[16] Concurrently the civil war also filtered into the secretariat when it was decided not to recruit any additional Chinese nationals until the situation had clarified itself. Cordier, who was opposed to this step, observed that Lie thought it was "practical politics" to avoid employment of additional secretariat members "who might soon be considered unacceptable" by the authorities in Peking. This policy decision, however, was soon rescinded. Chinese nationals would be recruited, Cordier explained to the Americans, equally with other nationals as circumstances permitted. He feared that if employment of Chinese nationals were deferred now, when some positions were available, it would mean that these positions would be occupied by Communists—the Nationalist forces were militarily on the defensive—to the United Nations' detriment.[17] The episode was an omen of things to come.

For about seven months no further developments affected the United Nations, while in China the enormous struggle waged uncontrolled. By late August 1949, Lie ascertained through Victor Hoo, the assistant secretary-general of trusteeship affairs, that China contemplated adding an item to the assembly's agenda accusing Soviet Russia of interfering in its affairs. Lie strongly opposed such a move since he believed the assembly could take no useful action. Hoo explained that China wanted to take this step both to inform the world and reduce the influence of the State Department's White Paper on recent Chinese-American relations, which had been critical of General Chiang Kai-shek's regime. In an attempt to head off such action, Lie admitted "he had deliberately raised the matter" in a meeting of the assistant secretaries-general (Price and Zinchenko, as well as Cordier) in order to let Washington and Moscow know of the intended Chinese move. Since a confrontation between the Chinese and the Russians would only contribute to increasing tension among the Big Five, especially if the Anglo-Americans supported the move, Lie emphasized that he would do everything possible to dissuade the Chinese from including the item on the assembly's agenda. State Department officers were less than pleased by Lie's action. They agreed that "Lie had been off-base in discussing this matter with his staff"; but Hickerson did not wish Lie to be called to task on the issue at that time, fearing that being forewarned the Russians would be in a stronger tactical position to handle the question. In private, Lie was very emotional over the issue, expressing "strong opposition" to putting the item on the agenda. He urged the Chinese to deal with the question in their general statement, if at all. [18]

The Anglo-Americans, like Lie, were interested in avoiding any formal assembly debate. Lie agreed that some action on the item could not be postponed [19] and therefore agreed with the American desire to refer the question to the Interim Committee for examination and study. [20] This was done by the assembly on December 8, 1949. [21] Quick footwork had circumvented, for the moment, confrontation. However, it could not be long avoided.

Indeed, even as the item was being shunted into the Interim Committee, Lie was contacted by Chou En-lai, foreign minister of the new communist regime in Peking—the Nationalists had been defeated and fled to Formosa (Taiwan). Chou En-lai held that his government was the country's only legal authority. The prior Nationalist regime had lost all rights to represent China and its delegation at the United Nations was the "tool of a handful of exiled elements." He demanded that the United Nations deprive the Nationalist delegation of any right to represent China there in accordance with the charter's principles and spirit. [22] Lie appears to have made no response to this message. If he thought any response might undercut the Anglo-American effort to sidetrack the agenda item or that the issue would soon be handled by the Western powers, making any reply superfluous, he was of course wrong.

Queried by the press in early January 1950 about the question of Chinese representation Lie indicated that he did not consider it "a serious threat" to the world organization. He thought the whole matter had to be decided by the council and the Interim Committee. As for himself, Lie observed, he would be guided by the action of the organs of the United Nations. [23] Two days later on January 8, whether in reaction to Lie's comments is unclear, Chou En-lai again returned to the fray in a message addressed not only to Lie but also to General Assembly President Romulo and to council members, except for the heretical Yugoslavia and Nationalist China. Peking, he maintained, considered "illegal" the continued presence in the United Nations of the Chinese Nationalist delegation, which had to be expelled. [24] This communication propelled the Russian representative, Yakov Malik, to request expulsion of the Chinese Nationalist representative from the council, as he had previously requested on December 29, 1949. If this were not done, he threatened, his delegation would not partake in the council's proceedings. When Malik's motion was defeated he left the chamber. The issue was now joined and there could be no turning back. When the council next convened there was some anxiety whether Malik would appear. He did and pressed his attack, which again was defeated. In a departing statement—he would not appear again in the chamber for six and a half months—Malik declared that his country would neither recognize the legality of any council decision adopted with the participation of the Chinese Nationalist representative nor consider itself bound by such decisions. In the weeks that followed Russian and other communist delegations similarly withdrew from a large number of United Nations bodies.

What did it mean? Was Moscow intent on establishing a rival world organization? Like others, Lie sympathized with those states that had recognized the new government in Peking. Recognition of a government, he correctly held, did not bestow one's approval; recognition was an act of political reality. Chiang Kai-shek was now isolated in Formosa; he did not control, and thus could not represent, China. True enough. Recognition of Peking also tied in with Lie's notion of universality of membership, although China was already a member. In addition, how could the world organization be the meeting ground of East and West in the world political struggle if the communist government that controlled China were excluded from the United Nations?[25] On January 19, Chou En-lai raised the ante. He once again contacted Lie, Romulo, and others, announcing the appointment of Chang Wen Tien as Peking's United Nations representative. He queried when the Nationalist Chinese would be expelled so Chang Wen Tien could attend the council. Lie responded that each United Nations organ was competent to pass upon the credentials of its members, and each one accordingly determined the representation and participation in its work. Lie's anxiety went undisguised. The United Nations' "stock was at its lowest ebb," because of the Chinese question, he observed to the Americans on the following day and opined that the world organization's work "should not be made to suffer because of this 'political struggle.' "[26] Lie had "side-stepped nimbly" Chou En-lai's communication, the Foreign Office's Paul Holmer observed, by treating the matter as a question of credentials; he could hardly have said anything else, and his conclusions dovetailed reasonably well with the procedure favored by Whitehall.[27]

Lie, unsure how he should navigate the maelstrom, wisely decided to consult the major powers. With Price in tow, he repaired to Washington on January 21 to talk to Secretary of State Acheson and his advisers. Lie expressed his deep concern over the situation caused by the Chinese question and the Russian walkout; and he did not know how to react. Unlike previous crises, such as Berlin, the new one was within the United Nations itself. Lie's entire work was based on the premise that Moscow did not want war and that it intended to remain in the United Nations. He now asked himself whether this was so. He thought that the American position on the Chinese question was "reasonable and correct"; namely, that when seven council members on a procedural motion voted to seat Peking's representative this would be done. He acknowledged that Peking's seizure of American and other foreign properties and Washington's understandable reaction, appeared to demonstrate that settlement of the question along lines he had previously envisaged would be neither easy nor soon achieved. Lie hesitatingly raised the possibility of a special assembly session on the question, but Acheson did not think one would be helpful.

Lie then noted that the Chinese Nationalist representative would withdraw from the United Nations whenever Peking was recognized by a majority of the members or if Washington, despite recent developments, recognized Peking. Acheson's reply was evasive but implied that there would be no immediate recognition. Lie asked whether Acheson had information that Moscow was contemplating the use of force. Acheson replied in the negative. Lie then inquired whether there was any information that Moscow was now thinking of leaving the United Nations. Rusk and Hickerson did not think so. What indication did Lie have that Moscow meant to withdraw, Rusk queried. None, Lie replied, but the possibility could not be excluded that its walkouts might lead to ultimate withdrawal unless something intervened. He feared that if Moscow did withdraw it could organize its own United Nations or some similar organization, which would include Peking and the satellite states of eastern Europe. In such an event the United Nations could only continue to function with its remaining members as best it could. Acheson and Rusk agreed.

The United Nations' great difficulty, Lie ruminated, was the failure of the Big Five to agree. He assessed no blame for the failure. No future solution, however, could be discovered except by direct talks between the top political leadership of England, Soviet Russia, and the United States. He admitted, and his hosts agreed, such talks would achieve nothing at that time. He had thought of going to Moscow, he noted, since Vyshinsky had invited him, but wondered whether such a visit could be helpful under current conditions. Acheson agreed that it would be unproductive.

A seemingly innocent comment by Hickerson, however, gave Lie an idea how the Chinese question might be solved and made his trip to Washington worthwhile. Hickerson noted that five states on the council had already recognized Peking—Soviet Russia, Norway, Yugoslavia, India, and England—thus France and Egypt held the key to the Chinese question. Their recognition of Peking would thus provide the seven votes needed in the council on a procedural motion to seat the Peking representative, a solution that Washington had already agreed to accept.[28]

Back at the United Nations, Lie closeted himself with Feller and Kerno to discover how he and the secretariat might affect the situation. Feller's and Kerno's legal opinion was that the Chinese question was procedural, being in the final analysis a question of whose credentials were accepted. The core of the Feller-Kerno argument, based on legal precedents and practice, was that representation in the United Nations had been joined with the question of recognizing a new government or state. This confused two processes that are superficially similar but essentially different. The two had to be separated. Recognizing either a new government or state was the prerogative of another state; whereas both admission to and acceptance of representation in an international organization like the United Nations are collective acts by the member states. It appeared to be legally inadmissible to condition admission or acceptance of representation in an international organization by a requirement that these acts be preceded by the recognition of a new government or state by another state. The obligations of United Nations membership in charter Article 4, could be executed only by governments that possessed the power to do so. If two governments claimed to represent a state, the only real issue was which of the two was in a position to harness the state's resources and its people to fulfill its membership obligations. This required ascertaining whether the new government exercised effective control within the state and was habitually obeyed by the larger part of the population. Appropriately by the membership's decision, United Nations organs would accord that government the right to represent the state in the world organization, even though individual members of the United Nations refused, and might continue to refuse in line with national interests, to accord that government diplomatic recognition. [29]

Armed with this legal opinion, Lie concluded that his four target states on the council were France, Cuba, Ecuador, and Egypt. On January 24, however, he first approached Cadogan, whose experience, sagacity, and service were second to none, and recapitulated the situation for him, as he had for Acheson. In particular he noted his alarm that the Chinese Nationalist representative might invoke the veto in the Chinese question and asked Cadogan point blank whether the British government would vote to unseat the Chinese Nationalist representative if a properly accredited communist representative appeared at the United Nations. Lie pointed out that in "ordinary circumstances" he would have considered that Chou En-lai's message of January 19 "constituted sufficient credentials for the individual named therein." The next council president, he observed, might feel himself bound to examine these credentials and wondered whether it was not possible for members, including those who had not recognized the Chinese communist regime, to vote to accept these credentials. Cadogan disagreed: the question was not only whether the credentials were properly issued by an authority to the individual named but whether this authority was actually the one entitled to issue them.

Lie then queried whether Cadogan thought that London would try to influence Paris and Cairo to recognize the Chinese communist regime. He noted that he had asked the State Department whether Washington would use its influence with Havana but received no assurances; accordingly, he would raise the matter directly with Cuba's council representative. Cadogan confessed that he shared Lie's concern about the course of events, especially since he believed Moscow's policy was calculated to discourage recognition of the Chinese communist regime by Washington and Paris. It seemed peculiar to Cadogan that Moscow, having declared it would stay away as long as the Chinese Nationalists sat in the council, was instigating the Chinese Communists to do everything possible to sustain that very situation. What explanation could one offer for Peking's occupation of American properties in China and its recognition of the Viet-Minh movement, which was in open conflict with the French-supported Indochinese government? Sir Alexander doubted therefore that one could expect any response from Moscow, or Peking, to any probes meant to prepare the way for recognition of the Chinese communist regime. He believed that London would authorize him to vote to unseat Nationalist China, if a properly accredited Communist representative appeared at the United Nations. He understood that Cairo would shortly recognize the Communists. But he was unsure that London would attempt to influence Paris in recognizing them. He agreed with the Americans that no useful purpose would be served by a special assembly session and had no clue what might happen if the Chinese question were dealt with inconsistently by different United Nations organs acting separately. The solution, he held, should be found in the council. He hoped that the Chinese Nationalist representative would step down once a decision had been made favoring the Peking regime. When Lie asked whether he would attend a private Four Power meeting with American, Russian, and Chinese Nationalist representatives to discuss the situation, Cadogan did not refuse but expressed skepticism concerning such a caucus in view of prior experience with Malik's attitude and tactics. Cadogan offered Lie "no special advice" but agreed to keep in touch.[30]

Lie's comment about Chou En-lai's January 19 message being examined by the council's next president obviously bothered Cadogan, and several days later he asked for instructions should this occur. Under the rules of procedure, he warned, Lie reported to the council on credentials. If required to do so in the Chinese question, he would presumably state that according to his standard procedure he would regard Chou En-lai's message as sufficient. If Lie so reported and the matter was voted on, Cadogan did not see how he could refuse to accept the credentials of the Chinese communist representative. This scenario was somewhat different from any resolution proffered to expel the Chinese Nationalist representative from the council. Any motion to accept the Chinese communist credentials would probably be rejected even if the Russians returned and voted in favor. Cadogan understood that Lie was "trying to persuade members" of the council whose governments had not yet recognized the Peking regime that they could nevertheless vote to accept the credentials of the communist representative. It was rumored that these arguments had affected the

Ecuadorian representative, but Cadogan doubted that he would support such a motion. Minister of State McNeil's response was pithy and to the point: He found Lie's argument about Chou En-lai's message "unimpressive."[31] The Foreign Office's initial reaction was that Cadogan should abstain in any vote on the Chinese communist credentials,[32] but this was subsequently reversed.[33] Lie's conversation with Cadogan was followed by discussions with the Cuban, French, Ecuadorian, Egyptian, Indian, Norwegian, and Yugoslavian representatives.[34]

On January 26, he talked with Ross and Ernest Gross of the American mission. His stance was now more frantic than before: unless the Chinese question were solved within four to six weeks, Moscow would depart from the United Nations, take Peking with it, and establish a rival organization comprising hundreds of millions of people. Other United Nations members would also depart, including states like India, which would avoid both organizations in an attempt to maintain neutrality. The world would split in two, destroying the unity and universality upon which the organization was founded. This would increase the probability of war. The problem was very serious and preyed on his mind to the point that he felt it necessary to share his concern with the member states. It was his duty, Lie felt, to devise some way out of the current impasse. When pressed by the Americans, however, Lie had to admit that he had no hard facts to support his assertions about Russia's future tack. He had merely discussed the matter with Yugoslav Deputy Foreign Minister Bebler to ascertain the communist perception and Bebler shared this view. It was a frivolous explanation for what Lie had correctly described as a serious problem; Ross and Gross abstained from comment. The Russian walkouts, Lie continued, were probably based on a desire to obscure Yugoslavia's election to a council seat; the propaganda value of posing as China's friend in getting her into the United Nations; and the desire to return to the council together with China and her veto. Ross and Gross inferred from Lie's "obscure comments" that, if these goals were not achieved by Moscow in four to six weeks, their value would sufficiently diminish from Moscow's viewpoint as to force it to withdraw from the United Nations completely.

Queried whether Moscow's objective might not be a permanent departure, regardless of what occurred in the Chinese question, Lie was evasive. He believed that Moscow's move might be partially to prepare the Russians for a permanent withdrawal. If after a partial walkout nothing serious occurred, like a war, nothing more would develop in the event of a complete walkout. In the possibility of a rival world organization, Lie attached importance to Sobolev's apparent association with Mao Tse-tung's delegation visiting Moscow. Sobolev, then serving in the Foreign Ministry, would be in a position, based on his San Francisco and United Nations experience, to develop such a new organization. Although Lie believed some in Moscow might want to withdraw from the United Nations, Malik and

Zinchenko appeared anxious to settle the Chinese question quickly. Lie's comment was akin to the belief then circulating in some quarters that Stalin was reasonable but Molotov was the Kremlin's real villain.

Following Malik's first walkout Lie asked him why Moscow had posed the matter as the unseating of the Chinese Nationalist representatives rather than the seating of the representatives of the new communist government. Several days before seeing Ross and Gross he had again contacted Malik (although in his memoirs Lie denied talking to him) to outline his proposed interpretation of charter Article 22 so as to guide the council in determining what was meant in the current circumstances by the phrase "Republic of China." Lie would interpret this phrase to mean Communist China, which Malik naturally liked. Lie was unclear, however, on exactly what legal acrobatics he would employ to establish this interpretation, which derived from the Feller-Kerno memorandum. It was designed, he frankly admitted, to overcome in particular the difficulties that the council's Latin American members would encounter, enabling their governments to maintain nonrecognition of Peking but still support this charter interpretation. Lie was optimistic that his argument would sway Ecuador and Cuba, which could be the sixth and seventh votes needed to settle the matter. Lie hoped, in conclusion, that Washington would respond positively to his ideas when consulted by others.

Ross and Gross did not so respond. Instead, Gross observed that the matter involved perceptions of Moscow's "motives and objectives," and a "wise judgment" had to be "based on [a] most careful estimate of this factor." Both "questioned whether Lie's approach was not premature . . . and cautioned against getting jittery in [this] situation." (Sunde's view that Lie was the "jittery" type had registered itself with the American mission.) The mission and the State Department, they assured him, were studying the matter carefully and wished further discussions with him. Gross informed the State Department that the mission thought Lie's proposal was "impractical."[35]

The Nationalist Chinese soon became aware of Lie's lobbying, and on February 9 their council representative, Tingfu Tsiang, called on him. Tsiang was irate over Lie's interviews with other council representatives but assumed that the secretary-general had not attempted to persuade them to support the seating of the Communist Chinese. Lie admitted to the interviews but then misrepresented his conversations, certainly with the Americans and British, by claiming that there had been no need to attempt to persuade anyone because all those whom he had spoken to shared much of his opinion on the juridical and political aspects of the problem. Tsiang asked that Lie remain neutral for the next three months because the situation would reverse itself: the communist regime would collapse as a result of the famine stalking China. Lie responded that wherever Article 99 applied—his now well-worn standby—he could not remain neutral. He could not relinquish any of the duties and rights that the charter bestowed on him. If the Chinese situation endangered world peace he would alert the council. When he acted officially, however, he would contact Tsiang.

When Tsiang observed that Peking would be unable to conquer Formosa for some time, Lie indelicately asked how long it would take Chiang Kai-shek to reconquer the mainland. He understood from Tsiang's comments in and out of the council, that the only possibility of the Nationalist government returning to the mainland rested on the hope of another world war resulting in the defeat of both Russian and Chinese Communists. He had to prevent local wars and world war, Lie insisted; his job was peacemaking.[36] The tone of Lie's comments in his initial version of this interview do not disguise his animus toward the Chinese Nationalists.

Within a week, Moscow announced that Russia and China had concluded a thirty-year treaty of alliance, friendship, and mutual assistance. Moscow placed at Peking's disposal $300 million in credits and returned Port Arthur and Dairen to China as well as the Changchum Railway. Lie viewed this as a Russian diplomatic success that greatly increased the latent strength confronting the democratic states in Sir Halford Mackinder's Eurasian heartland.[37] Ten days later Lie gave Ross the Feller-Kerno memorandum and reiterated his arguments about Russian withdrawal and the seating of Communist China. In view of American policy regarding Communist China's recognition and seating in the United Nations, Lie did not ask or expect Washington's support in his own endeavors. He had learned to his annoyance, however, that Ecuador had been urged by the American ambassador to stall on the Chinese recognition question. Lie said he did not see how this stance was in any way essential to Washington's policy, although it damaged the execution of his own responsibilities. After reiterating some of the American arguments Ross added that the disadvantages to Moscow of a permanent withdrawal were so great that it might well have second thoughts before taking such a step. He did not see the situation as so serious that it necessitated quick action.

To tackle the problem of Russian absence from the United Nations, Lie now proposed, in response to high-level American and British statements, that there be no separate discussions with the Russians outside the United Nations and that any resumption of discussions be within its framework. He believed that world public opinion, especially in Great Britain and the United States, would demand it and that President Truman would discover the political wisdom of backing such discussions. Lie thought that a special council meeting should be convoked under charter Article 28, an idea he appears to have picked up from the Yugoslav representative. This provides for periodic meetings of that organ at which representatives may be government members or other specially designated surrogates. Lie proposed that such representatives be the foreign ministers. For obvious reasons he thought the meeting should be convened in Paris or Geneva rather than New York, for about a month or longer, before the assembly's autumn session. It could handle such complex questions as the control of atomic energy and the hydrogen bomb. Lie explained that he had approached Malik, who was without instructions but appeared personally partial to the proposal. Lie wanted to caucus with Ross and Gross and his "think tank" of Cordier, Feller, Foote, and Gjesdal in the immediate future to discuss the idea.

Ross's reaction was measured, and his comments were well taken: What did Lie hope could be accomplished by such a council meeting? If its chances of success were slim, would there be any reason to hold it? Could one consider such a meeting unless there was a reasonable belief that the Russians would attend "with genuine willingness to seek agreement and intention to live up to any agreement that might be reached?" Moreover, such a council meeting would be a dramatic move that would capture the public's attention; would it not arouse perhaps false hopes? If such a meeting ended in failure, people might interpret it as the complete collapse of the United Nations and lose hope of coming to any agreement with the Russians. Lie held that there had to be give and take, that Moscow and Washington could not maintain inflexible positions. He claimed, and Ross thought sincerely, that the Russians and their policies both inside and outside the world organization had exhausted his patience. As to the meeting's failure, Lie observed that it would mirror the world's condition, which should not be hidden from the people. He would wish this condition to be known by the meeting's failure even if this risked jettisoning the United Nations and commencing the establishment of a new world organization. His ideas would be studied, Ross said, but in the interim he asked Lie to consider carefully the questions just raised.[38]

Press leaks about Lie's proposal soon developed, and the Foreign Office anxiously instructed the mission in New York to ascertain if they were well founded.[39] When approached by Cadogan's deputy, Sir Terence Shone, Lie explained his anxieties and his proposal for the special council meeting. He had complained strongly to the Russians about their behavior, he claimed. He gave Shone the Feller-Kerno memorandum and observed that he had occasionally been "criticized for making statements which were not regarded as proper for the Secretary-General" to make. He argued that his position was different from that of his League of Nations predecessors and referred specifically to Article 99.

Shone, like Ross, raised some questions. How would such a meeting be effective under present conditions? Would the Russians agree to sit with Tsiang, if the Chinese question were on the council's agenda? If the Russians did partake in the discussions, was the council likely to come to a solution that would allow continued Russian participation? Lie admitted the difficulties: the meeting would have to be very carefully prepared. Shone thought Lie appreciated that a failure might cause the situation to deteriorate even more.

Shone suspected that Lie's proposal "was hardly likely to commend itself" to Bevin. Various considerations, however, dictated that he say nothing to Lie except to point out some of the more obvious pitfalls that lay ahead. According to Shone both the Ecuadorian and Norwegian representatives, whom Lie contacted personally, thought that everything had to be arranged in advance so that the meeting would achieve something concrete, otherwise it would likely "do more harm than good." Obviously the Chinese question, they believed, would be the first roadblock.

Based on information conveyed to Shone, Lie's proposal and discussions had raised great speculation in the secretariat, which felt obliged to slip something to the press. Supposedly the assignment was delegated to a junior officer to downplay its importance. Shone viewed the procedure as somewhat improper, considering that Lie had not yet broached the matter with the American and British missions.[40] Shone, of course was unaware that Lie had approached Ross but it did not make his criticism any less valid. Even if the press leak had been an innocent mistake, and one suspects that it was an attempt to ginger up the Americans, the whole performance was another example of Lie's and perhaps one could say his staff's inability to deal wisely and soberly with the important minutia of confidential exchanges. The whole operation was splitting at the seams. A greater snarl up, however, was right down the road.

In response to all this information and speculation, Bevin saw no purpose in activating Article 28 unless Moscow could be induced to attend such a meeting, and it appeared that Lie could not promise this. Nevertheless, in view of the intensive interest being manifested in the possibility of arranging high-level East-West talks, Bevin did not want overly to discourage Lie or to suggest that he saw little advantage in his idea. A solution to the problem was urgently needed, and Bevin did not want it said that he had turned down Lie's proposal. The Russians, he observed, were chiefly to blame for the current impasse, and he wanted to ensure that the onus for this was placed squarely on their shoulders. Lie was therefore to be informed that Bevin was always prepared to consider any proposal that could recommence council discussions; but with the Russians boycotting all United Nations organs, he doubted that invoking Article 28 would exempt such a council session from the boycott. The Chinese question, Bevin continued, had to be dealt with separately.[41]

The State Department's thoughts on the matter moved in the same direction,[42] albeit circuitously, as we shall see. Its initial position was that no meeting be held under Article 28 while Moscow continued to absent itself from the council. The State Department assumed that Moscow would not agree to such a caucus while Tsiang represented China, and Washington naturally could not modify its stance and vote in favor of Chinese communist representation just to make the meeting possible.

At Rusk's initiative the question was discussed by a number of senior officials and a new position agreed to by March 3: that Washington would be willing to partake in periodic council meetings under Article 28 but that there could be no guarantee that the Secretary of State would represent the United States. Moreover, three points were to be discussed with Lie, but with care so as not to indicate that Washington's reply was in any way conditional. First, agenda items could be raised by any council member and whenever possible agreed upon in advance of a meeting. Second, every effort would be made not to raise public expectations. Last, any meeting should be a legitimate effort to help solve the question at issue not primarily for propaganda purposes. In talking with Lie, the problem of Chinese representation should not be raised. Indeed, the ball was to be thrown back into his court, as it was his idea to activate Article 28. Lie was to be told that it was his problem to work out, and that the American position was unchanged. If Lie's proposal had some chance of success, prior consultation by the permanent members might be considered to agree on agenda items. An Article 28 meeting could also provide an opportunity to consult on matters not within the United Nations' purview and include questions better handled through Four Power consultations than in the council.

This recommended approach was inconclusively discussed on March 6. In subsequent discussion with Rusk, it was agreed that Gross should assume an "exploratory attitude in discussing the matter" with Lie. Without revealing Washington's position, Gross was to attempt to develop Lie's ideas on such a meeting and discover what Lie specifically wanted to discuss and "what he considered to be the possibilities and objectives of such a periodic meeting of the Council."[43]

The Gross-Ross encounter with Lie and his American secretariat aids Cordier, Feller, and Foote quickly followed. Gross and Ross did not allow themselves to be drawn into an exchange on Washington's China policy but left with Lie the clear idea that they did not agree with his ruminations. Lie resented American pressure on other governments to prevent the seating of Communist China and appeared confident that France, Ecuador, and Cuba "would see the light as he saw it." The current impasse, Gross declared, was not one that arose from American mistakes but rather from "illegal action by the Russians" in abstaining from the work of the council and other United Nations organs. The bottom line was what price would be paid to "avoid Russian blackmail." If the price was paid and the "Russians returned to the United Nations, what blackmail might they not attempt next?" As Gross later pointed out to Sir Terence Shone he "doubted whether Lie had thought of this." Washington's position, Gross emphasized to Lie, remained unchanged: it continued to support the Chinese Nationalist representative and rejected the seating of any communist one. Washington's vote would not be considered a veto; unlike the Russians, the Americans would accept the council's majority decision. Concerning other governments, no pressure would be brought to bear. American opinion, however, would be expressed frankly; it was realized that this would influence other governments, but they would be told that how they voted would be entirely their own affairs. Lie and his associates appeared gratified by Gross's comments. To avoid any misunderstanding, Gross emphasized that Washington's position should not be misinterpreted. Lie and the secretariat should not, in their desire to have Peking seated and Moscow return, misinterpret Washington's position as a change in policy. It was not a "benevolent neutrality" nor one "more or less sympathetic" to Lie's endeavors to settle the question. Gross strongly implied that the State Department would take a very dim view of any possible misinterpretation of the American position, however innocent that misinterpretation might be.

On Lie's proposal to activate Article 28, Gross and Ross, in line with their instructions, attempted to raise questions rather than respond to Lie's comments or those of his associates. In effect they held that they had displayed a "sincere even-handed open-mindedness" toward Lie's proposal. In their questioning Gross and Ross pressed the notion that perhaps Lie and the secretariat unnecessarily stressed the need for agreement at a periodic council meeting on at least some of the important problems separating East and West. Agreement was desirable, Gross and Ross admitted, but they queried whether there was not the danger of misleading others into thinking that it was a quick and easy road. On the Chinese representation question, Lie and his associates appeared to think that this problem might be formally placed on the agenda, provided agreement to settle the matter was previously arrived at outside the council. Their consensus seemed to be that Chinese representation and a special council meeting should not be intertwined. When asked by the Americans what they thought of an informal Four Power dinner meeting at Lie's home, simply to ruminate and provide an opportunity for talk, they responded favorably. Lie concluded the meeting with the hope that Washington would take the lead and develop his proposal, especially with other states. A veiled warning, through repeated comments about Lie's responsibilities under Article 99, indicated that Lie would not consider it improper to invoke this article to propose a special council meeting.[44]

On the day following this conversation, March 8, the *New York Times* learned of the Feller-Kerno memorandum on the Chinese question. When questioned about the memorandum, Acheson explained the American position: continued recognition of the Chinese Nationalists, resistance to any effort to unseat them but recognition that each United Nations member should decide for itself, and Washington's acceptance of the council's majority decision.[45] Gross believed that the leak had occurred in Washington,[46] a plausible inference in view of the previous leak of Lie's earlier conversation with Eleanor Roosevelt and the attitude that had developed about him in American government circles since 1946. Up to this point Lie's actions behind the scenes had been known to a very small circle. His endeavors could not really be objected to if, like Bagehot's British monarch, one is willing to argue that at the minimum the secretary-general in private has the right to advise, warn, and recommend. However, Lie like Captain Ahab pursuing the White Whale, appeared to lack moderation on this issue, as in so many others. He went public and, in doing so, eroded what credibility he still possessed.

Lie immediately released a letter, explaining his conversation with council members on the Chinese question and the origins of the Feller-Kerno memorandum. Since the memorandum had been referred to in the press, he felt it appropriate to release the full text and make it available to everyone.[47] The storm soon broke. The Nationalist Chinese reaction was quick and sharp. Two hours after Lie circulated the memorandum, Tsiang protested and reserved his right to comment on the memorandum subsequently.[48] Publicly he claimed that the Feller-Kerno memorandum was a "deliberate attempt to prejudice China's case" before the world organization and that it overstepped the secretary-general's duties and undermined "public confidence in his impartiality." The present impasse, Tsiang maintained, stemmed from the Russian walkout, which was illegal. If Lie desired to use his influence to ameliorate the situation he should contact Moscow. The memorandum, Tsiang argued, was "both bad law and bad politics." The Nationalist Chinese ambassador in Washington, the experienced Wellington Koo, likewise let go with a blast, as did segments of the American press that Lie claimed were "isolationist." He had to seek a solution in the world organization's best interests, Lie maintained; he had held many discussions on the question and intended to have many more. He declined comment on Tsiang's remarks since he wished to avoid a controversy, thus failing to realize that a controversy had already erupted. Whether the memorandum was bad law, as Tsiang claimed, Lie left to the legal experts to decide; whether it was bad politics, he left to the members of the world organization and posterity.[49]

Gross declined detailed comment on the memorandum but endorsed Lie's right to make suggestions that he considered helpful in a question that obviously concerned him. Whether these suggestions should be private or public he left unclear. Shone noted to London that one journalist appeared to regard the issue as more political than legal and, accordingly, that the Feller-Kerno memorandum was unlikely to contribute to an early settlement of the question.[50] The journalist was right on both counts.

Cadogan suggested that he tell Lie that while London accepted some of his arguments it had doubts about others. In particular, it did not believe that a government's ability to execute its charter obligations, however much this applied in the case of Nationalist China, should be accepted as a general rule or as a norm for the resolution of Chineselike disputes that might develop in the future.[51] The Foreign Office's Cecil Parrott, head of the United Nations Department, believed that the entire Feller-Kerno memorandum despite "its somewhat false premises and its unrealistic conclusion," had probably achieved some good and might have had a curative effect, at the minimum, on the independent vote at the next assembly. It might also have contributed to easing the difficulty for some council members in modifying their attitude toward accepting Communist China.[52] The British mission enlarged on Cadogan's views by pointing out that the memorandum held that United Nations members could decide the representation issue in an international organization irrespective of their policies regarding recognition of a new state or new government. This argument, however, was built on sand because the criteria advanced—control of the country and the ability to fulfill charter obligations—were exactly those on which recognition would or should be based. Indeed, it was illogical for a state to vote for Peking's seating in the United Nations while it continued to maintain diplomatic relations with the Nationalist Chinese.[53] The legal arguments were endless; the resolution of the question could only be political.

Gross and the French representative, Jean Chauvel, concluded that Lie was "inclined to allow wishful thinking to colour his ideas and utterances." The result was that Lie "was sometimes apt to discount the views of others and factors which it might seem to him convenient to ignore." Shone thought that Gross and Chauvel felt Lie's understandable anxiety for the United Nations' future "led him to seek to influence delegations on the question of Chinese representation to an extent which was hardly proper."[54]

Gross dwelt on this theme when he asked the State Department to take stock immediately of the Chinese question, which had now become important in view of Lie's current actions and statements that threatened to "cause confusion." As to Lie's actions, there was little to be said beyond the fact that he was "admittedly waging [a] campaign designed" to seat Communist China in the council and other United Nations organs. In the mission's judgment, Lie's activities presented a serious problem regarding its relations with him and other delegations. The approach had been and, unless the State Department instructed otherwise, would remain to avoid anything that could be interpreted as contentiousness between the United States and Lie. Privately, the mission had attempted to explain clearly to Lie the American position. Because of the publicity given to Lie's approach to the Chinese question and his press conference of March 10, the mission assumed that he would probably continue to press his views on everyone at the United Nations.[55]

Analyzing the Feller-Kerno memorandum the Chinese Nationalists thought it was an "attempt to influence public opinion in favor of the Soviet Union whose stooge" Lie was. In addition, they held that Lie had disregarded charter Article 100, which enjoined him and the secretariat from any step that might reflect on their status as international civil servants responsible only to the United Nations. Moreover, Lie had also shown bad faith inasmuch as, on February 9, he had promised to take no steps on the

Chinese question without first consulting Tsiang. They admitted that the Feller-Kerno memorandum was "clever," but although correct in noting that each state decided for itself whether to recognize a new government or state, it neglected to note that this right was limited by the rights of other states and that "premature recognition" was considered an unfriendly act under international law. Likewise correct was the memorandum's contention that representation in an international organization was divorced from whether the state was recognized. However, two points were neglected: membership covered not only the "ability and willingness" to execute charter provisions but also whether the prospective member was peace loving; and premature action favoring a rival government, especially when that very matter was before the United Nations, would be as unpardonable for the world organization, as premature recognition of a new government or state is for other states. Legal arguments, of course, like those of Lie or the Nationalist Chinese are meant to justify or disguise positions of political substance, but the Nationalist Chinese arguments were not without legal merit.

These thoughts were incorporated by the Nationalist Chinese into a memorandum and dispatched to Tsiang, should he desire to issue a rejoinder to Lie's letter and the Feller-Kerno memorandum. The concluding sentence contended that Lie could be thinking only of Soviet Russia's interests, not those of the United Nations, when he circulated his letter and the Feller-Kerno memorandum.[56] Tsiang's public rejoinder of March 13 to Lie's letter of March 8 was a bitter attack on Lie. If it was too much to have expected Lie to use his influence against communism, Tsiang declared, it was certainly not too much to have expected him to "remain at least neutral in this world struggle." Soviet Russia used the United Nations only for obstructionist and propaganda purposes. Nevertheless, Lie had circulated the Feller-Kerno memorandum to appease the Russian delegation at the expense of the Chinese Nationalist one. For these reasons, Tsiang repeated, Lie's letter and the Feller-Kerno memorandum were "bad politics." Tsiang's note repeated the points conveyed to him by his superiors and went on to question whether Article 99 even applied. Nobody could believe, he argued, that the Chinese question threatened world peace and security. Even if it did, Lie should not have distributed the Feller-Kerno memorandum only to certain council representatives and exclude the sitting Chinese representative. All this, Tsiang reiterated, constituted "bad law." In addition, Lie had intervened against the interests of his country, Tsiang complained, and tomorrow might repeat his performance "against the interests of other countries." The world security orgnaization, he concluded, was "vitiated by an element of insecurity at its very centre, particularly for the smaller and weaker countries."[57] Iranians, Greeks, and no doubt others noted that telling comment.

Following Tsiang's missives, Lie's concern intensified.[58] He explained to the Americans that his objective was not to bring the Russians back but

rather to get the Chinese Communists seated in the United Nations. Contact with Peking would thus be established, and perhaps it might be won
over. Indeed, he proposed that a representative from Peking come to New
York for a "couple of weeks." He was unsure whether he had either the
"authority or responsibility to do this." What did Lie have specifically in
mind? the Americans asked. He wanted to establish contact with Peking,
he responded. The only contact he had at present was through the Russian
representative. Lie thought he might be able to make it clear to Peking
that Moscow's behavior in this question was not in its interest. He observed that he might be able to convince the Communist Chinese how
important it was for them to conduct their foreign affairs according to
internationally recognized standards.[59] To others Lie proposed to bring
Communist China into the United Nations through the back door, so to
speak, by having the Nationalist Chinese excluded from the Economic and
Social Council's Economic Commission for Asia and the Far East, accompanied perhaps by an invitation to the Communist Chinese to represent
China on the commission. The British fended off this proposal with the
argument that any such move should be taken in one of the world organization's major bodies, like the council.[60]

The Nationalist Chinese were not slow in offering Lie tit for tat. They
proposed to introduce two resolutions in the assembly's Interim Committee: one condemning Lie for intervening in the Chinese question by circulating the Feller-Kerno memorandum; the other attacking Moscow for
its walkout from various United Nations bodies. Feeling that there was
more than enough vituperation, the Americans unofficially advised the
British that the Interim Committee was probably not competent to handle
either resolution: its terms of reference hardly empowered it to criticize
Lie, and the Feller-Kerno memorandum had been circulated to the council,
not to the Interim Committee which could not make recommendations to
member states. Moreover, any recommendation to the assembly about
Moscow's behavior would be meaningless, even if the committee had the
right to make it. The British were prepared, if necessary, to defend Lie's
right to assume an initiative on a matter of such obvious concern to the
United Nations, but warned that this certainly did not mean that London
necessarily agreed with all his opinions. The British were prepared to support the condemnation of Moscow, however, since any abstention could be
interpreted as condoning Russian tactics.[61] London hoped that the Nationalist Chinese could be discouraged from offering their two resolutions or,
if this was not possible, that they would be ruled beyond the Interim
Committee's purview.[62] Since none of these contingencies developed the
Nationalist Chinese were presumably dissuaded from tendering their
resolutions.

As to invoking Article 28, Lie agreed with Bevin that a special council
meeting would be useless without Soviet Russia's presence and that Moscow was mainly to blame for the present impasse. Nevertheless, Lie still

sought to resolve the dispute. From some of his bitter comments, it is clear that he regarded the Americans as largely responsible for the continuance of the deadlock. The question left Lie in a "mood of angry gloom." Quito and Havana's attitude he blamed on Washington. He even voiced his regret that he had pressed to have the United Nations headquarters located in the United States rather than in Europe. He was obviously irritated by congressional and press attitudes and, Shone thought, had "an unfair and unreasoning resentment against the Americans." Lie thought London had been wise in recognizing the Peking regime. He hoped that when it established diplomatic relations with Peking, which he understood the Chinese Communists were foolishly obstructing, London would use its influence to urge other governments to follow suit, for example, Australia, the Benelux states, Canada, and New Zealand.[63]

Lie's attempts to influence the council votes of Cuba, Ecuador, Egypt, and France had been a dismal failure. Cuba's immediate reaction had been a firm no. The Egyptian representative had criticized Lie for exceeding his duties and informed him that Cairo's policy was unchanged.

France likewise decided to continue her policy, as did Ecuador. For the moment, Tsiang informed his embassy in Washington, Lie had succeeded only in generating controversy; he intended, however, to continue his efforts and therefore Nationalist China had to be alert. Tsiang understood that Washington did not share Lie's concern that Soviet Russia might exit permanently from the United Nations over the Chinese question and was committed to carrying on in the world organization without Moscow, if necessary. He reported that Gross emphasized the State Department's position on the connection between recognition of a new state or government by another state and its representation in an international organization—a stance at variance with that of the Feller-Kerno memorandum. In general, Tsiang observed, other representatives also thought that the Feller-Kerno memorandum's legal hypothesis was "untenable." The Latin American representatives were especially opposed to Lie, not only on the memorandum but on a long history of conflict[64]—an allusion, perhaps, to Lie's opposition to the internationalization of Jerusalem, which the Vatican and the Latin American states strongly favored.

Despite the attitude of Cuba, Ecuador, Egypt, and France, Lie insisted to Shone that if a vote were forced on whether Tsiang represented China's millions, only Cuba and the United States would support Tsiang, whereas India, Soviet Russia, and Yugoslavia would oppose. Egypt, Ecuador, and France, he presumed, would abstain. He wondered how Great Britain and Norway would vote, but noted that in any case the seven votes necessary to invalidate Tsiang's council status would be lacking.[65] Whether this erroneous analysis of the situation reflected Lie's inability to admit defeat or was an attempt to elicit information from Shone is unclear. Shone observed to Jebb that, of all those involved in the question, Lie had "taken the most extreme line." Indeed, he had "been in a state bordering on panic owing" to his fear that Moscow would exit permanently and establish a rival world organization. Shone had discovered no one else equally anxious, with the possible exception of the Indian representative. [66]

Even Lie had by now concluded that some other way had to be discovered to resolve the difficulty. Could the parties be brought together once more on issues other than that of Chinese representation, he asked himself, and his thoughts turned to what eventually became his ten-point, twenty-year peace program, [67] which we will examine later. He unexpectedly [68] aired some of these latest thoughts, as well as his proposal for a special meeting of the council, in an address before the B'nai B'rith organization in Washington. [69] When pressed by Hickerson about his peace program, however, Lie was unable to offer any concrete suggestions aside from that of a Security Council special session. [70] Once Lie had raised such a program publicly, he should have been prepared to proffer practical steps to implement it; but he had committed the unpardonable sin of being ill-prepared.

On the day following this speech, March 22, Lie visited the State Department for a requested interview with Hickerson, Jessup, and Rusk, to do what he could, he later wrote, to "direct" Washington's policy along lines proper for the United States, Asia, and the United Nations. Peking's recent confiscation of $30 million of American commodities, however, had not improved matters. Lie queried if Washington had direct contacts with Peking and repeated his earlier impractical suggestion that a Chinese communist representative be invited to establish contact with Washington. This would supposedly make it possible for Washington to ascertain conditions in China and also to express its disapproval directly rather than through a third party. No doubt to fend him off, the Americans promised to contact him about it later. Lie's contention that a council majority favored the removal of Tsiang surprised his hosts and caused Rusk to remark, perhaps to avoid argument, that Washington was still closely examining the question. The mistake of isolating Russia should not be repeated, Lie emphasized, contending that its earlier extended isolation had made possible the communist liquidation of all intellectual, liberal, and social-democratic elements in the society. If Peking were recognized, there would be a chance to contact these same Chinese elements, but speed was important. His hosts said nothing. Lie's Alice-in-Wonderland peep into Russia's Marxist past and into China's Marxist future was enough to cause aphasia in anyone.

Lie then branched out to China's famine and the whole of Asia. Regarding French Indochina, Lie believed that the United States could do nothing there outside the United Nations. He cited South Korea and Greece as cases in point where a handful of men with United Nations arm bands were able to achieve more toward maintaining the peace and stopping communist penetration than military ships and planes. The casting of council vetoes on French Indochina or other southeast Asian issues would only bring these questions before the assembly, he observed. As far as he could understand, Lie thought his hosts all agreed to this, but since his comments were utterly divorced from reality, discretion probably dictated this lack of American reaction.

Lie also thought that Chiang Kai-shek would not last more than a year on Formosa. The problem of the island, Lie held, could best be handled through a United Nations trusteeship, with its eventual disposition by a plebiscite. Lie failed to consider Communist China's reaction to all this. His impression still was that the Americans believed that the Chinese question had to be solved, that Soviet Russia and Communist China had to be seated in the United Nations, and that Asian problems had to go through the United Nations within the charter's framework. The whole conversation, if one can judge from Lie's less than coherent original memorandum of this meeting (he gives us only a pithy excerpt in his memoirs), was certainly one of the oddest ever recorded by a secretary-general.[71] The following month he returned to his proposal for a trusteeship over Formosa if Washington wished to avoid seeing it turned into a communist base, but he warned that the possibility of doing this would be virtually nil if the Communist Chinese continued to be kept out of the United Nations.[72] However, the State Department like the Foreign Office concluded that any United Nations trusteeship for Formosa would be "utterly unworkable."[73]

Lie aptly summed up his stance when he told the political gossip columnist Drew Pearson that he was "going to put the heat on other countries" in order to get Communist China seated in the council and thus break the existing deadlock.[74] Although he was apparently unaware of it, Lie by this point had shot his bolt. Resistance by Washington and others to any such step, plus Communist China's genius for taking actions that aggravated foes and alienated potential friends, foreclosed any success for Lie in the question. Failure in this direction in turn debarred any successful invocation of a special council meeting under Article 28. Accordingly, Lie's behind-the-scenes initiative to this end was a nonstarter.

Lie nonetheless returned to the question in late April, after a trip to Moscow. The suggestion tendered at the time, that the foreign ministers of the Big Five might meet in the council when they attended the assembly's autumn session in New York, he found inadequate. London was most anxious not to raise false hopes, he was told, by supporting a conference that had little prospect of progress.[75] Washington shared London's view. The United Nations' reputation, Hickerson argued, would suffer if such a meeting achieved nothing important. In any case, Washington counted on Moscow's objections to scuttle the proposal, which would enable it to avoid the blame for rejection.[76] Why Lie persisted in pressing the proposal is something of a mystery in view of the continued stalemate over Chinese representation. Perhaps he was mesmerized, as have been countless others, by the notion that mere movement is progress.

Lie again raised the issue just prior to the assembly session of 1950. By this point, the Korean fighting was in full swing and the Americans were even more adamant than before. To make certain that Lie fully comprehended Washington's position, Gross and Ross indicated its "strong opposition to unseating" Nationalist China while the Korean struggle continued. Lie appeared very distressed. If Washington insisted on this stance, he held, it would shatter the unity of the fifty-three-nation block supporting United Nations' actions in Korea. It would give the Russians another excuse to exit from the United Nations—they had returned the previous month. The State Department was unimpressed by his arguments.[77] At one point Lie wondered whether the Korean fighting would have erupted at all if Peking had been seated in the United Nations in the spring of 1950.[78] There is not a shred of evidence that seating Peking would have prevented the struggle. Indeed, one can argue that the decision to attack South Korea was never influenced by Communist Chinese desires but was a matter solely between Soviet Russia and North Korea. What one can say with some certainty is that Lie's decison to go public on the Chinese question had pretty well exhausted American patience, antagonized the Nationalist Chinese and others, and wrecked any other initiatives he might have undertaken on other matters. This certainly applied to his self-generated mission to Moscow and other capitals to sell his twenty-year peace program.

Mission to Moscow

The State Department's first inkling during the Chinese representation exchanges that something else might be afoot in the upper levels of the secretariat was a report in late February 1950 from Stockholm: the lead story in the *Dagens Nyheter* cited United Nations rumors that Lie was actively preparing for a fresh East-West mediation effort. It was believed that he planned a personal initiative when visiting European capitals in the spring to promote a conference of the great powers, in particular to seek a settlement between Moscow and Washington. In view of Washington's attitude, that any discussions which failed would only worsen matters, the *Dagens Nyheter*'s correspondent noted that Lie would have to proceed cautiously rather than try any dramatic steps.[79] Lie, as we have seen, soon aired some of his thoughts on March 21 in his address before the B'nai B'rith in Washington.[80] By mid-April his European tour was announced, with indications that he would also visit Moscow.[81]

Senior secretariat officials were far from sanguine about the Moscow trip but thought that it was worth a try. Despite professing "confidence in Lie's common sense," they simultaneously were "worried that he might be trapped into an unwise move." Since Russian Assistant Secretary-

General Zinchenko was to accompany Lie, these officials were particularly uneasy about his role—in the past he had proved both timid and ineffective.[82]

On April 17, Lie, with the secretariat's most senior officials, examined a draft memorandum on his proposed ten-point, twenty-year peace program,[83] which had already gone through several revisions to which Feller had contributed.[84] The constructive use of United Nations' potentialities, Lie's memorandum argued, could bring to the world a "real and secure peace." Such an effort would be attractive to small states that had much to contribute in conciliating the great powers and toward developing constructive and "mutually advantageous political and economic cooperation." Lie suggested certain points to be considered in formulating a United Nations peace program, some requiring urgent action, others requiring a twenty-year effort. The adoption, he claimed, of such a peace program would hasten settlement of the Austrian, German, and Japanese peace settlements. Periodic council meetings of high officials under Article 28 headed the list. Also included were international control of atomic energy to prevent its use in war and promote its peaceful uses; control of both atomic and conventional armaments; agreement on military forces to be made available to the council under Article 43; acceptance of universality of United Nations membership; a program of technical assistance for economic development that would include private, government, and intergovernment resources; a more vigorous use by member states of the United Nations' autonomous specialized agencies to promote greater economic and social development; continued development of United Nations' work in the human rights field; peaceful advancement of non-self governing people toward equality, and use of the United Nations to accelerate the development of international law.[85]

Lie's first step in selling his program was to proceed to Washington. The risks involved in Lie's seeing President Truman just before departing on a European trip that might lead to Moscow, Hickerson observed, were "outweighed by the benefits to be gained from granting Mr. Lie's request."[86] Accordingly on April 20, accompanied by Price, he talked to President Truman and Secretary of State Acheson. While waiting to be received by Truman, Lie gave Acheson his memorandum. Acheson, after quickly glancing at it, correctly observed that to solve all the problems of arms control would require "an atmosphere of confidence" that clearly could not develop as long as the Russian communist system had aggressive designs on Austria, East Germany, and French Indochina. Lie did not disagree but appeared to believe that somehow the proposed program would help. Although Acheson avoided arguing the matter, it was an inauspicious beginning.

In his talk with Truman, Lie surveyed the by-now standard political terrain, namely, Formosa, Chinese representation, and so on. His program, he pointed out to Truman, could not be executed until the Chinese question was settled. When pressed on this Lie, according to Acheson, admitted that he was unsure of the Russian position: whether mere termination of the Chinese Nationalist United Nations' membership would be adequate or whether Moscow would return only to vote for acceptance of the Chinese Communists. Lie then extolled the United Nations' role in stopping communism in Greece, Korea, and Indonesia. Acheson kept his tongue although he felt that Lie had failed to mention the most salient point; namely, Washington's economic and political assistance to these states. Lie ruminated that Stalin was misinformed about Washington's "policy and intentions" and that a meeting between Stalin and Truman would therefore be of immense help. Truman was unmoved: he had met the Russian at Potsdam, he observed. He had gone there desiring to settle problems, but the whole experience had "disillusioned [him] on the usefulness of such meetings." He would be happy to invite Stalin, as he had invited other state leaders, to be his guest; but he was not going beyond Washington to meet the Russian. Acheson interjected that Washington's difficulties with Moscow were of such a character that "changing the level of discussion was [not] going to produce solutions"; the political environment had to be changed. Although an anodyne press statement was then agreed upon,[87] it had clearly not been a fruitful meeting.

Having touched based with Washington Lie, almost as an afterthought, dispatched Cordier to Ottawa with a copy of his program.[88] This was a wise decision in view of the increasing influence of the Canadian mission, and Pearson personally, in the corridors of the United Nations. Pearson, however, cautioned Prime Minister Louis St. Laurent that although Lie was making a "very creditable" attempt to reinstitute East-West contacts, he had to admit that Lie did not advance "any specific proposals" that would settle any question.[89]

Lie's conversations with the British began with newly appointed Minister of State Kenneth Younger on April 28 (Bevin was ill). They were no more fruitful than those in Washington. Lie argued that it was essential that he take this initiative in order to tackle some of the questions underlying the Cold War. If the Great Powers' intent was simple victory in the Cold War, the struggle would intensify and eventually lead to a shooting war. He proposed that Great Britain, either alone or with France, be the necessary "balancing force" between the Americans and the Russians. Lie feared that, without such a force, tensions inside and outside the United Nations would heighten. According to Lie, Younger agreed in principle but pointed out that the Russians were unreceptive to mediatory or conciliatory efforts. Lie then raised the question of Chinese representation and its importance in regulating the situation in French Indochina. He thought Formosa would be occupied by Communist China, the only way to avoid this being for Washington to arrange a United Nations trusteeship over the island. As a step toward Communist China's recognition, he proposed that

London assist in excluding Nationalist China from the forthcoming meeting of the Economic Commission for Asia and the Far East. Younger was unreceptive, nor did he encourage Lie to believe that his government would support the proposal for a special council meeting under Article 28. What did Lie hope to accomplish in Moscow? Younger queried. Lie responded that he was not optimistic but felt duty bound to speak frankly to Stalin and Vyshinsky about the consequences of their policy. His principal purpose was to persuade them to be cooperative members in the world organization. He would emphasize the danger that faced them in a hardening world public opinion. If Moscow continued to boycott United Nations meetings, he wanted to ascertain how far it would cooperate along the lines outlined in his peace program. Younger wished him luck but sagely observed that many others who had discussed world affairs with Stalin departed from Moscow buoyed by their discussions, only to be subsequently disappointed by the practical results. At the minimum, Molotov and Vyshinsky had to be impressed; but it was possible that a far more influential but little-known foreign policy elite existed—perhaps an allusion by Younger to the higher echelon of the Russian armed forces and intelligence services. Lie acknowledged the difficulties ahead but said he would try his best.[90] Lie also contacted Jebb, who was to succeed Cadogan at the United Nations, but he was no more forthcoming.[91] Again, in his interview with Prime Minister Attlee, Lie, who appears to have done the talking, covered all the familiar problems. The responses of the cautious Attlee were pithy and anodyne.[92] Lie's reception in London had thus been cool but correct.[93] With American Ambassador Lewis Douglas, Lie argued that Washington should persuade Chiang Kai-shek to "withdraw" in favor of a United Nations trusteeship over Formosa. As to his Moscow trip, he told Douglas he intended to proceed unless the Russians said otherwise and counted on the help of Gromyko and Sobolev.[94] Lie was not deterred by the Russian lack of assurance in New York that he would see Stalin, since it was unclear whether he would be in Moscow or the Crimea.[95]

Across the channel in Paris, Lie again explained his Moscow trip and lobbied, as he had in London, for an Anglo-French combination independent of the United States and Soviet Russia. If he seemingly struck a response, it was mainly on the question of Chinese representation, which was intertwined with the issue of French Indochina. As Prime Minister Georges Bidault admitted, Peking's support of the Communists in Indochina had precluded Paris's recognition of the communist government, although such recognition might be given if Peking did not threaten Paris's interests in the area. As to Lie's Moscow trip, the French wished him luck. On the surface the Paris visit had apparently gone well, and Lie was more sanguine as he proceeded to Moscow.[96]

He stopped over in Prague, but his inability to lay wreaths at the graves of Beneš and Masaryk or to achieve the repatriation to Greece (in accord with resolutions of the assembly) of children spirited to Czechoslovakia by the Greek communist guerrilla forces must have alerted Lie that his reception in Moscow might be cooler than anything he had experienced in the West.[97] The State Department's fear, however, was that his trip would present Moscow with an "outstanding opportunity" for "spectacular propaganda,"[98] but the absence of any Russian press notice on Lie's visit was an ominous sign.[99] Although Gromyko met him at the airport when he arrived on May 11, the occasion was only briefly noted in the press. British Ambassador Sir David Kelly learned that Lie's "reception and accommodation [fell] clearly into the category reserved for visitors of secondary importance."[100] Sir David's American counterpart came to the same conclusion.[101] All details of Lie's stay in Stalin's regimented Russia were in the hands of state organs, the Canadian chargé d'affaires reported to Ottawa, and the arrangements strongly suggested "a calculated attitude of indifference."[102] The Kremlin had demonstrably registered its annoyance with Lie's peace mission.

This Russian reception must be contrasted with Lie's first postwar visit to Moscow in June 1946, on Russian invitation. He had then been wined, dined, and entertained. He had hoped during his visit to smooth over difficulties that prevented Sweden from applying for United Nations membership; to induce the Russians to nominate as many candidates for the secretariat as they were entitled to; to establish a United Nations information center in Moscow; to persuade them that their unrestrained use of the veto was not only not in their interests but was harming them; as well as to discuss the possibility of the United Nations' taking over the work of the postwar emergency United Nations Relief and Rehabilitation Administration. Lastly, he wanted to broach the general international situation, which left him uneasy, although he had to be optimistic in his public pronouncements.[103]

Following this 1946 meeting with Molotov and Stalin, Lie informed the press that he was "well satisfied" with his talks and believed that Moscow "intended to be co-operative." In private, however, he was "more pessimistic," complaining that Molotov and Vyshinsky had not been prepared to "talk seriously" about the Russian attitude toward the world organization and that they had attempted to turn his visit primarily into a social event. Moreover, he was treated as a Norwegian, and Norwegian-Russian questions were discussed with him. Both Molotov and Stalin complained of Norway's friendship with Great Britain. Vyshinsky, whose sensitivity was matched by his polemical manner, raised the question of the Svalbard archipelago and the island of Byørnøya, which was the last thing that Lie wanted to hear since it reminded him of his painful Moscow visit of 1944. Incredibly, Vyshinsky asked Lie's advice on what Moscow should do about this question. Lie wisely recommended that it do nothing, if only to avoid Western reactions over Iceland, which the Russians might find distasteful.[104] The staff members accompanying Lie on this 1946 visit thought he displayed none of his previous "pro-Russian sympathies."[105] The best that Lie could say about the whole trip was that Stalin appeared to be partial to children! This was also true of Hitler, the British ambassador at The Hague, ironically noted.[106]

Lie's first discussion was with Vyshinsky on May 12. He explained his fear that the Cold War might heat up and described the labyrinth of the Chinese representation question. He also expressed displeasure at Moscow's boycott of the world organization, which was, he held, contrary to the charter and had undermined Peking's case. In a rare show of tolerance Vyshinsky smiled and observed that Lie had the right to advance these arguments.

Lie conveyed his peace program saying he felt, from conversations in Washington, London, and Paris, that they lacked confidence in Moscow. He asked Vyshinsky for advice on how to restore confidence among the great powers. Vyshinsky's replies were standard Moscow fare: Moscow's struggle to uphold the charter could not be called a boycott; the lack-of-confidence argument was only a façade to justify the continuation of the Cold War. Soviet Russia, he maintained, conducted a peace-loving foreign policy, of which support for the United Nations was part.[107] This discussion got Lie nowhere. A shorter conversation on the following day with Gromyko about a number of questions including the kidnapped Greek children, new admissions to the world organization, and a United Nations trusteeship over Formosa, was equally unproductive. He likewise saw his former éminence grise, Sobolev, now in charge of American affairs at the Foreign Ministry, but nothing of substance developed beyond agreement that there was no immediate likelihood of war.[108] These talks, Lie admitted to an officer of the American embassy, had proved "unproductive."[109]

A laryngitis infection prevented Lie from having any further discussions, so he did not meet Stalin, together with Molotov and Vyshinsky, until late on the evening of May 15. Although Lie had prepared for the interview, he foolishly took no member of his staff with him, thus facing his hosts across a table with only the link of the Russian interpreter. Lie explained that he was on a lonely mission, representing no government, but only as secretary-general of the world organization. There was no reaction. He observed that he had first come to Moscow in 1921 and that much had occurred in the intervening years. Molotov nodded his approval to Stalin, who now showed greater interest. Lie denied ever having been a Communist and held that he had always attempted to be objective concerning Soviet Russia. He dwelt on Soviet Russia's development and remarkable postwar reconstruction, which no doubt pleased the Generalissimo. Lie then raised the possibility of a meeting of the Anglo-American-Soviet Russian heads of state. Stalin was unmoved: in the current situation, with all its accumulated difficulties, a single meeting among the leaders would not contribute to any solutions within a reasonable period.

In any case, one needed thorough preparation, the practical Stalin con-tinued, through established diplomatic channels over an extended period of time.

Lie then presented a copy of his peace program. Stalin surrendered the floor to Molotov because of his expertise on the United Nations. Molotov considered the program slanted toward the American viewpoint. Lie de-nied this and defended himself by pointing out that he had been attacked by the Nationalist Chinese, the Americans, and others. He not only acted as a mediator, he insisted, but also as a secretary-general. In this latter capacity he could not avoid the thoughts of others, especially on the ques-tion of the veto.

Playing Mr. Nice Guy to Molotov's Mr. Bad Guy, Stalin interjected that although he agreed with Molotov, he recognized that a mediator would always be attacked by both parties. Various points in the program were then scrutinized by both Molotov and Stalin, with Lie constantly on the defensive. On the question of the kidnapped Greek children, Lie appealed to Stalin to use his influence to have the children return to Greece. Chil-dren belonged with their parents, Stalin benignly reflected, and instructed Vyshinsky to furnish him with the necessary details so he could inform himself on the subject—as though he did not know about it already. Lie then touched on the Austrian and German peace treaties, the neutraliza-tion of Germany, and elections in Berlin. His hosts made no substantive comments. The interview terminated and Lie returned to his hotel,[110] having made no dent in the Kremlin's monolithic façade.

The next day, in line with his London comments that he would insist on seeing the Communist Chinese ambassador in Moscow,[111] Lie spoke with Wan Chiahsiang about Peking's possible representation in some of the United Nations' specialized agencies. Lie urged that Peking accredit representatives to meetings of these autonomous international agencies, perhaps thus obtaining a seat, if no Nationalist Chinese representatives were present. As to the situation in the United Nations, Lie argued that Moscow's tactics had not facilitated Peking's case in New York. The am-bassador disagreed. Lie appealed to Peking to show greater tact in dealing with governments that recognized it or were on the verge of doing so. Its abrasive conduct, especially toward England, France, and the United States, he noted, had not contributed to solving Peking's relations with the world organization.[112] Lie had offered Peking some sound advice.

Later that same day Lie closeted himself with Sobolev. They spoke about Austria, Germany, Berlin, and the general European situation. He urged Sobolev to use his influence to improve relations between Washing-ton and Moscow, stressing that America's enormous power should not be underestimated by Soviet Russia; America had never lost a war. Construc-tive forces—obviously Lie placed himself under that rubric—in both the East and West had to do everything possible to avoid a global catastrophe.[113] Lie's approach to Sobolev, whom he knew to be a dedicated Communist, was a desperate and somewhat naive attempt to salvage something from the Moscow visit.

Lie took leave of Vyshinsky on May 18. A recent decision by Acheson, Bevin, and Schuman to postpone consideration of the Chinese question until late August or early September disturbed Lie, and he told Vyshinsky that he would raise the question on his return to Paris and London. Vyshinsky naturally encouraged him to do so. Lie, seemingly buoyed by his visits to Washington, London, Paris, Prague, and Moscow despite the absence of results, hoped that they had brought him more respect in world affairs, he observed to Vyshinsky—perhaps, a reflection of feelings of insecurity and subconscious doubts of his adequacy. Accordingly he would insist on a reply, Lie noted to Vyshinsky, from the four governments to his peace program.[114]

In a departing statement to the Moscow press corps, Lie guardedly held that "he had no reason to be dissatisfied" with his Kremlin conversations. Final judgment would take at least several months. To the British ambassador he was more candid, confessing that there had been no "positive results" despite his correct reception, which was in line with the fact that he was not a Communist. Some believed that merely coming to Moscow meant you were sympathetic to communism, but *Pravda* had criticized him as an imperialist tool. Lie emphasized that he had been right to visit Moscow. His talks convinced him that the Kremlin was as afraid of the West as the West was afraid of the Kremlin. Lie conveyed a strong impression that "he was disappointed with his visit and that he had expected, if not immediate results, at least a more cordial reception,"[115] reported the ambassador. Lie made similar comments to the American ambassador.[116]

Backtracking

In Paris, Lie recounted his Moscow conversations, telling Schuman, with some exaggeration, that conditions appeared to favor informal and private discussions between the Four Powers and other members of the council.[117] Although Lie was "optimistic" that something good would flow from his visit, Schuman was far less sanguine and "did not think from what Lie had told him that anything significant had been accomplished."[118] On May 22 Lie saw Bidault and more correctly admitted that Moscow had not committed itself to anything; but he hoped the Russians might be more forthcoming if they were met with a modicum of understanding, and that the Cold War might thus abate. Bidault was skeptical that periodic meetings of the council under Article 28 would be productive since the veto could be used.[119] According to Alexander Parodi, the former French council representative who took a "somewhat poor view" of the secretary-general, Lie's conversation with Schuman "had been very vague" and

insubstantial. To the Norwegian ambassador in Paris, Lie was more optimistic than when he departed for Moscow,[120] although the ambassador
admitted to his American counterpart that Lie's hopeful signs were not of
a "concrete nature."[121] Lie was proving to be consistently inconsistent in
view of the contrary impressions he conveyed in Moscow and Paris. He
was laying a smoke screen to mask a failed mission before he crossed the
channel to London.

On the afternoon of May 23, Lie called on Bevin who was clearly ill and
apparently unattentive. Lie's impression was that the conversation was being recorded and that this largely explained Bevin's seeming lack of interest. Bevin gave a cool response to Lie's peace program and opposed any
periodic meetings of the council. Instead he emphasized the importance of
the North Atlantic Pact, which he equated with power, the only thing the
Russians understood. He eschewed negotations or even discussions with
Moscow unless it showed by action a changed attitude. When Lie contrasted the recent communique by the Western foreign ministers, declaring they were ready to grasp any opportunity to achieve a genuine and
lasting solution to international problems, with Bevin's comments, his
English host refused to budge. The North Atlantic Pact, he insisted, superseded everything else and could maintain the peace; but he did not oppose
discussions within the United Nations when the occasion allowed. He
concluded by observing that, although Great Britain gave "full support" to
the world organization, it "wanted equality of treatment."[122] The value of
Lie's talk with Bevin, the Foreign Office noted, was the impression generated by his comments that Moscow was "not, at this stage, contemplating
staying out permanently" from the United Nations.[123]

Later that day Lie called on Prime Minister Attlee, who, as usual, was
less than loquacious. He gave Lie the impression that he understood and
agreed with him in general but was unspecific, which annoyed Lie immensely. Lie was disappointed with Bevin's attitude, he explained to Attlee. It was unexpected, he held, following his prior exchanges in London.
Bevin's insistence that Moscow consent to concessions before London
agreed to periodic meetings of the council reminded Lie of Doubting
Thomas, who needed to see Christ's wounds before he believed in the res-
urrection. Since Lie lacked such wounds, Bevin disbelieved him when he
suggested that there was a basis for discussions that might lead to greater
understanding with the Russians.

Attlee appeared, on the other hand, to understand Lie's position that no
one could prove that compromise was possible before talks were held, but
he maintained the British government's position although offering to discuss it further with Bevin. Lie, however, demurred that since Bevin was ill
further discussion might adversely affect his health. Lie agreed to draft a
communique on his London visit that would not harm Bevin or the Labour
government, positing that no door had been closed to genuine discussions;

while Attlee assented that Lie could contact him directly, if necessary. They agreed that a summit meeting was unlikely for the time being. Lie again harped, in conclusion, on the need for periodic meetings of the council and repeated his prior suggestion that London assume an independent role in the struggle between East and West—comments that he conveniently excised from his memoirs.[124]

Lie then had a happier interview with Attorney General Sir Hartley Shawcross, whose views dovetailed with his on the questions of periodic council meetings and Communist Chinese representation. Lie voiced his discontent with Bevin's stance. Despite skepticism about Bevin's health allowing him to continue, Shawcross thought that he could carry on as foreign secretary until the next election. Lie thought that the attorney general would use the information he had imparted to work effectively to change London's future attitude.[125] It was the start of an ambitious attempt by Lie to undermine Bevin's position.

Lie returned to this offensive the following day in a talk with Minister of State Younger. He was dissatisfied with the conversation he had with Bevin, Lie blurted out, and pressed Younger on the need for periodic council meetings. There was no other route to lasting peace, Lie argued, than negotiations and stabs at compromise; otherwise the Cold War would persist and perhaps lead to open hostilities. Lie did not solicit Younger's opinion, and Younger did not advance any.[126]

Keeping up his brave front, Lie also saw Canada's Pearson in London. He claimed that his mission had not collapsed and that he was not as discouraged when he left Moscow as he had expected he would be. When Pearson asked whether he was satisfied with the publicity given to his visit by the Russians, Lie answered in the affirmative, although the Canadian and British reports showed this had not been the case. Pearson thought Lie sincere in hoping that something might develop from his mission. But at the same time, Lie claimed that he was not unaware of the dangers and misunderstandings that might be created, that Moscow might attempt to use both his peace program and his mission to further its own interests, but that he was doing everything possible to prevent this.[127]

Following this talk Lie lunched with Jebb and lobbed some additional shells in Bevin's direction.[128] Before departing for New York he called on Eden. Up to this point Lie had kept his comments about Bevin within government circles, but he now dropped them into the lap of one of the leaders of the parliamentary opposition. Vyshinsky, he nonchalantly observed, had declared he much preferred to negotiate with Churchill and Eden than with their successors Attlee and Bevin.[129] Whether these alleged remarks by Vyshinsky were true or not was immaterial: they were potentially dangerous and could be used against the Labour government by Eden and the Conservative party opposition, which was probably what Lie wanted.

While still in London, Lie had arranged an interview with Acheson and President Truman. This took place on May 29, covering his coversations in Moscow, Paris, and London. To forestall a negative reaction like Bevin's on the question of periodic meetings of the council, Lie urged Acheson not to answer that proposal at once but merely assure him that Washington would consider the matter. Acheson agreed.[130] The talk with Truman went quickly, since Lie had nothing additional of substance to offer. Lie's antennae, however, were insensitive, and he continued to confuse politeness with interest: his hosts were tired and annoyed with Lie and his public, unsolicited peace mission. When he proposed another meeting in the near future for a longer talk, Truman claimed his busy schedule would not permit one for awhile. Although Lie raised the proposal again, he was again rebuffed.[131]

Hickerson, who was present during the interview with Acheson, thought that Lie "had been personally exhilarated by the popular acclaim of his mission" and that his position had undoubtedly been enhanced within the world organization[132]—a not unimportant consideration, especially if Lie had his mind set on being reappointed to the office. Acheson took a dim view of Lie's public and unsolicited peace initiative and European jaunt, an attitude no doubt shared by Truman. The secretary-general, Acheson wrote to his daughter, was "more eager than aware." Despite Lie's protestations that his peace program and tour were no attempt at appeasement but only to foster negotiations between East and West, to Acheson it "sounded very much like appeasement."[133] The fact that Lie's endeavors coincided with the Russian-inspired and led Partisans for Peace campaign[134] that culminated in the Stockholm Peace Appeal of March 1950 to ban the atomic bomb,[135] activities Lie obliquely backed in his parting statement in Moscow,[136] was added grist to Acheson's mill. Lie's public peace initiative, although seemingly well intentioned, had gone awry. He was again back at square one.

Despite this, Lie was "feeling a little *exalté* about the popular recognition" of his peace efforts, Pearson wrote to the Canadian ambassador in Washington, but he did not think that this had obscured in Lie's mind the difficulties ahead.[137] Having gone through the ritual of private discussions, Lie was keen on staging a public performance about his peace mission. He probably thought that by doing this he could hold the initiative and give impetus to his endeavors. According to the *New York Times*, his public account might be given outside the United States, a possibility Ottawa could not ignore since Lie had suggested an official visit to Canada.[138]

Lie however, finally decided that rather than have a public discussion of his mission, he would simply transmit to the United Nations members his ten-point peace program, since he knew it was only a matter of time before it leaked to the press and became public knowledge. Nevertheless objections were raised. Hickerson informally took exception to the wording of Lie's draft letter of transmission, which he thought projected an erroneously optimistic impression of what had transpired on his mission. Specifically, on the proposal to prohibit atomic weapons, Hickerson emphasized that without "an effective control system" to make the prohibition truly effective, it was fraught with danger and disingenuous.[139]

Naturally, in view of the errant and optimistic thrust of Lie's draft letter, Moscow raised no objections to it. Indeed, Moscow asserted it showed some small "progress" when compared to the original peace program discussed in the Kremlin. Grasping at straws, Lie responded that he appreciated this qualified recognition of forward movement and pointed out that his task would be helped immeasurably if Moscow resolved a few problems. Nothing could be done to end the Cold War, he stressed, unless Moscow was more accommodating.[140]

Lie's letter, when released along with his peace program, was only marginally amended to take in Hickerson's demurrings.[141] When questioned on the subject Acheson noted that neither Lie nor anybody else could produce magic "with a wave of a wand to remove suddenly the tensions that now exist"—which would be true as long as Moscow continued its current stance.[142]

Lie had thus momentarily grabbed the headlines but not contributed substantively to bringing the parties closer together. By his unsolicited but public politicking he had surrendered substance for form and had once more confirmed in the eyes of Western governments that he lacked the necessary stature for the job.

Hickerson suggested to the British that discussions including the French might be useful at their United Nations missions about the tactics they should adopt in the light of Lie's recommendations.[143] The British thought no response was needed, but if replies were to be made there should be "close consultation" to coordinate them.[144] None of this proved necessary, however. Lie's whole peace campaign ended abruptly when the armed forces of Communist North Korea invaded the Republic of South Korea on June 25. By late August, Lie had wisely decided not to press his peace program while the Korean fighting raged.[145]

Nonetheless, led by the Americans, the British and French agreed to associate themselves with the "broad objectives" of Lie's proffered peace program and use it to foil Moscow's propagandistic peace initiatives. The approach decided upon was not to refer Lie's program for committee consideration but to discuss it during the assembly's plenary session. When contacted by the Americans Lie was willing "to accept any treatment" that Washington thought appropriate.[146]

Thus, in mid-November the three Western powers stroked Lie's feathers by generally supporting the program and resolution submitted by others commending Lie for his initiative. A resolution adopted on November 20, much to Vyshinsky's disgust, called on the world organization's appropriate bodies to consider portions of the program that particularly concerned them.[147] By this point, of course, thanks to the Russians and North Koreans, Lie's rose-colored glasses had lost some of their tint.

8

THUNDER
IN
THE
EAST

Staying on: Limited Options

American dissatisfaction with Lie's performance as secretary-general manifested itself as early as June 1946, when Stettinius observed to President Truman that Washington "had made a mistake in picking a dud as secretary-general." Truman agreed.[1] Stettinius had crossed swords with Lie over the Iranian-Russian dispute as well as the Spanish question, and the animus was undisguised. During this early period, the question of Lie's inadequacies and his replacement had also surfaced in the Foreign Office.[2] The French were equally negative: their United Nations representative, Jean Chauvel, was unenthusiastic;[3] his associate, Guy de la Tournelle, thought that Lie was both "cunning" and "stupid." By appearing to be reasonable with the Anglo-Americans on a broad range of secondary matters, Tournelle claimed, Lie managed to camouflage the fact that in important questions—like appointing the secretary of a significant commission—he favored the Russians.[4] Though Tournelle did not elaborate, he probably had the antics of Lund and the Balkan commission secretariat in mind.

Especially excruciating for the French, the Nationalist Chinese, and the Canadians was Lie's handling of Sobolev's withdrawal from the secretariat in the spring of 1949, and the appointment of Konstantin Zinchenko as his replacement. Neither the French nor the Nationalist Chinese appear to have been consulted in advance, Lie's press statement notwithstanding.[5] Not only was Lie incompetent to run the secretariat, Pierre Ordonneau, counsellor of the French mission exclaimed, but secretariat performance would never improve while Lie ruled the roost. His government, Ordonneau insisted, "would under no circumstances agree" to Lie's reappointment.[6]

Disenchantment with Lie likewise produced unease among the smaller states. This was reflected in the May 1949 comments of Thanassis Aghnides, Greek Chairman of the General Assembly's Committee on Administrative and Budgetary Questions. His intelligence, diplomatic and long-time League of Nations Secretariat experience, and commitment to the West lent weight to his comments that there was much speculation among the smaller states on what should be done when Lie's term expired in early 1951. Lie had said to him that he did not believe that he would continue in the office but, at the same time, indicated that he would be open to a second contractual term. Aghnides thought Lie would be supported by Moscow and some of the small states intent on not offending any great power.

Aghnides personally thought it "would be a very great tragedy" if Lie were reappointed since he had "not contributed the statesmanship and political craft required" to turn the United Nations into an effective instrument for peace. He could, however now retire with grace, on a comfortable pension, secure in the knowledge that he had contributed in building the United Nations headquarters in New York. Aghnides held that someone like the wartime Canadian ambassador in Moscow, Dana Wilgress, who had good rapport with the Russians, would probably be the candidate most acceptable to them. Aghnides hoped that fear of a stalemate in the selection process would not lead to Lie's automatic reappointment, which would only mean a "further deterioration" in the quality of secretariat personnel. On the contrary, a stalemate would not be a disaster, especially if one of the assistant secretaries-general, or Cordier, could assume interim direction. In reporting this conversation to Washington, Aghnides' interlocutor suggested that it was not premature to begin considering the American position for the 1950 assembly. If Lie's reappointment was not to be supported, he should be contacted, to avoid embarrassment by becoming a candidate and then facing Washington's opposition.[7]

Aghnides' comments made an impact. Dean Rusk was concerned, Ottawa learned in late June, lest Lie's term expire without his successor having been chosen. The new secretary-general would be selected in 1950 and Rusk thought difficulties might be circumvented if the assembly then resolved that Lie continue in office until his successor was selected; that would avoid Lie's committing himself to depart by a specific date. The only two candidates for the office the State Department had heard of—Sweden's Myrdal, and Australia's Evatt—"gave them cold shivers"; Rusk thought that, of those tested in the United Nations arena, only Canada's Pearson and Belgium's Spaak stood out. [8]

When the Americans and Canadians caucused prior to the 1949 assembly, Rusk explained that Washington did not intend to raise the issue at that session but would possibly do so at the 1950 session along the lines he had earlier suggested. The Canadians cautioned, however, that their legal experts held that a Security Council recommendation, subject to the veto, and an assembly recommendation, would be necessary even to extend Lie's appointment. [9] Time and necessity would erode attitudes toward Lie and charter requirements. The old adage about politics making strange bedfellows was never more apt than in this matter.

Like the State Department, the Foreign Office was uneasy over Myrdal's and Evatt's possible candidacies. Cadogan, aware of Myrdal's unacceptability in London while the reverse was true in Moscow, asked, Did not Lie deserve equal Russian support? Lie, he suspected, would pretend disinterest in seeking the office; but Cadogan would bet that during the coming months Lie would devote all his energy to assuring his reappointment. What would happen in a Lie-Myrdal contest, Cadogan could not guess; it was a pity that both were undesirable.

From every direction Cadogan heard complaints about Lie, who he thought had been a disaster. He was "very timid, and easily terrorised by the Russians." He attempted to shirk all responsibility; when pressed, he never defended his staff. He lacked administrative ability and never attended seriously to administrative questions. Since Lie rarely attended meetings of the United Nations' principal bodies, Cadogan was at a loss to explain what Lie did with his time; he thought Lie spent most of it lobbying for the votes of the Latin Americans on questions that he fancied. Naturally, one of these would be his reappointment.

Cadogan was sure that Lie would be supported by Soviet Russia, the eastern European satellites, and the Latin Americans. Regarding the United States it was reported that Washington would support Lie, which surprised Cadogan, as he did not think that it was "blind to his defects"; indeed, Austin had tangled with Lie more than once. Lie, Cadogan speculated, no doubt relied on London not exercising its veto; perhaps the time had come to make clear that he could not count on this. If there was deadlock on Lie's successor, Cadogan envisaged a system whereby the assistant secretaries-general plus Cordier might run the Secretariat, which would be no worse than the current situation. He regretted that Lie had proved disappointing; personally he liked him.

Evatt's name had also been mentioned. Although he would have supporters, Cadogan thought, he would also have many opponents; if he was wise, he would hold back until a deadlock developed and then place himself in the running as the desirable solution. It was all a matter of timing: he hoped Evatt would "miss the bus." Cadogan, who had experienced the league secretaries-general, then added a judicious postscript: the only thing that Lie really enjoyed doing was "cutting capers in public" and making policy pronouncements, which was the "one thing that the Secretary-General should avoid."[10]

Cadogan's suggestion of a hint to Lie that London might cast a veto generated a mixed reaction in the Foreign Office. Jebb for one hoped that London would veto Lie's candidacy—if, in fact, he had the "face to present it"—but doubted whether any hint should be dropped. Minister of State Hector McNeil was equally circumspect; he was confident that Lie would offer his candidacy, and like everyone else had "no use for him." He found Lie "cowardly, inept and vain"; he had "brought no ability or morality to his job." Since the future could not be predicted, McNeil thought London should not commit itself beforehand. He recalled that Moscow had "completely out-manoeuvred" London the first time round. If London let it be known in advance that it would veto Lie, Moscow might for tactical purposes renominate him. If Lie were blocked, London might find itself confronted with someone far worse. As for Myrdal, McNeil would let it be known that he was absolutely unacceptable; sharing all of Lie's weaknesses, he was "much more pointedly anti-British and [had] an ability and energy" that Lie never displayed. Evatt was more of a problem. McNeil was sure that he would not offer his candidacy before the Australian elections; if the Labour party won and Evatt acquired high office, he would not be interested. If the Labour party lost, however, McNeil doubted that any conservative government would support Evatt. In that event London would have the excuse it needed.

Wilgress, mentioned by Aghnides, was also considered. It was thought he "would certainly clean up the Secretariat," but Jebb's reaction was terse and to the point: "I imagine he hasn't a chance."[11] Ralph Bunche's name also surfaced, since an element in the State Department, somewhat naively, toyed with the idea that because Bunche was a negro, it would be almost impossible for the Russians to veto his candidacy.[12] The Mexican director-general of the United Nations Educational, Scientific, and Cultural Organization, Jaime Torres Bodet, also attracted British interest in view of Mexican lobbying to get him the job.[13]

Cadogan's prediction that Lie would be a candidate appeared well-founded when Vyshinsky publicly commented, in early October, that Lie was the only person he could imagine Moscow supporting.[14] Accordingly Lie, in mid-December, was being coy when he informed the press that after his present term expired he would not seek reappointment; but he declined comment on who might succeed him or what might be done if there was a deadlock about a successor.[15] Despite somewhat similar comments to his family at that time, he did not specifically state that he would reject the office if it were again offered.[16] He was, in fact, off and running.

Rusk's unease was reflected in a talk with Canada's Ambassador Hume Wrong. Rusk believed that, despite his public statements, Lie probably would accept another tour of duty or at least soldier on until his successor was appointed. He opined that Lie's tenure could be extended by an assembly resolution without any referral to the council since the latter organ had played no role in limiting Lie's contractual term of office to five years—an interesting comment in view of future events. Rusk was also sure that Spaak would be unacceptable to the Russians and assumed that Pearson would not want the post; even if he did, the Russians would likely veto him. Rusk thought that every effort had to be made by the council's permanent members either to extend Lie's term or to choose a successor.[17]

If Rusk's comments were an attempt to feel out Pearson they were partially successful. Pearson responded that Lie would have to be persuaded to continue in office, and he expected no difficulty in doing so. He interpreted Lie's recent statement as an attempt to strengthen his position respecting reappointment and to make it easier for him to set conditions as his price for continuing in office. Pearson said he sympathized with Lie's ploy and would do the same in his position. Obviously Lie would be in a stronger position if the council unanimously asked him to carry on. Pearson considered agreement on a suitable successor would be virtually impossible; in fact, any agreed successor was likely to be "colourless and relatively ineffective." He thought it, therefore, essential that Lie remain, but this might be on a year-to-year basis. Likewise Evatt should be informed that he had no chance of being appointed. A Latin American candidate was also a danger. The Latins might press for one of their own who would generate no objections, but who would possess only this "negative quality to commend him."

If asked by the council to stand for the office, Pearson said that he would do so but only on the understanding that Moscow had agreed beforehand to his appointment. Since this was unlikely the question was purely academic. He certainly did not want to be proposed by the West and then vetoed by the Russians; but if the occasion arose, he would be willing to surrender his political career for the office.[18]

In early 1950, a CIA informant reported that although, in the early days of the United Nations, the Russians had held Lie in "high esteem," their attitude had cooled somewhat following Lie's support of the Marshall Plan. However, in view of his current stand favoring Communist China's admission to the world organization, the informant thought Moscow would accept his reappointment, as there was nothing to indicate it had decided on someone else. This informant considered it of great importance that Lie serve again, for it would prove extremely difficult to obtain agreement on another candidate by the council's permanent members. Without a consensus candidate the United Nations would come to a grinding halt. If the Chinese representation problem were not settled by the autumn, the Nationalist Chinese "could and must be expected to veto Lie's nomination."[19] Naturally the informant was unaware that Lie had learned that when the Norwegian ambassador in Moscow had asked Sobolev who Soviet Russia would support for secretary-general, he had responded that it entertained only one name for the office and that was Lie's.[20]

Lie indirectly flashed his own signal in mid-April, when Cordier and Bunche passed word to the Canadians that Lie "could be counted upon to reconsider his intention of retiring": any renewal of his contract, they discreetly mumbled, from two to five years appeared acceptable.[21] In view of the question's importance the State Department had been primed to raise it in January 1950, when the problem of Chinese representation developed and Soviet Russia stalked out of the United Nations. Hence, the State Department had postponed action.[22] Serious American thinking about the question, which had been delayed in preparation for a May conference of the three Western foreign ministers, now recommenced. The salient points in the State Department's consensus were that preliminary talks should occur first with England and France and then with Soviet Russia and Nationalist China; that Lie be reappointed for another five years, since he appeared to be the only consensus candidate; that, although his tenure had had "certain shortcomings," it had "been generally satisfactory"; that other candidates might be proposed and considered, depending on ability and acceptability to the five states; that for tactical reasons the consultations be based on a list of candidates that included Lie's name; and that, if the consultations led to a deadlock, the assembly could be "empowered" by a simple resolution to continue Lie in office until a successor were selected or Lie reappointed. Moreover, Lie should be made aware of this contemplated assembly procedure and "urged as a matter of public duty to acquiesce" in it.[23]

By mid-May the three Western foreign ministers agreed that their United Nations representatives begin discussions.[24] Concurrently in Moscow, where Lie had arrived on his peace mission, Vyshinsky reiterated privately Russia's support of his candidacy.[25] Probably Vyshinsky's comment explained the confident posture of Norway's United Nations representative, Arne Sunde, who believed that Lie "would succeed himself," envisaging no alternative candidate. Lie's denial that he was a candidate, Sunde opined to the Americans, did not signify that he would not continue in the office "if he seemed to be the only person on whom agreement could be reached."[26]

Lie, however, was a Hobson's choice, and the Foreign Office was dissatisfied. Jebb reflected this on May 23 when he speculated to Cadogan on whether there was a possibility of any other consensus candidate or if Lie's term would have to be extended and on legal difficulties that might develop if one or more of the permanent members were absent when the council voted—an allusion to Soviet Russia's continued absence and the possible absence of Nationalist China. Perhaps, Jebb observed, a provisional interim arrangement would have to be worked out.[27]

When Lie lunched with Jebb on May 24, as he retraced his steps to New York from Moscow, he told Jebb he wanted to resign when his term expired. Lie thought the person to replace him was Pearson and said he had so informed the Russians (there is no evidence that he did so). Jebb queried Lie whether Moscow had agreed to this and concluded it had not. Indeed, Jebb decided from Lie's comments that he knew very well that, if he did not seek reappointment, there was no chance that the council's permanent members could agree on any other person.[28]

In reaction to this conversation, Cecil Parrott of the Foreign Office's United Nations Department noted that it appeared reasonably clear that Lie's trip to Moscow was in part something of an electoral tour. Despite remarks to the contrary, Lie was certainly interested in having himself reappointed and was lobbying the Latin Americans to bring this about. If Lie sincerely wanted to depart in 1951 he surely could have offered the Russians a "more palatable alternative" than Pearson. Aside from his unacceptable position as a Commonwealth foreign minister, Pearson a number of times had rapped the Russians "across the knuckles" during the previous year on the Palestine question.[29] Although Parrott did not say it specifically, Pearson was Lie's straw man in any discussions about his successor.

Western discussions at the United Nations about Lie's successor commenced on June 13, when Austin approached his French counterpart, Jean Chauvel. He pointed out that if an agreement on a candidate was unobtainable, some other course had to be considered. Washington did not wish to assume any position in the matter, Austin explained, except on the basis of the three-power discussions. Although he insisted he was "speaking personally" and not for the American government, Austin released his trial balloon: they should agree on Lie since it appeared that he would be the only candidate acceptable to the Russians. The potential fly in the ointment was abstention or opposition to Lie by Nationalist China, whose representative Tingfu Tsiang, had recently denounced him. If agreement proved impossible, Austin suggested the State Department's contemplated procedure of the assembly extending Lie's term.

The French, Chauvel imparted, also inclined to the notion that the only candidate acceptable to Moscow was Lie. The whole question was one of expediency, Chauvel rightly maintained, and accordingly the Quai d'Orsay did not dismiss the contemplated procedure of an assembly extension of Lie's term by one year. Chauvel's deputy emphasized that this procedure might be unacceptable to Lie, who, based on statements made in Paris and London, "had an aggressive take-it-or-leave-it attitude toward the Secretary-Generalship." Much, Chauvel correctly observed, would depend on whether Soviet Russia attended the assembly session. If the Russians departed from the United Nations for good, then probably someone other than Lie should be appointed. The only names that Chauvel offered were the Mexicans: Torres Bodet, or the United Nations representative, Luis Padilla Nervo.[30]

The discussions continued on the same lines the next day between Cadogan and Gross and Ross of the American mission. Objections by Nationalist China, Gross observed, "could be overcome." Cadogan saw no real alternative to Lie; but, on the other hand, he wanted some effort made to seek "another and probably better candidate." Personally, Cadogan was convinced that Lie wished to continue in office, despite his public stance, and was doing all he could to achieve this. He implied that Whitehall did not think highly of Lie and would undoubtedly prefer someone else if this were possible. Cadogan indicated it "thought Lie was an 'intriguer' and that he was a poor and costly administrator." Many had been mentioned as possible successors to Lie. Cadogan echoed Chauvel that, if Soviet Russia quit the United Nations, someone might be considered superior to Lie in the new situation. If circumstances compelled the acceptance of Lie as the compromise candidate, consideration might be given to limiting his second term to two years. The Americans, Cadogan reported to the Foreign Office, were convinced that Lie would have to be reappointed; and they might well be right. He was, however, unsure whether Lie's reappointment should be actively sought. This meant "expressing support for Lie and endorsing his record as Secretary-General," which Cadogan was very reluctant to do. He suggested that serious consideration be given to alternative candidates. If the Western states could agree on a list of names this could be used in private conversations with the Russians and Nationalist Chinese. In any case, Cadogan advised delay until the situation in the assembly was clarified.[31]

That night, June 14, Assistant Secretary of State for United Nations Affairs John Hickerson informed Lie confidentially that the United States supported his candidacy as secretary-general. He would serve, Lie responded, only if United Nations interest demanded it, and then only for two more years; another five year term was out of the question.[32] Accordingly, with American and Russian support in his hip pocket, not to mention the grudging support of the British and French, Lie could sit back and relax. However, the horizon had some dark clouds. There was a rising clamor from certain United States senators that Lie was a Communist and Moscow's tool, a stance largely triggered by his support of Peking's claim to China's seat. In addition, there was the statement of Nationalist China's Tsiang that he would veto Lie's full reappointment but would consent to a one year extension of his present term.[33] Unbeknownst to Lie a kaleido-scopic realignment was right round the corner as a result of Communist North Korea's invasion of South Korea on June 25.

Moscow's Pariah

The invasion of South Korea was the great watershed in Lie's tenure as secretary-general. His support of United Nations action in behalf of the Republic of South Korea generated Soviet Russia's implacable enmity.[34] This new state of affairs was soon confirmed by a report to the Foreign Office that a bellwether of Moscow's thinking, Poland's representative, Ju-liusz Katz-Suchy, had remarked that "Lie had outlived his usefulness."[35] Like it or not, to use the rhetorical parlance of the Left, Lie had become a lackey of the Western camp.

His conversation at this juncture with Jebb, who had replaced Cadogan at the United Nations, reflected his new unsolicited role. Lie's anti-Russian and other comments were interpreted by Jebb as an oblique ad-mission that he was in the running for secretary-general. Lie's point of view appeared to be that Moscow had definitely left the United Nations; that it would soon establish its own world organization, tempting away as many United Nations members as possible. According to Lie, the only hope for peace lay in the West realizing the danger it faced and showing Soviet Russia in no uncertain terms that it was far stronger. Jebb concluded that Lie discerned that he had burnt his bridges with Moscow; that, should Russia return to the United Nations, he would not be reappointed, even if there was no consensus on a successor; that, although he sought to give the impression he wanted to retire, he really wanted to continue in office; that he thought the chances were that Moscow would not return to the organization; and lastly, that without Soviet Russia, Lie felt there was a good chance that "his recent *satisfactory* conduct over Korea [might] result in securing the necessary votes on the part of the other powers concerned" to continue as secretary-general.[36]

Since the State Department was not keen on Mexico's Padilla Nervo or the Philippines' Romulo and thought that Myrdal "might be too inclined to look for compromises" with the Russians, Lie almost by default contin-ued to be the West's plausible candidate. Accordingly, the State Depart-ment informed Ottawa that, as there were no prospects that the permanent members could agree on any candidate, including Lie, assembly authoriza-tion would be sought to extend Lie's term of office.[37]

Despite Lie's public declaration that "he would not continue" in the post,[38] the Foreign Office fell in step with Washington's approach, which seemed to circumvent the wording of the assembly resolution of January 1946, which suggested both council and assembly votes were necessary to renew an incumbent's tenure. In the current situation the operative word was not "renewal," but "extension" of Lie's existing appointment.[39] Lie's support of South Korea caused the French to accept the American ploy "as a necessary evil."[40] The Canadians had been thinking along the same lines and likewise rejected Myrdal on the ground that "he would probably be less tractable and more sympathetic to Soviet views" than Lie. If and when the Russians and the West rejected each others' alternative candidates, an extension of Lie's term, or its renewal, could be broached as the obvious solution.[41]

The whole situation became more complex when in August Soviet Russia returned to the council, which it had boycotted since January, and assumed the presidency. The American tack now was to press in the council for a renewal of Lie's contract for another five years, since his "strong support of UN action in [the] Korean crisis ha[d] contributed appreciably to UN accomplishments in this matter and ha[d] greatly increased his personal status." In view of Moscow's hostility toward Lie this was optimism of a high order, and one suspects it was proffered with the specific purpose of embarrassing the Russians by forcing them to cast a veto. If no agreement were reached, the State Department believed that the assembly could then extend Lie's term for two years with further extension of up to five.[42]

Jebb admitted to the Americans that London had only contemplated a simple extension of Lie's term by the assembly but that the Russian return made it difficult to justify withholding the item from the council agenda. However, voting in a private meeting of the council should be avoided, where Russian rejection of Lie might make it difficult to justify subsequent assembly extension of his term. Though the Anglo-American discussion was inconclusive, it was agreed that, for tactical purposes, it would be useful to have alternative candidates available if needed in discussions with the Russians.[43]

The French again advanced the candidacies of Torres Bodet and Padilla Nervo and were likewise partial to extending Lie's contract albeit with indefinite terminology. The Nationalist Chinese, however, were not to be budged; Tsiang reiterated that he would veto any renewal of Lie's term but not oppose its extension. The Foreign Office suggested to Jebb that if informal discussions among the permanent members showed that the "Russians were either negative or evasive" about reappointing Lie, then a short-term extension of his contract by the assembly should be sought. Of course, the problem at this juncture was not just the Russians but also the Nationalist Chinese. Unless the situation changed, Jebb responded, the assembly procedure should be followed. The Foreign Office's basic desire, however, continued to be to delay matters until the situation in the United Nations crystallized, without committing London to Lie. London's views on Moscow's future participation in the world organization and on who should be secretary-general were intertwined.[44]

By September the British and American positions were basically the same: if Moscow withdrew London and Washington would review their positions on the secretary-generalship.[45] Broad strategy on this question among the Western powers converged; divergencies were merely tactical in nature.[46] As the Acting Head of the United Nations Division of Canada's External Department correctly pointed out to the British High Commissioner, the solution of the question would, in the "last analysis, be based on political considerations and not on a legal interpretation" of the assembly resolution of January 1946.[47]

A new tour of duty was so close that Lie could almost taste it. He badgered Gross about it on three occasions, and gave the impression that his term should be extended for five years. He professed a desire to retire but qualified it with references to an unsettled world and the need to maintain a strong United Nations, and "other similar statements dripping with virtue which were undoubtedly sincere but which at the same time were consistent with a manifest desire to remain available for public duty." In view of the Anglo-French wish to limit any extension of Lie's term, Gross dissuaded him from insisting on five years. After some "huffing and puffing" the great man agreed. No doubt to assuage his ego, Lie emphasized that the matter had to be handled discreetly and suggested that he be offered the opportunity to reject any services beyond two years. He insisted on this "face-saving technique" so much, Gross informed the State Department, that it was uncertain whether he would accept a two-year offer unless the matter were more or less handled in this manner.[48]

The Foreign Office, however, sought to delay the matter in order to discover the positions of Soviet Russia and Nationalist China. If the Russians proved difficult London would accept at the most a two-year extension of Lie's term. It desired to avoid a commitment to five years since Moscow's departure might cause Whitehall to seek a more desirable candidate. The French shared the British position and Jebb observed that if the Russians suggested an acceptable alternative to Lie he thought that London would accept that candidate.[49]

In mid-September Jebb discussed the question at lunch with Russia's Deputy Foreign Minister Yakov Malik. Jebb raised the possibility of extending Lie's term, solicited Malik's views on alternative candidates, and noted that only recently Moscow had favored Lie more so than the West, while perhaps the reverse was now true. At any rate, the West was open to "any possible solution." Malik asked about Lie's attitude. Jebb thought that, if pressed, he would accept a two year extension despite his public attitude on retirement. What other candidates had been put forward? the Russian queried. Torres Bodet, Padilla Nervo, and others, Jebb responded. What other delegations favored the extension of Lie's term? The Americans and the French shared this view, Jebb obliged. Malik explained he could not tender any views since he did not know Moscow's thoughts, which he would discuss when Vyshinsky arrived. Jebb appears to have talked too much and Malik not enough. In the Foreign Office's United Nations Department, Archibald Mackenzie's notation was to the point: I hope, he wrote, that "Malik got more out of his oysters" than Jebb got out of Malik.[50] The Russian enigma continued, however, for some days later when Jebb requested a meeting to discuss the question Vyshinsky failed to reply.[51] Lie was likewise unsuccessful in ascertaining Moscow's attitude through sounding out Russian Assistant Secretary-General Zinchenko. Certainly, from comments made to Lie by Acheson, Bevin, and Schuman, it was clear that he was the choice of the Western powers. Under these circumstances he decided he would have to accept an extension of his contract, if only to defend his stand on Korea, but cautiously stayed his hand.

As October neared and Jebb appeared unresponsive to Lie's desire to resolve the problem, Lie decided to announce to the assembly his determination to retire. Cordier, Feller, and Foote argued that, instead, identical letters be sent to Jebb, as president of the council, and Nasrollah Entezam, the Iranian president of the assembly, calling their attention to the termination of his contract, to an assembly agenda item dealing with the secretary-general's appointment, and to his December 1949 statement that he was not a candidate for reappointment. When Gross saw the draft letter he strongly recommended that it not be sent officially to Jebb and Entezam, or commented on publicly, since it would complicate the American task of his reappointment.[52] Under Secretary of State Hickerson agreed.

When approached by Gross Malik fended him off, as he had Jebb. He had no information to offer, Malik explained; Vyshinsky would handle it. Gross and Hickerson agreed that since Austin was president of the council for October, it be polled on whether to tackle the matter or to take it straight to the assembly. Regardless of the approach, and in line with Lie's wishes, Hickerson felt that he should be offered a five year contract, whereas Lie's counteroffer should be for three years. This shorter period would be contingent upon the consent of the other interested parties, who envisaged only a two year term.[53] Understandably, Lie wanted the assembly to resolve the matter as soon as possible, because the "uncertainty in his own status was causing him difficulty." Moreover, he pointed out that the Russians were attempting to "arouse" the Latin American and Arab states against him.[54]

On October 5, the American delegation decided that, after discussing a staff paper summarizing the options, a private meeting of the council should be convened and the question of a consensus candidate raised. If the council could not agree on a candidate, the matter would be taken immediately to the assembly to obtain a decision to extend Lie's contract.[55] On October 9, the council convened privately.[56] The Yugoslav representative proposed that Lie's term be extended by the assembly. Malik strongly objected that any appointment to the office required the concurrence of the council with the veto applicable and that action by only the assembly violated the charter, thus anyone elected in this fashion would be an illegal incumbent.[57] Of the alternative candidates raised during this meeting, Entezam, Jebb later reported, seemed a likely choice.[58]

Lie was angry: Jebb and Chauvel had hedged; Austin continued to support him; but the Western powers were less united on his candidacy than he had thought. He wished to avoid being a "political football," he later wrote, which would harm him personally. He felt he had been misled and was the current Russian whipping boy for merely doing his duty, the political struggle now extended beyond his reappointment. He cornered Jebb and in "unvarnished terms" unleashed his sentiments: he wanted to know the British position; he was not a pawn; his patience had limits; and so on. He also contacted Austin who was distressed by the lack of Western unity. Lie made it clear that if the situation persisted he was prepared to withdraw his name.[59] The Foreign Office was likewise dissatisfied with the situation. The Russians had still not committed themselves, it signaled Jebb: Was this a maneuver to corner London into proclaiming a willingness to consider alternative candidates? Would Moscow then declare its support for Lie and claim London was trying to dismiss him? Jebb was instructed to seek an extension of Lie's appointment and not let it be known that Great Britain would consider alternative candidates.[60]

By inference, Jebb had done exactly that, and his inclination therefore was to say nothing initially when the council again convened privately and to reject any Russian candidate who was clearly unacceptable. If, by some miracle, Malik pressed the candidature of someone like Entezam, Jebb proposed to request time to consult with Bevin. Only if it proved impossible to come to any agreement with the Russians in private, London responded, should the assembly be approached, with the recommendation that, to ensure United Nations working efficiency, a resolution be passed—minus the agreement of the council—extending Lie's term for another two years.[61]

Despite Jebb's own inclination initially to remain silent at the council's private meeting of October 12, he appears to have been the first to speak. He queried whether, in principal, a majority wished to continue Lie in office. If they did, the details could be worked out and the matter left to the assembly. He pointed out that it was unlikely a consensus candidate would emerge from the council. If Jebb's remarks were an attempt to smoke out Malik they succeeded. His straw man was Zygmunt Modzelewski, Poland's Foreign Minister. The Americans, Norwegians, and Yugoslavs supported Lie. Chauvel wondered if the question could be resolved, since Austin rejected Modzelewski and Malik opposed Lie. He doubted whether Modzelewski would show that impartiality Malik indicated was needed for the office, and he would therefore abstain. The Indian representative, Sir Benegal Rau, feigned that he needed instructions and that, if pressed, he would also have to abstain. Malik's proposal to defer the discussion until the representatives received instructions and his subsequent attempt to recommend Modzelewski were rejected. Malik then vetoed Lie's reappointment. Austin observed that he would write to General Assembly President Entezam what had transpired. But Jebb sewed it up by suggesting that the letter simply point out that the council was unable to make any recommendation.[62] Malik's tender of so unacceptable a candidate as Modzelewski had been an inept move.

As Minister of State Younger pointed out to Bevin there was no choice but to extend Lie's term, since the Russians offered no reasonable alternative, although he was uncertain that they had uttered their last word on the subject. Indeed, if they proffered a more acceptable candidate, at least he had to be considered impartially. Many, including the Indians and the Israelis, were afraid of the cumulative impact of assembly resolutions that Moscow strongly opposed. If the West now forced on Moscow a secretary-general it had publicly censured, Younger thought it might go far to drive the Russians out of the United Nations. If Russian actions forced the West to do this, then it could not be helped; but he thought London should manifest "just sufficient reserve" in its support for Lie to keep the door open to any more suitable candidate Moscow might suggest.[63] Along these lines Jebb made it clear to Gross, and the Foreign Office concurred, that the assembly's extension of Lie's term for two or three years was more acceptable; and besides neither the French nor the Indians would consent to a five year extension. Gross agreed to the shorter term.[64]

In an attempt to stave off the situation that had developed, Malik called on John Foster Dulles late on the night of October 16 to outline the Russian position; and the next day he saw Austin and Gross. Lie, he held, was a Janus in his dealings with Washington and Moscow: he bad mouthed the former to the latter and vice versa, according to Russian information. Lie's continuance in office would neither improve relations between the two states nor contribute to peace. It was important to have a consensus secretary-general, and Malik strongly believed that further discussions would bring this about.

Austin and Gross were not receptive. Austin observed that Washington had publicly committed itself to Lie and would need good cause to change its position. Soviet Russia stood alone in the council in opposing Lie; it was thwarting the majority will; and only concrete proposals by Moscow strengthening peace might lead Washington to consider a change of position. Malik responded that the United Nations would be damaged by a secretary-general whose legality was questioned: assembly appointment of

Lie without council concurrence would be a violation of the charter and the 1946 assembly resolution.

Austin pointed out that it would have helped if Moscow had consulted earlier on the issue. Malik retorted that it had not realized the issue would be tackled so quickly and asserted that both sides were to blame in not consulting earlier. Gross denied this: Jebb had tried in September with Vyshinsky but never received a reply; he himself had broached it to Malik, who held there was more than enough time. When Gross demurred, pointing out that it would come up early in the assembly, Malik had responded that Vyshinsky was dealing with the issue, and there was no rush. Malik had given a similar reply to Gross when he raised the issue a week later. Faced with this litany of missed opportunities, Malik conceded that perhaps the Russians had been at fault.

When Malik pressed the argument that an agreement could be reached on a candidate other than Lie, Austin suggested the matter could be solved by unanimously agreeing to Lie's reappointment thus acknowledging the majority will. This, Malik insisted, was out of the question, and he requested another private meeting of the council.[65] The discussion had been unproductive.

Jebb's information was that Malik might press for an Indian to replace Lie and had closeted himself with Padilla Nervo. If he offered a plausible Indian, the British position would be very difficult, Jebb pointed out to the Foreign Office; in such a case, should he broach the possibilities of reopening the whole question before requesting adjournment for consultation? Of course, the principal object of Malik's ploy might be to "muddy the waters" and prevent the assembly from extending Lie's term. Further delay might lead to a Latin American attempt to engineer an assembly blocking vote of one-third plus one against Lie, in hope of foisting their own candidate on the United Nations. Jebb doubted that any Indian candidate could obtain the seven votes needed in the council, since the United States, Cuba, Ecuador, Norway, and probably Nationalist China would abstain.[66] Nevertheless, Lie felt that the British were "complicating matters" by toying with the idea of having an Indian replacement.[67]

Moscow had to be given time to reconsider, the Foreign Office responded, to reduce the risk of an accusation that the West had forced the issue. Should a Russian offer appear reasonable, London could not dismiss it out of hand, especially if an Indian candidate was reputable, even though initially unable to garner the seven votes needed. London would have to support him anyway; moreover, the candidature of Padillo Nervo was not excluded.

There was, of course, the problem of controlling the assembly, should there be further delays. Assuming that an extension of Lie's contract would secure wide support, Jebb was also instructed to endorse it, if the Russian step turned out to be a mere delaying tactic. He was not to propose an alternative candidate but await the Russian offer. Further action would be decided in light of the Russian move, and Jebb should, if necessary, request an adjournment to consult London, which would give added time.[68]

Obviously, some elements in the Labour government and the Foreign Office for varied reasons preferred an Indian secretary-general rather than Lie. This sentiment, however, was not shared by the Americans, and the Foreign Office was soon made aware of this fact. The first secretary of the American embassy thought Washington "would treat with some reserve any proposal for the nomination of an Indian" as secretary-general. The State Department, Peter Hope of the Foreign Office's United Nations Department was unofficially informed, was "very sceptical of the political maturity of Indian figures." India's intervention during the Korean crisis "had left a deplorable impression of this in the minds of the State Department." The only Indian who might be acceptable was Sir Girja Bajpai, secretary-general of the Indian Foreign Ministry; but being secretary-general of the United Nations was not the same thing, and the State Department feared that he might not possess the "necessary strength of character for the latter job."[69]

The private meeting of the council requested by Malik was preceded by extensive lobbying, which reflected the Russian desire to avoid Lie's selection. To the Latin Americans Russia indicated a willingness to accept one of their own provided that person "was also acceptable" to Washington. Malik likewise showed interest in Indian candidates. Keeping in mind Lie's activities during the Palestine question, the Arabs shared the Russians' abhorrence of Lie.[70] The inability to agree on a candidate, Malik insisted during the private meeting of the council on October 18, did not mean that an attempt to concur on some other candidate was excluded. He saw various possibilities, especially from Latin America and Asia, and declared that extending Lie's term illegally would create the unwanted impression that the council was incapable of agreeing even on this question.

Perhaps playing the puppet at the end of Malik's string, the Indian representative, Rau, proposed that each council member submit, by secret ballot, the names of two candidates, resulting at the most in a list of twenty-two names. Before the list was submitted to the council, it would be examined by the five permanent members, who would eliminate unacceptable candidates. This would shorten the list, help avoid the veto, and maximize the possibility of an agreement. If a deadlock persisted it would have to be reported to the assembly.

In line with his instructions, Jebb noted the need to consult the Foreign Office. His initial reaction was that Rau's scheme was imaginative and a possible way out of the current difficulty. However, the possibility of a deadlock still existed if a candidate failed to receive the required seven votes—an allusion to possible abstentions by the United States and others.

Jebb was supported by France's Chauvel and Nationalist China's Tsiang, whose hostility to Lie went undisguised. Latin American support was tendered by Ecuador and Cuba. To no one's surprise Malik also put in his supporting oar. The Egyptians followed suit.

Austin was not amused by this performance. Which would be the first name stricken from the list? he asked. At the previous private meeting nine members had agreed on Lie; "did they now want to march downhill, he asked, and adopt a plan that would strike him off the list? Is the spoken word without value, he continued; is there no integrity?" He reserved the right to plead strongly with Lie's previous backers to maintain their position and not be moved by the notion that one state could thwart the votes of nine. The American mission had decided, Washington learned later, to oppose Rau's "proposal on the ground that it involved reopening the question and a series of secret nominations . . . [and that the] Russians should make their proposals publicly," since the proposed new procedure would liquidate Lie's candidacy.

Although the Norwegian representative, Arne Sunde, conceded Rau's plan had merit, he noted that Tsiang's opposition to Lie was based on his China policy, whereas Malik's was based on Lie's support of the South Koreans. Lie was Moscow's candidate in 1946, Sunde pointed out, and was persona grata until the North Koreans invaded South Korea. The council discussion quickly degenerated into an acrimonious exchange.[71] The Rau-Malik, Jebb-Chauvel-Tsiang, and so on combination was smarter by half: to reject Lie, after having selected him only days before would have been an awfully large pill to swallow even in a United Nations capable of adjusting to anything, but it was a pill absolutely unacceptable to Washington. American countermeasures inside and outside the United Nations quickly followed.

London could not oppose the Rau proposal, Jebb opined to the Foreign Office, without generating criticism in India, France, and elsewhere. Although he thought it would fail, Jebb believed it should be tested. Indeed, if the Indian proposal were turned down, the assembly might simply refuse to extend Lie's term and urge the council to rethink the question. The Americans, the Norwegians, and the Yugoslavs would undoubtedly vote against the proposal, but Jebb thought it unwise for London likewise to do so. If the necessary seven votes could not be acquired in favor of any candidate that emerged from the secret ballot, London would show that it had attempted to be as conciliatory as possible and had done everything conceivable to find a candidate acceptable to all the permanent members. If the whole procedure misfired, as seemed likely, the assembly would be more likely to reach a nearly unanimous decision recommending an extension of Lie's term, which otherwise seemed uncertain.[72]

Latin American support for the Rau proposal was conveyed to Austin by the Cuban Carlos Blanco, as offering a way out of the current difficulty.

Cuba would continue to support Lie, because it felt nothing would develop from the Indian proposal and that the result would be to return to the initial choice of Lie. The question was more than purely administrative, as appeared on the surface, Austin responded; it had "broad and deep political and moral implications." The present ploy to eliminate Lie was a Russian attack on the United Nations and, if it succeeded, would have immense impact. It would adversely affect morale in Korea, since Lie was a symbol of resistance against aggression, and undermine support for Korean reconstruction and rehabilitation in Congress, which would not have the same confidence in an untried successor. Moreover, states that had initially supported Lie would be accused of lacking "integrity and stability." Washington was therefore willing to face Moscow's charge of "intransigence or high-handedness" and would oppose the proposal. The Latin Americans, Blanco observed, felt that a conciliatory gesture was necessary. He suggested amending the proposal: to exempt Lie and Modzelewski from the list, thus leaving Lie available should the other candidates be rejected. Austin would have none of it: the Russians wanted to confuse the matter and get the council to give in after it had thoroughly defeated them on Lie's continuation. To conciliate "was sweet, but in this case it was the sweetness of arsenic, which kills." The entire Russian maneuver "was a trick and a trap and we should not be blinded to its danger by words having a high appeal."[73] Austin's emotive response was no feigned reaction to the Rau-Malik two-step: New Englanders of his generation often viewed events in a Calvinist perspective rather than a choice of lesser evils.

In London, Bevin drew the cabinet's attention to Bajpai's possible candidacy, pointing out it would prove embarrassing since support for Lie had already been voiced. In the discussion that followed it was suggested that Moscow's advocacy of Bajpai was based less on his merits and more on India's policy over Korea, which differed from the West's.[74]

Before Bevin could consult with anyone Acheson sent him a personal message.[75] Acheson was convinced that Russian approaches to the Latin Americans and Indians for candidates, and a recent attempt by Vyshinsky to recruit Romulo, were maneuvers to defeat Lie. In view of the earlier Anglo-American inability to consult with the Russians on this issue and Moscow's transparent and "obvious design" in instituting these last-minute moves, Acheson believed it was too late to reopen the issue in view of the objections Austin had raised. Acheson understood that the Austin-Jebb-Chauvel consensus had been that there was "no practical alternative" to Lie's redesignation, and this was still the case.

Acheson had little doubt that Moscow's strong objections to Lie could be traced largely, and perhaps decisively, to his attitude on the Korean question. Prior disagreements with Lie by everyone on various matters were perhaps natural because of the nature of his office and the difficult times; but Moscow now seemed determined to treat Lie's reappointment "as a test of the validity" of United Nations actions in Korea. Many whom the Russians had approached at the United Nations understood this, including even some who might seemingly gain by the selection of one of their nationals or someone from their region, as a candidate for the office. Acheson appreciated Bevin's delicate position because of the possibility of a Commonwealth candidate; yet he was convinced that Lie's initial selection had to be supported in face of Moscow's apparent determination to quash it as a demonstration of Russia's ability to thwart the majority consensus. Unless the line was held, the future selection of a new secretary-general was unpredictable; the new person might be regarded, perhaps unjustly, as a coerced choice and would be continuously open to similar pressures. Acheson therefore hoped Bevin would instruct Jebb not to support the Indian proposal.[76] It was a cogent message. Bevin agreed and Acheson was very grateful.[77]

He had decided, Bevin explained to Jebb, to continue supporting Lie, who represented a small and friendly European state, and had "withstood the test of . . . office reasonably well"; whereas the Indian proposal read "like a Soviet-inspired manoeuvre" directed less against Lie himself than against the Free World's policy. Since it required that those who had supported Lie drop his candidacy, any alternative candidate selected under the Indian proposal would be in a difficult position. Jebb was therefore directed to vote against the Indian proposal. He was to inform Rau and the Indian mission that whereas normally London would have supported a Commonwealth candidate all the way, a "question of principle" was involved here, requiring the maintenance of support for Lie.[78]

The State Department also transmitted copies of Acheson's missive to America's missions in Havana, Mexico City, Oslo, New Delhi, and Paris. In response to the American advocacy the first three capitals agreed to continue supporting Lie. Paris neatly sidestepped the issue by giving Chauvel "complete discretion," which evoked the restrained American reaction that Acheson "would undoubtedly be disappointed that [Foreign Minister] Schuman had not seen fit" to instruct Chauvel to oppose the Indian proposal.[79] In New Delhi, however, Prime Minister Pandit Nehru already instructed Rau to stand for the office, claiming that unanimous support was not essential, only a majority.[80] How Rau could hurdle an American or Nationalist Chinese veto, Nehru did not elucidate. The private meeting of the council on October 20 led nowhere. The Cubans, British, and Yugoslavs opposed the Indian proposal; the French and Russians endorsed it; Ecuador abstained.[81]

Because the proposal was sure to be defeated at the next day's formal meeting if not withdrawn, Jebb signaled Bevin, Malik had implied he would introduce alternative candidates who would doubtlessly include an Indian and a Latin American. In this event he thought it would be difficult to press for an adjournment as Bevin desired, since the Americans and others insisted on a quick decision. Unless instructed otherwise, therefore, he proposed to abstain from any "reasonable candidate" offered by Malik; since no alternative candidate could receive the necessary seven votes. If any Indian were offered, Nationalist China would veto, so London need not worry about Commonwealth implications.[82] Bevin agreed; "unfortunately the Russians [had] bedevilled the situation," he noted, and when contacted Bajpai thought London "quite right not to give way" to them.[83]

As Jebb had foreseen, at the council meeting of October 21, Rau withdrew the proposal. Malik, down but not out, did not offer alternative candidates, as Jebb prophesied, but proposed additional informal consultation by the permanent members; the results to be reported by October 24 and considered by the council the following day. Although Malik's proposal was accepted, the Americans, British, Norwegians, and Yugoslavs abstained.[84] He would advance no names, Jebb observed to London, and would indicate that, in any future council vote on a "reasonable candidate," Great Britain would abstain.[85] Bevin agreed that no other course of action was open.[86]

The informal meeting convened on October 23. The Russians proposed the candidacies of Padilla Nervo, Rau, and Lebanon's representative, Charles Malik; the Nationalist Chinese proposed Romulo, but found Padilla Nervo and Lebanon's Malik acceptable. Jebb indicated his preference for Lie; he would abstain on other candidates. His country, Austin declared, would support no one but Lie. The Russians naturally supported any other candidate. Chauvel implied no objections to those nominated, although he preferred Lie.[87] There was still no consensus.

In view of the French position, Jebb noted to London, it looked as if Padilla Nervo, provided there was no American veto, might receive the necessary seven votes to be selected.[88] Bevin speculated on alternative candidates, including Pearson, but concluded that Jebb "should continue to abstain on any reasonable alternative candidate to Lie."[89]

On this issue the Americans were adamant, the State Department even asking the Quai d'Orsay that Chauvel vote for Lie or at least abstain on any other candidate.[90] Acheson was indifferent whether the United States' decision to use the veto became public knowledge. Washington was not going to permit Moscow's maneuver to succeed, he informed the mission in New York, and would support Lie with whatever power was needed; tactics could be decided by the mission. Acheson disliked the idea of a series of votes on different candidates, preferring to "kill the whole thing off at one stroke by using the threat of the veto." He felt that if Washington "used the threat, it would not be necessary to use the veto."

Acheson considered the Good Neighbor Policy a two way street: Padilla Nervo should withdraw his candidacy and was to be informed that, if necessary, Washington would invoke the veto against any other candidate than Lie. No Latin American candidate was acceptable to the United States, and in fact the Latin Americans should not "embarrass themselves" by running one and triggering an American veto. Washington's position was a matter of principle: Moscow could not be permitted to punish Lie for his Korean stand. President Truman had pointed out that Lie had been Russia's candidate and that Korea was the only reason for its about-face; the United States was therefore "prepared to make a real fight on this matter."

Acheson bluntly instructed the mission thus to advise all concerned. The French had been informed in no uncertain terms and urged to "stick to their guns and support Lie"; Padilla Nervo and the Latin Americans would similarly be advised. Malik's and Vyshinsky's tactics based on Moscow's instructions to divide and conquer, delay and procrastinate, as these comments show, had backfired and whipped the fury of patient men.

The Latin Americans and the French soon heaved to. The steamroller continued: Lebanon's Malik was assured that the American veto of anyone but Lie would not be directed against him personally, against Lebanon, or against the Arab states generally, but would be "directed to the high principle and moral question involved."

Disagreement at the second informal meeting of the permanent members on the morning of October 25 was such that they could not even concur on the form of the report to the imminent private meeting of the council. There, although the votes had already been lined up, another repetitive, long, and bitter discussion pitted Russia's Malik against the Western powers and especially Austin. After some procedural hurdles, but in separate votes, Lebanon's Malik and Romulo were rejected, both by seven abstentions including all the Western powers. Rau withdrew his candidacy, and Padilla Nervo's was not pressed. The council then approved by seven votes to one, with three abstentions (Nationalist China, Egypt, and India) a letter to the presidents of the council and the assembly reporting the council's inability to agree on a recommendation.[91] The campaign orchestrated by the Americans to extend Lie's contract and the Russian resistance it generated accurately reflected the abysmal state that East-West relations had reached by the autumn of 1950.

Jebb reported it likely that Russia's Malik would request one more private council meeting to consider another, as yet unspecified, candidate.[92] But Bevin had had enough: continued discussion of this issue, he informed the British embassy in Washington, was "doing us no good and merely playing into Russian hands." Accordingly, "we should forthwith seek to terminate [the] discussion" on the grounds that the council had already reported to the assembly two previous failures to agree. Though Moscow might make propaganda value out of closure, the risk had to be assumed. If the Americans agreed but were reticent to act, Jebb was to assume the initiative.[93]

It proved unnecessary. When Russia's Malik was pressed for a date on another private council meeting, he declined to give one. It was rumored, Jebb reported, that the Russians could find no candidate who would allow

himself to be nominated and accordingly they had decided to abandon re-
convening the council. Even if a meeting was called for October 30, any
proposed alternative candidate would be rejected, and Jebb would then
seek a decision that the council had exhausted consideration of the question. If Malik did not request such a meeting, Moscow's ability to cause
additional delay would automatically lapse.[94]

On October 30, at Russian request, the council convened for its last
private meeting on this question. Malik warned that Moscow would consider any assembly reappointment of Lie illegal and propose that the assembly postpone consideration of the agenda item so additional candidates
could be considered. Malik's was the only affirmative vote on the proposal.
There were three abstentions (Egypt, Nationalist China, and India) and
seven votes opposed. Moscow's Fabian tactics had finally been brought to
an end. Malik then warned that if Lie was imposed on the world organization by the assembly, Moscow would not consider him the United Nations
secretary-general.[95]

Later that same day Vyshinsky, whose poisonous rhetoric was second to
none, publicly lambasted Lie. The performance was vintage Vyshinsky,
such as he had demonstrated as chief prosecutor in the Moscow purge
trials (1936–1938). But this was merely an hors d'oeuvre to the assembly
debates that raged for the next two days. Led by Vyshinsky and supported
by the representatives of the eastern European satellite states, the West's
attempt to extend Lie's term was vigorously opposed. The choice of secretary-general was the first agenda item. The next step was to find cospon-
sors for the draft resolution extending his term.[96] In the end, fourteen were
found. Lie had spoken "half seriously of getting fifty-three co-sponsors,"[97]
the American mission reported. In view of Lie's uneasy inner self, the
comment was probably more than half serious. While something of an
anticlimax, the debates mirrored the animosity dividing the two camps.
The Russians interestingly appear to have approached Pearson in a desperate bid to head off Lie, but with the curtain about to fall it was too late to
rewrite the last scene.

The resolution extending Lie's term for three more years was adopted
by forty-eight votes to five with eight abstentions. The opposing votes
were cast by Soviet Russia and her satellites. Nationalist China's abstention was self explanatory. The Arabs who had decided to support Lie also
abstained, following an Israeli statement urging the extension of Lie's term
on the grounds that he had assumed a favorable position during the Palestine question. Australia likewise abstained voicing legal doubts; though
Evatt was no longer in power, his designs for the post might partially explain this abstention. Lie was disappointed with the vote. He had looked
forward to fifty votes in support of the resolution and naively thought that
somehow the Arabs and the Nationalist Chinese would see the light and
give him their vote.[98] He was politically myopic to the very end.

Lie, of course, knew where his bread was buttered and sent Austin an obsequious letter of thanks for his and his government's support.[99] Moscow's bitter opposition to Lie's reappointment, however, and the manner by which it was accomplished, led it after February 1951 to the refusal to recognize him as secretary-general. This boycott rankled Lie immensely. One suspects that Lie's annoyance was due as much to the political isolation from the East that the boycott generated as to its social ostracism.[100] There was one last footnote to the whole affair. Myrdal, it was reported to the Foreign Office, had admitted that the Russians approached him near the end of the struggle and asked if he would agree to be nominated. Myrdal alleged that he refused and emphasized his support of Lie, all of which the British found "too good to be true."[101] The British mission had little doubt that Myrdal had hung around New York "in the vain hope that he might possibly be nominated" for the post.[102] Archibald Mackenzie of the United Nations Department neatly summed it up: "I think we are better off with Mr. Lie with all his limitations than with the rather sinister and very ambitious Mr. Myrdal."[103]

Korea: The Far East's Norway

With the exception of Lie's proposal in November 1946 that Hong Kong be transferred to the United Nations as a trusteeship, thus settling the political question between China and Great Britain,[104] Asian affairs had, in fact, taken little of Lie's attention during his first years as secretary-general,[105] including the question of Korea.[106]

When the war ended Japanese forces in Korea north of the 38th parallel surrendered to Soviet Russia and those south of it to the United States. To facilitate the surrender, the 38th parallel therefore had thus been selected as a temporary demarcation line between the two allied armies. The breakdown of the wartime consensus between East and West blocked the unification of the country and soon led to the establishment of two separate administrative and government structures. What had initially been a convenient geographical device to help round up the Japanese forces in Korea soon evolved into two Korean entities, dependent on their respective overlords for survival—client states of either Moscow or Washington.

The years following this division of the Korean peninsula were marked by frustrated attempts by the Western powers, led by the United States against Soviet Russian opposition, to unite the country under United Nations auspices. In 1947 the assembly set up a United Nations Temporary Commission on Korea to establish through nationwide elections a national government for the entire country. Moscow contended the assembly action had no legal basis; accordingly, it would not cooperate with the United Nations action not even to serve on the commission. Elections took place, therefore, only in the south under the aegis of the commission in May 1948, and the government of the Republic of South Korea was formed under the presidency of Syngman Rhee. In 1948 and again in 1949, the assembly declared the Rhee government the lawful, freely chosen government of Korea. It likewise established a United Nations Commission on Korea to facilitate Korea's peaceful unification. Concurrently in the north, elections were also held without United Nations supervision, and a government of the Democratic Peoples Republic of Korea was established under the presidency of Kim Il Sung. Russian and American troop withdrawals from North and South Korea soon followed. Continued political tensions between the two Koreas as well as border incidents, however, left the United Nations Commission on Korea increasingly uneasy, and it responded by expanding its observation groups south of the 38th parallel since it was not allowed to operate to the north. [107]

North Korea's attack on South Korea on June 25, 1950, was well prepared and executed. The report of the United Nations commission left no doubt as to the aggressor. The fury of the attack, which took everyone by surprise, reminded Lie of Nazi Germany's invasion of Norway on April 9, 1940. The trauma of the surprise attack was shared by the leaders of the American government who had lived through the Japanese attack on Pearl Harbor. Lie, like so many others, saw a replay of the 1930s: premeditated aggression, swiftly executed. [108] The charter had been blatantly violated, and no amount of sophistry could circumvent that naked fact. If the United Nations were to survive, there had to be a military response. [109] Given Lie's partiality toward small states, [110] the attack by a Russian surrogate upon a small state whose birth the United Nations had midwifed [111] was a lethal combination. Moscow soon discovered all this in Lie's passionate commitment to the South Koreans. Yet the decision to support the South Koreans, as Lie admitted to the Greek Aghnides, did not come easily: [112] once he crossed the Rubicon, Moscow's wrath would soon follow and his bridge-building efforts would collapse.

Perhaps equally important, his reappointment as secretary-general would prove impossible. If an additional impetus caused Lie to assume the position he did, it may have been a fractured ego. He intended to contact the Russians, Lie told the American mission soon after the North Korean attack, to communicate his disappointment that despite "all the talk of peace" he had had in Moscow the previous month, hostilities erupted. [113] As he wrote to the Norwegian chargé d'affaires in Moscow, it was far from pleasant traveling to the Russian capital on his peace mission, assuring everyone on the way of Soviet Russia's desire for peace, when in the middle of his mediation efforts, her Korean minion began an armed attack. [114]

When news of the North Korean attack was conveyed to Acheson on the night of June 24 (because of the international date line it was June 25 in Korea), he instructed Assistant Secretary John Hickerson to contact Lie and the acting American representative, Ernest Gross, and arrange an emergency meeting of the council. Unable to contact Gross immediately, Hickerson spoke to Lie first. The North Korean attack was an assault on the charter was Lie's flashpoint reaction. He asked that Washington assist him to maintain contact with the United Nations Commission on Korea in order to receive its authentic field reports and requested that the commission immediately furnish him with an estimate of the military situation. During the course of this momentous night, Gross subsequently contacted Lie about four times and at 3 A.M. on June 25 read to him Washington's formal request that the council convene in emergency session to consider the Korean situation.[115]

Lie assured Hickerson that he was prepared to convene the council. Naturally, Hickerson understood that any initiative by Lie along these lines based on Article 99 had to rest on information furnished by an impartial United Nations body, rather than simply in response to information conveyed by an interested state.[116] Lie's desire for unhindered contact with the United Nations Commission on Korea therefore made sense. Gross's subsequent communication of Washington's formal request that the council convene in emergency session obviated any invocation by Lie of Article 99. Nevertheless, Lie's request for a report from the commission, its reply confirming Washington's information, and the commission's suggestion that Lie invoke Article 99[117] went far to strengthen the West's case in the council and to legitimize its subsequent actions in Korea under a United Nations mantle.

At noon, with the commission's reply in hand, Lie caucused with Cordier and Feller. He resolved to act as the tip of the United Nations spear for reasons already discussed and because the council's response "would be more certain and more in the spirit of the Organization as a whole" were he to do so. Lie then contacted the Egyptian, Indian, and Norwegian council representatives, crediting himself with influencing their subsequent decision to support the resolution finally adopted. When the council convened that afternoon, June 25, by prior arrangement with its president, India's Rau, Lie was called upon to be the first speaker.[118] Citing the commission's report, he held that in violation of the charter the North Koreans had commenced a military action that threatened international peace, which the council was competent to tackle. He considered it duty bound to do what was necessary to reestablish peace in Korea.[119]

His actions earned Lie Moscow's implacable hostility. In retrospect, as noble as Lie's deeds appear from a Western perspective, given the nature of politics at any level, trade-off considerations also doubtlessly surfaced in Lie's mind. In a position to know, Cordier, frankly pressing the "view that this would help Lie in the light of his present troubles with American public opinion," let slip an allusion to Lie's recent Moscow peace mission and his support of Communist China in the United Nations. Cordier hoped that Lie's stance "would get good publicity"—it did. Both Cordier and Feller "indicated that this event had made it possible for Lie to prove that he was a United Nations man right down the line regardless of which way the chips fell."[120]

The result of the day's debate was the adoption of the American tendered resolution, subsequently amended, whereby the council declared the North Korean military action to be a breach of the peace and called for the hostilities to cease immediately and the North Koreans quickly to withdraw their military forces to the 38th parallel. In addition, it provided that the United Nations Commission on Korea monitor developments and that all member states assist the United Nations and refrain from aiding the North Koreans. The absence of a Russian veto was made possible by Moscow's continuing boycott of the council. Although the Russian representative had been informed that the council would convene, his truancy was in line with Moscow's January withdrawal in protest against the presence of the Nationalist Chinese in China's seat.[121]

Lie's "unusually strong language" to the council was noted by Sir Terence Shone, Jebb's deputy, Lie appearing "pleased" at the council's action and "at the general tone of the debate." He was likewise pleased that no "offensive reference" to Soviet Russia had been made. Thus, Lie optimistically observed, if Moscow wanted to divorce itself from Korean events it would still be able to do so.[122]

The council resolution, however, did not faze the North Koreans in the least, as the reports of the United Nations Commission on Korea clearly showed.[123] Asked if armed force could be used in Korea by the council, Lie responded affirmatively, provided its call for a cease-fire was ignored.[124] At a luncheon preceding the next meeting of the council, Lie, Gross, and Russian representative Yakov Malik discussed what had transpired. Lie was gratified by the "firm tone" of President Truman's recent statement justifying American support of the South Koreans on the basis of the council's June 25 resolution. The North Korean attack, Truman held, clearly showed that the Communists had gone beyond the "use of subversion" to conquer free states and were now resorting to military force and war. Under these circumstances, Formosa's occupation by the Communists would be a "direct threat to the security of the Pacific area." Accordingly, Truman ordered the U.S. Seventh Fleet to protect Formosa from attack and invited the Nationalist Chinese to call off their military operations against the mainland, which the Seventh Fleet would now see to. Malik maintained that Lie was partial, characterized the council session of June 25 as one sided, and pronounced its resolution as illegal because of his absence and that of a Communist Chinese representative. Naturally, Lie and Gross took the reverse tack. Malik's attempt to explain away the North Korean attack was not pursued further when Lie and Gross pointed out that the attack was more than a riposte to a border skirmish.

At this point, Lie asked for their reaction to the Korean commission's suggestion that a mediator be appointed—thinking of himself perhaps? Gross quickly shot the suggestion down on the grounds that the precondition for any such procedure would be a cease-fire and North Korean withdrawal to the 38th parallel. Lie saw the point, but Malik remained silent. When Malik queried Lie whether Peking would be seated as China's representative before the assembly convened, Lie said he hoped so. He ruminated that Truman's instructions to the Seventh Fleet to prevent the Nationalist Chinese from attacking the mainland constituted a species of recognition of Communist China. Gross denied this; the only thing it recognized, he argued, was that the Nationalist Chinese did not currently control the mainland. Gross asked if Malik had any thoughts on how to terminate the present situation; but Malik gave an evasive reply, though Lie pressed him to respond. [125]

The Russian representative's performance was vintage Malik and should have alerted Lie that the road ahead would be long and pitted by shell fire. As they came to their coffee and dessert Lie, without it appears consulting anyone, impulsively asked Malik if he would like to join them at the council meeting that would soon convene. He was insistent and repeated the suggestion. No doubt Lie felt that unless Moscow was drawn back into the council's political process, his own peacemaking initiatives would be foiled and the chances diminished for any meaningful discussions to end the crisis.

A long-time bureaucrat of the Stalinist regime, Malik knew his marching orders and declined the invitation. Gross did not disguise his relief at Malik's rejection of the invitation nor was he amused by Lie's antics. In view of American intentions for the council's afternoon meeting, Gross sarcastically expressed his solace that Lie had pressed his invitation so poorly that Malik had not been persuaded to accompany them. Could Lie imagine, Gross exclaimed, alluding to the veto, what would have occurred if Malik had accepted the invitation? Lie's politically unsophisticated response was that it would have made things more difficult, but the battle would have continued into the assembly. [126] The point was, however, that speed was of the greatest importance as far as the West, led by the Americans, was concerned. Its ploy was to legitimize any response to the North Korean attack through the council, which under charter Article 24 has "primary responsibility for the maintenance of international peace and security." To carry the struggle to the larger and less Western-dominated assembly would have required convening a special session, which would have courted delay—at that juncture, to be avoided at all costs. It was, to quote the Duke of Wellington, "the nearest run thing" one ever saw; but thanks to Malik's obedience to instructions, Moscow had outsmarted itself.

The council convened as scheduled, and though it did not adjourn until late that same night, it formally sat for only two hours and forty minutes. Nevertheless, during this relatively brief period it adopted an American-sponsored draft resolution, which only Yugoslavia rejected—Egypt and India did not vote, and Soviet Russia was, of course, absent. Under this resolution, the council determined that the North Korean attack was a breach of the peace; called for an immediate cease-fire and the withdrawal of North Korean forces to the 38th parallel; noted the Korean commission's report on the continuing advance of North Korean forces and the urgent need for military measures to restore international peace and security, as well as South Korea's appeal; and most important, recommended that United Nations member states furnish to South Korea "such assistance . . . as may be necessary to repel the armed attack and to restore international peace and security in the area."[127]

Claiming an executive role in implementing decisions of United Nations organs, in this case the council resolution of June 27,[128] Lie proposed a circular telegram requesting that all member states advise him of the specific assistance they intend to offer to the council. Subsequently, it appears, he instructed that the message not be conveyed to Soviet Russia, the satellite states of eastern Europe, and Yugoslavia. Although the State Department thought it "was a good idea to use the United Nations umbrella as much as possible," it also felt that "Lie should function as no more than a post office." The State Department had no objection to the idea of such a message, but its "form" would be very important. Since some member states, France for example, would be able to contribute little, the message should be drafted so as to assist them to reply without embarrassment. The State Department recommended that Lie indicate he would be pleased to have the member states inform him of any specific assistance they might wish to make available, for communication by him to the South Koreans. Washington thought it important to make clear that the offer of assistance was to be to South Korea as the victim of aggression.

The Americans considered it impractical for the world organization to get involved with "the actual use and control of assistance." As Gross explained to Jebb, they did not wish any offers of assistance to be conveyed directly to the council. Likewise, it was to be made very clear to Cordier and Lie that it would be "unthinkable" to involve the Military Staff Committee, which was incapable of practical contribution and, moreover, the Russians could demand to see any of its plans. Neither did the Americans want, formally or informally, any designation of the United States as agent of the United Nations nor of General Douglas MacArthur as the commander in Korea of United Nations forces. The State Department envisaged that in practice offers of assistance would be communicated to Lie, who would pass them on to the South Koreans, while the offering state would thrash out the details directly with Washington. In effect, the

United States would handle things, with MacArthur as commander for the United Nations. [129]

Although initially Cordier concurred with the State Department's views, it appears that, after consulting Lie, he was reluctant to include any reference to Lie merely transmitting replies from member states to the South Koreans. Gross, however, insisted on this point indicating that other governments, like the British and French, "would probably object" to the notion that Lie should be the recipient of the offers of assistance. [130] The Foreign Office shared the State Department's view, and Jebb was instructed to "persuade" Lie to "suspend" any action on his proposed message. [131]

Jebb replied that Lie would "suppress" his draft message [132] and that his attitude appeared to be "completely sound." He took the view that there could be no mediation or meeting with the Russians until the preceding status quo had been restored and the North Koreans forced back to the 38th parallel. Lie admitted that he was keen to have the Egyptians and Indians vote in favor of the June 27 resolution. This would counter Moscow's claim that the council decision was illegal because the resolution was adopted by only six votes, rather than the required seven, in view of the illegitimacy of the Nationalist Chinese representative. [133] Although the Indians later accepted the resolution of June 27, the Egyptians abstained, which "upset" Lie a great deal. What influence Lie had on the Indian decision is unclear. [134]

Despite the impression given that he would suppress his proposed message, Lie sent it on June 29. It noted that, should the member states be able to provide assistance to South Korea, the resolution of June 27 could more easily be implemented if he were provided with a timely response on the assistance to be given. Lie would then transmit the reply to the council and the South Korean government. [135] The American and British pressures nonetheless appear to have had their impact. Compared to Lie's initial draft, the message gave Lie only half of what he had wanted. Jebb's pithy observation to the Foreign Office was that its final form was "obviously much less objectionable" than what Lie had first proposed. This was so; but it should have alerted everyone that in the Korean question, as in so many others, Lie wanted loose reins, as though caution should not be exercised even on what appeared to be the flattest track.

As the replies began to filter in—the Latin Americans thought Lie's message a "great mistake politically, militarily and legally" [136]—Lie felt that some sort of mechanism was needed to coordinate United Nations efforts in Korea. [137] Cordier and Feller broached the question with the American mission on June 30. Cordier also suggested the designation of a United Nations commander in Korea (namely, General MacArthur) and that the combined forces there should fly the United Nations flag, on which point Lie was particularly keen. [138] Lie proffered the pertinent draft resolution on July 3. Under its terms the United States government was requested to assume responsibility for directing whatever military forces member states might furnish under the resolution of June 27, as well as the South Korean forces. It also authorized the flying of the United Nations flag for the combined forces in Korea—the latter proposal disapproved of by France. In particular, the draft resolution proposed a Committee on Co-ordination of Assistance for Korea, which would include the United States and others. Lie would serve as its rapporteur. Although the apparent purpose of the committee was to encourage and coordinate offers of assistance to South Korea, its real purpose was to place the United Nations in the forefront of the Korean drama, fostering its participation in and supervision of the international military response in a manner that the council could never provide. Although France's Chauvel and Norway's Sunde were partial to the idea of such a coordinating committee, Great Britain's Jebb was not, contrary to what Lie tells us. [139]

When queried by the State Department about Lie's coordinating committee, the American Joint Chiefs of Staff strongly objected. They pointed out that the positioning of such a committee in the "chain of command could seriously interfere with the strategic and tactical control of operations" by the United Nations commander and his subordinates in the field. Indeed, despite the State Department's initial qualms about designating the United States either formally or informally as the United Nations' agent in Korea, the Joint Chiefs of Staff favored a "command arrangement" with Washington in such a role. However, they wanted nothing "interposed" between the United Nations commander and the United Nations in New York. The State Department bowed to these military suggestions, which meant the rejection of Lie's coordinating committee. [140] London also thought the establishment of such a committee would "only raise awkward problems." [141]

On July 7, the council took another step to structure the United Nations response to Korea. Although Lie's coordinating committee had been rejected, other aspects of his proffered resolution were accepted, and these were presented in a joint Anglo-French draft resolution. It recommended that the military forces and assistance made available to South Korea be placed under an American-directed unified command; that the Americans designate the commander of this force; and that this unified command use the United Nations flag in its military operations against the North Koreans, concurrently with the flags of the various participating nations. With Russia still absent, the resolution was adopted by seven votes: Egypt, India, and Yugoslavia abstaining. Following this meeting Lie presented the United Nations flag to Austin, thus assuring the visual and symbolic presence of the world organization in Korea. On July 14 the flag was conveyed to General MacArthur, who was also appointed United Nations commander by General J. Lawton Collins, the United States' Army Chief of Staff. [142]

Lie later traced, with the rejection of his coordinating committee in mind, Washington's subsequent complaints that it was carrying the greater part of the burden in the Korean fighting, to its reticence during this early period to accord the United Nations a larger role in the direction of the crisis. By its stance, Lie argued, Washington "no doubt contributed to the tendency" of member states to let the Americans assume most of the Korean burden. Perhaps he was right. During those July days, Lie's actions up front and behind the scenes propelled Gromyko to castigate him publicly. To fend off Moscow, Lie directed the secretariat's Legal Department to draw up a memorandum to counter its arguments. Lie then circulated the memorandum, "Legal Aspects of the Security Council Action in Korea," privately among the important missions and principal persons at the United Nations.[143]

The memorandum's impact, however, is difficult to gauge. The British mission, for example, cautiously approved it. Likewise, the Foreign Office agreed "with most of its reasoning" and, subject to amendment, recommended its publication.[144] The memorandum, it is now clear, had a tangible impact on the internal American political scene. On July 8 Lie contacted Henry Wallace, former vice-president and cabinet officer then leader of the Progressive party, under which banner Wallace had campaigned unsuccessfully for the presidency in 1948. The party's leftist orientation was the closest thing to a political ally, excluding the American Communist party, that Moscow had on the American scene. Lie gave Wallace a copy of the memorandum, which convinced him that United Nations actions against North Korea "were justified on both legal and moral grounds."[145] Lie, despite a very low opinion of Wallace's political acumen,[146] noted his position in world opinion and asked him to speak out against the North Korean attack. Wallace, already at odds with the party's executive committee about events in Korea, then read Lie a statement that he had prepared. Lie enthusiastically approved it and urged him to release it immediately. Based on Lie's comments Wallace amended the statement on matters dealing with the United Nations and Lie's ten-point, twenty-year peace program[147] and issued it on July 15. He blamed Soviet Russia for events in Korea and declared his support for the United States and the United Nations. When the Progressive party failed to assume a similar stance, Wallace resigned,[148] thereby sounding the party's death knell.

July 8 was a busy day for Lie. After his discussion with Wallace, he informed Jebb that he would chair a meeting on July 10 that would include Austin, Security Council President Sunde, and South Korean Ambassador John Chang to consider the coordination of offers by member states of nonmilitary assistance to South Korea. Chauvel and Jebb had not been invited, Lie explained, as it would have appeared an attempt by him to prop up his proposal for a coordinating committee, which had not been embodied in the resolution of July 7. Gross confirmed the meeting but thought nothing

would develop from it until a scheme for dealing with the supply problem had been hammered out between Washington and MacArthur. He agreed with Jebb that "any tendency" by the secretariat to assume essentially operational functions should be prevented, and that, at the meeting, Austin should offer some anodyne proposal that Lie could convey to member states offering assistance, noting that they had been transmitted to Washington, which was considering how they could best be utilized.[149]

Lie's disclaimer notwithstanding, it would appear that the whole purpose of the July 10 meeting was to achieve through the backdoor what had been kept out of the resolution of July 7; namely, an up-front United Nations presence in the Korean drama. Although Lie admitted that in Korea the United States acted for the United Nations, he referred to the responsibilities of his office. Many representatives had approached "him for advice about possible offers of assistance," he alleged and stressed the importance of keeping to the fore the United Nations aspect of the Korean operation. At this point, Lie wanted concrete evidence that member states would support United Nations action in order to show Soviet Russia and North Korea that the world organization would back up South Korea. Member states wanted to offer assistance neither to the United States nor to South Korea but to the United Nations. He denied that he wanted the secretariat involved in administering anything; Washington and Seoul had to decide how to handle the offers of assistance, but Lie desired support in order to do a good job.

Austin placated Lie by assuring him that he had done a "fine job," and thought any discussions had to be "exploratory" until more was known about needs. For the moment the question was basically military, and word from the unified command was necessary, before any decisions could be made. Lie should therefore carry on as secretary-general, chief administrative officer and representative of the entire United Nations membership. Machinery to tackle the military problem was being developed in Washington. Chang and Sunde agreed with Austin. Lie, although appearing to agree, observed that "he took a political view of the matter." The opposition's clever propaganda had to be met politically, by pointing out the United Nations character of South Korea's defense. Alluding to the American political scene, he held that the United Nations must not lay itself open to the charge that Washington was providing all the personnel and assistance to South Korea. Promises, "definite and specific," had to be obtained from member states. They came to no conclusion.[150] For the moment, Lie was stymied.

Lie's desire, however, for "definite and specific" promises was not too dissimilar from the desire of the State and Defense Departments, and Austin was instructed to suggest that Lie send another communication to the member states. He should note that the replies received in response to his June 29 communication had been transmitted to the American-directed unified command, which he ascertained would contact member states regarding their offers of assistance to South Korea, and most important, that member states should "consider without delay" what more "effective assistance" they could offer, "including wherever possible combat forces, particularly ground forces." On the dispatch of Lie's message Washington would immediately approach those countries it considered in a "position to offer effective economic or military assistance, particularly combat forces." Lie was to be told of this proposed step by Washington. Although Washington recognized that militarily most member states could not offer effective assistance, there were "compelling political and psychological reasons for stimulating offers of assistance, particularly combat troops."[151]

Austin approached Lie on July 13, proposing that, for security reasons offers of assistance, including military assistance, should be transmitted in general terms by the member states to Lie, the detailed arrangements to be ironed out between the member state and the unified command.[152] One suspects that Austin had added the clause about Lie to his instructions, not solely on security grounds but because like Lie he wanted to give the United Nations through the secretary-general a more prominent role in the unfolding drama. Indeed, he appears to have argued that the matter was of the highest importance and that effective backing, in Congress and elsewhere, of America's support of the United Nations in Korea would be jeopardized if it appeared that Washington's action was "isolated and unsupported" by member states. Any wavering in the American position, Austin warned, would endanger the entire United Nations. He requested that Washington's message be transmitted to the member states but observed that the appeal would be more effective coming from Lie as secretary-general. Lie apparently agreed to do this and without referring to the fact that it had been requested by the Americans.[153]

Austin appears to have convinced Washington of this ploy, for in its circular message to fifty-six diplomatic missions on their bilateral approach to their respective host government, the State Department observed that "in order to maximize [the] UN effort" member states offering assistance should do so through Lie.[154] Lie it appears then had second thoughts. He correctly pointed out to Austin that the council had entrusted this task to the American-directed unified command and not to the secretary-general. Accordingly he argued, it would have to be made clear to member states that he was acting with the full consent of the unified command, namely the United States. Washington had to assure them, as well as their United Nations missions, that the secretary-general and the unified command were moving in tandem. Austin concurred, but Lie later maintained that this understanding was not executed as agreed. Confusion resulted and he, Lie claimed, was exposed to public criticism for sending his message without prior consultation.[155] In point of fact, on the morning of July 14 the member states were contacted by the State Department, so that the first part of the agreement appears to have been executed.[156] However, as we shall see, for unexplained reasons, the United Nations missions were not contacted. Nevertheless, Lie deserved the criticism he received. That Austin contributed to what had occurred is no less true and was unpardonable in view of Lie's adventurous initiatives on prior matters, which dictated caution in dealing with him. Canadian evidence, Pearson observed, indicated that Lie had been "subjected to strong and, I think unwise pressure" by the American mission, and Lie had been "weak enough to yield to it."[157]

With what appears to have been a green light from Austin,[158] Lie called a press conference on the morning of July 14 to announce the dispatch of his second communication.[159] On Austin's suggestion Lie's request to the member states had been amended to read that any assistance be "effective assistance . . . including combat forces, particularly ground forces."[160] Sir Terence Shone, Jebb's deputy, was puzzled;[161] but Paul Holmer, in the Foreign Office's United Nations Department, correctly assumed that Lie's move was due to an urgent American request, which lent weight to the communist claim that he was in America's pocket. "To spread the 'UN umbrella' a little more widely," Holmer noted, "it may still be necessary to reconsider the advisability of setting up some extra-Security Council machinery." The head of the United Nations Department, Cecil Parrott, was inclined to agree with Holmer's suggestion but wondered whether it was desirable to bestow on Lie such responsibility since he gave the impression of acting as Washington's agent and did not handle this kind of matter well. For example, at the press conference, he was confused and held that the Arabs had offered assistance until contradicted by the Egyptian representative. Lie's redeeming quality was his commitment to the cause, and London, Parrott noted, should be "duly grateful."[162]

Shone expressed his "surprise" to Gross at Lie's request for additional assistance, particularly armed forces, which he first heard about following Lie's press conference. Gross was in an uncomfortable position and declared that there was no connection between the meeting of July 10 and that of Lie-Austin on July 13. Shone observed that other missions besides the British "had been taken aback" by the secretary-general's "request and by the manner in which it had been made." He reminded Gross that, in prior discussions about Korea and the establishment under the council of some body to handle offers of assistance, everyone had been "concerned as to the danger, for security reasons, of giving the Secretariat too much of a hand in these matters." Despite Lie's statement that offers of military assistance should be transmitted to him in general terms, Shone could not help feel that "all this might result in the Secretariat assuming wider functions than were desirable or perhaps even proper." Gross appeared "distressed" and very upset that he could give no details about what had transpired between Lie and Austin.[163]

Further talks by Shone made it clear that although an attempt was made to show the messages dispatched by Lie to Security Council President Sunde—the texts varied depending on what offers of assistance had been received initially—he was not consulted about their contents. Indeed, all evidence showed that the American mission, presumably Austin, and the secretariat had decided to issue the messages after Lie's press conference. Shone also found Ambassador Sunde in agreement "that the whole proceedings had been most unusual and apt to embarrass the governments of member nations." [164] It had all been done, Holmer noted, "in the boldest possible way," which could only support the communist contention that the "whole thing [was] an American racket aided and abetted by that tool of American imperialism," Secretary-General Lie. His action of informing the press prior to informing the member governments was "tactless and misguided." "It certainly got badly out of hand," Parrott pithily noted. [165]

In addition, whether by design or discombobulation, the implication in Lie's press statement that there was a connection between the meeting of July 10 and the subsequent discussion with Austin alone, which resulted in his second communication, was "misleading." The whole episode appeared to be, Jebb reported, the "result of overhasty action by the Secretariat" and the American representative; the rest of the American mission being kept in the dark. According to press reports, the American mission had been swamped by countless letters emphasizing the need to stress the United Nations military response in Korea and by complaints that the United States was bearing both the military and nonmilitary burden virtually single-handedly. In such a situation the secretariat naturally was "apt to do all it [could] to assume a leading role . . . and to gain the maximum publicity for itself." As to Austin, Jebb felt, he had "a strong sense of 'mission' insofar as the United Nations [was] concerned which [was] apt to outweigh his judgment." Jebb thought it all a publicity stunt, with no evidence that it was meant to accomplish a real military purpose. Lie's moves, especially the "premature" press release, had "surprised and embarrassed" a great many missions, who pondered what might be foisted on them in the future. [166] Lie's action instigated by the Americans was "overprecipitate," Holmer thought, especially if, as Jebb suggested, it was all a publicity stunt. [167]

The Norwegian mission queried the American whether, in view of Oslo's contributions to the North Atlantic Pact, Washington really wished it to provide armed forces for Korea. The officer who responded was "embarrassed and admitted that Lie's appeal had been due to over-hasty action by the Secretariat" and the mission. [168] Holmer summed it up: this "ill-judged and hasty action [had] put many Govt's in a difficult position." [169]

Great Britain was a case in point. The cabinet discussed it on July 17 and felt that Lie's request "might prove embarrassing, in view of the publicity given to it." [170] British ire rose several days later, when the *New York*

Herald Tribune reported that London, among others, had expressed an interest in supplying additional aid to the unified command. Shone admonished Cordier, since the British mission had received no such instructions and made no such communication to the secretariat, that such statements "were both tendentious and embarrassing." Cordier admitted that the report lacked substance and was pure invention.[171] All this resulted from "allowing the Secretariat too much scope to dabble in this affair," Holmer noted. Parrott agreed.[172]

Shone pointed out that the Australian, Canadian, and French missions were no less annoyed by the story in the *New York Herald Tribune*. The Canadian John Holmes thought that, despite the difficulties of establishing some body under the council to deal with offers of assistance to South Korea, "this might well be preferable to leaving to the Secretariat the functions which they appear to have assumed" and by "hook or crook" were intent on keeping.[173] The whole episode was an embarrassment to many governments including his own, Pierre Ordonneau of the French mission explained to the Americans. How were they to answer Lie's message? Many governments might not answer at all. Lie had taken a "very serious and unwise step on his own responsibility." Any French troops to Korea would have to come from Indochina, which produced difficulties. Lie's dispatch to South Korea of South African Colonel Alfred G. Katzin as his "personal representative" was also questioned by Holmes and Ordonneau.[174] In the Foreign Office Holmer raised the question whether "alternative machinery" to handle offers of assistance might now be broached by the British mission with other missions.[175]

Lie's attempt to move himself and the United Nations to center stage in the Korean crisis, abetted by Austin, was best described by the Australian representative, Keith Shann. The North Korean invasion, he noted to Canberra, had led Lie to establish a War Office within the secretariat, staffed by the Americans Cordier, Feller, and Foote, who reflected respectively the executive, legal, and public information aspects of the secretariat's endeavors. In addition, an around-the-clock shift had been instituted to monitor events. Those in Canberra who had served at the United Nations, Shann observed, would appreciate that the composition of this group was "not such as to inspire the greatest confidence." Lie's press conference and the dispatch of his message was a case in point. Although there was general agreement that Lie's action was taken at American insistence, "the manner in which it was taken reflects a desire on the part of the Secretariat to indicate publicly widespread and effective activity on its part in relation to Korea." Actually "this activity [was] largely spurious and manufactured" at the United Nations. Following the decisions of its various organs and bodies, there was for the moment "nothing particularly effective or useful that [could] be done by the Secretariat." The suggestion that Assistant Secretary-General Zinchenko was mischievously involved in this, Shann correctly dismissed, on the grounds that Lie had "specifically excluded" him from any role in the secretariat's Korean work. In view of what occurred and in order for mission representatives to achieve better control, Shann thought reconsideration might be given to establishing a council subcommittee to receive offers of assistance and coordinate their transmission to Washington. This proposal, when first broached, had foundered over the question of the subcommittee's composition and the feeling by some that the "Secretariat might overdo its part" in such a body.

Shann did not suggest that Lie was "directly responsible" for the manner in which the secretariat then appeared to be acting; but Lie's "administrative weakness and lack of control" were contributing factors. If the United Nations had had a first-rate secretary-general these things could probably be avoided. But, generally, the secretariat had a conception of its role "which could do nothing but alarm" those accustomed to civil services like Great Britain's and the states of western Europe. The secretariat appeared to think it was a "unit with specific and independent functions separate from the interests of the governments which it serves." This notion was endemic throughout the United Nations system. Activities that showed bias against member states or disregarded their convenience and proper consultation with them, Shann thought, should be resisted as strongly as possible. Shann observed that Lie should be approached at the highest level and careful government consideration given to the attitude to be assumed toward the question of the secretariat at the next assembly session. [176]

Meeting July 21, the Americans, British, French, and Norwegians considered Lie's and the secretariat's conduct. Chauvel thought that Security Council President Sunde, while "honest and well-intentioned," was not able to "stand up to Lie" and that Austin, acting alone and in "cahoots" with Lie, had contributed to the current situation, with which the State Department was far from pleased. [177] Understandably, Austin defended the secretariat and "disagreed with the opinion that [the] SYG [had] exceeded his responsibility under [the] Charter." [178]

One could argue that Lie's endeavors, largely instigated by Austin, had been superfluous: member states committed to assisting South Korea militarily did not need prompting from the secretary-general. Occasionally states like Canada and France no doubt were gingered along by Lie's message. On the whole, it is probably fair to say that the response was less than enthusiastic and that most member states, although faced with a clear cut act of aggression, were unwilling or unable to back their rhetoric with concrete military assistance.

Lie complained to Norwegian Foreign Minister Lange about the lethargic response. [179] The foot dragging had certainly begun to crystallize by July 19 and partially explains Lie's proposal on that date to the Americans that a volunteer force be raised, which apparently was triggered by superabundant offers of voluntary service conveyed to the secretariat. These left Lie and Cordier perplexed as to how to respond. Their only idea was to advise potential volunteers to join the American military services or to suggest that circumstances might eventually make it possible for them to serve the world organization in the military services of their own countries. This suggested in turn a possible United Nations force. Initially the secretariat envisaged a volunteer force akin to the French Foreign Legion to be drawn from the United Nations membership. They wanted, however, to avoid mere adventurers and modern-day condottieri and accordingly were eager from the beginning to secure the backing of member states in the recruitment process. [180] Lie thought a division of troops could be raised in this manner and invoked the questionable analogies of the Swedish volunteers who had fought with the Finns against the Russians in the Winter War of 1939 and the Norwegians who had fought with the Loyalists against Franco in the Spanish Civil War in 1936. He admitted that he had no idea whether such a volunteer force was permissible under the charter, which point, he quipped, the lawyers could decide. [181]

Lie's idea, baptized the United Nations Legion, "was not seriously debated" in the assembly, which set up no special organ to study it. The Collective Measures Committee, established under the Uniting for Peace Resolution, examined it but took no action. Lie must have realized the immense legal, political, organizational, and other hurdles that lay in the path of any such force, for he "did not resourcefully struggle for the acceptance of even a modified version of his plan, as he had in the case of the United Nations Guard," [182] proposed during the postpartition fighting in Palestine.

Thwarted Mediation

Lie's commitment to the United Nations during this period did not ebb, [183] although he foresaw a long struggle and doubted whether MacArthur could hold the beachhead indispensable for any counteroffensive. [184] In the midst of this gloomy situation Assistant Secretary-General Zinchenko advised Lie not to depart for his planned Norwegian holiday, a not too subtle hint that something was afoot. [185] The surprise was sprung the next day, July 27, when Russia's Malik informed Lie of his intention to assume the council presidency, as he was entitled to, on August 1. [186]

After seven months absence, Moscow had decided that its interests dictated a return to the United Nations, the continued presence of the Nationalist Chinese notwithstanding. Lie interpreted this policy reversal as a Russian setback. [187] His initial reaction was that Malik's imminent return made it desirable that the next council meeting adopt a resolution on Korean relief. [188] This was done on July 31. [189]

Lie's track record on Korea and other questions prompted Acheson to describe him "as an honest man but one without too much common sense." Pearson, to whom this remark was directed, disagreed. He thought that Lie had performed very well under the difficult circumstances of the preceding weeks.[190] August was to prove a trying month. With Malik in the council chair, discussion of the Korean question was now subjected to every delay, frustration, and obstruction that his position allowed. His tactics would have put to shame a Quintus Fabius Maximus; they effectively paralyzed the council. The other members soon caucused on tactics for controlling Malik. In an attempt to forestall any demand by Lie to attend these discussions, as well as to learn his views on the current impasse, Jebb called on him. Lie objected to the idea of deposing Malik or convening the assembly, claiming that Malik was "rattled" and should be challenged in debate. If Malik was "particularly objectionable," adjournment of the meeting could be requested; should Malik refuse, the other members could simply leave the chamber. Lie suggested that he could secretly arrange to have the electricity cut off should Malik continue to preside![191]

Lie's analysis of the new situation, however, proved incorrect: he thought Moscow was on an "appeasement tack." Accordingly, he enthusiastically suggested that the Russians might be asked to cosponsor an American draft resolution to establish a council fact-finding and observation committee. Gross, less sanguine about Moscow's latest about-face, doubted that such a move would prove useful; but Lie held to his idea, maintaining that Moscow's "objection to many commissions and to the [General Assembly] Interim Committee had been based upon the fact that they had not been established" by the council. Moscow's return to the United Nations had apparently caused a lapse of memory on Lie's part about recent Russian machinations in Korea. Nevertheless, aside from this divergent approach, Gross observed to the State Department, Lie was very much committed to the draft resolution and "would privately express disagreement with any member opposed to it or reluctant to vote for it." The lack of a consensus among the western powers about the draft resolution, however, led Washington to withdraw it from consideration.[192]

With the coming of September, Lie anticipated the new assembly would be less than tranquil but devoid of any successes.[193] He was correct about the former prediction and incorrect about the latter. On the eve of the assembly, MacArthur's forces landed at Inchon, and the North Koreans were virtually annihilated by the United Nations forces breaking out of the Inchon beachhead and the Pusan perimeter. The West was resurgent. Lie actually got Acheson and Vyshinsky together at his home but without results.[194] Then in late September, the British proposed a new Commission on the Unification and Rehabilitation of Korea, to replace the existing United Nations commission, to supervise the unification of the country and the establishment of an independent and democratic government.[195] Lie complained that he had not been consulted about the British proposal and suggested that Jebb ascertain from Malik whether Moscow would use its influence to see that prior assembly and council decisions on Korea were executed. Although Lie anticipated a negative response from the Russians, he wanted it on record at the assembly's opening debate.

John Ross of the American mission argued that Washington wanted the Korean question dealt with by the United Nations in a broad and open manner not by private understandings with Moscow. It also wanted to avoid confusion between council and assembly actions. Ross therefore suggested that, if the Russians were to be cross-examined, it might be best done in open United Nations debate. Lie agreed.

Lie proposed terms for a Korean settlement, based on prior council and assembly decisions. In a proposed assembly resolution drafted by Feller, he suggested that North Korea agree to a cease-fire, withdraw to the 38th parallel, and demilitarize its forces under United Nations supervision. In addition, the United Nations Commission on Korea would enter North Korea to execute its reunification task while United Nations relief personnel would supervise the distribution of relief. Lastly, Koreanwide free elections were to be promulgated by the United Nations Commission within the year.

If the North Koreans accepted these conditions, Lie thought their jurisdiction over the northern area should be preserved until after the elections, when United Nations troops would enter the North. At that time authority would be handed over by the United Nations Commission to the new all-Korean government. The South Koreans should be asked to accept these electoral conditions. Likewise, general amnesty would be granted by both sides. If the North Koreans refused, the assembly would recommend that hostilities recommence with the purpose of destroying the North Korean regime. Once this was achieved North Korea would be placed under United Nations jurisdiction (details to be worked out) until the assembly or the council decided that elections for the whole country should be held.[196]

Lie's proposal that United Nations forces enter North Korea only after supervised elections did not dovetail with Washington's desire that MacArthur be "unhampered tactically and strategically to proceed north of the 38th parallel."[197] Accordingly, he was "apparently outdistanced" by American discussions with other missions on a draft resolution recommending that everything be done to ensure peaceful conditions throughout Korea, with elections under United Nations auspices to bring about a unified, independent, and democratic government for the whole country. The American draft indirectly authorized United Nations troops to enter North Korea for the time needed to achieve these objectives.

The resolution actually adopted by the assembly on October 7, was based on a somewhat toned down version of the American draft. It disbanded the United Nations Commission on Korea and established the United Nations Commission for the Unification and Rehabilitation of Korea.[198]

Lie "was unhappy in the abandonment" of his own proposal, especially as the Communists through the Czech foreign minister had manifested some interest in its approach. This communist interest was no doubt sparked by the North Korean military collapse and Lie's proposed exclusion of United Nations troops from North Korea until elections had been held. Lie failed to grasp this connection, although he "shared" the assembly's "dominant feeling" that North Korea's continued resistance was only prelude to another thrust southward, offering MacArthur's forces no choice but to advance north of the 38th parallel.[199]

To preclude paralysis of the United Nations should another Koreanlike aggression occur, the West under American leadership promoted the assembly adoption of the Uniting for Peace Resolution (November 3, 1950), which provided that an emergency session of the assembly could be called for by a majority of either the council or the assembly, should the council be incapable of responding to an act of aggression. It also established a Peace Observation Commission to report on any future situation of international stress, as well as a Collective Measures Committee to study (in consultation with the secretary-general and member states) methods to maintain and strengthen international peace and security. Lie naturally supported this proposal,[200] which seemingly strengthened the world organization's peace-keeping machinery and enhanced as well his own role in the peace-keeping process.

On November 29, the Communist Chinese intervened militarily and disastrously in the Korean conflict. In mid-November, the situation had moved Canada's Pearson to suggest that the council might authorize Lie to contact Peking (through a member of the secretariat) to ascertain its views on some sort of "transitional arrangements" that would safeguard Communist Chinese interests and also permit an end to the fighting. Jebb thought the possibility might be explored but doubted whether the council could come to a consensus on what instructions to issue to Lie. The Russians might either object to the whole procedure or attempt to twist the instructions to their own ends. Pearson then suggested that Lie might contact Peking on his own initiative; the important thing was to have someone like Bunche or Colonel Katzin contact Peking. Jebb's past experience with Lie's uninvited initiatives no doubt explained his cool reaction to Pearson's proposal and warning of "real difficulties" in the way of its adoption.[201]

Whether Lie decided to press his own case or was urged to do so by Pearson is unclear. However, some days later Lie broached the idea through the Americans that he be appointed council rapporteur in the Korean question and, accompanied by Colonel Katzin (his envy of Bunche made Katzin more acceptable), undertake an on-the-spot investigation in Korea. Naturally he would consult the United Nations Commission for the Unification and Rehabilitation of Korea but insisted that "one man could do [a] quicker, better job" than the commission, which had really been established to handle a different matter. He noted Katzin's warm and amicable relations with MacArthur and held that a "report on the facts" by the council's own rapporteur "might be more persuasive" to many United Nations members than unilateral reports from the unified command. He asked the State Department to mull it over.[202] The notion of Lie traipsing around the Korean landscape as council rapporteur apparently struck the State Department dumb, as it does not appear to have responded to the idea.

The presence at this time of a Communist Chinese delegation at the United Nations led by General Wu Hsiu-chuan now offered Lie a different opportunity to approach Peking. Wu and his associates had arrived ostensibly to participate in the council discussion of Peking's complaint alleging that Washington had threatened its security by invading Korea and Formosa and by bombing mainland China.[203] Initially Lie and the Yugoslav council president, Deputy Foreign Minister Aleš Bebler, failed to get the Communist Chinese to agree to enter into private talks with anyone outside the council.[204] This rebuff no doubt strengthened Lie's belief that Wu's delegation "would be neither helpful nor enlightening."[205] Several days later, November 29, came the massive Communist Chinese intervention. Although Lie, behind the scenes, admitted that he had no confidence in any information imparted by MacArthur,[206] he publicly affirmed his support of the general; and, to stave off a proposed evacuation of United Nations personnel to Tokyo with its disheartening impact, he instructed them to remain at their posts.[207] Feller signaled that something might be afoot on November 30—the day following Lie's proposal that he be appointed rapporteur—when he informed the Americans that Lie was "most anxious to be helpful."[208]

Presumably to Lie's surprise on December 1, Wu took the initiative, thanking Lie for the secretariat's assistance in getting the delegation to New York. Wasting no time, Lie assured him that the secretariat would continue to render whatever logistical support was needed to make their stay comfortable. However, he disingenuously continued, political questions were not his concern, even though he might occasionally be able to assist. To show his credentials, Lie recapitulated his stand on Peking's right to represent China in the United Nations. In view of his hoped-for role, Lie pointed out that he was not a fellow communist. Hoping no doubt to drive a wedge between Peking and Moscow, Lie observed that the Russian boycott of the United Nations had not assisted the Communist Chinese case. Wu, however, did not rise to the bait, and stressed that Soviet Russia was Communist China's friend.[209]

From Lie's own record of this meeting the discussion appears to have been polite, pro forma, and devoid of any substantive discussion of the Korean question or communist intervention. The version that he conveyed to the Anglo-Americans, however, was far different. He spent his time, Lie informed Jebb, trying to convince Wu to announce that Communist China would no longer continue its advance in Korea and to propose a cease-fire. The atmosphere created by such a gesture, Lie thought, could be used by Peking to advance its case in other directions. [210]

With the Americans, who with the South Koreans were doing the brunt of the fighting, Lie adjusted his story. He claimed that he told Wu bluntly that Communist China was committing an act of aggression in Korea and that the killing had to stop immediately with a cease-fire. Americans and Chinese served no useful purpose by killing each other. He said he had urged Wu to have greater contacts with other United Nations representatives, including those whose countries did not recognize Peking; if Wu would do so he would discover that everyone agreed with Lie's approach. The course pursued by Peking would not facilitate seating it in the United Nations. When Wu indicated a willingness to see other representatives, Lie arranged a dinner for this purpose, inviting representatives of countries that had recognized Peking. Because the assembly president, Iran's Nasrollah Entezam, was trying to contact Wu, Lie also appeared anxious to talk to Entezam. Gross, however, unlike Jebb, was not taken in by Lie's act. The "strong impression" that Lie conveyed throughout his talk with Gross, Austin informed the State Department, "without expressly saying so" was that "he considered himself to be [the] logical chosen instrument for mediation." Gross naturally did not commit himself. [211]

Lie's memorandum of his conversation with Wu (dated December 18) details no substantive comments about the Korean conflict nor does his account of the meeting in his memoirs. [212] It is difficult to believe that his alleged comments to Wu about Korean events could have skipped Lie's mind. The explanation of this curious discrepancy probably lies in Lie's desire to assume the mediating role of "honest broker" between Communist China and the West, especially the Americans. That he might help drive a wedge between Peking and Moscow made the initiative even more attractive. But to have spoken to Wu, in the manner he reported to Jebb and Gross, would have undermined his position with the Communist Chinese and ruined whatever chances he had of assuming a mediating role. His allegedly blunt language to Wu was probably aimed to show that he was still firmly in the Western camp and to be trusted implicitly. Because of the abysmal relations between Communist China and the West, Lie could be sure that the two sides would never compare notes.

It therefore can be cogently argued that Lie's own memorandum of the conversation was probably reasonably accurate, that his comments about Communist Chinese actions in Korea were never uttered, and that his hosting of any dinner was an attempt to begin unofficial and informal discussions on Korea but in a way not to raise the ire or suspicions of the West. Unfortunately, Lie never appears to have considered the possibility that his own past track record made any independent political endeavors by him absolutely unacceptable to the Western powers.

After his first conversation with Wu on December 1, Lie was "pessimistic" but did not feel that an "approach [was] hopeless."[213] Accompanied by the Yugoslav Bebler, Lie again saw Wu the following day. Bebler offered to mediate; the Chinese politely refused.[214] Their rejection of Bebler's offer could only have pleased Lie, since it enhanced his own possible role.

On December 4, Lie was contacted by Czech Foreign Minister Viliam Siroky. Whether Siroky's visit was a spontaneous attempt to ascertain Lie's views or a fishing expedition is unclear. Siroky assured Lie that the Communists desired peace in Korea, which meant that foreign troops should leave the country and its future be decided by the Koreans alone, although this did not exclude a cease-fire. Did it include the withdrawal of Communist Chinese troops? Lie asked. It did was the reply. Did the withdrawal of foreign troops pertain to all Korea or merely the North? Siroky explained that the situation should revert to the status quo of June 25, before the fighting erupted, and that all foreign troops should withdraw from the country. Was he reflecting Vyshinsky's views? Lie queried. He was not speaking for Vyshinsky, Siroky responded, but maintained, confusedly, that Vyshinsky shared his views. Lie responded favorably since a return to the previous status quo would mean a continued United Nations presence in South Korea. He urged the proposal as conciliatory to the Western representatives. Austin, however, was unimpressed, noting that the United Nations had achieved its purpose in restoring South Korea to its territory; all subsequent fighting could be charged to communist aggression.[215]

Making a major move, Lie also talked with Wu on December 4. He might go to Japan and Korea, he said, and believed such a trip important. He suggested that on either his outward or his return journey he could consult the government in Peking. A formal invitation, Lie opined, might create difficulties for the Peking authorities, who had to be loyal to Moscow, which now had a low opinion of him. The situation in Asia, however, would improve enormously if a cease-fire agreement could be reached as quickly as possible. The Chinese–North Korean forces would have to stop shooting. Indeed, a cease-fire agreement would go far to facilitate Peking's seating in the United Nations and would improve immensely the chances of obtaining a favorable settlement of the question of Formosa. If, on the other hand, a cease-fire was made conditional on Peking being seated in the United Nations and Formosa being returned to it, Lie believed Wu's mission would not succeed. They had their instructions that had to be followed, Wu responded. Lie harbored little hope that there could be real negotiations leading to an acceptable agreement.[216]

To the Americans, Lie claimed that he had suggested that Chinese forces might pull back to the Yalu River, while MacArthur's forces withdrew below the 38th parallel. He also indicated to the Americans that "he had made an independent cease-fire proposal to General Wu" who assured him that he would pass it on to Peking and would contact him again when he received a reply.[217] It is not absolutely clear, however, in Lie's record of the conversation that he made any such concrete proposal. Nevertheless, the Americans were disconcerted to learn from Lie post-facto that he had apparently made such an independent proposal without previously advising them.[218]

The scheduled dinner that Lie hosted that night, December 4, proved more productive than any of his conversations with Wu. This was largely due to the fertile political imagination of the Israeli foreign minister, Moshe Shertok, who in conversation with Wu broached the principles upon which a cease-fire resolution might be based—which were in fact subsequently adopted by the assembly.[219] In the days that followed Lie continued to be pessimistic about any settlement with Peking, which he viewed as intransigently communist. Since the Communist Chinese aimed at victory in Korea, United Nations seating, and the return of Formosa, Lie was perplexed at a country that flagrantly violated the charter yet expected to get what it wanted. Peking's objectives would put Asia under its influence, while it remained more or less under Moscow's sway. World communism, Lie thought, was closer than most people realized. A future Peking-Moscow rift was possible, but what could the Communist Chinese do if the Russians invaded?

Lie thought Moscow's game was to bleed the democracies white in the Far East. He did not foresee war in the near future or use of the atom bomb in Korea. The problem was not the United Nations per se but the lack of sufficient force to tackle a great power combination like Soviet Russia and Communist China. Lie was not among those who used Korean events to criticize the Americans. By a settlement in Korea leading to a solution of the United Nations question, negotiations among the Big Five might be renewed, contributing to relaxation of international tensions. Without this, an enormous armaments race might ensue, although that did not necessarily imply a world conflagration. The collapse of future negotiations to improve the international picture, Lie observed to his family, would finally lead to an armed struggle between communist and democratically ruled societies.[220] In retrospect, Lie's analysis was more than a little prophetic.

As negotiations inched forward to effect a cease-fire in Korea, Wu sought a talk with Lie on Saturday, December 9. Since Lie, as we have seen, was not committed to the Calvinist work ethic, he was less than keen on a Saturday outing. Nevertheless he answered the call to duty. When they met, Wu soon got to his salient point: Peking was committed to peace and was most interested in effecting a cease-fire. He mentioned no preconditions—for example, being seated in the United Nations or discussions about Formosa. He inquired about the conditions for a cease-fire sought by the United Nations and the United States. Lie assumed these conditions had been discussed in a conversation earlier that day between Wu and India's Sir Benegal Rau, who was acting as an intermediary. The general, however, wanted to know if Lie could assist in ascertaining such cease-fire conditions and thought, with his contacts, he could be helpful in the matter.

Wu's comments were the green light Lie had been hoping for. Wu had never previously asked him directly for help. But before giving an affirmative reply, Lie wanted to determine what had unfolded in the earlier Rau-Wu conversation. He therefore wisely asked for time to consider what, if anything, he could do to assist in the current difficult situation. Perhaps, Lie suggested, a peaceful settlement in Korea and of other political questions would prove impossible unless the leaders of the great powers met. Wu and his associates "smiled delightedly" and agreed with the necessity of such a meeting.

Lie told Gross what had transpired and discovered that Wu had spoken in the same sense to Rau. Gross strongly pressed Lie to bide his time until there were further developments; confusion might result if Lie and Rau both attempted to till the same soil. Gross's request was hard on Lie, who indicated "a real anxiety to 'get into the act.' "[221]

By the time Lie and Wu met again on December 14 things had changed. The earlier, amenable Communist Chinese stance was now reversed. The meeting, called by Lie, had been sparked by a British request that the secretary-general informally approach Wu to ensure the United Nations prisoners-of-war in Korea received humane treatment, in particular, to have Peking permit an official of the International Red Cross Committee to visit them in North Korea and to have Wu discuss details with a committee representative. In appealing for Wu's help, Lie pointed out that Peking had promised to abide by the Geneva Convention on prisoners-of-war. This question, Wu replied, was not the concern of Communist China, which was not responsible for the armed forces fighting in Korea; Lie had erred in approaching him, since there were no prisoners-of-war in mainland China. When Lie pointed out that Communist Chinese prisoners-of-war had fallen into the hands of MacArthur's forces, Wu maintained they were volunteers and therefore not his concern, but that of the North Korean government. When Lie asked to be put in contact with the North Korean authorities, Wu continued his pretence, asserting he did not know where they were and could not put Lie in contact with them. He doubted that Peking could help Lie in this matter. When Wu expressed dissatisfaction with the slow pace of the negotiations, Lie, in line with Gross's desire, explained that he could assume no initiatives in view of Rau's role.[222] Lie suspected that Wu's new tack foreshadowed additional difficulties and credited it to Vyshinsky or to pressure from Moscow on Peking.[223]

Lie told Gross he had also discussed with Wu the resolution sponsored by thirteen Asian states and adopted that day by the assembly. This established a three-man committee "to determine the basis [for] a satisfactory cease-fire," composed of the assembly president, Iran's Entezam, Canada's Pearson, and India's Rau. He asked for Wu's reaction, explaining that as secretary-general he would have to arrange for a meeting between the cease-fire committee and Wu's delegation. The committee, Wu claimed, was illegal and not binding on his government. He insisted that the preconditions to negotiate a cease-fire were stated by Russia's Malik the previous day: evacuation of all foreign forces from Korea, allowing the Koreans to settle all issues among themselves. Wu also insisted the question of Formosa had to be solved in connection with the cease-fire, and Lie got the impression that Peking would have to be seated in the United Nations. Wu and the delegation, he opined, were under Moscow's thumb.

Lie suggested to Gross and Entezam that Wu be forwarded a copy of the resolution establishing the cease-fire committee and asked to meet it to discuss the conditions for a cease-fire. Based on his conversation with Wu, Lie was pessimistic about a cease-fire, and the sooner the matter was disposed of, the better. Instead, he wanted a vote on a proposal submitted by six Western powers on December 7, calling on everyone not to assist the North Koreans, upholding the inviolable nature of the Chinese-Korean frontier, and protecting legitimate interests there endangered by Communist Chinese intervention. It also requested the United Nations Commission for the Unification and Rehabilitation of Korea to assist in settling any frontier problems.

Entezam disagreed with this suggestion. Gross thought him dissatisfied with Lie's initiatives on the eve of the cease-fire committee's endeavors. Entezam said with feeling that, if Lie envisaged using the cease-fire committee as a "political tool" publicly to force a negative response from the Communist Chinese, he would not consent. When Gross agreed with Entezam, Lie withdrew his proposal but said, with some annoyance, that the assembly should adjourn that week. Gross and Entezam held that it had to be on standby until the committee reported to it. Subsequently Cordier confidentially admitted to the American mission that Lie "was not in [a] good mood, to some extent because he was not a member of the cease-fire committee and, more particularly, since he was very anxious to go to Norway for Christmas."[224] Gross noted Lie obviously resented his exclusion from a salient effort that his office should have spearheaded.[225] Lie was nevertheless invited to the committee's deliberations on December 15 when MacArthur's command presented its conditions for a cease-fire. Lie offered the committee the services of Feller and Colonel Katzin but voiced to Pearson his low opinion of Rau, who, he claimed, was unable to handle or talk to Communists effectively. Rau's role, which obviated his own desire to mediate, clearly irked him.

Any possible mediation, however, was dashed when Wu informed Lie that same day that the delegation would shortly return to Peking, before which he wanted to hold a press conference at the United Nations. Lie was flabbergasted; he remonstrated with Wu that a press conference for the following day was ill-timed, while the cease-fire committee was trying to establish contact with the delegation. Wu refused to be swayed, however; he had received his instructions and that was that. Anyway, the committee was illegal and any cease-fire negotiations had to be based on the conditions mentioned by Malik along with simultaneous discussions on the questions of Formosa and Communist China's seat in the United Nations. They would leave on Tuesday, December 19.

The conversation had left Lie "excited and depressed," Pearson recorded. The exchange reminded Lie of his conversation with the German ambassador in Oslo just before Norway was invaded. Undaunted, the committee now accepted Lie's prior proposal (rejected by Entezam and Gross) formally to contact Wu. In addition, Lie recommended that the next committee session be held at the United Nations at the same time that Wu was holding his press conference, when Lie would attempt to have Wu meet its members.[226] This suggestion, as we shall see, was adopted.

On December 16 when Wu and his associates appeared at Lie's office prior to the scheduled press conference, Lie attempted to persuade them to change their plans. Since during the course of the press conference they did not, in fact, mention that they were about to depart for Peking, Lie thought they might still stay, making it possible to establish contact with the cease-fire committee; but nothing had changed, Wu assured him. Would they at least stop in London, as he recommended? Lie inquired. That would have to be considered, Wu replied. Lie then pointed out that the cease-fire committee was in the building and had listened to their press conference over the loudspeaker. The members had been pleased at the way the press conference went and continued to believe that there was a chance for negotiations, despite Rau's inability to contact Wu the previous day. Would Wu like to meet the committee members? No, he responded, the committee did not concern him, and he wanted nothing to do with it. However, he was willing to meet Entezam, but only in his capacity as assembly president. The two subsequently spoke, although nothing of substance was discussed; but Lie was rather pointedly not invited to be present.

Before his interview with Wu ended, Lie again tried to change his mind. He read a letter from the committee to Wu, offering to convene a meeting to discuss the basis for an agreed cease-fire and expressing its willingness to meet with the Communist Chinese and North Koreans at any place convenient to them. But the letter did not affect the Chinese decision to depart. They had their instructions and were obdurate. Faced with the likelihood that the delegation itself would announce its departure, Lie finally succumbed and agreed to make its decision public through the cease-fire committee's press officer.

Lie's subsequent comments to Gross were less than candid. To throw Gross off the scent, he fibbed that he did not have the text of the committee's note addressed to Wu. Indeed, he claimed that the committee had not kept him advised of its intentions nor used him to assist it administratively—annoyed, perhaps, that his offer of seconding Feller and Colonel Katzin to the committee had not been picked up. He "sarcastically characterized" the committee's note to Wu as a bid for a Peking junket. He feared that the cease-fire committee, and especially Rau, would now attempt to delay as much as possible further action by the United Nations in the "vain hope" that Peking would assume a different stance. Lie reiterated his "strong view" that the resolution sponsored by the six Western powers should be pressed for United Nations adoption, convinced that Peking did "not intend to cooperate in any way."[227]

The next day, Lie made the same points to Pearson and argued that failure had to be admitted and the cease-fire negotiations terminated. The whole question of what to do if the Communist Chinese continued their military intervention should be referred to the Collective Measures Committee established by the Uniting for Peace Resolution.[228] Since that committee was to act in consultation with the secretary-general and member states, the suspicion is strong that, unable to play a leading mediatory role because of the activities of Rau and the cease-fire committee, Lie saw the possibility of a new opportunity under the aegis of the Collective Measures Committee. In any event, he subsequently, but unsuccessfully, attempted to convene the Collective Measures Committee.[229]

Pearson, however, was not receptive to these arguments and speculated whether Lie was moved "more by his desire to spend Christmas in Norway, or to strike another blow for collective security in the United Nations." Lie repeatedly warned that the cease-fire committee had to be very cautious not to convey the impression that it was committed to appeasement of the Communist Chinese. Pearson, who had thought of inviting Lie to that night's meeting of the cease-fire committee, had second thoughts after this conversation and concluded that he would not be helpful.[230]

On December 19, despite these comments, Lie called on Wu and the delegation to say goodbye but once again was rebuffed when he raised the possibility of their remaining in New York and establishing contact with the cease-fire committee. Lie regretted his inability to assist in the political aspects of the Korean question, since mediation was indivisible and he had to remain in the background so long as the cease-fire committee's work was incomplete. The Communist Chinese said they understood. Lie again offered his assistance to Peking to secure peace in the Far East; he could always be contacted confidentially. Wu promised to convey the offer to Peking. The atmosphere was friendly but unproductive at this last meeting.[231]

He often pondered, Lie later wrote, whether subsequent developments might have been different, had some direct contact been continued by the United Nations (read here, Lie) with Peking in order to bypass communicating "through indirect channels."[232] But Wu and his delegation, like Gross and Pearson, most likely considered Lie's behavior somewhat bizarre. Moscow, no doubt, added its own poison to the well, stirred by Lie's anti-Russian comments to Wu. In choosing a mediator, Peking was not likely to settle on a self-declared noncommunist, and Westerner to boot. Far better intermediaries were the Indian ambassador in Peking, Kavalam Pannikar, and Rau in New York, despite their joint inadequacies. New Delhi's contacts with Washington were at least as good as Lie's. In addition, India was an Asian country, part of the anticolonialist crusade, which was not unimportant. The failure to bridge a political settlement of the Korean question at this time had little to do with techniques of negotiation or the availability and effectiveness of United Nations instruments of mediation. It had more to do with the very simple reality that the Communist Chinese militarily had the upper hand in Korea, and Peking saw little need to commit itself to any settlement not consistent with its declared terms.

9

THWARTED HOPES

Seeking a Cease-Fire

Lie's Korean stance and his improved image in the West was reflected in the Foreign Office's January 1951 recommendation and Bevin's concurrence, in spite of his dislike of Lie, to entertain him during a visit to London.[1] Lie's star in the West was clearly in the ascendent, which may help explain his decision to tackle India's formidable prime minister, Pandit Nehru. One could not envisage a more ill–matched pair: Lie, less than smooth and lacking intellectual credentials, and Nehru, who had both qualities and, especially in certain Western circles, an image as Asia's Diogenes-cum-philosopher king, all-knowledgeable about world affairs. (The fact that Nehru was less than altruistic where Western interests were concerned was ignored.)

Lie's rejection of a proposal by Rau for a Korean cease-fire that was not too dissimilar from Peking's position signaled a trying interview between Lie and Nehru in Paris on January 18. Rau's reports about Lie can be imagined and may help account for Nehru's disinterest and near reversion to a state of slumber when Lie tried to recount his peace mission to Moscow. Nehru struck Lie, as he did others, as egotistical and vain. If Lie thought that their shared values as Marxists of the democratic Left would produce a consensus on how to handle the Korean question, he was soon disappointed. Nehru's animus was directed not at the Communist Chinese and the North Koreans but at the Americans and those who followed their lead. When Lie spoke of defending principles and not rewarding aggression in Korea, they were on different wave lengths. [2]

After this, Lie was a marked man in New Delhi. In the spring, his possible arrival in the Indian capital moved the secretary-general of the Foreign Ministry, Sir Girja Bajpai, to express the hope that Lie would not come. He announced that such a trip would serve no useful purpose; and, as "Lie had been singularly inept during visits [to] other countries," it was not the time for a bull in the Indian china shop. Few Indians respected him, said Bajpai, and they found it difficult to understand his reappointment. Since he obviously reflected Nehru's views, the State Department warned Lie that "he might receive a cool reception" in India and suggested that it might not "be an opportune time for such a visit." [3] Lie got the point, and India was removed from his itinerary. A subsequent, unguarded comment, that "Nehru—despite his smooth talk—is a dictator" [4] showed the secretary-general's reaction.

As the Communist Chinese and North Koreans continued to roll up the United Nations line, Washington took the offensive in the General Assembly with a draft resolution denouncing Communist China for committing aggression and establishing a new committee of member states to consider additional measures to be adopted to meet the Communist Chinese–North Korean aggression and to report to the assembly. The proposed resolution also established a Good Offices Committee (the president of the assembly and two persons appointed by him) to help bring about a cease-fire and the achievement of United Nations objectives in Korea by peaceful means. [5]

Concurrently Lie proposed that he and Pearson go to the Far East to consult with MacArthur, the American ambassador to South Korea, and the United Nations Commission for the Unification and Rehabilitation of Korea. [6] Visiting Korea had been on his mind for some time, he informed MacArthur, in order to consult with the United Nations commission there. Since President Syngman Rhee had invited him, Lie inquired whether such a visit would be opportune. [7] MacArthur was forthcoming: he "heartily" favored the trip and assured Lie of the "warmest possible welcome." [8] Despite all this Lie never went; presumably the State and Defense Departments torpedoed the proposal.

Convening the Collective Measures Committee (or the new one the Americans were proposing) would have dovetailed with Lie's desire, and a Good Offices Committee would open an additional avenue through which he might influence a Korean settlement. He consequently gave unqualified support to Washington's draft resolution and was furious at the British who opposed it. "He harnessed himself to the American carriage and campaigned" enthusiastically to get out the vote in their behalf, the Israeli mission informed Tel Aviv. Lie had argued with the Israelis that the Korean problem could not be settled peacefully, that a military victory was imperative, and that a foreign ministers conference would be useless until American forces in Korea were strengthened. Since Lie regarded Israel as his "protege," he did not want it to oppose the United States on this issue. Washington's draft resolution had to be adopted as formulated, he argued: American public opinion would not accept any failure at the United Nations, which might even affect Washington's continued membership in the world organization. Without the Americans, Lie held, the United Nations would collapse.[9]

The Israelis ignored Lie's advice and, in conjunction with the British, worked to modify the American draft to the effect that the report of the special Additional Measures Committee could be deferred if the Good Offices Committee reported satisfactory progress in its work. The resolution was adopted on February 1, and some days later General Assembly President Entezam appointed Sweden's Sven Grafström and Mexico's Padilla Nervo as the other members of the Good Offices Committee.[10]

As MacArthur's forces fell back in Korea, Lie, it appears, tinkered with the possibility of formally diluting Russian political influence in the upper echelon of the secretariat by appointing a French national to replace Assistant Secretary-General Zinchenko, whose contract had expired: he would detail Zinchenko to social affairs. The Americans and the British strongly objected that this might induce the Russians to leave the United Nations, while the French declined to name a candidate until the Russians had spoken. Moscow naturally invoked the prior agreement among the Big Five on the division of senior secretariat positions.[11]

By early March 1951 the communist steamroller in Korea had been checked, the front line stabilized, and a series of successful attacks with limited objectives had passed the initiative to the United Nations forces. In this setting, Lie proposed that the North Koreans be approached through Gromyko. The notion to use Gromyko for this purpose had been tendered by Zinchenko.[12] Lie argued that, since Entezam's Good Offices Committee had elicited no reaction from Peking, the time was ripe to bypass the Communist Chinese, end the fighting, and postpone for subsequent discussion all other Far East questions. What Lie envisaged was a United Nations approach either through Entezam's committee or "otherwise" (read here, possibly Lie) to the North Koreans; a direct approach might prove fruitful.

The disadvantage of a direct approach, which might seem to confirm North Korea's de facto position, Lie considered would be offset by the advantage of removing from the Korean issue the notion of a "horse-trade with the Chinese over their own demands." Much would depend on whether Peking had wearied of the fighting, which Lie thought possible. He proposed that Ambassador at Large Philip Jessup informally approach

Gromyko in Paris and ascertain whether Moscow had any objections to negotiations for settlement between the United Nations and the North Koreans. If so, did it have an alternative approach in mind?

Lie's proposal, it appears, was based on information he had received that the Communist Chinese had been unsuccessful in acquiring war materiel from the Russians. He thought that there was sufficient tension between some factions in Peking and Moscow to justify an approach to the North Koreans through the Russians. If Moscow was interested in liquidating the drain of the Korean issue, it might grasp this dodge to achieve a settlement. Likewise the proposal might offer Peking a way to withdraw its so-called "volunteers," now that the North Koreans no longer needed them. Padillo Nervo, Lie claimed, was interested in his suggestion, but Entezam held that the Good Offices Committee was authorized to deal only with Peking.

Gross informed Assistant Secretary of State Henderson that Lie realized his ploy would succeed only if Peking and Moscow wanted to "cut their losses and liquidate the affair." Henderson was unreceptive, although he found Lie's proposal of interest. He had no faith in its efficacy since he saw no evidence that Moscow and Peking wanted to settle the matter. Lie's December talks with Czech Foreign Minister Siroky and General Wu were dated, and the fighting since then gave no reason to hope the Communists were ready to negotiate. Henderson also doubted that such a move would lead to friction between them; indeed, Lie's proposal could be interpreted as an attempt to separate the North Koreans and the Communist Chinese, which would complicate even more the work of the Good Offices Committee. However, Gross was authorized to make known that Washington would not object, if the committee believed it useful, to approach the North Koreans, as the committee's mandate would cover such a move.

When Gross outlined these thoughts to Lie, he argued that the recent successes of MacArthur's forces offered a fine opportunity to assume the initiative and press for a settlement. The alternative was a stalemate and continued United Nations casualties, especially among American troops. How long would American public opinion accept this? he asked. He thought that the State Department concentrated too much on Communist China and too little on Soviet Russia. He interpreted a recent press statement by Stalin as indicating that Moscow wished to wash its hands of the Korean venture. Lie argued that, if Communist Chinese and Russian interests did not dovetail, Moscow would not hesitate to use the North Koreans to achieve a peaceful settlement. Lie queried about the possibility of a de facto cease-fire now or later that would lead to a negotiated settlement. He held that Washington should accept less than a 100 percent achievement of United Nations objectives in Korea and that a reestablishment of the status quo before June 25 would be the best way out of the current predicament. Gross pointed out the dangers of any provisional cease-fire and any status quo situation that left the Communists uncontrolled or unsupervised by the United Nations, thus permitting them to prepare a new attack.[13] Lie then asked for a meeting with Henderson and was enraged when it did not take place.[14]

Jebb thought Lie's proposal "ingenious though rather far fetched" and doubted that Moscow would facilitate any contacts with the North Koreans.[15] Like Henderson, the Foreign Office was unreceptive; the proposal was "unlikely to yield results," Jebb was informed. If the Communist Chinese were not ready to negotiate, he was told, it was difficult to fathom how an approach to the North Koreans would change their attitude; in fact, it might be construed "as a sign of weakness or disunity"; nor could an approach independent of the Good Offices Committee be endorsed, at least until the committee had failed in its task.[16] Anglo-American disapproval was echoed by the French and sealed the fate of Lie's proposal.[17]

During the spring of 1951 developments in Korea appeared to signal—or so Lie thought—that the time was finally "ripe for a realistic agreement" on Korea. On April 11, President Truman, because of General MacArthur's unauthorized political pronouncements, summarily dismissed him as commander of United Nations forces in Korea and the American forces in the Far East. In the weeks that followed, MacArthur's replacement, Lieutenant General Matthew Ridgway, and the field commander, Lieutenant General James Van Fleet, pushed the communist forces slightly north of the 38th parallel, inflicting heavy losses in men and materiel.

Lie selected Ottawa to commence publicly his new initiative. It was a shrewd move, since Pearson's own thoughts on a Korean settlement ran somewhat parallel to Lie's. Because United Nations forces had driven the communist forces across the 38th parallel, Lie orated, a cease-fire along that parallel would implement the body of the Security Council resolutions of June and July 1950, provided it was followed by the reestablishment of peace and security in the area.[18]

Lie had privately broached his new thoughts to Jebb a week before, but they "were so disjointed and indeed confused" that Jebb "did not take them seriously." Only later were he and his French counterpart, Francis Lacoste, able to piece together the proposal.[19] Lie, who claimed that Pearson favored the proposal, thought that the assembly's Political Committee could convene and dissolve the Good Offices Committee on the basis of the latter's admission of failure. Once it was dissolved, he wanted the assembly to activate the Special Committee on Chinese Representation and ask it to report in the autumn to the 6th General Assembly; lastly, the current assembly could formulate settlement aims, including a cease-fire along the 38th parallel as well as necessary guarantees, and then dissolve itself.[20]

Lie, Jebb reported, was inspired to make this proposal because he believed that Washington was using the Good Offices Committee in order to avoid pursuing any "'peace feelers'" itself. Moreover, the 5th General Assembly, including that committee, was "anathema" to Peking, which would do nothing until it was prorogued. On the other hand, the Special

Committee on Chinese Representation had not incurred Peking's wrath and therefore might be more acceptable. Lie was convinced that the time was right to end the fighting on the basis of the status quo before June 25 and believed that Moscow shared this view. He wanted his proposal to be jointly examined by the British and French, who, if they agreed, might persuade the Americans to accept it also.

Jebb was partial to adjourning the current assembly, provided that the Additional Measures Committee continued, even if the Good Offices Committee were dissolved. However, some brake on the former would be necessary to forestall any idea that the search for a peaceful solution had been dropped. He doubted that the Special Committee on Chinese Representation would be any more successful than Entezam's committee. Moreover, its terms of reference would have to be revised to allow a mediatory role, or the Americans might think it a ploy to drag the representation issue into the Korean settlement. If Peking really desired a cease-fire, he thought it could use New Delhi as an intermediary; but it was dubious that Peking would officially pursue any cease-fire proposal. [21]

Herbert Morrison, who had replaced the very ill Bevin as foreign secretary, had no objection to adjourning the assembly, but he did not want the Good Offices Committee to report failure, thus leaving the Additional Measures Committee unchallenged and possibly creating the "false impression" that there was no hope of a negotiated settlement. He also agreed with Jebb that there were difficulties in giving the Special Committee on Chinese Representation the mediatory functions of Entezam's committee. [22]

The French likewise were unenthusiastic about Lie's suggestion. Lacoste felt that Lie should not press it and should even be prepared to drop it, if need be. [23] The Americans, whom Lie had not approached directly, "took a dim view" of the proposal, in particular, the idea of adjourning the assembly: Lacoste observed correctly that "Lie was motivated to a considerable degree by jealousy of Entezam," and his desire to abolish the Good Offices Committee stemmed from his belief that it was an American tool, not committed to making peace. The American Ross thought it clear that Lie had been "very busily engaged in building backfires around us and in a manner which could hardly increase any confidence we might feel in him." He proposed with Gross to attempt to get Lie "straightened out." [24] Objections were also raised by the Good Offices Committee, which certainly was not going to dissolve itself and admit failure. The Swedish member Grafström characterized Lie's position on the Special Committee on Chinese Representation as "'stupid,'" and laughed at the secretary-general's view that Entezam's committee was an obstacle to peace, which angered Lie. [25]

Thus stymied, Lie came up with a revised proposal for a cease-fire on or about the 38th parallel, to be arranged through the opposing military commanders: the United Nations command could issue a public statement addressed to the North Korean commander, pointing out that acceptance of a cease-fire would neither affect political questions nor prejudice the position of any party thereon. Addressing the statement to the North Koreans would emphasize the military nature of the statement and avoid Peking's smoke screen that its troops in Korea were volunteers. As earlier proposed, the assembly would adjourn and the Good Offices Committee be dissolved with additional efforts made for a cease-fire and peace settlement through other United Nations bodies.

The Additional Measures Committee would be authorized to report to the council, the next assembly, or in an emergency to a special assembly. The Special Committee on Chinese Representation would report to the next assembly. If a cease-fire did not develop additional troops could be arranged outside of the Additional Measures Committee, and some other procedure for negotiating would have to be found, such as "informal approaches through diplomatic and other channels, . . . preferable to the creation or revival of any formal United Nations machinery." The "other channels" by implication were Lie himself.[26]

Jebb saw some value in Lie's revised proposal regarding a cease-fire, but he suspected "personal considerations" in the idea of dissolving Entezam's committee, which would be unlikely to affect the Communist Chinese in any event.[27] Again, moreover, the United States and France were not receptive. In fact Gross and Lacoste, like Jebb "formed a very definite opinion that Lie's primary objective was to eliminate the Good Offices Committee and particularly Entezam, so that Lie himself could assume more responsibility for any peace negotiations."[28]

Moscow had received the revised proposal through Zinchenko, at a time when communist forces were retreating in Korea under heavy pressure, with enormous losses in men and materiel. Perhaps as a result Malik suggested on June 23 in a radio broadcast that, as a first step toward a Korean settlement, discussions commence between the two sides for a cease-fire and armistice, which should provide for reestablishment of the status quo ante of June 25. At this momentous moment Lie had just arrived in Norway on his annual holiday,[29] an absence from his office that was privately criticized.[30] Appraised of Malik's statement, Lie publicly suggested that discussions for a cease-fire commence immediately; once attained, the political issues of restoring peace and security could then be discussed in the United Nations[31]—which would obviously open possibilities for Lie's involvement.

Jebb personally thought that Lie should have remained silent on Malik's statement. Gross objected to Lie's initial draft, which requested that the "political authorities" instruct the military commanders on both sides to commence negotiations, and thought it "undesirable" for Lie to "indicate any kind of *procedure*." Gross therefore did not actually approve the pronouncement but simply refrained from raising any objections, so the pronouncement was issued, and Lie managed to keep quiet that he had consulted prior to its issue.[32]

At London airport, on his hurried return to New York, Lie opined that Malik's broadcast showed that Moscow seriously desired a cease-fire. It dovetailed with several "informal approaches" made to him previously through Zinchenko, he claimed, and even maintained that "Malik had lifted some ideas" from his own revised proposal to use in the broadcast. The salient point, he insisted, was to dissolve the present assembly, in part because Moscow was very hostile to it and in part because Entezam was in a difficult situation due to the Anglo-Iranian oil dispute—this stemmed from Iran's April nationalization of the Anglo-Iranian Oil Company—and the "sooner he ceased to be President of the Assembly the better." If the Korean negotiations were fruitful, they should be referred to the council since any settlement required Moscow's consent.[33]

Likewise in New York Lie continued to emphasize the significance of Malik's statement. He saw the Good Offices Committee, strenuously opposed a new approach to Peking as suggested by Padilla Nervo, and was doubtlessly pleased that Entezam "appeared embarrassed by Malik['s] refusal to see him and wished to beat a graceful retreat to Washington," which Lie encouraged. Gross sought to dampen Lie's ardor,[34] while Lie denied to Ross that he was pressuring Washington. In talking with the Good Offices Committee, Lie held that Ridgway "had full authority" to commence cease-fire negotiations on the United Nations' behalf, which would obviate the need for an assembly meeting or other United Nations action as many had been pressing for, but would entail delay.[35] In this setting, Lie reinforced his stance publicly, after consultations with senior secretariat officials, by a legal memorandum written by Feller, supporting Ridgway's authority to lead a delegation from the United Nations command in negotiations for the world organization.[36]

On the eve of the communist acceptance of Ridgway's invitation to commence cease-fire negotiations, Lie felt forced by American pressure to request United Nations members to express their willingness to supply troops should a cease-fire and armistice not be obtained.[37] However, when the Greeks offered to double their forces in Korea, he said he should not be informed officially, in view of the current cease-fire negotiations—a stance that the Americans rejected.[38] Concurrently Lie suggested to Washington that the Palestine precedent might be followed using a Bernadotte-like mediator[39]—perhaps thinking of himself in that role. He had had Dragon Protitch, the Yugoslav director of the Department of Security Council Affairs, prepare a memorandum[40] proposing, on the basis of prior United Nations endeavors, that a single mediator would offer more hope of success than a commission in Korea. He proposed the mediator have "the broadest possible mandate" and responsibility to the assembly (or to a committee appointed by it when it was not in session), which would play the policy-making role on Korea. To avoid "confusion and overlapping," moreover; on the mediator's appointment, the United Nations Commission for the Unification and Rehabilitation of Korea would be dissolved. The mediator would control the truce supervision machinery and the problem of Korean unification as well as other political matters.[41]

Lie "was virtually certain," Jebb informed London, that a Korean cease-fire or armistice would be negotiated but was far from sanguine about the "prospects of any real political settlement." He felt that the Communists would never consent to a unified, non-Communist Korea and had "no real interest in bringing about a political settlement in the area." Despite this, he felt that a determined effort should be made to secure a solution. The use of a mediator, he argued, would help save the faces of Moscow and Peking and assist the Truman administration in its internal difficulties by avoiding direct negotiations with Peking. Lie had in mind as the possible mediator, Erik Boheman, the Swedish ambassador in Washington, as well as others.

Jebb thought Lie's proposal "worth serious consideration," although he also was sceptical about the possibility of a sound political solution; but it should be attempted and, at some point, the United Nations associated with this attempt. The notion of a mediator appeared to offer distinct advantages; its implementation might deflect attention from Korea and avoid, or at least postpone, issues like Formosa and Chinese representation. Of the possible mediators, Jebb was partial to Boheman or Sir Ramaswami Mudaliar, the Indian representative, since he doubted that Moscow would consent to a Dutch national or a Dane, however qualified the person might be. He was, however, unsure about Lie's suggested policy-making committee, which he felt might detract from the mediator's authority. Perhaps, without tieing him down too much, the mediator might be made responsible to the council or the assembly. One possibility offered by the committee, he thought, was that, once constituted minus any Chinese representation, the committee might lead to a situation enabling Washington to withdraw recognition from the Nationalist Chinese without necessarily according it to Peking.[42]

Other Western reaction to Lie's proposal was mixed. The State Department felt it was "premature," as Korea's long-term problems could only be tackled after a cease-fire.[43] France's foreign minister, Robert Schuman, raised no objections to the notion of a single mediator.[44] Initial consensus in the Foreign Office was to support Lie's proposal, even though there was little hope Moscow would accept a mediator; although Boheman was highly rated, Mudaliar was thought probably to be more acceptable to the Russians; and anyway they thought it wiser to have an Asian mediator in Korea.[45] Depending on how the cease-fire talks went, the Russians might be approached during the latter phase of the negotiations. The council might also pass on the proposal, which arrangement might secure limited

Russian cooperation, although the Americans might be annoyed by this. Much depended on Moscow's "sincerity and intentions."[46]

Commonwealth representatives at the United Nations, however, raised objections.[47] Specifically, the Indians inexplicably wanted to avoid any involvement in appointing a mediator and therefore frowned on the possible selection of Mudaliar.[48] The Australians, like the Americans, felt it was "premature" and feared it might raise false hopes. They also doubted the desirability of an Indian mediator; but irrespective of the person chosen, they foresaw possible difficulties within the United Nations, should the person chosen refuse to accept South Korea's continued integrity as a primary United Nations objective. This would be true even if the mediator were convinced that there was no assurance that a unified Korea would be democratic and independent.[49]

By early August, these and other objections caused the Foreign Office to have second thoughts on the matter. Morrison now saw greater obstacles in the way of Lie's proposal than he originally did, in particular the fundamental problem that the United Nations itself was a participant in the Korean fighting, which made it doubtful that the mediator "could operate effectively or produce a plan acceptable to both sides as a basis for discussion."[50] In the end, Lie's proposal was stillborn. Although cease-fire negotiations commenced at Kaesong, in communist-controlled territory, they soon collapsed. After the United Nations military successes, they were renewed at Panmumjom in October. They were to drag on, punctured by intermittent fighting, until July 1953, well after Lie had departed as secretary-general.

The autumn of 1951 brought Lie additional disappointment. He "wanted to avoid exacerbating the Russians further" for the duration of his tour of duty. At the assembly in Paris it was generally known that he favored electing a Russian satellite to replace Yugoslavia on the council,[51] but the seat went to Greece. Concurrently Lie called on Acheson, apparently moved by the idea that Moscow "wanted to make 'contact' but in a face-saving manner," although he did not elaborate on why he thought so. Lie therefore mentioned the German question and membership in the United Nations as possible contact points,[52] but this brought no response from Acheson. There is some evidence that Lie's notion about the Russians came from Gromyko's positive response to an invitation by Gunnar Myrdal to a preliminary meeting of government experts for the preparation of a European trade conference under the Economic Commission for Europe.[53] Along these lines, Lie also tried again to get Vyshinsky and Acheson together, which led to nothing except perhaps a modicum of civility in the assembly debates.[54]

Whether Lie's numerous proposals to effect a cease-fire were sound can be questioned, but he cannot be criticized for tendering them or for the manner in which this was done. At the minimum, the secretary-general was entitled to offer privately, either officially or unofficially, ways and means to end the Korean fighting that might lead to a solution of broader Asian problems, in particular the question of Communist China's position in the United Nations. Experience had perhaps taught him that public exposure and open initiatives were counterproductive and led to his relative avoidance of the public forum; his press comments about Malik's radio broadcast can perhaps be explained as a case where exuberance and optimism got the upper hand over wisdom and caution. He can be criticized, however, over his undisguised hostility to the Good Offices Committee in general and to assembly President Entezam in particular. This attitude had less to do with conflicting personalities than with Lie's perception of the committee and Entezam as competitors who complicated his own initiatives, and mediatory desires and thus detracted from the chances of obtaining a peaceful settlement in Korea. In fact, although Lie may have been oblivious to it, his animus contributed toward the negative reaction to his own peace efforts.

Loyalty in the Secretariat

Problems closer to home also undercut Lie's position and hastened the desire of many to see him go as soon as possible. A central issue was the political reliability of the secretariat and Washington's belated contention that some of its American members posed a risk to the security of the United States.

Questions on the nature of the secretariat had been raised from the beginning, despite the charter provisions as to its international character. Lie decided in the spring of 1946 to ask the State Department for comments on the Americans Cordier, Feller, and David Vaughan and was criticized by Cordier who considered it a "mistake." Cordier's view was supported by others, who held that Lie should be unfettered in his choice of secretariat members even if he wanted to hire nationals not inscribed by their governments on some recommended list, for lack of political influence or some other reason. A State Department official who was present voiced his doubts and tellingly pointed out that it "might be unrealistic to assume that a person could be hired who would be persona non grata to his Government." Cordier and his colleagues agreed that such a case should naturally be avoided and should be tackled informally by the secretary-general rather than be based on some "formal procedure."[55]

Cordier's comments reflected his ignorance of standard procedure in recruiting personnel in the League of Nations Secretariat. It was naive to believe that a multinational civil service of a world organization dealing mainly with political questions could be entirely divorced from the politics of those questions; and the secretariat simply could not be like an ideal, nonpolitical national civil service on the Weberian model. Even the best of national civil services, in fact, had fallen prey to the political factor; so had the league secretariat, even though it had been relatively homogeneous. No international secretariat could possess the characteristics and shared values that contributed to cohesiveness in an ideal bureaucratic model. Inevitably the political nature of its multinational civil service had manifested itself in the league secretariat from the beginning despite Secretary-General Sir Eric Drummond's myth-making on the subject, which persisted during the tenure of his French successor, Joseph Avenol. Indeed, Drummond had, as a matter of course, quietly ascertained the attitude of prospective candidates' governments, especially of the more powerful states.[56]

Lie's decision therefore to solicit State Department views about Cordier and other Americans was both the better part of valor and in line with prior practice. Nevertheless, during Lie's 1946 discussions with Secretary of State Byrnes, the latter indicated that Washington would neither tender any recommendations, support officially, nor give clearance on the appointment of American nationals to subordinate positions in the secretariat. This excluded the post of assistant secretary-general, reserved for an American, initially awarded to John Hutson and later assumed by Byron Price. What role Alger Hiss played in this policy decision is difficult to assess, although there is no doubt that he was involved.[57] In view of league practice, it was a naive stance.

Lie also solicited nominations from other member states, checked with them on appointments to the secretariat, but reserved to himself the ultimate decision on hiring.[58] The collapse of the wartime coalition and the development of the Cold War generated a suspicion in Lie's mind that some members of the American Communist party might have infiltrated the secretariat.[59] Their ability to do so would have been aided by Washington's lackadaisical initial attitude toward secretariat recruitment. Needless to say, American Communists in the secretariat would have been an unacceptable idea to any American administration and certainly to the Congress. This idea that a secretariat official's political loyalty had to be acceptable to his or her national government was common to most member states, especially communist ones. Thus, Gromyko raised objections even to the employment of White Russian émigrés and their children, a position Lie rejected; within a year of the 1948 Czech coup d'état he likewise rejected that communist regime's pressure on him to dismiss all but three officials of Czechoslovakian nationality on the ground that they were personae non gratae to Prague.[60]

Since no secretariat official could properly function with strong government opposition and since the secretary-general had to maintain good relations with the member governments, the secretary-general would be under overwhelming pressure to sacrifice an official who came under governmental displeasure. Any such move, however, had to navigate some difficult rapids: the contractual arrangements made when hiring the official concerned, the charter stipulations, staff regulations dealing with secretariat tenure, and the myth inherited from the league that secretariat officials were nonpolitical civil servants. The uninvited burden was Lie's.

In 1946, and again in 1947, Lie "informally" asked Washington to supply personnel information about Americans serving in the secretariat.[61] In line with Byrnes's comments to Lie there appears to have been no response to these requests. By the spring of 1947, possible infiltration of the secretariat by communist agents had to be squarely faced by Lie, following complaints raised about the antics of members of the Balkan Commission secretariat:[62] Stanley Ryan's activities in particular, as Pearson reported to Ottawa, had attracted Lie's attention.[63] So did those of the Pole Gustav Gottesman, whose improper conduct on the commission Lie could not forgive and was consequently pleased when Gottesman subsequently resigned.[64]

In Washington, in 1948, the issue of Communists in the secretariat surfaced when a State Department official from the Visa Division testified before staff members of the Senate Judiciary Subcommittee on Immigration that secretariat appointments had been used as a cover to introduce subversive foreign agents into the United States. Secretary of State Marshall appeared to contradict this testimony by declaring that he knew of no case where American security had been threatened by any foreign official in the secretariat.[65] In fact, although this was rarely done, Washington had had no compunction in pressing Lie to reject the appointment of a foreign national whose presence might be detrimental to national security—as it had in the case of the Pole Stefan Littauer.[66]

On the specific instance of the Senate Judiciary Subcommittee testimony, Marshall privately informed Lie that a junior officer had testified without the State Department's permission and would probably retract his statements in subsequent testimony. However, the important point Marshall wanted conveyed to Lie was that the State Department could not muzzle its officials appearing before a congressional committee nor was it "possible to make the kind of diplomatic disavowal which might be made under other circumstances."[67] This ex post facto explanation, however, could not erase the damage already done.

Washington's attitude toward American personnel in the secretariat had already begun to change following President Truman's decision in the spring of 1947 to establish a loyalty review program for American federal employees. By the end of 1948, the Federal Bureau of Investigation had been authorized to institute "discreet inquiries" regarding American secretariat personnel "who might be applying for U.S. Government jobs or otherwise be the subject of investigations." Under this arrangement, David Vaughan, principal director of the United Nations Department of Conference and General Services, would be contacted and would make inquiries about American secretariat officials on behalf of the Federal Bureau of Investigation and, moreover, indicate those who could be interviewed directly by the Federal Bureau of Investigation "without embarrassment or difficulty" for the United Nations. In Vaughan's absence only Price or Feller would be contacted. The State Department hoped that this procedure would avoid embarrassment from the "natural reactions of the alien members of the Secretariat" or by the "investigation by an American police agency at [the] UN."[68] A discreet investigation by Washington of its own nationals might perhaps have been rationalized on the grounds that Americans in the secretariat had no immunity from investigation by their own government. For American senior United Nations officials to assist in these investigations, even if nominally to save the amour-propre of the secretariat and the United Nations, was questionable indeed.

Matters hardened by the spring of 1949. Washington refused to issue a passport to a secretariat official of American nationality, which led Lie to issue orders that the official in question be discharged. Similarly he discharged another American, subpoenaed to appear before the House of Representatives Un-American Activities Committee. Lie told the American mission through Feller that he wanted to remove such secretariat personnel who were "unable to be effective members of his staff and [brought] him public embarrassment." As far as was known, Austin was informed, Lie's action had not been suggested to him by any American official. In this case, Lie asked for a postponement of the hearing. If it appeared, Lie held, that the dismissal had occurred because the official was under suspicion as a communist agent, "he would have to reverse himself and stand by his staff." On the other hand, if the official were let go immediately any subsequent testimony before the House committee would be looked upon as coincidental.[69] Although the official in question did not appear before the House committee until several months later, accused of being a communist courier, his removal from the secretariat, for unexplained reasons, did not occur until January 1951.[70]

Following the decision to dismiss the two Americans, Lie instructed Assistant Secretary-General Price to approach the Federal Bureau of Investigation and explain that the secretary-general did not want foreign spies in the secretariat. Lie, the bureau was to be told, regarded such activity as contrary to Article 100 of the charter, which holds that the secretary-general and the secretariat shall neither seek nor receive instructions from any government and shall refrain from any action that might undermine their status as international officials. Specifically, Lie did not want American Communists in the secretariat. Only Communists from communist states could be countenanced. Price emphasized that the secretariat lacked any investigative machinery and needed assistance in such matters. Would it be possible, he asked, for the Federal Bureau of Investigation either to screen American applicants for secretariat positions or, at a minimum, to indicate informally whether it had any derogatory information on an American applicant?

The proposal was rejected[71] at the time but, by late July 1949, the pressure on Washington increased to institute some sort of procedure for clearance of American applicants. The Senate judiciary subcommittee released testimony by a mystery informant, who testified in broken English and was identified only as "Witness No. 8"; he urged the senators to seek Lie's ouster and the appointment of an able successor, claiming that the secretariat was terrorized by communist agents who forced other officials to do their bidding. The secretariat protested to Lie, who foisted the matter off on Price and Cordier. They, in turn, categorically denied the veracity of the testimony.[72]

Following this unseemly fracas, on August 3, Feller approached the American mission on whether "some more regular and responsible way" could not be devised to inform the United Nations about American applicants before a crisis developed.[73] This time the State Department was receptive to Feller's probe, concerned "over the situation which investigative reports were disclosing." Hickerson discussed the matter informally with one of Lie's principal assistants, probably Price. Their mutual concern led to a secret agreement in September 1949 whereby Washington would identify for Lie American nationals in, or being considered for, the secretariat who appeared to be either Communist party members or under communist discipline. Washington formally understood that under the charter only Lie could employ and discharge secretariat personnel, for whose appointment he was beholden exclusively to the assembly. Any adverse comment to Lie about any American national would be by word of mouth. Lie professed to understand that this procedure did not constitute a clearance of the individual in question. These byzantine and hypocritical proceedings were apparently justified on the grounds that public admission that American nationals were being scrutinized by Washington would have made it difficult for Lie to fend off demands for a similar procedure to cover secretariat officials of eastern European nationality, appointed before a communist take-over of their countries and consequently personae non gratae to the new governments.[74]

The informal and secret 1949 arrangement was pragmatically no worse than most "practical politics" but hardly added to United States luster in its shining knight role. The agreement hammered out had eroded the position of both sides: the establishment of a "responsible and loyal" secretariat "not nominated or directed by any national states."[75] Understandably the arrangement has been attacked polemically,[76] as though the act itself, as one astute writer has noted, took "on the character of original sin."[77] "Practical men" Acheson has observed, "could have solved the problem easily."[78] This was not to be. In the fall of 1962, the Senate Judiciary Subcommittee on Internal Security and a federal grand jury met in

New York to investigate the loyalty of Americans in the secretariat. Some of the subpoenaed witnesses invoked their Fifth Amendment right under the American Constitution against self-incrimination, which resulted in jaundiced views of the United Nations in the United States and vice versa. Although the secretariat officials invoking this right were a very small percentage of the total American nationals employed in the secretariat, the American public reaction that it generated seemingly alarmed Lie, who not surprisingly felt a strong need for American government and public support. His attitude, he later wrote, was that those Americans who had pleaded the Fifth Amendment had "gravely and irresponsibly" breached United Nations' staff regulations and helped discredit the entire secretariat. Moreover, although the United Nations was not bound by American precedent, the invocation of the Fifth Amendment under American law, at all levels of government, could lead to dismissal from the public service. Lie's decision therefore was to dismiss those officials who had only temporary contracts with the United Nations and to place on compulsory leave those with permanent contracts, as he was unsure of his legal right to dismiss them.[79]

This action came easily enough; indeed, one could argue that the whole situation was something of a godsend as far as Lie was concerned, since it went far to solve some of the "administrative problems" he claimed to be "beset by." As he explained to Jebb his "first task was to make a clean sweep of the Communists" from the secretariat; second, "to weed out" of the secretariat as many officials as possible over sixty years of age; and lastly, to discharge the temporary secretariat staff or convert them into permanent members.[80] Although both Lie and the assembly desired an increase in permanent staff, and Lie had declared publicly that he wanted young talent to enter the secretariat,[81] his "resolve to weed out Communists" was doubtlessly strengthened by American pressure, David Royce of the Foreign Office observed, but was not in response to any assembly decision.[82] In September, as the Senate Judiciary Subcommittee geared up to take on the American nationals in the secretariat, the British embassy in Washington reported that the assembly was pressing Lie to improve secretariat efficiency and organization and that the State Department suspected he might be using the few cases that attracted public attention—the Senate Judiciary Subcommittee had not yet held any open hearings—"as a stalking horse for some of his other very considerable staff problems." The embassy noted that Lie was "not the most tactful of operators in personality issues" and had collided with the United Nations Administrative Tribunal over some of his dismissals. The State Department thought that the decisions of the tribunal had "been overweighted in favour of the staff," complicating Lie's task even more than it was intrinsically. Some of the tribunal's decisions had angered Lie, and although the State Department sympathized with him, it was "convinced that he [was] riding off one grievance on the back of another." The embassy thought it unwise for the moment "to stick our oar in any deeper" with the Americans on this very sensitive issue.[83] Not only did the British government keep mum, but so did everyone else.[84]

After consulting Feller and the assistant secretaries-general as well as some delegations, presumably those of the Western powers, Lie decided it would be wise to ascertain the opinion of an international commission of jurists as to his rights in this question. After some difficulty a three-man panel was constituted, composed of Sir Edwin Herbert, a well-known British solicitor; William Mitchell, President Hoover's former attorney general; and Paul Veldekens, a professor of civil law at the Catholic University of Louvain. The charge was later raised, which Lie strongly denied, that he had packed the commission. On the day before the jurists convened Feller committed suicide, driven to self-destruction by the accumulated strain of grappling with the legal and other problems stemming from the secretariat loyalty issue. The loss of one of his closest advisers left Lie shattered and grief stricken.[85] Feller's defenestration "gave rise to much speculation and a good deal of sympathy for members of the United Nations staff," the Foreign Office was informed.[86]

Following two weeks of deliberations the Commission of Jurists submitted what has been labeled its "jesuitical 'host country' formula."[87] According to the commission, the refusal by secretariat officials of American nationality to answer questions about Communist party membership or any subversive activity, on the ground of possible self-incrimination, constituted a breach of the staff regulations. Lie had the authority, it held, to discharge those Americans with permanent contracts who had invoked the Fifth Amendment and recommended that he do so.[88] When the officials in question continued their refusal to testify, even after Lie had given them the opportunity to do so, he dismissed them.[89] Lie was very "aware of the seriousness of the problem," Price later told the Senate Subcommittee, "presented by the presence in the Secretariat, within the borders of the United States, of American citizens which their Government felt it had ground to suspect of subversive activities."[90] Although in private conversation during this period Jebb made no secret of his disdain for some of the Neanderthal types that stalked the American political landscape,[91] in reporting to Eden, by then foreign secretary in Churchill's second government, his comments were measured.

After discussing the commission's report with Sir Edwin Herbert, Jebb thought that "as a statement of the strict legal position the report [was] probably correct"; but whether the problem should be approached from a purely legal standpoint was another matter. The jurists, in fact, recognized that the establishment and maintenance of friendly relations with Washington depended on understanding the needs of the United Nations and the secretariat, on the one hand, and the United States, on the other.

Although the report was legally sound, Jebb felt, its "tone" was "unduly biased" in favor of the Americans. Much was said about United Nations obligations toward the United States but little in the reverse to ensure that the "United Nations [was] allowed to function effectively as an international organisation." Sir Edwin had readily admitted that the current problem was due far less to the vagaries of the secretariat than to American law on internal security and the way it was applied. Nevertheless, the law itself and congressional methods were facts that had to be accepted, however much one disagreed with them. If the situation was considered entirely intolerable, the only remedy would be to remove the United Nations headquarters from the United States. In addition, the jurists' report offered no greater protection to non-American nationals of the secretariat, for example, if British nationals were charged with engaging in activities directed against the host government, despite London's denials that this was so. "If we accept the legal conclusions of the report," Jebb observed, "I do not see how this position can be challenged, however unpalatable we may feel it to be" since "the document as a whole [was hardly] open to serious challenge on technical grounds."[92]

An unofficial British objection was raised, however. Lord Reginald Crook, a member of the United Nations Administrative Tribunal, accompanied by Jebb and Minister of State Selwyn Lloyd, called on Lie. Crook voiced his disagreement with the jurists' report and suggested that Lie do nothing until the tribunal could review the individual cases. He accused Lie of acting under American pressure, which Lie denied categorically, pointed out that the question was his responsibility, and admonished Crook to mind his business. Was Crook speaking in behalf of the British government? Lie queried. Lloyd said no—the only substantive remark that Lloyd or Jebb made during this meeting. Lie resented it and protested Crook's partiality to the tribunal. (Crook subsequently failed to attend the tribunal's hearings, which was credited to his wife's illness.) The British performance had been irregular, but the Foreign Office reacted strongly on learning that Lie had "admitted quite shamelessly" that he had tape recorded the conversation, which was also irregular.[93]

The jurists' report was presented to Lie at the same time the federal grand jury ended its New York investigations. Although it returned no indictment, it concluded that there had been large-scale infiltration of the secretariat by disloyal Americans, which constituted a threat to the United States. No figures or names were given to support these allegations.[94]

When Lie asked for either the records of the grand jury or an official accounting of the evidence on which the presentment was based (a request that the State Department supported), both were denied. But in line with draft legislation sponsored by Senator Pat McCarran of Nevada, chairman of the Senate Judiciary Subcommittee, and with no prior consultation with Lie, Washington informed him in early January 1953 that an Executive

Order had been issued spelling out procedures for making available to him certain government information concerning Americans employed or being considered for employment by the secretariat. This was intended to assure that the United Nations would neither employ nor continue to employ Americans engaged, previously engaged, or likely to be engaged in any subversive activities against the United States. The evidence gathered by the United States government agencies would be submitted to Lie, and he would make the ultimate decision.

Lie welcomed the Executive Order as giving him the assistance he had previously sought, and he sanctioned the fingerprinting and interviewing of Americans within the headquarters building by Washington's agents. Lie defended this not on the "host country" thesis adumbrated by the jurists' report but on its conclusion: that he already had authority to expel from the secretariat or to deny employment to any subversive. The British mission thought that Lie had placed the problem in a "better perspective" than the jurists' report, and in doing so emphasized the "independence of the Secretariat, and the need for adequate evidence to enable the Secretary-General to arrive at sound conclusions in individual cases." Lie successfully defended his position before the assembly, which in effect supported his policies—thanks largely to the backing of the United States, Great Britain, Norway, and various other member states.[95]

Washington, however, had not been oblivious to the impact that all this might have. Hickerson acknowledged in mid-February 1953 that Washington had been "fully alive to the difficulties, dangerous implications and precedents" that its actions might raise and that "only after long and serious consideration" had it decided to act. He admitted the security issue had been exaggerated in the public mind. At the same time, he observed that other states had to consider the "depth of the emotional feeling on this matter" in the United States. The State Department, he divulged to Dutch and French interlocutors, had decided that its actions were "necessary to forestall more drastic unilateral action which might have been demanded [by American public opinion] and to help restore the necessary measure of confidence" in the world organization throughout the United States. Hickerson maintained that Washington had no intention to pass judgment on non-American nationals in the secretariat, with the possible future exception of those few officials who, although aliens, had permanent immigration status and were in the process of acquiring American nationality.[96] Not until Lie was succeeded by Hammarskjöld was use of the headquarters building denied to Washington's agents for fingerprinting and interviewing Americans.[97] By this time, however, both American and world scenes had changed.

The events of these years reinforced by the continued fighting in Korea, with Americans dying in an undeclared war, demanded absolute loyalty from all Americans, even if this required reaching into the United Nations.

A resolute and less pliant secretary-general might have handled the situation better, but it is doubtful that anyone could have long resisted the enormous pressure felt both from Congress and the American public. Washington's belated decision, after ignoring Lie's earlier prodding, to guarantee the loyalty of Americans employed in the secretariat would have been less shocking and more understandable to well-meaning people, if the myth of a nonpolitical multinational secretariat, first cultivated by Drummond in 1919, had not been oversold. That a nonpolitical secretariat would have been desirable goes without saying; that it could have been obtained, in view of the increasing postwar political, military, and ideological struggle, is clearly unlikely. The tragedy of this period was that, when the myth of an impartial secretariat was exposed to scrutiny, its fragility became obvious. Lie had not decked himself with glory, but the Truman administration, by not vetting Americans being recruited for the secretariat, had failed to give Lie the initial assistance he had requested. Compounded by demagoguery and the impact of the Korean war on American public opinion, events overtook both Lie and the Truman administration. On this matter, wisdom had been in short supply everywhere.

Lowering the Pilot

As the cease-fire negotiations ground away unprofitably at Panmunjom, Lie returned to his idea of organizing a United Nations Legion composed of volunteers prepared to serve in support of collective action under the aegis of the organization. In renewing this proposal, he was stimulated by the growing impatience of Washington and American public opinion over the Korean deadlock, with the possible consequent American adoption of extreme measures, like bombing targets in Communist China. Lie did not believe that assembly action on either economic or political measures would be of practical value but thought the only meaningful action that could help maintain United Nations solidarity, as well as impress Moscow and Peking, would be to dispatch additional ground forces to Korea. He wanted the British and French to supply about 20,000 such troops and to urge other western European states to do likewise, so that an equivalent number of American troops could be released.

Washington doubted the political "wisdom" of a trip to London and Paris by Lie to press his arguments but felt it could raise no objection, since it was "first broached to us in [the] form of [a] decision already taken." Lie, however, was advised to avoid implying that he was acting as Washington's "agent" although he could stress the seriousness with which the Korean problem was viewed in the United States. Hortatory resolutions by the assembly would be unacceptable to Washington, although for many reasons it thought stronger measures should be taken by the assembly once it was clear that the Communists would not agree to an armistice. Washington welcomed whatever Lie could do to obtain additional ground forces but doubted that London or Paris would furnish them; it thought Lie should approach countries that had not yet contributed any forces. Lie thought he could probably persuade Eden more easily than Pearson, who would also be in London and who Lie considered the "'weaker of the two.'" His proposal, however, was rejected by both Eden and the French.[98]

These off-stage endeavors by Lie were tolerated by the powers, which was not the case when he sought to effect publicly other issues in world politics, such as Iran's nationalization of the Anglo-Iranian Oil Company. The Foreign Office felt that Lie's public comments on the question were not in themselves harmful but that it would be unfortunate if the Iranian authorities interpreted his words "as an offer to mediate." Accordingly, Lie was discouraged from making any public comments about the affair and, although he feigned that he understood London's desire, he probably was less than pleased by it.[99] His pronounced, if private, anti-British stance on the matter certainly made him unfit to dabble in the question.[100]

In the midst of these political endeavors, Lie decided after discussion with his family to resign as secretary-general. The British had little doubt that his difficulties with Washington over Americans in the secretariat was a factor in his decision. Moscow's animosity and his difficulties with the Administrative and Budgetary Committee were also important. Ostensibly, however, Lie maintained that a change was needed, although his term did not expire until February 1954. Eden and Pearson were informed in September, during a visit to London. Eden, it appears, did not think the decision well-timed. Pearson was sympathetic. The French thought Lie meant to resign in February 1954 rather than immediately. Lie asked the Norwegian prime minister to inform King Haakon that he would announce his resignation in November 1952. On the day following the American presidential elections and the victory of General Dwight Eisenhower, Lie also informed Acheson, who expressed his regrets but said he understood.[101] He might also have been surprised, for Gross had earlier predicted that Lie would no doubt sound out Washington on its "attitude toward his re-election."

Just before making his announcement to the assembly on November 10[102] and inscribing the appointment of a successor on its agenda, Lie informed senior secretariat officials of his decision. According to Lie his words left "some . . . numb and shocked, others looked desperate."[103] However, a Canadian witness tells us there "were a few conventional murmurs of regret but no strong objections or even any suggestions that he should reconsider." No one else, it appears, offered to resign. When the meeting adjourned, some held that perhaps Lie's resignation was all for the good, and that all "should hope for a man of stronger character and more effective abilities" in his place. There was no apparent joy but neither was there significant evidence of regret.[104] Assistant Secretary-General David Owen pointed out to Jebb that, "rightly or wrongly," the secretariat had lost confidence in Lie and longed for the council to agree on an appropriate successor.[105] Eden, echoed by others, told the assembly that Lie should reconsider his decision,[106] which left Foreign Office's Assistant Under-Secretary Paul Mason uneasy: he assumed that Eden's words were "purely formal and that we have no intention (or indeed prospect) of preventing Mr. Lie's resignation"[107]—a supposition confirmed by Jebb.[108]

On November 11, the day following his announcement Lie told Jebb he would be pleased if his successor could be picked quickly; but if necessary, he would shoulder the burden until the 1953 assembly session. His own preferred candidate was Pearson, Entezam, Romulo, or the Swede Eric Boheman, although he expected Romulo and Boheman would be opposed by Moscow. He was not partial to any Latin American candidates on the grounds that they lacked the "qualities required." Bunche, he opined, although clearly "very good" would be vetoed by Soviet Russia. If Pearson were similarly vetoed, Lie thought it would be a "splendid gesture" on London's part to support Entezam, who he believed was qualified but an unlikely possibility since the dispute over Iranian nationalization of the Anglo-Iranian Oil Company was in full swing. Lie thought Acheson, Eden, and Schuman should confer jointly, and then if they agreed on a list of candidates, Eden should talk to Vyshinsky.

According to Dragon Protitch, the Yugoslav director of the Department of Security Council Affairs, who was present when Lie's resignation was drafted and supposedly argued against it, the secretary-general did not want a deadlock to develop over his successor followed by a request for him to serve until the following year, and then for shorter periods if the deadlock persisted. What Lie contemplated, was a deadlock followed by an offer from the Western powers, if need be against Moscow's opposition, for another three-year reappointment. In view of the discrepancy between Protitch's and Lie's comments to Jebb, the latter was uncertain what would transpire if a stalemate did develop by the end of the current assembly session and "if it were then simply suggested" that Lie should continue for another year (presumably withdrawing his resignation).[109] With all these contradictory statements, Pearson also began to have doubts whether Lie would really leave.[110]

As to Gromyko he wanted "informal consultations" on Lie's successor. Acheson, however, was in no rush; he liked the line Eden suggested, that Lie's formal announcement that he would resign did not mean his resignation was final and should be investigated before jumping into any agreement on his successor. Acheson did not credit the possibility that Lie would reconsider his resignation but felt that Eden's ploy "would be a useful maneuver at this time." Eden agreed and raised the probability that

Moscow would attempt to cause trouble by suggesting candidates in no way qualified for the post.

Several days later an American mission official informally observed that Washington was in "no great hurry" to Manfred Lachs of the Polish mission, who raised the names of Entezam or Padilla Nervo and dismissed (but did not rule out) Romulo. The Soviet bloc, Lachs noted, was partial to a private meeting of the Big Four—excluding the Nationalist Chinese, who were "only a shadow state" that would follow in Washington's wake. Agreement on Lie's successor, he held, would be seen by the Soviet bloc as an important step in reducing tension between the Americans and Russians. When pressed by his American interlocutor, however, Lachs admitted that such an agreement could only be a "very small step forward." Lachs stressed the importance to the Soviet bloc of having at the United Nations' "helm a capable man . . . acceptable to the major interested powers." The American held that he was without instructions but personally saw Lie's recent moves as "only an intention to resign rather than an actual and irrevocable resignation." If no successor could be agreed on, he assumed that Lie would continue as secretary-general with the assembly's full support. The American's analysis upset Lachs, who interpreted Lie's resignation as irrevocable and challenged the notion that the assembly would give him its confidence. From Lachs's comments, the American concluded that Moscow "strongly opposed" Lie's continuance in office and that, "if properly played by the US, Soviet aversion to Lie [might] be an important trump card" for Washington in agreeing with Moscow on his successor. He thought, however, that Lachs's insistence on private conversations among the Big Four only was "probably bluff," since Russia had had no qualms in sitting down with the Nationalist Chinese in the past to discuss the membership question. He recommended that Washington be "very cautious" about instituting Big Four or Big Five conversations on Lie's successor, since it might turn out to be the one question on which it could allow Moscow to make the initial approach.

No doubt on Lie's prodding, Price conveyed to the American mission his "strong recommendation" that Washington oppose the selection of a Latin American or Arab as Lie's successor; any difficulties he had experienced with Lie would be child's play compared to those to be expected if the next secretary-general were from Latin America or the Middle East: the "spoils system" would hold sway, and the organization's financial structure would collapse if the governmental notions of either of these two areas gained ascendency. Any doubts about this would be dispelled by a look at the United Nations Educational, Scientific and Cultural Organization. Price thought Lie's resignation gave the Western powers the upper hand in the matter. He believed Moscow "would be willing to agree to almost anyone to avoid the continuation of Mr. Lie on an acting basis."

This was the developing American consensus at the United Nations, which Jebb shared. Accordingly, a report from the American embassy in New Delhi on the possible candidature of Sir Girja Bajpai found Washington unreceptive; it instructed the embassy not to discuss the question with the Indians.[111]

The Foreign Office considered that Moscow's objections would rule out a national of any North Atlantic Pact member; Nationalist Chinese and American objections would preclude an Indian, whereas Russian-bloc candidates would obviously be unacceptable to London. This left only Arab, Asian, and Latin American possibilities; but none of those raised by the press, however, was thought to be an especially attractive candidate. Sweden's Myrdal had also been mentioned[112] and, despite the stricture on Indians, Sir Ramaswami Mudaliar; also Boheman might be acceptable "though ideally one Scandinavian should not succeed another."[113] Perhaps Mudaliar's name was proffered on the notion that he would be the one Indian palatable to the Americans. Personally Jebb felt that things might be worse with anyone mentioned "than with the Devil we know except for Pearson or some good Scandinavian candidate."[114] Indeed, he warned Gross that the British would veto any candidates but Pearson or Boheman; he admitted that Entezam would be a very fine candidate but said London "could not support him"—no doubt because of the Anglo-Iranian oil dispute.[115]

In Washington, Lebanon's Malik, who the Central Intelligence Agency had learned was favored by Moscow and the pro-Soviet bloc[116] and considered by some Arabs as a possible candidate,[117] pressed his own candidacy with Hickerson. Hickerson fended him off by feigning ignorance of whether Lie could be persuaded to serve out his term and with the anodyne comment that Malik's candidacy and those of others would be given very earnest consideration.[118]

Malik's candidacy reflected the political realignment occurring worldwide, and consequently in the United Nations. As yet, there had been no marked increase in United Nations membership from states outside the European area, but the shadow of coming events caused the assistant under-secretary of the Foreign Office, Paul Mason, some concern. He saw possible difficulties in naming a suitable successor to Lie developing also in the assembly, if the "frequent unholy alliance between Arabs, Asians and Latin Americans" prevented any strong candidate selected by the council from obtaining the two-thirds majority needed in the assembly.[119] In the end this difficulty did not occur, but Mason's concern was prophetic.

To coordinate Anglo-American tactics, Gross approached Jebb. As expected, Gromyko had played his opening gambit by raising with the Western Big Three the candidacy of Polish Foreign Minister Stanislaw Skrzeszewski. Gross urged Jebb that London and Washington agree on candidate or candidates before any private council meeting was convened. Washington, Gross explained, would accept "any good and outstanding" Canadian,

European, or Latin American candidate or Romulo from the Philippines. It would join any consensus on Entezam also but would not support a candidate from the Middle East, or especially one from India. Moreover, Washington would not support any candidate opposed by London. It would be best, Gross noted, if none of the Big Three used the veto; although nothing could be done to prevent a Russian or Nationalist Chinese veto. The important point was a common Western line. Gross conceded that although the Big Three could agree on Pearson, it would serve no useful purpose to press his candidacy except as a "stalking horse" to hide the West's real candidate, who should only be unveiled when a deadlock developed. Jebb urged that Pearson's name be placed in nomination, with it being made clear that under no circumstances would any other name be agreed to, in the hope that the Russians would finally accept him out of their animus toward Lie. Gross did not think this would be a productive approach.[120]

To Eden, only Pearson or Dirk Stikker, the Dutch foreign minister, were really suitable candidates. Moreover, he was in no rush to resolve the question and held that, if the West gave the impression that it would be content to see Lie continue in office, the Russians might be forced to accept either Pearson or Stikker. Understandably, Jebb wanted to know London's short list of candidates and the tactics to be pursued. Personally, he thought and Eden agreed that Romulo "would make a bad Secretary-General," although the Americans might favor him and he might generate considerable assembly support. Entezam he viewed as well qualified; he had been a very good president of the 1950 assembly, and once secretary-general, he could probably be counted on "to stick to his real job of administration instead of trying to play politics as Lie had been inclined to do and Romulo would certainly do." While there was the political difficulty of accepting an Iranian at that point, Jebb inquired whether London would veto Entezam if a council majority, including the Big Four, favored him. Aside from American objections, Jebb was also unsure whether London really wanted an Indian in a post where he could cause Great Britain considerable trouble on colonial questions. Were New Delhi to nominate someone, the pressure to support him would be strong; perhaps it could be agreed that, if London did not support an Indian, Washington would not support Romulo.

If there were no agreed candidate, Lie would probably continue for another year, which solution, Jebb thought, should be accepted only in extremis, since Lie had never been "a good Secretary-General and his position and ability have both been greatly weakened by recent events." The secretariat had lost faith in him, and Jebb did not know what its reaction would be if he continued in office. The inability to come to an agreement on Lie's successor would be a body blow to the United Nations' prestige, so soon after a number of reverses, including Feller's suicide. Jebb thought the best approach would be to agree with the Americans and the French on about three names to be placed before the council early on. They should be supported firmly until the Russians vetoed them, at which point the West might fall back on some lesser candidate, if one could be found acceptable to both sides. [121]

Eden agreed and was willing to stand fast on Pearson, Stikker, and Boheman, especially the first two, and dismissed all the others mentioned so far. Since Moscow would vigorously press Skrzeszewski, that was all the more reason for London to tender its best candidate. Eden believed that by doing so it would "succeed in wearing the Russians down." Since the Russians might not veto Boheman, keeping his name in reserve might amount, in effect, to sacrificing Pearson and Stikker in his favor. Eden therefore preferred to announce immediately and publicly that the three of them were London's candidates and avoid an early council meeting with the risk of an immediate Russian veto so that it would "sink in on the Russians" that there was no chance that London could be "induced to wobble off on to some of the other names . . . being canvassed." Rather than accepting anyone else, Eden preferred to keep Lie in the office, possibly for another year, although he did not consider this a satisfactory arrangement. However, if the Russians learned that failure to accept one of London's candidates would lead to Lie's continuance "it would soften them up in favour of one of London's [three] candidates." [122]

The problem, however, was now complicated by the change of administration in Washington. When Hickerson had proposed settling the question by December 23 or postponing it until the next assembly meeting, Senator Henry Cabot Lodge, Jr., of Massachusetts, nominated to represent the Eisenhower administration at the United Nations, had demurred. [123] If Washington backed Pearson at this juncture, Gross lamely explained to Jebb, it would be in trouble with Romulo and the Latin American and Middle East candidates; if it agreed to someone proposed by the Western Big Three as a kind of stalking horse, it would be in even greater trouble. Instead, he proposed a private meeting of the council; they should not press any candidate then but should make it clear that no Russian candidate would be accepted and that further consideration of the question should be delayed until the assembly convened.

Obviously unaware of Washington's new tack, the French representative, Henri Hoppenot, was canvassing vigorously on Entezam's behalf, although warned by Jebb that this was "ill-advised" as he could give "no assurance" that in the last resort Entezam might not be vetoed by London. [124] The British consensus in New York to postpone matters [125] dovetailed with Eden's opposition to an early council meeting. If the Russians forced a meeting, Jebb was to maintain that Moscow's candidate was unacceptable and that London would offer its own candidate later; if Washington argued that, because of the change in administration, it could not then propose candidates, this need not debar London from doing so. [126] The

Foreign Office rejected the notion of circumventing a Russian veto in the council by taking the question to the assembly, maintaining that the appointment of a new secretary-general was a substantive not a procedural matter. Although the assembly could appoint as secretary-general only someone recommended by the council, it could reject the person tendered and ask the council to reconsider its recommendation. Circumventing the council, on the other hand, would undermine the veto, lead to a Russian withdrawal from the organization, militate against London's current tactics, and be contrary to the government's policy of supporting the charter. [127] Only if an impasse developed in the council did the Foreign Office envisage the adoption of a procedure whereby the assembly would select someone to run the organization provisionally. [128] The State Department's position was not too dissimilar. [129]

When the West's representatives met, France's Hoppenot observed that Lie insisted "he was serious regarding his resignation" but would continue "until a 'suitable' successor was found"; yet when Hoppenot had mentioned possible successors, Lie found them all unsuitable. Jebb and Hoppenot argued to postpone discussion; and if the Russians forced a council meeting, proposing Skrzeszewski and pressing for a vote, he urged they vote against him. Jebb and Hoppenot preferred Pearson as first choice but thought Stikker, Boheman, and Spaak were also possible. When Gross raised Romulo's name, Jebb and Hoppenot were unenthusiastic. [130]

Reviewing the whole situation Pearson was uncertain that Lie would actually depart; if there were no agreement on a successor, he might be persuaded to continue for another, longer tour of duty. Cynics even suggested that this was what Lie had had in mind when he resigned, with the inability to agree on a successor making it "possible for him to lay down his own conditions for a renewed contract." Pearson admitted this possibility, but he thought Lie's resignation announcement was sincere. The two were "not necessarily incompatible." The Russians, he suggested to Prime Minister St. Laurent, were so keen to replace Lie that they might possibly accept almost anyone nominated, even Pearson himself, if pressed hard by London and Washington and if he were the only alternative to Lie's reappointment. In this event, Pearson did not see how he could refuse to accept the post. [131]

Despite Washington's aversion to any Indian candidate, the new year found the Foreign Office discussing the possible candidacy, raised by Jebb, of India's ambassador in Moscow, Krishna P. S. Menon. Doubt that he was friendly, and a consensus that he was a weak individual, led to his rejection; Eden opposed any compromise candidate like Menon, Jebb was informed, and firmly held to his list of Pearson, Stikker, and Boheman. [132]

By mid-January 1953, the Canadians began to accumulate circumstantial evidence that the Russians might not be averse to Pearson after all, such as comments by a Russian member of the secretariat and remarks made to the Israelis by an adviser to the Russian delegation. Jebb was unaware of the Israeli source, Gideon Rafael, who "understood Pearson might be satisfactory" to the Russians. However, he admitted to the Americans that "he had not been informed directly by any Soviet delegate, . . . [but] that there seemed to be good reason to think the Soviet government would not object too strenuously" to Pearson. For Pearson to be accepted, Rafael noted to the Canadians, he should not be offered as the American candidate. Likewise, Cordier personally thought that Moscow would accept Pearson; and although Cordier tended to be "rather optimistic," Jebb noted "his opinions are usually fairly sound."

In view of the Russian caveat, Jebb proposed that Pearson be nominated by a nonpermanent member of the council. This question and the tactics to be followed would have to be discussed with the French and the Americans as soon as the Eisenhower administration had taken over. If offered the job, Jebb speculated, there was no doubt that Pearson would accept. [133] From Washington, British Ambassador Sir Roger Makins reinforced all this. In a conversation with Georgiy Zarubin, his Russian counterpart, the question of the new secretary-general had been raised, and Zarubin "rather went out of his way to comment favourably on Mike Pearson," which Makins interpreted as a possible hint that Moscow would accept him. [134]

Concurrently, information reached Pearson that Lie's resignation had been less than sincere. Despite Lie's assurances that he would relinquish the post if he could leave it to a competent person—and he had been alluding to Pearson—Lie had presumably decided now that Moscow might not after all veto Pearson's candidacy. He was therefore telling the Americans and John Foster Dulles, the new Secretary of State, in particular, that Pearson would be a dangerous successor because he was considerably to the Left and unsound on Far Eastern questions. Pearson was unwilling to believe that Lie could be so duplicitous and wanted to check the information, which had come from a well-placed Canadian source. [135] Jebb had similarly ascertained in early January, from a fellow countryman and senior official in Lie's office, that he thought that Lie was determined to continue as secretary-general and that, in line with this, he was going to exceed Senator Pat McCarran in persecuting alleged Communists within the secretariat. By so doing, he hoped to make himself so persona grata to the Eisenhower administration that it would strive to retain him as secretary-general. [136]

Pearson attempted to confirm the story in London and Washington that Lie wanted to stay on. [137] Indeed, it appeared that his own acceptance by the Russians hinged on their need "to do so in order to prevent Lie from continuing." [138] In conversation with the Canadian High Commissioner Norman Robertson, Assistant Under-Secretary Paul Mason frankly spelled out London's pro-Pearson stance. Mason indicated, however, that rather than accept a compromise candidate, it might be more productive to advocate Lie's "temporary continuation in office," not as an ideal solution "but [because] a judicious use of the threat . . . might render the Russians more amenable."[139]

In Washington, Ambassador Wrong reported to Pearson that his probe drew the comment from Hickerson that there was "no intention to let the matter end in an indefinite continuance of Lie in office"; Washington was "fed up" with him. Like Pearson, Hickerson suspected Lie's "motives in presenting his resignation, but if the resignation was bluff," he thought the bluff should be called.[140] Even before this, the first move in meshing Anglo-American policy on the question had occurred in a conversation between Jebb and his new American counterpart, Henry Cabot Lodge. The prevailing rumors that Moscow might find Pearson acceptable surprised Lodge, who queried Russia's partiality to Pearson. Based on his own experience, Jebb responded, he had the impression that the Russians would find almost anyone preferable to Lie, "for whom they had conceived a violent dislike." Why Pearson over Stikker, Lodge questioned, since both were important figures in Western defense and had made clear publicly they would not tolerate added Russian aggression. Jebb offered no insight into Russian motives but thought that, based on Pearson's record, Moscow perhaps believed he might be more sensitive than other Western candidates to the desire, in certain circumstances, of compromising Far Eastern issues to arrange a Korean armistice.[141]

Pearson was soon informed of the Makins-Zarubin and Jebb-Lodge conversations. A member of the British delegation reported that Lodge, on hearing of Zarubin's comments to Makins in Washington, personally believed that there should be no obstacle to a Big Five consensus on Pearson's selection, although he was careful not to commit the State Department, which at that point was still undecided.[142] Whether conveying this information to Pearson was an attempt to spur him along to accept the post if offered or whether it was the optimistic exuberance of the British informant is unclear. Lie was not optimistic. He would be greatly surprised, he declared to Lodge, if Pearson was acceptable to the Russians and thought the "British might be floating this story," but if well founded then Pearson should be selected.[143]

Since the first rumors surfaced about Moscow's pro-Pearson stance, additional circumstantial evidence had been uncovered, tending to show that the Russians would not oppose Pearson's appointment if pressed by the Western Big Three. The source was again the perceptive Israeli Rafael; Russia's Malik in conversation with him had indicated that, although Moscow recognized Pearson's commitment to the West, it also knew exactly where he stood and was satisfied that he would follow a "reasonably independent line" toward Washington. Because of Soviet Russia's desire to replace Lie, it realized, Malik admitted, that a price would have to be paid, namely, the selection of someone committed to the Western camp. Rafael heard virtually the same comments from another party, who he felt he could not identify; he was not a member of a Soviet bloc delegation but had acquired his information from an official of the Russian delegation. [144] The realization that he just might be offered the gilded throne disturbed Pearson, since he personally thought the call to serve would never come. [145]

Pearson might have been less uneasy if he had known that Lodge felt himself under pressure and wanted to avoid suggesting anyone for the post. Romulo was watching him "'like a lynx,'" he told Jebb, and explained that, although Washington had a high regard for Pearson with whom he personally could cooperate, he was not in a position to canvass on Pearson's behalf. Jebb construed this to mean that Lodge would not veto Pearson, but for the moment could do nothing more. [146]

When Jebb attempted to arrange a meeting of the Big Three, Lodge refused to attend, seemingly "terrified" at assuming any stance until Dulles could be consulted. Hoppenot agreed with Jebb to vote for Pearson and was pleased by the indications that Moscow would accept him. The two also agreed that Pearson's name should be proposed by the Pakistani representative, Ahmed Bokhari, who likewise favored Pearson but understandably had to consult his government. When Bokhari raised Entezam's possible candidacy, Jebb expressed doubt whether Entezam or anyone except Pearson could receive the necessary seven votes, irrespective of whether a veto might be cast. [147] As to Lodge, he pointed out to Dulles that the British were "pursuing" Pearson's selection in the belief that he "would be acceptable" to Moscow. If his name were offered there would be an attempt to have him "recommended" avoiding a vote on the ground that there was no objection. Accordingly, Lodge thought it "would be desirable to vote for and not oppose" Pearson's selection if the issue was raised in this manner. Dulles agreed, noting if the Russians vetoed Pearson, Lodge then might indicate to Jebb his hope that London would support a candidate of Washington's choice. [148] Lodge observed to the Canadian representative, David Johnson, that Pearson would be fine for the post and Lodge would support him if proposed but believed his appointment most unlikely. [149] Obviously Lodge and Dulles would accept Pearson, but they were less than keen in leading the phalanx. In fact, it is probable that their belief that Pearson's chances were minimal helps explain Lodge's attempt to ascertain the availability of Boheman; but the responses from both Stockholm and Boheman himself were not encouraging. [150] In an attempt to smoke out Dulles, Ambassador Makins was instructed to approach him on the question and did so on the evening of February 19. He explained London's awareness of Washington's difficulty in giving public support to Pearson. London hoped, however, that Washington could lend its support behind the scenes. Dulles frankly responded that he personally was very partial to Pearson—the United States had supported Pearson in 1946 and thought it would again do so—but he would not make a firm commitment then. [151]

Concurrently, a story in the *New York Times* that Moscow was unlikely to reject Pearson, quoting a very embarrassed Zarubin as its source, further complicated matters. Pearson believed that the story undermined his chances. Some suspected it had been planted for this very purpose, perhaps by Lie; others saw the Americans as the culprits, but this appeared out of step with Dulles's comments to Makins. On the other hand, Jebb learned that Lie had recently been ingratiating himself with Lodge. Ominously, when Bokhari had approached the Russian representative, Valerian Zorin, he proved "uncommunicative." Zorin, Bokhari informed Lodge, "refused to give a yes or no answer" and was only willing to say that he "would 'consider' Pearson's name." When Bokhari attempted to see him again, he was fended off by Zorin, who claimed that he was ill, but the malaise had developed only after publication of the *New York Times* story.

He was uneasy, Jebb observed to Eden. If Pearson were blackballed by the Russians, he raised the possibility of casting a veto, should it be uncertain that there were sufficient abstentions to deny the selection of Entezam or Romulo.[152] Lie, however, insisted that he would retire and that Pearson should succeed him;[153] but by this point, anything Lie said had to be discounted. Lodge appears to have been given a completely free hand in the negotiations in New York; and Lodge, Jebb had discovered, did not necessarily share Dulles's favorable view of Pearson. Evidence had continued to accumulate that Lie was doing everything possible to ensure his continuance as secretary-general, including buttering up Lodge. By kowtowing to the Eisenhower administration, it was reported on the "best authority," Lie had destroyed whatever "small respect" the secretariat had had for him, an attitude now unfortunately extended into many United Nations missions. It even appeared possible he might withdraw his resignation.

All this, Jebb assumed, strengthened the case for selecting Pearson. Despite his previous suggestions, he now thought the best procedure would be to convene the council as soon as Bokhari contacted Vyshinsky. Further delay might lead to the success of Lie's intrigues, so that the seven votes needed to select Pearson might prove unobtainable. Should Moscow veto Pearson, which was uncertain, Jebb thought, additional nominations might be offered; but unless the necessary abstentions could be arranged, he again asked for authority to veto anyone except Pearson, even including Stikker and Boheman, although selection of either was remote. Eliminating all other candidates might bring the discussion back to Pearson, with some hope that Moscow would finally accept him. Jebb therefore proposed to resist any immediate vote except on Skrzeszewski, Pearson, Stikker, or Boheman, which would give time for consultation about the veto.[154]

Lie's recent activities placed him "in a very bad light," the Foreign Office's Michael Williams noted, and he was "rapidly losing his claim to be regarded as an adequate Secretary-General." Williams doubted London would now "wish to see Mr. Lie withdraw his resignation," even if no successor could be selected. Paul Mason agreed.[155] Jebb was to propose an early council meeting, but London had never used the veto and Eden thought it would be wrong to do so at that point. Accordingly, Jebb was to do everything possible to ensure that no candidate received the requisite seven votes. However, if this did occur, Jebb was to refer to London.[156]

In an attempt to form a consensus around Pearson, Jebb lobbied with members of the council, except for the Americans, Nationalist Chinese, Russians, and the absent Lebanese. After this exchange, Jebb claimed that only Pearson could garner the requisite seven votes and regretted Lodge's foot dragging. Gross, now Lodge's deputy, disagreed and emphasized that Pearson did not want his candidacy bandied about, his name offered for the post only to be rejected. Jebb wavered but held that, if Pearson and others were initially rejected, Pearson's candidacy could possibly again be pressed successfully. Gross thought this poor tactics.[157]

Canadian fears about Moscow's possible objections to Pearson were confirmed when Vyshinsky, in a meeting of the General Assembly's First Committee (Political and Security), attacked Pearson for pro-Western partiality. Lie was amused and somewhat pleased that Pearson had now been subjected to the same kind of abuse he had endured. Pearson interpreted Vyshinsky's words as merely an attempt to make it clear that Moscow would not automatically accept his candidacy, but would undoubtedly drive a hard bargain. In this case, he would be the winner if not nominated.[158]

The first substantive evidence on the Russian position was furnished by Bokhari. Vyshinsky's candidate, he reported, was still Skrzeszewski, and Bokhari thought he would veto all Western candidates but might settle for Pearson on the second round, if there was no other way of replacing Lie. Bokhari also thought that Jebb's clumsy tactics had not furthered Pearson's cause, which moved Pearson to retort that he had "no cause."[159]

Jebb's suspicions were heightened when an agitated Lodge approached him, proposing that the assembly debate secretariat personnel policy before the council convened to select a secretary-general. Lodge argued that he had induced Lie to take measures on Americans in the secretariat that would keep Congress at bay; he was "terrified" lest Lie's successor might interfere with this arrangement. If so, Lodge noted, he would be forced to educate a new secretary-general. He feared Lie's emotional reaction should the council select his successor before the assembly debate on secretariat personnel policy. Moreover, if the council selected a new secretary-general before the assembly debate, there would possibly be confusion, since the incumbent's policy would be unknown.

Jebb refused to budge: Eden wanted to press ahead, he explained, before the debate on personnel policy. If Pearson were selected, the "edge" would be off the debate and "acrimonious" speeches could likely be avoided. Jebb suspected the Americans might be intent on continuing Lie in office, which seemed borne out by Lodge's argument on reeducating a new secretary-general. Everything possible should be done to get Pearson appointed, Jebb recommended, since the United Nations would otherwise suffer. Accordingly he urged that the plan be held to and surmised that Hoppenot would insist on this arrangement,[160] which was accurate.[161]

Selecting Hammarskjöld

In the midst of these negotiations, Stalin died. The great tyrant's death and the struggle within the Kremlin over a successor added to an already complicated situation. In the assembly's First Committee Vyshinsky eulogized his late chief, whose "immortal name would live forever in the hearts of the peoples of the USSR and all of mankind." But when Lie offered his hand in condolence, Vyshinsky refused to shake it, which blatant insult, Lie claimed, moved him unofficially to withdraw his resignation. Pearson, informed of Lie's about-face by Cordier, thought it an odd way to react and suspected that Lie would soon change his mind.[162] This was wishful thinking on Pearson's part. Vyshinsky's snub was merely a convenient pretext for Lie to enter the fray once more, probably in the belief that Stalin's death portended new political alignments that might mean a call that he continue to serve the world organization: the known might be far preferable to the unknown. On whom else, he must have theorized, could there be a consensus?

The first collective attempt to tackle the question, initiated by Jebb and Hoppenot with Zorin concurring but without indicating Moscow's line,[163] was in a private council meeting on March 11. The predictable nominations were advanced: Romulo, Skrzeszewski, and Pearson.[164] The merits of those nominated were virtually undiscussed. Nationalist China's Tsiang supported Romulo and opposed Skrzeszewski, but did not commit himself on Pearson. Russia's Zorin was silent about both Pearson and Romulo. Jebb's attempt to force a vote failed, some members claiming they required instructions.[165] With the Americans openly supporting Romulo, Jebb's colleagues began to waver in their support for Pearson, especially the Latin Americans. Even the five abstentions necessary to avoid casting a veto against Romulo became doubtful. Hoppenot was willing to veto Romulo, if Jebb joined him, and both agreed to press for a secret ballot. If Romulo failed to acquire the necessary votes, Jebb was certain Pearson would. Even if the Russians vetoed him initially they might abstain the second time around—Jebb's familiar refrain.[166]

Pearson was the right choice, Minister of State Selwyn Lloyd nonetheless emphasized, and Jebb was to do everything possible to impress on the others that London did not acquiesce in Washington's support of Romulo. Were Skrzeszewski rejected, Moscow would veto Romulo but might settle for Pearson. Backing Romulo would lead to a stalemate, Selwyn Lloyd thought, and thus presumably continue Lie in office. The important point was to urge Lodge strongly not to pressure other representatives to support Romulo. The political motives moving the Americans to nominate Romulo were appreciated, but once this was done they should be content.

Tactics in New York were left to Jebb, especially encouraging abstentions on Romulo and avoiding a veto that was not thought proper in a question of this nature, even if he was joined by the French.[167] A probe by Makins at the State Department disclosed it was unwilling to dictate to Lodge "either policy or tactics," since the question had so far been largely in his hands. Makins's encouraging news, however, was that the Americans had no intention of pressing for Romulo's selection; although Lodge had nominated him, it would be up to Romulo to make his own way.[168]

Jebb and Hoppenot called on Lodge to smoke him out on how much Washington was committed to Romulo. Washington supported Romulo, Lodge indicated, but was not opposed to Pearson. Because of Romulo's stand on colonial questions, Hoppenot raised the possibility of a French veto. The two men emphasized in the strongest terms that Pearson would raise no problem on secretariat personnel policy but could be relied upon to carry on from Lie's initial steps. Indeed, Pearson might assume the post in June, giving Lie additional time to move the personnel question along.

As to Skrzeszewski, Lodge disclosed he had considered a veto, since Washington "did not want to run the slightest risk that a Communist would be elected as Secretary-General." Such a development would signal the death knell of the organization so far as Washington was concerned. The possible nomination of other candidates, for example, Madame Viyaya Lakshmi Pandit, Nehru's sister, left all three uneasy.[169]

Lodge later explained to Pearson that American support of Romulo was tactical and it was not expected that the general could garner the necessary votes. Once he was rejected, Washington would support Pearson. Pearson noted that the American stance had surprised everyone at the United Nations, provoking various interpretations. With Romulo lobbying for votes and Jebb pressing everyone to support him, Pearson—operating on the notion of "out of sight, out of mind"—hurried back to Ottawa to avoid being selected for a post he did not want.[170]

Prior to the next private meeting of the council on March 13, Jebb and Hoppenot caucused to coordinate tactics.[171] In the event, Romulo and Skrzeszewski failed to secure the required seven affirmative votes and Pearson was vetoed by the Russians.[172] Jebb, supported by a majority of the council, had insisted on an immediate vote despite the Russian and Nationalist Chinese desire to postpone it.[173] In off-record remarks Zorin appeared apprehensive that, if Pearson was vetoed, the council could not reconsider him at a later session. Jebb denied this and asked Zorin to inform

Moscow that, if no other candidate proved acceptable, reconsideration in a later meeting could be given to those already rejected. He also warned that Zorin's obstruction of the proceedings might lead to Lie's withdrawing his resignation, an alarming thought to both of them. Jebb optimistically held to the belief that, once it was apparent that only Pearson had the slightest chance of acceptance, the Russians might well abstain on his candidacy. Moreover, he thought Lodge's partiality toward Pearson pretty well scotched numerous journalistic stories about an Anglo-American rift over the matter.[174]

The Foreign Office was undismayed over Pearson's rejection: Jebb was told to "stand firm," refuse to accept any "weak compromise candidate," and thus wear Soviet Russia down to agree to a Western candidate[175]—the unmentioned, creditable threat being that Lie would otherwise be asked to continue. In New York, things were perceived differently, the general opinion appearing to be that Jebb's heavy-handed tactics had virtually forced Moscow to veto Pearson whereas if the vote had been postponed until the following week, Zorin might have abstained. When Pearson returned to the United Nations on March 16, Jebb in fact expressed mea culpa: he had thought that, by forcing the vote, Romulo would be removed from consideration, thus making clear Pearson's strong position. Jebb continued to hold, however, that the latest Russian veto was not necessarily Moscow's final say. Others did not agree that, once having vetoed Pearson, Moscow would have second thoughts, even if initially it might have agreed to abstain. Lie also held this position, congratulating Pearson on sharing with him Moscow's rejection and even indicating his satisfaction that Jebb's tactics left virtually no chance of Pearson's election. Pearson's impression was that Lie appeared to "relish" the probability of now being beseeched to continue.[176] As to Romulo, his hopes died slowly: if the Americans pressed his candidacy with the Russians, he wrote to Dulles, and told Moscow to choose either him or Lie, he thought his selection would be assured.[177]

Pearson emphasized that the question had to be brought quickly to a head or the world organization would look ridiculous. He suggested that the Big Five caucus before another private meeting of the council, when all possible candidates should be considered and decided on, one way or another. If no candidate commanded the required votes, then Moscow should be told that Lie would continue in office, which might break the logjam. Jebb was partial to the suggestion, since he thought that it might result in Moscow's reconsideration of Pearson; Lodge was not convinced; contending Moscow would have no worries if Lie stayed on, as it would then have his continued presence as a grievance.[178]

Accordingly a meeting of the Big Five representatives was tentatively arranged. Jebb worried that Moscow might bring up the name of Madame Pandit,[179] as press reports suggested she was gaining favor over Pearson.[180]

He was instructed to be discreet in commenting on the lady, who was not regarded "as an adequate candidate." London also considered it too early to raise any alternatives to Pearson, Stikker, or Boheman. In fact, the Indians were being cautious in pressing Pandit's candidacy and really hoped for Pearson's appointment; only if the Anglo-Americans agreed, would they put forward Pandit's name.[181] London explained its intention to persevere with Pearson to the Indian High Commissioner, since the Foreign Office thought Pearson would inevitably garner the necessary votes.[182]

On March 17, Jebb and Hoppenot called on Lodge to prepare for the next meeting of the Big Five. With Hoppenot in the chair, the two agreed that Jebb should query Zorin about the private meeting of March 13; they would then attempt to ascertain Moscow's intentions. They thought Zorin might table a new list of candidates, including perhaps Colombia's Eduardo Zuleta, Thailand's Prince Wan Waithayakon, and others. If the names were tabled there should be no decision on them. In that case, the next private session of the council should be convened without additional consultation.[183]

The Five Power meeting was duly held the next day, March 18, with Zorin making it clear that neither Pearson nor Romulo was acceptable and offering instead either Madame Pandit or Sir Benegal Rau. Jebb doubted that anyone other than Pearson could garner the necessary votes and, with Lodge, indicated that if Moscow nonetheless continued to reject Pearson the result would be Lie's continuance. Zorin declared such a move would be "illegal and unacceptable," which made agreement among the Big Five all the more urgent.[184]

Moscow's options were limited indeed, since none of the names raised, as Pearson afterwards observed, could make it through the council.[185] Press reports that Moscow would accept either Pandit—who was annoyed that her name had been raised without prior consultation[186]—or Rau caused the Nationalist Chinese to warn the Americans that they would veto either one and hoped that Washington would prevent the situation from formally rising. Dulles likewise took a dim view of these Indian candidates, who lacked executive and administrative experience and whose government favored neutralism; the immediate problem of communist aggression in Korea could not be solved by Indian advocacy of passive resistance. A veto was undesirable but Lodge could cast one if necessary to prevent either being selected. As most council members apparently would abstain, Lodge could probably do likewise.[187]

Ultimately Zorin formally proposed Madame Pandit at the private council meeting of March 19. His attempts to refer her candidacy to a Big Five caucus, to adjourn that meeting, or to have an open vote on her were all defeated. With eight abstentions, she could not garner the seven votes needed, let alone those of the permanent members.[188]

It was obvious that Zorin was stalling for time. Pearson speculated that he was waiting for instructions that Vyshinsky would be bringing from Moscow. On the other hand, by dragging out the discussions the Russian mission might exploit the situation and divide its opponents. It might also gain some propaganda value for Moscow by proposing Pandit and Rau and indicating that others from the Third World would be acceptable, while simultaneously forcing London and Washington to reject them. Jebb's insistence on Pearson alone assisted the Russian ploy and probably even irritated his friends. In fact, one American friend hinted that Pearson was being badly served by Jebb's management of his campaign, which was actually preventing his selection. Since Pearson was uninterested in being selected, however, he refused to intervene with Jebb.[189]

Apparently at about this point Lie let it be known if no consensus candidate could be found, he would continue to soldier on.[190] Concurrently, Jebb finally began to realize that perhaps Moscow's insistence that there could be no reconsideration of earlier votes, and that a candidate acceptable to all sides had to be found might mean that Pearson was precluded even if it meant the continuance of Lie indefinitely. Consequently he wondered whether Stikker's name should not be pressed forward, and since Boheman had declared he was not a candidate for the office, he also raised the names of Rolf Sohlman, Swedish ambassador in Moscow, and, for the first time, of Dag Hammarskjöld, Swedish minister of state in the Foreign Ministry. Although Sohlman had his faults, Jebb thought, he would be better than Lie; whereas Hammarskjöld would be "excellent" in every respect and would probably find it difficult to refuse the office if offered to him. Jebb urged that the time was fast approaching when the possibility should be explored of an agreement on candidates not heretofore raised. He warned that Lie was "capable of withdrawing his resignation at any moment," and once this was done, a more difficult situation would develop.[191]

Eden accepted the Foreign Office opinion that Moscow might really have decided to reject Pearson and still doubted whether alternative names should be raised. But Jebb was on the spot and could see the situation better, so he was given the option to raise Stikker's name if convinced that Zorin would not budge. However, Eden rejected Sohlman as likely to be "weak and subservient to Russian influence" and was not for the moment prepared to sponsor Hammarskjöld.[192]

At this juncture, and before receiving Eden's new instructions, Jebb approached Hoppenot on a personal basis and voiced his doubts about Zorin accepting Pearson, concurrently raising Hammarskjöld's name. He thought that a Scandinavian, "in principle, [had] a better chance than most" of unanimous acceptance by the Big Five. Since he had no instructions to propose Hammarskjöld himself, he suggested this to Hoppenot, who readily accepted.[193]

At a second meeting of the Big Five on March 23, therefore, the inability to agree on either Pearson or Pandit moved Hoppenot to raise four possible candidates, including Hammarskjöld. He asked whether Zorin would veto any of them, but Zorin refused to give a direct answer. When pressed, he held that none offered a "prospect of compromise or agreement." In view of the failure of acceptance of Skrzeszewski and Pandit, would Moscow prefer Lie to continue? he was asked. He was in office illegally, Zorin insisted, and there had to be agreement on a replacement. He refused to be budged, and it was decided to inform the council president that they had failed to agree.[194]

Jebb was disconcerted when Hoppenot proffered his four candidates, since he thought he had suggested it unlikely that any of them would receive the necessary votes, save by implication Hammarskjöld. He was disconcerted even more when Hoppenot later told him that if Entezam now became the proposed candidate he would vote for him. Jebb retorted that Eden would regard such French action seriously and urged that the question be ironed out between London and Paris. Jebb surmised that the Russians preferred to nourish a great grievance about Lie's legality "rather than agree to the appointment of anyone less harmless from their own point of view than Mrs. Pandit."[195]

At another council private meeting on the following day, March 24, there was no substantive discussion of the question; indeed, Zorin said nothing at all, and it was simply agreed that the council would meet again on Friday, March 27. In the interim the Big Five should reconvene if any developments offered hope for agreement. The council accepted that fruitless consideration of the issue could not continue indefinitely, and unless there was a breakthrough soon, the council would have to inform the assembly that it had failed to select a successor to Lie.[196]

Considering the nadir that Anglo-Iranian relations had reached following Teheran's nationalization of British oil interests, the possibility of French support for Entezam went unappreciated at the Foreign Office, which made representations at the Quai d'Orsay.[197] The Russians proceeded to hint that Hammarskjöld—or any Swede for that matter—was unacceptable. Sweden, Gromyko opined, was an "honorary member" of the North Atlantic Pact.[198]

Despite these comments, Jebb thought the Russian position "a little less rigid than previously," at another Big Five meeting on March 27. Asked by Jebb whether he would veto any candidate other than Skrzeszewski or Pandit, Zorin would only say he could only consider candidates who were raised officially. The same roster of names was again discussed, and again there was no consensus. Zorin nonetheless suggested further Five Power consultation. However, Zorin flashed a signal at the private council meeting that afternoon, observing, somewhat surprisingly, that the "permanent members were embarking on a path of joint agreement."[199]

Jebb was almost certain, he informed the Foreign Office, that Zorin would veto Stikker. The question to be faced was Entezam: if Zorin did not veto him and his name was put forward, Jebb thought he would garner four certain votes and likely the Russian one. Four members would likely abstain. The doubtful votes were Chile and Colombia, who might well also support Entezam, thus giving the needed majority, unless both were subjected to strong American pressure. To avert Entezam's selection the French had to be urged to abstain. In addition, the Americans might also be urged to pressure the Chileans and Colombians. Padilla Nervo's selection was remote as there would be so many abstentions. In view of Gromyko's comments Jebb thought Hammarskjöld would be vetoed. Although he thought it very unlikely, there was also the remote possibility of reverting to London's original plan of reconsidering those candidates already rejected, which might influence Moscow to abstain on Pearson. Most probably the perpetuation of Lie had to be contemplated. Jebb thought Lie had "retired to bed" on learning that the Big Five discussions had led to "'certain progress.'"[200]

The Foreign Office sprang into action. Pearson and Stikker were still Eden's choices, Jebb was informed, and he refused alternative candidates despite the risk of Lie's continuance. Indian candidates were unacceptable to the Americans and Nationalist Chinese. Eden was as opposed to Entezam as ever, and Jebb was told to continue his endeavors to ensure that he was not selected. Failing modification of the Russian stance, Eden thought the best course would be to continue Lie until the end of 1953, when his appointment would lapse. Eden was aware that Lie had lost his standing with the secretariat and member states but would still be better than anything now offered. Similar thoughts were conveyed to Paris with added emphasis that London had very strong views on Entezam's selection and hoped that Paris would support London's position. Pressed this hard, the Quai d'Orsay succumbed, and the "appropriate instructions" were issued to Hoppenot, for which Eden was thankful.[201]

Since Skrzeszewski and Pandit were unacceptable to the West, and Pearson and Stikker unacceptable to the East, Indian candidates were unacceptable to the Americans and Nationalist Chinese, and with Padilla Nervo an unlikely starter, another stalemate was in the offing. Despite Gromyko's comments, the one conceivable candidate now was Hammarskjöld. His rejection by Moscow would lead to a deadlock and Lie's continuance, which it was obvious no one wanted.

Suffice it to note that, when the Big Five representatives convened on the morning of March 30, to everyone's surprise Zorin announced that Moscow was now prepared to accept the Swede. Jebb credited the Russian reversal to his reiterated statements that Entezam would not mobilize the necessary votes. Hoppenot said he would accept Hammarskjöld. Jebb, with the others, wanted to obtain instructions. The fly in the ointment appeared to be a possible veto by the Nationalist Chinese. Jebb recommended that London accept Hammarskjöld. It was just possible that he might get the organization's machinery working once more. Lie had "forfeited the confidence" of many delegations and the secretariat would probably function far better under "some new and more respected chief." As Jebb subsequently wrote to Churchill, he had little doubt that Hammarskjöld's record as secretary-general would "be not only a significant improvement on that of Mr. Lie, but generally admirable by any standard."[202] He was to be proved right.

Based on the "sketchy information" available to him, Lodge likewise supported Hammarskjöld and informed Washington that the Swede might "be as good as we can get." Interestingly, he thought Zorin had appeared in a big rush to settle the question. The State Department's reaction was uniformly positive. In particular, the former ambassador in Sweden, H. Freeman Matthews, "spoke in high terms of Mr. Hammarskjöld's ability and pro-Western views"; he thought the United Nations would be lucky to get him, it could do far worse. Lodge was instructed to accept him.[203] In the past, the Foreign Office had perceived Hammarskjöld as the "most friendly and western-minded" of Sweden's ministers and a "man of outstanding ability and culture."[204] Eden accepted him as an "excellent candidate" and gave Jebb appropriate instructions.[205] Prodded by Eden, the State Department obtained Nationalist China's assurances that it would abstain.[206]

Why Moscow finally accepted a pro-Westerner like Hammarskjöld cannot be answered with certainty. His orientation and background were no mystery to the Russians. In fact, the previous year he had had a heated exchange with them when two Swedish aircraft had been shot down over the Baltic. The scenario of rejecting him and being saddled once again with Lie was a Damoclean sword wisely to be avoided.[207] Events in Russia no doubt played a role: the death of Stalin probably led his cynical political heirs to present a more moderate image of themselves in world affairs, thus winding down the tensions racking the international community and giving time to settle among themselves the vital succession issue. Then again Hammarskjöld's background as a long-time civil servant gave the hope that, unlike Lie, and more like the league's first holder of the office, Sir Eric Drummond, he would be a technocrat and administrator and prove benign politically, at least in public—a view that dovetailed with western perceptions and desires.[208]

When the Big Five representatives convened on March 31, all but Nationalist China's Tsiang, who was ordered to abstain, had received instructions to accept Hammarskjöld. By this point, the news was rapidly leaking, and Jebb, fearful that additional delay "would prove unfortunate," was able to convince everyone that a private meeting of the council and an immediate vote were desirable. Since Hoppenot had first raised Hammarskjöld's name, he was tapped to propose him for the post. Except for Tsiang's abstention the vote was unanimous, and Hammarskjöld's fate was sealed.[209] The remorseless Vyshinsky was no doubt relieved by Hammarskjöld's selection, because later that day he went out of his way to smile, shake Lodge's hand, and inquire about his health.[210] For Lie, the selection of Hammarskjöld was traumatic. His reaction was predictable: he took the Swede's selection with "ill grace." Lie paled when Lodge informed him, probably on his way to the last meeting of the Big Five, that it would be a quick session since a consensus had formed around Hammarskjöld.[211] He undoubtedly had hoped that the stalemated negotiations on a successor would lead to his reappointment, to new opportunities for bridge-building between East and West, and to a vindication of his political isolation from the East following his support of South Korea in June 1950. Lie understandably speculated and unsuccessfully probed how Hammarskjöld was chosen and his own possible reelection undercut.[212]

Lie's vilification of his successor, which can only be called sordid, now commenced. At his politest, he observed that Hammarskjöld would allow the office's political functions to "wither" and that, if Hammarskjöld were an American, he would belong to the Republican party's conservative wing.[213] He complained, incorrectly, that Hammarskjöld "had little political and no administrative experience; his knowledge of economics was largely theoretical, his tastes literary, and his record that of a dilettante."[214] Less charitably, he observed to Pearson, Hammarskjöld would be nothing more than a clerk.[215]

Lie hit his nadir when he circulated a rumor that Hammarskjöld was a homosexual, although there is not a shred of evidence to prove the allegation.[216] For example, he approached the Greek representative, Alexis Kyrou, and queried whether he was going to support the "fairy."[217] What reply the experienced Kyrou gave is unrecorded. That Hammarskjöld was an unusual, complex, and gifted individual is attested to by those who served with him in the United Nations and by others, as well as by his posthumously published *Markings*.[218] Unfortunately, the rumor lingered.[219] It was not one of Lie's finest hours.

The changing of the guard soon followed on April 7, when the assembly adopted by an overwhelming vote the council's recommendation that Hammarskjöld be appointed secretary-general.[220] Although Lie was diplomatically eulogized by many member states during this plenary session, Vyshinsky to the bitter end refrained from praising him, as did the French, the Arab states, and others.[221] Several days later Hammarskjöld arrived in New York. He was met at the airport by Lie who prophetically warned him that he was assuming the world's "most impossible job."[222]

At the assembly session of April 10, Hammarskjöld was sworn into office.[223] Vyshinsky finally succumbed and shook Lie's hand,[224] no doubt relieved, as were others, that Lie was finally leaving. But was he? He continued to use an office on the thirty-eighth floor of the headquarters building. Hammarskjöld, who longed for his departure, found the situation embarrassing, since he was aware that Lie was slandering him. As Jebb laconically observed to the Foreign Office, "the old boy has frankly been doing a great deal of damage during the last few days of his stay." Finally, in early May, Hammarskjöld gently eased him out.[225]

During these last days, Lie suggested to Lodge that he make a farewell visit to Washington to pay his respects to President Eisenhower and Secretary of State Dulles before departing for Norway.[226] Pearson was uneasy, as rumor had it that Lie hoped to address Congress or the Washington Press Club. Hickerson and Lodge were fully aware of the potential dangers should Lie be officially received as a guest and granted special honors. Neither was under any "illusions about Lie's deportment in New York recently"—his comments about Hammarskjöld had come home to roost. Hickerson, in particular, was careful to see that no arrangements were made other than the two requested interviews.[227] The interview with the president, in particular, was pro forma.[228]

Lie's departure for Oslo did not go as smoothly, however. His announced intention to syndicate his memoirs as secretary-general caused great unease among the Americans, who feared he might reveal facts that they thought still should be kept secret for reasons of state. His yearly retirement pension of $10,000 was specifically intended to obviate the necessity to earn money by such means.[229] Unlike the British, Hammarskjöld opposed raising the question of the memoirs officially and hoped to persuade Pearson to approach Lie on the matter.[230] Whether Lie was so approached is unclear, but his eventual book caused no earth tremors.

Equally unnerving at the time was Lie's threat to return the following year as a member of the Norwegian delegation to the assembly and, in any case, to go on the lecture circuit. If this proved to be the case, Jebb recommended, Lie's pension should be stopped immediately as it would be in contravention of the London Preparatory Commission's recommendations.[231] The Foreign Office agreed that Lie's attendance as a member of the Norwegian delegation was impolitic but doubted that Oslo would ever appoint him; however, it was unsure that public lectures were prohibited, "inappropriate and discourteous to Hammarskjöld as they would undoubtedly be." While the Foreign Office hoped that Lie would have the "good sense" to eschew any such lecturing well into the future, it authorized Jebb to mention to his Norwegian counterpart the deplorable impression any comments by Lie in the United States would have, especially on sensitive issues such as the secretariat.[232] Whatever was said obviously had an impact, for Lie, who it was reported was "itching" to reenter the political arena,[233] declared that he had no intention of returning to Norwegian politics for some time. This had been the king's advice and also his own wish, he claimed.[234]

The Canadian representative, David Johnson, assessing Lie for Ottawa, found him well stocked in both merits and deficiencies. "Perhaps," Johnson wrote, "what chiefly detracted from his status was his personal vanity and sensitivity." Considering his size Lie was not a placid person, which was not surprising in view of the burdens of his office. All in all, Johnson thought he bore them well. The Canadian mission had sent Lie and his wife flowers on their departure, Johnson observed, and they "carried our very genuine good wishes."[235] Lie sailed to Norway.

There was only desultory contact between Lie and Hammarskjöld until the spring of 1955.[236] Then, in May, Hammarskjöld invited Lie to a planned meeting at the San Francisco Opera House, sponsored by the assembly to commemorate the tenth anniversary of the signing of the United Nations Charter. Although plans for the meeting were not completed, they had reached a point where it was possible formally to invite Lie to participate. Hammarskjöld and the advisory committee for the occasion had agreed that it would be incomplete without Lie, who would make a statement at an appropriate moment in the meeting. Lie's expenses would be paid by the United Nations. It was a warm letter, and Lie was delighted. But then came a second missive, and it was obvious that there was a fly in the ointment. There was, Hammarskjöld informed Lie, a strong desire in the advisory committee to restrict participation at the meeting to persons with an official connection to the organization. Hammarskjöld had argued that the addresses at the meeting should include some persons not in the official delegation, but this had not been accepted. Nevertheless, he looked forward to seeing Lie in San Francisco. Naturally, Hammarskjöld's letter disappointed Lie, who correctly suspected the fingers of Moscow, and perhaps others in the denial; but what he feared most was perhaps to be insulted or neglected in San Francisco. Nevertheless, his desire to see old associates and friends was so great that at first he was willing to take the risk, while hoping that Hammarskjöld and the secretariat would see that he was not shunted aside. He desperately hoped that some occasion would arise during the meeting so he could air his views, and in a letter to Cordier, Lie remained curious about why Hammarskjöld's initial invitation had been altered.[237]

Cordier responded that objections had been raised by one delegation on the advisory committee, although he did not mention it was the Russian, despite Hammarskjöld's strong argument that Lie had rendered the world organization yeoman service and that, at a commemorative meeting, bygones should be bygones. This original objection was soon followed by others, some from the Arab states because of Lie's propartition stance on the Palestine question and his public support of the Zionist cause. Another group opposed to Lie's participation was moved by his allegations concerning his successor's homosexuality. Those who approached Hammarskjöld on this particular point felt that he had handled it in a dignified manner, sustained as he was by a "clear conscience." Despite these objections, everything would be done, Cordier assured him, to avoid any unpleasantness, and he begged Lie to attend.[238] But Lie adamantly refused,[239] much to Hammarskjöld's and Cordier's regrets.[240] Cordier and Wilder Foote subsequently cabled that they had missed him very much at the meeting.[241] Hammarskjöld's generosity was not reciprocated; from the beginning of his tenure, Lie displayed animus toward him.[242] Later, dissatisfied with American policies, Lie also complained to Adlai Stevenson about those of his successor.[243] It was all very sad.

In 1959, based on an assembly resolution, Lie was appointed by the king of Norway to mediate the delimitation of the boundary between Ethiopia and the Trust Territory of Somaliland (Somalia), which was then under Italian administration. Throughout, Lie kept Hammarskjöd informed of the negotiations.[244] Alas, for reasons beyond Lie's control, his endeavors led nowhere.[245]

Lie's desire to see a silver lining wherever Moscow was concerned was jolted when Stalin's successor, Nikita Khrushchev, paid an official visit to Norway in the summer of 1964. Lie and Prime Minister Gerhardsen "believed that a fundamental change in Soviet Foreign Policy had developed"; but the "uncompromising stance" of Khrushchev and his entourage soon disabused them of that notion. Khrushchev had nothing but scorn for the United Nations and treated Lie in a condescending manner. He likewise ill-treated Gerhardsen and other members of the cabinet. Both Lie and Gerhardsen admitted to Foreign Minister Halvard Lange, whose policies they had sometimes opposed, that Khrushchev's visit had spotlighted their errors, and they promised Lange their unqualified future support. Lie declared to the Labor party's secretary, Haakon Lie, that although in the past he had opposed the latter's "uncompromising anti-communist views," he would not do so in the future. Khrushchev's visit had taught everyone a lesson, Lie admitted.[246]

During his last years Lie assumed a number of important government posts. He also wrote four volumes of memoirs. Lie died on December 30, 1968, at seventy-two years of age.

As in 1951, when the assembly observed a symbolic minute of silence following the death of the league's first secretary-general, Sir Eric Drummond,[247] there was a similar ceremony in the Security Council for Lie. Secretary-General U Thant eulogized his predecessor as someone "frequently criticized from many sources, as often for doing too much as for doing too little." The French representative, Claude Chayet, noted that Lie had "imparted the first lustre to the hazardous office of Secretary-General."[248]

What had commenced with zeal and guarded optimism in early 1946 as a great trek, had foundered on the realities of international politics. Perhaps, as secretary-general, Lie could have steered a safer course had he heeded Janius's observation that there is a "holy mistaken zeal in politics as well as in religion. By persuading others, we convince ourselves."

Lie and Hammarskjöld, April 9, 1953, with police escort prior to the induction ceremony (photo courtesy of UNATIONS).

10

THE
OFFICE
Then
and
Now

As secretaries-general go, Lie was middling. Despite his personal inadequacies, one can cogently argue that he was better than some others who both preceded and succeeded him. These would certainly include France's Joseph Avenol and Burma's U Thant. Avenol had preceded Lie as second secretary-general of the League of Nations. Although he held intellectual and administrative credentials far better than Lie's, he was a political disaster of the first order. His swan song as secretary-general was his unsuccessful attempt, after the fall of France in the early summer of 1940, to be the secretary-general of the new Hitlerian order and to legitimatize the Nazi conquest of Europe through the League of Nations.[1] As to U Thant, his undisguised partialities and conception of the United Nations were formulated largely from the vantage point of the Afro-Asian world. Thant perceived his role as secretary-general with colonialism in mind and gave his office a narrower focus than the catholic one developed by Lie.[2]

If Lie had one overwhelming virtue, it was his wholehearted commitment to the United Nations and its success in world affairs. This commitment had deep roots. They included his sensitivity, as a national of a small state, to the insecurity that such states are subject to in world affairs. Certainly the Nazi invasion of Norway had seared him as it had all Norwegians. It was compounded by wartime exile, albeit as foreign minister in a refugee government residing in a friendly and allied country. In addition, as a young man in a neutral Norway he had undoubtedly agonized over the bloodletting of the First World War and the postwar political, economic, and social dislocation it had engendered. The league's failure to help manage world affairs during the interwar period and prevent another worldwide conflagration, as well as Lie's social democratic dedication to the horizontal brotherhood of man, were added factors in his commitment to the United Nations' success.

Accordingly an institution like the United Nations appeared to offer people of good intention, like Lie, some hope that the endemic insecurity in world affairs, especially for small states, might be mitigated, primarily by keeping the rogue elephants of international relations, the more powerful states, under some sort of constraint or control. United States membership in the world organization and the active role it had played in instituting it, unlike its rejection of the League of Nations in 1919, augured well that the interwar failure of the league would not be repeated in the postwar world of the United Nations. Provided Lie's commitment to the United Nations was matched by that of the permanent members of the Security Council—France, Great Britain, Nationalist China, Soviet Russia, and the United States—the road ahead might lead to a less Hobbesian international order. The keystone to this arch of commitment and international restraint was postwar consensus among the permanent members of the council. This was not to be.

The breakdown of the wartime Allied consensus soon manifested itself when the Axis coalition was defeated; it led to divergent perceptions of the organization in line with the differing foreign policy desires of the powers involved, which in turn led to varying commitments to the organization. The primary postwar status quo power was the United States. Based on its geographic location, initial nuclear bomb monopoly, a vast industrial and agricultural capacity undamaged by war, and other socioeconomic and political factors, Washington could well afford to dovetail its foreign policy desires with the requirements of the United Nations. It was easy to argue smugly that it alone among the great powers had hitched itself to the charter; this lent itself to moralizing about the political defects and shortcomings of others, a stance that neatly fitted certain calvinist-puritan aspects of the American political culture.

Great Britain was also a status quo power. Unlike the United States, however, Great Britain was a great power in form but not in substance. The body blows of the Second World War added to those of the First signaled the dissolution of a great empire and the slow decline of the metropolitan power. London's forte was multilateral diplomacy through international organizations as developed during the League of Nations years. It avidly reactivated this instrument in the postwar period in the pragmatic belief that the far-reaching disagreements and tensions that racked the former allies, might in some situations be better managed through the United Nations. Certainly logomachy was the preferable option that the United Nations offered: in the arena of the world organization London was willing and capable of playing Athens to Washington's Rome.

France sought to play an active role in the United Nations commensurate with its weakened position in world affairs; but a state once pivotal in the international balance when forced by events to play a scaled-down version of the same role will find the adjustment difficult, even in the best of times. In the immediate postwar era, to paraphrase the old quip about the Monroe Doctrine, France was a cheese box floating in the wake of an American man-of-war. Far more difficult was the position of Nationalist China whose chaotic political condition made it an object of concern and debate rather than coequal with the other permanent members of the council. The fact that Soviet Russia had assisted the Chinese Communists to come to power and was the source of their ideology was grist for the mill of political confrontation and hostility.

The alleged culprit in this dissolution of the wartime consensus was, of course, Soviet Russia. A controlled society, as only modern totalitarian states can be, and presided over by a leader who put to shame Machiavelli's Prince, it was perceived by others as an expansionist state. To many the driving force was Soviet Russia's ideological bent, although others saw this as a mere façade. They discerned Stalin's foreign policy desires and those of the czars to be analogous. Soviet Russia was therefore no different from Czarist Russia, they argued, except that the ideological harp plucked by Moscow made it easier to disguise its aggressive designs.

In this worldwide confrontational setting Lie's role was made far more difficult. Factors beyond his control placed him in the unenviable position of being not the secretary-general of a consensus organization but someone bobbing and weaving to keep the organization from foundering on the rocks of political disagreement. To keep the ship afloat Lie grasped the organization's administrative helm to help navigate these political shoals. Without hesitation he invoked the powers granted to him under the charter; he interpreted these powers and other provisions of the charter liberally, as well as the rules of procedure of the organization's various bodies; he insisted on the right to assume private and especially unsolicited public political initiatives, even though he had not been invited to do so by member states; he pressed for symbolic and formal respect for his office and its incumbent, in order to elevate the office's prestige in world affairs; and he invoked the need to have access to, and consult with, national political leaders. Lie wanted the office of secretary-general to be in the front rank of the United Nations attempt to keep the peace. The actions he took and the precedents he set blazed a trail that would be expanded by his immediate successor, Dag Hammarskjöld.

The rub is that spontaneous movements or initiatives by a secretary-general whether public or private do not necessarily always lead to progress. Lie failed to take note of the fact that, although the secretary-general had a certain political role to play, this role could never outpace or outdistance the desires of the more powerful states in world affairs to resolve their political differences through accommodation. This partially explained the nature of the veto on substantive questions enjoyed by the council's permanent members. Moreover, the need for political accommodation between member states should have cautioned the wise that in certain issues unsolicited private and especially public political initiatives by the secretary-general might aggravate his relations with the powers concerned. Thus in taking an initiative his ability to influence the mediation and the settlement process might prove nil, if not counterproductive. Indeed, the short-term and long-term damage might lead the concerned powers to become hostile to Lie and his initiative, to his continuance in office, and to any actions or other political initiatives that he might undertake in the future. Lie, however, was not the wisest of persons.

Time and experience taught Lie that perhaps the most productive initiative and the one least likely to cause trouble or expose him to criticism should be private; he certainly was entitled, at the minimum, to undertake private initiatives in view of the expanded powers that he enjoyed under the charter as opposed to those his league counterparts enjoyed under the covenant. However, Lie's initial adventurous initiatives both public and private in the Iranian, Spanish, and Greek questions, the Berlin blockade, the establishment of the North Atlantic Treaty Organization, and so on inspired little faith within Western circles in either his impartiality or political acumen. This was reenforced by his administrative inefficiency and slipshod diplomatic methods. His personality failures, accentuated by a self-defeating ego, were added to the burdens he carried and helped undermine initiatives he inaugurated. This is not to say that *ab initio* all his endeavors were without merit; indeed, one can argue that this was reflected in his 1951 spring initiative to end the fighting in Korea, as well as other proposals that he tendered in various questions. But trust by Western powers in Lie, in his methods, and most important in his proposals just was not there. They perceived him, rightly or wrongly, as partial to Soviet Russia, as a meddling bumbler, and a loose cannon on the heaving deck of postwar politics.

The North Korean invasion of South Korea, and Lie's open support of the victim, reversed the perception: to Moscow he was now anti-Russian. Lie's "defection" over the Korean crisis was unforgiveable in Moscow's eyes following what it perceived as previous public and private initiatives favoring its cause in a number of questions. He was an apostate; someone

whose youthful, strong Marxist orientation, although occasionally ambivalent, was mirrored in an understanding attitude, nourished perhaps by
feelings of fear and awe. Lie crossed the Rubicon in the summer of 1950,
when he took issue with a permanent member of the council. Although
initially he was able to have his way, in the long-run he lost. This scenario
was repeated by his successor, Hammarskjöld, whose public and private
initiatives in the Congo crisis clashed with Russian desires but dovetailed
with Western interests. In the case of U Thant, the aggrieved parties were
Great Britain and the United States. Although the confrontation was not
as direct, they both undoubtedly perceived his opposition in a number
of issues and probably correctly credited it to the disguised resentment
against the Western powers harbored by the first non-Western secretary-
general.

Khrushchev's pithy observation that while countries were neutral men
were not, certainly applied to Lie. By his commitment to the United
Nations Lie was neither impartial nor neutral. The actions of any state
that he perceived as detrimental to the interests or survival of the organization placed him in an adversarial relationship. How he reacted, the attitude he assumed, drew him, almost inextricably, into a political vortex
where the choices he made furthered the political drives and desires of one
supplicant state over another. Although he might rationalize his choices
on legal or administrative grounds, Lie was nevertheless involved in what
were essentially political acts. Accordingly, unsolicited public initiatives,
as in the Korean crisis, often led him into situations where discretion
would have been the sagacious policy. These situations automatically
placed him on a collision course. The public confrontation that followed
was sometimes dramatic, flashy, and newsy, but whether it helped solve
the political question at issue is open to discussion. In addition, Lie failed
to see that, as the hub of the multinational secretariat's administrative
wheel whose task it was to service the organization and to keep world
events under surveillance, approaches would be made by member states to
use him, his office, or the secretariat, to further their policies.[3] Caution
and restraint had to be exercised in all such approaches, but Lie was by
temperament and his own interpretation of the office not one committed
to either caution or restraint.

If unsolicited public initiatives had their danger, private initiatives were
no less dangerous. Lie's activities in the Palestine question are a case in
point. His support of the Zionists, first behind the scenes and then publicly, may have been affected by the atmosphere of the times: the general
consensus of a guilt-ridden Christian world that the Holocaust could be
redeemed by accepting the Zionist argument for partition. For Lie, it was
an easy tack to take in view of the general consensus on the question mirrored by the report of the General Assembly's Palestine Committee and
buttressed by the supporting attitudes of Soviet Russia and the United

States. Moreover, Lie's stance was made easier by the Palestine Arabs who undermined their own position by refusing to cooperate with the Palestine Committee and by rejecting the partition plan that envisaged a Zionist state much smaller than the one finally established after the partition fighting. Lie's pro-Zionist stance is open to criticism, predicated as it was on increasing the powers of his office and having the United Nations play an important role in a tangled and emotional problem that would bestow needed prestige on the organization. His actions may have ingratiated him with Israel's leaders, but it certainly destroyed forever whatever chance he had of developing an Arab constituency. After 1948 the Arab bloc, which increased in strength and influence in world affairs and within the United Nations specifically, was Lie's implacable foe, and when support or assistance was needed Lie could never approach them. He had burned his bridges.

Obviously unsolicited public or private political initiatives had their risks. To engage in activities of this nature exposes Lie and anyone else who holds the office to political retribution. High-level politics in international organization is never a zero-sum game. Russian hostility to Lie over Korea and to Hammarskjöld over the Congo, or Anglo-American hostility to U Thant on a range of issues, clearly reflects the dangers that face any secretary-general who wishes to assume an activist role in world affairs. The ability to assume such a role is enshrined in the charter, but there is a price to pay in doing so.

In the immediate postwar era Lie's activist interpretation of his office drew kudos from the well meaning. In a world recovering from a six-year conflagration and striving for some sort of peace and order, the activities of a Lie appeared a step in the right direction. But a secretary-general devoid of armed forces has little leverage in world politics except through the prestige of the office and the confidence of others. Lie certainly lacked the latter and thus lacked influence that is a direct outgrowth of confidence. Mistrusted by all sides, his ability to influence or affect the flow of events even through private initiatives was badly compromised. If Hammarskjöld seemed a more successful secretary-general, as perceived through Western eyes, much of his success could be traced to the confidence he generated in others, the influence that accrued from it, and the diplomatic methods that cleverly amalgamated the "old diplomacy" with the "new" multilateral diplomacy through international organization.

Like those who have held the office since U Thant, Lie learned with time and experience that despite the wording of the charter perhaps the most practicable approach is for the secretary-general to restrict action to private initiatives and eschew the public forum. The problem here is that private initiatives by a secretary-general require endless perseverance. They lead to tedious negotiations and are by definition outside the limelight. Private initiatives require self-control, endless imagination, and a grasp of world politics, as well as a familiarity with the topic under discussion equal to, or greater than, the secretariat's experts. Lie enjoyed none of these virtues. One gets the impression that private initiatives were a strain on him. They were not his "style" of doing things, as the public and dramatic were. The quiet private "style" was the virtue of someone who had been trained as a civil servant, which, of course, he had never been. The private approach demands the ability to gain and to hold the confidence of others, but alas this was not one of Lie's strong cards. The built-in liability of the unsolicited public approach circumscribed Lie from the beginning, regardless of the powers he enjoyed under the charter. His own shortcomings and inadequacies went far to limit his ability to act effectively in private. Lie's major virtue, already mentioned, was his commitment to the United Nations and what it was attempting to achieve in world affairs. This said, Lie had little else going for him. He was the wrong man, in the wrong job, at the wrong time. Being charitable, one might argue that even men far more gifted than Lie would have stumbled during this period in executing what he labeled the world's "most impossible job."

NOTES

Abbreviations

ADEAC	Archives, Department of External Affairs, Ottawa, Canada
BL	British Library, British Museum, London
CCL	Churchill College Library, Cambridge University, Cambridge, England
CIA Files	Central Intelligence Agency Files, Washington, D.C.
CU	Columbia University, New York
CUC	Cambridge University, Cambridge, England
CZAJ	Central Zionist Archives, Jerusalem
DCER	Canada, Department of External Affairs, *Documents on Canadian External Relations* (Ottawa: Queen's Printer, 1967–)
DFPI	Israel Ganzakh ha-Medinah, *Documents on the Foreign Policy of Israel* (Jerusalem: Israel Ganzakh ha-Medinah, 1981–)
EL	Dwight David Eisenhower Library, Abilene, Kansas
FBI Files	Federal Bureau of Investigation Files, U.S. Department of Justice, Washington, D.C.
FDRL	Franklin Delano Roosevelt Library, Hyde Park, New York
FO	Foreign Office records, Public Record Office, London
FRUS . . .	U.S. Department of State, *Foreign Relations of the United States* . . . (Washington, D.C.: Government Printing Office)
FUL	Flinders University Library of South Australia, Bedford Park
GAOR	General Assembly of the United Nations, Official Records

INS Files	Immigration and Naturalizarion Service Files, U.S. Department of Justice, Washington, D.C.
LSEPS	London School of Economics and Political Science
ISAJ	Israel State Archives, Jerusalem
KB	Kungliga Biblioteket (Royal Library), Stockholm
MANV	Douglas MacArthur Archives, Norfolk, Virginia
NA	National Archives of the United States, Washington, D.C.
NLC	Newberry Library, Chicago
NMFA	Norwegian Ministry of Foreign Affairs, Oslo
PAC	Public Archives of Canada, Ottawa
PDD, December 1947–May 1948	Israel Ganzakh ha-Medinah, *Political and Diplomatic Documents, December 1947–May 1948* (Jerusalem: Israel Ganzakh ha-Medinah, 1979)
PP	Private Papers
PRO	Public Record Office, London
PU	Princeton University, Princeton, New Jersey
RHLOU	Rhodes House Library, Oxford University, Oxford, England
SCOR	Security Council of the United Nations, Official Records
SHSW	State Historical Society of Wisconsin, Madison
TL	Harry S. Truman Library, Independence, Missouri
UI	University of Iowa, Iowa City
UM	University of Michigan, Ann Arbor
UN Doc. . . .	United Nations Document . . .
UNA	United Nations Archives, New York
UV	University of Virginia, Charlottesville
UVt	University of Vermont, Burlington
WAR	Chaim Weizmann Archives, Rehovot, Israel
YUN . . .	*Yearbook of the United Nations* . . . (New York: Department of Public Information United Nations)

Notes for Chapter 1: Consensus Candidate

1. James Barros, *Office without Power: Secretary-General Sir Eric Drummond 1919–1933* (Oxford: The Clarendon Press, 1979), and James Barros, *Betrayal from Within: Joseph Avenol, Secretary-General of the League of Nations, 1933–1940* (New Haven: Yale University Press, 1969).
2. Barros, *Betrayal from Within*, pp. 14–22, 198–205.
3. Stevenson (London) to the Sec. of State, No. 618, Dec. 22, 1945, File 500.CC (PC)/12–2245, RG 59, NA.
4. Halifax (Washington) to the Foreign Office, No. 1828, Mar. 28, 1945, FO/371/50686.
5. *FRUS, 1945*, I, p. 1439.
6. See Barros, *Betrayal from Within*, p. 269.
7. Ibid., pp. 1–14; Barros, *Office without Power*, pp. 1–19.
8. Calendar notes, Sept. 7, 1945, Box 247, Stettinius Papers, UV. Also see Edward R. Stettinius, Jr., *The Diaries of Edward R. Stettinius, Jr., 1943–1946*, ed. Thomas W. Campbell and George C. Herring (New York: New Viewpoints, 1975), p. 416.
9. Stettinius to Hiss, July 3, 1945, Box 694; Stettinius to Hiss, Sept. 19, 1945; and Hiss to Stettinius, Oct. 4, 1945, Box 424, Stettinius Papers, UV. Also see Allen Weinstein, *Perjury: The Hiss-Chambers Case* (New York: Alfred A. Knopf, 1978), pp. 346, 352–56.
10. A note from C[harles] K. W[ebster] to the Min. of State, no date, Section 15/4, Webster Papers, LSEPS.
11. James Barros, "Alger Hiss and Harry Dexter White: The Canadian Connection," *Orbis*, 21, no. 3 (Fall 1977): 593–605. Also see H. Montgomery Hyde, *The Atom Bomb Spies* (London: Hamilton, 1980), p. 33 and n.
12. Minutes of a meeting of the Big Five at Claridge's Hotel, London, Sept. 17, 1945, Section 15/4, Webster Papers, LSEPS. Also see Memo. of Con. (Stettinius, Gromyko, Massigli, et al.), Sept. 17, 1945, Box 247, Stettinius Papers, UV.
13. *FRUS, 1945*, I, pp. 1449–50.
14. Ibid., pp. 1448–49. The question of a secretary-general's reemployment after retirement was undoubtedly raised by Acheson because of the stir that was created in 1933 following Drummond's resignation from the league. He was immediately reappointed to the Foreign Office and posted as ambassador in Rome. Barros, *Betrayal from Within*, pp. 2–3 n.
15. C[harles] K. W[ebster] to the Min. of State, Sept. 21, 1945, Section 15/4, Webster Papers, LSEPS. Also see Memo. of Con. (Webster, Stevenson), Sept. 20, 1945, Box 247, Stettinius Papers, UV; and Philip A. Reynolds and E. J. Hughes, *The Historian as Diplomat. Charles Kingsley Webster and the United Nations 1939–1946* (London: Robertson, 1976), pp. 76–77.
16. C[harles] K. W[ebster], Meeting between Mr. Stettinius and the Min. of State, Sept. 25, 1945, FO/371/50739. Also see Memo. of Con. (Noel-Baker, Webster, Stettinius, Stevenson, et al.), Sept. 25, 1945, Box 247, Stettinius Papers, UV, as well as Reynolds and Hughes, p. 77. The proposal to make Eisenhower secretary-general appears to have had public support in Great Britain. See Geoffrey de Frietas to the Prime Minister, Oct. 26, 1945, PREM/8/119, PRO.
17. Acheson (Washington) to Stettinius, No. 8345, Sept. 22, 1945, File 500.CC (PC)/9–1945, RG 59, NA.
18. United Nations Preparatory Commission, Informal Five Power Meeting, Sept. 26, 1945, FO/371/50883; *FRUS, 1945*, I, p. 1452. Also see Memo. of Con. (Gromyko, Massigli, Stettinius, Stevenson, Noel-Baker, Webster, et al.), Sept. 26, 1945, Box 247, Stettinius Papers, UV.

19. Memo. of Con. (Fouques-Duparc, Rothwell), Sept. 27, 1945, Box 247, Stettinius Papers, UV.

20. Record of a Meeting Held at the Foreign Office, Sept. 28, 1945, FO/371/50885.

21. Winant for Stettinius (London) to the Sec. of State, No. 10221, Oct. 1, 1945, File 500.CC (PC)/10–145, RG 59, NA. Also see calendar notes, Sept. 28 and 30, 1945, Box 247, Stettinius Papers, UV.

22. Stettinius (London) to the Sec. of State, No. 10349, Oct. 4, 1945, File 500.C (PC)/10–445, RG 59, NA. Also see calendar notes, Oct. 3, 1945, Box 247, Stettinius Papers, UV.

23. Gore-Booth (Washington) to Falla, Oct. 9, 1945, FO/371/50740.

24. Byrnes (Washington) to Stettinius, No. 8965, Oct. 10, 1945, File 500.CC (PC)/10–445, RG 59, NA; Memo. of Con. (Hasluck, Stevenson), Oct. 9, 1945, Box 247, Stettinius Papers, UV.

25. Charles K. Webster diary, Mon., Oct. 8, 1945, Part II, Webster Papers, LSEPS.

26. Meeting at Mr. Stettinius's flat at Claridge's Hotel on Monday, Oct. 8, [1945], PREM/8/119, PRO; Memo. of Con. (Gromyko, Massigli, Stettinius, Stevenson, Webster, et al.), Oct. 8, 1945; and Memo. of Con. (Byrnes, Stevenson, Noyes), Oct. 22, 1945, Box 247, Stettinius Papers, UV; Charles K. Webster diary, Mon., Oct. 8, 1945, Part II, Webster Papers, LSEPS; *FRUS, 1945*, I, pp. 1455–56. Also see Lord Gladwyn, *The Memoirs of Lord Gladwyn* (London: Weidenfeld and Nicolson, 1972), pp. 182–83 and Reynolds and Hughes, pp. 78–79.

27. [Calendar notes], Oct. 8, 1945, Box 247, Stettinius Papers, UV.

28. Weinstein, pp. 355, 356. For Hiss's activities at the Preparatory Commission as perceived by a Canadian participant see Paul Martin, *A Very Public Life* (Ottawa: Deneau, 1983), I, p. 405.

29. Charles K. Webster diary, Thurs., Oct. 12, 1945; and Mon., Oct. 15, Wed., Oct. 17; Thurs., Nov. 1; Sun., Dec. 30, 1945; and Sun., Jan. 20, 1946, Part II, Webster Papers, LSEPS, as well as Noel-Baker to Webster, Oct. 9, 1945, Section 15/5, ibid.

30. [Charles K. Webster], Seat of the United Nations Organization and the Choice of the Secretary-General [Oct. 10, 1945?], Section 15/5, ibid.

31. P[hilip] N[oel-]B[aker] to the Sec. of State, Oct. 12, 1945, PREM/8/119, PRO.

32. [Stettinius] to the Sec. of State, No. 10711, Oct. 13, 1945, File 500.CC (PC)/10–1345, RG 59, NA; Memo. of Con. (Mackenzie King, Stettinius, Noyes), Oct. 12, 1945, Box 247, Stettinius Papers, UV; William Lyon Mackenzie King, *The Mackenzie Record*, ed. J. W. Pickersgill and D. F. Forster (Toronto: University of Toronto Press, 1970), III, p. 62.

33. P[hilip] N[oel-]B[aker], Record of Conversation with the Prime Minister of Canada, Oct. 13, 1945, Section 15/5, Webster Papers, LSEPS. Also see Lester B. Pearson, *Mike: The Memoirs of the Right Honourable Lester B. Pearson* (Toronto: University of Toronto Press, 1972), I, pp. 280–81.

34. *FRUS, 1945*, I, p. 1461.

35. Department of State, Division of European Affairs to [Alger] Hiss, Oct. 24, 1945, and the marginal minute by [John] H[ickerson], File 501.BA/10–2445, RG 59, NA.

36. E[rnest] B[evin], Site of the United Nations Organisation, Oct. 29, 1945, FO/371/50741. Also see Memo. of Con. (Noyes, McNeil), Oct. 4, 1945, Box 247, Stettinius Papers, UV.

37. A[lexander] C[adogan] to Jebb, Oct. 30, 1945, Section 15/4, Webster Papers, LSEPS.

38. Jebb to Cadogan, Nov. 1, 1945, Section 15/4, ibid.

39. Minutes by P[hilip] N[oel-]B[aker], Nov. 6, 1945, Section 15/4, ibid. Also see

Cyrus L. Sulzberger, *A Long Row of Candles; Memoirs and Diaries* [*1934–1954*] (New York: Macmillan, 1969), p. 270.
40. *FRUS, 1945*, I, pp. 1477–78.
41. Ibid., p. 1488. Also see Memo. of Con. (Stone, Hiss, Armstrong), Dec. 7, 1945, Box 247, Stettinius Papers, UV.
42. Also see Memo. of Con. (Stettinius and Gromyko), Oct. 11, 1945, Box 247, Stettinius Papers, UV.
43. *FRUS, 1945*, I, pp. 1491–92.
44. Stevenson (London) to the Sec. of State, Dec. 19, 1945, File 500.CC (PC)/12–1945, RG 59, NA.
45. Acheson to the London embassy, Dec. 19, 1945, File 500.CC (PC)/12–1945, ibid.
46. *FRUS, 1945*, I, pp. 1492–93.
47. Ibid., p. 1504.
48. Acheson to Stevenson, Dec. 21, 1945, File 500.CC (PC)/12-2145, RG 59, NA.
49. *FRUS, 1945*, I, p. 1478.
50. Ibid., pp. 1504–1509. Also see Charles K. Webster diary, Mon., Dec. 24, 1945, Part II, Webster Papers, LSEPS; and Trygve Lie, *In the Cause of Peace* (New York: Macmillan, 1954), pp. 2–3.
51. Memo. of Con. (Noyes, McNeil), Oct. 4, 1945; and calendar notes, Jan. 8–9, 13, 1946, Box, 247, Stettinius Papers, UV; Oliver Harvey diary (July 24, 1943–April 29, 1946), Xmas 1945, Harvey Papers, Add. MS. 56400, BL; Charles K. Webster diary, Sun., Jan. 20, and week beginning Sun., Jan. 27, 1946, Part II, Webster Papers, LSEPS; Anthony Eden, *The Reckoning* (London: Cassell), p. 554; Lie, pp. 11–12.
52. Private information.
53. *FRUS, 1945*, I, p. 1507 n.
54. *FRUS, 1946*, I, p. 159 n. Also see calendar notes, Jan. 13, 1946, Box 247, Stettinius Papers, UV.
55. *FRUS, 1945*, II, p. 778.
56. *DCER*, 12, pp. 622–23; Mackenzie King, pp. 123–24; Charles K. Webster diary, Mon., Oct. 15, 1945, Part II, Webster Papers, LSEPS.
57. Department of External Affairs to [Pearson], No. 123, Jan. 14, 1946, File 211-A(s), ADEAC.
58. *FRUS, 1946*, I, p. 139.
59. Eden to Oliphant, No. 59, Mar. 23, 1944; and a memorandum from Spaak to Eden, Mar. 24, 1944, FO/371/38868. Aveling (Brussels) to the Foreign Office, No. 335, Oct. 19, 1945, FO/371/49025.
60. Lie, p. 5.
61. Charles K. Webster diary, Sun., Dec. 30, 1945, Part II, Webster Papers, LSEPS. As to Spaak's desire for the post, see Martin, I, p. 403.
62. Lie, pp. 2–4; *FRUS, 1945*, I, p. 1509.
63. *FRUS, 1946*, I, pp. 140–42; Minutes by A[lexander] C[adogan], Jan. 9, 1946, FO/371/57035.
64. Paul-Henri Spaak, *Combats inachevés* (Paris: Fayard, 1969), I, pp. 199–200.
65. *FRUS, 1946*, I, pp. 1448–49; [Alexander Cadogan], to the S[ec.] of S[tate], [Jan. 10, 1946], FO/371/57038.
66. Minutes by P[hilip] N[oel-]B[aker], [Jan. 10, 1946], FO/371/57038. In an obvious mistake Noel-Baker had written in the minutes that the Latin Americans would vote for Lie. Cadogan scribbled "Spaak," in querying the error.
67. Minutes by J[ohn] G. Ward, Jan. 12, [1946], FO/371/57032.
68. *FRUS, 1946*, I, pp. 152–53. Byrnes became aware of Stevenson's activities only

on the morning of January 10, 1946. See Calendar notes, Jan. 10, 1946, Box 247, Stettinius Papers, UV.

69. E[rnest] B[evin], Minutes by the Sec. of State, Jan. 11, 1946, FO/371/57032. Also see Reconstruction Department to the Chancery, British Embassy, Washington, Jan. 25, 1946, FO/371/57038.

70. Lie, pp. 4–6; V[alentine] G. L[awford], to the Sec. of State, Jan. 10, 1946, FO/371/57038.

71. GAOR, 1st Plen. Mtg., Jan. 10, 1946, pp. 43–46; Lie, pp. 7–10; [Gladwyn Jebb?], United Nations Assembly, Mar. 27, 1946, FO/371/57052; Minutes by P[hilip] Noel-Baker, Jan. 12, 1946, FO/371/57053. Also see Frances Williams, *Ernest Bevin* (London: Hutchinson, 1952), p. 246.

72. *FRUS, 1946*, I, p. 152.

73. Spaak, I, p. 201.

74. Paul Gore-Booth, *With Great Truth and Respect* (London: Constable, 1974), p. 154.

75. Calendar notes, Jan. 10, 1946, Box 247, Stettinius Papers, UV; Lie, pp. 10–11.

76. *FRUS, 1946*, I, p. 152.

77. Charles K. Webster diary, Sun., Jan. 20, 1946, Part II, Webster Papers, LSEPS.

78. Wilson (Ankara) to the Sec. of State, No. 133, Jan. 30, 1946, and also the corrected version, File 501.BA/1–3045, RG 59, NA.

79. These various communications can be found in File 501.BA/1-, ibid.

80. *DCER*, 12, p. 623; Robertson to Pearson, No. 155, Jan. 16, 1946; and Robertson to Pearson, No. 180, Jan. 21, 1946, File 211-A(s), ADEAC.

81. Calendar notes, Jan. 18, 1946, Box 247, Stettinius Papers, UV.

82. Roberts (Moscow) to the Foreign Office, No. 206, Jan. 17, 1946, FO/371/57034.

83. After his appointment as secretary-general, Lie received Moscow's public imprimatur when it noted that he appeared to be "a suitable man for the job." *New Times* (Moscow), no. 5 (March 1, 1946), p. 21.

84. Robertson to Pearson, No. 155, Jan. 16, 1946, File 211-A(s), ADEAC.

85. *DCER*, 12, pp. 624–25.

86. *FRUS, 1946*, I, pp. 161–63, 166–69 and n.; calendar notes, Jan. 20 and 23, 1946, Box 147, Stettinius Papers, UV; *DCER*, 12, pp. 625–27. During this period the irrepressible Manuilsky's solution to the problem was that, if a military man was to be chosen secretary-general, "he thought there should be three Secretaries, [General Dwight] Eisenhower, [General Georgi] Zhukov and [General Bernard] Montgomery." This early prototype of the "troika" secretary-general that Nikita Khruschchev subsequently unveiled at the fifteenth session of the General Assembly belies Manuilsky's assurances that this was not a serious proposal. It obviously was an idea percolating inside the Russian delegation. Foote to Stevenson, Jan. 21, 1946, Box 427, Stettinius Papers, UV.

87. Calendar notes, Jan. 23, 1946, Box 247, Stettinius Papers, UV.

88. Calendar notes, Jan. 24, 1946, Box 247, ibid.

89. *DCER*, 12, pp. 625–27. Also see Douglas G. Anglin, "Lester Pearson and the Office of Secretary-General," *International Journal*, 17, no. 2 (Spring 1962): 146.

90. *FRUS, 1946*, I, pp. 172–82. Also see calendar notes, Jan. 22, 1946, Box 247, Stettinius Papers, UV.

91. Lie, pp. 13–15; Martin, I, p. 404.

92. [Lie] (Oslo) to Stoneman, June 10, 1953, Box 1, Stoneman Papers, Bentley Historical Library, UM.

93. Lie, pp. 15–16.

94. Eleanor Roosevelt diary, Fri., Jan. 25, 1946, Box 4561, FDRL.
95. [Stettinius] to the Sec. of State, No. 1396, Feb. 5, 1946, File 501.BA/2–546, RG 59, NA; Calendar notes, Jan. 27–28, 1946, and Telephone Conversation, Jan. 28, 1946, Box 247, Stettinius Papers, UV.
96. FRUS, 1946, I, pp. 183–84.
97. Lie, pp. 16–17.
98. Osborne (Oslo) to the Sec. of State, No. 73, Jan. 25, 1946, File 501.BA/1–2546, RG 59, NA. Also see Osborne (Oslo) to the Sec. of State, No. 84, Jan. 29, 1946, File 501.BA/1–2946, ibid.
99. Osborne (Oslo) to the Sec. of State, No. 80, Jan. 28, 1946, File 857.00/1–2846, ibid.
100. Collier (Oslo) to the Foreign Office, No. 48, Jan. 29, 1946, FO/371/56302.
101. Lie, p. 17.
102. SCOR, 1st Yr., 1st Ser., 4th Mtg., Jan. 29, 1946, p. 44; and ibid., 1st Yr., Supp. 1, Annex 6, p. 80; GAOR, 12th Plen. Mtg., Feb. 1, 1946, pp. 303–304.
103. Charles K. Webster diary, Sun., Feb. 3, 1946, Part II, Webster Papers, LSEPS. Also Alexander Cadogan diary, Sat., Feb. 2, [1946], CCL.
104. Charles K. Webster diary, Sun., Feb. 3, 1946, Part II, Webster Papers, LSEPS.
105. P[hilip] N[oel-]B[aker] to Webster, Oct. 17, [1945], Section 15/4, Webster Papers, ibid. Lie "seems to be no better than second-rate," was one Canadian view. Escott Reid, On Duty. A Canadian at the Making of the United Nations 1945–46 (Toronto: McClelland and Stewart, 1983), pp. 140, 151. Also see Brian Urquhart, A Life in Peace and War (New York: Harper and Row, 1987), p. 99.
106. In view of this attitude one can ask whether it was by chance or by design that there began to circulate in London a pun on Lie's name, to wit, that it was unfortunate to appoint as secretary-general a man called "Tricksy" Lie. Harold Nicolson, Diaries and Letters 1945–1962, ed. Nigel Nicolson (London: Collins, 1968), p. 53.
107. Osborne (Oslo) to the Sec. of State, No. 86, Jan. 29, 1946, File 501.BA/1–2946, RG 59, NA.
108. Charles K. Webster diary, Sun., Jan. 26, 1946, Part II, Webster Papers, LSEPS; Williams, p. 246.
109. FRUS, 1946, I, p. 159.

Notes for Chapter 2: Persona and Politics

1. Wrong (London) to the Sec. of State for External Affairs, No. 264, Jan. 30, 1946, File 211-A(s), ADEAC and DCER, 12, pp. 627–28.
2. Winant (London) to the Sec. of State, No. 1227, Feb. 1, 1946, File 501.BA/2–146, RG 59, NA. On Lie's ambition see also [Stoneman] to [Binder], Nov. 14, 1952, Binder Papers, NLC; and [George M. Warr], Monsieur Lie, [Mar. 8, 1946?], FO/371/57053.
3. [Warner] to Collier, Feb. 2, 1946, FO/371/56302. For Lie's speech see GAOR, 9th Plen. Mtg., Jan. 16, 1946, pp. 141–44. The speech was favorably commented on by Pravda (Jan. 17, 1946), p. 5. On Lie and the Russians at San Francisco, see Walter R. Crocker, "Memoir about the United Nations" (typescript), p. 274, Evatt Collection, FUL.
4. Collier (Oslo) to Bevin, No. 26, Feb. 5, 1946, FO/371/57237. Also see [Lawford] to Ward, May 10, 1946, FO/371/57060; Walter R. Crocker, Travelling Back (Melbourne: Macmillan, 1981), p. 165; and Crocker, "Memoir about the United

Nations," pp. 274–76, 283. For Prime Minister Einar Gerhardsen's complementary views about Lie, see his *Samarbeid og strid: Erindringer 1945–1955* (Oslo: Tiden, 1971), pp. 190–91.

5. Minutes by C[lifford] Heathcote-Smith, Feb. 20, [1946], FO/371/57237.
6. Minutes by P[hillip] N[oel-]B[aker], Mar. 5 [1946], ibid.
7. Collier (Oslo) to Warner, Feb. 12, 1946, FO/371/56302.
8. Minutes by C[hristopher] F. A. W[arner], Mar. 1, 1946, ibid.
9. Bowker (Oslo) to Eden, No. 9, Jan. 7, 1937, FO/371/21087; Dormer (Oslo) to Eden, No. 2, Jan. 1, 1938, FO/371/22281; Dormer (Oslo) to Halifax, No. 213, July 1, 1939, FO/371/23675.
10. Hugh S. Cumming, Jr., to Hickerson and Matthews, Jan. 30, 1946, File 501.BA/1–3046, RG 59, NA.
11. Lester B. Pearson, *Mike: The Memoirs of the Right Honourable Lester B. Pearson* (Toronto: University of Toronto Press, 1972), I, p. 280 and II, p. 124.
12. Trygve Lie, *In the Cause of Peace* (New York: Macmillan, 1954), p. 18. Also see Hugh L. Keenleyside, *Memoirs* (Toronto: McClelland, Stewart, 1982), II, p. 366.
13. Findlay (Christiania) to the Foreign Office, No. 3487, Oct. 1, 1918, FO/371/3336.
14. "The Reminiscences of Thanassis Aghnides" (typescript), pp. 336–37, Oral History Collection, CU. According to Erik-Wilhelm Norman, head of the Archives Division of the Norwegian Foreign Ministry, the relevant file on the Litvinov-Lockhart exchange, which might have yielded additional information on Lie's role, appears to be missing. Norman to the author, Mar. 20, 1981. Likewise Lie's police file in the National Archives in Oslo also appears to be missing. The reader can ruminate over these documentary disappearances, keeping in mind that Lie was Minister of Foreign Affairs (1941–1946) and Minister of Justice (1935–1939) and would have had access to these materials.
15. It is odd, but this dispatch and the relevant enclosures are missing from their proper place in the State Department papers in the National Archives in Washington, D.C. (File 861.00/5434, RG 59, NA). Their disappearance leaves room for conjecture. They were traced only by examining the legation's files. See C[harles] B[oyd] C[urtis] (Christiania) to the Sec. of State, No. 1351, Sept. 23, 1919, Enclosure 7, Records of the American Legation, Christiania [Oslo], Vol. XI, File 800 (3), RG 84, NA; also the Oslo telephone directories 1919–1939. Lie's speech was a leftist-tinged view of the Russian revolution and an appeal to abolish compulsory military service in Norway. See *Social Demokraten* (July 23, 1919), p. 1. For the general strike, see France: Ministère des Affaires Étrangères, *Bulletin Périodique de la Presse Scandinave*, No. 73: 1–2.
16. Schmedemann (Christiania) to the Sec. of State, No. 1768, Feb. 28, 1921, and enclosure, File 857.00B/31, RG 59, NA.
17. Findlay (Christiania) to Curzon, No. 202, Nov. 3, 1919, and enclosures, FO/371/4076.
18. Under Secretary for Thomson, No. 10, 1919, and Director of Intelligence to Under-Secretary for Foreign Affairs, No. 18, 1919, ibid.
19. Sir Basil Thomson, *The Scene Changes* (Garden City, N.Y.: Doubleday and Doran, 1937), p. 424.
20. [Memo. of Con.] (Belt, Walker), Jan. 24, 1947, Box 112, US Mission UN 1945–49, RG 84, NA.
21. McClintock to Walker, Feb. 7, 1947, Box 112, ibid.
22. Tittman (Port-au-Prince) to the Sec. of State, No. 269, Feb. 1, 1947, File 033.0038/2–147, RG 59, NA. Also see *Weekly Report on the American Re-*

publics, Office of American Republic Affairs, Department of State (Feb. 8–14, 1947), CIA Files; and Lie, *Cause of Peace*, pp. 125–32.

23. Matthews (Stockholm) to the Sec. of State, No. 805, Aug. 12, 1949, File 501/8–1249, RG 59, NA.
24. Coyne to Ladd, July 15, 1947, FBI Files.
25. Hoover to Scheidt, July 18, 1947, ibid.
26. O'Donnell to Hoover and the attached list, Aug. 8, 1921, ibid.
27. Hoover to Scheidt, July 18, 1947, ibid.
28. S[pecial] A[gent in] C[harge] to Director, Aug. 4, 1947, ibid.
29. Director to S[pecial] A[gent in] C[harge], Aug. 12, 1947, ibid.
30. S[pecial] A[gent in] C[harge] to the Director, Aug. 28, 1947, ibid.
31. Coyne to Ladd, Sept. 27, 1947, ibid.
32. Martin M. Wise, memo Article in *Plain Talk* about Trygve Lie and other members of the Secretariat (Oct. 30, 1947), Box 50, US Mission UN 1945–49, RG 84, NA.
33. Clark to the Sec. of State, Sept. 2, 1948 and the attached memorandum; Rusk to the Sec. [of State], Sept. 9, 1948, and Marshall to Clark, Sept. 14, 1948, File 501.BA/9–248, RG 59, NA.
34. Keay to Fletcher, Oct.1, 1948, FBI Files.
35. Keay to Fletcher, Oct. 21, 1948, *ibid.*
36. An unsigned memorandum re Trygve Lie, Secretary-General of the United Nations, Oct. 22, 1948, ibid.
37. On this point, see "The Reminiscences of Thanassis Aghnides," pp. 334, 336.
38. Hoover to Nicholson, Sept. 20, 1950; Hoover to Nicholson, Feb. 23, 1951; Hoover to McInerney, June 19, 1952, Hoover to Nicholson, June 19, 1952, FBI Files.
39. Durand to Marcosao, Jan. 21, 1952, CIA Files.
40. Farrell to Devaney, June 11, 1953, and MacKey to the Sec. of State, July 1, 1953, INS Files.
41. Devaney to Habberton, June 18, 1953, ibid.
42. Habberton to Devaney, June 19, 1953, ibid.
43. A. C. Devaney, memorandum for the file, Sept. 10, 1953; and Devaney to Maney, [Sept. 17, 1953?]; and Argyle R. Mackey, re Trygve Lie. In Consideration Under Section 212 . . . of the Immigration and Nationality Act, Sept. 11, 1952, ibid.
44. A scribbled noted dated Sept. 23, 1953 on a letter from Devaney to Maney, [Sept. 17, 1953?], ibid.
45. Devaney to Shaughnessy, Sept. 11, 1953, and Marks to the Immigration and Naturalization Service, Sept. 30, 1953, ibid.
46. CIA and FBI files.
47. "The Reminiscences of Thanassis Aghnides," pp. 336, 337; Aghnides to the author, Dec. 4, 1978.
48. Bay (Oslo) to the Sec. of State, No. 555, Aug. 11, 1949, File 501/8–1149, RG 59, NA.
49. Memo. of Con. (Lie, Hall), Oct. 11, 1949, Box 66, US Mission UN 1945–49, RG 84, NA.
50. Philip M. Burgess, *Elite Images and Foreign Policy Outcomes: A Study of Norway* (Columbus: Ohio State University Press, 1968), pp. 61–62; Lie, *Cause of Peace*, p. 19.
51. Gladwyn Jebb, Report on the Secretariat of the United Nations, Feb. 3, 1947, CAB/134/435, PRO. Also see Robertson (London) to Pearson, Apr. 14, 1947, vol. 429, King Papers, MG 26, J1, PAC.
52. Trygve Lie, *Oslo-Moskva-London* (Oslo: Tiden, 1968), pp. 11–34; Hans

Amundsen, *Trygve Lie; Gutten fra Grorud som ble General-Sekretaer i FN* (Oslo: Tiden, 1946), pp. 9–44; Arthur W. Rovine, *The First Fifty Years; The Secretary-General in World Politics 1920–1970* (Leyden: Sijthoff, 1970), pp. 207–208; *Who Was Who, 1961–1970* (London: Adam and Black, 1972), pp. 674–75; *Current Biography 1946*, ed. Anna Rothe (New York: Wilson, 1947), p. 342.

53. Collier to Eden, No. 51, Apr. 21, 1943, FO/371/36888.
54. Lie, *Cause of Peace*, pp. 19, 294.
55. Franz Borkenau, *World Communism; A History of the Communist International* (Ann Arbor: University of Michigan Press, 1962), pp. 67–68, 167; Trond Gilberg, *The Soviet Communist Party and Scandinavian Communism: The Norwegian Case* (Oslo: Universitetsforlaget, 1973), pp. 23–58.
56. Lie, *Oslo-Moskva-London*, pp. 34–44; Amundsen, pp. 55-59; Isaac Deutscher, *The Prophet Outcast: Trotsky, 1929–1940* (London: Oxford University Press, 1963), p. 293.
57. Borkenau, pp. 260–61; Gilberg, 35–58.
58. Ralph Hewins, *Quisling: Prophet Without Honour* (London: Allen, 1965), p. 85.
59. Lie, *Oslo-Moskva-London*, pp. 83–84; also see Amundsen, pp. 77–79.
60. Findlay (Christiania) to Curzon, No. 146, Apr. 1, 1921, Enclosure 15, FO/419/7; Lindley (Oslo) to Chamberlain, No. 110, Feb. 21, 1928, and Lindley (Oslo) to Chamberlain, No. 175, Mar. 22, 1928, FO/371/13229; Swenson (Oslo) to the Sec. of State, No. 1155, Mar. 23, 1928, File 857.00B/89, RG 59, NA.
61. Deutscher, pp. 292–94, 331–37.
62. Dormer (Oslo) to Eden, No. 380, Sept. 14, 1936, FO/371/20354. Also see Deutscher, p. 337.
63. Deutscher, pp. 337–45, 350–55. For Lie's version of the events see Lie, *Oslo-Moskva-London*, pp. 64–79. Amundsen, pp. 94–101; Dormer (Oslo) to Hoare, No. 262, June 20, 1935, FO/371/19470. Dormer (Oslo) to Eden, No. 338, Aug. 8, 1936, Dormer (Oslo) to Eden, No. 345, Aug. 15, 1936; Dormer (Oslo) to the Foreign Office, No. 47, Sept. 4, 1936; Dormer (Oslo) to Eden, No. 361, Sept. 7, 1936, Dormer (Oslo) to Eden, No. 434, Nov. 2, 1936, Bowker (Oslo) to Eden, No. 506, Dec. 24, 1936, FO/371/20354. James Barros, "Trygve Lie: De mortius nil nisi bonum," *International Journal*, 25, no. 2 (Spring 1970): 409–10; and Jane Degras, ed., *Soviet Documents on Foreign Policy* (London: Oxford University Press, 1953), III, pp. 204–206.
64. Lie, *Cause of Peace*, p. 20.
65. Ibid. and Collier to Eden, No. 55, Apr. 30, 1943, FO/371/36888. Also see Trygve Lie, *Leve eller dø Norge i krig* (Oslo: Tiden, 1955), pp. 73–86.
66. "Trygve Halvdan Lie under Norway in the Report Prepared by the Political Biographic Section of the Department of State for the San Francisco Conference," vol. II, Box 311, Stettinius Papers, UV.
67. Dowling (Vienna) to the Department of State, No. 63, July 10, 1952, File 315/7–1052, RG 59, NA.
68. Lie, *Cause of Peace*, p. 5.
69. Gladwyn Jebb, Report on the Secretariat of the United Nations, Feb. 3, 1947, CAB/134/435, PRO.
70. Eden to Collier, No. 124, July 17, 1941, Eden to Collier, No. 13, July 18, 1941, Eden to Collier, No. 17, July 23, 1941, Eden Papers, Pt. 2, FO/954/23; A[lexander] C[adogan], Memo. of Con., July 24, 1941; Foreign Office to Moscow, No. 888, July 25, 1941, FO/371/29432; Trygve Lie, *Med England i ildlinjen 1940–42* (Oslo: Tiden, 1956), pp. 263–72; Trygve Mathisen, *Svalbard in*

the Changing Arctic (Oslo: Gyldendal, 1954), pp. 33–35; Willy Østreng, *Politics in High Latitudes: The Svalbard Archipelago* (London: Hurst, 1977), pp. 46–47, Nils M. Udgaard, *Great Power Politics and Norwegian Foreign Policy* (Oslo: Universitetsforlaget, 1973), pp. 43–44.

71. Eden to Collier, No. 24, Aug. 6, 1941, Eden to Collier, No. 38, Sept. 18, 1941, and Eden to Collier, No. 56, Nov. 14, 1941, Eden Papers, Pt. 2, FO/954/23.
72. Eden to Collier, No. 17, July 23, 1941, Eden Papers, Pt. 2, FO/954/23; Lie, *Med England i ildlinjen 1940–42*, pp. 268–70; Udgaard, p. 44.
73. Collier to Eden, No. 19, Feb. 5, 1943, FO/371/36867.
74. Collier to Eden, No. 61, Oct. 5, 1942, FO/371/32853.
75. Collier to Eden, No. 55, Apr. 30, 1943, FO/371/36888. Also see Collier to Warner, Dec. 17, 1943, FO/371/36868; and Trygve Lie, *Hjemover* (Oslo: Tiden, 1958), p. 97–101.
76. Broadcast to Norway by the Norwegian Foreign Minister—Mr. Trygve Lie, Jan. 15, 1944, FO/371/43234; Schoenfeld (London) to the Sec. of State, No. 74, Jan. 21, 1944, and enclosure, File 840.50/3489, RG 59, NA; Udgaard, p. 94. On the clandestine press see Johnson (Stockholm) to the Sec. of State, No. 3491, June 7, 1944, File 857.9111/6–744, RG 59, NA.
77. Minutes by C[hristopher] F. A. Warner, Jan. 29, 1944, FO/371/39020.
78. Sargent to Hollis, Mar. 10, 1944, FO/371/43248.
79. O[rme] Sargent, untitled memorandum, Feb. 19, 1944, ibid.
80. Lie, *Hjemover*, pp. 126–27; Udgaard, p. 58.
81. Udgaard, pp. 58, 62–63.
82. Norwegian government memorandum to the Russian government, [December 1944?], FO/371/47503; A[rchibald] C[lark] K[err] to Eden, Nov. 20, 1944, Inverchapel Papers, FO/800/302; Lie, *Hjemover*, pp. 155–59; Rolf Andvord, *Med hånden på hjertet* (Oslo: Cappelen, 1964), pp. 237–38; Østreng, p. 50; Mathisen, pp. 46–48; Udgaard, pp. 67–68.
83. Norwegian government memorandum to the Russian government, December 1944?, FO/371/47503; Lie, *Hjemover*, pp. 162–65; Østreng, pp. 50–51; Mathisen, pp. 48–51; Udgaard, p. 87.
84. Molotov to Andvord, Jan. 29, 1945; Anderson to Collier, July 16, 1945; and Collier (Oslo) to Eden, No. 31, July 24, 1945, FO/371/47503. Lie, *Hjemover*, pp. 166–72; Mathisen, pp. 51–53; Østreng, p. 51; Udgaard, pp. 87–88.
85. Sargent to the Chiefs of Staff Committee, Dec. 27, 1944, FO/371/47503. Eden to [Churchill], Jan. 19, 1945, Eden Papers, Pt. 2, FO/954/23.
86. Eden to Collier, No. 16, Jan. 16, 1945; and Eden to Collier, No. 84, Mar. 7, 1945, Eden Papers, Pt. 2, FO/954/23.
87. Collier to Eden, No. 12, Feb. 2, 1945, and the enclosed aide-mémoire, Feb. 1, 1945, FO/371/47506. Udgaard, pp. 88, 89.
88. Udgaard, p. 136; Collier (Oslo) to Eden, No. 31, July 24, 1945, FO/371/47503.
89. Collier (Oslo) to the Foreign Office for Sargent, No. 92, July 4, 1945, FO/371/47503.
90. Minutes by O[rme] Sargent, Mar. 7, 1945, ibid.
91. Ross to the Sec. [of State], Feb. 26, 1947 and Reams to Cumming, Feb. 27, [1947], File 501.BA/2–2647, RG 59, NA.
92. Collier (Oslo) to Hankey, Jan. 24, 1947, FO/371/66021 and Collier (Oslo) to Bevin, No. 107, Apr. 9, 1947, FO/371/66022. Also see Bay (Oslo) to the Sec. of State, No. 845, Apr. 2, 1947, File 501.BA/4–247, RG 59, NA, and Udgaard, p. 293 n. 38.
93. Schoenfeld (London) to the Sec. of State, No. 125, Aug. 9, 1944, File 857.00/8–944, RG 59, NA.

94. Collier (Oslo) to Churchill, No. 5, June 14, 1945, FO/371/47521; Osborne (Oslo) to the Sec. of State, No. 110, June 25, 1945, File 857.00/6–2545, RG 59, NA; Osborne (Oslo) to the Sec. of State, No. 121, July 9, 1945, File 857.00/7–945, ibid.; Lie, *Hjemover*, pp. 127–28; Udgaard, p. 120. It would appear that Lie was also hard pressed at this time in the Labor party, for in May he was dropped from the National Executive, which he had joined in 1926, and was not reelected until September. Udgaard, p. 278 n. 7.

95. Collier (Oslo) to Churchill, No. 10, June 27, 1945, FO/371/47521; Lie, *Hjemover*, p. 218; Udgaard, p. 120.

96. Collier (Oslo) to the Foreign Office, No. 54, June 20, 1945, FO/371/47521; Udgaard, p. 120.

97. Collier (Oslo) to Churchill, No. 10, June 27, 1945, FO/371/47521. Also see Collier (Oslo) to the Foreign Office, No. 54, June 20, 1945, ibid.

98. Osborne (Oslo) to the Sec. of State, No. 53, Aug. 24, 1945, File 857.00/8–2445, RG 59, NA.

99. Udgaard, p. 121.

100. Collier (Oslo) to Bevin, No. 57, Aug. 28, 1945, FO/371/47521; Udgaard, pp. 121–24, 128–29.

101. Osborne (Oslo) to the Sec. of State, No. 535, Oct. 12, 1945, File 857.00/10–1245. RG 59, NA.

102. Collier (Oslo) to the Foreign Office, No. 241, Sept. 8, 1945, FO/371/47905; Roberts (Moscow) to the Foreign Office, No. 4054, Sept. 12, 1945, Collier (Oslo) to the Foreign Office, No. 253, Sept. 13, 1945, Roberts (Moscow) to the Foreign Office, Sept. 16, 1945, FO/371/47513; Lie, *Hjemover*, pp. 222–25; Udgaard, p. 135.

103. Osborne (Oslo) to the Sec. of State, No. 502, Nov. 28, 1945, File 861.415/11–2845, RG 59, NA.

104. Collier (Oslo) to Bevin, No. 149, Nov. 20, 1945, FO/371/47503. Also see Cyrus L. Sulzberger, *A Long Row of Candles; Memoirs and Diaries [1934–1954]* (New York: Macmillan, 1969), pp. 171–72, and the *New York Times* (Nov. 15, 1945), p. 7, and (Nov. 16, 1945), p. 18.

105. Collier (Oslo) to Bevin, No. 149, Nov. 20, 1945, FO/371/47503.

106. Wardrop (Oslo) to Bevin, No. 166, Dec. 7, 1945, FO/371/47503; *FRUS, 1945*, V, pp. 100–108; Udgaard, pp. 138–39.

107. Osborne (Oslo) to the Sec. of State, No. 819, Dec. 27, 1945, File 501.BB/12–2745, RG 59, NA.

108. Osborne (Oslo) to the Sec. of State, No. 601, Dec. 28, 1945, File 857.00/12–2845, RG 59, NA.

109. Udgaard, pp. 195–96.

110. "Trygve Halvdan Lie under Norway in the Report Prepared by the Political Biographic Section of the Department of State for . . ."

111. *The Times* (London) (Dec. 31, 1968), p. 10.

112. [George M. Warr], Monsieur Lie, [Mar. 8, 1946?], FO/371/57053.

113. Noted earlier in this chapter.

114. Collier (Oslo) to Scarlett, Feb. 1, 1950, FO/371/88443.

115. Mathews (Oslo) to the Department of State, No. 612, Mar. 12, 1954, File 857.41/3–1254, RG 59, NA.

116. Minutes by C[ecil] C. Parrott, Feb. 8, 1950, FO/371/88443.

117. Leon Gordenker, *The UN Secretary-General and the Maintenance of Peace* (New York: Columbia University Press, 1967), p. 47. Also see [Stoneman] to [Binder], Nov. 14, 1952, Binder Papers, NLC. Keenleyside, II, pp. 366–67 and Brian Urquhart, *A Life in Peace and War* (New York: Harper and Row, 1987), p. 100.

NOTES TO PAGES 45–46 • 367

118. "Trygve Halvdan Lie under Norway in the Report Prepared by the Political Biographic Section of the Department of State for . . ." For the Foreign Office attitude see this chapter p. ooo. Also see "The Reminiscences of Thanassis Aghnides," p. 418.
119. "Trygve Halvdan Lie under Norway in the Report Prepared by the Political Biographic Section of the Department of State for . . ."
120. Lithgow Osborne, *Mission to Norway* (Auburn: Auburn Publishing Co., 1946), p. 5, and Byron Price, "Memoir" (typescript), Book IV (Section 1), p. 493, Folder 5, Box 5, Price Papers, SHSW.
121. Gordenker, p. 47; Dowling (Vienna) to the Department of State, No. 63, July 10, 1952, File 315/7–1052, RG 59, NA. Also see Lord Gladwyn, *The Memoirs of Lord Gladwyn* (New York: Webright and Talley, 1972), p. 258.
122. [George M. Warr], Monsieur Lie, [Mar. 8, 1946?], FO/371/57053; [Lawford] to Ward, May 10, 1946; and minutes by C[hristopher] F. A. Warner, June 9, [1946], FO/371/57060; "The Reminiscences of Thanassis Aghnides," pp. 419, 422; Sulzberger, p. 650.
123. "The Reminiscences of Thanassis Aghnides," p. 459; Kathleen Teltsch, *Crosscurrents at Turtle Bay* (Chicago: Quadrangle, 1970), p. 39. Also see Urquhart, p. 107.
124. Dowling (Vienna) to the Department of State, No. 63, July 10, 1952, File 315/7–1052, RG 59, NA.
125. "The Reminiscences of Thanassis Aghnides," pp. 418–19, 434; Lord Gladwyn, p. 258.
126. Helm (Tel Aviv) to Furlonge, May 1, 1951 and minutes by Peter Hope, May 9, [1951], FO/371/91717, as well as Jebb (New York) to Mason, Aug. 22, 1951, FO/371/95728. Also see Keenleyside, II, p. 373.
127. Woodward to Connelly, Mar. 6, 1946, Official File, Truman Papers, TL; Hiss to Connor, Mar. 4, 1946, Memo. of Con. (Cordier, Hiss), Mar. 4, 1946, Sweetser to Foote, Mar. 7, 1946, Ross to Stokes, Mar. 12, 1946, File 501/3–746, RG 59, NA; Memo. of Con. (Cordier, Hiss), Mar. 8, 1946, [Memo. of Con.] (Woodward, Spruks, Muir, McClintock), Mar. 18, 1947, Memo. of Con. (Noue, Rusk, Power), Aug. 11, 1947, Power to Rusk, Feb. 24, 1949, Sandifer to Rusk, Feb. 25, 1949, Sandifer to Ingram, Feb. 25, 1949, Power to Ingram, Mar. 1, 1949, Box 112, US Mission UN 1945–49, RG 84, NA; Collier (Oslo) to Warner, July 14, 1947 and minutes by Edgar Light, July 21, [1947] and P[aul] Mason, July 25, [1947], FO/371/66018. The Norwegian Foreign Ministry's Protocol Section held that if the secretary-general were the guest of honor he would rank "second only to the King." However, he would not be treated as the head of a state or government but ranked as an ambassador. Normally, the secretary-general would be ranked below the king, the Storting's president, the prime minister and foreign minister, and foreign ambassadors, but higher than other Norwegian cabinet members and ambassadors to international organizations. Tibbetts (Oslo) to the Sec. of State, No. 862, June 17, 1966, CIA Files.
128. "The Reminiscences of Thanassis Aghnides," p. 427.
129. [George M. Warr], Monsieur Lie, [Mar. 8, 1946?], FO/371/57053.
130. [E. E. Tomkins], The Soviet Attitude at the General Assembly of the United Nations, October–December, 1946, [Dec. 31, 1946?], FO/371/67533.
131. Price, "Memoir," Book IV (Section 1), p. 493; "The Reminiscences of Andrew Cordier" (typescript), p. 334, Oral History Collection, CU; also Stephen M. Schwebel, *The Secretary-General of the United Nations* (Cambridge: Harvard University Press, 1952), p. 54. Also see Keenleyside, II, p. 366 and Urquhart, p. 101.

132. Price, "Memoir," Book IV (Section 1), p. 494.
133. Minutes by [William] D[enis] Allen, Jan. 14, 1946, FO/371/57035; and [Lawford] to Ward, May 10, 1946, as well as minutes by C[hristopher] F. A. Warner, June 9, [1946], FO/371/57060.
134. Walter R. Crocker, *Australian Ambassador* (Melbourne: Melbourne University Press, 1971), pp. 78, 80; Teltsch, p. 40; Price, "Memoir," Book IV (Section 1), pp. 510–11; "The Reminiscences of Thanassis Aghnides," p. 419; "The Reminiscences of Andrew Cordier," p. 334; Keenleyside, II, p. 366; Urquhart, p. 100.
135. Teltsch, p. 40; "The Reminiscences of Thanassis Aghnides," pp. 414–15.
136. Amundsen, pp. 80–86.
137. Crocker, "Memoir about the United Nations," p. 278.
138. Confidential biographic data on Trygve Halvdan Lie, prepared by Winthrop S. Greene of the American embassy in Oslo, Nov. 1, 1945 and Feb. 7, 1946, CIA Files. Also see Keenleyside, II, p. 366; and Urquhart, p. 100.
139. Crocker, "Memoir about the United Nations," p. 278.
140. Teltsch, pp. 38–40.
141. Byron Price to the author, Nov. 7, 1978.
142. Lie, *Cause of Peace*, pp. 70–72; Crocker, *Australian Ambassador*, pp. 73–81; Sulzberger, p. 680; Oscar Schacter to the author, Sept. 20, 1978, and Lord Gladwyn, p. 258.
143. Alexander Cadogan diary, Sat., Mar. 23 [1946], CCL; Teltsch, p. 38; Crocker, *Australian Ambassador*, p. 78; Schwebel, p. 54.
144. Alexander Cadogan diary, Sat., Mar. 23, [1946], CCL; "The Reminiscences of Thanassis Aghnides," p. 445.
145. Collier (Oslo) to Sargent, Nov. 15, 1945, FO/371/47528.
146. Gladwyn Jebb, Report on the Secretariat of the United Nations, Feb. 3, 1947, CAB/134/435, PRO; Lord Gladwyn, p. 258.
147. [Stoneman] to [Binder], May 16 and July 1, 1946 and Nov. 9, 1953, Binder Papers, NLC; Crocker, "Memoir about the United Nations," pp. 278–80; Teltsch, p. 38; Crocker, *Australian Ambassador*, pp. 78–79; Sulzberger, p. 650; also Byron Price to the author, Nov. 7, 1978. Also see Urquhart, p. 100.
148. Gladwyn Jebb, Report on the Secretariat of the United Nations, Feb. 3, 1947, CAB/134/435, PRO. Also see [Lawford] to Ward, May 10, 1946, FO/371/57060.
149. "The Reminiscences of Andrew Cordier," p. 365.
150. Crocker, "Memoir about the United Nations," pp. 284–85. For the contrary view see Urquhart, p. 104.
151. Paul Hasluck, *Diplomatic Witness* (Melbourne: Melbourne University Press, 1980), pp. 265–66, 284.
152. Memo. of Con. (Pelt, Power), Dec. 11, 1949, Box 55, US Mission UN 1945–49, RG 84, NA. Also see Gladwyn Jebb, Memorandum on the State of the Secretariat and Suggestions for its Improvement, Oct. 26, 1946, FO/371/59757.
153. "The Reminiscences of Andrew Cordier," pp. 328–29. Also see Sulzberger, p. 651; and Urquhart, p. 100.
154. Gladwyn Jebb, Report on the Secretariat of the United Nations, Feb. 3, 1947, CAB/134/435, PRO.
155. "The Reminiscences of Andrew Cordier," p. 328.
156. Morton to Evans, Feb. 2, 1950, FO/371/88451.
157. Memo. of Con. (Cordier, Rothwell), May 1, 1946, Box 110, US Mission UN 1945–49, RG 84, NA.

158. Teltsch, p. 51.
159. Crocker, *Australian Ambassador*, p. 79. Also see Urquhart, pp. 103–104.
160. Byron Price to the author, Nov. 7, 1978.
161. "The Reminiscences of Thanassis Aghnides," pp. 422–27, 443; Crocker, *Australian Ambassador*, p. 82; Lie, *Cause of Peace*, p. 48. Also see Gladwyn Jebb, Report on the Secretariat of the United Nations, Feb. 3, 1947, CAB/134/435, PRO; Gladwyn Jebb, Memorandum on the State of the Secretariat and Suggestions for Its Improvement, Oct. 26, 1946, FO/371/59757. Also see Ross to Winslow and Power, June 7, 1949, Box 110, US Mission UN 1945–49, RG 84, NA.
162. Jean Chauvel, *Commentaire d'Alger à Berne (1944–1952)* (Paris: Fayard, 1972), II, p. 227.
163. [Lawford] to Ward, May 10, 1946, FO/371/57060; Gordenker, p. 48; Lord Gladwyn, p. 258; Crocker, *Australian Ambassador*, pp. 80–81; Sulzberger, p. 650. Lie was "quick, rather than profound," it was noted in the Foreign Office. Minutes by C[hristopher] F. A. Warner, June 9, [1946], FO/371/57060; Keenleyside, II, p. 366.
164. Lie, *Cause of Peace*, pp. 39–42. Also see Lie's comments in United Kingdom Delegation (United Nations) to the Foreign Office, No. 274, Mar. 3, 1950, FO/371/88507.
165. Minutes by P[eter] Hope, Apr. 21, 1951, FO/371/91207.
166. James Barros, *Office without Power: Secretary-General Sir Eric Drummond 1919–1933* (Oxford: The Clarendon Press, 1979), pp. 250–53, 401.
167. Lie, *Cause of Peace*, pp. 41–42; Teltsch, p. 41.
168. *Morgenposten* (Feb. 27, 1946) enclosed in American embassy (Oslo) to the Department of State, No. 788, Mar. 1, 1946, File 501.BA/3–146, RG 59, NA.
169. Austin (New York) to the Sec. of State, No. 115, Jan. 31, [1949]; and Jessup (New York) to the Sec. of State, No. 122, Feb. 2, [1949], Box 150, US Mission UN 1945–49, RG 84, NA.
170. Acheson (Washington) to the Sec. of State, No. 1040, Aug. 23, [1946], Box 157, ibid.; Bancroft to Johnson, Sept. 19, 1946, Box 112, ibid.
171. Amundsen, pp. 45–53.
172. [Austin] (New York) to the Sec. of State, No. 972, Dec. 16, [1946], Box 137, US Mission UN 1945–49, RG 84, NA. Also see *Aftenposten* (Dec. 31, 1946), enclosed in American embassy (Oslo) to the Department of State, No. 472, Jan. 10, 1947, File 501/1-1047, RG 59, NA.
173. Lie, *Cause of Peace*, pp. 99–103, 254–63, 280, 301, 319, 428.
174. Alexander Cadogan diary, Wed., Aug. 14, [1946], CCL.
175. [Lie] to [Guinness], June 7, 1946, Guri Lie Zeckendorf Papers, PP.
176. John Hohenberg, *Foreign Correspondence: The Great Reporters and their Times* (New York: Columbia University, 1964), p. 387. Also see [Lie] (Oslo) to [Stoneman], July 12, 1949, Stoneman Papers, Bentley Historical Library, UM.
177. Lie, *Cause of Peace*, pp. 14, 175, 201, 202, 210, 373, 394, 412; "The Reminiscences of Thanassis Aghnides," pp. 419–20; Urquhart, p. 100.
178. Lie (London) to Fosdick, Feb. 15, 1946, Gilchrist to Pelt, Mar. 14, 1946, Fosdick (New York) to Lie, Mar. 25, 1946, Fosdick Papers, PU.
179. Lie to Attlee, Oct. 21, 1949, Dag-1/1.1.2.2–1, UNA.
180. Alexander Cadogan diary, Thurs., Sept. 29, [1949], CCL.
181. Tittmann (Port-au-Prince) to the Sec. of State, No. 269, Feb. 1, 1947, File 033.0038/2–147, RG, NA.
182. Robertson (London) to Pearson, Apr. 14, 1947, vol. 429, Mackenzie King Papers, MG 26, J1, PAC.

183. Memo. of Con. (Lie, Power), Feb. 24, 1949, Box 71, US Mission UN 1945–49, RG 84, NA; and Ross (New York) to the Sec. of State, No. 232, Feb. 25, 1949, File 501.A Summaries/2–2549, RG 59, NA. Also see Lie, *Cause of Peace*, p. 230.

184. Austin (New York) to the Sec. of State, No. 334, Mar. 25, [1948], Box 143, US Mission UN 1945–49, RG 84, NA.

185. See John A. Armstrong, "The Soviet Attitude Toward UNESCO," *International Organization*, 8, no. 2 (Spring 1954): 217–33; Harold K. Jackson, *The USSR and the UN's Economic and Social Activities* (Notre Dame: University of Notre Dame Press, 1963), passim; Alvin Z. Rubinstein, *The Soviets in International Organizations* (Princeton: Princeton University Press, 1964), passim.

186. Lie to Eleanor Roosevelt, Feb. 8, 1946, and [Eleanor Roosevelt] to Lie, Feb. 9, 1946, Box 4563, Eleanor Roosevelt Papers, FDRL.

187. Lie to Malik, Feb. 15, 1949, Cordier Papers, CU; Austin (New York) to the Sec. of State, No. 186, Feb. 15, 1949; and Austin (New York) to the Sec. of State, No. 207, Feb. 18, 1949, Box 150, US Mission UN 1945–49, RG 59, NA. Also see Austin (New York) to the Sec. of State, No. 407, Apr. 9 [1948], Box 144, ibid.

188. Conversation with the Vice Minister for Foreign Affairs of the USSR, Mr. Gromyko, May 13, 1950, and Interview with Generalissimo Stalin, Vice-Minister of State Molotov and Minister of Foreign Affairs Vyshinsky in the Kremlin, May 15, 1950, Box 1, Lie Papers, NMFA. Also see Lie, *Cause of Peace*, pp. 303–304.

189. This chapter, pp. 37–38.

190. Leland M. Goodrich, Edvard Hambro, and Anne Patricia Simons, *Charter of the United Nations: Commentary and Documents*, 3d ed. (New York: Columbia University Press, 1969), pp. 121–22.

191. Memo. of Con. (Kiang, Fabregat, Matienzo, Johnson), June 26, 1948, Box 112; and Jessup (New York) to the Sec. of State, No. 827, June 28, [1948], Box 145, US Mission 1945–49, RG 84, NA.

192. Johnson to Jessup and Ross, June 26, 1948, Box 112, ibid.

193. Marshall to U.S. Mission, No. 444, July 2, 1948, Box 158, ibid.

194. Johnson to Ross, July 14, 1948, Box 110, and Memo. of Con. (Lie, Stoneman, Ross), July 15, 1948, Box 112, ibid.

195. Jessup (New York) to the Sec. of State, No. 914, July 19, [1948], Box 146, ibid.

196. Memo. of Con. (Cordier, Johnson), Aug. 4, 1948, Box 112, ibid.

197. Austin (New York) to the Sec. of State, No. 118, Sept. 13, 1949, File 501.BB/9–1349, RG 59 NA.

198. Calendar notes, Feb. 8, 1946, Box 247, Stettinius Papers, UV.

199. Moore to Cadogan, Feb. 8, 1946; and [Chiefs] O[f] S[taff], 23rd Mtg., Feb. 11, [1946], FO/371/57064.

200. Hollis to Cadogan, Feb. 12, 1946 and Cadogan to Hollis, Feb. 14, 1946, ibid.

201. Comments by the Secretary-General on the Report of the Military Staff Committee, [Feb. 27, 1946?], ibid.

202. Memo. of Con. (Johnson, Hiss), May 10, 1946, File 501.BC/5–1046, RG 59, NA; Stettinius (New York) to the Sec. of State, No. 169, May 11, 1946, File 501.BC/5–1146, ibid.

203. Stettinius (New York) to the Sec. of State, No. 183, May 15, 1946, File 501.BC/5–1546, ibid.; Stettinius (New York) to the Sec. of State, No. 186, May 15, File 501.BC/5–1546, ibid.; United Kingdom Delegation (United Nations) to the Foreign Office, No. 210, May 15, 1946, FO/371/57247.

204. Minutes by J[ohn] G. Ward, May 21, [1946], G[ladwyn] J[ebb], May 21, [1946], P[hilip] N[oel-]B[aker], [May 21, 1946], Ward to the Min. of State, May 21, [1946], and minutes by G[erald] G. Fitzmaurice, (no date), FO371/57247.
205. Foreign Office to the United Kingdom Delegation (United Nations), No. 440, May 22, 1946, ibid.
206. Schwebel, pp. 84–86, 252–53.
207. United Kingdom Delegation (United Nations) to the Foreign Office, No. 29, May 30, 1946, FO/371/59714; and United Kingdom Delegation (United Nations) to the Foreign Office, No. 199, May 10, 1946, FO/371/57247.
208. Minutes by J[ohn] G. Ward, June 12, [1946], FO/371/59714.
209. [Johnson] (New York) to the Sec. of State No. 276, June 4, 1946, Box 135, US Mission UN 1945–49, RG 84, NA.
210. SCOR, 1st Yr., 1st Ser., 44th Mtg., June 6, 1946, pp. 310–11; and 1st Yr., Supp. 2, Annex 1G, p. 41. For Lie's version of the events, see Lie, *Cause of Peace*, pp. 87–88.
211. Lie, *Cause of Peace*, p. 88.
212. UN Doc. S/115, Aug. 1, 1946 (Restricted).
213. SCOR, 1st Yr., 2nd Ser., 53rd Mtg., Aug. 28, 1946, p. 44.
214. United Kingdom Delegation (United Nations) to the Foreign Office, No. 849, Aug. 29, 1946, FO/371/59733.
215. Minutes by J[ohn] H. Peck, Sept. 17, [1946], and W[illiam] E. Beckett, Sept. 18, 1946, ibid.
216. Gore-Booth to Jebb, Sept. 27, 1946, ibid.
217. Jebb to Gore-Booth, Oct. 1, 1946, FO/371/59718.
218. Minutes by J[ohn] H. Peck, Oct. 10, [1946], W[illiam] E. Beckett, Oct. 11, [1946], and Gore-Booth, Oct. 12, [1946], ibid.
219. SCOR, 1st Yr., 2nd Ser., 70th Mtg., Sept. 20, 1946, p. 404.
220. Lawford to Mason, Oct. 3, 1946, FO/371/59719.
221. Minutes by J[ohn] H. Peck, Oct. 24, 1946, P[aul] Mason, Oct. 24, [1946], and W[illiam] E. Beckett, Oct. 26, 1946, ibid.
222. Delegation to the Department, May 8, 1948, FO/371/72734.
223. Minutes by P[aul] Mason, Aug. 23, [1948], and Hector McNeil, [Aug. 23, 1948?], FO/371/72701.
224. [Lawford] to Ward, May 10, 1946, FO/371/57060.
225. Schwebel, pp. 94–95; Joseph P. Lash, *Dag Hammarskjold Custodian of the Brushfire Peace* (New York: Doubleday, 1961), pp. 9–10; Lie, *Cause of Peace*, p. 86.
226. Hasluck, pp. 265, 267. Also see Urquhart, p. 103.
227. Gladwyn Jebb, Report on the Secretariat of the United Nations, Feb. 3, 1947, CAB/134/435, PRO. See Lie's version of the events in Lie, *Cause of Peace*, pp. 39–54.
228. Although the prose is purple and the tone strident, the most succinct description of this hectic period is Crocker, *Australian Ambassador*, pp. 73–82. For the introduction of American managerial concepts see "The Reminiscences of Thanassis Aghnides," p. 413.
229. Thanassis Aghnides to the author, Dec. 4, 1978.
230. A. R. K. MacKenzie, Memorandum on the United Nations' First Year, Sept. 20, 1946, FO/371/59718.
231. Gladwyn Jebb, Memorandum on the State of the Secretariat and Suggestions for Its Improvement, Oct. 26, 1946, FO/371/59757.
232. This chapter, pp. 63–64.
233. Calendar notes, Feb. 8 and 10, 1946, Box 247, Stettinius Papers, UV.

234. Lie, *Cause of Peace*, p. 47. Also see "The Reminiscences of John Hutson" (typescript), pp. 520–24, Oral History Collection, CU; and Urquhart, p. 103.

235. Gladwyn Jebb, Memorandum on the State of the Secretariat and Suggestions for Its Improvement, Oct. 26, 1946, FO/371/59757. On Hutson's failure, also see Byron Price, "Notebooks" (Unnumbered) Feb. 1948–July 1950, p. 1, Folder 2, Box 4, Price Papers, SHSW.

236. Johnson (New York) to the Sec. of State for Austin, No. 23, Jan. 9, 1947, Box 137, US Mission UN 1945–49, RG 84, NA.

237. Chester Bowles, *Promises to Keep; My Years in Public Life 1941–1969* (New York: Harper and Row, 1971), p. 245.

238. Lie, *Cause of Peace*, p. 50; John B. Martin, *Adlai Stevenson of Illinois* (New York: Doubleday, 1976), p. 261; Kenneth S. Davis, *The Politics of Honor: A Biography of Adlai E. Stevenson* (New York: Putnam's Sons, 1967), p. 174; "The Reminiscences of Henry A. Wallace" (typescript), pp. 4580, 4871, Oral History Collection, CU.

239. Price, "Notebooks," pp. 1–3; Price, "Memoir," Book IV (Section 1), pp. 495–97; Lie, *Cause of Peace*, pp. 50–51.

240. Memo. of Con. (Cordier, Rothwell), May 1, 1946, Box 110, US Mission UN 1945–49, RG 84, NA.

241. Perm. United Kingdom Rep. (United Nations) to the Foreign Office, No. 967, Mar. 24, 1947, FO/371/67564.

242. [Gladwyn Jebb], Circular No. 011, Jan. 24, 1947, FO/371/67533.

243. Cabinet Steering Committee on International Organisations, Mar. 4, 1947, FO/371/67563.

244. H[ector] McN[eill], Proceedings of the General Assembly of the United Nations 1947, Dec. [no date], 1947, CAB/129/22, PRO.

245. *New York Times* (Mar. 12, 1947), pp. 1, 12; *New York Herald Tribune* (Mar. 11, 1947), p. 11 and (Mar. 12, 1947), p. 12; [Austin] (New York) to the Sec. of State, No. 225, Mar. 11, 1947, and Austin (New York) to the Sec. of State, No. 230, Mar. 12, [1947], Box 138, US Mission UN 1945–49, RG 84, NA; Cadogan to Jebb, Mar. 24, 1947, FO/371/67485A.

246. Cadogan to Attlee, Apr. 11, 1947, FO/371/67485A. On Lie's lack of administrative abilities see Price, "Notebooks," pp. 4–5.

247. Price, "Notebooks," pp. 5–7.

248. Memo. of Con. (Schachter, Stokes), Dec. 2, 1947, File 501.BA/12–247, RG 59, NA.

249. Lie to Noel-Baker, June 24, 1946, FO/371/59675; [Austin] (New York) to the Sec. of State, No. 225, Mar. 11, 1947, Box 138, US Mission UN 1945–49, RG 84, NA.

250. Barros, *Office without Power*, pp. 60–74 and passim.

251. Gladwyn Jebb, Memorandum on the State of the Secretariat and Suggestions for Its Improvement, Oct. 26, 1946, FO/371/59757.

252. United Kingdom Delegation to the General Assembly (United Nations) to the Foreign Office, No. 1545, Nov. 9, 1946; and Jebb to the Sec. of State, Nov. 8, 1946, ibid.

253. United Kingdom Delegation (New York) to the Foreign Office, No. 1640, Nov. 13, 1946, File 4/741, Noel-Baker Papers, CCL. Also see Bevin's unsigned Memo. of Con., Nov. 9, 1946, Bevin Papers, FO/800/508.

254. Memo. of Con. (Jebb, Raynor), Oct. 20, 1947, Box 71, US Mission UN 1945–49, RG 84, NA.

255. Memo. of Con. (Jebb, Raynor), Nov. 25, 1947, Box 71, ibid.

256. Alexander Cadogan diary, Thurs., Dec. 18, [1947], CCL.

257. Memo. of Con. (Cordier, Power), Dec. 18, 1947, Box 110, US Mission UN 1945–49, RG 84, NA.
258. Alexander Cadogan diary, Mon., Jan. 5, [1948], CCL. Also see Urquhart, p. 116.
259. Hector McNeil, Untitled Memorandum of a Conversation with Trygve Lie, [Feb. 2, 1948?], FO/371/72645.
260. Alexander Cadogan diary, Mon., Jan. 5 [1948], CCL. Also see Crocker, "Memoir about the United Nations," p. 297.
261. United Kingdom Delegation (United Nations) to the Foreign Office, No. 15, Jan. 5, 1948, United Kingdom Delegation (United Nations) to the Foreign Office, No. 31, Jan. 6, 1948, Foreign Office to the United Kingdom Delegation (United Nations), No. 61, Jan. 6, 1948, FO/371/72645.
262. P[aul] Mason, Commander Jackson, Apr. 1, 1948, ibid.
263. Typed minutes to the above by E[dmund] Hall-Patch, Apr. 2, 1948, ibid.
264. R. G. A. Jackson, Note of a Meeting between the Foreign Secretary, the Minister of State and Commander Jackson, Apr. 2, 1948, Hector McNeil, Untitled Memorandum of a Conversation with Trygve Lie, Apr. 3, 1948, ibid.
265. Foreign Office to Washington, No. 466, Apr. 9, 1948, ibid.
266. Cadogan to Hall-Patch, Jan. 12, 1948, ibid. Also see Urquhart, p. 116.
267. Sandifer to Hickerson, Apr. 21, 1948, File 501.AA/4-1448, RG 59, NA.
268. Inverchapel (Washington) to the Foreign Office, No. 155, Apr. 28, 1948, FO/371/72645.
269. Stettinius [London] to the Sec. of State, No. 1304, Feb. 2, 1946, Box 34A, US Mission UN 1945–49, RG 84, NA.
270. Thanassis Aghnides to the author, June 27, 1979; interview with Thanassis Aghnides, Nov. 7, 1980.
271. Salter to Lie [no date] and [Lie] to Salter, Feb. 5, 1946, Guri Lie Zeckendorf Papers, PP.
272. United Nations Conference on International Organization (New York: United Nations Information Organizations, 1945), I, pp. 149–50, 154, 215, 256, 261, 314, 388, 395, 462, 467, 490, 494, 526, 536, 542, 581–82, 591–592, 597, 600, 608, 667; ibid., XII, pp. 309–10, 322–23. For Smuts's comments see ibid., I, p. 461.
273. Thanassis Aghnides to the author, Dec. 3, 1980.
274. For the attitude toward the league, see Crocker, Australian Ambassador, p. 74.
275. Beith (Geneva) to the United Nations Department, Mar. 1, 1951. FO/371/95649.
276. James Barros, Betrayal from Within: Joseph Avenol, Secretary-General of the League of Nations, 1933–1940 (New Haven: Yale University Press, 1969), pp. 198–205.
277. Ibid., p. 257.
278. "The Reminiscences of Thanassis Aghnides," pp. 337–39, 398–400; also, Thanassis Aghnides to the author, Jan. 19, 1979. For Lie's version of Kerno's appointment, see Lie, Cause of Peace, p. 49.
279. Minutes by Roger Allen, Sept. 6 [1948], FO/371/72722.
280. A scribbled marginal note with illegible initials to Eric [Beckett], probably written in early June 1951, FO/371/95615.
281. D[avid] F. Duncan, Assistant Secretaries-General in the United Nations, Sept. 29, [1950], FO/371/88452. Czechoslovakian interviewees in 1953 inferred that Kerno's silence following the communist coup against the Prague government in 1948 until his retirement in 1952, "demonstrated a lack of

moral courage." John M. Littell, Report of Investigation, July 31, 1953, INS Files.

282. Memo. of Con. (Papanek, Ganem, Beer, Auger, Johnson), July 2, 1948, Box 69, US Mission UN 1945–49, RG 84, NA; Memo. of Con. (Kerno, Feller, Ross), Apr. 8, 1949, Box 52, ibid.

283. Lie, Cause of Peace, p. 49.

284. Interview with Thanassis Aghnides, Nov. 7, 1980.

285. "The Reminiscences of Thanassis Aghnides," p. 431; Udgaard, p. 147.

286. [Henry A. Wallace], Korea, Trygve Lie and the Progressive Party from July 6 to 12, 1950, Microfilm Reel 67, Frame Nos. 199–202, Wallace Papers, UI. Soon after Lie's appointment as secretary-general, I "remember being unpleasantly impressed," Lawford of the British mission to the United Nations wrote, "by his attitude towards the Secretary of State [for Foreign Affairs] personally, which was critical and jealous." [Lawford] to Ward, May 10, 1946, FO/371/57060. For Lie's description of Bevin's unionist debating skills and their inappropriateness in United Nations discussions, see Lie, Cause of Peace, pp. 31–32.

287. Roderick Barclay, Ernest Bevin and the Foreign Office 1932–1969 (London: Latimer: the author, 1975), p. 79. Also see Alan Bullock, The Life and Times of Ernest Bevin (London: Heinemann, 1960), II, passim. For Bevin's unconcealed anticommunism see Lie, Cause of Peace, pp. 31–32.

288. [Henry A. Wallace], Korea, Trygve Lie and the Progressive Party from July 6 to 12, 1950, Microfilm Reel 67, Frame Nos. 199–202, Wallace Papers, UI.

289. As Lawford wrote, "you will not have forgotten certain other indications we had of what [Lie] really thought about our country," soon after his appointment as secretary-general. [Lawford] to Ward, May 10, 1946, FO/371/57060. Also see Sulzberger, pp. 409, 680, 716; Bay (Oslo) to the Sec. of State, No. 555, Aug. 11, 1949, File 501/8–1149, RG 59, NA.

290. "The Reminiscences of Thanassis Aghnides," p. 483.

291. Lie, Cause of Peace, pp. 11–12, 13, 14, 21, 261, 412, 413; Udgaard, p. 147.

292. Lie, Med England i ildlinjen, p. 127.

293. Sec. of State for Dominion Affairs to the Sec. of State for External Affairs, Canada, No. 834, Sept. 7, 1946, Vol. 415, Mackenzie King Papers, MG 26, J1, PAC.

294. Dixon (Prague) to the Foreign Office, No. 41, Jan. 27, 1948; and the minutes by J[ohn] H[enniker-Major], Jan. 28, [1948], FO/371/72675.

295. Rubinstein, p. 281 n.

296. Calendar notes, Jan. 31, 1946, Box 247, Stettinius Papers, UV.

297. Calendar notes, Feb. 8, 1946, Box 247, ibid.; Lie, Cause of Peace, pp. 45–46.

298. Gladwyn Jebb, Report on the Secretariat of the United Nations, Feb. 3, 1974, CAB/134/435, PRO; Crocker, "Memoir about the United Nations," p. 287; Department of State Biographic Brief No. 230, Sept. 13, 1954, CIA Files; Urquhart, p. 103.

299. Gladwyn Jebb, Memorandum on the State of the Secretariat and Suggestions for Its Improvement, Oct. 26, 1946, FO/371/59757. Also see Crocker, "Memoir about the United Nations," p. 287.

300. Interview with Byron Theodoropoulos, Dec. 4, 1981.

301. Gladwyn Jebb, Report on the Secretariat of the United Nations, Feb. 3, 1947, CAB/134/435, PRO. See also Crocker, "Memoir about the United Nations," p. 287.

302. Lie, Cause of Peace, p. 46.

303. Memo. of Con. (Biddle, Hall), Oct. 16, 1946, File 501.BD/10–1646, RG 59, NA.
304. "The Reminiscences of Thanassis Aghnides," pp. 428, 429, 443.
305. Gladwyn Jebb, Report on the Secretariat of the United Nations, Feb. 3, 1947, CAB/134/435, PRO.
306. Memo. of Con. (Lie, Power), Feb. 24, 1949, Box 71, US Mission UN 1945–49, RG 84, NA; Ross (New York) to the Sec. of State, No. 232, Feb. 25, 1949, File 501.A Summaries/2–2549, RG 59, NA.
307. Gladwyn Jebb, Report on the Secretariat of the United Nations, Feb. 3, 1947, CAB/13/435, PRO. On Sobolev toeing the Communist party line, see Gladwyn Jebb, Record of Conversation with M. Sobolev, Oct. 31, 1946, FO/371/59793; Memo. of Con. (Tournelle, Maffitt), Jan. 17, 1949, Box 110, US Mission UN 1945–49, RG 84, NA. Also see Crocker, "Memoir about the United Nations," p. 287 and Urquhart, p. 103.
308. Gladwyn Jebb, Memorandum on the State of the Secretariat and Suggestions for Its Improvement, Oct. 26, 1946, FO/371/59757.
309. Johnson (New York) to the Sec. of State, No. 514, Aug. 23, 1946, Box 136, US Mission UN 1945–49, RG 84, NA; Johnson (New York) to the Sec. of State, No. 515, Aug. 23, 1946, File 501.AA/8–2346, RG 59, NA; *FRUS, 1946*, I, p. 436.
310. Perm. United Kingdom Rep. (United Nations) to the Foreign Office, No. 967, Mar. 24, 1947, FO/371/67564. Also see Schwebel, p. 58; and A. R. K. MacKenzie, Memorandum on the United Nations' First Year, Sept. 20, 1946, FO/371/59718.
311. Memo. of Con. (Jebb, Raynor), Oct. 7, 1947, Box 38, US Mission UN 1945–49, RG 84, NA.
312. Goodrich, Hambro, and Simsons, p. 122.
313. Memo. of Con. (Lie, Cordier, Feller, Wainhouse), Nov. 5, 1947, Box 38, US Mission UN 1945–49, RG 84, NA.
314. Memo. of Con. (Cordier, Achilles), Nov. 7, 1947, ibid.; Memo of Con. (Cordier, Noyes), Nov. 8, 1947, Box 39, ibid.
315. Memo. of Con. (Papanek, Ganem, Beer, Auger, Johnson), July 2, 1948, Box 69, ibid.
316. Jessup (New York) to the Sec. of State, No. 777, June 14, 1948, File 501.A Summaries/6–1448, RG 59, NA; Memo. of Con. (Cordier, Power), June 14, 1948, Box 51, US Mission UN 1945–49, RG 84, NA. Also see Ross (New York) to the Sec. of State, No. 232, Feb. 25, 1949, File 501.A Summaries/2–2549, RG 59 NA.
317. Memo. of Con. (Lie, Power), Feb. 24, 1949, Box 71, US Mission UN 1945–49, RG 84, NA; Ross (New York) to the Sec. of State, No. 232, Feb. 25, 1949, File 501.A Summaries/2–2549, RG 59, NA; Memo. of Con. (Cordier, Power), Feb. 28, 1949, Box 111, US Mission UN 1945–49, RG 84, NA.
318. Austin (New York) to the Sec. of State, No. 941, Aug. 17, 1949, File 501.A Summaries/8–1749, RG 59, NA; Memo. of Con. (Lie, Cordier, Austin, Ross, Power), Aug. 17, 1949, Box 53, Austin Papers, UVt.
319. Lyon (Berlin) to the Sec. of State, No. 932, Jan. 17, 1952, File 762A.52/1–1752, RG 59, NA. Sobolev was "'one of our best agents,'" Molotov told Lie when Sobolev was appointed to the Secretariat. Whether Molotov meant this in the sense of an intelligence agent is unclear. Memo. of Con. (Tournelle, Maffitt), Jan. 17, 1949, Box 110, US Mission UN 1945–49, RG 84, NA.
320. Memo. of Con. (Lie, Jessup), Nov. 14, 1951, File 330/11–1451, RG 59, NA.
321. Calendar notes, July 19, 1945, Box 247, Stettinius Paper, UV.

322. Calendar notes, Jan. 31, 1946, Box 247, ibid.
323. Crocker, *Australian Ambassador*, p. 80.
324. [Stoneman] to [Binder], Nov. 14, 1952 and Nov. 9, 1953, NLC; "The Reminiscences of Ernest Gross" (typescript), p. 577, Oral History Collection, CU; "The Reminiscences of Andrew Cordier," p. 301.
325. Ross to Winslow and Power, June 7, 1949, Box 110, US Mission UN 1945–49, RG 84, NA.
326. Crocker, *Australian Ambassador*, pp. 80–81. Also see Stoneman to [Binder], Nov. 14, 1952, Binder Papers. NLC.
327. Meeting of the Executive (American Section) of the Jewish Agency, Sept. 18, 1947, p. 4, File Z5/56, CZAJ.
328. [Stoneman] to [Binder], Nov. 14, 1952, Binder Papers, NLC.
329. Crocker, *Australian Ambassador*, p. 81; Belmont to Ladd, Nov. 14, 1952, FBI Files. There is often a fine line and thus confusion between communist leanings and the "high ideals" that Feller was credited with by one senior Canadian secretariat official. Keenleyside, II, p. 342. Also see Urquhart, p. 123.
330. Feller to the Editor, *Plain Talk*, Oct. 14, 1947, Box 2, Lie Papers, NMFA. Feller's letter appeared in the December issue.
331. Belmont to Ladd, Nov. 13, 1952, and Nichols to Tolson, Nov. 13, 1952, FBI Files.
332. Cadogan to Jebb, Mar. 24, 1947, FO/371/67485A. On Sobolev, also see Price, "Memoir," IV (Section 1), p. 504; for Jebb's comment on Lund, see Gladwyn Jebb, Report on the Secretariat of the United Nations, Feb. 3, 1947, CAB/134/435, PRO.
333. Perm. United Kingdom Rep. (United Nations) to the Foreign Office, No. 967, Mar. 24, 1947, FO/371/67564.
334. When the secretariat was established Elisabeth Poretsky, widow of the important Russian intelligence agent "Ignace Reiss" (who had defected and been murdered in Switzerland by Moscow's gunmen) asked Spaak to assist her in being appointed to the secretariat. Spaak, who had attempted to aid her to escape Moscow's assassins in 1937, thought her chances of being appointed were nil since too many of her "old friends [were] in powerful positions in the Secretariat" and the various missions. Spaak was right, she was not appointed. Elisabeth K. Poretsky, *Our Own People: A Memoir of 'Ignace Reiss' and His Friends* (London: Oxford University Press, 1969), pp. 255–56.

Notes for Chapter 3: Postwar Fissures

1. Sargent to [Churchill], May 9, 1945 and Churchill's scribbled note, May 10, 1945; and O[rme] G. S[argent] to [Churchill], May 10, 1945, Eden Papers, Pt. 2, FO/954/23. Also see Forrest C. Pogue, *The Supreme Command. The United States Army in World War II: The European Theater of Operations* (Washington, D.C.: Government Printing Office, 1954), p. 509.
2. Bevin to Randall, No. 148, Aug. 28, 1945, Bevin Papers, FO/800/500.
3. *FRUS, 1945*, IV, pp. 579–81.
4. Lithgow Osborne, *Mission to Norway* (Auburn: Auburn Publishing Co., 1946), p. 33.
5. Nils M. Udgaard, *Great Power Politics and Norwegian Foreign Policy* (Oslo: Universitetsforlaget, 1973), p. 135.
6. Minutes by [Christopher] Warner, Jan. 30, 1946, FO/371/56106; Foreign Office to Washington, No. 1191, Feb. 5, 1946, FO/371/57211; *FRUS, 1946*, V, p. 390.

On Sweden's uneasiness and suspicions see Mallet (Stockholm) to the Foreign Office, No. 879, May 17, 1945, FO/371/47239; Lee (Gothenburg) to Labouchere, May 23, 1945, FO/188/504; Mallet (Stockholm) to Eden, No. 249, May 26, 1945, FO/371/48045.

7. *FRUS, 1946*, V, p. 392.
8. Ibid., p. 393 n.
9. Lord Gladwyn, *The Memoirs of Lord Gladwyn* (New York: Webright and Talley, 1972), p. 184.
10. Trygve Lie, *In the Cause of Peace* (New York: Macmillan, 1954), p. 75.
11. Record of Con. between the Sec. of State and Mr. Marshall at the United States Embassy in Paris, Oct. 4, 1946, FO/371/73109. On the British assurances see Record of the Informal Meeting held in the Kremlin, Dec. 23, 1945, FO/371/57088; British Delegation (Moscow) to the Foreign Office, No. 142, Dec. 26, 1945, Bevin Papers, FO/800/489; Suggested International Control of Entrances to the Baltic, Dec. 31, 1945, CAB/129/5 PRO; CAB/128/5, Jan. 3, 1946, PRO; Foreign Office to Washington, Nos. 1191 and 1192, Feb. 5, 1946, FO/371/57211; Great Britain, Parliament, *Parliamentary Debates* (Commons), 5th Ser., Vol. 419, Feb. 21, 1946, col. 1356; CAB/128/5, Mar. 13, 1946, PRO.
12. Lord Gladwyn, p. 185; and Brian Urquhart, *A Life in Peace and War* (New York: Harper and Row, 1987), p. 105.
13. Bevin to Roberts, No. 469, Mar. 15, 1946, FO/371/57054; Lie, p. 37.
14. Lord Gladwyn, p. 185.
15. *YUN, 1946–1947*, pp. 327–29; *FRUS, 1946*, VII, pp. 304, 306–12, 314–17, 320–26.
16. Osborne (Oslo) to the Sec. of State, No. 144, Feb. 21, 1946, File 891.00/2–2145, RG 59, NA. Also see Lie, p. 30.
17. Lie, pp. 30, 75.
18. Ibid., pp. 74–76.
19. Edward R. Stettinius, Jr., *The Diaries of Edward R. Stettinius, Jr., 1943–1946*, ed. Thomas W. Campbell and George C. Herring (New York: New Viewpoints, 1975), pp. 460–61.
20. Calendar notes, Mar. 25, 1946, Box 247, Stettinius Papers, UV.
21. *YUN, 1946–1947*, pp. 329–30; *FRUS, 1946*, VII, pp. 381–85.
22. Lie, p. 77.
23. *YUN, 1946–1947*, p. 330–32; *FRUS, 1946*, VII, pp. 381–85, 388–93, 396–98, 402–403, 407–12.
24. Telephone Conversation, Apr. 8, 1946, Box 247, Stettinius Papers, UV.
25. *YUN, 1946–1947*, p. 332; *FRUS, 1946*, VII, pp. 415, 418–19, 421–26.
26. Lie, pp. 79–81.
27. Calendar notes, Apr. 17, 1946, Box 248, Stettinius Papers, UV.
28. Lie, p. 82; [Stoneman] to [Binder] Nov. 14, 1952, Binder Papers, NLC.
29. SCOR, 1st Yr., 1st Ser., 33rd Mtg., Apr. 16, 1946, pp. 143–45.
30. Calendar notes, Apr. 17, 1946, Box 248, Stettinius Papers, UV.
31. Lie, p. 83.
32. *YUN, 1946–1947*, pp. 332–33; *FRUS, 1946*, VII, pp. 427–32.
33. Charles E. Bohlen, *Witness to History 1929–1969* (New York: Norton, 1973), p. 252.
34. *FRUS, 1946*, VII, p. 429 n.
35. Calendar notes, Apr. 17, 1946, Box 248, Stettinius Papers, UV.
36. Stephen M. Schwebel, *The Secretary-General of the United Nations* (Cambridge: Harvard University Press, 1952), p. 94. Also see Lie, p. 85.
37. Bohlen to Stettinius, Apr. 18, 1946, Box 248, Stettinius Papers, UV.

38. *New York Times* (Apr. 20, 1946), pp. 1, 4; Halifax (Washington) to the Foreign Office, No. 2550, Apr. 20, 1946, FO/371/52673. Also see Lie, p. 85.
39. Halifax (Washington) to the Foreign Office, No. 2525, Apr. 20, 1946, FO/371/51607. Among Lie's critics was the *Washington Post*, which "skinned" him, Byrnes informed Stettinius, Calendar notes, Apr. 17, 1946, Box 248, Stettinius Papers, UV.
40. Reiff to Sandifer, Apr. 19, 1946, File 501.BC/4–1946, RG, 59, NA. Also see *FRUS, 1946*, VII, pp. 431–34.
41. Minutes by G[erald] G. Fitzmaurice, Apr. 17, 1946, FO/371/52673.
42. *YUN, 1946–1947*, pp. 333–34, 410; Lie, pp. 84–85.
43. Minutes by J[ohn] G. Ward, Apr. 25, 1946, FO/371/57246.
44. Calendar notes, Apr. 22, 1946, Box 248, Stettinius Papers, UV.
45. *YUN, 1946–1947*, p. 334; *FRUS, 1946*, VII, pp. 435–37.
46. Ward to [Lawford], Apr. 30, 1946, FO/371/57058.
47. Hall to Ward, May 2, 1946, FO/371/57246.
48. [Lawford] to Ward, May 10, 1946, FO/371/57060.
49. Minutes by J[ohn] G. Ward, May 23, [1946], Gladwyn Jebb, May 25, [1946], G[eorge] M. Warr, May 28, [1946], C[hristopher] F. A. Warner, June 9, [1946], P[aul] Mason, May 31 [1946], E[dmund] Hall-Patch, June 23, [1946], ibid.
50. Stettinius (New York) to the Sec. of State, No. 130, May 1, 1946, Box 135, US Mission UN 1945–49, RG 84, NA; United Kingdom Delegation (United Nations) to the Foreign Office, No. 158, May 1, 1946, and United Kingdom Delegation (United Nations) to the Foreign Office, No. 168, May 5, 1946, FO/371/52674.
51. Minutes by J[ohn] G. Ward, May 3 [1946] and May 7, 1946, FO/371/52674.
52. Foreign Office to the United Kingdom Delegation (United Nations), No. 19, May 4, 1946, ibid.
53. Foreign Office to the United Kingdom Delegation (United Nations), No. 284, May 4, 1946, ibid.
54. United Kingdom Delegation (United Nations) to the Foreign Office, No. 168, May 5, 1946, ibid.
55. Minutes by P[hilip] N[oel-] B[aker], May 16, 1946, FO/371/57060.
56. Calendar notes May 3 and 4, 1946, Box 248, Stettinius Papers, UV; United Kingdom Delegation (United Nations) to the Foreign Office, No. 166, May 4, 1946, FO/371/52674; *FRUS, 1946*, VII, pp. 445–46.
57. *YUN, 1946–1947*, pp. 334–35; *FRUS, 1946*, VII, pp. 450–53, 456–57.
58. [Stettinius] (New York) to the Sec. of State, No. 206, May 20, 1946, Box 135, US Mission UN 1945–49, RG 84, NA; Stettinius (New York) to the Sec. of State, No. 207, May 20, 1946, File 501.BC/5–2056, RG 59, NA.
59. Alexander Cadogan diary, Wed., May 22, [1946], CCL. Also see *YUN, 1946–1947*, p. 335; *FRUS, 1946*, VII, pp. 473–77.
60. Foreign Office to the United Kingdom Delegation (United Nations), No. 477, May 27, 1946, FO/371/52677.
61. Memo. of Con. (Lie, Cohen), June 4, 1946, File, 501/6-446, RG 59, NA.
62. Lie, p. 33.
63. *YUN, 1946–1947*, pp. 345–46.
64. [Lawford] to Ward, May 10, 1946, FO/371/57060.
65. *YUN, 1946–1947*, p. 346.
66. Calendar notes, Apr. 26, 1946, Box 248, Stettinius Papers, UV; Stettinius (New York) to the Sec. of State for Acheson, No. 199, Apr. 28, 1946, File 501.BC/4-2846, RG 59, NA.

67. Stettinius (New York) to the Sec. of State for Acheson, No. 120, Apr. 28, 1946, File 501.BC/4–2846, RG 59, NA. On Argentina's loan see the *New York Times* (Apr. 27, 1946), p. 6.
68. *YUN, 1946–1947*, pp. 346–48.
69. Stettinius (New York) to the Sec. of State, No. 196, May 17, 1946, Box 135, US Mission UN 1945–49, RG 84, NA.
70. Stapleton to Hoyer Millar, May 19, 1946, FO/371/60358.
71. Memo. of Con. (Lie, Cohen), June 4, 1946, File 501/6-446, RG 59, NA.
72. Johnson (New York) to the Sec. of State for Matthews, No. 278, June 5, 1946, File 501.BC Spain/6–546, ibid.; and Johnson (New York) to the Sec. of State, No. 280, June 5, 1946, File 501.BC/6–546, ibid.
73. Stettinius (San Francisco) to the President, May 23, 1945, President's Secretary File, Truman Papers, TL. Also see Urquhart, p. 117.
74. Abba Eban, *Abba Eban: An Autobiography* (New York: Random House, 1977), p. 91. Also see Cyrus L. Sulzberger, *A Long Row of Candles; Memoirs and Diaries [1934–1954]* (New York: Macmillan, 1969), p. 427 and Urquhart, p. 117.
75. [Dening] to Machtig, May 25, 1948, Sargent Papers, FO/800/277.
76. See Sulzberhger, p. 427.
77. *YUN, 1946–1947*, pp. 348–51.
78. Johnson (New York) to the Sec. of State, No. 330, June 18, 1946, File 501.BC/ 6–1846, RG 59, NA.
79. *YUN, 1946–1947*, p. 351.
80. Alexander Cadogan diary, Wed., Aug. 14, [1946], CCL.
81. GAOR, 35th Plen. Mtg., Oct. 24, 1946, p. 700.
82. Memo. of Con. (Lie, Sobolev, Shawcross, Lopez, Stevenson), Nov. 19, 1946, Box 37, US Mission UN 1945–49, RG 84, NA; Austin (New York) to the Sec. of State, No. 829, Nov. 20, [1946], File 501.BB Summaries/11–2046, RG 59, NA.
83. [Austin] (New York) to the Sec. of State, No. 705, Oct. 24, 1946, File 501.BB Summaries/10–2446, RG 59, NA; United Kingdom Delegation (United Nations) to the Foreign Office, No. 1306, Oct. 25, 1946, FO/371/60364.
84. Minutes by John Wilson, Oct. 30, 1946, and William Hogg, Oct. 31, [1946], FO/ 371/60364.
85. Bonsal (Madrid) to the Sec. of State, No. 1565, Oct. 25, 1946, File 852.00/ 10–2546, Bonsal (Madrid) to the Sec. of States, No. 1572, Oct. 26, 1946, File 852.00/10–2646, and Bonsal (Madrid) to the Sec. of State, No. 3064, Nov. 1, 1946, File 852.00/11–146, RG 59, NA. Foreign Office to the United Kingdom Delegation (United Nations), No. 1708, Oct. 29, 1946, File 4/738, Noel-Baker Papers, CCL; Mallet (Madrid) to the Foreign Office, No. 835, Nov. 1, 1946, FO/ 371/60365.
86. Randall (Copenhagen) to the Foreign Office, No. 307, Oct. 29, 1946, FO/371/ 60364.
87. Mallet (Madrid) to Harvey, Oct. 25, 1946, FO/371/60365.
88. [Hoyer Millar] to Harvey, Oct. 28, 1946, ibid.
89. Minutes by John Wilson, Oct. 31, [1946], ibid.
90. Mallet (Madrid) to the Foreign Office, No. 824, Oct. 28, 1946, ibid.
91. Minutes by Hoyer Millar, Nov. 1, 1946, J[ohn] H. Peck, Nov. 5, 1946, Hoyer Millar, Nov. 6, 1946, and G[eorge] M. Warr, Nov. 8, [1946], ibid.
92. *YUN, 1946–1947*, pp. 126, 351; *FRUS, 1946*, V, p. 1078.
93. Jebb to the Sec. of State, Nov. 8, 1946, FO/371/59757.
94. Austin (New York) to the Sec. of State, No. 785, Nov. 9, 1946, File 501.BB

Summaries/11–946, RG 59, NA; Memo. of Con. (Lie, Stevenson), Nov. 9, 1946, Box 37, US Mission UN 1945–49, RG 84, NA. See the extract from the letter of Hoyer Millar to Harvey, Nov. 13, [1946], FO/371/60364.

95. [Austin] (New York) to the Sec. of State, No. 808, Nov. 14, [1946], File 501.BB Summaries/11–1446, RG, 59, NA; *New York Times* (Nov. 15, 1946), p. 10.

96. Memo. of Con. (Lie, Sobolev, Shawcross, Lopez, Stevenson), Nov. 19, 1946, Box 37, US Mission UN 1945–49, RG 84, NA; Austin (New York) to the Sec. of State, No. 829, Nov. 20, 1946, File 501.BB Summaries/11–2046, RG 59, NA.

97. [Bay] (Oslo) to the Sec. of State, No. 699, Nov. 19, 1946, File 501/11–1946, RG 59, NA.

98. Austin [New York] to the Sec. of State, No. 803, Nov. 13, 1946, Box 136, US Mission UN 1945–49, RG 84, NA; William Dawson, Memo. (Hohenberg's Article in *New York Post*, Nov. 12, . . . and Article in same paper, Nov. 13, . . .), Nov. 13, 1946, Box 37, ibid.

99. Austin (New York) to the Sec. of State, No. 820, Nov. 18 [1946], Box 136, ibid. Also see Belt's speech GAOR, 41st Plen. Mtg., Oct. 29, 1946, p. 830; and Dodds (Havana) to the United Kingdom Delegation (United Nations), No. 1, Oct. 30, 1946, FO/371/60365.

100. Austin (New York) to the Sec. of State, No. 836, Nov. 21, [1946], Box 136, US Mission UN 1945–49, RG 84, NA.

101. *YUN, 1946–1947*, pp. 126–28.

102. Austin (New York) to the Sec. of State, No. 946, Dec. 7 and 8, 1946, File 501.BB Summaries/12–746, RG 59, NA.

103. *YUN, 1946–1947*, pp. 128–30; *FRUS, 1946*, V, pp. 1081–82.

104. Perm. United Kingdom Rep. (United Nations) to the Foreign Office, No. 2714, Dec. 20, 1946, FO/371/60371.

105. Minutes by R. K. W. Sloan, Dec. 23, [1946], ibid.

106. Byron Price, "Memoir" (typescript), Book IV (Section 1), p. 498, Folder 5, Box 5, Price Papers, SHSW.

107. Inverchapel (Washington) to the Foreign Office, No. 2989, May 20, 1947, FO/371/67868, PRO.

108. Roger E. Sanders, *Spain and the United Nations 1945–1950* (New York: Vantage Press, 1966), p. 64; *YUN, 1946–1947*, p. 130.

109. [Austin] (New York) to the Sec. of State, No. 405, Apr. 30 [1947], Box 138, US Mission UN 1945–49, RG 84, NA.

110. Inverchapel (Washington) to the Foreign Office, No. 3270, June 5, 1947, and the attached minutes by W[illiam] Hogg, June 6, 1947, and Gladwyn Jebb, June 10, 1947, FO/371/67868.

111. UN Doc. A/315, July 14, 1947. Also see Perm. United Kingdom Rep. (United Nations) to the Foreign Office, No. 2266, Aug. 16, 1947, FO/371/67870.

112. *YUN, 1947–1948*, pp. 47–52.

113. *FRUS, 1948*, III, p. 1027.

114. Lie to Gerhardsen, Apr. 5, 1948, Box 2, Lie Papers, NMFA.

115. Bay (Oslo) to the Sec. of State, No. 555, Aug. 11, 1949, File 501/8–1149, RG 59, NA; Austin (New York) to the Sec. of State, No. 941, Aug. 17, 1949, File 501.A Summaries/8–1749, ibid.; Memo. of Con. (Lie, Cordier, Austin, Ross, Power), Aug. 17, 1949, Box 53, Austin Papers, UVt; Ross (New York) to the Sec. of State, No. 1006, Aug. 27, 1949, Box 153, US Mission UN 1945–49, RG 84, NA.

116. Austin (New York) to the Sec. of State, Ross to Sandifer, No. 1074, Sept. 8, 1949, File 501.BB/9–849, RG 59, NA.

117. Meade (Washington) to Parrott, Mar. 30, 1950, FO/371/88619. Also see Lie's comments to Acheson on Jan. 21, 1950, in an untitled memorandum of conversation dated Jan. 23, 1950, Box 1, Lie Papers, NMFA, as well as *FRUS, 1950*, II, p. 227.
118. Sanders, p. 99.
119. Ibid., pp. 105–106.

Notes for Chapter 4: War by Other Means

1. Trygve Lie, *In the Cause of Peace* (New York: Macmillan, 1954), pp. 31–33; Edward R. Stettinius, Jr., *The Diaries of Edward R. Stettinius, Jr., 1943–1946,* ed. Thomas W. Campbell and George W. Herring (New York: New Viewpoints, 1975), p. 453; Record of the Secret Session . . . of the Security Council, Tuesday, Feb. 5, 1946 . . . , Box 247, Stettinius Papers, UV; *YUN, 1946–1947,* pp. 336–38. Also see *FRUS, 1946,* VII, pp. 99, 104–15.
2. *YUN, 1946–1947,* pp. 351–60.
3. See Chapter 2, pp. 57–58.
4. Cadogan to Jebb, May 27, 1948, FO/371/72676.
5. *FRUS, 1946,* VII, pp. 219–20.
6. Ibid., pp. 267–68.
7. *YUN, 1946–1947,* pp. 361–62.
8. Byrnes to Johnson, Dec. 20, 1946, File 868.00/12–2046, RG 59, NA.
9. Johnson (New York) to Byrnes, Dec. 21, 1946, File 501.BC Greece/12–2146, ibid. Also see Edgar F. Puryear, Jr., *Communist Negotiating Techniques: A Case Study of the United Nations Security Council Commission of Investigation Concerning the Greek Frontier Incidents* (Ann Arbor: University Microfilms, 1961), p. 169, and the *New York Times* (April 3, 1947), p. 4, as well as H.M. Consul General (Salonika) to the Foreign Office, No. 108, Mar. 12, 1947, FO/371/61858.
10. [Lawford] to Mason, Jan. 10, 1947, FO/371/66996.
11. Minutes by D[aniel] J. McCarthy, Feb. 13, 1947, FO/371/67602.
12. Mason to Lawford, Feb. 19, 1947, FO/371/66996. On the Australian dubbing of Gottesman see Alexis Kyrou, *Dreams and Reality: Years of Diplomatic Life (1923–1953)* [in Greek] (Athens, 1972), p. 271.
13. Kyrou, p. 271; interview with Byron Theodoropoulos, Dec. 4, 1981.
14. Ethridge to Baxter, Sept. 26, 1947, attached to C[yril] E. Black, Memo. (Appraisal of the United Nations Secretariat Attached to the Balkan Commission), July 21, 1947, Box 68, US Mission UN 1945–49, RG 84, NA. It would appear that the secretariat also seconded into their ranks Greek communists, whom they hired as local employees of the commission. Kyrou, p. 271.
15. George to Reilly, Mar. 20, 1947, FO/371/67065. For Canadian complaints about Ryan's reporting see Canadian Consulate General (New York) to the Sec. of State for External Affairs, No. 1271, Oct. 9, 1947, Asdel Telegrams, Pt. 1, Vol. 1056, RG 25, F6, PAC.
16. [LaFleche] to the Sec. of State for External Affairs, Feb. 26, 1947, FO/371/67065.
17. Memo. from the Greek embassy to the Department of State, May 5, 1947, File 501.BA/5–547, RG 59, NA.
18. Once he retired from the secretariat, the United States Immigration and Naturalization Service proscribed Ryan's entry into the country as an "undesirable person" under provisions of the Immigration and Nationality Act. Letter to Lega[l] at[taché] (Ottawa) re Stanley Ryan, [autumn 1968], FBI Files.

19. Norton (Athens) to the Foreign Office, No. 358, Feb. 11, 1947, FO/371/67062; Puryear, pp. 182–83.
20. Dendramis to the Secretary-General, Feb. 7, 1947, SCOR, 2nd Yr., Supp. 4, Annex 10, pp. 52–54. The British commissioner pointed out that the commission secretariat had "shown favorable inclinations towards EAM and the left; and criticism of the middle and right . . . [and had] started the business of asking the Greek Govt to stay executions on its own, without informing all the commissioners." Gallman (London) to the Sec. of State, No. 1194, Feb. 21, 1947, File 501.BC Greece/2–2147, RG 59, NA.
21. Norton (Athens) to the Foreign Office, No. 317, Feb. 27, 1947, FO/371/66999. Also see Lund to the Secretary-General, Feb. 6, 1947, SCOR, 2nd Yr., Supp. 4, Annex 9, pp. 51–52.
22. FRUS, 1947, V, pp. 817–18. Also see MacVeagh (Athens) to the Sec. of State, No. 168, Feb. 7, 1947, File 501.BC Greece/2–747 RG 59, NA.
23. FRUS, 1947, pp. 818–20.
24. See Dendramis's two letters to Lie, Feb. 9, 1947, SCOR, 2nd Yr., 100th Mtg., Feb. 10, 1947, pp. 180–82.
25. Foreign Office to Athens, No. 364, Feb. 15, 1947, FO/371/67075.
26. Norton (Athens) to the Foreign Office, No. 434, Feb. 19, 1947, ibid.
27. Ethridge to Baxter, Sept. 26, 1947 attached to C[yril] E. Black, Memo. (Appraisal of the United Nations Secretariat Attached to the Balkan Commission), July 21, 1947, Box 68, US Mission UN 1945–49, RG 84, NA. Also see H.M. Majesty's Consul-General (Salonika) to Athens, No. 88, Feb. 26, 1947, Foreign Office to Salonika, No. 64, Mar. 3, 1947, and H.M. Majesty's Consul-General (Salonika) to the Foreign Office, No. 75, Mar. 5, 1947, FO/371/67075, as well as H.M. Consul General (Salonika) to the Foreign Office, No. 63, Mar. 1, 1947, FO/371/67062. Also see Gibson (Salonika) to the Sec. of State, No. 11, Feb. 28, 1947, File 501.BC Greece /2–2647, RG 59, NA.
28. Gibson (Salonika) to the Sec. of State, No. 12, Mar. 6, 1947, File 501.BC Greece/3–647, RG 59, NA. Also see H.M. Majesty's Consul-General (Salonika) to the Foreign Office, No. 63, Mar. 1, 1947, FO/371/67062.
29. H.M. Majesty's Consul-General (Salonika) to the Foreign Office, No. 63, Mar. 1, 1947, FO/371/67062.
30. Ethridge to Baxter, Sept. 26, 1947 attached to C[yril] E. Black, Memo. (Appraisal of the United Nations Secretariat Attached to the Balkan Commission), July 21, 1947, Box 68, US Mission UN 1945–49, RG 84, NA.
31. H.M. Majesty's Consul-General (Salonika) to the Foreign Office, No. 63, Mar. 1, 1947, FO/371/67062.
32. C[yril] E. Black, Memo. (Appraisal of the United Nations Secretariat Attached to the Balkan Commission), July 21, 1947, Box 68, US Mission UN 1945–49, RG 84, NA.
33. Porter (Geneva) to the Sec. of State, Dec. 15, 1948, File 111.20A/12–1548, RG 59, NA.
34. D[avid] P. Aiers, Fifth Session of E.C.C., Apr. 27, 1950, FO/371/87347.
35. Matthews (Stockholm) to the Sec. of State, No. 805, Aug. 12, 1949, File 501/8–1249, RG 59, NA.
36. Berthoud to Beith, Jan. 18, 1950, FO/371/87346.
37. To say, wrote the head of the Economic Department, that Myrdal was "prone to wishful thinking on East-West liaison [was] an understatement: he wants to prove to himself that the principal stumbling block is not in the East." Minutes by R[oger] S[tevens], Jan. 5, [1948], FO/371/68866.

38. Porter (Geneva) to the Sec. of State, Dec. 15, 1948, File 111.20A/12–1548, RG 59, NA. On the shared British view, see Beith to Berthoud, Jan. 19, 1950, FO/371/87346.
39. Extract from Record of Conversation between Mr. Hector McNeil and Trygve Lie, late Jan. or early Feb. 1948, ibid.
40. Hickerson to Thorp and Rusk, Feb. 25, 1948, File 501.BD Europe/2–2548, RG 59, NA.
41. McNeil to Cadogan, Mar. 4, 1948, FO/371/71779.
42. Cadogan to McNeil, Mar. 12, 1948, ibid.
43. Lie, p. 104.
44. Byron Price, "Memoir" (typescript), Book IV (Section 1), pp. 498–99, Folder 5, Box 5, Price Papers, SHSW.
45. Lie, p. 104.
46. George T. Mazuzan, *Warren R. Austin at the U.N. 1946–1953* (Kent, Ohio: Kent State University Press, 1977), pp. 71–72.
47. Stephen G. Xydis, "The Truman Doctrine in Prospective," *Balkan Studies*, 8, no. 2 (1967): 253. Also see Dean Acheson's testimony in U.S. Congress, Senate, Committee on Foreign Relations, *Executive Sessions of the Senate Foreign Relations Committee*, 81st Congress, 1st and 2nd Sessions, 1949–1950 (Washington, D.C.: Government Printing Office, 1976), II, pp. 9–13; Joseph M. Jones, *The Fifteen Weeks* (New York: Viking Press, 1955), p. 160; James Barros, "Alger Hiss and Harry Dexter White: The Canadian Connection," *Orbis*, 21, no. 3 (Fall 1977): 593–605; Allen Weinstein, *Perjury: The Hiss Chambers Case* (New York: Alfred A. Knopf, 1978), p. 368; H. Montgomery Hyde, *The Atom Bomb Spies* (London: Hamilton, 1980), p. 33.
48. [Wrong] to Pearson, Mar. 17, 1947, Vol. 3, Pearson Papers, MG 26, N1, PAC.
49. [Mayhew] to McNeil, Mar. 17, 1947, FO/371/67509A.
50. Minutes by E[dward] E. Tomkins, Mar. 29, [1947] and D[aniel] J. McCarthy, Apr. 14, [1947], ibid.
51. Ross to Rusk, Mar. 19, 1947, File 868.00/3–1347, RG 59, NA.
52. Questions posed by Vandenberg to Acheson, Mar. 20, 1947; and Acheson's answers Mar. 28, 1947, File 868.00/3–2047, ibid.
53. SCOR, 2nd Yr., 123rd Mtg., Mar. 28, 1947, pp. 617–24.
54. [Austin] (New York) to the Sec. of State, No. 290, Mar. 26, [1947], Box 138, US Mission UN 1945–49, RG 84, NA; and the *New York Times* (Apr. 1, 1947), p. 12.
55. SCOR, 2nd Yr., 126th Mtg., Apr. 7, 1947, pp. 697–702.
56. Ibid., 122nd Mtg., Mar. 25, 1947, pp. 610–11.
57. Ibid., Supp. 12, Annexes 34 and 35, pp. 130–32.
58. Perm. United Kingdom Rep. (United Nations) to the Foreign Office, No. 1029, Mar. 27, 1947, FO/371/67064.
59. Foreign Office to the Perm. United Kingdom Rep. (United Nations), No. 1015, Mar. 28, 1947, ibid.
60. Austin (New York) to the Sec. of State, No. 338, Apr. 10, 1947, File 501.BC/4–1047, RG 59, NA.
61. Alexander Cadogan diary, Wed., Apr. 16, [1947], CCL.
62. Alexander Cadogan diary, Thurs., Apr. 17, [1947], ibid.
63. [Austin] (New York) to the Sec. of State, No. 290, Mar. 26, [1947], Box 138, US Mission UN 1945–49, RG 84, NA. Also see Bay (Oslo) to the Sec. of State, No. 842, Apr. 2, 1947, File 501.BA/4–247, RG 59, NA.
64. Patterson to Austin, Mar. 29, 1947, File 501.BC Greece/3–2947, RG 59, NA.

65. [Austin] (New York) to the Sec. of State, No. 310, Apr. 2, [1947], Box 138, US Mission UN 1945–49, RG 84, NA.
66. Rusk to Acheson, Mar. 31, 1947, File 501.BC Greece/3-3147, RG 59, NA.
67. Acheson to Geneva for Ethridge, No. 91, Apr. 3, 1947, File 501.BC Greece/4–347, ibid.
68. Troutman from Ethridge (Geneva) to the Sec. of State, No. 93, Apr. 7, 1947, File 501.BC Greece/4–747, ibid.
69. Perm. United Kingdom Rep. (United Nations) to the Foreign Office, No. 1069 Apr. 1, 1947, FO/371/67064. Also see the minutes by E[dward] E. Tomkins, Apr. 24, 1947, FO/371/67585.
70. The United Nations Commission in Greece [meeting in Sir Orme Sargent's room at 11 A.M. on Apr. 11, 1947], FO/371/67065.
71. Acheson (Washington) to Athens, No. 351, Mar. 22, 1947, File 501.BC Greece/3–2247, RG 59, NA.
72. Norton (Athens) to the Foreign Office, No. 739, Mar. 30, 1947, FO/371/67064.
73. Perm. United Kingdom Rep. (United Nations) to the Foreign Office, No. 1069, Apr. 1, 1947, ibid.
74. Austin (New York) to the Sec. of State, No. 327, Apr. 8, 1947, File 501.BA/4–847, RG 59, NA. Also see Austin (New York) to the Sec. of State, No. 328, Apr. 8, [1947], Box 138, US Mission UN 1945–49, RG 84, NA.
75. Perm. United Kingdom Rep. (United Nations) to the Foreign Office, No. 1118, Apr. 8, 1947, FO/371/67065. Also see Alexander Cadogan diary, Mon., Apr. 7, [1947], CCL.
76. Minutes by D[aniel] J. McCarthy, Apr. 10, [1947], FO/371/67065.
77. Austin (New York) to the Sec. of State, No. 327, Apr. 8, 1947, File 501.BA/4–847, RG 59, NA. Also see Austin (New York) to the Sec. of State, No. 328, Apr. 8, [1947], Box 138, US Mission UN 1945–49, RG 84, NA.
78. Acheson to New York, No. 137, Apr. 9, 1947, File 501.BC/4–947, RG 59, NA. Also see this chapter p. 101.
79. [Austin] (New York) to the Sec. of State, No. 333, Apr. 9, [1947], Box 138, UN Mission UN 1945–49, RG 84, NA.
80. Acheson to Geneva for Ethridge, No. 126, Apr. 11, 1947, File 501.BC Greece/4–1147, RG 59, NA.
81. Acheson to Geneva for Ethridge, No. 134, Apr. 12, 1947, File 501.BC Greece/4–1247, ibid.
82. Chancery, British Embassy (Athens) to the Southern Department, May 3, 1947, FO/371/67066.
83. Aide-mémoire by the Permanent Greek Delegation to the United Nations, Apr. 12, 1947, Box 3, Lie Papers, NMFA.
84. Minutes by D[aniel] J. McCarthy, May 12, [1947], FO/371/67066.
85. When Lie queried about Lund, Kyrou replied that he preferred to forget the unpleasant past but that Lie knew that the commission secretariat had not behaved like Caesar's wife. Kyrou, p. 271 n.
86. [William Stoneman], Summary of Report on the Balkans Commission, Apr. 22, 1947, Box 3, Lie Papers, NMFA.
87. Austin (New York) to the Sec. of State, No. 383, Apr. 23, [1947], and [Austin] (New York) to the Sec. of State, No. 384, Apr. 23, [1947], Box 138, US Mission UN 1945–49, RG 84, NA.
88. Clutton (New York) to Mason, Aug. 7, 1947, and Mason (London) to Lawford, Sept. 11, 1947, FO/371/67590B.
89. YUN, 1946–1947, pp. 365–75.

90. Ibid., *1947–1948*, pp. 337–52.
91. Perm. United Kingdom Rep. (United Nations) to the Foreign Office, No. 117, Aug. 14, 1947, FO/371/67072; Weekly Political Intelligence Summary, No. 405 (Aug. 27, 1947), FO/370/1441. See pp. 57–58, 93.
92. Julian Huxley, *Memories* (London: Allen and Unwin, 1973), II, p. 37.
93. *YUN, 1947–1948*, pp. 63–75.
94. Memo. of Con. (Kyrou, Noyes), Nov. 1, 1947; and Memo. of Con. (Kyrou, Raynor), Nov. 5, 1947, Box 50, US Mission UN 1945–49, RG 84, NA.
95. United Kindgom Delegation (United Nations) to the Foreign Office, No. 3182, Nov. 3, 1947, FO/371/67074. For Lie's attitude toward Aglion see Memo. of Con. (Lie, Drew, Ross, Power), June 15, 1949, Box 57, US Mission UN 1945–49, RG 84, NA.
96. Memo. of Con. (Jebb, Beckett, Gore-Booth, Rusk, Sandifer, Raynor), Nov. 3, 1947, Box 50, US Mission UN 1945–49, RG 84, NA.
97. Memo. of Con. (Lawford, Noyes), Nov. 6, 1947, Box 50, ibid.
98. Memo. of Con. (Cordier, Achilles), Nov. 7, 1947, Box 57, ibid. Also see the *New York Times* (Nov. 8, 1947), p. 6.
99. *YUN, 1948–1949*, p. 238.
100. Memo. of Con. (Gouras, Baxter), June 17, 1948, File 501.BB Balkan/6–1748, RG 59, NA.
101. Gibson (Salonika) to the Sec. of State, No. 472, June 23, 1948, File 501.BB Balkan/6–2348, ibid.
102. *YUN, 1948–1949*, p. 244.
103. Geoffrey A. Wallinger, Greece at the General Assembly, Dec. 3, 1948, FO/371/72365; Kylie Tennant, *Evatt: Politics and Justice* (Sydney: Angus and Robertson Ltd., 1970), p. 233.
104. Marshall (Paris) to the Sec. of State, No. 786, Nov. 16, 1948, Box 149, US Mission UN 1945–49, RG 84, NA; Memo. of Con. (Kyrou, Drew, Howard), Nov. 14, 1948, Box 43, ibid. Also see [Harry N. Howard], An Attempt at Conciliation between Greece and Albania, Bulgaria and Yugoslavia, [Jan. 1949?], Box 80, ibid.
105. Memo. of Con. (Lie, Cordier, Power), Feb. 23, 1949, Box 52, ibid.
106. Wallinger to the Min. of State, Nov. 16, 1948, FO/371/72365.
107. Memo. of Con. (Sarper, Wainhouse), Dec. 3, 1948, Box 56, US Mission UN 1945–49, RG 84, NA.
108. Memo. of Con. (Sarper, Howard), Apr. 28, 1949, Box 52, ibid.
109. Memo. of Con. (Gouras, Baxter), May 4, 1949, File 501.BB Balkan/5–449, RG 59, NA.
110. Minor (Athens) to the Sec. of State, No. 865, May 2, 1949, File 501.BB Balkan/5–249, ibid.; Acheson (Washington) to New York, No. 244, May 3, 1949, File 501.BB Balkan/5–349, ibid. Also see [Harry N. Howard], Greece: The Evatt Conciliation Discussions, May 27, 1949, Box 80, US Mission UN 1945–49, RG 84, NA.
111. Austin (New York) to the Sec. of State, No. 559, May 4, 1949, File 501.BB Balkan/5–449, RG 59, NA. Also see [Harry N. Howard], Greece: The Evatt Conciliation Discussions, May 27, 1949, Box 80, US Mission UN 1945–49, RG 84, NA.
112. Memo. of Con. (Howard, Baxter), May 9, 1949, File 501.BB Balkan/5–949, RG 59, NA.
113. Memo. of Con. (Lie, Drew, Ross, Power), June 15, 1949, Box 57, US Mission UN 1945–49, RG 84, NA.

114. Power to Austin, May 23, 1949, Box 80, ibid.
115. [Harry N. Howard], Greece: The Evatt Conciliation Discussions, May 27, 1949, Box 80, ibid. Also see *FRUS, 1949*, VI, pp. 321–22.
116. *European Affairs; Independent Monthly Review of International Events*, No. 3 (June 1949), p. 6.
117. Lie to Kyrou, June 9, 1949; and Lie to Kyrou, June 23, 1949, Dag 1/1.1.2.2–1, UNA.
118. Memo. of Con. (Lie, Drew, Ross, Power), June 15, 1949, Box 57, US Mission UN 1945–49, RG 84, NA.
119. Bay (Oslo) to the Sec. of State, No. 555, Aug. 11, 1949, File 501/8–1149, RG 59, NA.
120. Memo. of Con. (Lie, Cordier, Austin, Ross, Power), Aug. 17, 1949, Box 53, Austin Papers, UVt; Austin (New York) to the Sec. of State, No. 941, Aug. 17, 1949, File 501.A Summaries/8-1749, RG 59, NA.
121. Ross (New York) to the Sec. of State, No. 953, Aug. 22, 1949, File 501.BB Balkan/8–2249, RG 59, NA; Ross (New York) to the Sec. of State, No. 962, Aug. 22, 1949, Box 153, US Mission UN 1945–49, RG 84, NA; United Kingdom Delegation (United Nations) to the Foreign Office, No. 1709, Aug. 22, 1949, FO/371/78458.
122. Alexander Cadogan diary, Mon., Aug. 22 [1949], CCL.
123. Ross (New York) to the Sec. of State, No. 953, Aug. 22, 1949, File 501.BB Balkan/8–2249, RG 59, NA; United Kingdom Delegation (United Nations) to the Foreign Office, No. 1709, Aug. 22, 1949, FO/371/78458.
124. Ross (New York) to the Sec. of State, No. 957, Aug. 22, 1949, Box 153, US Mission UN 1945–49, RG 84, NA; Ross (New York) to the Sec. of State, No. 970, Aug. 23, 1949, File 501.A Summaries/8–2349, RG 59, NA.
125. United Kingdom Delegation (United Nations) to the Foreign Office, No. 1709, Aug. 22, 1949; and Bevin's scribbled note, FO/371/78458.
126. Minutes by E[dward] H. Peck, Aug. 25, 1949; and Foreign Office to the United Kingdom Delegation (United Nations), No. 2714, Aug. 26, 1949, ibid.
127. Minutes by E[dward] H. Peck, Aug. 30, 1949; D[enis] James, Aug. 31, [1949], G[ladwyn] J[ebb], Sept. 1, [1949], and F[rancis] A. Vallat, Sept. 3, [1949], ibid.
128. Ross (New York) to the Sec. of State, No. 1006, Aug. 27, 1949, Box 153, US Mission UN 1945–49, RG 84, NA.
129. Ross (New York) to the Sec. of State, No. 1011, Aug. 29, 1949, Box 153, ibid.
130. Austin (New York) to the Sec. of State, No. 1067, Sept. 7, 1949, File 501.BB/9–749, RG 59, NA; Austin (New York) to the Sec. of State, No. 1076, Sept. 8, 1949, File 501.A Summaries/9-849, ibid.
131. Austin (New York) to the Sec. of State, No. 1074, Sept. 8, 1949, File 501.BB/9–849, ibid.; Austin (New York) to the Sec. of State, No. 1076, Sept. 8, 1949, Box 153, US Mission UN 1945–49, RG 84, NA.
132. Acheson (New York) to the Sec. of State, No. 1185, Sept. 25, 1949, Box 153, US Mission UN 1945–49, RG 84, NA; Memo. of Con. (Lie, Cohen, Howard), Sept. 24, 1949, Box 41, ibid.
133. Memo. of Con. (Lie, Romulo, Pearson, Cohen, Howard), Sept. 26, 1949, Box 41, ibid.; Acheson (New York) to the Sec. of State, No. 1190, Sept. 27, 1949, File 501.A Summaries/9–2749, RG 59, NA.
134. *YUN, 1948–1949*, p. 247.
135. Power to Hickerson, Oct. 5, 1949, Box 80, US Mission UN 1945–49, RG 84, NA.
136. Memo. of Con. (Dendramis, Kyrou, Howard), Oct. 5, 1949, Box 41, ibid.

137. Memo. of Con. (Romulo, Lie, Sarper, Pearson, Cohen, Drew, Howard), Oct. 13, 1949, Box 41, ibid.
138. *YUN, 1948–1949*, pp. 247–48.
139. Austin (New York) to the Sec. of State, No. 1284, Oct. 22, 1949, Box 154, US Mission UN 1945–49, RG 84, NA.
140. Austin (New York) to the Sec. of State, No. 1357, Nov. 21, 1949, Box 154, ibid.
141. *YUN, 1948–1949*, pp. 251–52.
142. Memo. of Con. (Lie, Cordier, Howard), Dec. 2, 1949, Box 55, US Mission UN 1945–49, RG 84, NA.
143. Verbatim Record of an Informal Meeting with the Secretary-General, Wed., Apr. 18, 1951. At the headquarters of the UN Special Committee on the Balkans, Athens, Greece, and Con. with Marshal Tito, Apr. 13, 1951, Box 2, Lie Papers, NMFA. Also see Lie, pp. 235, 243, 245, 289–90, 304–305.
144. Interview with Byron Theodoropoulos, Dec. 4, 1981. Also see Lie, pp. 245–46.

Notes for Chapter 5: A Plunging Mercury

1. *Department of State Bulletin*, 16 (1947): 1159–60.
2. [Austin] to the Sec. of State, No. 570, June 13, [1947], Box 139, US Mission UN 1945–49, RG 84, NA.
3. Chapter 4, pp. 102–4.
4. Dreyfus (Stockholm) to the Sec. of State, No. 664, July 29, 1947, File 840.50 Recovery/7–2947; and Cumming (Stockholm) to the Sec. of State, No. 928, Nov. 14, 1947, File 501.BD Europe/11-1447, RG 59, NA.
5. Record by Gore-Booth of Telephone Conversation with Martin Hill Special Assistant to the Secretary-General of the United Nations, June 15, 1947; and Minutes by W. B. Stevens, FO/371/62399.
6. Johnson (New York) to the Sec. of State, No. 577, June 17, 1947, File 501.BD/6–1747, RG 59, NA.
7. Memo. of Con. (Price, Ross), June 17, 1947, Correspondence File, June 1947 Folder, Austin Papers, UVt. Also see George T. Mazuzan, *Warren R. Austin at the U.N. 1946–1953* (Kent, Ohio: Kent State University Press, 1977), p. 89.
8. Thorp and Rusk to the Secretary [of State, June 17, 1947?], File 501.BD/6–1747, RG 59, NA.
9. Perm. United Kingdom Rep. (United Nations) to the Foreign Office, No. 1645, June 18, 1947, FO/371/62400.
10. Hall to Cadogan, June 18, 1947, FO/371/62403.
11. Foreign Office to the Perm. United Kingdom Rep. (United Nations), No. 1782, June 19, 1947, FO/371/62400.
12. Perm. United Kingdom Rep. (United Nations) to the Foreign Office, No. 1665, June 20, 1947, FO/371/62401.
13. Cooper (Paris) to Moscow, No. 56, June 18, 1947, FO/371/62400. Also see *FRUS, 1947*, III, pp. 262–63.
14. [Austin] to the Sec. of State, No. 587, June 19, [1947]; and Austin to the Sec. of State, No. 597, June 23, [1947], Box 139, US Mission UN 1945–49, RG 84, NA; Inverchapel (Washington) to the Foreign Office, June 20, 1947, FO/371/62400.
15. [Austin] to the Sec. of State, No. 602, June 25, [1947], Box 139, US Mission UN 1945–49, RG 84, NA; Perm. United Kingdom Rep. (United Nations) to the Foreign Office, No. 1698, June 25, 1947, FO/371/62402.
16. Minutes by B. C. Cook, June 26, 1947, FO/371/62405.

17. [Austin] to the Sec. of State, No. 626, July 2, [1947], Box 139, US Mission UN 1945–49, RG 84, NA.
18. Cooper (Paris) to the Perm. United Kingdom Rep. (United Nations), No. 43, July 3, 1947, FO/371/62404.
19. Perm. United Kingdom Rep. (United Nations) to the Foreign Office, No. 1769, July 3, 1947, FO/371/62405.
20. Bay (Oslo) to the Sec. of State, No. 1208, July 11, 1947, File 501/7–1147, RG 59, NA.
21. Trygve Lie, *In the Cause of Peace* (New York: Macmillan, 1954), pp. 368, 370; and Smith (Moscow) to the Sec. of State, No. 2205, Sept. 17, 1948, File 501.BA/ 9–1748, RG 59, NA.
22. Collier (Oslo) to Warner, July 14, 1947, FO/371/66018.
23. Chapter 3, p. 90.
24. Porter (Geneva) to the Sec. of State, No. 17, Jan. 13, 1948, File 501.BD Europe/ 1–1348, RG 59, NA.
25. Lie to Gerhardsen, Apr. 5, 1948, Box 2, Lie Papers, NMFA.
26. See Chapter 6, p. 198.
27. *New York Times* (Apr. 13, 1948), pp. 1, 12.
28. Memo. of Con. (Lie, Cordier, Austin, Ross, Power), Aug. 17, 1949, Box 53, Austin Papers, UVt; Austin (New York) to the Sec. of State, No. 941, Aug. 17, 1947, File 501.A Summaries/8–1749, RG 59, NA.
29. Fleischer (Oslo) to the United States Information Agency, No. 19, Dec. 22, 1953; and Anderson (Oslo) to the Sec. of State, No. 495, Jan. 22, 1957, CIA Files.
30. Tibbetts (Oslo) to the Sec. of State, No. 3460, Apr. 7, 1967, ibid.
31. Memo. of Con. (Lie, Bovey), May 23, 1967 in Tibbetts (Oslo) to the Department of State, No. A673, June 9, 1967, ibid.
32. Conversation with Jan Masaryk: Czernin Palace, Jan. 26 and 27, 1948; and Conversation with President Beneš, Jan. 27, 1948, Box 2, Lie Papers, NMFA; Lie, pp. 230–34. Also see [Stoneman] to [Binder], Feb. 28, 1948, Binder Papers, NLC; and Dixon (Prague) to the Foreign Office, No. 42, Jan. 27, 1948, FO/371/ 72698.
33. Byron Price, "Memoir" (typescript), Book IV (Section 3), pp. 551A–553, Folder 6, Box 5, and Byron Price, "Notebooks" (unnumbered), Feb. 1948–July 1950, pp. 26–27, Folder 2, Box 4, Price Papers, SHSW; Lie, pp. 230–34.
34. "The Reminiscences of Jan Papánek" (typescript), pp. 327–28, Oral History Collection, CU.
35. Price, "Memoir," Book IV (Section 3), pp. 554–58, and Price "Notebooks," pp. 27–29.
36. Price, "Notebooks," pp. 29–30.
37. Cyrus L. Sulzberger, *A Long Row of Candles; Memoirs and Diaries [1934–1954]* (New York: Macmillan, 1969), p. 410. Also see Lie, p. 235.
38. "The Reminiscenses of Jan Papánek," pp. 330–31.
39. *Documents on American Foreign Relations*, ed. Raymond Dennett and Robert K. Turner (Princeton: Princeton University Press, 1950), X, pp. 625–27.
40. Alexander Cadogan diary, Wed., Mar. 10, [1948], CCL.
41. *FRUS, 1948*, I, pp. 167–69.
42. Austin (New York) to the Sec. of State, No. 269, Mar. 10, 1948, File 501.BC/ 3–1048, RG 59, NA.
43. Austin to the Sec. of State, No. 272, Mar. 10, [1948], Box 143, US Mission UN 1945–49, RG 84, NA.
44. *FRUS, 1948*, I, pp. 169–70.

45. Sandifer to Lovett, Mar. 11, 1948, File 501.BC/3–1148, RG 59, NA. Also see "The Reminiscences of Jan Papánek," pp. 332–33.
46. United Kingdom Delegation (United Nations) to the Foreign Office, No. 860, Mar. 11, 1948, FO/371/71303.
47. Canadian Perm. Delegate (United Nations) to the Sec. of State for External Affairs, No. 317, Mar. 11, 1948, Vol. 440, Mackenzie King Papers, MG 26, J1, PAC. Also see Macdonnell (Ottawa) to the Sec. of State for External Affairs, No. 252, June 29, 1948, File 2/11/o, Vol. 2614, RG 25, F6, PAC.
48. Austin to the Sec. of State, No. 277, Mar. 11, [1948], Box 143, US Mission UN 1945–49, RG 84, NA.
49. Price, "Memoir," Book IV (Section 3), pp. 557, 559–60; and Price, "Notebooks," pp. 29, 31–32. On Lie's plea that the press eliminate nationality references when discussing the secretariat, see Austin (New York) to the Sec. of State, No. 308, Mar. 17, 1948, File 501.A Summaries/3–1748, RG 59, NA.
50. Bancroft to Sandifer, Mar. 11, 1948, File 501.BC/3–1148, RG 59, NA.
51. UN Doc. S/694, Mar. 12, 1948.
52. Marshall (Washington) to New York, No. 142, Mar. 16, 1948, and the attached amended page of instructions, File 501.BC/3–1648, RG 59, NA.
53. Bacon to Butterworth and Penfield, Mar. 18, 1948, File 501.BA/3–3048, ibid.
54. Butterworth to Rusk, Mar. 18, 1948, File 501.BC/3–1848, ibid.
55. Rusk to Butterworth, Mar. 30, 1948, File 501.BA/3–3048, ibid.
56. YUN, 1947–1948, pp. 451–58.
57. Italics added. Memo. of Con. (Ordonneau, Knox), Mar. 19, 1948, Box 68, US Mission UN 1945–49, RG 84, NA. Also see Austin (New York) to the Sec. of State, No. 322, Mar. 22, 1948, File 501.A Summaries/3–2248, RG 59, NA.
58. Memo. of Con. (Cordier, Power), Mar. 31, 1948, Box 68, US Mission to UN 1945–49, RG 84, NA. Also see Austin (New York) to the Sec. of State, No. 367, Apr. 1, 1948, File 501.A Summaries/4–148, RG 59, NA.
59. Austin to the Sec. of State, No. 169, Feb. 11, 1949, Box 150, US Mission UN 1945–49, RG 84, NA.
60. An unaddressed and unsigned letter, June 28, 1948, Cordier Papers, CU. For a slightly varied version see 12/1, Microfilm copy Cordier Papers, UNA. Also Memo. of Con. (Price, Jessup, Ross), June 29, 1948, Box 69, US Mission UN 1945–49, RG 84, NA.
61. Alexander Cadogan diary, Mon., June 28, [1948], CCL.
62. Memo. of Con. (Price, Jessup, Ross), June 29, 1948, Box 69, US Mission UN 1945–49, RG 84, NA. Also see Jessup (New York) to the Sec. of State, No. 832, June 29, 1948, File 501.A Summaries/6–2948, RG 59, NA.
63. United Kingdom Delegation (United Nations) to the Foreign Office, No. 1839, June 28, 1948, FO/371/70497.
64. P[aul] Mason, Possible Reference of Berlin Situation to the United Nations, June 28, 1948, and Jebb's minutes, no date, FO/371/70498.
65. Foreign Office to Paris, No. 1993, June 30, 1948, ibid.
66. Foreign Office to Berlin (Military Governor), No. 1396, June 30, 1948, ibid.
67. Foreign Office to the United Kingdom Delegation (United Nations), No. 2839, June 28, 1948, FO/371/70497.
68. Douglas (London) to the Sec. of State, No. 2877, June 29, 1948, File 501.BC/6–2948, RG 59, NA.
69. Deputy Director for European Affairs to Lovett, June 29, 1948, File 501.BC/6–2948, ibid.
70. Jessup (New York) to the Sec. of State, No. 830, June 29, 1948, File 501.BC/

6–2948, ibid.; Jessup (New York) to the Sec. of State, No. 832, June 29, 1948, File 501.A Summaries/6-2948, ibid.

71. Canadian Perm. Delegate (United Nations) to the Sec. of State for External Affairs, No. 720, June 29, 1948, Vol. 440, Mackenzie King Papers, MG 26, J1, PAC.

72. United Kingdom Delegation (United Nations) to the Foreign Office, No. 1850, June 30, 1948, FO/371/70498.

73. Jessup (New York) to the Sec. of State, No. 832, June 29, 1948, File 501.A Summaries/6–2948, RG 59, NA.

74. Memo. of Con. (Cordier, Feller, Ross), July 2, 1948, Box 79, US Mission UN 1945–49, RG 84, NA.

75. [Memo. of Con.] (Ross, McClintock), June 30, 1948, Box 4, Rusk-McClintock Papers, RG 59, NA.

76. [Memo. of Con.] (Ross, McClintock), July 1, 1948, Box 4, Rusk-McClintock Papers, ibid. For Lie's cancelled note see [Lie] to Austin and the other permanent members of the Security Council, June 30, 1948, Dag 1/1.1.1.3, UNA. It would appear that the Russians were likewise annoyed with Lund. Although appointed Norwegian military attaché to Moscow in the autumn of 1948, he had still not been issued a visa to proceed by June 1949. Bay (Oslo) to the Sec. of State, No. 421, June 9, 1949, File 501.5761/6–949, RG 59, NA.

77. Jessup to the Sec. of State, No. 892, July 16, [1948], Box 146, US Mission UN 1945–49, RG 84, NA.

78. Minutes by Orme Sargent, Aug. 4, 1948, FO/371/72677.

79. UN Doc. A/565, Supp. 1, July 30, 1948.

80. Lie to his wife and daughter Mette, No. 3, Aug. 16, 1948, Guri Lie Zeckendorf Papers, PP. Also see Canadian Perm. Delegate (United Nations) to the Sec. of State for External Affairs, No. 881, Aug. 16, 1948, File 2/16/0, Vol. 2614, RG 25, F6, PAC.

81. Bay (Oslo) to the Sec. of State, No. 524, Sept. 16, 1948, File 501.BB/9–1648, RG 59, NA.

82. Smith (Moscow) to the Sec. of State, No. 2002, Sept. 16, 1948, File 501.BA/9–1648, ibid.; Harrison (Moscow) to the Foreign Office, No. 1232, Sept. 16, 1948, FO/371/70515.

83. Heath (Sofia) to the Sec. of State, No. 1199, Sept. 22, 1948, File 501/9–2248, RG 59, NA; Crocker (Warsaw) to the Sec. of State, No. 1273, Sept. 27, 1948, File 501/9–2748, ibid.

84. Smith (Moscow) to the Sec. of State, No. 2004, Sept. 17, 1948, File 501.BA/9–1748, RG 59, NA; Harrison (Moscow) to the Foreign Office, No. 1232, Sept. 16, 1948, FO/371/70515.

85. Minutes by D[onald] M. Gordon, Sept. 16 and 22 [1948], A[ndrew] G. Gilchrist, Sept. 17, [1948], and D[avid] Hildyard, Sept. 24, [1948], FO/371/70515.

86. Memo. of Con. (Lie, Jessup), Sept. 29, 1948, File 501.BC/9–2948, RG 59, NA; and Canadian Delegation (United Nations) to the Sec. of State for External Affairs, No. 89, Sept. 30, 1948, File Telegrams to External, Vol. 1063, RG 25, F6, PAC.

87. Lie, p. 202, and especially Memo. 1, Box 2, Lie Papers, NMFA.

88. Lie, pp. 201–202.

89. YUN, 1948–1949, pp. 284–85.

90. Chapter 3, p. 83.

91. Alan Watt, Australian Diplomat (Sydney: Angus and Robertson, Ltd., 1972), p. 140; Kylie Tennant, Evatt; Politics and Justice (Sydney: Angus and Robert-

ertson, Ltd., 1970), p. 237; Brian Urquhart, *A Life in Peace and War* (New York: Harper and Row, 1987), p. 117.

92. Memo. of Con. (Marshall, Evatt), Oct. 4, 1948, File 501.BC/10–448, RG 59, NA.

93. Lie, pp. 202–203. On Lie's pro-Zionist orientation see Chapter 6. In view of the senior State Department positions that Cohen held, the highly confidential information to which he was privy, and especially the trust placed in him by the American government, Cohen's close liaison with the Jewish Agency and its higher officials, the privy and confidential information that he conveyed to them, and his activities behind the scenes in their behalf are open to the severest criticism. See Meetings of the Executive (American Section) of the Jewish Agency, Sept. 17, 1947, p. 11, File Z5/59, and Sept. 18, 1947, p. 5, File Z5/56, CZAJ. Also see *PDD, December 1947–May 1948*, pp. 294–96; and *DFPI*, I, pp. 86, 487, 516, 637.

94. Sulzberger, p. 409.

95. Dulles to Lie, Oct. 21, 1948, Lie to Dulles, Oct. 22, 1948, and Dulles to Lie, Oct. 22, 1948, Dulles Papers, PU.

96. *YUN, 1948–1949*, p. 286.

97. Memo. I and Memo. II, Box 2, Lie Papers, NMFA; Lie, pp. 203–205.

98. Lie, pp. 205–207.

99. *FRUS, 1948*, II, pp. 1236–37.

100. Lovett for Bohlen and Jessup, No. 4215, Oct. 29, 1948, Box 191, US Mission UN 1945–49, RG 84, NA.

101. Memo. III and Memo. IV, Box 2, Lie Papers, NMFA; Lie, pp. 207–10.

102. Gross to Jessup, Oct. 31, 1948, File 740.00119 Control (Germany)/10–3148, RG 59, NA.

103. Memo. V and Memo. VI, Box 2, Lie Papers, NMFA; Lie, pp. 210–11.

104. *FRUS, 1948*, II, pp. 1247–48.

105. Memo. VI, Box 2, Lie Papers, NMFA; Lie, p. 211.

106. Alexander Cadogan diary, Wed., Nov. 3, [1948], CCL.

107. United Kingdom Delegation (United Nations) to the Foreign Office, No. 286, Nov. 3, 1948, FO/371/70520.

108. Foreign Office to the United Kingdom Delegation (United Nations), No. 384, Nov. 4, 1948; and minutes by P[atrick] Dean, Nov. 4, 1948, ibid.

109. Memo. VII, Box 2, Lie Papers, NMFA; Alexander Cadogan diary, Fri., Nov. 5, [1948], CCL; Lie, p. 212.

110. United Kingdom Delegation (United Nations) to the Foreign Office, No. 316, Nov. 5, 1948, FO/371/70521.

111. *FRUS, 1948*, II, pp. 1248–49.

112. Holmes (London) to the Sec. of State, No. 4767, Nov. 6, 1948, File 740.00119 Control (Germany)/11–648, RG 59, NA.

113. Lovett to Jessup and Bohlen, No. 4337, Nov. 8, 1948, Box 192, US Mission UN 1945–49, RG 84, NA.

114. United Kingdom Delegation (United Nations) to the Foreign Office, No. 325, Nov. 6, 1948, FO/371/70521; Alexander Cadogan diary, Sat., Nov. 6, [1948], CCL.

115. Memo. VII, Box 2, Lie Papers, NMFA; Lie, p. 212.

116. Alexander Cadogan diary, Sun., Nov. 7, [1948], CCL.

117. Memo. VII, Box 2, Lie Papers, NMFA; Lie, pp. 212–13.

118. Memo. VIII, Box 2, Lie Papers, NMFA; Lie, p. 214.

119. United Kingdom Delegation (United Nations) to the Foreign Office, No. 346, ·Nov. 9, 1948; and minutes by Donald Gordon, Nov. 11, 1948, FO/371/70521;

Memo. VII, Box 2, Lie Papers, NMFA; Alexander Cadogan diary, Tues., Nov. 9, [1948], CCL.

120. Memo. VII, Box 2, Lie Papers, NMFA; Lie, p. 213.
121. [Lie] to his wife and daughter Mette, Nov. 10, 1948, Box 3, Lie Papers, NMFA.
122. Memo. of Con. (Cordier, Power), Nov. 14, 1948, Box 79, US Mission UN 1945–49, RG 84, NA.
123. *FRUS, 1948*, II, pp. 1249–51; Canadian Delegation (United Nations) to the Acting Sec. of State for External Affairs, No. 396, Nov. 16, 1948, File Telegrams to External, Vol. 1063, RG 25, F6, PAC; Memo. IX, Box 2, Lie Papers, NMFA; Marshall (Paris) to the Sec. of State for Lovett, No. 138, Nov. 16, 1948, File 501.BC/111–1648, RG 59, NA; Lie, p. 214.
124. [Stoneman] to [Binder], Jan. 28, 1949 and Nov. 14, 1952 as well as Apr. 29 and May 7 and 11, 1948, Binder Papers, NLC. Lie subsequently arranged to have Stoneman receive a Norwegian decoration in order to give the impression that he and Stoneman had never had a falling out. Stoneman was furious. [Stoneman] to [Binder], Feb. 18, 1954, Binder Papers, ibid.
125. Marshall (Paris) to the Sec. of State, No. 786, Nov. 16, 1948, Box 149, US Mission UN 1945–49, RG 84, NA; Memo. of Con. (Kyrou, Drew, Howard), Nov. 14, 1948, Box 43, ibid. Also see [Harry N. Howard], Attempt at Conciliation between Greece and Albania, Bulgaria and Yugoslavia, [Jan. 1949?], Box 80, ibid.
126. *Documents on American Foreign Relations*, X, pp. 100–101.
127. Watt, p. 136.
128. Tennant, p. 234.
129. United Kingdom Delegation (United Nations) to the Foreign Office, No. 403, Nov. 14, 1948, Fo/371/70700.
130. James V. Forrestal, *The Forrestal Diaries*, ed. Walter Millis (New York: Viking Press, 1951), p. 532.
131. Marshall (Paris) to the Sec. of State for Lovett, No. 138, Nov. 16, 1948, File 501.BC/11–1648, RG 59, NA.
132. Marshall (Paris) to the Sec. of State for Lovett, No. 140, Nov. 16, 1948, File 501.BC/11–1648, ibid.
133. Villard (Oslo) to the Sec. of State, No. 708, Nov. 15, 1948, File 501.BC/11–1548, ibid.
134. Marshall (Paris) to the Sec. of State for Lovett, No. 140, File 501.BC/11–1648, ibid.
135. Strang to the Min. of State, Nov. 14, 1948, FO/371/70522.
136. [Lie] to his wife and daughter Mette, Nov. 15, 1948, Guri Lie Zeckendorf Papers, PP.
137. CAB/128/13, Nov. 15, 1948, PRO.
138. *Documents on American Foreign Relations*, X, pp. 101–103; Lie, p. 215.
139. [Lie] to his wife and daughter Mette, Nov. 19, 1948, Box 3, Lie Papers, NMFA.
140. Memo. X, Box 2, Lie Papers, NMFA; Lie, p. 216.
141. *YUN, 1948–1949*, p. 286.
142. Marshall to the Sec. of State, Jessup for Lovett, No. 822, Nov. 18, 1948, Box 191, US Mission UN 1945–49, RG 84, NA.
143. Memo. X, Box 2, Lie Papers, NMFA; Lie, p. 216.
144. *YUN, 1948–1949*, p. 286.
145. United Kingdom Delegation (United Nations) to the Foreign Office, No. 125, Feb. 15, 1949, FO/371/76544.
146. Kirkpatrick to the Sec. of State, Feb. 16, 1949; and Foreign Office to the United Kingdom Delegation (United Nations), No. 595, Feb. 16, 1949, ibid.

147. Douglas (London) to the Sec. of State, No. 588, Feb. 16, 1949, Box 192, US Mission UN 1945–49, RG 84, NA.
148. United Kingdom Delegation (United Nations) to the Foreign Office, No. 372, Feb. 17, 1949, FO/371/76545.
149. *YUN, 1948–1949*, p. 286.
150. Ross (New York) to the Sec. of State, No. 232, Feb. 25, 1949, File 501.A Summaries/2–2549, RG 59, NA.
151. Lie, p. 217.
152. *FRUS, 1949*, III, pp. 666–67, 694–98 and passim; Lie, p. 217. Also see Philip C. Jessup, "Park Avenue Diplomacy—Ending the Berlin Blockade," *Political Science Quarterly*, 87, no. 3 (Fall 1972): 377–400; and Philip C. Jessup, "The Berlin Blockade and the Use of the United Nations," *Foreign Affairs*, 50, no. 1 (Oct. 1971): 163–73.
153. Austin to the Sec. of State, No. 372, Mar. 19, 1949, Box 151, US Mission UN 1945–49, RG 84, NA.
154. Austin to the Sec. of State, No. 376, Mar. 19, 1949, Box 151, ibid.
155. Memo. of Con. (Cordier, Power), Apr. 22, 1949, Box 52, ibid.
156. *FRUS, 1949*, VI, pp. 301–302.
157. *YUN, 1948–1949*, pp. 286–87.
158. Bay (Oslo) to the Sec. of State, No. 555, Aug. 11, 1949, File 501/8–1149, RG 59, NA.
159. Austin to the Sec. of State, No. 931, Aug. 16, 1949, Box 153, US Mission UN 1945–49, RG 84, NA.
160. Lie, p. 218.
161. Memo. of Con. (McKeever, Brown), Feb. 12, 1948, and Marshall to Sofia, No. 103, Feb. 14, 1948, File 501.AA/1–3048, RG 59, NA.
162. Memo. of Con. (Cordier, Power), Mar. 31, 1948, Box 68, US Mission UN 1945–49, RG 84, NA.
163. Lie to Gerhardsen, Apr. 5, 1948, Box 2, Lie Papers, NMFA.
164. *New York Times* (Apr. 13, 1948), pp. 1, 12.
165. Ibid. (April 16, 1948), p. 22.
166. Memo. of Con. (Foote, Raynor), Apr. 20, 1948, Box 112, US Mission UN 1945–49, RG 84, NA.
167. Rusk to Raynor, Apr. 24, 1948, Box 112, ibid.
168. Halvard M. Lange, *Norges vei til NATO* (Oslo: Pax, 1966), pp. 28–29, 49–50.
169. Inverchapel (Washington) to the Foreign Office, No. 451, June 16, 1948, FO/371/51608.
170. Austin to the Sec. of State, No. 169, Feb. 11, 1949, Box 150, US Mission UN 1945–49, RG 84, NA.
171. Harvey (Paris) to the Foreign Office, No. 164, Feb. 14, 1949, FO/371/79225.
172. Austin (New York) to the Sec. of State, No. 365, Mar. 18, 1949, File 840.20/3–1849, RG 59, NA.
173. Austin to the Sec. of State, No. 372, Mar. 19, 1949, Box 151, US Mission UN 1945–49, RG 84, NA.
174. Austin to the Sec. of State, No. 379, Mar. 19, 1949, Box 151, ibid.
175. United Kingdom Delegation (United Nations) to the Foreign Office, No. 625, Mar. 19, 1949; Mayhew to the Sec. of State, Mar. 22, 1949; and the Minutes by R[obert] M. A. Hankey, Mar. 24, 1949, FO/371/77612. Also see the Minutes from the head of the United Nations Department, Roger Allen to Sir Gladwyn Jebb, Mar. 23, 1949, FO/371/78784.
176. Troutman (Geneva) to the Sec. of State, from Porter to Harriman, No. 293, Mar. 31, 1949, File 501.BA/3–3149, RG 59, NA.

177. Memo. of Con. (Kerno, Feller, Ross), Apr. 8, 1949, Box 52, US Mission UN 1945–49, RG 84, NA.
178. Memo. of Con. (Nielsen, Bell, Rogers), May 2, 1949, File 840.20/5–249, RG 59, NA.
179. Villard (Oslo) to the Sec. of State, No. 233, July 11, 1949, File 501.BA/7–1149, ibid.
180. UN Doc. A/930, July 7, 1949.
181. The Times (London) (Aug. 9, 1949), p. 5.
182. Wadsworth (Ankara) to the Sec. of State, No. 346, Aug. 10, 1949, File 501.BB/8–1049, RG 59, NA.
183. Kirk (Moscow) to the Sec. of State, No. 1993, Aug. 9, 1949, File 501/8–949, ibid.; and Lyon (Warsaw) to the Sec. of State, No. 538, Aug. 12, 1949, File 501/8–1249, ibid.
184. Collier (Oslo) to Allen, Aug. 18, 1949, FO/371/78791, PRO.
185. Villard (Oslo) to the Sec. of State, No. 272, Aug. 12, 1949, File 501/8–1249; and Laureys (Copenhagen) to the Sec. of State for External Affairs, No. 161, Aug. 17, 1949, File 501/9-949, RG 59, NA.
186. Mason (Oslo) to the Western European Information Department, Aug. 13, 1949, FO/371/78791.
187. [Stoneman] to [Binder], Nov. 14, 1954, Binder Papers, NLC.
188. Coulson to Parrott, May 30, 1951, A. J. Williams, Presidency of the Forthcoming General Assembly, July 2, 1951; and Mason to Steel, July 11, 1951, FO/371/95728.
189. Wright (Oslo) to the Foreign Office, No. 25, Oct. 17, 1951, FO/371/95729.
190. Mason (Oslo) to the Western Europe Information Department, Aug. 13, 1949, FO/371/78791; Sparks (Copenhagen) to the Sec. of State, No. 568, Aug. 10, 1949, File 840.20/8–1049, RG 59, NA; Villard (Oslo) to the Sec. of State, No. 272, Aug. 12, 1949, File 501/8–1249, ibid., Lyon (Warsaw) to the Sec. of State, No. 538, Aug. 12, 1949, File 501/8–1249, ibid.; Laureys (Copenhagen) to the Sec. of State for External Affairs, No. 161, Aug. 17, 1949, File 501/9–949, ibid.; Matthews (Stockholm) to the Sec. of State, Nos. 784 and 794, Aug. 9 and 10, 1949; and Douglas (London) to the Sec. of State, No. 3161, Aug. 10, 1949, Box 53, Austin Papers, UVt.
191. Mason (Oslo) to the Western European Information Department, Aug. 13, 1949, FO/371/78791. On Lie's Arbeiderbladet interview, also see Villard (Oslo) to the Sec. of State, No. 272, Aug. 12, 1949, File 501/8–1249, RG 59, NA.
192. Laureys (Copenhagen) to the Sec. of State for External Affairs, No. 161, Aug. 17, 1949, File 501/9–949, RG 59, NA.
193. Collier (Oslo) to Allen, Aug. 18, 1949, FO/371/78791.
194. Matthews (Stockholm) to the Sec. of State, No. 800, Aug. 11, 1949, File 840.20/8–1149, RG 59, NA.
195. Lambert (Stockholm) to Bevin, No. 233, Aug. 19, 1949, FO/371/78791; and also Matthews (Stockholm) to the Sec. of State, No. 805, Aug. 12, 1949, File 501/8–1249, RG 59, NA.
196. Matthews (Stockholm) to the Sec. of State, No. 332, Aug. 25, 1949, File 501.BA/8–2549, RG 59, NA.
197. Randall (Copenhagen) to Bevin, No. 220, Aug. 18, 1949, FO/371/78791; Sparks (Copenhagen) to the Sec. of State, No. 574, Aug. 15, 1949, File 501/8–1549, RG 59, NA; Laureys (Copenhagen) to the Sec. of State for External Affairs, No. 161, Aug. 17, 1949, File 501/9–949, ibid.; Sparks (Copenhagen)

to the Sec. of State, No. 202, Aug. 19, 1949, File 501/8–1949, ibid.; Hughes (Bern) to the Sec. of State, No. 537, Aug. 25, 1949, File 501.BA/8–2549, ibid.
198. Memo. of Con. (Lie, Cordier, Austin, Ross, Power), Aug. 17, 1949, Box 53, Austin Papers, UVt.
199. Matthews (Stockholm) to the Sec. of State, No. 332, Aug. 25, 1949, File 501.BA/8–2549, RG 59, NA.
200. Memo. of Con. (Lie, Cordier, Ross, Power), Aug. 29, 1949, Box 92, US Mission UN 1945–49, RG 84, NA.
201. Ross to the Sec. of State, No. 1013, Aug. 29, 1949, Box 153, ibid.
202. Austin to the Sec. of State, No. 1067, Sept. 7, 1949, Box 153, ibid.; Austin (New York) to the Sec. of State, No. 1076, Sept. 8, 1949, File 501.A Summaries/9–849, RG 59, NA.
203. Note, Wed., Mar. 23, 1950, Box 1, Lie Papers, NMFA.
204. Note, Wed., May 24, 1950, Box 1, Lie Papers, ibid.
205. *FRUS, 1951*, II, p. 492 n.; Fleischer (Oslo) to the United States Information Agency, No. 19, Dec. 22, 1953, and Wahl (Oslo) to the Department of State, No. 449, Jan. 4, 1954, CIA Files.
206. Wright (Oslo) to Mason, June 23, 1953, FO/371/106362.

Notes for Chapter 6: Palestine

1. Over the years voluminous and hitherto confidential documentation has been released, but the most lucid, factual, and objective work is still J. C. Hurewitz, *The Struggle for Palestine* (New York: Norton, 1950), passim.
2. Abba Eban, *Abba Eban: An Autobiography* (New York: Random House, 1977), pp. 90–91.
3. Brian Urquhart, *A Life in Peace and War* (New York: Harper and Row, 1987), p. 118.
4. Robert St. John, *Eban* (New York: Doubleday, 1972), pp. 183, 273; and Report of the Representative of Israel at the United Nations to the Foreign Minister, May 15–July [1948], File 92/28, ISAJ. Also see Eban, p. 91, as well as David Horowitz, *State in the Making*, trans. Julian Meltzer (New York: Alfred A. Knopf, 1953), pp. 278, 280, 330.
5. Weizmann (Geneva) to Lie, Sept. 27, 1948, Box 2, Lie Papers, NMFA. Also see *DFPI*, I, p. 637.
6. Lie to Sharett, Oct. 27, 1950, Dag 1/1.1.2.2–1 UNA.
7. [Unsigned Message] (Geneva) to the Sec. of State from Porter, No. 17, Jan. 13, 1948, File 501.BD Europe/1–1348, RG 59, NA.
8. Hugh L. Keenleyside, *Memoirs* (Toronto: McClelland, Stewart, 1982), II, p. 369. One high secretariat official who served under Lie and one former national representative claimed he was anti-Jewish. On Jewish sufferings, see Trygve Lie, *In the Cause of Peace* (New York: Macmillan, 1954), p. 159; and Eban, p. 91.
9. Lie, p. 159 and also pp. 197–98.
10. Cordier to Lie, June 5, 1955, Microfilm 37/10, Cordier Papers, UNA.
11. Two memoranda by Adelson to Goldmann, July 2, 1946, File Z5/1291, CZAJ. Also see L. M. G[elber] to Goldmann, June 20, 1946, Z6, Box 6, File 13, Goldmann Papers, CZAJ.
12. Bancroft, Gerig, and Sanders to Ross, Feb. 20, 1947, Box 8, Rusk-McClintock Papers, RG 59, NA.

13. Perm. United Kingdom Rep. (United Nations) to the Foreign Office, No. 637, Feb. 26, 1947, FO/371/61769. Also see Alexander Cadogan diary, Wed., Feb. 26, [1947], CCL.
14. Austin (New York) to the Sec. of State, No. 184, Feb. 27, 1947, File 501.BB Summaries/2–2747, RG 59, NA.
15. Foreign Office to the Perm. United Kingdom Rep. (United Nations), No. 681, Mar. 3, 1947, FO/371/61769. Also see Sec. of State for Dominion Affairs (London) to the Sec. of State for External Affairs, No. 227, Mar. 8, 1947, Vol. 430, Mackenzie King Papers, MG 26, J1, PAC.
16. Alexander Cadogan diary, Mon., Mar. 3, [1947], CCL.
17. *FRUS, 1947*, V, p. 1060; Austin (New York) to the Sec. of State, No. 193, Mar. 3, 1947, File 501.BC/3–347, RG 59, NA; Perm. United Kingdom Rep. (United Nations) to the Foreign Office, No. 711, Mar. 4, 1947, and Perm. United Kingdom Rep. (United Nations) to the Foreign Office, No. 739, Mar. 6, 1947, FO/371/61769.
18. Minutes by E[dward] E. Tomkins, Mar. 18, [1947], and P[aul] Mason, Mar. 18, [1947], FO/371/61769.
19. Gelber to the Members of the Executive of the Jewish Agency, Mar. 5, 1947, File Z5/1323, CZAJ.
20. [Dorothy Adelson], Conversation with Raoul Aglion . . . [written sometime between March 13 to 25, 1947], File Z5/458 (I), ibid.
21. Austin, Memo. on Palestine (Referring to my Telegram No. 192 . . .), Mar. 4, 1947, Box 86, US Mission UN 1945–49, RG 84, NA.
22. Minutes by E[dward] E. Tomkins, Mar. 6, [1947]; W[illiam] E. Beckett, Mar. 6, [1947]; and Gladwyn Jebb, Mar. 7, [1947], FO/371/61769.
23. Memo. of Con. (Merriam, Wilkins, McClintock, Johnson, Bechhoefer, Green, Taylor, Mangano), Mar. 4, 1947, Box 8, Rusk-McClintock Papers, RG 59, NA.
24. McClintock to Henderson and Fahy, Mar. 4, 1947, File 867N.01/3–347, ibid.
25. *FRUS, 1947*, V, p. 1061 n.
26. Telephone Conversation between Senator Austin and Ross, Mar. 5, 1947, Box 86, US Mission UN 1945–49, RG 84, NA.
27. McClintock to Ross, Mar. 6, 1947, Box 8, Rusk-McClintock Papers, RG 59, NA.
28. *FRUS, 1947*, V, p. 1061.
29. Memo. of Con. (Noyes, McClintock), Mar. 7, 1947, File 501.BB Palestine/ 3–747, RG 59, NA.
30. *FRUS, 1947*, V, pp. 1062–63; Austin (New York) to the Sec. of State, No. 219, Mar. 8, 1947, File 501.BC/3–847, RG 59, NA; Perm. United Kingdom Rep. (United Nations) to the Foreign Office, No. 767, Mar. 7, 1947; and minutes by H[arold] Beeley, Mar. 11, [1947], FO/371/61769. Also see Alexander Cadogan diary, Fri., Mar. 7, [1947], CCL.
31. McClintock to Rusk, Mar. 10, 1947, Box 8, Rusk-McClintock Papers, RG 59, NA.
32. Foreign Office to the United Kingdom Delegation (Council of Foreign Ministers), No. 58, Mar. 12, 1947, FO/371/61769.
33. Gallman (London) to the Sec. of State, No. 1582, Mar. 12, 1947, Box 8, Rusk-McClintock Papers, RG 59, NA.
34. Acheson (Washington) to New York, No. 98, Mar. 19, 1947, Box 157, US Mission UN 1945–49, RG 84, NA. Partially reproduced in *FRUS, 1947*, V, p. 1063 n.
35. *FRUS, 1947*, V, pp. 1063–64. Also see Sec. of State for Dominion Affairs (London) to the Sec. of State for External Affairs, No. 268, Mar. 21, 1947, Vol. 430, Mackenzie King Papers, MG 26, J1, PAC.

36. Acheson (Washington) to New York, No. 105, Mar. 22, 1947, Box 157, US Mission UN 1945–49, RG 84, NA. Partially reproduced in *FRUS, 1947*, p. 1067 n.
37. Memo. of Con. (Johnson, Rusk), Mar. 25, 1947, File 501.BB/3–2547, RG 59, NA.
38. Telephone Conversations between Johnson and Lie, Mar. 26, 1947; and between Johnson and Rusk, Mar. 26, 1947, Box 86, US Mission UN 1945–49, RG 84, NA.
39. *FRUS, 1947*, V, pp. 1066–67.
40. Dorothy Adelson, The Plans to Date for Special UN Session to Discuss Palestine, Mar. 26, 1947, File 2266/5, ISAJ.
41. Memo. of Con. (Johnson, McClintock), Mar. 27, 1947, File 501.BB Palestine/3–2747, RG 59, NA; *FRUS, 1947*, V, p. 1067 n.
42. *YUN, 1946–1947*, pp. 276–78. For Lie's version of all these events, see Lie, pp. 160–61.
43. Shertok to the Members of the Executive of the Jewish Agency, Apr. 24, 1947, File A245N/207, CZAJ.
44. Austin (New York) to the Sec. of State, No. 359, Apr. 17, 1947, File 501.BB/4–1747, RG 59, NA. Partially reproduced in *FRUS, 1947*, V, pp. 1069–70. Also Austin (New York) to the Sec. of State, No. 361, Apr. 17, 1947, File 501.BC/4–1747, RG 59, NA; Perm. United Kingdom Rep. (United Nations) to the Foreign Office, No. 1181, Apr. 16, 1947, FO/371/67585.
45. Douglas (London) to the Sec. of State, No. 2289, Apr. 18, 1947, File 501.BB/4–1847, RG 59, NA.
46. Foreign Office to the Perm. United Kingdom Rep. (United Nations), No. 1181, Apr. 18, 1947, FO/371/67585. Also see [Memo. of Con.] (Lawford, Ross), Apr. 23, 1947, Box 84, US Mission UN 1945–49, RG 84, NA.
47. Memo. of Con. (Austin, Thompson), Apr. 18, 1947, File 501.BB/4–1847, RG 59, NA.
48. Sanders to Rusk, Apr. 24, 1947, and the two attached memoranda, File 501.BB Palestine/5–147, ibid.
49. Perm. United Kingdom Rep. (United Nations) to the Foreign Office, No. 1309, May 1, 1947, FO/371/61775.
50. Austin (New York) to the Sec. of State, No. 414, May 2, 1947, File 501.BB Summaries/5–247, RG 59, NA; Canadian Consulate General (New York) to the Sec. of State for External Affairs, No. 521, May 3, 1947, Vol. 428, Mackenzie King Papers, MG 26, J1, PAC. For an analysis of the World Federation of Trade Unions' approach to the General Committee in London, see Sanders to Rusk, Apr. 24, 1947, Annex A, Apr. 16, 1947, File 501.BB Palestine/5-147, RG 59, NA.
51. When asked in his press conference of April 9 about the Jewish Agency's representation before the assembly, Lie responded that that organ made its own rules. It was thought this comment could be interpreted as an encouragement for the Jewish Agency to appeal to be heard, which even if refused, would be favorable publicity for the Zionist cause. Adelson to [Gelber?], Apr. 10, 1947, File Z5/458 (1), CZAJ.
52. *YUN, 1946–1947*, pp. 278–90, 294–303. It would appear that the committee's Guatemalan member, Jorge García Granados, and Uruguayan member, Enrique Fabregat, were committed Zionists for family and other reasons. Memo. of Con. (Jamali, Kopper), Oct. 6, 1947, Box 57, US Mission UN 1945–49, RG 84, NA; Hadow to Mason, May 22, 1948, FO/371/72728.
53. Perm. United Kingdom Rep. (United Nations) to the Foreign Office, No. 1391, May 15, 1947, FO/371/67586. Also see *YUN, 1946–1947*, p. 294.

54. *YUN, 1946–1947*, p. 303.
55. Perm. United Kingdom Rep. (United Nations) to the Foreign Office, No. 1408, May 17, 1947, FO/371/61778.
56. *YUN, 1946–1947*, p. 303.
57. Perm. United Kingdom Rep. (United Nations) to the Foreign Office, No. 1391, May 15, 1947, FO/371/67586; Lie, p. 161.
58. Johnson to the Sec. of State, No. 516, May 29, [1947], Box 138, US Mission UN 1945–49, RG 84, NA.
59. [Austin] to the Sec. of State, No. 533, June 3, [1947], Box 138, ibid.; also see Lie, p. 161.
60. Austin (New York) to the Sec. of State, No. 551, June 9, [1947], Box 139, US Mission UN 1945–49, RG 84, NA.
61. Lie, p. 161.
62. *YUN, 1947–1948*, pp. 227–31; *YUN, 1946–1947*, p. 304.
63. Meeting of the Executive (American Section) of the Jewish Agency, Sept. 17, 1947, p. 18, File Z5/59, CZAJ.
64. Meeting of the Executive (American Section) of the Jewish Agency, Sept. 18, 1947, p. 4, File Z5/56, ibid.
65. Lie, p. 162. Also see Abba Eban, *The New Diplomacy* (New York: Random House, 1983), p. 270.
66. Austin to the Sec. of State, No. 218, Feb. 27, [1948], Box 143, US Mission UN 1945–49, RG 84, NA.
67. Johnson (New York) to the Sec. of State, No. 783, Aug. 27, 1947, File 501.BB Palestine/8-2747, RG 59, NA.
68. *YUN, 1947–1948*, pp. 231–56.
69. *FRUS, 1947*, V, pp. 1289–90, 1297; Alexander Cadogan diary, Tues., Dec. 2, [1947], CCL; United Kingdom Delegation (United Nations) to the Foreign Office, No. 3688, Dec. 19, 1947, FO/371/61783.
70. Austin to the Sec. of State, No. 1279, Dec. 3, [1947], Box 141, US Mission UN 1945–49, RG 84, NA.
71. Lie, pp. 163–64.
72. Horowitz, p. 330. Also see Lie, p. 165.
73. United Kingdom Delegation (United Nations) to the Foreign Office, No. 3688, Dec. 19, 1947, FO/371/61893.
74. *PDD, December 1947–May 1948*, pp. 110, 125.
75. Austin to the Sec. of State, No. 30, Jan. 8, [1948], Box 142, US Mission UN 1945–49, RG 84, NA; United Kingdom Delegation (United Nations) to the Foreign Office, No. 53, Jan. 9, 1948, FO/371/68528.
76. Foreign Office to the United Kingdom Delegation (United Nations), No. 100, Jan. 8, 1948; and United Kingdom Delegation (United Nations), to the Foreign Office, No. 53, Jan. 9, 1948, FO/371/68528.
77. Memo. of Con. (Lie, Feller, Ross), Jan. 8, 1948, and the attached Secretariat memoranda, Oct. 17 and 22, 1947, Box 1, Rusk-McClintock Papers, RG 59, NA.
78. Lie, pp. 164–65.
79. Memo. of Con. (Price, Austin, Ross), Jan. 27, 1948, Box 9, Rusk-McClintock Papers, RG 59, NA.
80. McNeil to the Sec. of State and Sargent, Feb. 2, 1948, FO/371/68531.
81. *FRUS, 1948*, V, p. 615.
82. *PDD, December 1947–May 1948*, pp. 325–26, 344–45.
83. Ibid., p. 321. Also Lie to Shertok, Feb. 11, 1948, Box 3, Lie Papers, NMFA.
84. *FRUS, 1948*, V, p. 615.

85. *YUN, 1947–1948*, p. 256.
86. Lie, p. 166.
87. Canadian Perm. Delegate (United Nations) to the Sec. of State for External Affairs, No. 223, Feb. 20, 1948, Vol. 440, Mackenzie King Papers, MG 26, J1, PAC.
88. United Kingdom Delegation (United Nations) to the Foreign Office, No. 611, Feb. 21, 1948, Box 60, File 2, Creech Jones Papers, RHLOU.
89. *YUN, 1947–1948*, pp. 403–407; Lie, pp. 166–68.
90. Minutes of the Executive (American Section) of the Jewish Agency, Feb. 25, 1948, pp. 17–18, File Z5/2377, CZAJ.
91. Austin to the Sec. of State, No. 218, Feb. 27, [1948], Box 143, US Mission UN 1945–49, RG 84, NA. Also see Lie, p. 168.
92. Zvi Ganin, *Truman, American Jewry, and Israel, 1945–1948* (New York: Homes and Meier, 1979), p. 129.
93. Austin to the Sec. of State, No. 239, Mar. 4, [1948], Box 143, US Mission UN 1945–49, RG 84, NA.
94. *YUN, 1947–1948*, p. 407.
95. Canadian Perm. Delegate (United Nations) to the Sec. of State for External Affairs, No. 309, Mar. 8, 1948, Vol. 440, Mackenzie King Papers, MG 26, J1, PAC; Lie, p. 169.
96. Lie, p. 169.
97. Meeting of the Executive (American Section) of the Jewish Agency, Mar. 9, 1948, pp. 1–3, File Z5/2380, CZAJ.
98. *FRUS, 1948*, V, p. 701. Also see *YUN, 1947–1948*, p. 404; and *New York Times* (Mar. 9, 1948), p. 3.
99. *FRUS, 1948*, V, pp. 718–19.
100. *PDD, December 1947–May 1948*, p. 467.
101. Memo. of Con. (Mahmoud Fawzi Bey, Kopper), Mar. 12, 1948, Box 68, US Mission UN 1945–49, RG 84, NA.
102. *YUN, 1947–1948*, pp. 407–409.
103. United Kingdom Delegation (United Nations) to the Foreign Office, No. 932, Mar. 19, 1948, FO/371/68539; Lie, p. 170.
104. Lie, p. 170–71.
105. On this policy reversal, see the documents, editorial comments, and footnotes in *FRUS, 1948*, V, pp. 744–50.
106. *YUN, 1947–1948*, pp. 409–412.
107. Marshall (Bogota) to the Sec. of State, No. 20, Apr. 3, 1948, File 501.BB Palestine/4–348, RG 59, NA.
108. Austin (New York) to the Sec. of State, No. 380, Apr. 5, 1948, File 501.A Summaries/4–548, ibid.; Memo. of Con. (Parodi, Lie, McClintock), Apr. 5, 1948, Box 68, US Mission UN 1945–49, RG 84, NA; Lie to Gerhardsen, Apr. 5, 1948, Box 2, Lie Papers, NMFA. For Lund's pro-Zionist machinations while in Palestine, see *PDD, December 1947–May 1948*, pp. 433–39, 451–54, 491–93, 524, 563–65, 574, 583–86, 660–63, 664, 689–91, 722–23, 757, 778–79, 784–85.
109. In mid-June it was recalled to Cordier "the unfortunate experiences" that Washington had had with Lund in the Balkan commission, explaining that it "did not want American officers serving under him" as military observers for the council's Truce Commission. Cordier was receptive and admitted that Lund had caused difficulties and bedeviled the secretariat in Palestine "because of his free-wheeling and confusing operations." Lie naturally refused

to recall Lund but superseded him with a Swedish officer. Memo. of Con. (Cordier, Power), June 14, 1948, Box 69, US Mission UN 1945–49, RG 84, NA.

110. Lie, p. 172.

111. Eban to Moe, Apr. 12, 1948, Weizmann Paper, WAR.

112. *PDD, December 1947–May 1948*, p. 565.

113. Memo. of Con. (Stavropoulos, Cargo), Apr. 16, 1948, Box 69, US Mission UN 1945–49, RG 84, NA; Austin (New York) to the Sec. of State, No. 468, Apr. 18, 1948, File 501.BB Summaries/4-1848, RG 59, NA.

114. Austin (New York) to the Sec. of State, No. 476, Apr. 20, 1948, File 501.BB Summaries/4–2048, RG 59, NA.

115. Lie, p. 172; Eban, *Abba Eban*, p. 109. Also see *YUN, 1947–1948*, pp. 261–63.

116. Meeting of the Executive (American Section) of the Jewish Agency, May 10, 1948, pp. 4–5, File Z5/2388, CZAJ.

117. *YUN, 1947–1948*, pp. 281, 415.

118. Dan Kurzmann, *Genesis 1948*, (New York: World Publishing, 1970), pp. 254–55.

119. Lie to Bowles, May 14, 1948, Dag 1/1.1.2.2–1, UNA.

120. Feller to Lie, May 3, 1948, and the attached memorandum Stavropoulos to Feller, Box 2, Lie Papers, NMFA; Lie, p. 174.

121. Lie, pp. 174–75. Also see *YUN, 1947–1948*, pp. 416–17.

122. Austin to the Sec. of State, No. 664, May 17, [1948], Box 145, US Mission UN 1945–49, RG 84, NA; Memo. of Con. (Cordier, Power), May 15, 1948, Box 69, ibid.

123. Contacts made by Cordier with State Department officials with regard to the Palestine issue, May 15–17, 1948, Box 2, Lie Papers, NMFA; Memo. of Con. (Cordier, Power), May 15, 1948, Box 69, US Mission UN 1945–49, RG 84, NA.

124. Lie, pp. 175–78.

125. *FRUS, 1948*, V, pp. 1000–1001; Lie, pp. 178–79.

126. [Austin] to Lie, May 17, 1948, Box 53, Austin Papers, UVt.

127. J[ackson], Notes on a Conversation with Sir Alexander Cadogan, May 16, 1948; and J[ackson], Memorandum, May 17, 1948, Box 2, Lie Papers, NMFA. United Kingdom Delegation (United Nations) to the Foreign Office, May 17, 1948, FO/371/68553; Alexander Cadogan diary, Sun., May 16, [1948], CCL. The Jackson-Cadogan conversation is partially reproduced in Lie, pp. 179–81.

128. Foreign Office to the United Kingdom Delegation (United Nations), No. 2112, May 17, 1948, FO/371/68553.

129. Alexander Cadogan diary, Mon., May 17, [1948], CCL. Also see Lie, p. 182.

130. *FRUS, 1948*, V, pp. 999–1000.

131. Rusk through Lovett to the [Sec.] of State, May 20, 1948, Box 10, Rusk-McClintock Papers, RG 59, NA.

132. Marshall (Washington) to New York, No. 310, May 17, 1948, File 501.BB Palestine/5–1748, RG 59, NA.

133. *FRUS, 1948*, V, p. 1018.

134. Contacts made by Cordier with State Department officials with regard to the Palestine issue, May 15–17, 1948, Box 2, Lie Papers, NMFA. Cordier's report on his Washington conversations is partially reproduced in Lie, pp. 181–82.

135. Alexander Cadogan diary, Tues., May 18, and Wed., May 19, [1948], CCL.

136. United Kingdom Delegation (United Nations) to the Foreign Office, No. 1530, May 19, 1948, FO/371/72676.

137. P[aul] Mason, Position of the United Nations: Views of the Secretary-

General, May 21, 1948; Minutes by Gladwyn Jebb, May 21, 1948, and O[rme] Sargent, May 21, [1948], ibid.

138. Austin to the Sec. of State, No. 670, May 18, [1948], Box 145, US Mission UN 1945–49, RG 84, NA.

139. [Jackson] to Cadogan, May 26, 1948, FO/371/72676.

140. *DFPI*, I, p. 56.

141. On cricket jargon, see Urquhart, p. 116.

142. Minutes by Gladwyn Jebb, July 8, 1948, FO/371/72677.

143. Makins to Sargent, May 21, 1948, FO/371/68650.

144. [Jackson] to Cadogan, May 26, 1948, FO/371/72676; Jackson to Lie, May 26, 1948, Box 2, Lie Papers, NMFA. Jackson's report on his London conversations is partially reproduced in Lie, pp. 183–84.

145. [Jackson], untitled memorandum, [May 21, 1948], FO/371/72676.

146. Minutes by M[artin] R. Wright, May 21, 1948, FO/371/68650.

147. E[rnest] B[evin], Record of Conversation with Commander Jackson, May 22, 1948; and Foreign Office to the United Kingdom Delegation (United Nations), No. 2265, May 25, 1948, FO/371/68650. [Jackson] to Cadogan, May 26, 1948, FO/371/72676; Jackson to Lie, May 26, 1948, Box 2, Lie Papers, NMFA. Jackson's report on his London conversations is partially reproduced in Lie, pp. 183–84.

148. Foreign Office to the United Kingdom Delegation (United Nations), No. 2265, May 25, 1948, FO/371/68650.

149. Jebb to Roberts, May 24, [1948], ibid.

150. Jackson to Lie, May 26, 1948, Box 2, Lie Papers, NMFA. Jackson's report on his London conversations is partially reproduced in Lie, p. 185.

151. Brian Urquhart, Points from Commander Jackson, [May 25, 1948?], Box 2, Lie Papers, NMFA.

152. [Jackson] to Cadogan, May 26, 1948, FO/371/72676.

153. Cadogan to Jebb, May 27, 1948; minutes by Gladwyn Jebb, May 29, [1948], M[artin] R. Wright, May 29, [1948] and O[rme] S[argent], no date, ibid.

154. Alexander Cadogan diary, Thurs., May 27, [1948], CCL.

155. United Kingdom Delegation (United Nations) to the Foreign Office, No. 1607, 1608, and 1617, May 27, 1948; Jebb to Wright, May 28, 1948; Foreign Office to the United Kingdom Delegation (United Nations), No. 2347 and 2356, May 28, 1948; United Kingdom Delegation (United Nations) to the Foreign Office, No. 1620, May 28, 1948; Falla to Urquhart, May 29, 1948; Jacko [Jackson] to Jebb, June 2, 1948; United Kingdom Delegation (United Nations) to the Foreign Office, No. 1650, June 2, 1948; Falla to Mason, June 3, 1948, FO/371/72676.

156. Douglas (London) to the Sec. of State, No. 2315, May 28, 1948, File 501.BB Palestine/5–2848, RG 59, NA.

157. Lovett to London, No. 1964, May 28, 1948, File 501.BB Palestine/5–2848, ibid.

158. "Reminiscences of Loy W. Henderson" (typescript), pp. 137–39, Oral History Collection, TL; and "Reminiscences of Spruille Braden" (typescript), p. 2934, Oral History Collection, CU. Also see Evan M. Wilson, *Decision on Palestine* (Stanford, Calif.: Hoover Institution Press, 1979), pp. 11, 56, 58, 70, 78, 89, 94, 116, 127, 136, 142.

159. Meeting of the Executive (American Section) of the Jewish Agency, Oct. 8, 1947, p. 35, File A5/2371, CZAJ.

160. Minutes by Gladwyn Jebb, July 8, 1948, FO/371/72677.

161. Roberts to Jebb and Sargent, July 15, 1948, FO/371/72677.

162. Urquhart, p. 116.
163. Minutes by O[rme] S[argent], Aug. 4, 1948, FO/371/72676. If Lie had known of Jackson's serious doubts regarding the practicability of using United Nations guards in Palestine, even to defend United Nations personnel and equipment, it undoubtedly would have been additional lament by Lie about Jackson's alleged inadequacies. See Canadian Perm. Delegate (United Nations) to the Sec. of State for External Affairs, No. 813, July 28, 1948, File 2/16/0, Vol. 2614, RG 25, F6, PAC.
164. Lie to his wife and daughter Mette, No. 5, Aug. 19, 1948, Box 2, Lie Papers, NMFA.
165. [Jackson], untitled memorandum, Aug. 23, 1948, FO/371/72645, and Alexander Cadogan diary, Fri., Aug. 29, [1948], CCL.
166. Lie to Jackson, [Aug. 25, 1948], FO/371/72645.
167. Jackson to Cadogan, Aug. 25, 1948, ibid.
168. "Reminiscences of Andrew Cordier" (typescript), p. 304, Oral History Collection, CU.
169. Memo. of Con. (Cordier, Ross), Aug. 22, 1948, Box 111, US Mission UN 1945–49, RG 84, NA. Also see Walter R. Crocker, "Memoir about the United Nations" (typescript), p. 297, Evatt Papers, FUL; and Urquhart, p. 116.
170. Minutes by Gladwyn Jebb, July 8, 1948, FO/371/72677.
171. Robert McClintock, Memo. for the Files, June 29, 1948, Box 4, Rusk-McClintock Papers, RG 59, NA.
172. F. B. A. Rundall, Dismissal of Comm. Jackson, Sept. 2, 1948; and [Sargent] to Smith, Sept. 3, 1948, FO/371/72645.
173. Foreign Office to the United Kingdom Delegation (United Nations), No. 3530, Aug. 28, 1948; and United Kingdom Delegation (United Nations) to the Foreign Office, No. 2238, Aug. 29, 1948, ibid.
174. (Illegible initials) to Cordier, Sept. 14, 1948, 12/15, Microfilm copy of Cordier Papers, UNA.
175. McNeil to Lie, Sept. 22, 1948, Box 2, Lie Papers, NMFA.
176. Lie, p. 185.
177. DFPI, I, p. 119.
178. Rafael (Paris) to Shertok, Sept. 4, 1948, File 2404/3, ISAJ.
179. Cyrus L. Sulzberger, A Long Row of Candles; Memoirs and Diaries [1934–1954] (New York: Macmillan, 1969), p. 140. Lie's remarks may perhaps be traced to Bernadotte's activities during the last days of the war when he obtained the release of 20,000 Scandinavians, including Jews, as well as thousands of Jewish women from German camps in exchange for German military personnel interned in Sweden. Chaim Weizmann, The Letters and Papers of Chaim Weizmann, ed. Aaron Klieman (New Brunswick: Transaction Books, Rutgers University, 1980), Ser. A, XXIII, p. 160, n. 4. Also see Counte Folke Bernadotte, The Fall of the Curtain (London: Cassell, 1945), pp. 13, 24–26, 28–31, 34, 40–46, 48–49, 51, 53–54.
180. DFPI, I, pp. 186, 564. Also see Weizmann, Ser., A, XXIII, p. 160, n. 3.
181. DFPI, I, p. 569; and also Rafael (Paris) to Shertok, Sept. 4, 1948, File 2404/3, ISAJ.
182. DFPI, I, p. 312.
183. Lie to his wife, Sept. 23, 1948, Guri Lie Zeckendorf Papers, PP; Lie, pp. 190–91.
184. [Stoneman] to [Binder], Nov. 9, 1953, Binder Papers, NLC. On Lie's eulogy see GAOR, 136th Plen. Mtg., Sept. 21, 1948, pp. 20–23.
185. DFPI, I, p. 637.

186. Rafael (Paris) to Shertok, Sept. 4, 1948, File 2404/3, ISAJ.
187. *DFPI*, I, pp. 75, 568, 586; Rafael to Shertok, Sept. 4, 1948, File 2404/3, Rafael to Eytan, Apr. 8, 1949, File 2329/6, and Rafael to Eban, Apr. 8, 1949, File 64/1, ISAJ.
188. Eban to Eytan, Mar. 3, 1949, File 64/1, ISAJ; and Eban, *Abba Eban*, pp. 137–38. Also see Sulzberger, p. 110. Lie rationalized that the Negev's disposition as a "land bridge between Egypt and Jordan was based on outmoded strategic thinking," which explains his 1951 silence when informed that both countries might sign a peace treaty with Israel, provided Tel Aviv surrendered the whole of the Negev to Jordan. Memo. of Con. (Lie, Cordier, Porter, Tomlinson, Power), Aug. 18, 1949, Box 36, US Mission UN 1945–49, RG 84, NA; and Record of Con. with the Secretary-General . . . on the Middle East (Lie, Feller, Bowker, Oliver), May 3, [1951], FO/371/95589.
189. United Kingdom Delegation (United Nations) to the Foreign Office, No. 60, Jan. 10. 1949, FO/371/75400; Jessup (New York) to the Sec. of State, No. 25, Jan. 11, 1949, File 501.A Summaries/1–1149, RG 59, NA; *FRUS, 1949*, p. 687.
190. McNeil to the Sec. of State, Jan. 14, 1949, FO/371/75337.
191. Power to Ross, Feb. 24, 1949, Box 7, Rusk-McClintock Papers, RG 59, NA.
192. Eytan to Shibah, Apr. 1, 1949, File 2431/2, ISAJ.
193. Kohn to Sharett, Apr. 28, 1949, File 2454/10, ibid.
194. As late as August 1949 Lie was still making "disparaging remarks regarding British actions both in and out of [the] UN, stating [that the] UK [was] motivated by self-interest and almost as difficult to work with as [the] Soviets." Bay (Oslo) to the Sec. of State, No. 555, Aug. 11, 1949, File 501/8–1194, RG 59, NA.
195. Eban's comments in the Meeting of the Israeli Delegation to the United Nations, Oct. 21, 1948, File 183/1, ISAJ.
196. Lie, p. 192.
197. Urquhart, p. 119.
198. Ibid., pp. 118–19.
199. Power to Ross, Feb. 24, 1949, Box 7, Rusk-McClintock Papers, RG 59, NA; Memo. of Con. (Cordier, Power), Jan. 27, 1949, Memo. of Con. (Cordier, Power), Feb. 8, 1949, and Power to Austin, June 29, 1949, Box 87, US Mission UN 1945–49, RG 84, NA.
200. *FRUS, 1949*, VI, p. 931.
201. Memo. of Con. (Ordonneau, Ross), June 7, 1949, Box 87, US Mission UN 1945–49, RG 84, NA. Also see the *New York Times* (June 7, 1949), p. 5.
202. Power, Memo. for Files, June 20, 1949, Box 87, US Mission UN 1945–49, RG 84, NA.
203. Memo. of Con. (Cordier, Power), June 21, 1949, Box 87, ibid.
204. Bay (Oslo) to the Sec. of State, No. 555, Aug. 11, 1949, File 501/8–1149, RG 59, NA.
205. Memo. of Con. (Lie, Cordier, Porter, Tomlinson, Power), Aug. 18, 1949, Box 36, US Mission UN 1945–49, RG 84, NA.
206. Austin (New York) to the Sec. of State, No. 124, Oct. 21, 1949, File 501.BB/10–2149, RG 59, NA.
207. Austin (New York) to the Sec. of State, No. 1297, Oct. 29, 1949; and Austin (New York) to the Sec. of State, No. 1299, Oct. 28, 1949, Box 154, US Mission UN 1945–49, RG 84, NA.
208. *YUN, 1948–1949*, pp. 209–12.
209. Minutes by Orme Sargent, Aug. 4, 1948, FO/371/72677.
210. Memo. of Con. (Lie, Hall), Oct. 26, 1948, US Mission UN 1945–49, RG 84,

NA. Also see Memo. of Con. (Hill, Seymour, Tomlinson), Oct. 5, 1949, Box 41, ibid.; Austin (New York) to the Sec. of State, No. 1266, Oct. 18, 1949, Box 154, ibid.; Memo. of Con. (Lie, Cordier, Rockwell), Nov. 4, 1949, Box 36, ibid.; Note on a Conversation between the Secretary-General and Anthony Eden, Paris, Nov. 22, 1951, Box 2, Lie Papers, NMFA.

211. Stevenson (Cairo) to the Foreign Office, No. 306, Apr. 19, 1951, FO/371/91207.
212. Lie, pp. 195–96.
213. DFPI, I, pp. 250, 277; and [Eban] to [Weizmann], July 16, 1948, WAR.
214. Rafael to Eytan, Apr. 8, 1949, File 2329/6; and Rafael to Eban, Apr. 8, 1949, File 64/1, ISAJ.
215. Memo. of Con. (Lie, Ross), Nov. 7, 1949, Box 36, US Mission UN 1945–49, RG 84, NA; Austin (New York) to the Sec. of State, No. 1325, Nov. 9, 1949, Box 154, ibid.
216. Memo. of Con. (Atyeo, Howard), Nov. 24, 1949, Box 37, ibid.
217. Memo. of Con. (Cordier, Power), Nov. 26, 1949, Box 37, ibid.
218. YUN, 1948–1949, pp. 190–93.
219. Alexander Cadogan diary, Fri., Dec. 9, [1949], CCL.
220. YUN, 1948–1949, pp. 196–97.
221. Memo. of Con. (Lie, Noyes), Dec. 12, 1949, Box 55, US Mission UN 1945–49, RG 84, NA; Austin (New York) to the Sec. of State, No. 1426, Dec. 13, 1949, Box 155, ibid.
222. Lie, pp. 195–98.
223. Franks (Washington) to the Foreign Office, No. 1164, Apr. 17, 1951, and Foreign Office to Cairo, No. 369, Apr. 18, 1951, FO/371/91373; minutes by James C. Wardrop, and R[eginald] J. Bowker, Apr. 18, 1951, FO/371/91374; Stevenson (Cairo) to the Foreign Office, No. 306, Apr. 19, 1951, and minutes by Peter Hope, Apr. 21, 1951, FO/371/91207.
224. Chancery (British Legation, Damascus) to the Eastern Department, Apr. 28, 1951, FO/371/91854.
225. Bruins (Beirut) to the Department of State, No. 581, May 4, 1951, File 033.83A11/5–451, RG 59, NA. Also see FRUS, 1951, V, p. 649.
226. Failure of Plot to Kill Trygve Lie, May 1, 1951, CIA Files.
227. Kahany (Geneva) to Hachutz, No. 153, Jan. 17, 1951; Eytan to Kahany, Jan. 24, 1951; [Lie] to [Sharett], Mar. 20, 1951; Zinder to Bendor, Apr. 10, 1951, File 2404/3, ISAJ.
228. Weizmann to Lie, May 7, 1951, Weizmann Papers, WAR.
229. Helm (Tel Aviv) to the Foreign Office, No. 157, Apr. 30, 1951, FO/371/91374. Also see Helm (Tel Aviv) to Morrison, No. 192, Apr. 30, 1951, FO/371/91717.
230. Bovey (Oslo) to the Department of State, No. 211, Oct. 24, 1967; and Memo. of Con. (Lie, Bovey), May 23, 1967, in Tibbetts (Oslo) to the Department of State, No. 673, June 9, 1967, CIA Files.
231. Memo. of Con. (Lie, Jessup), Nov. 14, 1951, File 330/11–1451, RG 59, NA. Also see Philip C. Jessup, The Birth of Nations (New York: Columbia University Press, 1974), p. 107.

Notes for Chapter 7: Initiatives Everywhere

1. Ross (New York) to the Sec. of State, No. 1006, Aug. 27, 1949, Box 153, US Mission to UN 1945–49, RG 84, NA.

2. *FRUS, 1949*, II, p. 246; Memo. of Con. (Lie, Cohen, Howard), Sept. 24, 1949, Box 41; and Acheson (New York) to the Sec. of State, No. 1180, Sept. 24, 1949, Box 153, US Mission UN 1945–49, RG 84, NA.

3. Trygve Lie, *In the Cause of Peace* (New York: Macmillan, 1954), p. 253.

4. Memo. of Con. (Lie, Romulo, Pearson, Cohen, Howard), Sept. 26, 1949; and Acheson (New York) to the Sec. of State, No. 1190, Sept. 27, 1949, Box 153, US Mission UN 1945–49, RG 84, NA.

5. *FRUS, 1949*, II, pp. 253–54.

6. Austin (New York) to the Sec. of State, No. 1209, Oct. 1, 1949, File 501.A Summaries/10–149, RG 59, NA; and *FRUS, 1949*, II, 256–57.

7. *FRUS, 1949*, II, pp. 257–58; Austin (New York) to the Sec. of State, No. 1218, Oct. 4, 1949, Box 153, US Mission UN, 1945–1949, RG 59, NA.

8. *FRUS, 1949*, II, pp. 259–60. Also see Lie, pp. 367–68.

9. *FRUS, 1949*, II, pp. 280–81; and Austin (New York) to the Sec. of State, No. 1284, Oct. 22, 1949, File 501.A Summaries/10–2249, RG 59, NA.

10. Lie, passim.

11. Memo. of Con. (McNeil, Nervo, Pearson, Lie, Jessup), Nov. 30, 1949, Box 55, US Mission UN 1945–49, RG 84, NA.

12. Dai-Ming Lee, Chinese Democratic Constitutionalist Party to Lie, May 27, 1948, Microfilm Reel No. 45, Frame Nos. 934–935, Wallace Papers, UI.

13. Ross (New York) to the Sec. of State, No. 4, Jan. 5, 1949, File 501.BC/1–549, RG 59, NA; *New York Times* (Jan. 6, 1950), p. 15.

14. Jessup (New York) to the Sec. of State, No. 8, Jan. 6, 1949, Box 150, US Mission UN 1945–49, RG 84, NA.

15. Stuart (Nanking) to the Sec. of State, No. 304, Feb. 3, 1949, File 501/2–239, RG 59, NA.

16. Austin (New York) to the Sec. of State, No. 135, Feb. 4, 1949, File 501/2–449, ibid.; Austin to the Sec. of State, No. 142, Feb. 4, 1949, Box 150, US Mission UN 1945–49, RG 84, NA.

17. Memos. of Con. (Cordier, Power), Feb. 2 and 9, 1949, Box 111, US Mission UN 1945–49, RG 84, NA.

18. *FRUS, 1949*, II, pp. 154–55, 158, 163, 175–76, 185; United Kingdom Delegation (United Nations) to the in Foreign Office, No. 741, Aug. 30, 1949, FO/371/75832; Alexander Cadogan diary, Wed., Aug. 31, [1949], CCL.

19. Memo. of Con. (Romulo, Lie, Jessup), Nov. 20, 1949, Box 42, US Mission UN 1945–49, RG 84, NA.

20. Memo. of Con. (Cordier, Power), Nov. 26, 1949, Box 37, ibid.

21. *YUN, 1948–1949*, pp. 294–98.

22. *FRUS, 1949*, IX, p. 195.

23. Austin (New York) to the Sec. of State, No. 9, Jan. 6, 1950, File 310.5/1-650, RG 59, NA.

24. *FRUS, 1950*, II, pp. 189–90.

25. Lie, pp. 249–54.

26. *FRUS, 1950*, II, pp. 200–201.

27. Minutes by P[aul] C. Holmer, Jan. 31, [1950], FO/371/88503.

28. *FRUS, 1950*, II, pp. 205–206; an untitled memorandum of conversation dated Jan. 23, 1950, Box 1, Lie Papers, NMFA. Lie's published version of this interview should be approached with caution. Lie, pp. 254–55.

29. Lie, pp. 225–57. The Feller-Kerno memorandum is in UN Doc. S/1466, Mar. 9, 1950.

30. Note of Con. between Trygve Lie and Sir Alexander Cadogan on the Chinese

Question, Jan. 24, 1950, Box 1, Lie Papers, NMFA; United Kingdom Delegation (United Nations) to the Foreign Office, No. 100, Jan. 25, 1950, FO/371/88502; Alexander Cadogan diary, Tues., Jan 24, [1950], CCL; Lie, pp. 258–59.

31. United Kingdom Delegation (United Nations) to the Foreign Office, No. 105, Jan. 26, 1950; and minutes by H[ector] Mc[Neil], Jan. 30, 1950, FO/371/88503.

32. R[osamund] Benson, Chinese Representation in the Security Council, Feb. 2, 1950, FO/371/88504.

33. *FRUS, 1950*, II, p. 226; United Kingdom Delegation (United Nations) to the Foreign Office, No. 21, Feb. 17, 1950, FO/371/88504.

34. Lie, p. 259.

35. *FRUS 1950*, II, pp. 210–14, 217. On Lie's denial that he spoke to Russia's Malik, see Lie, p. 260.

36. Note of a conversation with Ambassador Tsiang on Feb. 9, [1950]. Box 1, Lie Papers, NMFA. For Lie's scrubbed version of this conversation, see Lie, p. 260.

37. Lie, p. 261.

38. *FRUS, 1950*, II, pp. 227–31. See Lie, p. 261; and Memo. of Con. (Lie, Ross), Feb. 25, 1950, File 330/2–2550, RG 59, NA. On the Yugoslav origins of Lie's proposal, see Shone to an unknown addressee, Mar. 9, 1950, and United Kingdom Delegation (United Nations) to the Foreign Office, No. 307, Mar. 9, 1950, FO/371/88507.

39. Foreign Office to the United Kingdom Delegation (United Nations) No. 361, Mar. 2, 1950, FO/371/88507.

40. United Kingdom Delegation (United Nations) to the Foreign Office, No. 274 and Nos. 275, Mar. 3, 1950, and 286, Mar. 4, 1950, ibid.

41. Foreign Office to the United Kingdom Delegation (United Nations), No. 404, Mar. 10, 1950, ibid.

42. [Franks] (Washington) to the Foreign Office, No. 145, Mar. 14, 1950, ibid.

43. *FRUS, 1950*, II, pp. 231–33; Under Secretary's Meeting, Mon. Mar. 6, 1950, General Records of the Department of State, Office of the Executive Secretariat, RG 59, NA. Also see Franks (Washington) to the Foreign Office, No. 817, Mar. 10, 1950, FO/371/88507.

44. *FRUS, 1950*, II, pp. 233–37. For Gross's comment to Shone, see United Kingdom Delegation (United Nations) to the Foreign Office, No. 307, Mar. 9, 1950, FO/371/88507.

45. Franks (Washington) to the Foreign Office, No. 782, Mar. 8, 1950, FO/371/88504. Also see Memo. of Con. (Hoyer Miller, Sandifer, Raynor, Bancroft), Mar. 10, 1950, File 310.2/3–1050, RG 59, NA; Lie, p. 261; *New York Times* (Mar. 8, 1950), pp. 1, 12; and (Mar. 9, 1950), p. 16.

46. Shone to an unknown addressee, Mar. 9, 1950, FO/371/88507.

47. UN Doc. S/1466, Mar. 9, 1950.

48. UN Doc. S/1470, Mar. 15, 1950.

49. *New York Times* (Mar. 9, 1950), p. 16; and (Mar. 10, 1950), p. 13; Lie, pp. 261–62.

50. United Kingdom Delegation (United Nations) to the Foreign Office, No. 308, Mar. 9, 1950, FO/371/88504.

51. United Kingdom Delegation (United Nations) to the Foreign Office, No. 155, Mar. 31, 1950, FO/371/88508.

52. Parrott to Laskey, Apr. 19, 1950, FO/371/88414.

53. Laskey to Parrott, Apr. 21, 1950, FO/371/88416.

54. Shone to an unknown addressee, Mar. 9, 1950, FO/371/88507.

55. *FRUS, 1950*, II, pp. 238–43.

56. Memo. of Mar. 10, 1950; and Memo. of Mar. 12, 1950, Box 149, Koo Papers, CU.
57. UN Doc. S/1470, Mar. 15, 1950.
58. United Kingdom Delegation (United Nations) to the Foreign Office, No. 338, Mar. 14, 1950, FO/371/88504.
59. Popper to Bacon and Meeker, Mar. 17, 1950, File 310.2/3-1750, RG 59, NA.
60. Younger to Cadogan, No. 104, Apr. 28, 1950, FO/371/88619; and Shone to Jebb, Apr. 13, 1950, FO/371/88415.
61. [Laskey] to Parrott, Apr. 4, 1950, FO/371/88608.
62. Parrott to Laskey, Apr. 17, 1950, ibid.
63. United Kingdom Delegation (United Nations) to the Foreign Office, No. 343, Mar. 15, 1950, FO/371/88507.
64. Tsiang to Chih-mai, Mar. 16, 1950, Box 149, Koo Papers, CU. On the American attitude toward the connection between recognition and representation, see *FRUS, 1950*, II, p. 244. As to Lie's pressure on Cairo, see Caffery (Cairo) to the Sec. of State, No. 262, Mar. 18, 1950, File 310.2/3–1850; and Caffery (Cairo) to the Sec. of State, No. 278, Mar. 22, 1950, File 310.2/3–2250, RG 59, NA.
65. United Kingdom Delegation (United Nations) to the Foreign Office, No. 375, Mar. 20, 1950, FO/371/88505.
66. Shone to Jebb, Mar. 21, 1950, FO/371/88420.
67. Lie, pp. 262–63.
68. Meade (Washington) to Parrott, Mar. 30, 1950, FO/371/88619.
69. Text, *United Nations Bulletin*, 8, no. 9 (Apr. 1, 1950), pp. 286–88, 313.
70. Meade (Washington) to Parrott, Mar. 30, 1950, FO/371/88619.
71. Note, Wed., Mar. 23, 1950, Box 1, Lie Papers, NMFA; Lie, p. 263.
72. Younger to Cadogan, No. 104, Apr. 28, 1950, FO/371/88619. Also see Douglas (London) to the Sec. of State, No. 2337, Apr. 28, 1950, File 320/4–2850, RG 59, NA.
73. Meade (Washington) to Parrott, May 19, 1950, FO/371/88508.
74. Drew Pearson, *Diaries 1949–1959* (New York: Holt, Rinehart, and Winston, 1974), p. 115.
75. Younger to Cadogan, No. 104, Apr. 28, 1950, FO/371/88619.
76. Meade (Washington) to Parrott, May 19, 1950, FO/371/88508.
77. *FRUS, 1950*, II, pp. 268–69, 285–86.
78. Kathleen Teltsch, *Crosscurrents at Turtle Bay* (Chicago: Quadrangle, 1970), p. 44.
79. Matthews (Stockholm) to the Sec. of State, No. 251, Feb. 27, 1950, File 958.61/2750, RG 59, NA.
80. This chapter, p. 236.
81. *New York Times* (Apr. 15, 1950), pp. 1–2; Acting Canadian Perm. Delegate (United Nations) to the Sec. of State for External Affairs, No. 258, Apr. 17, 1950, File 5475-6-40, ADEAC.
82. Holmes (New York) to Heeney, May 11, 1950, Vol. 7, Pearson Papers, MG 26, N, PAC.
83. Lie, p. 264.
84. "Reminiscences of Andrew Cordier" (typescript), p. 319, Oral History Collection, CU.
85. Lie, pp. 278–83.
86. Hickerson to Webb, Apr. 17, 1950, File 315/4–1750, RG 59, NA.
87. *FRUS, 1950*, II, pp. 371–73. Also see Price's memorandum of the conversation dated Apr. 21, 1950, Box 1, Lie Papers, NMFA; and used by Lie, pp. 283–85.

88. Sec. of State for External Affairs to the Acting Canadian Perm. Delegate (United Nations), No. 216, Apr. 25, 1950, Vol. 7, Pearson Papers, MG 26, N, PAC.

89. Pearson for the Prime Minister, Apr. 27, 1950; Pearson to Heeney, Apr. 27, 1950; and Riddell to Holmes, Apr. 28, 1950, ibid.

90. This conversation is reconstructed from Younger to Cadogan, No. 104, Apr. 28, 1950, FO/371/88619; and interview with Kenneth Younger, Minister of State, at the Foreign Office, London, Apr. 28, 1950, Lie Papers, Box 1, NMFA. Also see Lie, p. 266.

91. Interview with Sir Gladwyn Jebb, at the Foreign Office, London, Apr. 28, 1950, Box 1, Lie Papers, NMFA. Also see Lie, pp. 265–66.

92. Interview with Prime Minister C. R. Attlee, No. 10 Downing Street, London, Apr. 28, 1950, Lie Papers, Box 1, NMFA; note by C[lement] R. Attlee, Apr. 29, 1950, FO/371/88619. Also see Lie, p. 266.

93. Foreign Office to British diplomatic missions, No. 89, May 9, 1950, FO/371/88391.

94. Douglas (London) to the Sec. of State, No. 2337, Apr. 28, 1950, File 320/4–2850, RG 59, NA.

95. Austin (New York) to the Sec. of State, No. 352, Apr. 19, 1950, File 310.5/4–1950, RG 59, NA.

96. Henri Laugier's minutes on a conversation with Vincent Auriol, May 1, 1950, Memorandum of a Conversation with Robert Schuman, May 2, 1950, interview with Georges Bidault at the Palais Matignon, May 2, 1950, interview with Robert Schuman, May 4, 1950, interview with Alexander Parodi, May 4, 1950, Box 1, Lie Papers, NMFA. Lie, p. 266.

97. Interview with Chiroky [Siroky], Minister of Foreign Affairs, May 10, 1950, Box 1, Lie Papers, NMFA; Lie, pp. 235–36.

98. Thompson to the Acting Secretary [of State], May 9, 1950, File 661.00/5–950, RG 59, NA.

99. Kelly (Moscow) to the Foreign Office, No. 396, May 5, 1950, FO/371/88393; Stansfield (Moscow) to the Sec. of State for External Affairs, No. 180, May 19, 1950, File 5475-6-40, ADEAC.

100. Kelly (Mosocw) to the Foreign Office, No. 417, May 12, 1950, FO/371/86836. Also see Stansfield (Moscow) to the Sec. of State for External Affairs, No. 180, May 19, 1950, File 5475-6-40, ADEAC.

101. Kirk (Moscow) to the Sec. of State, No. 1361, May 12, 1950, File 310.5/5–1250, RG 59, NA.

102. Stansfield (Moscow) to the Sec. of State for External Affairs, No. 180, May 19, 1950, File 5475-6-40, ADEAC.

103. Nielson (Oslo) to the Sec. of State, No. 208, July 16, 1946, File 501.BA/7–1646, Nielson (Oslo) to the Sec. of State, No. 473, July 22, 1946, File 501.BC/7–2246, Smith (Moscow) to the Sec. of State, No. 2253, July 23, 1946, File 501.BC/7–2346, RG 59, NA; Wardrop (Oslo) to Bevin, No. 237, July 16, 1946, Collier (Oslo) to Warner, July 19, 1946, Peterson (Moscow) to the Foreign Office, No. 2461, July 22, 1946, FO/371/59754; Lie, pp. 221–26.

104. Peterson (Moscow) to the Foreign Office, Nos. 2506 and 2507, July 25, 1946, FO/371/56287; Lie, pp. 226–30.

105. Memo. of Con. (Cordier, Rothwell), Aug. 14, 1946, Box 71, US Mission UN 1945–49, RG 84, NA.

106. Bland (The Hague) to the Foreign Office, No. 308, July 26, 1946, FO/371/59754.

107. Conversation with Vyshinsky, May 12, 1950, Box 1, Lie Papers, NMFA. Also see Lie, p. 267.

108. Conversation with the Vice-Minister for Foreign Affairs of the USSR, Mr. Gromyko, May 13, 1950; and untitled note, May 13, 1950, Box 1, Lie Papers, NMFA. Also see Kirk (Moscow) to the Sec. of State, No. 1428, May 19, 1950, File 661.00/5–1950, RG 59, NA.
109. Kirk (Mosocw) to the Sec. of State, No. 1379, May 13, 1950, File 310.5/5–1350, RG 59, NA.
110. Interview with Generalissimo Stalin, Vice-Minister of State Molotov and Minister of Foreign Affairs Vyshinsky in the Kremlin, May 15, 1950, Box 1, Lie Papers, NMFA. Also see Lie, pp. 267, 291–307.
111. Douglas (London) to the Sec. of State, No. 2337, Apr. 28, 1950, File 320/4–2850, RG 59, NA.
112. Untitled note, May 16, 1950, Box 1, Lie Papers, NMFA; Lie, pp. 267–69.
113. Untitled note, May 13, 1950, Box 1, Lie Papers, NMFA.
114. Conversation with Vyshinsky, May 18, 1950, ibid. Also see Lie, p. 270.
115. Kelly (Moscow) to the Foreign Office, No. 432, May 18, 1950, FO/371/86836. Also see Stansfield (Moscow) to the Sec. of State for External Affairs, No. 180, May 19, 1950, File 5475-6-40, ADEAC.
116. Kirk (Moscow) to the Sec. of State, No. 1413, May 17, 1950, File 315/5–1750, RG 59, NA.
117. Untitled note, June 12, Box 1, Lie Papers, NMFA. See Lie, pp. 307–309.
118. Bruce (Paris) to the Sec. of State, No. 2504, May 25, 1950, File 850.33/5–2550, RG 59, NA.
119. Untitled note, June 12, 1950, Box 1, Lie Papers, NMFA. See Lie, pp. 307–309.
120. [Harvey] (Paris) to the Foreign Office, No. 188, May 24, 1950, FO/371/88393.
121. Bruce (Paris) to the Sec. of State, No. 2504, May 25, 1950, File 850.33/5–2550, RG 59, NA.
122. Untitled note, May 23, 1950, Lie Papers, NMFA; Bevin (London) to Cadogan, No. 129, May 23, 1950, FO/371/88620. Also see Lie, pp. 309–11.
123. Minutes by P[aul] C. Holmers, May 25, [1950], FO/371/88620.
124. Untitled note, May 23, 1950, Box 1, Lie Papers, NMFA. For Lie's promised statement, see UN Press Release SG/93, May 24, 1950. Also see Lie, pp. 312–14.
125. Untitled note, May 23, 1950, Box 1, Lie Papers, NMFA.
126. Untitled note, Wed., May 24, 1950, Box 1, Lie Papers, ibid.; Younger to the United Nations (Political) Department, May 29, 1950, FO/371/88508.
127. [Pearson], Memo. to the Prime Minister, May 24, 1950, File 5474-6-40, ADEAC.
128. Untitled note, Wed., May 24, 1950, Box 1, Lie Papers, NMFA. Also see Jebb to Strang, May 24, 1950, FO/371/88391.
129. Note, May 24, 1950, Box 1, Lie Papers, NMFA.
130. FRUS, 1950, II, pp. 379–83; [Byron Price], An untitled memorandum, May 31, 1950, Box 1, Lie Papers, NMFA. Also see Lie, pp. 314–15.
131. FRUS, 1950, II, pp. 383–84 and IV, pp. 1200–1201; [Byron Price], Untitled memo., May 31, 1950, Box 1, Lie Papers, NMFA. Also see Lie, pp. 315–16.
132. [George Ignatieff?], Mr. Hickerson's Account of the Results of Trygve Lie's Mission to Moscow, June 3, 1950, File 1950, UN General (A) Pt., I, RG 25, B3, Vol. 2155, PAC.
133. Dean Acheson, Present at the Creation (New York: Norton, 1969), p. 378.
134. FRUS, 1950, II, p. 396 n., and IV, pp. 261–62.
135. Royal Institute of International Affairs, Documents on International Affairs 1949–1950, ed. Margaret Carlyle (London: Oxford University Press, 1953), p. 139.

136. UN Doc., Press Release SG/88, May 19, 1950. Also see the *New York Times* (May 18, 1950), p. 4.
137. Pearson to Wrong, June 7, 1950, File 5475-6-40, ADEAC.
138. Acting Canadian Perm. Delegate (United Nations) to the Sec. of State for External Affairs, No. 347, June 2, 1950, File 5475-6-40, ibid. Also see the *New York Times* (June 2, 1950), p. 6.
139. *FRUS, 1950,* II, pp. 385–89.
140. Lie, pp. 316–17.
141. GAOR, 5th Sess., Annexes Vol. II, agenda item 60, UN Doc., A/1304.
142. *Department of State Bulletin,* 22 (1950): 1050–1951.
143. Franks (Washington) to Younger, No. 460, June 6, 1950, FO/371/88620.
144. *FRUS, 1950,* II, p. 390.
145. United Kingdom Delegation (United Nations) to the Foreign Office, No. 334, August 28, 1950, FO/371/88397; *FRUS, 1950,* III, p. 1128.
146. *FRUS, 1950,* II, p. 391 n.; and III, pp. 1117–19, 1128–29, 1183–84; Peter Hope, Mr. Lie's Peace Program, Sept. 6, 1950, FO/371/88622.
147. Lie, pp. 316–22; *YUN, 1950,* pp. 214–20.

Notes for Chapter 8: Thunder in the East

1. Edward R. Stettinius, Jr., *The Diaries of Edward R. Stettinius, Jr., 1943–1946,* eds. Thomas W. Campbell and George C. Herring (New York: New Viewpoints, 1975), p. 474.
2. Chapter 3, p. 000.
3. Jean Chauvel, *Commentaire d'Alger à Berne (1944–1952)* (Paris: Fayard, 1972), II, p. 227.
4. Memo. of Con. (Tournelle, Maffitt), Jan. 17, 1949, Box 110, US Mission UN 1945–49, RG 84, NA.
5. Memo. of Con. (Lapie, Ordonneau, Noyes, Maffitt), Apr. 29, 1949, Box 71, US Mission UN 1945–49, RG 84, NA; Austin (New York) to the Sec. of State, No. 543, Apr. 30, 1949, File 501.A Summaries/4–3049, RG 59, NA; Memo. of Con. (Tsiang, Stein), Apr. 30, 1949, Memo. of Con. (Riddell, Raynor), Apr. 29, 1949, Box 71, US Mission UN 1945–49, RG 84, NA; Austin (New York) to the Sec. of State, No. 548, May 1, 1949, File 501.A Summaries/5–149, RG 59, NA; Memo. of Con. (Ordonneau, Crawford), May 3, 1949, Box 71, US Mission UN 1945–1949, RG 84, NA; [Austin] (New York) to the Sec. of State, No. 558, May 4, 1949, File 501.A Summaries/5–449, RG 59, NA.
6. Austin (New York) to the Sec. of State, No. 589, May 13, 1949, File/501.A Summaries/5–1349, RG 59, NA.
7. Memo. of Con. (Aghnides, Hall), May 23, 1949, Box 112, US Mission UN 1945–49, RG 84, NA. With Soviet Russia as a neighbor, Turkey's preference for Lie was understandable. Memo. of Con. (Dendramis, Howard), Dec. 8, 1949, Box 55, ibid.
8. J[ohn] W. Holmes, Memo. for the Deputy Under-Secretary of State for External Affairs, July 26, 1949, File 5475-1-40, ADEAC.
9. Power to Hickerson, Sept. 1, 1949; and Ross to Hickerson, Sept. 6, 1949, Box 112, US Mission UN 1945–49, RG 84, NA; Canadian Perm. Delegate (United Nations) to the Sec. of State for External Affairs, No. 1015, Sept. 7, 1949, File 5475-1-40, ADEAC.
10. Cadogan to [Jebb], Aug. 11, 1949, FO/371/78794.
11. Minutes by D. J. Speares, Aug. 24, [1949], C[ecil] C. Parrott, Aug. 26, [1949],

Gladwyn Jebb, Aug. 28, [1949], H[ector] McNeil, Sept. 1, 1949, Roger Allen, Sept. 2, 1949, G[ladwyn] J[ebb], Sept. 5, [1949], ibid.

12. Salt to Jebb, Oct. 1, 1949, ibid.

13. Malcolm to Allen, Nov. 28, 1949, and Allen to Malcolm, Dec. 14, 1949, ibid.; Lewis to Allen, Jan. 10, 1950, FO/371/88488.

14. Trygve Lie, *In the Cause of Peace* (New York: Macmillan, 1954), pp. 367–68.

15. Austin (New York) to the Sec. of State, No. 1437, Dec. 16, 1949, Box 155, US Mission UN 1945–49, RG 84, NA. Also see *New York Times* (Dec. 16, 1949), p. 5; and Lie, p. 369.

16. Lie, p. 369.

17. Wrong to Pearson, Dec. 22, 1949, Vol. 4, Pearson Papers, MG 26, N1, PAC.

18. [Pearson] to Wrong, Dec. 29, 1949, Vol. 4, Pearson Papers, MG 26, N1, PAC.

19. Soviet Appraisal of Trygve Lie, Apr. 3, 1950, CIA Files.

20. Lie, p. 368.

21. [Pearson], Memo. for the Prime Minister, Apr. 14, 1950, Vol. 17, Pearson Papers, MG 26, N1, PAC.

22. Meade (Washington) to Parrott, June 7, 1950, FO/371/88448.

23. *FRUS, 1950*, II, pp. 87–89.

24. Ibid., pp. 98–99; and Alexander Cadogan diary, Mon., May 15, [1950], CCL.

25. Untitled note, May 15, 1950, Box 1, Lie Papers, NMFA; and Lie, p. 368.

26. Ross (New York) to the Sec. of State, No. 487, June 7, 1950, File 310.5/6–750, RG 59, NA.

27. [Jebb] to Cadogan, May 23, 1950, FO/371/88394.

28. Jebb to Strang, May 24, 1950, FO/371/88391.

29. Minutes by C[ecil] C. Parrott, June 2, 1950, ibid.

30. *FRUS, 1950*, II, pp. 99–100. On Tsiang's statement denouncing Lie, see the *New York Times* (June 1, 1950), p. 9.

31. United Kingdom Delegation (United Nations) to the Foreign Office, No. 237, June 15, 1950, FO/371/88448; *FRUS, 1950*, II, pp. 101–102; and Gross (New York) to the Sec. of State, No. 517, June 16, 1950, File 310.5/6–1650, RG 59, NA.

32. Lie, pp. 368–69.

33. *New York Times* (June 23, 1950), p. 14, and (June 24, 1950), p. 4; *New York Herald Tribune* (June 19, 1950), pp. 1–2.

34. Lie, pp. 335, 342, 369–70.

35. Ledward to Lasky, July 6, 1950, FO/371/88513.

36. Jebb (New York) to Dixon, July 10, 1950, FO/371/88448.

37. Wrong (Washington) to the Sec. of State for External Affairs, No. 1764, July 13, 1950, File 5475-1-40, ADEAC. Also see Memo. of Con. (Ignatieff, Raynor), July 12, 1950, File 315.3/7–1250, RG 59, NA.

38. Sparks (Copenhagen) to the Sec. of State, No. 178, Aug. 14, 1950, File 310.357/8–1450, RG 59, NA.

39. Foreign Office to the United Kingdom Delegation (United Nations), No. 562, July 21, 1950, FO/371/88448.

40. Austin (New York) to the Sec. of State, No. 75, July 18, 1950, File 310.5/7–1850, RG 59, NA.

41. United Kingdom High Commissioner (Canada) to the Commonwealth Relations Office, No. 124, Aug. 15, 1950, FO/371/88448.

42. Acheson (Washington) to USUN, No. 162, Aug. 17, 1950, File 315.3/8–1750, RG 59, NA.

43. United Kingdom Delegation (United Nations) to the Foreign Office, No. 874, Aug. 22, 1950, FO/371/88448.

44. *FRUS, 1950*, II, p. 1132; Foreign Office to the United Kingdom Delegation (United Nations), No. 1071, Aug. 28, 1950, and the United Kingdom Delegation (United Nations) to the Foreign Office, No. 338, Aug. 29, 1950, FO/371/88448.

45. *FRUS, 1950*, II, pp. 112–15; and Cabinet Steering Committee on International Organisations. Sept. 12, 1950, CAB/134/402, PRO.

46. *FRUS, 1950*, II, pp. 119–20.

47. Holmes to Shannon, Oct. 3, 1950, and the enclosed instructions on Lie's appointment to the Canadian delegation at the United Nations, File 5475-1-40, ADEAC.

48. *FRUS, 1950*, II, p. 121. See p. 370 in Lie's disingenuous memoirs.

49. Austin (New York) to the Sec. of State, No. 469, Sept. 7, 1950, File 310.5/9–750, RG 59, NA.

50. Jebb to Younger, No. 35, Sept. 16, 1950; and minutes by A[rchibald] R. Mackenzie, Sept. 26, [1950], FO/371/88404.

51. Austin (New York) to the Sec. of State, No. 613, Sept. 27, 1950, File 310.5/9–2750, RG 59, NA.

52. Lie, pp. 370–73.

53. *FRUS, 1950*, II, p. 128.

54. Austin (New York) to the Sec. of State, No. 651, Oct. 5, 1950, File 310.5/10–550, RG 59, NA.

55. *FRUS, 1950*, II, pp. 129–34.

56. SCOR, 5th Yr., 509th Mtg., Oct. 9, 1950.

57. Lie, pp. 374–75.

58. United Kingdom Delegation (United Nations) to the Foreign Office, No. 1347, Oct. 9, 1950, FO/371/88448.

59. Lie, pp. 375–76.

60. Foreign Office to the United Nations Delegation (United Nations), No. 1619, Oct. 10, 1950, FO/371/88448.

61. United Kingdom Delegation (United Nations) to the Foreign Office, No. 1366, Oct. 11, 1950, and the Foreign Office to the United Kingdom Delegation (United Nations), No. 1637, Oct. 12, 1950, ibid.

62. *FRUS, 1950*, II, pp. 136–38; and Lie, pp. 376–77. Also see SCOR, 5th Yr., 510th Mtg., Oct. 12, 1950. Rau certainly had received instructions by October 9 to extend Lie's term. United Kingdom Commissioner (India) to the Commonwealth Relations Office, No. 2855, Oct. 9, 1950, FO/371/88448.

63. Younger to Bevin, Oct. 16, 1950, FO/371/88495.

64. United Kingdom Delegation (United Nations) to the Foreign Office, No. 1423, Oct. 16, 1950, and Foreign Office to the United Kingdom Delegation (United Nations), No. 1696, Oct. 17, 1950, FO/371/88448.

65. *FRUS, 1950*, II, pp. 138–41.

66. United Kingdom Delegation (United Nations) to the Foreign Office, No. 1438, Oct. 17, 1950, FO/371/88448.

67. Austin (New York) to the Sec. of State, No. 678, Oct. 13, 1950, File 310.5/10–1350, RG 59, NA.

68. Foreign Office to the United Kingdom Delegation (United Nations), No. 1704, Oct. 18, 1950, FO/371/88448.

69. Peter Hope, Secretary-General of the United Nations, Oct. 18, 1950, FO/371/88449.

70. Austin (New York) to the Sec. of State, No. 692, Oct. 18, 1950, File 310.5/10–1850, RG 59, NA.

71. *FRUS, 1950*, II, pp. 141–46, 147–48; and Lie, pp. 377–78. Also see SCOR, 5th Yr., 512th Mtg., Oct. 18, 1950.

72. United Kingdom Delegation (United Nations) to the Foreign Office, No. 1450, Oct. 18, 1950, FO/371/88448; and United Kingdom Delegation (United Nations) to the Foreign Office, No. 1463, Oct. 19, 1950, FO/371/88449.
73. *FRUS, 1950*, II, pp. 150–51.
74. CAB/128/18, Oct. 19, 1950, PRO.
75. Douglas to Bevin, Oct. 19, 1950, FO/371/88449.
76. *FRUS, 1950*, II, pp. 146–50.
77. Foreign Office to Washington, No. 4652, Oct. 20, 1950, and Franks (Washington) to the Foreign Office, No. 2830, Oct. 20, 1950, FO/371/88449. Also see *FRUS, 1950*, II, p. 153.
78. Foreign Office to the United Kingdom Delegation (United Nations), No. 1731, Oct. 20, 1950, FO/371/88449. Also see *FRUS, 1950*, II, p. 153 n.
79. *FRUS, 1950*, II, pp. 151–56.
80. United Kingdom High Commissioner (India) to the Commonwealth Relations Office, No. 2963, Oct. 20, 1950, FO/371/88449.
81. Austin (New York) to the Sec. of State, No. 713, Oct. 21, 1950, File 310.5/10–2150, RG 59, NA. Also see *FRUS, 1950*, II, p. 156; and SCOR, 5th Yr., 513th Mtg., Oct. 20, and 21, 1950.
82. United Kingdom Delegation (United Nations) to the Foreign Office, No. 1490, Oct. 20, 1950, and the Foreign Office to the United Kingdom Delegation (United Nations), No. 1738, Oct. 20, 1950, FO/371/88449.
83. Foreign Office to the United Kingdom Delegation (United Nations), No. 1746, Oct. 21, 1950, and United Kingdom High Commissioner (India) to the Commonwealth Relations Office, No. 2996, Oct. 26, 1950, ibid.
84. Austin (New York) to the Sec. of State, No. 716, Oct. 22, 1950, File 310.5/10–2250, RG 59, NA. Also see *FRUS, 1950*, II, p. 156; and SCOR, 5th Yr., 513th Mtg., Oct. 20 and 21, 1950.
85. United Kingdom Delegation (United Nations) to the Foreign Office, No. 1500, Oct. 21, 1950, FO/371/88449.
86. Foreign Office to the United Kingdom Delegation (United Nations), No. 1759, Oct. 23, 1950, ibid.
87. *FRUS, 1950*, II, pp. 156–57.
88. United Kingdom Delegation (United Nations) to the Foreign Office, No. 1506, Oct. 23, 1950, FO/371/88449.
89. Foreign Office to the United Kingdom Delegation (United Nations), No. 1778, Oct. 24, 1950, ibid. Also see Bevin's comments to the Cabinet, CAB/128/18, Oct. 23, 1950, PRO.
90. *FRUS, 1950*, II, p. 157.
91. *FRUS, 1950*, II, pp. 158–71, especially Austin's informal description and explanation of the events, pp. 172–75; Lie, pp. 379–82. Also see SCOR, 5th Yr., 515th Mtg., Oct. 26, 1950.
92. United Kingdom Delegation (United Nations) to the Foreign Office, No. 1529, Oct. 25, 1950, FO/371/88449.
93. Foreign Office to Washington, No. 4766, Oct. 27, 1950, ibid.
94. United Kingdom Delegation (United Nations) to the Foreign Office, No. 1565, Oct. 28, 1950, ibid.
95. Austin (New York) to the Sec. of State, No. 752, Oct. 31, 1950, File 310.5/10–3150, RG 59, NA; Lie, p. 382; *FRUS, 1950*, II, p. 178 n. Also see SCOR, 5th Yr., 516th Mtg., Oct. 30, 1950.
96. United Kingdom Delegation (United Nations) to the Foreign Office, No. 1565, Oct. 28, 1950, FO/371/88449.
97. *FRUS, 1950*, II, p. 177.

98. Lie, pp. 382–85. Also see *YUN, 1950*, pp. 125–29. On the Arab abstention, see Austin (New York) to the Sec. of State, No. 765, Nov. 2, 1950, File 310.5/11–250, RG 59, NA.

99. Lie to Austin, Nov. 6, 1950, Box 53, Austin Papers, UVt.

100. Lie, 385, 408–409; Kathleen Teltsch, *Crosscurrents at Turtle Bay* (Chicago: Quadrangle, 1970), p. 35; Arthur W. Rovine, *The First Fifty Years. The Secretaries-General in World Politics 1920–1970* (Leyden: Sijthoff, 1970), p. 266.

101. Beith (Geneva) to Berthoud, Nov. 14, 1950, FO/371/88449.

102. Coulson to Berthoud, Dec. 5, 1950, ibid.

103. Minutes by A[rchibald] R. K. Mackenzie, Dec. 12, [1950], ibid.

104. Wellington Koo, "The Reminiscences of Wellington Koo," (typescript), VII, Pt. A, Sec. 1 and 2, p. A-44, Oral History Collection, CU.

105. See Chapter 7, p. 217.

106. Bland (The Hague) to the Foreign Office, No. 309, July 26, 1946, FO/371/53805; Austin (New York) to the Sec. of State, No. 30, Jan. 8, [1948], Box 142, US Mission UN 1945–49, RG 84, NA; Austin (New York) to the Sec. of State, No. 398, Apr. 7, 1948, File 501.A Summaries/14–748, RG 59, NA; Ross to Wainhouse, June 22, 1948, Box 84; Dulles to the Sec. of State, No. 978, Nov. 27, 1948, Box 149, and Ross (New York) to the Sec. of State, No. 1006, Aug. 27, 1949, Box 153, US Mission UN 1945–49, RG 84, NA. *FRUS, 1950*, VII, pp. 68–76; Leon Gordenker, *The United Nations and the Peaceful Unification of Korea* (The Hague: Nijhoff, 1959), pp. 222–25; Lie, pp. 323–27.

107. Lie, pp. 323–27. Also see *YUN, 1947–1948*, pp. 81–88, 282–84, 302–304; and *YUN, 1948–1949*, pp. 287–94.

108. Lie to Nygaardsvold, July 25, 1950, Guri Lie Zeckendorf Papers, PP; Lie, p. 329; Teltsch, p. 45.

109. Lie to his family, July 5, 1950, and Lie to Gjesdal, July 17, 1950, Guri Lie Zeckendorf Papers, PP.

110. See Chapter 2.

111. The North Korean attack on South Korea "was an affront to the United Nations more than to anyone else," according to Lie, "since the United Nations had been so very largely responsible for the formation of the Republic." United Kingdom Delegation (United Nations) to the Foreign Office, No. 250, June 26, 1950, FO/371/84057. Also see Lie, p. 329.

112. "The Reminiscences of Thanassis Aghnides," (typescript), pp. 429, 482–83, Oral History Collection, CU.

113. Austin (New York) to the Sec. of State, No. 569, June 30, 1950, File 330/6–3050, RG 59, NA.

114. Lie to Akre, July 3, 1950, Guri Lie Zeckendorf Papers, PP. Also see Lie, p. 329; and Lester B. Pearson, *Mike: The Memoirs of the Right Honourable Lester B. Pearson* (Toronto: University of Toronto Press, 1973), II, p. 154.

115. *FRUS, 1950*, VII, pp. 126–27; "The Reminiscences of John D. Hickerson," (typescript), pp. 94–95, Oral History Collection, TL; Lie, pp. 327–28; Gaddis Smith, *Dean Acheson. The American Secretaries of State and Their Diplomacy*, ed. by Robert Bemis and Samuel Flagg Bemis (New York: Cooper Square Publishers, Inc., 1972), XVI, pp. 179–80; George T. Mazuzan, *Warren R. Austin at the U.N. 1946–1953* (Kent, Ohio: Kent State University Press, 1977), pp. 141–42; Merle Miller, *Plain Speaking* (New York: Berkley Publishing, 1974), pp. 271–72; Glenn D. Paige, *The Korean Decision June 24–30, 1950* (New York: The Free Press, 1968), pp. 90–91; UN Doc. S/1495, June 25, 1950.

116. Lie, p. 328.

117. UN Doc. S/1496, June 25, 1950.
118. Lie, pp. 328–29.
119. SCOR, 5th Yr., 473rd Mtg., June 25, 1950, p. 3.
120. *FRUS, 1950*, VII, p. 146 and 193.
121. *YUN, 1950*, pp. 221–22.
122. United Kingdom Delegation (United Nations) to the Foreign Office, No. 250, June 26, 1950, FO/371/84057.
123. UN Docs. S/1503, S/1504, S/1505 Rev. 1, and S/1507, June 26, 1950.
124. Lie, p. 331.
125. *FRUS, 1950*, VII, pp. 208–209. For President Truman's statement of June 27, see Harry S. Truman, *Memoirs: Years of Trial and Hope* (New York: Doubleday, 1956), II, pp. 338–39.
126. Ernest Gross, "The Reminiscences of Ernest Gross," (typescript), pp. 693–96, Oral History Collection, CU; Miller, pp. 279–80; Lie, p. 333; Arnold Beichman, *The "Other" State Department* (New York: Basic Books, 1968), pp. 184–85.
127. *YUN, 1950*, pp. 222–24.
128. Lie, p. 333.
129. *FRUS, 1950*, VII, pp. 221–22; United Kingdom Delegation (United Nations) to the Foreign Office, No. 629, June 28, 1950, FO/371/84080.
130. *FRUS, 1950*, VII, pp. 225–26.
131. Foreign Office to the United Kingdom Delegation (United Nations), No. 727, June 29, 1950, FO/371/84080.
132. United Kingdom Delegation (United Nations) to the Foreign Office, No. 631, June 29, 1950, ibid.
133. United Kingdom Delegation (United Nations) to the Foreign Office, No. 632, June 29, 1950, ibid. Also see Lie, p. 335.
134. *YUN, 1950*, p. 224; *FRUS, 1950*, VII, pp. 230–31, 234–35, 233, 261–62, 266.
135. *FRUS, 1950*, VII, p. 221 n.; also see Lie, p. 333.
136. Austin (New York) to the Sec. of State, No. 30, July 6, 1950, RG 59, NA.
137. Lie, p. 333.
138. *FRUS, 1950*, VII, pp. 263–65.
139. Gross (New York) to the Sec. of State, July 4, 1950, File 330/7–450, RG 59, NA; Lie, pp. 333–34. On Chauvel's disapproval of flying the United Nations flag, see Memo. of Con. (Gross, Wainhouse), July 4, 1950, File 795B.5/7–450, RG 59, NA. As to Jebb's attitude, see United Kingdom Delegation (United Nations) to the Foreign Office, No. 656, July 3, 1950, FO/371/88512; and United Kingdom Delegation (United Nations) to the Foreign Office, No. 660, July 5, 1950, FO/371/88513.
140. J. Lawton Collins, *War in Peacetime* (Boston: Houghton Mifflin, 1969), p. 34. Also see Lie, p. 334.
141. Foreign Office to the United Kingdom Delegation (United Nations) No. 774, July 6, 1950, FO/371/88512.
142. *YUN, 1950*, p. 230; Lie, pp. 334–35.
143. Lie, pp. 334–35. For the memorandum, see "Legal Aspects of the Security Council Action in Korea," July 7, 1950, Noncorrespondence, Wallace Papers, UI.
144. Jebb to Lie, July 13, 1950; and Hope to Laskey, Aug. 11, 1950, FO/371/88514.
145. Edward L. Schapsmeier and Frederick H. Schapsmeier, *Prophet in Politics: Henry A. Wallace and the War Years, 1940–1965* (Ames: Iowa State University Press, 1970), p. 204.
146. Pearson, II, p. 156.

147. [Henry A. Wallace], Korea, Trygve Lie and the Progressive Party from July 6 to 12, 1950, Microfilm Reel 67, Frame Nos. 109–202, Wallace Papers, UI; J. Samuel Walker, *Henry A. Wallace and American Foreign Policy* (Westport, Conn.: Greenwood Press, 1976), pp. 208–209; Lie, p. 341.
148. Walker, p. 209.
149. Jebb to Bevin, No. 127, July 10, 1950, FO/371/88513.
150. *FRUS, 1950*, VII, pp. 355–57; Memo. of Con. (Lie, Cordier, Chang, Sunde, Stabell, Austin, Gross, Ross), July 10, 1950, Box 1, Lie Papers, NMFA. Also see Lie, p. 336.
151. *FRUS, 1950*, VII, pp. 368–69.
152. Austin (New York) to the Sec. of State, No. 57, July 13, 1950, File 357.AD/7–1350, RG 59, NA; Lie, p. 337.
153. Pearson, II, p. 155.
154. *FRUS, 1950*, VII, pp. 377–78.
155. Lie, p. 337. Also see Memo. of Con. on Korea enclosed in Laskey to Parrott, July 27, 1950, FO/371/88515; and Pearson, II, pp. 155–56.
156. *FRUS, 1950*, VII, pp. 377–78.
157. Pearson to Wrong, July 20, 1950, Vol. 10, Pearson Papers, MG 26, N1, PAC.
158. Laskey to Parrott, July 27, 1950, FO/371/88515.
159. *New York Times* (July 15, 1950), pp. 1, 4.
160. Austin (New York) to the Sec. of State, No. 60, July 14, 1950, File 357.AD/7–1450, RG 59, NA. Also see the circular message to the member states UN Doc. S/1619, July 14, 1950.
161. United Kingdom Delegation (United Nations) to the Foreign Office, Nos. 705 and 706, July 14, 1950, FO/371/88514.
162. Minutes by P[aul] C. Holmer, July 15, [1950], and C[ecil] C. Parrott, July 17, [1950], ibid.
163. United Kingdom Delegation (United Nations) to the Foreign Office, No. 273, July 17, 1950, ibid.
164. United Kingdom Delegation (United Nations) to the Foreign Office, No. 274, July 17, 1950, ibid.
165. Minutes by P[aul] C. Holmer, July 20, [1950], and C[ecil] C. P[arrott], July 21, [1950], ibid.
166. United Kingdom Delegation (United Nations) to the Foreign Office, No. 713, July 17, 1950, ibid.
167. Minutes by P[aul] C. Holmer, July 17, and 20, [1950], ibid.
168. United Kingdom Delegation (United Nations) to the Foreign Office, No. 717, July 18, 1950, ibid.
169. Minutes by P[aul] C. Holmer, July 20, [1950], ibid. Also see Austin (New York) to the Sec. of State, No. 70, July 17, 1950, File 330/7–1750, RG 59, NA.
170. CAB/128/18, July 17, 1950, PRO.
171. United Kingdom Delegation (United Nations) to the Foreign Office, No. 724, July 19, 1950, FO/371/88515.
172. Minutes by P[aul] C. Holmer and C[ecil] C. Parrott, July 21, [1950], ibid.
173. United Kingdom Delegation (United Nations) to the Foreign Office, No. 725, July 19, 1950, ibid. On Canada's annoyance, see Denis Stairs, *The Diplomacy of Constraint: Canada, the Korean War, and the United States* (Toronto: University of Toronto Press, 1974), pp. 71–72.
174. *FRUS, 1950*, VII, pp. 416–17.
175. Minutes by P[aul] C. Holmer, July 21, [1950], FO/371/88515.
176. Shann's report of July 21, 1950, enclosed in Canadian Acting Perm. Delegate (United Nations) to the Sec. of State for External Affairs, No. 377, July 27, 1950, File 5475-6-40, ADEAC. Also see Lie, p. 343. On Zinchenko's exclu-

sion, see Zinchenko to Lall, July 28, 1950, Cordier to Price, Owen, Laugier, Hoo, Cohen, and Kerno, July 28, 1950, Box 2, Lie Papers, NMFA; and Lie, p. 343.

177. Shone to Dixon, No. 126, July 22, 1950, FO/371/88509.
178. *FRUS, 1950*, VII, p. 491 n.
179. Bay (Oslo) to the Sec. of State, No. 200, Aug. 25, 1950, File 795B.5/8–2550, RG 59, NA.
180. R. G. Riddell, Note for Mr. Pearson, July 28, 1950, Vol. 10, Pearson Papers, MG 26, N1, PAC.
181. Memo. of Con. (Lie, Price, Cordier, Austin, Gross, Hickerson, Merchant, Ross, Hyde, McKeever, Winslow, Bender), July 20, 1950, Box 1, Lie Papers, NMFA. Also see Lie, pp. 338–39.
182. Stephen M. Schwebel, "A United Nations 'Guard' and a United Nations 'Legion,'" in William R. Fyre, *A United Nations Peace Force* (New York: Oceana, 1957), p. 212.
183. Pearson, II, p. 154.
184. Lie to his family, July 24 and 27, 1950, Guri Lie Zeckendorf Papers, PP.
185. Lie, p. 341. Also see Gideon Rafael, *Destination Peace* (London: Weidenfeld and Nicolson, 1981), p. 26.
186. UN Doc. S/1643, July 27, 1950.
187. Lie to his family, Aug. 2, 1950, Guri Lie Zeckendorf Papers, PP.
188. United Kingdom Delegation (United Nations) to the Foreign Office, July 27, 1950, FO/371/88505; and Austin (New York) to the Sec. of State, No. 143, July 27, 1950, File 310.5/7–2750, RG 59, NA.
189. *YUN, 1950*, pp. 266–67.
190. L. B. P[earson], Memo. for the Prime Minister, Discussions on Korea, Aug. 1, 1950, Box 234, St. Laurent Papers, MG 26, L, PAC.
191. United Kingdom Delegation (United Nations) to the Foreign Office, No. 812, Aug. 9, 1950, FO/371/88516.
192. *FRUS, 1950*, II, pp. 307–308, 311–14.
193. Lie to his family, Sept. 4, 1950, Guri Lie Zeckendorf Papers, PP. Also see Austin (New York) to the Sec. of State, No. 465, Sept. 6, 1950, File 320/9–650, RG 59, NA.
194. Dean Acheson, *Sketches from Life of Men I Have Known* (New York: Harper Bros., 1960), pp. 94–96.
195. *FRUS, 1950*, VII, pp. 807–808.
196. Ibid., pp. 824–25. Also see Lie, pp. 344–45.
197. *FRUS, 1950*, VII, p. 826.
198. Lie, p. 345; *YUN, 1950*, pp. 257–66.
199. Lie, p. 345.
200. Ibid., pp. 346–47.
201. United Kingdom Delegation (United Nations) to the Foreign Office, No. 1763, Nov. 16, 1950, FO/371/84115. Also see Memo—Canada and Korea, Sept. to Dec. 1950, Vol. 10, Pearson Papers, MG 26, N1, PAC.
202. Austin (New York) to the Sec. of State, No. 898, Nov. 29, 1950, File 795B.5/11–2950, RG 59, NA.
203. Lie, p. 351; *YUN, 1950*, p. 241.
204. United Kingdom Delegation (United Nations) to the Foreign Office, No. 1856, Nov. 26, 1950, FO/371/83308.
205. Austin (New York) to the Sec. of State, No. 891, November 28, 1950, File 310.5/11–2850, RG 59, NA.
206. United Kingdom Delegation (United Nations) to the Foreign Office, No. 1895, Nov. 29, 1950, FO/371/84104.

207. Lie, pp. 350–51.
208. *FRUS, 1950*, VII, p. 1269.
209. The Chinese Communist Delegation's Stay in New York 1950 (Conversation, Fri., Dec. 1), Box 1, Lie Papers, NMFA. Also see Lie, pp. 351–52.
210. United Kingdom Delegation (United Nations) to the Foreign Office, No. 1915, Dec. 1, 1950, FO/371/83309.
211. *FRUS, 1950*, VIII, pp. 1341–42. Also see "The Reminiscences of Ernest Gross," pp. 813–15.
212. Lie, pp. 351–52.
213. *FRUS, 1950*, VII, p. 1343.
214. Den Kinesiske Kommunistdelegasjonens New York Opphold 1950 (Samtale lordag, Dec. 2), Box 1, Lie Papers, NMFA; Lie, p. 352.
215. The Chinese Communist Delegation's Stay in New York 1950 (Conversation, Mon., Dec. 4), Box 1, Lie Papers, NMFA; *FRUS, 1950*, VII, pp. 1414–15; United Kingdom Delegation (United Nations) to the Foreign Office, No. 1938, Dec. 4, 1950, FO/371/84105; Lie, p. 353.
216. The Chinese Communist Delegation's Stay in New York 1950 (Conversation, Mon., Dec. 4), Box 1, Lie Papers, NMFA. Also see Lie, p. 352.
217. *FRUS, 1950*, VII, pp. 1378–79.
218. "The Reminiscences of Ernest Gross," pp. 827–28.
219. Rafael, pp. 27–29; Lie, p. 353.
220. Lie to his family, Dec. 8, 1950, Gury Lie Zeckendorf Papers, PP.
221. The Chinese Communist Delegation's Stay in New York 1950 (Conversation, Sat., Dec. 9), Box 1, Lie Papers, NMFA; *FRUS, 1950*, VII, pp. 1494–96; "The Reminiscences of Ernest Gross," pp. 859–60. Also see Lie, pp. 353–54.
222. Record of Con. (Secretary-General and Members of the Communist Chinese Delegation), Dec. 14, 1950 and the *Aide-Mémoire*, Dec. 11, 1950, Box 1, Lie Papers, NMFA; *FRUS, 1950*, VII, p. 1546; Lie, p. 354.
223. Lie, p. 354.
224. *FRUS, 1950*, VII, pp. 1546–48. For the cease-fire committee resolution, Malik's comments, and the six power proposal, see *YUN, 1950*, pp. 244–50.
225. "The Reminiscences of Ernest Gross," pp. 879–81.
226. Lester B. Pearson diary, Fri., Dec. 15, 1950 (Korean Cease-Fire Negotiations at the United Nations), Vol. 2, Pearson Papers, MG 26, M8, PAC; Pearson, II, pp. 280–82; The Chinese Communist Delegation's Stay in New York, 1950 (Conversations, Fri., Dec. 15), Box 1, Lie Papers, NMFA; Lie, pp. 354–56; *FRUS, 1950*, VII, pp. 1556–58.
227. The Chinese Delegation's Stay in New York 1950 (Conversation, Sat., Dec. 16), Box 1, Lie Papers, NMFA; Lie, pp. 356–57; Pearson, II, pp. 282–83; *FRUS, 1950*, VII, pp. 1560–61. For the cease-fire committee's letter to Wu, see UN Doc. A/C.1/643, Jan. 2, 1951.
228. Pearson, II, p. 284.
229. Coulson to Parrott, Jan. 11, 1951, FO/371/95631.
230. Pearson, II, p. 284.
231. The Chinese Communist Delegation's Stay in New York 1950 (Conversation, Tues., Dec. 19), Box 1, Lie Papers, NMFA. Also see Lie, p. 357.
232. Lie, p. 357.

Notes for Chapter 9: Thwarted Hopes

1. Minutes by C[ecil] C. Parrott, Jan. 9, 1951, P[ierson] D[ixon], Jan. 10, [1951], and E[rnest] B[evin], (no date), FO/371/95589.

2. Con. with Prime Minister Nehru in Paris, Jan. 18, 1951, Box 1, Lie Papers, NMFA. Also see Trygve Lie, *In the Cause of Peace* (New York: Macmillan, 1954), pp. 359–62. Under direct and indirect Russian threats, Yugoslavia's Marshal Tito, unlike Nehru, could ill-afford to reject anyone's outstretched hand, Lie's included, which goes far to explain their friendly encounter in April when Lie boldly raised the possibility of Yugoslavia contributing combat forces in Korea. Con. with Marshal Tito, Apr. 13, 1951, Box 2, Lie Papers, NMFA; and Lie, pp. 239–44. Also see Memo. of Con. (Feller, Bancroft), June 4, 1951, File 795B.00/6–451, RG 59, NA.
3. *FRUS, 1951*, VI, p. 1766.
4. Cyrus L. Sulzberger, *A Long Row of Candles; Memoirs and Diaries [1934–1954]* (New York: Macmillan, 1969), p. 680.
5. *YUN, 1951*, pp. 216–17.
6. Austin (New York) to the Sec. of State, No. 1058, Jan. 25, 1951, File 795.00/1–2551, and Austin (New York) to the Sec. of State, No. 1364, April 4, 1951, File 310.5/4–451, RG 59, NA.
7. Cordier to Ribes, No. 69, Jan. 26, 1951, MacArthur Papers, MANV.
8. Bunker to Ribes, Jan. 26, 1951, ibid.
9. [Rafael] (New York) to Shertok, Feb. 9, 1951, File 2384/21, ISAJ.
10. *YUN, 1951*, pp. 217–25.
11. K[enneth] G. Younger, Untitled Memo. of Con., Jan. 22, 1951, FO/371/95589; Canadian Perm. Delegate (United Nations) to the Sec. of State for External Affairs, No. 270, Mar. 1, 1951, Sec. of State for External Affairs to the Canadian Perm. Delegate (United Nations), No. 209, Mar. 2, 1951, and Canadian Perm. Delegate (United Nations) to the Sec. of State for External Affairs, No. 304, Mar. 13, 1951, File 5475-1-40, ADEAC. Also see Williams (New York) to Hope, Nov. 4, 1952, FO/371/101308.
12. *FRUS, 1951*, VII, Pt. 1, p. 241; Rafael to Shertok, Apr. 5, 1951, File 2384/21, ISAJ.
13. *FRUS, 1951*, VII, Pt. 1, pp. 223–26, 227–28, 240–41. Also see Lie to his family, Mar. 22, 1951, Guri Lie Zeckendorf Papers, PP; and Lie, p. 362.
14. Rafael to Shertok, Apr. 5, 1951, File 2384/21, ISAJ.
15. United Kingdom Delegation (United Nations) to the Foreign Office, No. 318, Mar. 9, 1951, FO/371/92778.
16. Foreign Office to the United Kingdom Delegation (United Nations), No. 333, Mar. 17, 1951, ibid.
17. *FRUS, 1951*, VIII, Pt. 1, p. 248 n.
18. Lie, p. 362; and Denis Stairs, *The Diplomacy of Constraint: Canada, the Korean War, and the United States* (Toronto: University of Toronto Press, 1974), p. 234.
19. United Kingdom Delegation (United Nations) to the Foreign Office, No. 168, May 30, 1951, FO/371/92782.
20. *FRUS, 1951*, VII, Pt. 1, p. 523.
21. United Kingdom Delegation (United Nations) to the Foreign Office, No. 168, May 30, 1951, FO/371/92782.
22. Foreign Office to the United Kingdom Delegation (United Nations), No. 665, June 5, 1951, ibid.
23. United Kingdom Delegation (United Nations) to the Foreign Office, No. 182, June 9, 1951, ibid. On the French attitude, see *FRUS, 1951*, VII, Pt. 1, p. 524 n.
24. Ross to Hickerson and Rusk, June 12, 1951, File 795.00/6–1251, RG 59, NA. Partially reproduced in *FRUS, 1951*, VII, Pt. 1, p. 524 n. Also see the memorandum by John MacVane, June 11, 1951, File 357.AK/6–1251, RG 59, NA.
25. *FRUS, 1951*, VII, Pt. 1, pp. 523–24.

26. Ideas Concerning Attainment of a Ceasefire in Korea, June 12, 1951, FO/371/ 92783. Also see Lie, pp. 362–63.
27. United Kingdom Delegation (United Nations) to the Foreign Office, No. 616, June 13, 1951, FO/371/92783.
28. United Kingdom Delegation (United Nations) to the Foreign Office, No. 212, June 23, 1951, FO/371/92784. Also see Foreign Office to the United Kingdom Delegation (United Nations), No. 883, June 18, 1951, FO/371/92783; and Lie, p. 363.
29. Lie, p. 363.
30. Sulzberger, pp. 650–51.
31. *New York Times* (June 25, 1951), p. 1.
32. United Kingdom Delegation (United Nations) to the Foreign Office, No. 654, June 24, 1951, FO/371/92784.
33. Foreign Office to the United Kingdom Delegation (United Nations), No. 928, June 27, 1951, FO/371/92783. Also see Lie, pp. 363–64.
34. *FRUS, 1951*, VII, Pt. 1, pp. 562–63, 566.
35. Gross (New York) to the Sec. of State, No. 1743, June 29, 1951, File 795.00/ 6–2951, RG 59, NA.
36. Lie to his wife and family, July 2, 1951, Guri Lie Zeckendorf Papers, PP; Lie, p. 364; *FRUS, 1951*, VII, Pt. 1, pp. 573–74.
37. Ambassador of Canada to Lie, June 21, 1951, Guri Lie Zeckendorf Papers, PP. Jebb (New York) to Parrott, June 22, 1951, and Laskey (New York) to Parrott, June 23, 1951, FO/371/95648; Lie, pp. 364–65.
38. Peurifoy (Athens) to the Sec. of State, No. 4690, June 30, 1951, and Acheson to New York, No. 4, July 3, 1951, File 795.00/6–3051, RG 59, NA.
39. *FRUS, 1951*, VII, Pt. 1, p. 676 n.
40. Memo. of Con. (Malania, Brown), July 5, 1951, Box 51, Austin Papers, UVt.
41. Note for the Secretary-General Concerning the Possible Appointment of a Mediator or Commission for the Korean Question, July 3, 1951, FO/371/92787.
42. United Kingdom Delegation (United Nations) to the Foreign Office, No. 227, July 4, 1951, FO/371/92787. Also see Lie to his wife and family, July 5, 1951, Guri Lie Zeckendorf Papers, PP.
43. United Kingdom Delegation (United Nations) to the Foreign Office, No. 239, July 10, 1951, FO/371/92788.
44. Harvey (Paris) to the Foreign Office, No. 255, July 10, 1951, ibid.
45. Minutes by J[ohn] O. Lloyd, July 6, 9, and 10, 1951, C[ecil] C. Parrott, July 6, [1951], R[obert] H. Scott, July 10, 1951, P[aul] M[ason], July 10, [1951], FO/371/ 92787.
46. Foreign Office to the United Kingdom Delegation (United Nations), No. 832, July 12, 1951, ibid.
47. United Kingdom Delegation (United Nations) to the Foreign Office, No. 256, July 20, 1951, FO/371/92789. Also see Shattock to Jebb, Aug. 8, 1951, ibid.
48. Austin (New York) to the Sec. of State, No. 115, July 19, 1951, File 795.00/ 7–1751, RG 59, NA.
49. United Kingdom Delegation (United Nations) to the Foreign Office, No. 865, July 20, 1951, FO/371/92787.
50. Foreign Office to Washington, No. 3859, Aug. 3, 1951, FO/371/92788.
51. *FRUS, 1951*, II, p. 100.
52. Ibid., pp. 45–46.
53. Myrdal to the Foreign Ministers of Hungary, Poland, and the USSR, June 14, 1951, Gromyko to Myrdal, July 15, 1951, Myrdal to Lie, July 16, 1951, Lie to Myrdal, July 18, 1951, and Lie to Cordier, July 18, 1951, Microfilm 12/05, Cordier Papers, UNA.

54. Dean Acheson, *Present at the Creation* (New York: Norton, 1969), p. 582.
55. Memo. of Con. (Cordier, Rothwell), May 1, 1946, Box 110, US Mission UN 1945–49, RG 84, NA.
56. James Barros, *Office without Power: Secretary-General Sir Eric Drummond 1919–1933* (Oxford: The Clarendon Press, 1979), pp. 60–74, 179–81, 192, 287–92, 391–94; and James Barros, *Betrayal from Within: Joseph Avenol, Secretary-General of the League of Nations 1933–1940* (New Haven: Yale University Press, 1969), passim.
57. U. S. Senate, Committee on the Judiciary, *Activities of United States Citizens Employed by the United Nations*, Hearings before the Subcommittee to Investigate the Administration of the Internal Security Act and Other Internal Security Laws, 82nd Congress, 2nd Session, October 13, 14, 15, 24; November 11, 12; December 1, 2, 10, 11 and 17, 1952, pp. 412, 415, 419. On Hiss's role see ibid., pp. 332–34, 415. Also see Lie, p. 387.
58. U. S. Senate, Committee on the Judiciary, *Activities of United States Citizens Employed by the United Nations*, p. 419.
59. Lie, pp. 386–88 and "The Reminiscences of John Hutson" (typescript), pp. 513–14, Oral History Collection, CU.
60. Memo. of Con. (Papánek, Power), Jan. 31, 1949, Memo. of Con. (Papánek, Hyde), Feb. 1, 1949, Memo. of Con. (Cordier, Power), Aug. 5, 1949, Box 111, US Mission UN 1945–49, RG 84, NA; H[ayden] R[aynor], Memo. for the Files, Feb. 1, 1949, and Austin (New York) to the Sec. of State, No. 113, Jan. 30, 1949, File 501.BA/1–3049, RG 59, NA; Lie, p. 394.
61. Lie, p. 389.
62. Chapter 4, pp. 109–13.
63. L. B. P[earson], Discussion with Trygve Lie, Mon., July 31, 1951, Box 234, St. Laurent Papers, MG 26, L, PAC.
64. Memo. of Con. (Lie, Power), Feb. 24, 1949, Box 111, US Mission UN 1945–49, RG 84, NA.
65. *New York Times* (July 21, 1948), pp. 1, 4; (July 22, 1948), p. 3; and (July 23, 1948), p. 6; Lie, p. 394.
66. Power to Raynor, Mar. 24, 1948, Memo. of Con. (Cordier, Power), Mar. 30, 1948, Power to Raynor, Feb. 1, 1949, Memo. of Con. (Cordier, Power), Feb. 23, 1949, Memo. of Con. (Lie, Power), Feb. 24, 1949, Box 111, US Mission UN 1945–49, RG 84, NA; Power to Austin, Feb. 7, 1949, Memos. of Con. (Cordier, Power), Feb. 7, 8, and 9, 1949, Box 193, ibid. Indeed, Washington had no qualms in denying a visa to a member of the Czech mission on the grounds of "national security." See *FRUS, 1952–1954*, III, pp. 211–19.
67. Memo. of Telephone Conversation (Rusk, Jessup), July 29, 1948, Box 111, US Mission UN 1945–49, RG 84, NA.
68. Memo. of Con. (Vaughan, Power), Jan. 20, 1949, Box 111, ibid.
69. Power to Austin, May 4, 1949, Box 111, ibid. For the State Department's refusal of a passport, see *New York Times* (Aug. 31, 1948), p. 9.
70. *New York Times* (July 26, 1949), p. 10; and (Feb. 26, 1952), p. 15.
71. Byron Price, Memo. of Con. with James G. Gray, June 28, 1949, Box 2, Lie Papers, NMFA; Lie, p. 389.
72. *New York Times* (July 24, 1949), p. 10; and (July 28, 1949), p. 8; *Evening Star* (Washington) (July 24, 1949), pp. 1, 5; Memo. of Con. (Lie, Cordier, Austin, Ross, Power), Aug. 18, 1949, Box 53, Austin Papers, UVt; [Lie] to [Stoneman], Aug. 3, 1949, Box 1, Stoneman Papers, Bentley Historical Library, UM. Also see Lie, pp. 394–95.
73. Power to Sandifer, Aug. 4, 1949, Box 111, US Mission UN 1945–49, RG 84, NA.

74. U.S. Senate, Committee on the Judiciary, *Activities of United States Citizens Employed by the United Nations*, pp. 411–16, 419. Also see *FRUS, 1952–1954*, III, pp. 327–28.
75. Acheson, p. 698.
76. Shirley Hazzard, *Defeat of an Ideal* (Boston: Little, Brown and Co., 1973), passim.
77. James P. Sewell, *UNESCO and World Politics* (Princeton: Princeton University Press, 1975), p. 288 n.
78. Acheson, p. 698.
79. Lie, pp. 395–97.
80. Laskey to Hope, Apr. 25, 1952, FO/371/101306.
81. *YUN, 1951*, pp. 115–17.
82. Minutes by D[avid] N. Royce, May 3, [1952], FO/371/101306.
83. Steel (Washington) to Strang, Sept. 23, 1952, FO/371/101307.
84. Lie, p. 398.
85. Lie, pp. 398–99; Hazzard, p. 43.
86. Chancery of the British Embassy (Washington) to the United Nations (Political) Department, Nov. 28, 1952, FO/371/101308.
87. Hazzard, p. 32.
88. UN Doc. A/2364, Jan. 30, 1953, Annex III.
89. Lie, p. 400.
90. U. S. Senate, Committee on the Judiciary, *Activities of United States Citizens Employed by the United Nations*, p. 422.
91. Lord Gladwyn, *The Memoirs of Lord Gladwyn* (New York: Webright and Talley, 1972), pp. 255–56.
92. Jebb (New York) to Eden, No. 31, Dec. 14, 1952, FO/371/101310. Jebb subsequently wrote the mission felt that the "legal findings" of the jurists' report "are in general sound though the way in which the report is presented tends to colour the whole picture in a way which is too favourable to the host country." Jebb (New York) to Mason, Jan. 7, 1953, FO/371/107038.
93. Trygve Lie, Record of Conversation, (no date), Sanasen to Bastid, Feb. 2, 1953, and minutes by A. A. Duff, Nov. 20, 1953, FO/371/107046.
94. *New York Times* (Dec. 3, 1952), p. 19.
95. Lodge to the President, Jan. 29, 1953, Box 327, Official File, Eisenhower Papers, EL; Laskey (New York) to Williams, Jan. 31, 1953 and the attached minutes by F. A. Vallat, Jan. 30, 1953, Jebb (New York) to Mason, Feb. 6, 1953, FO/371/107039; Williams to Laskey, Feb. 4, 1953, FO/371/107038; United Kingdom Delegation (United Nations) to the Foreign Office, No. 82, Feb. 25, 1953, United Kingdom Delegation (United Nations) to the Foreign Office, No. 128, Mar. 3, 1953, FO/371/107040; S[elwyn] L[loyd], United Nations Personnel Policy, Mar. 2, 1953, CAB/129/5 and CAB/128/26, Pt. I, PRO; Lie, pp. 401–405; *FRUS, 1952–1954*, III, pp. 317–20, 325–39; *YUN, 1953*, pp. 57–68.
96. Memo. of Con. (Van Roijen, Millet, Hickerson, Wainhouse, Allen), Feb. 12, 1953, File 795.00/2–1253, RG 59, NA.
97. Kathleen Teltsch, *Crosscurrents at Turtle Bay* (Chicago: Quadrangle, 1970), pp. 50–51.
98. Gross (New York) to the Sec. of State, No. 218, Sept. 8, 1952, File 795.00/9–852; Acheson to New York, No. 109, Sept. 8, 1952, File 795.00/9–852; Austin (New York) to the Sec. of State, No. 228, Sept. 9, 1952, File 795.00/9–952; and Gifford (London) to the Sec. of State, No. 1467, Sept. 12, 1952, File 795.00/9-1252, RG 59, NA; Laskey to Hope, Aug. 25, 1952, FO/371/101316; United Kingdom Delegation (United Nations) to the Foreign Office, No. 563, Aug. 27,

1952, FO/371/99583; United Kingdom Delegation (United Nations) to the Foreign Office, No. 582, Sept. 9, 1952, and C. H. Johnston, Brief for the Sec. of State's Interview with Trygve Lie, Sept. 10, 1952, FO/371/99584; Foreign Office to Washington, No. 3794, Sept. 12, 1952, FO/371/99583; M[ichael] S. Williams to Twiss, Sept. 13, 1952, and V. W. Street to Williams, Sept. 16, 1952, FO/371/101317.

99. Foreign Office to the United Kingdom Delegation (United Nations), No. 322, May 22, 1952, FO/371/98681; Jebb to Eden, No. 11, May 27, 1952, and Jebb to Lie, May 27, 1952, FO/371/98689; Lie to Jebb, May 29, 1952, and Jebb to Eden, No. 14, June 18, 1952, FO/371/98690.

100. Sulzberger, pp. 680, 716.

101. [Gladwyn Jebb], Annual Report [1952], FO/371/107023; Lie, pp. 411–12; Lester B. Pearson, *Mike: The Memoirs of The Right Honourable Lester B. Pearson* (Toronto: University of Toronto Press, 1973), II, p. 124.

102. *FRUS, 1952–1954*, III, pp. 420, 423–24.

103. Lie, p. 413.

104. Hugh L. Keenleyside, *Memoirs* (Toronto: McClelland, Stewart, 1982), II, pp. 369–70.

105. Jebb (New York) to Mason, Dec. 20, 1952, FO/371/107049.

106. Lie, p. 413.

107. Foreign Office to the United Kingdom Delegation (United Nations), No. 690, Nov. 13, 1952, FO/371/101311.

108. Jebb (New York) to Mason, Nov. 19, 1952, ibid.

109. Gladwyn Jebb, Record of a Con. between the Secretary-General and Sir Gladwyn Jebb, Nov. 11, 1952, FO/371/101311. On Protitch's presence, see Lie, p. 412.

110. Pearson, II, p. 324.

111. *FRUS, 1952–1954*, III, pp. 425–29. On Jebb's sharing the consensus, see Jebb (New York) to Mason, Nov. 19, 1952, FO/371/101311.

112. Minutes by A[nthony] J. Williams, Nov. 12, 1952, and C[harles] P. Hope, Nov. 13, 1952, FO/371/101311.

113. Foreign Office to the United Kingdom Delegation (New York), No. 690, Nov. 13, 1952, ibid.

114. Jebb (New York) to Mason, Nov. 19, 1952, ibid.

115. *FRUS, 1952–1954*, III, pp. 429–30.

116. Charles Malik a Candidate to Succeed Trygve Lie, June 15, 1951, CIA Files.

117. Acheson (New York) to the Sec. of State, No. 205, Nov. 18, 1952, File 320/11–1852, RG 59, NA.

118. *FRUS, 1952–1954*, III, p. 430. Also see the *note verbale* from the Lebanese Foreign Ministry to the British Embassy in Beirut proposing Malik's candidacy, Nov. 18, 1952, FO/371/101311.

119. Mason to Selwyn Lloyd, Nov. 19, 1952, FO/371/101311.

120. [Gladwyn Jebb], Extract from Minutes, Nov. 26, 1952, enclosed in Jebb (New York) to Mason, Dec. 1, 1952, ibid.

121. Jebb to Mason, Dec. 1, 1952, ibid.

122. Mason to Jebb, Dec. 5, 1952, ibid.

123. Lodge to Dulles, Dec. 5, Dulles Papers, PU.

124. United Kingdom Delegation (United Nations) to the Foreign Office, No. 941, Dec. 5, 1952, FO/371/101311.

125. United Kingdom (United Nations) to the Foreign Office, No. 942, Dec. 5, 1952, FO/371/101339.

126. Foreign Office to New York, No. 1116, Dec. 8, 1952, FO/371/101311.

127. Minutes by R[obert] S. Smith, Nov. 28 and Dec. 29, 1952, M[ichael] S. Williams, Dec. 23, 1952, and those of others, as well as Nutting to Noel-Baker, Jan. 6, 1953, FO/371/101311; Minutes by G[erald] G. Fitzmaurice, Jan. 23, 1953, and M[ichael] S. Williams, Jan. 27, 1953, as well as Fitzmaurice to Noel-Baker, Jan. 28, 1953, FO/371/107049.

128. Fitzmaurice to Vallat, Feb. 11, 1953, Vallat to Laskey, Feb. 24, 1953, an untitled note by Laskey, Feb. 27, 1953, Vallat (New York) to Williams, Mar. 5, 1953, and the minutes by G[erald] G. Fitzmaurice, Mar. 10, 1953, and P[aul] Mason, Mar. 11, [1953], FO/371/107049.

129. *FRUS, 1952–1954*, III, p. 436.

130. Ibid., p. 433. Also see Jebb to Mason, Dec. 8, 1952, FO/371/101311.

131. Pearson, II, pp. 125–26. Also see Lester Pearson diary, Fri., Feb. 6, 1953, Vol. 2, Pearson Papers, MG 26, N8, PAC.

132. Jebb (New York) to Mason, Dec. 20, 1952, minutes by R[obert] H. Scott, Dec. 22, 1952, F[rank] K. Roberts, Dec. 23, 1952, and P[aul] Mason, Jan. 5, 1952 [sic], Mason to Jebb, Jan. 6, 1952 [sic], and Nye (Ottawa) to Jebb, Jan. 20, 1953, FO/371/1097049.

133. Jebb (New York) to Mason, Jan. 13, 1953, ibid. On Rafael's discussions, see Austin (New York) to the Sec. of State, No. 388, Dec. 20, 1952, File 320/12–2052, RG 59, NA; and Pearson, II, p. 127.

134. [Makins] (Washington) to Strang, Jan. 24, 1953, FO/371/107034. Also see Gross (New York) to the Sec. of State, No. 464, Jan. 30, 1953, File 310.5/1–3053, RG 59, NA.

135. Lester Pearson diary, Sun., Jan. 18, 1953, Vol. 2, Pearson Papers, MG 26, N8, PAC. Also see Keenleyside, II, p. 370.

136. Jebb (New York) to Mason, Jan. 7, 1953, FO/371/107038.

137. Pearson to Robertson, Jan. 20, 1953, Vol. 64, Pearson Papers, MG 26, N1, PAC.

138. Pearson to Wrong, Jan. 20, 1953, ibid.

139. P[aul] Mason, Successor to Trygve Lie as Secretary-General of the United Nations, Jan. 28, 1953, FO/371/107049. Also see Robertson (London) to Pearson, Jan. 28, 1953, Vol. 64, Pearson Papers, MG 26, N1, PAC.

140. [Wrong] to Pearson, Jan. 29, 1953, Vol. 64, Pearson Papers, MG 26, N1, PAC.

141. Jebb (New York) to Eden, No. 6, Jan. 28, 1953, FO/371/107031.

142. Johnson to Pearson, Feb. 4, 1953, Vol. 16, Pearson Papers, MG 26, N1, PAC.

143. Gross (New York) to the Sec. of State, No. 464, Jan. 30, 1953, File 310.5/1–3053, RG 59, NA.

144. Johnson to Pearson, Feb. 4, 1953, Vol. 16, Pearson Papers, MG 26, N1, PAC.

145. Pearson, II, pp. 127–28.

146. Jebb (New York) to Mason, Feb. 5, 1953, FO/371/107049.

147. Jebb (New York) to Mason, Feb. 9, 1953, ibid.

148. *FRUS, 1952–1954*, III, p. 437.

149. Johnson to Pearson, Feb. 17, 1953, Vol. 16, Pearson Papers, MG 26, N1, PAC.

150. *FRUS, 1952–1954*, III, pp. 439–40.

151. Mason to Makins, Feb. 17, 1953, and Makins to Mason, Feb. 19, 1953, FO/371/107049.

152. Jebb (New York) to Eden, Feb. 20, 1953, ibid. Also see the *New York Times* (Feb. 18, 1953), pp. 1, 6. On Bokhari's discussions, also see Gross (New York) to the Sec. of State, No. 505, Feb. 12, 1953, File 315/2–1253; and Gross (New York) to the Sec. of State, No. 510, Feb. 12, 1953, File 310.5/2–1253, RG 59, NA.

153. Lester Pearson diary, Fri., Feb. 20, 1953, Vol. 2, Pearson Papers, MG 26, N8, PAC. Also see Johnson to Pearson, Feb. 11, 1953, Vol. 16, Pearson Papers, MG 26, N1, PAC.

154. United Kingdom Delegation (United Nations) to the Foreign Office, No. 76, Feb. 24, 1953, FO/371/107049.
155. Minutes by M[ichael] S. Williams, Feb. 25, 1953, and P[aul] Mason, Mar. 25, [1953], ibid.
156. Foreign Office to New York, No. 112, Feb. 26, 1953, ibid.
157. *FRUS, 1952–1954*, III, pp. 441–42.
158. Lester Pearson diary, Mon. 7, Mar. 2, 1953, Vol. 2, Pearson Papers, MG 26, N8, PAC; and Pearson, II, p. 129. Also see GAOR, 7th Sess., 1st Ctte., 561st Mtg., Mar. 2, 1953, pp. 368–69.
159. Lester Pearson diary, Tues., Mar. 3, 1953, Vol. 2, Pearson Papers, MG 26, N8, PAC. Also see Johnson to Pearson, Feb. 17, 1953, Vol. 16, Pearson Papers, MG 26, N1, PAC.
160. United Kingdom Delegation (United Nations) to the Foreign Office, No. 105, Mar. 4, 1953, FO/371/107041. Also see *FRUS, 1952–1954*, III, p. 334.
161. Foreign Office to New York, No. 137, Mar. 6, 1953, FO/371/107040.
162. Lester Pearson diary, Fri., Mar. 6, 1953, Vol. 2, Pearson Papers, MG 26, N8, PAC; Pearson, II, pp. 187–88; GAOR, 7th Sess., 1st Ctt., 566th Mtg., Mar. 6, 1953, p. 397.
163. United Kingdom Delegation (United Nations) to the Foreign Office, No. 117, Mar. 7, 1953, FO/371/107049.
164. United Kingdom Delegation (United Nations) to the Foreign Office, No. 157, Mar. 11, 1953, ibid.; SCOR, 8th Yr., 612th Mtg., Mar. 11, 1953.
165. United Kingdom Delegation (United Nations) to the Foreign Office, No. 158, Mar. 11, 1953, FO/371/107049; and Lodge (New York) to the Sec. of State, No. 453, Mar. 11, 1953, File 320/3–1153, RG 59, NA.
166. United Kingdom Delegation (United Nations) to the Foreign Office, No. 160, Mar. 12, 1953, FO/371/107049.
167. Foreign Office to New York, No. 195, Mar. 12, 1953, ibid.
168. Makins (Washington) to the Foreign Office, No. 574, Mar. 13, 1953, ibid.
169. *FRUS, 1952–1954*, III, pp. 442–43.
170. Pearson, II, pp. 129–30.
171. Jebb to the Sec. of State, Mar. 13, 1953, FO/371/107049.
172. SCOR, 8th Yr., 613th Mtg., Mar. 13, 1953.
173. United Kingdom Delegation (United Nations) to the Foreign Office, No. 181, Mar. 13, 1953, FO/371/107049.
174. Jebb (New York) to Eden, Mar. 14, 1953, ibid.
175. Minutes by M[ichael] S. Williams, Mar. 16, 1953, and P[aul] Mason, Mar. 16, [1953], ibid.
176. Lester Pearson diary, Mar. 8 to 19, 1953, Vol. 2, Pearson Papers, MG 26, N8, PAC; and Pearson, II, p. 130; as well as S. F. Rae, Note for Mr. Pearson, Mar. 14, 1953, Vol. 16, Pearson Papers, MG 26, N1, PAC. Also see Joseph P. Lash, *Dag Hammarskjöld, Custodian of the Brush-Fire Peace* (New York: Doubleday and Co., 1961), p. 8.
177. *FRUS, 1952–1954*, III, pp. 443–44, 447.
178. Pearson, II, p. 130.
179. United Kingdom Delegation (United Nations) to the Foreign Office, No. 184, Mar. 16, 1953, FO/371/107049.
180. Foreign Office to New York, No. 162, Mar. 10, 1953, ibid.
181. Foreign Office to New York, No. 224, Mar. 17, 1953; and also Kher to Eden, Mar. 16, 1953, ibid.
182. Minutes by Selwyn Lloyd, Mar. 18, 1953; and Williams to Fowler, Mar. 19, 1953, ibid.
183. *FRUS, 1952–1954*, III, p. 444.

184. United Kingdom Delegation (United Nations) to the Foreign Office, No. 195, Mar. 18, 1953, FO/371/107049; and Lodge (New York) to the Sec. of State, No. 472, Mar. 18, 1953, File 320/3–1853, RG 59, NA.

185. Lester Pearson diary, Mar. 8 to 19, 1953, Vol. 2, Pearson Papers, MG 26, N8, PAC.

186. Telephone Conversation with Ambassador Lodge, Mar. 24, 1953, Box 1, Dulles Papers, EL.

187. *FRUS, 1952–1954*, III, pp. 445–46.

188. United Kingdom Delegation (New York) to the Foreign Office, No. 201, Mar. 19, 1953, FO/371/107050; and Lodge (New York) to the Sec. of State, No. 475, Mar. 19, 1953, File 320/3-1953, RG 59, NA; and SCOR, 8th Yr., 614th Mtg., Mar. 19, 1953.

189. Lester Pearson diary, Mar. 8 to 19, 1953, Vol. 2, Pearson Papers, MG 26, N8, PAC.

190. Brian Urquhart, *Hammarskjold* (New York: Alfred A. Knopf, 1972), p. 11. Also see Keenleyside, II, p. 370.

191. United Kingdom Delegation (United Nations) to the Foreign Office, No. 204, Mar. 20, 1953, FO/371/107050.

192. Minutes by M[ichael] S. Williams, Mar. 21, 1953, and P[aul] Mason, Mar. 21, [1953], and Foreign Office to New York, No. 250, Mar. 21, 1953, ibid.

193. Jebb (New York) to Churchill, May 7, 1953, ibid.; and Lord Gladwyn, p. 257.

194. United Kingdom Delegation (New York) to the Foreign Office, No. 217, Mar. 23, 1953, FO/371/107050; and Lodge (New York) to the Sec. of State, No. 490, Mar. 24, 1953, File 320/3-2453, RG 59, NA.

195. United Kingdom Delegation (United Nations) to the Foreign Office, No. 218, Mar. 23, 1953, FO/371/107050.

196. United Kingdom Delegation (United Nations) to the Foreign Office, No. 224, Mar. 24, 1953, ibid.; and Lodge (New York) to the Sec. of State, No. 490, Mar. 24, 1953, File 320/3-2453, RG 59, NA; SCOR, 8th Yr., 615th Mtg., Mar. 24, 1953.

197. Minutes by M[ichael] S. Williams, March 24, 1953, and P[aul] Mason, Mar. 24, [1953], W[illiam] Strang, Mar. 25, [1953], Harvey (Paris) to the Foreign Office, No. 104, Mar. 25, 1953, and Mason to Harvey, Mar. 28, 1953, FO/371/107050.

198. United Kingdom Delegation (United Nations) to the Foreign Office, No. 238, Mar. 27, 1953, ibid.

199. United Kingdom Delegation (United Nations) to the Foreign Office, No. 239, Mar. 27, 1953, ibid.; and Lodge (New York) to the Sec. of State, No. 504, Mar. 27, 1953, File 320/3-2753, RG 59, NA; SCOR, 8th Yr., 616th Mtg., Mar. 27, 1953. On Zorin's signal, also see Urquhart, *Hammarskjold*, p. 12.

200. United Kingdom Delegation (United Nations) to the Foreign Office, No. 240, Mar. 27, 1953, FO/371/107050.

201. Mason to Jebb, Mar. 28, 1953, Mason to Harvey, Mar. 28, 1953, Foreign Office to Paris, No. 723, Mar. 28, 1953, Foreign Office to Paris, No. 325, Mar. 29, 1953, Harvey (Paris) to the Foreign Office, Nos. 111 and 112, Mar. 30, 1953, and Foreign Office to Paris, No. 342, Mar. 31, 1935, ibid.

202. United Kingdom Delegation (United Nations) to the Foreign Office, No. 249, Mar. 30, 1953, and Jebb (New York) to Churchill, May 27, 1953, FO/371/107050.

203. *FRUS, 1952–1954*, III, p. 448. Also see Lash, p. 7; and Urquhart, p. 14.

204. Makins to the Sec. of State, June 18, 1952, and H. A. F. Hohler, Visit of Dag Hammarskjöld, July 19, 1952, FO/371/100943.

205. Foreign Office to New York, No. 301, Mar. 31, 1953, FO/371/107050.
206. Foreign Office to New York, No. 301, Mar. 31, 1953, Foreign Office to Washington, No. 1466, Mar. 31, 1953, Makins (Washington) to the Foreign Office, No. 690, Mar. 31, 1953, ibid.; Dulles to Taipei, No. 756, Mar. 30, 1953, and Memo. of Con. (Tan, Allison, McConaughy), Mar. 30, 1953, File 315/3–3053, as well as Rankin (Taipei) to the Sec. of State, No. 1028, Mar. 30, 1953, File 315/3–3153, RG 59, NA; *FRUS, 1952–1954*, III, p. 449.
207. Lash, p. 9. As one Russian secretariat official laughingly noted, Pearson "would have been a big improvement" on Mr. Lie. [James George], Memo. for Mr. Pearson, Apr. 8, 1953, Vol. 10, Pearson Papers, MG 26, N1, PAC.
208. On this point see Abba Eban, *The New Diplomacy* (New York: Random House, 1983), p. 271; and Brian Urquhart, *A Life in Peace and War* (New York: Harper and Row, 1987), p. 124.
209. Jebb (New York) to Churchill, May 27, 1953, FO/371/107050; and Lodge (New York) to the Sec. of State, No. 516, Mar. 31, 1953, File 320/3–3153, RG 59, NA. Also see SCOR, 8th Yr., 617th Mtg., Mar. 31, 1953.
210. Lodge (New York) to the Sec. of State, No. 516, Mar. 31, 1953, File 320/3–3153, RG 59, NA.
211. Lash, pp. 8–10. Also see Wright (Oslo) to Mason, June 23, 1953, FO/371/106362; Teltsch, pp. 48–49; Keenleyside, II, p. 371, and Lie, p. 416.
212. *FRUS, 1952–1954*, III, p. 451.
213. Ibid.
214. Keenleyside, II, p. 371.
215. Urquhart, *Hammarskjold*, p. 15. Also see "The Reminiscences of Andrew Cordier" (typescript), pp. 2–3, Oral History Collection, CU.
216. Keenleyside, II, pp. 371–72; and Urquhart, *Hammarskjold*, pp. 25–27, 54. Also see Henry Van Dusen, *Dag Hammarskjold: The Statesman and His Faith* (New York: Harper and Row, 1967), pp. 78–83, 221–22.
217. "The Reminiscences of Thanassis Aghnides," p. 433.
218. Dag Hammarskjöld, *Markings*, trans. by Leif Sjoberg and W. H. Auden (London: Faber and Faber, 1965).
219. Indeed, the unsubstantiated allegation that Hammarskjöld was a pederast acquired respectability when it graduated into the world of the literati. Conor Cruise O'Brien, a former Irish delegate to the assembly, published a play about the Congo crisis, which he describes as a "play about real action, not real people." Nevertheless, Hammarskjöld is portrayed as a homosexual. He "could not convincingly represent him as anything other than a person of homosexual tendencies discreetly expressed," Cruise O'Brien tells us. In fact, a normal Hammarskjöld appeared "quite impossible and the entirely sublimated creatures posited by the hagiographers would be in danger of floating out of the theater altogether." Perhaps. Conor Cruise O'Brien, *Murderous Angels* (Boston: Little, Brown, and Co., 1968), pp. xxxi–xxxii.
220. GAOR, 423rd Plen. Mtg., Apr. 7, 1953, pp. 669–70.
221. Chairman, Canadian Delegation (United Nations) to the Sec. of State for External Affairs, No. 151, Apr. 7, 1953, File 5475-1-40, ADEAC; United Kingdom Delegation (United Nations) to the Foreign Office, No. 278, Apr. 7, 1953, FO/371/107050.
222. Urquhart, *Hammarskjold*, p. 15; and Richard I. Miller, *Dag Hammarskjold and Crisis Diplomacy* (New York: Oceana, 1961), p. 1.
223. GAOR, 426th Plen. Mtg., Apr. 10, 1953, p. 697.
224. Chairman, Canadian Delegation (United Nations) to the Sec. of State for External Affairs, No. 170, Apr. 10, 1953, File 5475-6-40, ADEAC.

225. Jebb to Mason, May 5, 1953, FO/371/107042; Urquhart, *Hammarskjold*, p. 54. Also see Bo Beskow, *Dag Hammarskjold: Strictly Personal* (New York: Doubleday, 1969), pp. 16–17.

226. A note about a call from Roderic O'Connor of the State Department (undated), Box 327, Official Files, Eisenhower Papers, EL; Can[adian] Del[egation] (United Nations) to Pearson, No. 53, Apr. 17, 1953, Vol. 7, Pearson Papers, MG 26, N1, PAC.

227. Can[adian] Del[egation] (United Nations) to Pearson, No. 53, Apr. 17, 1953, Vol. 7, MG 26, N1, Pearson Papers, PAC.

228. Memo. of Con. (The President, Lie, Simmons), Apr. 30, 1953, Box 41, Administration Series, Eisenhower Papers, EL.

229. Johnson to the Under-Secretary of State for External Affairs, No. 422, May 6, 1953, File 5475-1-40, ADEAC.

230. United Kingdom Delegation (New York) to the Foreign Office, No. 540, July 23, [1953], FO/371/107091.

231. Jebb to Mason, May 5, 1953, FO/371/107042.

232. Mason to Jebb, May 28, 1953, ibid.

233. Note for the Record (Conversation with Mme. Skaug), June 6, 1953, FO/371/106363.

234. Wright (Oslo) to Mason, June 23, 1953, ibid.

235. Johnson to the Under-Secretary of State for External Affairs, No. 442, May 6, 1953, File 5475-1-40, ADEAC.

236. [Hammarskjöld] to Lie, June 12 and Nov. 4, 1953, and Lie to Hammarskjöld, June 16, 1953, SD I (Personal and Private Correspondence 1953), Hammarskjöld Papers, KB.

237. Hammarskjöld to Lie, May 11, and May 21, 1955, Lie to Hammarskjöld, May 16 and May 24, 1955, and Lie to Cordier, May 23, May 24, and June 2, 1955, Microfilm 01/23, Cordier Papers, UNA.

238. [Cordier] to Lie, June 3, 1955, Microfilm 37/10, ibid. On the Russian opposition to Lie's participation, see Committee on Programme for the Commemoration of the 10th Anniversary of the Signing of the Charter, Minutes of the 7th Meeting (closed), May 20, 1955, Dag 1/1.1.1.2–4, ibid.

239. Lie to Hammarskjöld, June 15, 1955, and Lie to Cordier, June 18, 1955, Microfilm 01/23, Cordier Papers, ibid.

240. Hammarskjöld to Lie, June 16 and June 20, 1955, Microfilm 01/23, ibid.; and Cordier to Lie, June 16, 1955, Microfilm 37/10, ibid.

241. Cordier to Lie, June 25, 1955, Microfilm 37/10, ibid.

242. Wright (Oslo) to Mason, June 23, 1953, FO/371/106362.

243. [Lie] to Stevenson, Apr. 5, 1957, Stevenson Papers, PU.

244. Lie to Hammarskjöld, Aug. 29, Sept. 1, 3, 7, Oct. 12, 1959, and [Hammarskjöld] to Lie, Sept. 9, 14, Oct. 2, as well as Hammarskjöld to Lie, Oct. 15, 1959, SD II Part B, Folder b (Lie—Strictly Private), Hammarskjöld Papers. KB.

245. *YUN, 1959*, pp. 358–59. Also see the *New York Times* (June 22, 23), p. 4; (Oct. 17), p. 7; (Oct. 18), p. 10; and (Dec. 6, 1959), p. 8.

246. Norwegian Government Leaders Reaction to Khrushchev Visit, Aug 21, 1964, CIA Files.

247. GAOR, 356th Plen. Mtg., Dec. 20, 1951, p. 281.

248. SCOR, 23rd Yr., 1461st Mtg., Dec. 30, 1968, pp. 1–2; and 1462nd Mtg., Dec. 31, 1968, p. 3.

Notes for Chapter 10: The Office

1. James Barros, *Betrayal from Within: Joseph Avenol, Secretary-General of the League of Nations, 1933–1940* (New Haven: Yale University Press, 1969).
2. U Thant, *View from the UN: The Memoirs of U. Thant* (New York: Doubleday and Co., 1978).
3. See James Barros, "The Importance of Secretaries-General of the United Nations," in Robert S. Jordan, ed., *Dag Hammarskjold Revisited* (Durham: N. Car.: Carolina Academic Press, 1983), pp. 25–27.

BIBLIOGRAPHIC
NOTE

As the reader has observed, the materials that compose this study are overwhelmingly archival in nature. They were examined in public and private depositories as far apart as the National Archives in Washington, D.C., and the Central Zionist Archives in Jerusalem.

The indispensable official records were supplemented whenever possible with private materials to elucidate the official archival record. These private materials were scattered in various university libraries and other public depositories and included material in private hands.

The United Nations, which has one of the most liberal policies on access to official records, made available whatever Lie materials were to be found in its archives, but unfortunately most of these papers had been sanitized, probably by Lie, before his departure as secretary-general. Of special importance were the interviews of individuals involved with the United Nations during Lie's tenure as secretary-general. Most of the typescripts of these interviews were examined at the Oral History Collection at Columbia University in New York.

The United States Freedom of Information Act proved especially valuable in acquiring sensitive materials that would not ordinarily have been accessible. It was invoked against the Federal Bureau of Investigation, the Central Intelligence Agency, and the Immigration and Naturalization Service.

The archival record, public and private, was buttressed whenever possible with the officially published documentary collections of the involved states, as well as the published records of the United Nations. Lastly, memoirs, diaries, autobiographies, biographies, secondary works, newspapers, and so on were also used.

These published materials are clearly cited in the notes; if cited in acronym form they are clearly elucidated with the archival sources in the table of abbreviations found on the first page of the Notes section. The acronyms easily inform the reader what source is being cited, whose papers they are, and where they are found. Accordingly, it was thought unnecessary to list these materials in any detailed bibliography. Telegrams and dispatches are cited using only the surnames or titles of those involved.

INDEX